MW00890049

Mastering Etf Investing

How to Build Wealth with Lazy Portfolios
and Passive Investing Strategies

Agostino Carbone & Cosimo Palma

Mastering Etf Investing: How to Build Wealth with Lazy Portfolios and Passive Investing Strategies

© Copyright 2024 All rights reserved.

Written by Agostino Carbone & Cosimo Palma

Limited Liability - Legal Notice

Please note that the contents of this book are based on personal experience and various informational sources, intended solely for personal use. The information provided in this document is for educational and reflective purposes only and comes with no warranties, either explicit or implied.

Readers acknowledge that the author does not provide legal, financial, or professional advice. It is advisable to consult a licensed professional before attempting any technique described in this book.

Nothing in this book is intended to replace common sense or legal, accounting, or professional advice and is for informational purposes only. Your specific circumstances may not align with the examples in this book; in fact, it's likely they won't.

The information in this book is used at your own risk. The reader is responsible for their actions. The information provided here is stated as true and consistent, meaning that any responsibility, whether due to negligence or otherwise, arising from any use or misuse of any policy, process, or guidance contained herein is the sole and total responsibility of the reader recipient.

By reading this book, the reader agrees that under no circumstances shall the author be liable for any losses, direct or indirect, resulting from the use of the information contained in this document, including, but not limited to, errors, omissions, or inaccuracies.

Table of Contents

Preface

When approaching the world of investments for the first time, it's common to feel overwhelmed by the myriad of available solutions. From the numerous bank-offered funds to the large range of debt instruments issued by various entities, including national and international financial institutions, to global stocks and even the complex financial engineering products like derivatives.

Often, the result for newcomers to personal finance is feeling discouraged before even starting, entrusting their financial management to third parties. Unfortunately, those managing these finances don't always act in the investor's best interest, offering expensive solutions that may not be in agreement with investor financial plans. In case the investor decides to act on his/her own, it is common emotions lead decisions what to buy, with the result that a portfolio is filled with diverse instruments, lacking a well-defined logic.

In 1999, the renowned financial advisor and American political figure, Harry Browne, introduced a revolutionary concept to personal finance - the Lazy Portfolio. It was designed to be simple, cost-effective, and suitable to any economic scenario. His innovative proposal was intended for every investor, even those with limited resources. It represented the ultimate solution for those seeking a portfolio. This portfolio, known as the "Permanent", stood out in 2008 during the sub-prime mortgage crisis, demonstrating its effectiveness in the middle of a severe financial crisis, a real baptism by fire.

Although the path seemed paved towards Lazy Portfolios, the new challenge became sailing the countless lazy portfolio proposals that developed in the following years, each with its unique structure and own target.

That is where lazyportfolioetf.com website comes into play, conceived by Agostino and Cosimo, Italians with an international vision. Their project aims to collect and organize Lazy Portfolios, providing a well valuable data analysis tool accessible to both small investors and professionals.

Lazy Portfolios don't represent the endpoint but rather the starting point. Our Independent Financial Advisory Firm', during daily practice, makes our clients' investment choices on a Lazy Portfolio, easy to understand and suitable to any specific financial targets. Subsequently, more complex and active strategies are built upon this solid basis, much like a house's foundations provide stability to the building. The Lazy Portfolio forms the basis for a successful investment strategy, and lazyportfolioetf.com website stands as the excellence in this field.

This book aims to serve as a guide and reference for those looking to take by hands their finances, steering them towards their goals, both managing them directly and preferring the assistance of professional advisor, providing a clear awareness of the path to undertake. There's always a lazy portfolio out there waiting for us, ready to support us towards our financial targets!

Happy reading!

Gabriele BELLELLI

Francesco BRANCATISANO

Maurizio PAPI

Co-Founders of Zefiro SCF

Introduction

Welcome to the fascinating world of Lazy Portfolios and smart (even if "lazy") investing.

We are the team behind LazyPortfolioEtf.com, a website that started almost as a hobby in 2019, aiming to explore and share our passion for personal finance and ETFs.

What started as a personal project has now grown into something bigger than we could have ever imagined. Today, the site has become a go-to resource for financial professionals and investment enthusiasts worldwide.

We are two engineers with a fervent passion for financial analysis and investing in the world of ETFs. Our curiosity has driven us to delve deeply into the principles of Lazy Portfolios, that smart and low-maintenance approach that is gaining increasing attention.

This book is the result of our deep commitment and passion. All the information, including calculations, is already available on our website, freely accessible to everyone.

We will identify the metrics that should be carefully considered before undertaking any investment, and the ways in which to use and interpret them.

Our hope is that you can use this book as a reliable guide as you explore the paths of investment, and that the knowledge gained will help you make more informed and thoughtful financial decisions.

Let's embark on this journey together, exploring the potentials of Lazy Portfolios and identifying the metrics that define the right choice for you.

Your financial future is in your hands.

The introductory chapters of the book are intentionally short and illustrative. They get straight to the point.

We're referring, for instance, to concepts such as:

- Money management
- Inflation
- Goal and time horizon
- Asset class and financial instruments

These are all topics extensively covered by other authoritative texts and endless online blogs, so we won't bore you with subjects you may already be familiar with.

However, if these concepts are new to you, you'll find essential principles that will ease you into the subsequent chapters. It's a primer, so feel free to delve deeper into key concepts if you feel the need.

Starting from the basics, we will analyze a strategy that will help identify the right asset allocation for you. The book's focus will be on examining metrics tailored to your specific goals.

Don't worry, here you won't encounter the usual generic concepts often presented superficially when discussing investments.

To give you a little taste:

- We'll almost never talk about the performance of the last 5, 10, or 15 years of a portfolio. And if we do, it will never be our sole criterion for choice.
- Want to know how much equity should weigh in your ideal portfolio? Don't worry, you won't find oversimplifications like:
  - "To find the suitable percentage of equity for you, subtract your age from 100."

- o "Young? Then go all-in on stocks; they always go up in the long run."

Approaches like these can lead to dangerous approximations that could even harm you.

We believe that a numerical and statistical approach can be the key to helping you make informed choices. Once you grasp the concepts in the book, you'll always have access to the *LazyPortfolioEtf.com* website for any simulations you want. It's all online and open to everyone.

Currently, all the portfolios on the site are expressed in dollars and often tilted towards U.S. assets. This may not align with your ideal or practical portfolio, but no worries, because the strategy we'll present is valid regardless of the type of asset allocation you choose.

For Euro investors, we have added an appendix at the end of the book with the recalculation of statistics based on the currency exchange US Dollar -> Euro.

1. Money Management

There are many things in life more important than money, but they cost so much money!

GROUCHO MARX

A successful journey to financial stability begins with mastering the art of managing money.

In this chapter, we'll explore the fundamental concepts that allow us to take control of our finances and get to know the main adversary of every saver.

The Concept of 'Money Management'

Money management is not just a practical matter but a cornerstone on which our financial stability rests.

It's a concept that goes beyond mere bookkeeping and influences every aspect of our financial life, guiding everyday choices.

It means creating a solid path toward stability and well-being.

It's the skill of balancing short-term desires with long-term goals, creating a harmony between immediate gratification and future security.

Such an approach requires a holistic view, prompting us to question what we truly expect from our money and how we can maximize its potential, especially in our future.

The family budget thus becomes the foundation of this skill. Through a budget, we assign tangible value to our priorities and commit to honoring them. By monitoring income and expenses, we identify strengths and weaknesses and then adapt our financial path accordingly.

The art of saving is not just about setting aside a percentage of our earnings. It's an attitude that opens the doors to future possibilities. We learn to distinguish between needs and wants, to forgo small immediate gratifications for lasting benefits.

However, relying solely on savings leads us to face a pitfall, which we will explore in just a moment. Saving a lot throughout a lifetime without effective money management might not be the preferable solution.

Why Fear Inflation

Inflation is, in essence, a *general increase in prices* that occurs over time.

Imagine walking into a store and finding that things cost a bit more than the last time you saw them.

This happens because inflation means the money you have today can buy you fewer things in the future. Prices rise gradually, and your money has less purchasing power.

In other words, inflation causes your money to lose some of its value over time.

Imagine you have saved **$10,000 today**.

Let's assume the average annual inflation rate is 2%. It may seem like a small figure, but let's see how it impacts our savings over time:

Year 0: You have $10,000 in savings. With these savings today, you would be able to purchase some things you like. You can choose what.

Year 1: Due to the 2% annual inflation, to purchase the same things, you now need $10,200. It's inconvenient, but perhaps still acceptable. A small sacrifice can be made.

Year 10: Due to the 2% annual inflation, to purchase the same things, you now need about $12,190. That's a significant difference. But will your salary or income also appreciate in the same way? Or what you can afford today, will it be a distant dream in 10 years?

In recent months, in many countries around the world, we have witnessed a new surge in inflation. Depending on where you live, you have probably experienced a noticeable increase in prices that may have disheartened you, after relatively calm years.

As of July 2023, the annual inflation rate in the United States was 3.2%. One year earlier, in June 2022, it was even higher at 9.1%, on an annual basis. There have been much worse instances, for example, in 1980 when inflation in the United States exceeded 13%.

Similarly, in the Eurozone, the situation is not much different. The annual inflation rate in July 2023 was 5.3%, and in October 2022, it was 10.6%.

In short, to keep our financial outlook secure, it's crucial to take inflation into account in our financial planning.

In other words, it's not just about saving money; it's also about managing it wisely.

2. Investing in the Stock Market

There are mainly 3 ways to lose money:

- *At the casino, it's the most entertaining way.*
- *With women, it's the most pleasant way.*
- *In the stock market, it's the fastest way.*

ANONYMOUS

We couldn't find who coined this quote, which is quite amusing. You can save it for the next financial-themed get-together with friends.

But is it really true? Let's try to answer, at least for the third point.

Losing everything unexpectedly, and even quickly, is a clear sign of having invested in something not thoroughly understood and far riskier than initially thought.

Let's be clear: if you are well aware that an investment can go to zero, you have every right to allocate the portion of your wealth you prefer to it.

The important thing is that you have conducted a thorough analysis and consciously chosen to risk a part of your capital in pursuit of a potential significant gain.

Every financial investment should be aimed at achieving a specific goal and should be consistent with the timeline and methods for reaching that goal.

Easier said than done.

Clarity of Purpose

"I want to shield myself from inflation for the next 20 years": this is an objective.

"I want to invest and be confident in growing my capital within the next 7 years": this is also an objective.

"I want to double my capital in 3 years": this is also an objective, but perhaps more of a dream. We'll see what is achievable and what is not in due course.

"I want to earn more from my investments by investing in the instrument that everyone is making money from": if you invest in something just because many others are doing it and making money (maybe...), well, that certainly is not an objective.

Each of us has specific needs, and when we delve into studying Lazy Portfolios, we'll discover that there is no one-size-fits-all portfolio. Instead, there is a portfolio that suits your specific needs.

Put bluntly, an investment should solve a financial problem that you have or anticipate having. For instance, are you concerned that you won't have enough money when you retire? You need to address this issue in advance.

For this reason, entering an online forum and asking, "Can you recommend a good investment?" is like walking into a doctor's office and abruptly asking, "Can you prescribe me a good medication?"

Defining the Time Horizon

When it comes to planning your financial journey, one of the key points is the time horizon.

In essence, it's how long you think you need to wait before achieving your financial goals. Alternatively, from a different perspective, it's the time during which you don't believe you'll need the money you've invested.

Imagine wanting to save for a trip, a new car, or your retirement: each of these goals, based on the time frame and economic scope, should be associated with a tailored financial plan.

For a short time horizon, you'd prefer safer and more stable investments. In such a complex scenario, the primary focus should be on preserving capital, or even better, trying to withstand the impact of inflation.

It may seem like a too defensive attitude, but it is the wisest thing to do.

Let's anticipate some topics we will discuss later to make the concept clearer. *High returns become more 'likely' and conceivable only with an appropriate time horizon.*

Furthermore, to aspire to such returns, you must be prepared to endure potential declines (or crashes) in prices, which statistically can happen.

A short time horizon might not be sufficient to absorb such a crash. For this reason, if you truly need to liquidate the investment within a few years, it is not wise to take on this risk.

In finance, short, medium, and long-term horizons are frequently discussed. While there are no precise thresholds, approximately:

- A short-term horizon is at most 3-4 years.
- A medium-term horizon is between 5 and 10 years.
- A long-term horizon is beyond ten years.

You will see that there are asset allocations that fit better with specific time horizons. In the book, we will learn how to measure these aspects.

Informed Decision-Making

Making informed financial decisions is one of the crucial points for a successful journey in the world of investments.

The right approach can make all the difference.

When discussing Lazy Portfolios and lazy investing, we will explore the vital role of metrics and analyses based on concrete data.

Once you have a clear understanding of what is achievable and what is not, then you can:

- Have a benchmark (a reference) against which to assess the investments you make independently or that are recommended by your trusted advisor/financial coach.
- Understand if the tools you've used provide returns similar to the market's average.
- Determine if the promised returns from a particular financial instrument align with the markets or if they are significantly off scale (and might be considered outright scams).

In the following chapters, you will learn to evaluate an asset allocation based on your goal. And when we say evaluate, we mean that, numerically, in the truest sense of the term, you will know how to quantify how suitable an investment strategy is for a short/medium/long-term objective.

3. Asset Classes

Diversification is not a guarantee of success, but it is a good insurance policy against failure

PHILIP FISHER

When you choose to invest, you have the option to select from various Asset Classes.

Asset Classes are investment categories, each offering unique advantages and disadvantages determined by their nature and economic events.

Here is a quick overview of traditional Asset Classes. It's a brief introduction, and if you want to delve deeper, we encourage you to conduct further research.

Equities (Stocks)

Stocks represent ownership in a company. When you invest in stocks:

- You can profit when you sell them if the stock price increases.
- You may receive dividends if the company decides to distribute them.

On average, stocks offer higher returns compared to bonds, but they are usually riskier as their value can fluctuate significantly over time.

The life of a company is influenced by various factors such as the economic situation, corporate performance, market trends, and global events.

These factors can cause unpredictable fluctuations in prices. When investing in stocks, there is the possibility that the value may decrease significantly, resulting in the loss of part or all of the invested capital.

Real Estate (REITs)

It's the category that encompasses real estate proper.

When you operate in the stock market, you are actually making an indirect real estate investment. This means you don't directly acquire real estate but rather shares in a fund or stocks of real estate companies, which in turn hold the assets.

In simpler terms, you can view the Real Estate category as a sectoral equity investment, specifically focused on the real estate market. On LazyPortfolioEtf.com, we categorize it under 'Stocks'.

Bonds

Bonds are issued by governments and companies when they want to raise funds.

By purchasing a bond, you are providing a loan to the issuer, who agrees to repay the face value of the loan on a specific date (maturity), and may also pay periodic interest along the way (usually once or twice a year).

<u>Example</u>:

Face Value: $1000

Market Value: $990

Coupon Rate: 5% annually (paid in 2 semi-annual coupons)

Maturity: In 2 years

In this case, you buy the bond on the market for $990, and in two years, it will be repaid to you at $1000. In the meantime, every year, you will also receive 5% of $1000, which is $50, in semi-annual coupons of $25.

It's not mandatory to wait until the maturity of a bond; you can sell it earlier. However, you will sell it at the market price, which can be accidentally lower than what you bought it for.

Unlike stocks, bonds issued by companies do not confer ownership rights. Therefore, you may not necessarily benefit from the company's growth, but you also won't see as significant an impact when the company is not performing well, as long as it still has the resources to meet its debt obligations.

In the worst-case scenario, where the issuer is unable to honor the loan, your bond may be only partially repaid or, worse, not repaid at all.

Each issuer can be assessed through the so-called *Rating*, which is an evaluation of its reliability. Ratings are assigned by specialized companies (e.g., Fitch Investors Service, Moody's, Standard & Poor's).

Cash

In practical terms, liquidity is the portion of money you keep in your checking account or savings account.

In financial terms, liquidity refers to the portion of one's wealth invested mainly in fixed-income instruments (bonds) with a minimal remaining maturity and easily convertible to cash.

On *LazyPortfolioEtf.com*, when discussing liquidity, we envision that this portion of the portfolio is invested in so-called "ultra short-term bonds", i.e., high-rated government bonds with a remaining maturity of 1-3 months.

Commodities

Commodities represent one of the oldest and fundamental markets in the global economic landscape.

Even today, natural resources play a crucial role in the supply and production of essential goods.

Investors worldwide venture into the commodities market with the aim of diversifying their investment strategies and capitalizing on price dynamics.

This market provides the opportunity to profit from changes in supplies, global demand, and geopolitical events, thus playing a significant role in overall investment strategies.

The quintessential commodity, often invested in, is gold, also considered a *safe-haven* asset because its intrinsic value is believed to be relatively stable over time.

Why diversify

Certainly, you've heard it said in various ways that diversification is important.

Diversifying is a smart way to:

- protect your money
- survive stock market crashes and financial disasters
- rely on resilient returns

It's like putting many eggs in different baskets. If one basket falls, you haven't broken everything.

Warren Buffett puts it differently, but always brilliantly, as is his usual style. He says that *diversification is protection against ignorance*! So, if you're not capable of investing in the right companies at the right time, then it's advisable to diversify to avoid ruin in a short time.

If you have different asset classes in your portfolio, there's less likelihood of losing all your money.

It can happen that stocks rise when the economy is strong and fall when it's weak. Conversely, during periods of economic uncertainty, bonds may be more stable. The hope is that, regardless of the economic cycle and events, there's at least one asset class that balances the disaster of the others.

In the following paragraphs of the book, it will be much clearer, with numbers and examples, what the tangible benefits of diversification are.

Historical returns

On *LazyPortfolioEtf.com*, you can easily find the updated returns of various asset classes. Just navigate to the top menu and select THEMES > ASSET CLASSES.

You'll find the returns of numerous detailed asset classes (stocks divided by geographic areas, technology stocks, bonds from emerging countries and so on).

To have a more in-depth historical overview, you can enter the detailed page of each Asset Class.

Remember that metrics are calculated on instruments that invest in US Dollars (USD). If you invest in different currencies, you are subject to exchange rate risk.

Examining the complete historical series, what has been the annualized return, in USD, of the main Asset Classes?

Annualized Return (%) - USD - as of Aug 31, 2023		
US Total Stock Market	+9.08%	(since Jan 1871)
US REITs	+6.96%	(since Jan 1928)
US Total Bond Market	+4.48%	(since Jan 1871)
US Cash	+3.99%	(since Jan 1871)
Commodities	+2.64%	(since Jan 1871)

Remember that 'annualized' means that the return was achieved every year, starting from the capital reached in the previous year and always accumulating the interest.

An annualized return of 5%, starting with a capital of 100, leads to this progression: 100.00 -> 105.00 -> 110.25 -> 115.76 -> 121.55 -> 127.63 ...

From the table, you can see that US stocks have provided approximately a 9% compounded annual return. Sounds fantastic, right? A nice, calm 9% annualized return. Unfortunately, it's not all that rosy...

Do you know why?

- The annualized return you saw earlier is calculated retrospectively, but in reality, it's not constant year after year.
- There are better years and worse years. Stock prices can rise to a "maximum" value and then crash, sometimes significantly. It will then take time for them to recover and reach new highs.
- It's highly likely that, sooner or later, you will want/need to liquidate your investment and cash out. And what if you are forced to sell at a strongly negative moment?

Since we like numbers, let's define how much the "maximum damage" would be. This metric, the worst loss compared to a previous market peak, is known as *Maximum Drawdown*.

How did the same Asset Classes we saw before perform in this regard?

Maximum Drawdown (%) - USD - as of Aug 31, 2023		
US Total Stock Market	-84.60%	(since Jan 1871)
US REITs	-68.30%	(since Jan 1928)
US Total Bond Market	-17.28%	(since Jan 1871)
US Cash	-0.42%	(since Jan 1871)
Commodities	-74.54%	(since Jan 1871)

Now, imagine this: you've invested everything in US stocks, and unfortunately, you have to liquidate the investment just at the moment when you are at -84% from the previous market peak.

You're so happy to have reached your first million dollars, and then what happens? In a short amount of time, you lose $840,000, and, worse still, you're forced to sell due to unforeseen circumstances. It's not pleasant at all.

Perhaps you're still in profit because you had reached a million starting from $100,000, but nonetheless, the loss incurred in the final phase is substantial.

How do you feel after these numbers? You went from the euphoria of +9% annualized to the drama of -84%? Yet everyone says that, in the long term, stocks are always a breeze...

At this point, I urge you, don't make the opposite mistake. Don't forcibly seek refuge in "safer" investments.

If you've noticed that the *Maximum Drawdown* for the US Cash asset is only -0.42%, with an honest +3.99% annualized, know that there's a catch here as well.

Remember inflation? Do you know how the *Maximum Drawdown* becomes, in "real" terms, considering inflation? It turns into a hefty -48.08%. And do you know how long it took to return to the peaks, also in "real" terms? 795 months, which is more than 66 years. You can verify everything for yourself on *LazyPortfolioEtf.com*.

What can we say? Stay strong and keep reading: you'll learn to examine different metrics and find the right portfolio for you.

And, above all, you won't be deceived by the only metric everyone shows: the return of the last period.

4. Building a Portfolio

Predicting rain doesn't count, building an ark does

WARREN BUFFETT

Financial resilience is built through careful planning and the construction of a solid investment portfolio.

It's not about predicting the ups and downs of the markets; it primarily requires a smart and diversified strategy.

Portfolio *Asset Allocation* is an investment management strategy that involves dividing your funds among various asset classes.

The main goal is to create a mix that aligns:

- with your financial goals
- with your risk tolerance
- with your investment time horizon

The perfect portfolio for you should meet all three of these requirements and should not simply aim to maximize portfolio returns.

Instruments

We know that the object of an investment is the Asset Class. But how do you acquire it?

There are various instruments that allow its purchase.

It is possible to buy **individual securities** (stocks or bonds). For example, if you want to buy the stocks of a specific company that you like, you can do so. If you are lucky or skilled, you may have potentially high returns if your chosen company grows.

However, in the opposite scenario, you risk incurring significant losses.

Buying individual securities requires in-depth research and constant market monitoring.

If you want to diversify, you have the option to buy a **mutual fund**. Mutual funds are investment vehicles that pool money from many investors and invest it in a diversified portfolio of stocks, bonds, or other securities.

Such funds are typically *actively* managed, as fund managers make proactive decisions on selecting and managing assets within the portfolio. Managers seek to achieve returns superior to a market benchmark by leveraging their expertise, analyses, and research.

They allow for broad diversification and are suitable for less experienced investors; however, they often come with relatively high management fees. These high fees can erode overall returns for investors over the years.

From a statistical perspective, a fund manager may outperform the market in certain years due to their skill in stock selection, but they could also underperform in others.

This variability means that, on average, the manager may achieve returns similar to those of the market overall. However, due to management fees, the investor might ultimately receive a lower return than what the market naturally offers.

This is where John "Jack" Bogle comes into play with his innovative idea: to create the first index mutual fund in 1975. His idea was that, instead of trying to beat the index and charging high costs, this fund would simply track the performance of the index in the long term, providing better returns at lower costs compared to actively managed funds.

Thus, **Exchange-Traded Funds (ETFs)** and **Index Funds** are born, which, at low or nearly zero costs, simply replicate a benchmark index, aiming to deliver the exact return of the index itself. This marks the birth of **passive investing**.

If the index gains +2% in a year, then a passive instrument replicating it will also gain +2%, net of management fees, which on average are around 0.20 - 0.30% (and even much less for the most popular indices).

Of course, if the index loses 2%, the passive instrument will also incur a 2% loss.

5. Passive Investing

The big money is not in the buying or selling, but in the waiting

CHARLIE MUNGER

Just like the choice of financial instruments, the investment strategy can be active or passive.

Simply buying passive management instruments is not enough to fully benefit from their features.

For example, let's consider an investor who decides to allocate a portion of their capital to an ETF that tracks the S&P 500, a widely representative index of U.S. stocks.

The passive aspect of the strategy lies in the fact that the investor does not try to manually select stocks to buy or time the market based on predictions.

However, if the investor starts making frequent purchases and sales of the ETF in response to economic news or market movements, this active management strategy could incur additional costs in the form of trading commissions and potentially compromise the long-term goal of passively tracking the index.

If an investor wishes to diversify, they can choose to build a portfolio with various low-cost index funds, each representing a specific asset class (e.g., stocks, bonds, and commodities).

The passive management strategy here involves purchasing these funds, holding onto them for an extended period, and reallocating the allocation only occasionally to maintain the desired diversification. In contrast, an investor who constantly monitors the portfolio and tries to time the market by moving money from one fund to another in response to market fluctuations is adopting an active management strategy, which can prove to be inefficient and costly in terms of commissions.

In summary, a passive investment strategy involves:

- selecting passive index funds / ETFs
- holding them in a disciplined manner without frequent trading

The idea is to go along with the market and reap the natural rewards it offers. If, instead, you try to beat the market, you are likely to be the one beaten, overwhelmed by transaction costs and errors.

Let's explore the advantages of the Passive Investing - ETF combination.

Advantages

Reduced Costs

As we already know, passively managed index funds and ETFs have significantly lower management fees compared to actively managed funds. This means that investors can retain a larger portion of their returns. Let's illustrate this with an example and compare:

- a passively managed index fund with a 0.1% annual fee
- an actively managed mutual fund with a 1.5% annual fee

Let's assume both perfectly replicated an index that yielded a 5% annualized return over 20 years. Let's say you invested $1,000.

Capital Growth

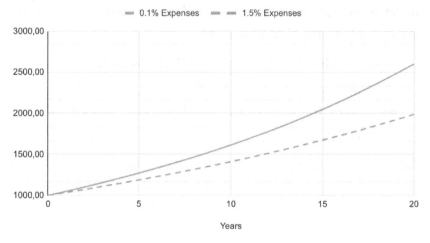

After 20 years, we would have reached:

- $2,603.21 for the passive fund
- $1,989.79 for the actively managed fund

The passive fund would have provided approximately 30% more.

Another aspect, still related to costs: a passive investment philosophy involves only a few transactions. For this reason, trading commission expenses will be very low.

Automatic Diversification

Indexed funds are designed to replicate the performance of a specific index, which means they offer automatic diversification within the portfolio.

Beyond the technicalities, and simplifying, it can be said that an ETF replicating the S&P 500 invests in all 500 companies included in that index, and therefore has the same performance as the index.

32

This way, you reduce the specific risk of investing in a single company and expose yourself to a broad category of assets, such as U.S. stocks in this case.

Transparency

ETFs and index funds provide complete transparency on their portfolios. Investors can easily see which assets are included in the fund and in what proportion. This transparency helps investors make informed decisions about the composition of their portfolios.

Reduction of Underperformance Risk

Many actively managed funds fail to consistently outperform the market in the long term.

Passive investing, by simply tracking the index, reduces the risk of underperformance compared to the benchmark market.

Ease of Access

ETFs and index funds are easily accessible through most online investment platforms.

This makes passive investing convenient and available to a wide range of investors, regardless of portfolio size.

Downsides

Limited Upside Potential / Outperformance

Passive investments simply track the performance of the index, so they cannot achieve higher returns.

If you aim to achieve returns superior to the market, you need to rely on an active fund manager who has the ability to select individual stocks or bonds that, in theory, could outperform the market.

Applying active management could make a difference during periods of generalized market crises.

Exposure to Declining Sectors

Indices may include companies or sectors that could be in decline or exposed to specific risks.

For example, if a company within an index is involved in a financial scandal, this news could negatively impact the index, and you will bear the consequences even if you have done nothing wrong in your investment strategy.

Inappropriate for all market conditions

As mentioned above, if we focus on the growth of the S&P 500 through an ETF, we may face challenges in a bearish market phase.

An active fund manager, on the other hand, might have the opportunity to manage short positions or remain in cash.

However, whether they can do so effectively at all times is subject to verification.

Risk of Overconcentration

If an index is heavily weighted in certain stocks or sectors, Passive Investing could lead to a potential overexposure to those assets.

The FTSE All-World stock index, covering the entire world, is exposed at the country level as follows:

Market allocation

United States	60.4%
Japan	6.3%
United Kingdom	3.9%
China	3.4%
France	2.9%
Canada	2.5%
Switzerland	2.4%
Germany	2.1%
Australia	2.0%
India	1.7%

(Source: Vanguard. As of 31 July 2023)

At the individual stock level, the exposure to individual stocks is as follows:

Holding Name	
Apple Inc.	4.36%
Microsoft Corp.	3.72%
Amazon.com Inc.	1.79%
NVIDIA Corp.	1.65%
Alphabet Inc. Class A	1.17%
Tesla Inc.	1.10%
Facebook Inc. Class A	1.05%
Alphabet Inc. Class C	1.03%
Berkshire Hathaway Inc. Class B	0.70%
UnitedHealth Group Inc.	0.70%

(Source: Vanguard. As of 31 July 2023)

An active fund, for example, would have the option to reduce exposure to the USA or Apple.

The choice between an active or passive investment strategy depends on your needs. Some investors may opt for a combination of both strategies to leverage the strengths of each based on market conditions.

We are not saying that active management is inherently bad: if you want to invest in niche or inefficient markets, the best choice is probably the active approach, as in this case, a manager's expertise could make a difference.

With a critical approach and a preliminary analysis of investments, you will surely be able to make the best choice or provide your trusted advisor with the right insights to assist you.

6. Lazy Portfolios

The ability to simplify means to eliminate the unnecessary so that the necessary may speak

HANS HOFMANN

It is vain to do with more what can be done with less

WILLIAM OF OCCAM

In the frenetic world of investments, where daily attention to markets and price fluctuations seems to be the norm, there is an approach that embraces tranquility and simplicity.

Lazy Portfolios are the epitome of passive investing. They have inspired us so much that we created a website to gather them, demonstrate how to implement them with ETFs, and share historical data.

What are they?

The term 'Lazy Portfolio' wasn't coined by a single individual or specific source but has become a common term in the investment world.

A Lazy Portfolio is a passive investment strategy that involves creating a relatively simple and well-diversified portfolio designed to require minimal effort on the part of the investor.

If you want to create a Lazy Portfolio, you need to follow some simple rules.

- Choose the assets that will make up your portfolio and the percentage weight of each (example: US Equities 40%, US Bonds 40%, Gold 20%). You can take inspiration from a famous Lazy Portfolio or create your own after thorough study. In the book, you'll find insights to make informed choices.
- Invest using passive instruments, low-cost ones, adhering to the percentages set in the previous step.
- At regular intervals (e.g., annually or every 6 months), reallocate the assets to their original percentages. In technical terms, this is called 'rebalancing' (we'll provide a numerical example shortly).

Quite lazy, isn't it? The points where your intervention is required are:

- At the beginning: when you need to invest for the first time, purchasing various ETFs or index funds.
- Every year (or every 6 months): when you need to rebalance the assets. Additionally, during this phase, you can invest new liquidity if you find it appropriate.

On your part, it requires a commitment of 1 or 2 days a year. Rebalancing is a crucial step in the strategy as it allows you to bring all assets back to their original weight, thus keeping the overall risk level of your portfolio intact.

How to rebalance your portfolio

Let's suppose your portfolio is composed as follows:

US Stocks: 40%

US Bonds: 40%

Gold: 20%

If, at the beginning of *Year 0*, you invest a total of $10,000, these would be the allocated amounts for each component:

US Stocks: $4,000 (40% of $10,000)

US Bonds: $4,000 (40% of $10,000)

Gold: $2,000 (20% of $10,000)

Suppose now that, as of December 31st, due to price fluctuations, these are the counter values of each asset in your portfolio.

		Year 0	
		Jan 1st	Dec 31st
Stocks	40%	4000	4600
Bonds	40%	4000	3800
Gold	20%	2000	1900
	SUM	10000	10300

The total portfolio value is now $10,300, and the weight of each asset is no longer the original one.

At this point, starting from the total of $10,300, we need to calculate the new amounts, still according to the proportions of 40%-40%-20%.

At the beginning of the new year, this should be the starting situation:

US Stocks: $4,120 (40% of $10,300)

US Bonds: $4,120 (40% of $10,300)

Gold: $2,060 (20% of $10,300)

		Year 0		Year 1	
		Jan 1st	Dec 31st	Jan 1st	Dec 31st
Stocks	40%	4000	4600	4120	.....
Bonds	40%	4000	3800	4120	.....
Gold	20%	2000	1900	2060	.....
	SUM	10000	10300	10300	.....

To achieve these amounts, it will be necessary to sell excess stocks and buy bonds and gold.

Thus, Year 1 will also pass, and by December 31st, we will once again have each asset with its new amount.

Let's assume that the new situation is as follows:

		Year 0		Year 1	
		Jan 1st	Dec 31st	Jan 1st	Dec 31st
Stocks	40%	4000	4600	4120	4080
Bonds	40%	4000	3800	4120	4300
Gold	20%	2000	1900	2060	2120
	SUM	10000	10300	10300	10500

The total portfolio is now worth $10,500. For the beginning of Year 2, we will once again need to calculate the correct amounts for the assets.

US Stocks: $4,200 (40% of $10,500)

US Bonds: $4,200 (40% of $10,500)

Gold: $2,100 (20% of $10,500)

		Year 0		Year 1		Year 2	
		Jan 1st	Dec 31st	Jan 1st	Dec 31st	Jan 1st	Dec 31st
Stocks	40%	4000	4600	4120	4080	4200	.....
Bonds	40%	4000	3800	4120	4300	4200	.....
Gold	20%	2000	1900	2060	2120	2100	.....
	SUM	10000	10300	10300	10500	10500	.....

You've understood by now; it's not complicated. All the simulations on *LazyPortfolioEtf.com* are done with this logic and involve rebalancing at the beginning of each year, as in the example we just provided.

On your end, if you prefer, you can also rebalance every six months or whenever you want. There is no inherently better strategy.

Remember that every time you buy or sell, you will likely pay a commission to your bank. Also, depending on the tax regulations in your country, selling for a profit may incur a tax on the gain, a factor not considered in the website's calculations.

In case you want to invest new capital, you have the option, during the purchase phase, to align the assets with the established weights. Let's take an example, again for the beginning of year 2.

At the end of year 1, your portfolio is worth, as we've seen, $10,500. Suppose you want to invest an additional $1,500. This means that, by the beginning of year 2, your invested capital will be $10,500 + $1,500 = $12,000. The weights of the assets should then be:

US Stocks: $4,800 (40% of $12,000)

US Bonds: $4,800 (40% of $12,000)

Gold: $2,400 (20% of $12,000)

You will need to buy the missing portion to reach these values. See the details below:

		Year 1				Year 2	
		Jan 1st	Dec 31st			Jan 1st	Dec 31st
Stocks	40%	4120	4080	Buy	720	4800	.....
Bonds	40%	4120	4300	Buy	500	4800	.....
Gold	20%	2060	2120	Buy	280	2400	.....
	SUM	10300	10500	Sum	1500	12000	.....

In practice, if your plan involves the periodic investment of new funds, this way you can balance the weights of the assets without being forced to sell (and therefore pay taxes).

This "trick" may not always be possible because if the new funds are limited, you may not have a sufficient budget to bring the weights back to the desired values. However, if you are in a position to do so, take advantage of it.

The most used assets

The most efficient tools for replicating broad market indices were born in the USA. Consequently, the majority of the most famous Lazy Portfolios also use assets related to the American market.

Talking about stocks, the most popular assets are:

- US Total Stock Market
- US Real Estate
- US Large Caps
- US Small Caps
- US Growth Stocks

- US Value Stocks
- US Dividend Stocks
- Total World Stocks
- World Developed Markets
- Emerging Markets

As for the bond market, we have:

- US Total Bonds Market
- US T-Bills (max 12 months maturity)
- US 1-3 Years Treasuries
- US 3-7 Years Treasuries
- US Long Term Treasuries (20+ years)
- US Inflation-Linked Bonds
- International Bonds
- Emerging Market Bonds
- Corporate Bonds
- High Yield Bonds

In the commodities sector, to conclude:

- Gold
- Commodity Basket

Passive replication instruments are ideal for replicating these types of broad and diversified indices.

With few exceptions, in the most famous Lazy Portfolios, you will never find sectoral or niche asset classes. Choosing such an asset would already imply a minimum level of "active" investment approach.

Nevertheless, nothing prohibits such an approach. On *LazyPortfolioEtf.com*, we also have portfolios exposed to specific sectors (e.g., Energy) or indices composed based on particular logics (e.g., momentum, equal weight).

The important thing is always to invest consciously, understanding the limits of each strategy.

Why implement a Lazy Portfolio?

In certain aspects, Lazy Portfolios prove to be fundamental in investment management.

Firstly, they can represent the backbone or the "core" part of a portfolio. Their well-diversified nature, composed of broadly representative asset classes, allows investors to build a solid foundation on which to base their strategy.

This central component of the portfolio provides a certain stability, which is often lacking in highly active strategies.

Stability, indeed, is the second key aspect offered by Lazy Portfolios. We don't mean to suggest that Lazy Portfolios always ensure low volatility or risk, but at least investors know they can rely on a reliable and quantifiable overall performance in the long term, given the extensive historical data on which these portfolios have been "put to the test."

Once the goal (or goals) for investing is set, the use of Lazy Portfolios allows investors to rely on a time-tested approach. On the *LazyPortfolioEtf.com* website, there are numerous assets for which a historical series dating back to 1871 is available.

The returns that these passive strategies have provided over the years, simply by following benchmark indices, should encourage investors not to take on additional risks due to individual choices of niche stocks/sectors or market timing.

An active approach often entails a series of challenges. Selecting individual stocks or allocating assets based on market forecasts requires in-depth knowledge and constant vigilance.

In these cases, the bet is twofold: firstly, you need to identify the asset or sector to invest in, and, non-trivially, you must do it at the right time and not too late. Delaying such an investment could mean entering a market where prices have already risen enough, and therefore, there is no longer anticipation of extra returns.

That being said, we absolutely do not want to demonize the active investment strategy. If the wealth allows for it, and for a limited portion of the capital, it is perfectly legitimate to seek higher returns based on personal speculations or suggestions from your financial coach or trusted advisor. The key is to be aware that this part of the portfolio is certainly subject to higher risk and the possibility of loss, even in relatively short periods.

Common Investor Mistakes

The true ally of every investor who invests wisely is time.

There is no investment that can make you rich quickly: if the prospects are such, either you are facing a monstrous risk or it's a scam.

The prime example in recent times has been Bitcoin. Those who invested when only the suburban nerds were talking about it are now tremendously wealthy. On the contrary, those who invested recently are deeply dissatisfied.

The future? No one knows.

We won't bore you with advanced psychology theories, but perhaps the weak point of many investors is that it's challenging to *let go* and admit that it's the market that provides returns, not human actions.

Fortunately, as human beings, we are curious and inclined to make hypotheses about the future, but often we don't realize that our predictions are based on our past experiences. Additionally, when evaluating the information available to us, we give more weight to those that confirm our initial hypothesis and beliefs.

If we want to embrace the theory of passive investing, we must resist the temptation to predict the future. Or, if we really want to do it, let's limit ourselves to sharing it during a friendly gathering, without putting our wealth at risk.

2022 was a peculiar year: it's not often that stocks and bonds experience such significant declines simultaneously. For this reason, the 60% stocks and 40% bonds portfolio, considered the quintessential balanced portfolio, yielded a -16.95% return for the year.

That's why the motto of recent times has been: 'the 60/40 portfolio is dead.' Have you heard it before? We conducted a search on Google (it was September 2023), and we typed 'Is 60/40 portfolio dead?' We got 348,000 results well distributed among articles, forums, and videos.

Should we think that we should no longer invest in the 60/40 portfolio?

Before 2022, another particularly negative year was 2008, with a -19.44%, in the midst of the subprime mortgage crisis. Contrary to the predictions of the time, we survived. Do you know what happened to the 60/40 portfolio from 2008 until 2022? All positive years and only one negative (2018, with -3.17%).

Another typical mistake is not adhering to the strategy in terms of time horizon and allocation.

Every day, while browsing through groups and online forums, we always find someone saying, "I want to start a decade-long investment plan. Which ETFs do you recommend?".

Firstly, it's already a mistake to seek financial advice from random strangers. How many of these people do you think are still carrying out the accumulation plan? Do you really believe that in 10 years, we'll all gather somewhere in the world for a reunion and there will be a lot of us?

Perhaps in 1-2-3 decades, they will still be investing, but on average, they will have changed their asset allocation every year. In contrast to the lazy investor, who only does calculations for rebalancing at the end of the year and goes to celebrate New Year's.

7. Interpreting Metrics

In God we trust; all others must bring data

W. EDWARDS DEMING

We are in love with data. It is a fundamental factor in choosing an investment, although not the only one.

Various important metrics can be derived from the data, allowing us to assess the effectiveness of a strategy.

This is something that everyone should consider, without distinction between passive and active investors. Whether you are a fan of ETFs or other instruments, it doesn't matter. It is always useful to know how to evaluate the results of an investment strategy for two reasons:

- to compare it with a benchmark (i.e., a "yardstick")
- to understand if, given past results, it might be suitable for you

That said, we already know the typical objection: past performance is not indicative of future results.

Of course, we completely agree with this, but we want to make you reflect with an example.

Suppose you are a skydiving enthusiast and love to do it whenever you can. You can choose, at the time of the jump, between two different parachute models:

- one that, based on past statistics, has encountered problems in 30% of cases
- another one that has never reported particular issues so far.

Which one do you choose?

There are no guarantees about the future, but we imagine that you would choose the second model. Even though you know that, unfortunately, it could happen that you might be the first to encounter issues...

The same goes for investments: would you choose one that, in the past, even in favorable market conditions, has performed poorly? And why should it perform better in the future?

But let's take it step by step and understand what "has performed poorly" means. Do we all have a unanimous answer on this issue? Let's see...

The most interesting metrics

Every metric is important because it provides its own "point of view."

Depending on your sensitivity and your goal, you will surely prefer some metrics over others.

There are investors who fear risk: they are willing to earn little but absolutely do not want to take risks. On the other hand, there are those who aim to maximize profit, knowing (hopefully) that they may endure significant temporary losses.

Do you know well which numbers to look at to precisely define which category you belong to? Do you know the odds of failing the goal based on your choice? Are you sure you've always examined the most effective metrics for you?

All the metrics you'll find in the book are easily retrievable on the *LazyPortfolioEtf.com* website. You can find them in the details of the portfolios and individual ETFs, and you can also obtain them through your own asset allocation simulation.

Let's start with the metrics we will use in our strategies when we analyze individual asset classes and their combinations in portfolios.

Compound Annual Growth Rate

The Compound Annual Growth Rate, often abbreviated as CAGR, is a financial measure that represents the growth rate of an investment over a specific period, taking into account compounded interest.

In other words, CAGR indicates how much an investment grows annually, assuming that all gains are reinvested and added to the capital.

Very often, it is the only metric presented when an investment is advertised. Sometimes, the only prominently visible information is: "*The ABC fund has yielded 3% compound annual growth over the last 3 years*".

This means that if you had invested $1,000 in that fund three years ago, you would now have $1,092.73. Every year, the capital increases by 3% compared to the previous year.

Capital Growth		
		1000.00
Year 1	3%	1030.00
Year 2	3%	1060.90
Year 3	3%	1092.73

The formula to calculate the CAGR (in percentage) is as follows:

$$CAGR = \left(\left(\frac{EV}{BV} \right)^{\frac{1}{n}} - 1 \right) \times 100$$

where:

EV = Ending value

BV = Beginning value

n = Number of years

(Source: *investopedia.com*)

This is the formula used on *LazyPortfolioEtf.com* to calculate the annualized compound return for periods greater than or equal to one year.

For periods shorter than one year, the annualized return is not calculated, but rather the overall return, which takes into account only the final and initial values of the capital.

$$\left(\left(\frac{EV}{BV} \right) - 1 \right) \times 100$$

If, for example, in one month, you invested $1,000 and now you have $1,100, then you have achieved a return of 10% (not annual but overall).

Let's take another example from *LazyPortfolioEtf.com*:

	Return (%) as of Aug 31, 2023						
	1M	6M	1Y	5Y	10Y	30Y	MAX (~153Y)
Warren Buffett Portfolio	-1.46	13.51	14.47	10.09	11.54	9.47	8.68
US Inflation Adjusted return	-1.89	11.22	10.42	5.84	8.55	6.77	6.42
Components							
VV USD Vanguard Large-Cap	-1.64	14.77	15.88	10.95	12.64	10.01	8.97
SHY USD iShares 1-3 Year Treasury Bond	0.41	1.73	0.98	0.86	0.68	2.97	4.42

Returns over 1 year are annualized | Available data source: since Jan 1871
US Inflation is updated to Aug 2023. Current inflation (annualized) is **1Y: 3.67%** , **5Y: 4.02%** , **10Y: 2.76%** , **30Y: 2.54%**

This portfolio, as of August 31, 2023, returned -1.46% in the last month and 11.54% annually over the last 10 years.

In other words, the story is as follows:

- You invest $1,000 on September 1, 2013
- After 10 years, on August 31, 2023, your capital is $2,980.

In practice, you would have tripled your capital in 10 years. Fantastic, right? If you thought only about this, be careful! You are judging a portfolio after examining only one time period (Sep 2013 - Aug 2023), which may have been particularly (or unusually) profitable.

Let's do a test: let's examine the same portfolio but choose another time frame. Let's take a trip back in time to December 31, 2008.

LazyPortfolioEtf.com didn't exist yet, but the page for the same portfolio would have looked like this:

	Return (%) as of Dec 31, 2008						
	1M	6M	1Y	5Y	10Y	30Y	MAX (~138Y)
Warren Buffett Portfolio	1.66	-25.09	-32.35	-0.97	-0.37	10.68	8.27
US Inflation Adjusted return	2.72	-22.03	-32.41	-3.54	-2.82	6.57	6.08
Components							
VV USD Vanguard Large-Cap	1.87	-28.86	-36.68	-1.83	-1.23	10.84	8.47
SHY USD iShares 1-3 Year Treasury Bond	0.56	4.53	6.62	3.98	4.83	7.72	4.82

Returns over 1 year are annualized | Available data source: since Jan 1871
US Inflation is updated to Dec 2008. Current inflation (annualized) is **1Y: 0.09%** , **5Y: 2.67%** , **10Y: 2.52%** , **30Y: 3.85%**

The story is very different in this case. On December 31, 2008, the annualized return over 10 years would have been -0.37%.

In practice, this would have happened:

- You invest $1,000 on January 1, 1998.
- After 10 years, on December 31, 2008, your capital is $963.

Same portfolio, different historical period... negative return over 10 years!

Back to our times. If you decide to invest today, what will the situation be in a decade? No one knows.

To decide if a portfolio suits you, it's not enough to look at the returns of the last period; always remember this!

What should you look at then? Let's find out right away.

Rolling returns

The rolling returns are an analytical technique used to evaluate the performance of an investment or portfolio over various consecutive periods, gradually shifting the evaluation period.

This analysis helps understand how the investment's performance may vary over time and provides a more in-depth view of its stability and consistency.

Here is how rolling returns are calculated:

- Choose the data source to use. For example, you can calculate rolling returns considering the entire available database or only the last 30 years.
- Decide on the period for calculating rolling returns: 3 years, 5 years, 10 years, ...

- For each month, calculate the rolling return for the specific period, gradually moving month by month.

Let's go through a practical example. We want to calculate the rolling returns over 10 years, considering the last 30 years of the database.

The goal is to discover the 10-year returns for all periods in the last three decades (remember earlier when we told you that it's not enough to look at just the latest?).

Suppose, for example, that the starting point of the database is September 1993 - August 2023 (30 years).

Let's calculate the returns for each 10-year interval. For example:

September 1993 - August 2003 → 5.4% annualized

October 1993 - September 2003 → 5.6% annualized

November 1993 - October 2003 → 5.1% annualized

- - - - - - - -

August 2013 - July 2023 → -0.8% annualized

September 2013 - August 2023 → -0.7% annualized

Once everything is calculated for each possible interval and duration, on *LazyPortfolioEtf.com*, we generate a graph like this. The returns are annualized (compounded).

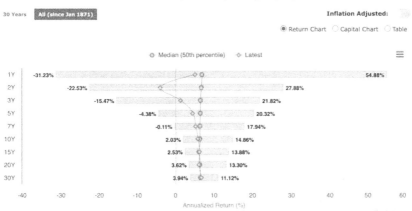

What does this graph tell us?

It tells us that, from 1871, the one-year return of the portfolio has been variable and ranged between -31.23% and +54.88%. We shouldn't be deceived by the fact that the latest year was positive (symbol "Latest"), as it is just one of the available measurements.

Let's look at the rolling returns for 10 years. It's nice to discover that, for this portfolio, the minimum return has been 2.03%. This means that it has never gone negative holding the investment for 10 years.

On the website, you can also view the information in tabular format. Here you can see something interesting.

Rolling Period	Worst Period			15th Percentile		50th Percentile		85th Percentile		Best Period			Latest	Negative Periods
	Ann. Return	From To	Growth of 1$	Ann. Return	Growth of 1$	Ann. Return	Growth of 1$	Ann. Return	Growth of 1$	Ann. Return	From To	Growth of 1$		
1Y	-31.23	07/1931 06/1932	0.68$	-1.20	0.98$	6.97	1.06$	15.02	1.15$	54.88	07/1932 06/1933	1.54$	5.14	18.45%
2Y	-22.53	06/1930 05/1932	0.60$	1.19	1.02$	6.73	1.13$	12.77	1.27$	27.88	07/1984 06/1986	1.63$	-3.92	10.83%
3Y	-15.47	07/1929 06/1932	0.60$	2.57	1.07$	6.51	1.20$	11.56	1.38$	21.82	08/1984 07/1987	1.80$	1.37	3.95%
5Y	-4.38	06/1927 05/1932	0.79$	3.55	1.19$	6.49	1.36$	10.40	1.63$	20.32	04/1982 03/1987	2.52$	4.58	2.26%
7Y	-0.11	07/1925 06/1932	0.99$	4.08	1.32$	6.36	1.54$	10.15	1.96$	17.94	04/1980 03/1987	3.17$	5.25	0.11%
10Y	2.03	09/1929 08/1939	1.22$	4.42	1.54$	6.41	1.86$	9.30	2.43$	14.86	10/1981 09/1991	3.99$	5.93	0.00%
15Y	2.53	09/1881 08/1896	1.45$	4.88	2.04$	6.22	2.47$	9.02	3.65$	13.88	08/1982 07/1997	7.02$	6.22	0.00%
20Y	3.62	07/1901 06/1921	2.03$	4.96	2.63$	6.41	3.46$	9.03	5.63$	13.30	04/1980 03/2000	12.14$	6.14	0.00%
30Y	3.94	06/1902 05/1932	3.18$	5.26	4.65$	6.49	6.59$	9.26	14.25$	11.12	07/1970 06/2000	23.63$	6.79	0.00%

Here, for each rolling period, you have the worst and best values, along with the period in which they occurred.

You also have the percentile values. For example, the 15th percentile means that in 15% of cases, the return was lower.

Take the row for the rolling 7-year return:

- in 15% of cases, the return was lower than 4.08% annualized. Or, if you prefer, the return was equal to or higher than 4.08% in 85% of cases.
- 6.36% is the median annualized return. In 50% of cases, the return was lower, and in 50%, it was equal to or higher.
- in 85% of cases, the return was lower than 10.15% annualized. In 15% of cases, it was at least equal to or higher.

The *15th percentile* is often called the **baseline return** (as on the excellent *PortfolioCharts.com* website). It is used when estimating future returns in pessimistic terms. It is a good parameter for assessing the resilience of returns, and we will use it for our evaluations later in the book.

The *50th percentile* is often called the **median return**. Be careful not to confuse it with the arithmetic mean. It tells us that in 50% of cases, the return was equal to or higher than that value, and in 50% of cases, it was lower.

The *85th percentile* is often called the **stretch return** (again, we borrow this definition from *PortfolioCharts.com*). In return analysis, it represents the "optimistic" estimate.

For each rolling return, in the "*Negative Periods*" column, you can see how many times you would have lost money for that time horizon. Let's take the example of the 7-year rolling return row: only in 0.11% of cases would you have lost money over a 7-year time horizon. We will use this metric and call it **%Fail**.

In conclusion, rolling returns are crucial for assessing performance over time. They provide a clearer view of performance consistency and allow you to evaluate whether the return has been consistently positive or has shown significant variations.

Standard Deviation

The standard deviation is a statistical measure that indicates the dispersion (variability) of a set of data relative to their mean.

In other words, it represents how much the data points in a sample tend to deviate from the mean.

A higher standard deviation indicates greater data dispersion, while a lower standard deviation indicates less variability.

In the evaluation of an investment, the standard deviation is calculated on the returns.

If you're interested, the formula we use is as follows:

$$\sigma = \sqrt{\frac{\sum_{i=1}^{n}(x_i - \bar{x})^2}{n}}$$

where:

x_i = Value of the ith point in the data set

$\bar{x}$ = The mean value of the data set

n = The number of data points in the data set

(derived by Investopedia.com)

In our case, the individual "data points" used for the calculation are the individual monthly returns. So, X(1) is the return for month 1, X(2) for month 2, and so on.

With the described formula, we measure the root-mean-square deviation (variability) of the returns relative to the mean return over a specified period.

Expanding on the topic, since we start with monthly returns, if we want to think about normalized and annualized results, we need to multiply by the square root of 12.

The higher the variability of returns, the higher the standard deviation. If returns are less variable, they tend to be closer to the mean value: in this sense, they are more "predictable." An investment with less variable returns is seen as "less risky."

That's a concise summary:

Variable returns → High standard deviation → More risk

Less variable returns → Low standard deviation → Less risk

Everything is fine, but there's a problem. The value of standard deviation is simply a number that measures risk in the classical sense. However, it is not a number that provides a clear idea of how prices have fluctuated. At most, we can use it to compare two investments and understand which one was riskier.

Furthermore, let's think about it for a moment: if an investment consistently provided a fixed -1% monthly return, then the returns would have a standard deviation of 0 because they never deviated from the mean (-1%, in this case). Would you still consider something like that a 'low-risk' investment?

For these reasons, on *LazyPortfolioEtf.com*, we have calculated and included standard deviation for the sake of completeness, but we do not consider it primary for choosing your preferred portfolio.

The purists are now setting the book on fire: forgive us, we hope to make up for it with the next metrics, which we believe are more effective.

Drawdown

A Drawdown is the measure of the loss in value of an investment relative to its previous peak.

Example: your portfolio reached a peak value of $10,000 and has now fallen to $8,000. In other words, it has lost 20% from the highs. This is the drawdown.

For each portfolio or ETF, on *LazyPortfolioEtf.com*, you will find a dedicated section that shows the main drawdowns, both graphically and in tabular form.

It's one of the most important metrics because a "large" drawdown indicates a significant loss from the previous peak, and this could suggest a higher level of risk or greater volatility in the investment's performance.

Let's try to simplify things with an example. In the following graph, the curve is the so-called *equity line* of an investment, representing the capital growth. The shaded areas, on the other hand, highlight some periods where the capital remains below the previously reached peak. Those are the drawdown periods.

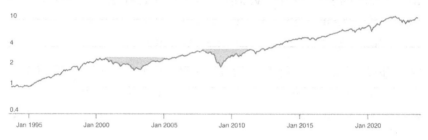

To get an idea of the actual loss and duration of drawdowns, the following representation, which you can always find on *LazyPortfolioEtf.com*, is more effective. We recommend taking a look at both the graph and the table.

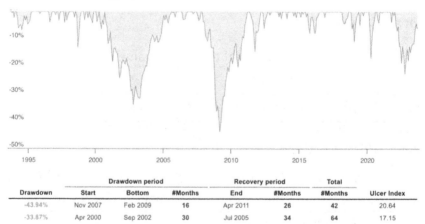

	Drawdown period			Recovery period		Total	
Drawdown	Start	Bottom	#Months	End	#Months	#Months	Ulcer Index
-43.94%	Nov 2007	Feb 2009	16	Apr 2011	26	42	20.64
-33.87%	Apr 2000	Sep 2002	30	Jul 2005	34	64	17.15

The most extended drawdown (maximum drawdown) started in November 2007 and hit its lowest point in February 2009 (-43.94%). For an inexperienced eye, these values were not so evident from the equity line graph.

Imagine what it means to experience such a drawdown: everything calm in November 2007, and then, after 16 months, you find yourself with a -43%. And not only that, it will take another 26 months to return to the levels of November 2007.

Using more specific terms:

- Drawdown time: 16 months
- Recovery time: 26 months
- Underwater period: 16+26=42 months

The term 'Underwater Period' perfectly captures the idea of the breath-holding that the worst drawdowns induce in the investor. This term is borrowed from *PortfolioVisualizer.com*, a fantastic site that allows for simulations of stock, ETF, and fund portfolios.

Not necessarily the drawdown with the most pronounced loss is also the longest. In the example above, we see that the second drawdown on the list reached a bottom of -33%, but it had a longer underwater period (64 months).

In evaluating an investment, therefore, always calculate or retrieve information on:

- Maximum Drawdown (the one with the worst loss)
- Longest Drawdown (the one with the longer underwater period)

For those who want more, it's interesting to examine the Ulcer Index as well. It is calculated very similarly to the standard deviation and is an indicator of how much the average deviation of drawdown points is from the previously reached peak.

The higher the Ulcer Index, the more the 'pain' caused by the drawdown in terms of depth and duration. It's not a numerical value that provides a clear and immediate idea, but it is useful for making comparisons between different investments.

Longest negative period

Based on what we've seen in the previous section, it might seem that the longest period of suffering corresponds to the underwater period of the longest drawdown.

Unfortunately, this is not the case: numerous drawdown periods can occur in sequence, so there's not even time to recover from the first before falling into the next.

Let's take the same graph shown earlier to have a clearer view:

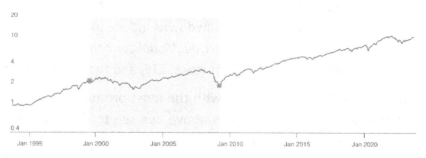

Let's consider the highlighted period and the two points marked on the graph. Investing at the beginning of the period and divesting at the end, it's clear that you would have experienced a negative return because the final capital is less than the initial capital (referring to the 2 highlighted points).

We intentionally chose a more extended period than a single drawdown to show you that it's possible to incur a loss even for longer periods than those indicated in the drawdowns.

We have named this metric 'Longest negative period', which corresponds to the longest period for which a negative overall return was recorded.

Let's take an example: if an investment had a longest negative period of 80 months, it means that there existed a time interval (of 80 months) that produced a negative return.

But it also means that:

- any interval of at least 81 months has always guaranteed a zero or positive return.
- rolling returns starting from 81 months have never been negative."

This last one is, in turn, an important metric. We can rename it the '*Safe Holding Period*': it tells us, historically, what has been the minimum period that has guaranteed us a non-negative return. Having held the investment for 81 months, you would never have lost money, according to past statistics.

If we want to be formal, we can say that:

Safe Holding Period = Longest Negative Period + 1

These metrics are challenging to find and are meaningful only for assets with a very extensive history. If you happen to study on *PortfolioCharts.com*, you'll find these concepts under the '*Drawdown*' section.

By choice, entirely legitimate, the author does not consider a drawdown closed until the quotations have permanently recovered. In his case, therefore, the longest negative period is that of the longest drawdown.

Risk-adjusted metrics

When you make purchases online or at the mall, have you ever looked at the quality/price ratio of a product? What does it mean?

It means that if a product doesn't have outstanding quality but still costs very little, then it can be a good buy.

Similarly, a not-so-impressive return can still be attractive if obtained with low risk. In this regard, there are metrics that relate return and risk.

Below, we list our favorite risk-adjusted metrics, and we'll let you know upfront that they're not the traditional metrics you often see.

Like all other metrics, they are calculated over a reference period. Suppose, for example, we want to calculate them over the last 50 years (but, of course, you can choose different periods).

Return / Maximum Drawdown

You take the annualized return of the last 50 years and divide it by the maximum drawdown, also from the last 50 years, in absolute value.

For example, return: 8.5% annualized; maximum drawdown: -35%. The ratio is 8.5/35 = 0.24.

Baseline 15Y Return / Maximum Drawdown

You take the 15-year rolling returns, calculated over the last fifty years. Then, you determine the baseline return, which is the rolling return corresponding to the 15th percentile (as you'll recall, it's the minimum rolling return, excluding the worst 15% of cases). After that, you divide the baseline return by the maximum drawdown, also from the last 50 years, in absolute value.

For example, baseline 15-year rolling return: 3.5% annualized; maximum drawdown: -35%. The ratio is 3.5/35 = 0.10.

If you prefer, in the same way, you can also use the baseline 10-year return as the numerator. You can do this if, for example, you have a more limited database.

You can use your imagination and calculate the risk-adjusted indicators that you prefer. You can use, for example, the standard deviation as the denominator. In that case, you would have the indicators:

Return / Standard Deviation

Baseline 15Y (10Y) Return / Standard Deviation

If you are wondering, instead, what the "classic" risk-adjusted performance metrics are:

Sharpe Ratio: it is the ratio of return (net of the risk-free rate) to standard deviation.

Sortino Ratio: it is like the Sharpe Ratio, but, in the denominator, it has the "negative" standard deviation (downside standard deviation), calculated only on values below the average of returns.

These metrics, for the classical study of return/risk associated with a return, are fundamental.

In our asset allocation choices, we have ignored them because we preferred more direct and clear metrics, but, of course, for your evaluations, you can consider them.

You can still find them on *LazyPortfolioEtf.com*, where, to evaluate the risk-free return, we used the performance of an ETF that replicates the ultra-short-term (1-3 months) US government bond yield.

8. The diversification effect

The only investors who shouldn't diversify are those who are right 100% of the time

SIR JOHN TEMPLETON

Diversification, a fundamental pillar of wealth management, is conceived as a strategic approach that goes beyond the mere distribution of investments.

In the financial context, diversification involves judiciously spreading investments across various assets or sectors. The evaluation and effectiveness of such a practice can be observed through specific metrics.

Such an approach, aimed at risk dispersion, represents an essential component in constructing a well-balanced and informed portfolio, capable of tackling the dynamics and uncertainties of financial markets in a more robust and calculated manner.

Individual assets

Let's consider 4 assets and some specific metrics. In this example, calculations are performed over the last 30 years and updated as of September 2023.

Data source: last 30Y - as of Sep 2023

Etf Ticker	Investment Theme	Max Draw-down (%)	Longest Negative Period	Baseline 15Y Roll. Return (%)	Median 15Y Roll. Return (%)	Stretch 15Y Roll. Return (%)
VTI	US Total Stock Market	-50.84	11Y 7M	5.30	7.55	9.95
BIL	US 1-3 Month T-Bills	-0.42	8Y 9M	0.86	1.33	3.17
TLT	US 20+ Year Treasury Bonds	-44.73	12Y 0M*	5.80	7.02	8.10
GLD	Gold	-42.91	12Y 1M*	6.27	8.84	10.48

* in progress

Examine the Longest Negative Period measured for each of these assets. In the best-case scenario (BIL), it was 8 years and 9 months, with a median annualized return of 1.33% over 15 years. Is it really worth it?

If we look at the other assets, the median return over 15 years increases, but Drawdown and Longest Negative Period worsen significantly.

Assets, taken individually, may have unsatisfactory metrics due to their intrinsic characteristics and market fluctuations. Each asset has its own risk and return profile, influenced by specific factors such as economic, political, or sectoral conditions.

However, when different types of assets are aggregated in a portfolio, diversification often allows for a more even distribution of the overall portfolio risk so that any losses associated with a particular asset can be offset by gains in others.

Asset mix

There is a very famous Lazy Portfolio, created by Harry Browne: the *Permanent Portfolio*. We will see it later.

This portfolio consists of the 4 assets mentioned in the previous example, each with a weight of 25%.

Let's see how the metrics change in this case:

Etf Ticker	Investment Theme	Max Draw-down (%)	Longest Negative Period	Baseline 15Y Roll. Return (%)	Median 15Y Roll. Return (%)	Stretch 15Y Roll. Return (%)
VTI	US Total Stock Market	-50.84	11Y 7M	5.30	7.55	9.95
BIL	US 1-3 Month T-Bills	-0.42	8Y 9M	0.86	1.33	3.17
TLT	US 20+ Year Treasury Bonds	-44.73	12Y 0M*	5.80	7.02	8.10
GLD	Gold	-42.91	12Y 1M*	6.27	8.84	10.48
	VTI - BIL - TLT - GLD	-15.92	3Y 3M*	6.62	7.18	7.55

* in progress

The maximum drawdown is astonishing when compared to that of individual assets (excluding BIL). We are at just over -16%.

Even more surprising is the Longest Negative Period, only 3 years and 3 months (although, as of September 2023, it was still in progress). This is far from the 8, 11, and 12 years of the other assets.

Over 15 years, considering all rolling returns, we have a baseline return of 6.62%, which is higher than that of all individual components.

Not to mention the median return (7.18%) and stretch return (7.55%), which are quite respectable.

With this example, you clearly understand how diversification is *fundamental*.

We also point out another detail: in the Permanent Portfolio, the *variability of returns* is more limited.

Let's explain this further by looking at the numbers: excluding the worst 15% and the best 15% of cases, the 15-year rolling return varies between 6.62% and 7.55%. In other words, in 70% of cases (100% - 15% - 15% = 70%), the return is between 6.62% and 7.55%.

Let's try to estimate this indicator, even in an approximate and non-academic way, to get an idea of what we are saying.

We can calculate the return delta between Baseline and Stretch return and relate it to the median return.

$$Return\ Variability\ =\ \frac{Stretch\ return - Baseline\ Return}{Median\ Return}$$

Etf Ticker	Investment Theme	Baseline 15Y Roll. Return (%)	Median 15Y Roll. Return (%)	Stretch 15Y Roll. Return (%)	Delta Baseline - Stretch (%)	Variability = Delta / Median
VTI	US Total Stock Market	5.30	7.55	9.95	4,65	61,59%
BIL	US 1-3 Month T-Bills	0.86	1.33	3.17	2,31	173,68%
TLT	US 20+ Year Treasury Bonds	5.80	7.02	8.10	2,30	32,76%
GLD	Gold	6.27	8.84	10.48	4,21	47,62%
	VTI - BIL - TLT - GLD	6.62	7.18	7.55	0,93	12,95%

The Permanent Portfolio, compared to individual assets, also provides a striking result in this case.

With low variability of returns, it is possible to estimate a long-term return with less likelihood of error (or with less 'dispersion'). And all of this doesn't even depend on the historical moment when you start investing: in 15 years (to cite the example), the return will likely be within a narrow range.

This last aspect, even if formulated differently, is a concept related to "*Start Date Sensitivity*", which you can find in the analyses on *PortfolioCharts.com*.

A well-diversified portfolio solves the eternal dilemma: when is the best time to invest? If you haven't invested yet, the best time is always now, little changes.

But then, to reap these benefits, is it enough to mix a few assets randomly? Clearly not. The best mix is created when the portfolio contains assets that are uncorrelated with each other

Correlation

Correlation is a statistical measure that expresses the relationship between two variables.

The correlation can be positive, negative, or zero, depending on how the two variables "move" together.

On *LazyPortfolioEtf.com*, to calculate correlation coefficients, we have used the *Pearson correlation coefficient*.

Without delving into the mathematical formula, we can say that this index measures the *strength* and *direction* of the linear relationship between two variables. Its value ranges from -1 to 1, where:

- 1 indicates a perfectly positive correlation: the two variables always move together. If A rises, B also rises. If A falls, B also falls.
- -1 indicates a perfectly negative correlation: the two variables always move in opposite directions. If A rises, B falls. If A falls, B rises.
- 0 indicates that there is no correlation between the two variables: the movements of A and B are uncorrelated. The variables are practically independent.

In the case of the Permanent Portfolio, these are the correlation indices among the various assets that make up the portfolio, calculated over the last three decades.

Asset	VTI	BIL	TLT	GLD
VTI	-	-0.03	-0.14	0.06
BIL	-0.03	-	0.04	-0.01
TLT	-0.14	0.04	-	0.21
GLD	0.06	-0.01	0.21	-

As you can see, all the coefficients are low in absolute value. Some are even slightly negative. This means that the assets are essentially decorrelated.

If you can find such a mix, diversification is likely to be effective.

Unfortunately, over time, correlation coefficients can change. Let's take the same assets and calculate the correlations over the last 12 months. The example is updated to September 2023.

Asset	VTI	BIL	TLT	GLD
VTI	-	-0.45	0.51	0.36
BIL	-0.45	-	-0.05	-0.14
TLT	0.51	-0.05	-	0.87
GLD	0.36	-0.14	0.87	-

Regarding BIL, the correlations have decreased, but in other cases, they have increased significantly. This means that, in the last 12 months, these assets have moved more often in the same direction (up or down).

If the direction is upward, that's not a problem; we don't complain. The issue arises when all assets decline simultaneously.

These negative periods are part of normal market behavior, as we have seen.

Statistically, there will be positive and less positive periods: history tells us that.

9. Time Horizons and Objectives

A goal properly set is halfway reached.

ZIG ZIGLAR

Certainly, you may have heard that for a short time horizon, you should necessarily consider bond investments. Conversely, for a long-term horizon, pure equities are the best choice.

We won't tell you that these indications are wrong, but we want to provide you with an additional perspective, a different methodology that will assist you in choosing asset allocation based on your time horizon.

You can then focus on the metrics most suitable for you.

Objective: Long Term (15+ years)

Are you interested only in long-term returns? Never focus on the performance of the last period! Instead, examine these metrics, always calculated over a historical period of at least thirty years:

- Long term (15Y) baseline rolling return
- Long term (15Y) median rolling return

If you prefer, also consider:

- Long term (15Y) worst rolling return
- Long term (15Y) rolling return - %fail
- Maximum drawdown
- Longest Negative Period

We consider 15 years as long term. The real challenge is to stay confident and patient throughout this time. Regarding returns, over such a horizon, the market will likely provide them naturally.

Do 15 years seem too long? Know that, if we consider the entire historical data, the Longest Negative Period for a US Total Stock Market investment was 188 months (= 15 years and 8 months) in nominal terms (without counting inflation).

If we include inflation, it was even 316 months!!!

Are you examining a portfolio or strategy and do not have such a long history? Then be aware of the risk and carefully evaluate how much to allocate to this investment.

Take, for example, megatrend-themed financial products: they will tell you that there will surely be ample profit margins in the future, but the historical data you'll see is, at best, for 2/3 years.

Objective: Medium term (~7 years)

Aiming for medium-term safety? In this case, you should focus on a portfolio that, over 7 years, statistically provided gains in the majority of cases.

Consider, always based on a historical period of at least thirty years:

- Medium term (7Y) baseline rolling return
- Maximum drawdown
- Longest Negative Period

For a more comprehensive picture, you can also look at:

- Medium term (7Y) worst rolling return
- Medium term (7Y) rolling return - %fail

With these additional metrics, you can see if there have ever been negative periods longer than your time horizon.

Objective: Short term (∼3 years)

Do you need your invested capital back in just 3 years? With such a short time horizon, you really need to be very cautious.

In this case, you should first focus on preserving your capital and only then try to understand the profit opportunities.

The metrics to study are those that tell you how much, statistically, you would have lost over the 3 years. <u>Always on a historical basis of at least thirty years</u>, look at:

- Maximum drawdown
- Longest Negative Period
- Short term (3Y) baseline rolling return

For greater awareness, the following metrics are also important.

- Short term (3Y) worst rolling return
- Short term (3Y) rolling return - %fail

It's not easy to find profitable investments with a 3-year time horizon. When conducting your simulations, you often find a Longest Negative Period exceeding 3 years. Alternatively, you may encounter an unsustainable *%fail* over the 3 years.

For example, if your time horizon is 36 months and the Longest Negative Period is 50-60 months, this is a red flag. It indicates that the portfolio has not historically provided certainty of gains over timeframes similar to yours. Consequently, for such a scenario, the *%fail* over 3 years could be a significant value.

Graphical Summary

Here is a summary of the metrics we consider, based on the time horizon.

	Objectives		
	Long Term ≥15Y	Medium Term ~7Y	Short Term ~3Y
Long term (15Y) rolling return			
Worst	O		
Baseline	X		
Median	X		
%fail	O		
Medium term (7Y) rolling return			
Worst		O	
Baseline		X	
%fail		O	
Short term (3Y) rolling return			
Worst			O
Baseline			X
%fail			O
Maximum drawdown	O	X	X
Longest Negative Period	O	X	X

X = recommended
O = optional

75

10. The Strategy

The difference between a castle and a house is not determined by the bricks; it's the skill of the builder

ChatGPT

The journey is getting interesting! Are you tired? Indeed, we have seen many things in a way that is rarely found in books or on the web.

Before continuing, let's recap the path we have taken.

In the introduction, we briefly saw what it means to manage and invest money.

We then identified the most common asset classes (stocks, real estate, bonds, cash, commodities) that will be the components of portfolios.

We saw that, despite appearances, if our portfolio is *Lazy*, then we can implement very effective investment strategies, at a low cost and without excessive commitment.

Then we took off and raised the level: we explained what the main metrics are that you need to examine in an investment. Few reach such a level of analysis, believe us.

We then focused on some particular metrics and associated them with a short/medium/long-term goal.

Now is the time to discover, with numbers in hand, which asset mixes are the most interesting.

76

Below, you will find many tables and numerous numbers. We wanted to create a real 'Catalog' that you can consult whenever you need it. Armed with colored pencils, you can highlight the combinations of assets that seem most interesting to you.

Always remember that on *LazyPortfolioEtf.com*, you can perform all your tests, replicating what you found in the book and working on your asset allocation ideas.

On the website, you will always have updated metrics: for this reason, you may notice different results from those presented here in the book.

Historical Series

All calculations are based on past statistics. For the assets we examine, we have access to significant, sometimes very deep, historical data.

A 'representative sample' is a portion of data that accurately reflects the characteristics of the entire population from which it is drawn. Similarly, a long and varied historical series serves as a representative sample of the past behavior of financial markets.

By covering different economic periods and market cycles, we obtain a more complete and reliable picture of possible future dynamics.

In particular, we are very interested in "crisis" periods because it is in these moments that markets suffer and trigger panic among investors.

Let's list some:

- The Great Depression of 1929
- The oil shock of 1973
- The dot-com bubble of 2000

- The recession of 2008
- The sovereign debt crisis of 2011
- The pandemic crisis of 2020

In these difficult periods, market prices, especially stocks, were heavily affected, and it took several years to return to pre-crisis levels.

On *LazyPortfolioEtf.com*, we have a historical dataset that starts from 1871 for various asset classes and from 1927 for many others.

In any case, all the "classic" portfolios you see on the homepage have a history of at least 30 years.

Our calculations are based on end-of-month values, and in periods where the considered ETF did not exist, we replaced the returns with those of the underlying index or comparable instruments.

To reconstruct the historical values of the indices, we consulted various online sources (American .edu sites or reputable information sources) and studies conducted by the excellent bogleheads.org community.

Details here: https://www.lazyportfolioetf.com/data-sources/

Methodology

The asset allocations will be composed exclusively of ETFs.

In particular:

- We will use ETFs traded on the U.S. market. If you do not have access to this market and want to invest in these assets, check if there are low-cost ETFs or instruments in your country that replicate the same benchmarks. Be careful because your instrument may have an annual management fee different from the original ETF.

- We will use ETFs traded in U.S. dollars (USD). This means that if your reference currency is not USD, you will need to take into account the exchange rate effect for your analyses. The results can be very different. In the appendix of the book, you will find analyses in EUR currency.
- Many ETFs pay dividends. When a dividend is paid, the investor receives the credit of the dividend in their account. At the same time, the ETF's price is reduced by the same value. For the calculation of metrics, it is assumed that dividends are reinvested immediately. This is not always possible in reality.

The portfolios are implemented and measured based on the following assumptions:

- An annual rebalancing is expected, done at the beginning of each year. Following a rebalancing, some ETF shares may need to be sold: it is possible that, depending on the tax regime to which you are subject, there may be a tax to pay. In the calculations, we do not consider any type of tax.
- Taxes due to the crediting of dividends are not considered.
- No commission costs of any kind applied by your bank or broker are considered. These are subjective costs that should be as low as possible for the benefit of your investments.

The assumptions we have outlined may seem restrictive and unrealistic, but in fact, they are the practice for calculations of this type.

It is the calculation methodology of *LazyPortfolioEtf.com* and countless other websites.

SIMULATIONS AND METRICS

The most dangerous words in investing are: "it's different this time"

SIR JOHN TEMPLETON

The simulations and metrics presented below are updated as of **November 30, 2023**.

All statistics refer to the past and provide no guarantees for the future. We have done our best, but we cannot exclude imperfections in the calculations or in the starting database.

Before investing, always study the updated analyses, which you can find on *LazyPortfolioEtf.com*. Over time, the metrics will take on different values: we do not expect upheavals in the rankings, but always verify with 'fresh' data.

Comparison of different Assets/Portfolios

For comparative analyses among various asset allocations, you will see tables like this:

Portfolio	3Y Rolling Annualized Return (%)			7Y Rolling Annualized Return (%)			15Y Rolling Annualized Return (%)				Max Draw-down (%)	Long Neg Period (Y.M) ▲
	Worst	Base	%Fail	Worst	Base	%Fail	Worst	Base	Median	%Fail		
Portfolio 1	0.33	2.84	0%	2.41	3.66	0%	3.44	4.40	5.09	0%	-12.91	2Y.10M
Portfolio 2	0.42	2.53	0%	2.32	3.12	0%	2.98	3.98	4.86	0%	-11.24	2Y.11M
Portfolio 3	0.35	4.03	0%	4.04	5.23	0%	4.92	6.03	6.62	0%	-14.72	3Y.2M

In the first column (Portfolio Column), you will find the list of asset allocations, which will be sorted based on the value of the metric under consideration. This way, you can identify which asset mixes have been the best performers so far, according to your goal.

The other columns, quite self-explanatory, contain the metrics we have associated with the objectives:

- 3Y Rolling Annualized Return (%):
  - Worst
  - Baseline
  - %Fail
- 7Y Rolling Annualized Return (%):
  - Worst
  - Baseline
  - %Fail
- 15Y Rolling Annualized Return (%):
  - Worst
  - Baseline
  - Median
  - %Fail
- Maximum Drawdown (%)
- Longest Negative Period (Y.M - years/months) - *if the symbol (*) is present, it means that the negative period is still in progress.*

3Y, 5Y, 15Y stands for, respectively, 3 years, 5 years, 15 years.

You already know that the *baseline rolling return* refers to the minimum rolling return obtained, excluding the worst 15% of cases. In other words, it is the 15th percentile of rolling returns, sorted in ascending order of performance.

The *median rolling return* is the 50th percentile, or the median of all rolling returns sorted in ascending order of performance. In 50% of cases, the return was lower, and in the other 50%, it was equal to or higher.

The *worst rolling* return is the all-time lowest rolling return over the considered historical period.

The *%fail* indicates, statistically, how many times that rolling return has been negative. In other words, it tells you how many times you would have lost money over that time horizon.

The *Maximum drawdown* measures the largest temporarily incurred loss compared to a previous peak.

The *Longest Negative Period* indicates the longest period for which an overall negative return was obtained.

If you need a review, feel free to go back to section 7. Take the time you need to thoroughly understand the metrics, and if you wish, you can also look at examples of real portfolios on *LazyPortfolioEtf.com*.

Inflation

A well-done analysis must necessarily consider inflation. As you have seen in the initial chapters, general price increases, which naturally occur, will erode your purchasing power, and you cannot afford to be unprepared for this eventuality.

The tables will be calculated for both of the following scenarios:

- in nominal terms (i.e., without considering inflation)
- in real terms (considering inflation)

Keep in mind that the inflation used for the calculations is that of the United States. Evaluate whether, in your case, it makes sense to consider it or if it is preferable to consider the inflation of the country where you live.

If you cannot make precise calculations, you can potentially deduct inflation from the metrics you see in the tables.

It's not a correct and rigorous calculation, but you can get an idea.

For example, if the inflation you are subject to has averaged 2% per year over the last 30 years, you can scale this value from all the metrics calculated over the same period.

So, if any baseline return calculated over the last 30 years is 4%, in your case, the real return, calculated based on the average inflation, would be:

$$\frac{1 + 4\%}{1 + 2\%} - 1 = 1.96\%$$

If you want to make an even more approximate calculation, you can subtract inflation from the nominal return. In the example above, therefore, 4% - 2% = 2% real.

Again, this calculation is absolutely not rigorous because it considers only the average value of inflation and does not take into account the exact inflation on each period (rolling period) of the last years. It's better than nothing if you don't have the possibility to make precise calculations.

The currency risk

The currency risk is a crucial variable that certainly deserves attention and in-depth analysis. Currency volatility can significantly impact the overall profitability of a portfolio: it is essential to examine strategies aimed at mitigating this type of risk.

All assets considered here in the book are expressed, as mentioned earlier, in US dollars (USD). If your reference currency is different, the final performance of the portfolio in your local currency could vary greatly, either positively or negatively. In the case of EUR currency, take a look at the book's appendix.

In calculating with your assets, it is preferable to retrieve exchange rate data so that you can quantify the resulting performance variations over all the rolling periods you will consider.

If you have difficulty obtaining such detailed information, you can also reason on an annual basis: the analysis will be less precise but still meaningful.

A common alternative is the use of currency-hedged instruments. These instruments provide protection against currency fluctuations, allowing investors to maintain a certain stability in the performance of their portfolio. However, this form of hedging comes at a cost, which is important to carefully evaluate during planning.

In general and as a first approximation, the hedging cost, which does not explicitly appear among the ETF costs, is related to the spread between the benchmark interest rates of the currency to hedge and the "local" currency.

Let's take an example: suppose the interest rate in the USA is 5% and that in the Eurozone it is 4.5%. An investor in the Eurozone would like to hedge the investment in dollars because their local currency is the Euro. The approximate annual hedging cost will be:

$$\frac{1 + 5\%}{1 + 4.5\%} - 1 = 0.4785\%$$

Note that, conversely, a dollar investor wishing to hedge an investment in Euros would have a negative hedging cost, effectively an extra return:

$$\frac{1 + 4.5\%}{1 + 5\%} - 1 = -0.4762\%$$

In practice, hedging a currency with a higher interest rate incurs a cost. The opposite incurs a negative cost, resulting in extra returns.

Generally, currency-hedged ETFs have a higher annual management cost, to which the aforementioned currency hedging cost must be added.

For Euro investors, a currently interesting website is Backtest by Curvo (https://curvo.eu/backtest/en), which allows simulating portfolios with ETFs traded on European markets, in Euros.

It does not cover all the metrics we use, but provides, for example, data on drawdowns (longest and deepest) and %Fail (in the "Minimum investment horizon" section).

Data Sources

The historical periods we will work with are:

- **the last 30 years**: this interval allows us to include some relatively "young" but interesting assets (as you will see in the summary table shortly). Considering the last 30 years means incorporating the dot-com bubble of the early 2000s and the 2008 subprime crisis into the study.
- **the last 60 years**: this is a fairly extensive time frame. It may be suitable if you prefer to include only the more "classic" assets with a deeper history. This time frame covers, for example, the 1973 oil crisis.
- **the entire available history**: going back to 1871/1927, depending on data availability. This is an extreme case, presented for completeness. As you have already seen, the results can be drastic in terms of drawdowns and the longest negative period because they include the period of the Great Depression that began in 1929. According to many, the world is different now, and such crashes are unlikely to happen again, but there is no certainty about the future.

Assets used

Below is a summary outline of the assets used for simulations, along with their respective historical data in our possession.

Etf Ticker	Investment Theme	Last 30Y	Last 60Y	More	Data Source (from)
VTI	US Total Stock Market	X	X	X	gen 1871
VEA	Ex-US Developed Markets Stock Index	X			gen 1970
EEM	Emerging Markets Total Stock Index	X			gen 1976
IJS	US Small Cap Value Stocks	X	X	X	gen 1927
VTV	US Large Cap Value Stocks	X	X	X	gen 1927
MTUM	US Momentum Factor Stocks	X			gen 1982
SCZ	Ex-US Develop. Markets Small Cap Stocks	X			gen 1975
VNQ	US Real Estate	X	X	X	gen 1928
BND	US Total Bond Market	X	X	X	gen 1871
BNDX	International Total Bond Index	X			gen 1985
BIL	US 1-3 Month T-Bills	X	X	X	gen 1871
SHY	US 1-3 Year Treasury Bonds	X	X	X	gen 1871
IEI	US 3-7 Year Treasury Bonds	X	X	X	gen 1871
TLT	US 20+ Year Treasury Bonds	X	X	X	gen 1871
TIP	US Treasury Inflation Protected Bonds	X			gen 1985
HYG	High Yield Corporate Bonds	X			gen 1979
LQD	Investment Grade Corporate Bonds	X	X	X	gen 1871
CWB	US Convertible Bonds	X			gen 1988
EMB	Emerging Markets Bonds	X			gen 1985
GLD	Gold	X	X	X	gen 1871

For your sense of security, it is understandable if you choose to use only assets with a broad historical data. However, for completeness, consider even those assets with a 'limited' database because, as you will see, they have led to very interesting results over the last thirty years.

You might be wondering why one of the most famous ETFs, the SPY, which tracks the S&P 500 index, is not among the considered assets. We chose to include the more generic VTI, which is much more diversified (replicating a basket of over 3500 companies) and still has very similar returns to the SPY (the correlation is close to 1).

Below, we list each ETF used, along with a brief description taken from *Etf.com*.

VTI - US Total Stock Market: *The fund is passively managed to provide vanilla exposure to approx. 100% of the US equity investable world.*

VEA - Ex-US Developed Markets Stock Index: *The fund is passively managed to provide exposure to the developed markets ex-US equity space.*

EEM - Emerging Markets Total Stock Index: *It tracks an index of emerging-market firms weighted by market cap.*

IJS - US Small Cap Value Stocks: *It tracks an index of small-cap US stocks.*

VTV - US Large Cap Value Stocks: *It tracks an index of large-cap stocks in the US, selected and weighed based on five value factors.*

MTUM - US Momentum Factor Stocks: *It aims to pick stocks that have steadily increased in price lately, scaled by the volatility of returns.*

SCZ - ex-US Developed Markets Small Cap Stocks: *It tracks a market-cap-weighted index of small-cap companies from Europe, Asia and the Far East.*

VNQ - US Real Estate: *It tracks an index of companies involved in the ownership and operation of real estate in the US.*

BND - US Total Bond Market: *It tracks a broad index of US investment-grade, fixed-income securities with maturities of 1+ year.*

BNDX - International Total Bond Index: *It tracks an investment-grade, non-USD denominated bond index, USD hedged.*

BIL - US 1-3 Month T-Bills: *It invests in Treasury bills with three months or less to maturity.*

SHY - US 1-3 Year Treasury Bonds: *It tracks a market weighted index of debt issued by the US Treasury with 1-3 years remaining to maturity.*

IEI - US 3-7 Year Treasury Bonds: *It focuses on the middle of the US Treasury note market, holding mostly notes maturing 3-7 years from now.*

TLT - US 20+ Year Treasury Bonds: *It tracks an index of debt issued by the US Treasury with remaining maturities of 20+ years.*

TIP - US Treasury Inflation Protected Bonds: *It seeks to track an index that holds a broad portfolio of TIPS - Treasury Inflation Protected Securities.*

HYG - High Yield Corporate Bonds: *It tracks a market-weighted index of US high-yield corporate debt.*

LQD - Investment Grade Corporate Bonds: *It tracks a market-weighted index of US corporate investment-grade bonds.*

CWB - US Convertible Bonds: *It tracks a market-cap weighted index of US convertible securities of any credit quality.*

EMB - Emerging Markets Bonds: *It tracks an index of US-dollar-denominated sovereign debt issued by emerging-market countries.*

GLD - Gold: *It tracks the gold spot price, less expenses and liabilities, using gold bars held in London vaults.*

Ranking

We will start with rankings of portfolios composed of a single asset. Then we will proceed with equally weighted portfolios consisting of 2-3-4-5 assets.

Finally, we will present an overall ranking, obtained by considering all the previous portfolios. You will notice that at the top, there are often portfolios composed of 3, 4, or 5 assets, attesting to the advantages of diversification.

If your budget is not high, you may encounter difficulties in purchasing a minimum number of ETF shares, especially if their unit cost is high. For the same reason, it might be challenging to rebalance the assets correctly. If this is your case, perhaps it's better to implement portfolios with a maximum of 3 assets.

Each simulation is conducted based on what was described earlier in the 'Methodology' section.

Single-Asset Lazy Portfolios

Below, we present, for single-asset portfolios, the rankings ordered based on the metrics considered.

You will see that individually, none of the assets provides exceptional *overall* results in terms of metrics.

This is why many investors abandon their investment plans, even when setting up an accumulation plan for a single asset.

Some aim for returns but are psychologically crushed by a significant drawdown. Others are ultra-conservative in terms of capital protection but then do not achieve an acceptable return.

Ranking: Baseline 3Y Return

Order by **Baseline 3Y Return - Last 30 Years** (from 1993-12 to 2023-11)

Portfolio	3Y Rolling Annualized Return (%)			7Y Rolling Annualized Return (%)			15Y Rolling Annualized Return (%)				Max Draw-down (%)	Long Neg Period (Y.M)
	Worst	Base ▼	%Fail	Worst	Base	%Fail	Worst	Base	Median	%Fail		
IJS	-18.25	3.65	10.8%	-1.42	6.00	0.7%	5.15	7.80	9.07	0%	-54.13	8Y.1M
EMB	-7.65	3.53	7.4%	-0.47	4.25	0.7%	3.08	5.67	10.28	0%	-31.43	8Y.2M
BNDX	-4.35	3.16	6.2%	0.18	3.98	0%	3.31	4.85	5.62	0%	-14.88	6Y.5M
LQD	-6.71	2.94	6.5%	0.33	4.15	0%	3.56	4.71	5.91	0%	-23.27	6Y.3M
CWB	-12.29	2.82	10.2%	0.04	5.07	0%	5.15	6.36	7.44	0%	-43.81	8Y.6M
TLT	-17.32	2.73	7.1%	-4.12	4.78	5.4%	1.81	5.76	7.02	0%	-47.74	12Y.1M
BND	-5.59	2.05	5.5%	-0.23	2.60	0.7%	2.36	3.62	4.64	0%	-17.28	7Y.6M
HYG	-7.69	1.64	5.5%	0.42	4.22	0%	3.43	4.97	5.62	0%	-30.85	5Y.10M
VNQ	-25.03	1.58	11.7%	-1.16	5.57	0.7%	3.84	6.51	9.52	0%	-68.30	7Y.8M
TIP	-2.68	1.49	6.2%	0.61	2.34	0%	2.51	3.78	5.31	0%	-14.76	6Y.5M
IEI	-4.27	1.24	6.2%	-0.11	1.77	0.7%	1.63	3.34	4.79	0%	-13.59	7Y.7M
SHY	-1.26	0.52	4.9%	0.39	0.72	0%	0.87	1.83	2.71	0%	-5.36	3Y.11M
BIL	-0.10	-0.03	19.7%	-0.05	0.16	7.9%	0.50	0.81	1.29	0%	-0.42	8Y.9M
VTI	-16.22	-1.94	16.9%	-2.98	3.78	2.2%	4.37	5.30	7.55	0%	-50.84	11Y.7M
VTV	-16.62	-2.60	17.5%	-3.00	4.01	1.4%	4.43	5.32	7.00	0%	-54.78	11Y.7M
SCZ	-20.24	-2.72	26.5%	-1.95	1.92	8.3%	1.82	5.17	7.62	0%	-63.26	9Y.4M
VEA	-19.64	-3.37	22.8%	-2.53	1.87	4.7%	0.92	3.21	4.48	0%	-57.00	12Y.6M
MTUM	-15.43	-3.44	19.1%	-0.57	5.24	0.7%	5.61	7.13	10.08	0%	-53.85	10Y.6M
EEM	-15.31	-4.00	33.9%	-6.71	-0.15	15.9%	-1.21	3.98	7.53	1.1%	-60.44	16Y.1M*
GLD	-15.02	-6.98	33.9%	-6.20	-2.30	24.2%	3.86	6.28	8.84	0%	-42.91	12Y.1M

Order by **Baseline 3Y Return - Last 30 Years** (from 1993-12 to 2023-11) - **US Infl. Adjusted**

Portfolio	3Y Rolling Annualized Return (%)			7Y Rolling Annualized Return (%)			15Y Rolling Annualized Return (%)				Max Draw-down (%)	Long Neg Period (Y.M)
	Worst	Base ▼	%Fail	Worst	Base	%Fail	Worst	Base	Median	%Fail		
EMB	-12.06	1.67	11.1%	-3.86	2.47	7.6%	0.67	3.63	8.01	0%	-35.97	13Y.3M
IJS	-20.02	0.94	13.9%	-3.83	3.54	2.2%	3.14	5.38	6.75	0%	-55.05	11Y.5M
BNDX	-9.52	0.78	10.5%	-3.24	2.03	8.3%	0.91	2.61	3.42	0%	-26.46	13Y.2M
CWB	-14.19	0.44	13.9%	-2.50	2.84	2.5%	2.76	3.91	5.11	0%	-45.00	11Y.5M
TLT	-21.79	0.37	12.9%	-7.37	2.55	7.9%	-0.68	3.59	4.79	1.1%	-55.99	18Y.5M
LQD	-11.76	0.32	12%	-3.07	2.18	7.6%	1.14	2.49	3.64	0%	-33.86	13Y.2M
BND	-10.69	0.09	14.5%	-3.61	0.84	8.3%	0.00	1.49	2.53	0.5%	-30.25	20Y.5M
TIP	-7.96	-0.43	20.3%	-2.39	0.10	13.7%	0.17	1.68	3.23	0%	-23.74	15Y.9M
IEI	-9.45	-0.57	23.7%	-3.52	0.10	13%	-0.85	1.21	2.67	7.7%	-26.99	21Y.1M
HYG	-9.89	-1.09	21.9%	-2.13	1.90	5.8%	0.87	2.68	3.33	0%	-32.45	12Y.2M
SHY	-6.65	-1.40	47.4%	-2.90	-1.02	35.4%	-1.59	-0.29	0.65	29.8%	-23.76	25Y.8M
VNQ	-26.58	-1.64	19.7%	-3.59	3.05	4.3%	1.31	4.37	6.98	0%	-69.76	12Y.2M
BIL	-4.61	-2.06	62.5%	-2.40	-1.62	66.4%	-1.84	-1.20	-0.68	71.8%	-25.55	30Y.0M*
VTI	-18.24	-4.37	20%	-5.40	1.18	6.9%	2.16	2.90	5.14	0%	-51.59	13Y.5M
VTV	-18.43	-4.60	22.8%	-5.42	1.48	4.7%	1.98	2.88	4.80	0%	-55.68	13Y.6M
SCZ	-21.97	-5.36	35.4%	-4.39	-0.11	17%	-0.55	2.91	5.27	1.7%	-63.82	16Y.6M
MTUM	-17.26	-5.53	23.4%	-3.05	2.60	2.2%	3.37	4.81	7.64	0%	-54.55	12Y.5M
VEA	-21.58	-5.93	31.7%	-4.84	-0.34	20.2%	-1.43	0.86	2.18	6.1%	-57.66	22Y.9M
EEM	-17.17	-6.03	44.6%	-9.04	-1.79	32.1%	-3.52	1.77	5.19	9.9%	-61.05	17Y.9M
GLD	-15.87	-8.89	42.5%	-8.11	-4.32	30.3%	1.46	3.82	6.62	0%	-45.57	13Y.3M

Order by **Baseline 3Y Return - Last 60 Years** (from 1963-12 to 2023-11)

Portfolio	3Y Rolling Annualized Return (%)			7Y Rolling Annualized Return (%)			15Y Rolling Annualized Return (%)				Max Draw-down (%)	Long Neg Period (Y.M)
	Worst	Base ▼	%Fail	Worst	Base	%Fail	Worst	Base	Median	%Fail		
IJS	-18.25	4.44	9.2%	-2.35	6.98	1.7%	5.15	8.94	14.42	0%	-54.13	8Y.1M
BND	-5.59	2.53	2.6%	-0.23	4.05	0.3%	2.36	4.28	7.03	0%	-17.28	7Y.6M
IEI	-4.27	2.12	2.9%	-0.11	3.38	0.3%	1.63	4.28	7.14	0%	-13.59	7Y.7M
LQD	-6.71	2.00	7.6%	0.33	4.15	0%	3.30	5.03	7.09	0%	-23.27	6Y.3M
VTI	-16.22	1.87	12.6%	-3.00	4.15	1.7%	4.37	6.49	10.48	0%	-50.84	11Y.7M
VNQ	-25.03	1.44	11.2%	-1.87	4.78	1.6%	3.84	8.22	10.82	0%	-68.30	11Y.1M
SHY	-1.26	1.29	2.3%	0.39	1.39	0%	0.87	2.34		0%	-8.52	3Y.11M
VTV	-16.62	1.09	12.4%	-3.00	4.15	1.6%	4.43	6.38	10.91	0%	-54.78	11Y.7M
TLT	-17.32	0.70	12.6%	-4.12	3.10	2.3%	1.81	5.52	8.25	0%	-47.74	12Y.1M
BIL	-0.10	0.60	9.3%	-0.05	0.68	3.5%	0.50	1.21	5.38	0%	-0.42	8Y.9M
GLD	-15.32	-6.07	32.9%	-6.75	-2.30	29.7%	-3.63	-1.12	7.05	19.6%	-61.78	27Y.5M

Order by **Baseline 3Y Return - Last 60 Years** (from 1963-12 to 2023-11) - **US Infl. Adjusted**

Portfolio	3Y Rolling Annualized Return (%)			7Y Rolling Annualized Return (%)			15Y Rolling Annualized Return (%)				Max Draw-down (%)	Long Neg Period (Y.M)
	Worst	Base ▼	%Fail	Worst	Base	%Fail	Worst	Base	Median	%Fail		
IJS	-20.02	0.29	14.6%	-8.11	3.86	5.5%	3.14	6.39	9.73	0%	-57.83	11Y.5M
SHY	-6.65	-1.57	36.2%	-3.25	-0.94	28.1%	-1.59	-0.10	2.29	16.8%	-23.89	25Y.8M
BIL	-4.61	-1.68	43.8%	-2.40	-1.35	43.3%	-1.84	-0.77	1.09	31.8%	-25.55	35Y.2M
BND	-10.69	-1.75	25.1%	-4.53	-0.74	19.9%	-2.30	0.30	3.30	11.8%	-35.11	20Y.8M
IEI	-9.45	-1.86	29.6%	-4.53	-0.85	22%	-2.31	0.13	3.47	14.2%	-35.11	21Y.1M
LQD	-14.61	-2.19	24.4%	-5.92	-1.09	24.2%	-3.58	1.18	3.95	12.9%	-45.79	21Y.3M
VNQ	-26.58	-2.46	23.2%	-7.33	0.76	11.5%	0.14	4.35	7.44	0%	-69.76	14Y.11M
VTI	-18.54	-2.55	20.6%	-8.51	0.01	14.9%	-1.47	2.39	6.97	2.2%	-54.53	18Y.1M
VTV	-18.43	-2.93	21%	-8.13	0.48	12.9%	-0.49	2.50	6.82	0.9%	-55.68	17Y.10M
TLT	-21.79	-3.83	26.6%	-7.37	-2.37	28.1%	-4.99	0.33	4.82	14.2%	-56.13	22Y.0M
GLD	-20.28	-9.47	51.1%	-11.38	-5.24	44.3%	-7.77	-4.24	3.96	33.1%	-82.57	43Y.11M*

Order by **Baseline 3Y Return - All data** (from 1871/1927 to 2023-11)

Portfolio	3Y Rolling Annualized Return (%)			7Y Rolling Annualized Return (%)			15Y Rolling Annualized Return (%)				Max Draw-down (%)	Long Neg Period (Y.M)
	Worst	Base ▼	%Fail	Worst	Base	%Fail	Worst	Base	Median	%Fail		
BND	-5.59	2.15	1.6%	-0.23	2.57	0.1%	1.40	2.67	4.00	0%	-17.28	7Y.6M
IEI	-4.27	2.02	1.7%	-0.11	2.47	0.1%	1.37	2.65	3.94	0%	-13.59	7Y.7M
LQD	-6.71	1.93	3.6%	0.33	2.46	0%	1.32	2.65	4.03	0%	-23.27	6Y.3M
SHY	-1.26	1.46	1.1%	0.39	1.52	0%	0.87	2.11	4.40	0%	-8.52	3Y.11M
TLT	-17.32	1.45	7.9%	-4.12	2.10	2.8%	0.07	2.44	4.28	0%	-47.74	14Y.2M
IJS	-49.09	1.17	13%	-7.75	5.98	4.3%	0.44	9.17	14.53	0%	-88.57	14Y.9M
BIL	-0.10	0.65	3.6%	-0.05	0.76	1.3%	0.29	1.18	4.72	0%	-0.42	8Y.9M
VTV	-43.29	-0.19	15.3%	-8.41	3.75	5.9%	-1.07	6.25	10.63	1.1%	-84.40	15Y.7M
VTI	-43.81	-0.56	15.9%	-9.49	3.29	4.2%	-0.35	5.49	8.60	0.1%	-84.60	15Y.8M
VNQ	-25.90	-0.81	17.8%	-7.36	1.29	7.9%	-1.75	2.31	8.05	1.8%	-68.30	19Y.5M
GLD	-15.32	-1.61	23.9%	-6.75	-1.32	22.2%	-3.63	-0.50	0.05	21.3%	-61.78	62Y.0M

Order by **Baseline 3Y Return - All data** (from 1871/1927 to 2023-11) - **US Infl. Adjusted**

Portfolio	3Y Rolling Annualized Return (%)			7Y Rolling Annualized Return (%)			15Y Rolling Annualized Return (%)				Max Draw-down (%)	Long Neg Period (Y.M)
	Worst	Base ▼	%Fail	Worst	Base	%Fail	Worst	Base	Median	%Fail		
IJS	-45.05	-1.91	17.5%	-8.11	3.63	6%	0.72	6.44	10.61	0%	-85.57	14Y.8M
BIL	-10.74	-1.91	33.8%	-6.82	-1.62	32.4%	-3.90	-0.88	1.22	24.4%	-48.08	92Y.5M
SHY	-12.29	-2.01	30.1%	-7.07	-1.41	25.7%	-3.27	-0.49	1.90	19.8%	-45.12	52Y.1M
BND	-13.89	-2.23	26.6%	-7.81	-1.23	25.1%	-3.27	-0.65	2.01	21.8%	-48.08	51Y.10M
IEI	-13.90	-2.29	28.3%	-7.82	-1.26	26%	-3.29	-0.68	1.92	22.6%	-48.09	51Y.11M
LQD	-14.61	-2.39	26.9%	-7.93	-1.41	26.9%	-3.58	-0.79	2.27	25.9%	-56.56	84Y.5M
VTI	-39.36	-2.49	20.7%	-8.51	0.77	12.6%	-2.10	2.40	6.93	2.5%	-80.55	26Y.4M
TLT	-21.79	-3.09	29.4%	-8.20	-2.33	31.4%	-4.99	-1.40	2.66	32.5%	-70.04	87Y.7M
VNQ	-26.58	-3.33	31%	-7.33	-0.56	22.1%	-3.71	0.18	3.85	13.2%	-69.76	48Y.0M
VTV	-38.79	-4.05	21.7%	-8.13	0.34	13.4%	-1.22	2.19	6.65	1.4%	-80.30	20Y.1M
GLD	-20.28	-5.84	58.4%	-11.38	-4.43	56.9%	-7.77	-3.77	-0.10	50.5%	-82.57	132Y.3M

Ranking: Maximum Drawdown

Order by **Maximum Drawdown - Last 30 Years** (from 1993-12 to 2023-11)

Portfolio	3Y Rolling Annualized Return (%)			7Y Rolling Annualized Return (%)			15Y Rolling Annualized Return (%)				Max Draw-down (%) ▼	Long Neg Period (Y.M)
	Worst	Base	%Fail	Worst	Base	%Fail	Worst	Base	Median	%Fail		
BIL	-0.10	-0.03	19.7%	-0.05	0.16	7.9%	0.50	0.81	1.29	0%	-0.42	8Y.9M
SHY	-1.26	0.52	4.9%	0.39	0.72	0%	0.87	1.83	2.71	0%	-5.36	3Y.11M
IEI	-4.27	1.24	6.2%	-0.11	1.77	0.7%	1.63	3.34	4.79	0%	-13.59	7Y.7M
TIP	-2.68	1.49	6.2%	0.61	2.34	0%	2.51	3.78	5.31	0%	-14.76	6Y.5M
BNDX	-4.35	3.16	6.2%	0.18	3.98	0%	3.31	4.85	5.62	0%	-14.88	6Y.5M
BND	-5.59	2.05	5.5%	-0.23	2.60	0.7%	2.36	3.62	4.64	0%	-17.28	7Y.6M
LQD	-6.71	2.94	6.5%	0.33	4.15	0%	3.56	4.71	5.91	0%	-23.27	6Y.3M
HYG	-7.69	1.64	5.5%	0.42	4.22	0%	3.43	4.97	5.62	0%	-30.85	5Y.10M
EMB	-7.65	3.53	7.4%	-0.47	4.25	0.7%	3.08	5.67	10.28	0%	-31.43	8Y.2M
GLD	-15.02	-6.98	33.9%	-6.20	-2.30	24.2%	3.86	6.28	8.84	0%	-42.91	12Y.1M
CWB	-12.29	2.82	10.2%	0.04	5.07	0%	5.15	6.36	7.44	0%	-43.81	8Y.6M
TLT	-17.32	2.73	7.1%	-4.12	4.78	5.4%	1.81	5.76	7.02	0%	-47.74	12Y.1M
VTI	-16.22	-1.94	16.9%	-2.98	3.78	2.2%	4.37	5.30	7.55	0%	-50.84	11Y.7M
MTUM	-15.43	-3.44	19.1%	-0.57	5.24	0.7%	5.61	7.13	10.08	0%	-53.85	10Y.6M
IJS	-18.25	3.65	10.8%	-1.42	6.00	0.7%	5.15	7.80	9.07	0%	-54.13	8Y.1M
VTV	-16.62	-2.60	17.5%	-3.00	4.01	1.4%	4.43	5.32	7.00	0%	-54.78	11Y.7M
VEA	-19.64	-3.37	22.8%	-2.53	1.87	4.7%	0.92	3.21	4.48	0%	-57.00	12Y.6M
EEM	-15.31	-4.00	33.9%	-6.71	-0.15	15.9%	-1.21	3.98	7.53	1.1%	-60.44	16Y.1M*
SCZ	-20.24	-2.72	26.5%	-1.95	1.92	8.3%	1.82	5.17	7.62	0%	-63.26	9Y.4M
VNQ	-25.03	1.58	11.7%	-1.16	5.57	0.7%	3.84	6.51	9.52	0%	-68.30	7Y.8M

Order by **Maximum Drawdown - Last 30 Years** (from 1993-12 to 2023-11) - **US Infl. Adjusted**

Portfolio	3Y Rolling Annualized Return (%)			7Y Rolling Annualized Return (%)			15Y Rolling Annualized Return (%)				Max Draw-down (%) ▼	Long Neg Period (Y.M)
	Worst	Base	%Fail	Worst	Base	%Fail	Worst	Base	Median	%Fail		
TIP	-7.96	-0.43	20.3%	-2.39	0.10	13.7%	0.17	1.68	3.23	0%	-23.74	15Y.9M
SHY	-6.65	-1.40	47.4%	-2.90	-1.02	35.4%	-1.59	-0.29	0.65	29.8%	-23.76	25Y.8M
BIL	-4.61	-2.06	62.5%	-2.40	-1.62	66.4%	-1.84	-1.20	-0.68	71.8%	-25.55	30Y.0M*
BNDX	-9.52	0.78	10.5%	-3.24	2.03	8.3%	0.91	2.61	3.42	0%	-26.46	13Y.2M
IEI	-9.45	-0.57	23.7%	-3.52	0.10	13%	-0.85	1.21	2.67	7.7%	-26.99	21Y.1M
BND	-10.69	0.09	14.5%	-3.61	0.84	8.3%	0.00	1.49	2.53	0.5%	-30.25	20Y.5M
HYG	-9.89	-1.09	21.9%	-2.13	1.90	5.8%	0.87	2.68	3.33	0%	-32.45	12Y.2M
LQD	-11.76	0.32	12%	-3.07	2.18	7.6%	1.14	2.49	3.64	0%	-33.86	13Y.2M
EMB	-12.06	1.67	11.1%	-3.86	2.47	7.6%	0.67	3.63	8.01	0%	-35.97	13Y.3M
CWB	-14.19	0.44	13.9%	-2.50	2.84	2.5%	2.76	3.91	5.11	0%	-45.00	11Y.5M
GLD	-15.87	-8.89	42.5%	-8.11	-4.32	30.3%	1.46	3.82	6.62	0%	-45.57	13Y.3M
VTI	-18.24	-4.37	20%	-5.40	1.18	6.9%	2.16	2.90	5.14	0%	-51.59	13Y.5M
MTUM	-17.26	-5.53	23.4%	-3.05	2.60	2.2%	3.37	4.81	7.64	0%	-54.55	12Y.5M
IJS	-20.02	0.94	13.9%	-3.83	3.54	2.2%	3.14	5.38	6.75	0%	-55.05	11Y.5M
VTV	-18.43	-4.60	22.8%	-5.42	1.48	4.7%	1.98	2.88	4.80	0%	-55.68	13Y.6M
TLT	-21.79	0.37	12.9%	-7.37	2.55	7.9%	-0.68	3.59	4.79	1.1%	-55.99	18Y.5M
VEA	-21.58	-5.93	31.7%	-4.84	-0.34	20.2%	-1.43	0.86	2.18	6.1%	-57.66	22Y.9M
EEM	-17.17	-6.03	44.6%	-9.04	-1.79	32.1%	-3.52	1.77	5.19	9.9%	-61.05	17Y.9M
SCZ	-21.97	-5.36	35.4%	-4.39	-0.11	17%	-0.55	2.91	5.27	1.7%	-63.82	16Y.6M
VNQ	-26.58	-1.64	19.7%	-3.59	3.05	4.3%	1.31	4.37	6.98	0%	-69.76	12Y.2M

Order by **Maximum Drawdown - Last 60 Years** (from 1963-12 to 2023-11)

Portfolio	3Y Rolling Annualized Return (%)			7Y Rolling Annualized Return (%)			15Y Rolling Annualized Return (%)				Max Draw-down (%) ▼	Long Neg Period (Y.M)
	Worst	Base	%Fail	Worst	Base	%Fail	Worst	Base	Median	%Fail		
BIL	-0.10	0.60	9.3%	-0.05	0.68	3.5%	0.50	1.21	5.38	0%	-0.42	8Y.9M
SHY	-1.26	1.29	2.3%	0.39	1.39	0%	0.87	2.34	6.67	0%	-8.52	3Y.11M
IEI	-4.27	2.12	2.9%	-0.11	3.38	0.3%	1.63	4.28	7.14	0%	-13.59	7Y.7M
BND	-5.59	2.53	2.6%	-0.23	4.05	0.3%	2.36	4.28	7.03	0%	-17.28	7Y.6M
LQD	-6.71	2.00	7.6%	0.33	4.15	0%	3.30	5.03	7.09	0%	-23.27	6Y.3M
TLT	-17.32	0.70	12.6%	-4.12	3.10	2.3%	1.81	5.52	8.25	0%	-47.74	12Y.1M
VTI	-16.22	1.87	12.6%	-3.00	4.15	1.7%	4.37	6.49	10.48	0%	-50.84	11Y.7M
IJS	-18.25	4.44	9.2%	-2.35	6.98	1.7%	5.15	8.94	14.42	0%	-54.13	8Y.1M
VTV	-16.62	1.09	12.4%	-3.00	4.15	1.6%	4.43	6.38	10.91	0%	-54.78	11Y.7M
GLD	-15.32	-6.07	32.9%	-6.75	-2.30	29.7%	-3.63	-1.12	7.05	19.6%	-61.78	27Y.5M
VNQ	-25.03	1.44	11.2%	-1.87	4.78	1.6%	3.84	8.22	10.82	0%	-68.30	11Y.1M

Order by **Maximum Drawdown - Last 60 Years** (from 1963-12 to 2023-11) - **US Infl. Adjusted**

Portfolio	3Y Rolling Annualized Return (%)			7Y Rolling Annualized Return (%)			15Y Rolling Annualized Return (%)				Max Draw-down (%) ▼	Long Neg Period (Y.M)
	Worst	Base	%Fail	Worst	Base	%Fail	Worst	Base	Median	%Fail		
SHY	-6.65	-1.57	36.2%	-3.25	-0.94	28.1%	-1.59	-0.10	2.29	16.8%	-23.89	25Y.8M
BIL	-4.61	-1.68	43.8%	-2.40	-1.35	43.3%	-1.84	-0.77	1.09	31.8%	-25.55	35Y.2M
BND	-10.69	-1.75	25.1%	-4.53	-0.74	19.9%	-2.30	0.30	3.30	11.8%	-35.11	20Y.8M
IEI	-9.45	-1.86	29.6%	-4.53	-0.85	22%	-2.31	0.13	3.47	14.2%	-35.11	21Y.1M
LQD	-14.61	-2.19	24.4%	-5.92	-1.09	24.2%	-3.58	1.18	3.95	12.9%	-45.79	21Y.3M
VTI	-18.54	-2.55	20.6%	-8.51	0.01	14.9%	-1.47	2.39	6.97	2.2%	-54.53	18Y.1M
VTV	-18.43	-2.93	21%	-8.13	0.48	12.9%	-0.49	2.50	6.82	0.9%	-55.68	17Y.10M
TLT	-21.79	-3.83	26.6%	-7.37	-2.37	28.1%	-4.99	0.33	4.82	14.2%	-56.13	22Y.0M
IJS	-20.02	0.29	14.6%	-8.11	3.86	5.5%	3.14	6.39	9.73	0%	-57.83	11Y.5M
VNQ	-26.58	-2.46	23.2%	-7.33	0.76	11.5%	0.14	4.35	7.44	0%	-69.76	14Y.11M
GLD	-20.28	-9.47	51.1%	-11.38	-5.24	44.3%	-7.77	-4.24	3.96	33.1%	-82.57	43Y.11M*

Order by **Maximum Drawdown** - **All data** (from 1871/1927 to 2023-11)

Portfolio	3Y Rolling Annualized Return (%)			7Y Rolling Annualized Return (%)			15Y Rolling Annualized Return (%)				Max Draw-down (%) ▼	Long Neg Period (Y.M)
	Worst	Base	%Fail	Worst	Base	%Fail	Worst	Base	Median	%Fail		
BIL	-0.10	0.65	3.6%	-0.05	0.76	1.3%	0.29	1.18	4.72	0%	-0.42	8Y.9M
SHY	-1.26	1.46	1.1%	0.39	1.52	0%	0.87	2.11	4.40	0%	-8.52	3Y.11M
IEI	-4.27	2.02	1.7%	-0.11	2.47	0.1%	1.37	2.65	3.94	0%	-13.59	7Y.7M
BND	-5.59	2.15	1.6%	-0.23	2.57	0.1%	1.40	2.67	4.00	0%	-17.28	7Y.6M
LQD	-6.71	1.93	3.6%	0.33	2.46	0%	1.32	2.65	4.03	0%	-23.27	6Y.3M
TLT	-17.32	1.45	7.9%	-4.12	2.10	2.8%	0.07	2.44	4.28	0%	-47.74	14Y.2M
GLD	-15.32	-1.61	23.9%	-6.75	-1.32	22.2%	-3.63	-0.50	0.05	21.3%	-61.78	62Y.0M
VNQ	-25.90	-0.81	17.8%	-7.36	1.29	7.9%	-1.75	2.31	8.05	1.8%	-68.30	19Y.5M
VTV	-43.29	-0.19	15.3%	-8.41	3.75	5.9%	-1.07	6.25	10.63	1.1%	-84.40	15Y.7M
VTI	-43.81	-0.56	15.9%	-9.49	3.29	4.2%	-0.35	5.49	8.60	0.1%	-84.60	15Y.8M
IJS	-49.09	1.17	13%	-7.75	5.98	4.3%	0.44	9.17	14.53	0%	-88.57	14Y.9M

Order by **Maximum Drawdown** - **All data** (from 1871/1927 to 2023-11) - **US Infl. Adjusted**

Portfolio	3Y Rolling Annualized Return (%)			7Y Rolling Annualized Return (%)			15Y Rolling Annualized Return (%)				Max Draw-down (%) ▼	Long Neg Period (Y.M)
	Worst	Base	%Fail	Worst	Base	%Fail	Worst	Base	Median	%Fail		
SHY	-12.29	-2.01	30.1%	-7.07	-1.41	25.7%	-3.27	-0.49	1.90	19.8%	-45.12	52Y.1M
BND	-13.89	-2.23	26.6%	-7.81	-1.23	25.1%	-3.27	-0.65	2.01	21.8%	-48.08	51Y.10M
BIL	-10.74	-1.91	33.8%	-6.82	-1.62	32.4%	-3.90	-0.88	1.22	24.4%	-48.08	92Y.5M
IEI	-13.90	-2.29	28.3%	-7.82	-1.26	26%	-3.29	-0.68	1.92	22.6%	-48.09	51Y.11M
LQD	-14.61	-2.39	26.9%	-7.93	-1.41	26.9%	-3.58	-0.79	2.27	25.9%	-56.56	84Y.5M
VNQ	-26.58	-3.33	31%	-7.33	-0.56	22.1%	-3.71	0.18	3.85	13.2%	-69.76	48Y.0M
TLT	-21.79	-3.09	29.4%	-8.20	-2.33	31.4%	-4.99	-1.40	2.66	32.5%	-70.04	87Y.7M
VTV	-38.79	-4.05	21.7%	-8.13	0.34	13.4%	-1.22	2.19	6.65	1.4%	-80.30	20Y.1M
VTI	-39.36	-2.49	20.7%	-8.51	0.77	12.6%	-2.10	2.40	6.93	2.5%	-80.55	26Y.4M
GLD	-20.28	-5.84	58.4%	-11.38	-4.43	56.9%	-7.77	-3.77	-0.10	50.5%	-82.57	132Y.3M
IJS	-45.05	-1.91	17.5%	-8.11	3.63	6%	0.72	6.44	10.61	0%	-85.57	14Y.8M

Ranking: Longest Negative Period

Order by **Longest Negative Period** - **Last 30 Years** (from 1993-12 to 2023-11)

Portfolio	3Y Rolling Annualized Return (%)			7Y Rolling Annualized Return (%)			15Y Rolling Annualized Return (%)				Max Draw-down (%)	Long Neg Period (Y.M) ▲
	Worst	Base	%Fail	Worst	Base	%Fail	Worst	Base	Median	%Fail		
SHY	-1.26	0.52	4.9%	0.39	0.72	0%	0.87	1.83	2.71	0%	-5.36	3Y.11M
HYG	-7.69	1.64	5.5%	0.42	4.22	0%	3.43	4.97	5.62	0%	-30.85	5Y.10M
LQD	-6.71	2.94	6.5%	0.33	4.15	0%	3.56	4.71	5.91	0%	-23.27	6Y.3M
BNDX	-4.35	3.16	6.2%	0.18	3.98	0%	3.31	4.85	5.62	0%	-14.88	6Y.5M
TIP	-2.68	1.49	6.2%	0.61	2.34	0%	2.51	3.78	5.31	0%	-14.76	6Y.5M
BND	-5.59	2.05	5.5%	-0.23	2.60	0.7%	2.36	3.62	4.64	0%	-17.28	7Y.6M
IEI	-4.27	1.24	6.2%	-0.11	1.77	0.7%	1.63	3.34	4.79	0%	-13.59	7Y.7M
VNQ	-25.03	1.58	11.7%	-1.16	5.57	0.7%	3.84	6.51	9.52	0%	-68.30	7Y.8M
IJS	-18.25	3.65	10.8%	-1.42	6.00	0.7%	5.15	7.80	9.07	0%	-54.13	8Y.1M
EMB	-7.65	3.53	7.4%	-0.47	4.25	0.7%	3.08	5.67	10.28	0%	-31.43	8Y.2M
CWB	-12.29	2.82	10.2%	0.04	5.07	0%	5.15	6.36	7.44	0%	-43.81	8Y.6M
BIL	-0.10	-0.03	19.7%	-0.05	0.16	7.9%	0.50	0.81	1.29	0%	-0.42	8Y.9M
SCZ	-20.24	-2.72	26.5%	-1.95	1.92	8.3%	1.82	5.17	7.62	0%	-63.26	9Y.4M
MTUM	-15.43	-3.44	19.1%	-0.57	5.24	0.7%	5.61	7.13	10.08	0%	-53.85	10Y.6M
VTI	-16.22	-1.94	16.9%	-2.98	3.78	2.2%	4.37	5.30	7.55	0%	-50.84	11Y.7M
VTV	-16.62	-2.60	17.5%	-3.00	4.01	1.4%	4.43	5.32	7.00	0%	-54.78	11Y.7M
TLT	-17.32	2.73	7.1%	-4.12	4.78	5.4%	1.81	5.76	7.02	0%	-47.74	12Y.1M
GLD	-15.02	-6.98	33.9%	-6.20	-2.30	24.2%	3.86	6.28	8.84	0%	-42.91	12Y.1M
VEA	-19.64	-3.37	22.8%	-2.53	1.87	4.7%	0.92	3.21	4.48	0%	-57.00	12Y.6M
EEM	-15.31	-4.00	33.9%	-6.71	-0.15	15.9%	-1.21	3.98	7.53	1.1%	-60.44	16Y.1M*

Order by **Longest Negative Period** - **Last 30 Years** (from 1993-12 to 2023-11) - **US Infl. Adjusted**

Portfolio	3Y Rolling Annualized Return (%)			7Y Rolling Annualized Return (%)			15Y Rolling Annualized Return (%)				Max Draw-down (%)	Long Neg Period (Y.M) ▲
	Worst	Base	%Fail	Worst	Base	%Fail	Worst	Base	Median	%Fail		
IJS	-20.02	0.94	13.9%	-3.83	3.54	2.2%	3.14	5.38	6.75	0%	-55.05	11Y.5M
CWB	-14.19	0.44	13.9%	-2.50	2.84	2.5%	2.76	3.91	5.11	0%	-45.00	11Y.5M
HYG	-9.89	-1.09	21.9%	-2.13	1.90	5.8%	0.87	2.68	3.33	0%	-32.45	12Y.2M
VNQ	-26.58	-1.64	19.7%	-3.59	3.05	4.3%	1.31	4.37	6.98	0%	-69.76	12Y.2M
MTUM	-17.26	-5.53	23.4%	-3.05	2.60	2.2%	3.37	4.81	7.64	0%	-54.55	12Y.5M
BNDX	-9.52	0.70	10.5%	-3.24	2.03	8.3%	0.01	2.61	3.42	0%	-26.46	13Y.2M
LQD	-11.76	0.32	12%	-3.07	2.18	7.6%	1.14	2.49	3.64	0%	-33.86	13Y.2M
EMB	-12.06	1.67	11.1%	-3.86	2.47	7.6%	0.67	3.63	8.01	0%	-35.97	13Y.3M
GLD	-15.87	-8.89	42.5%	-8.11	-4.32	30.3%	1.46	3.82	6.62	0%	-45.57	13Y.3M
VTI	-18.24	-4.37	20%	-5.40	1.18	6.9%	2.16	2.90	5.14	0%	-51.59	13Y.5M
VTV	-18.43	-4.60	22.8%	-5.42	1.48	4.7%	1.98	2.88	4.80	0%	-55.68	13Y.6M
TIP	-7.96	-0.43	20.3%	-2.39	0.10	13.7%	0.17	1.68	3.23	0%	-23.74	15Y.9M
SCZ	-21.97	-5.36	35.4%	-4.39	-0.11	17%	-0.55	2.91	5.27	1.7%	-63.82	16Y.6M
EEM	-17.17	-6.03	44.6%	-9.04	-1.79	32.1%	-3.52	1.77	5.19	9.9%	-61.05	17Y.9M
TLT	-21.79	0.37	12.9%	-7.37	2.55	7.9%	-0.68	3.59	4.79	1.1%	-55.99	18Y.5M
BND	-10.69	0.09	14.5%	-3.61	0.84	8.3%	0.00	1.49	2.53	0.5%	-30.25	20Y.5M
IEI	-9.45	-0.57	23.7%	-3.52	0.10	13%	-0.85	1.21	2.67	7.7%	-26.99	21Y.1M
VEA	-21.58	-5.93	31.7%	-4.84	-0.34	20.2%	-1.43	0.86	2.18	6.1%	-57.66	22Y.9M
SHY	-6.65	-1.40	47.4%	-2.90	-1.02	35.4%	-1.59	-0.29	0.65	29.8%	-23.76	25Y.8M
BIL	-4.61	-2.06	62.5%	-2.40	-1.62	66.4%	-1.84	-1.20	-0.68	71.8%	-25.55	30Y.0M*

Order by **Longest Negative Period - Last 60 Years** (from 1963-12 to 2023-11)

Portfolio	3Y Rolling Annualized Return (%)			7Y Rolling Annualized Return (%)			15Y Rolling Annualized Return (%)				Max Draw-down (%)	Long Neg Period (Y.M) ▲
	Worst	Base	%Fail	Worst	Base	%Fail	Worst	Base	Median	%Fail		
SHY	-1.26	1.29	2.3%	0.39	1.39	0%	0.87	2.34	6.67	0%	-8.52	3Y.11M
LQD	-6.71	2.00	7.6%	0.33	4.15	0%	3.30	5.03	7.09	0%	-23.27	6Y.3M
BND	-5.59	2.53	2.6%	-0.23	4.05	0.3%	2.36	4.28	7.03	0%	-17.28	7Y.6M
IEI	-4.27	2.12	2.9%	-0.11	3.38	0.3%	1.63	4.28	7.14	0%	-13.59	7Y.7M
IJS	-18.25	4.44	9.2%	-2.35	6.98	1.7%	5.15	8.94	14.42	0%	-54.13	8Y.1M
BIL	-0.10	0.60	9.3%	-0.05	0.68	3.5%	0.50	1.21	5.38	0%	-0.42	8Y.9M
VNQ	-25.03	1.44		-1.87	4.78	1.6%	3.84	8.22	10.82	0%	-68.30	11Y.1M
VTI	-16.22	1.87	12.6%	-3.00	4.15	1.7%	4.37	6.49	10.48	0%	-50.84	11Y.7M
VTV	-16.62	1.09	12.4%	-3.00	4.15	1.6%	4.43	6.38	10.91	0%	-54.78	11Y.7M
TLT	-17.32	0.70	12.6%	-4.12	3.10	2.3%	1.81	5.52	8.25	0%	-47.74	12Y.1M
GLD	-15.32	-6.07	32.9%	-6.75	-2.30	29.7%	-3.63	-1.12	7.05	19.6%	-61.78	27Y.5M

Order by **Longest Negative Period - Last 60 Years** (from 1963-12 to 2023-11) - **US Infl. Adjusted**

Portfolio	3Y Rolling Annualized Return (%)			7Y Rolling Annualized Return (%)			15Y Rolling Annualized Return (%)				Max Draw-down (%)	Long Neg Period (Y.M) ▲
	Worst	Base	%Fail	Worst	Base	%Fail	Worst	Base	Median	%Fail		
IJS	-20.02	0.29	14.6%	-8.11	3.86	5.5%	3.14	6.39	9.73	0%	-57.83	11Y.5M
VNQ	-26.58	-2.46	23.2%	-7.33	0.76	11.5%	0.14	4.35	7.44	0%	-69.76	14Y.11M
VTV	-18.43	-2.93	21%	-8.13	0.48	12.9%	-0.49	2.50	6.82	0.9%	-55.68	17Y.10M
VTI	-18.54	-2.55	20.6%	-8.51	0.01	14.9%	-1.47	2.39	6.97	2.2%	-54.53	18Y.1M
BND	-10.69	-1.75	25.1%	-4.53	-0.74	19.9%	-2.30	0.30	3.30	11.8%	-35.11	20Y.8M
IEI	-9.45	-1.86	29.6%	-4.53	-0.85	22%	-2.31	0.13	3.47	14.2%	-35.11	21Y.1M
LQD	-14.61	-2.19	24.4%	-5.92	-1.09	24.2%	-3.58	1.18	3.95	12.9%	-45.79	21Y.3M
TLT	-21.79	-3.83	26.6%	-7.37	-2.37	28.1%	-4.99	0.33	4.82	14.2%	-56.13	22Y.0M
SHY	-6.65	-1.57	36.2%	-3.25	-0.94	28.1%	-1.59	-0.10	2.29	16.8%	-23.89	25Y.8M
BIL	-4.61	-1.68	43.8%	-2.40	-1.35	43.3%	-1.84	-0.77	1.09	31.8%	-25.55	35Y.2M
GLD	-20.28	-9.47	51.1%	-11.38	-5.24	44.3%	-7.77	-4.24	3.96	33.1%	-82.57	43Y.11M*

Order by **Longest Negative Period** - All data (from 1871/1927 to 2023-11)

Portfolio	3Y Rolling Annualized Return (%)			7Y Rolling Annualized Return (%)			15Y Rolling Annualized Return (%)				Max Draw-down (%)	Long Neg Period (Y.M)
	Worst	Base	%Fail	Worst	Base	%Fail	Worst	Base	Median	%Fail		
SHY	-1.26	1.46	1.1%	0.39	1.52	0%	0.87	2.11	4.40	0%	-8.52	3Y.11M
LQD	-6.71	1.93	3.6%	0.33	2.46	0%	1.32	2.65	4.03	0%	-23.27	6Y.3M
BND	-5.59	2.15	1.6%	-0.23	2.57	0.1%	1.40	2.67	4.00	0%	-17.28	7Y.6M
IEI	-4.27	2.02	1.7%	-0.11	2.47	0.1%	1.37	2.65	3.94	0%	-13.59	7Y.7M
BIL	-0.10	0.65	3.6%	-0.05	0.76	1.3%	0.29	1.18	4.72	0%	-0.42	8Y.9M
TLT	-17.32	1.45	7.9%	-4.12	2.10	2.8%	0.07	2.44	4.28	0%	-47.74	14Y.2M
IJS	-49.09	1.17	13%	-7.75	5.98	4.3%	0.44	9.17	14.53	0%	-88.57	14Y.9M
VTV	-43.29	-0.19	15.3%	-8.41	3.75	5.9%	-1.07		10.63	1.1%	-84.40	15Y.7M
VTI	-43.81	-0.56	15.9%	-9.49	3.29	4.2%	-0.35	5.49	8.60	0.1%	-84.60	15Y.8M
VNQ	-25.90	-0.81	17.8%	-7.36	1.29	7.9%	-1.75	2.31	8.05	1.8%	-68.30	19Y.5M
GLD	-15.32	-1.61	23.9%	-6.75	-1.32	22.2%	-3.63	-0.50	0.05	21.3%	-61.78	62Y.0M

Order by **Longest Negative Period** - All data (from 1871/1927 to 2023-11) - **US Infl. Adjusted**

Portfolio	3Y Rolling Annualized Return (%)			7Y Rolling Annualized Return (%)			15Y Rolling Annualized Return (%)				Max Draw-down (%)	Long Neg Period (Y.M)
	Worst	Base	%Fail	Worst	Base	%Fail	Worst	Base	Median	%Fail		
IJS	-45.05	-1.91	17.5%	-8.11	3.63	6%	0.72	6.44	10.61	0%	-85.57	14Y.8M
VTV	-38.79	-4.05	21.7%	-8.13	0.34	13.4%	-1.22	2.19	6.65	1.4%	-80.30	20Y.1M
VTI	-39.36	-2.49	20.7%	-8.51	0.77	12.6%	-2.10	2.40	6.93	2.5%	-80.55	26Y.4M
VNQ	-26.58	-3.33	31%	-7.33	-0.56	22.1%	-3.71	0.18	3.85	13.2%	-69.76	48Y.0M
BND	-13.89	-2.23	26.6%	-7.81	-1.23	25.1%	-3.27	-0.65	2.01	21.8%	-48.08	51Y.10M
IEI	-13.90	-2.29	28.3%	-7.82	-1.26	26%	-3.29	-0.68	1.92	22.6%	-48.09	51Y.11M
SHY	-12.29	-2.01	30.1%	-7.07	-1.41	25.7%	-3.27	-0.49	1.90	19.8%	-45.12	52Y.1M
LQD	-14.61	-2.39	26.9%	-7.93	-1.41	26.9%	-3.58	-0.79	2.27	25.9%	-56.56	84Y.5M
TLT	-21.79	-3.09	29.4%	-8.20	-2.33	31.4%	-4.99	-1.40	2.66	32.5%	-70.04	87Y.7M
BIL	-10.74	-1.91	33.8%	-6.82	-1.62	32.4%	-3.90	-0.88	1.22	24.4%	-48.08	92Y.5M
GLD	-20.28	-5.84	58.4%	-11.38	-4.43	56.9%	-7.77	-3.77	-0.10	50.5%	-82.57	132Y.3M

Ranking: Baseline 7Y Return

Order by **Baseline 7Y Return - Last 30 Years** (from 1993-12 to 2023-11)

Portfolio	3Y Rolling Annualized Return (%)			7Y Rolling Annualized Return (%)			15Y Rolling Annualized Return (%)				Max Draw-down (%)	Long Neg Period (Y.M)
	Worst	Base	%Fail	Worst	Base ▼	%Fail	Worst	Base	Median	%Fail		
IJS	-18.25	3.65	10.8%	-1.42	6.00	0.7%	5.15	7.80	9.07	0%	-54.13	8Y.1M
VNQ	-25.03	1.58	11.7%	-1.16	5.57	0.7%	3.84	6.51	9.52	0%	-68.30	7Y.8M
MTUM	-15.43	-3.44	19.1%	-0.57	5.24	0.7%	5.61	7.13	10.08	0%	-53.85	10Y.6M
CWB	-12.29	2.82	10.2%	0.04	5.07	0%	5.15	6.36	7.44	0%	-43.81	8Y.6M
TLT	-17.32	2.73	7.1%	-4.12	4.78	5.4%	1.81	5.76	7.02	0%	-47.74	12Y.1M
EMB	-7.65	3.53	7.4%	-0.47	4.25	0.7%	3.08	5.67	10.28	0%	-31.43	8Y.2M
HYG	-7.69	1.64	5.5%	0.42	4.22	0%	3.43	4.97	5.62	0%	-30.85	5Y.10M
LQD	-6.71	2.94	6.5%	0.33	4.15	0%	3.56	4.71	5.91	0%	-23.27	6Y.3M
VTV	-16.62	-2.60	17.5%	-3.00	4.01	1.4%	4.43	5.32	7.00	0%	-54.78	11Y.7M
BNDX	-4.35	3.16	6.2%	0.18	3.98	0%	3.31	4.85	5.62	0%	-14.88	6Y.5M
VTI	-16.22	-1.94	16.9%	-2.98	3.78	2.2%	4.37	5.30	7.55	0%	-50.84	11Y.7M
BND	-5.59	2.05	5.5%	-0.23	2.60	0.7%	2.36	3.62	4.64	0%	-17.28	7Y.6M
TIP	-2.68	1.49	6.2%	0.61	2.34	0%	2.51	3.78	5.31	0%	-14.76	6Y.5M
SCZ	-20.24	-2.72	26.5%	-1.95	1.92	8.3%	1.82	5.17	7.62	0%	-63.26	9Y.4M
VEA	-19.64	-3.37	22.8%	-2.53	1.87	4.7%	0.92	3.21	4.48	0%	-57.00	12Y.6M
IEI	-4.27	1.24	6.2%	-0.11	1.77	0.7%	1.63	3.34	4.79	0%	-13.59	7Y.7M
SHY	-1.26	0.52	4.9%	0.39	0.72	0%	0.87	1.83	2.71	0%	-5.36	3Y.11M
BIL	-0.10	-0.03	19.7%	-0.05	0.16	7.9%	0.50	0.81	1.29	0%	-0.42	8Y.9M
EEM	-15.31	-4.00	33.9%	-6.71	-0.15	15.9%	-1.21	3.98	7.53	1.1%	-60.44	16Y.1M*
GLD	-15.02	-6.98	33.9%	-6.20	-2.30	24.2%	3.86	6.28	8.84	0%	-42.91	12Y.1M

Order by **Baseline 7Y Return - Last 30 Years** (from 1993-12 to 2023-11) - **US Infl. Adjusted**

Portfolio	3Y Rolling Annualized Return (%)			7Y Rolling Annualized Return (%)			15Y Rolling Annualized Return (%)				Max Draw-down (%)	Long Neg Period (Y.M)
	Worst	Base	%Fail	Worst	Base ▼	%Fail	Worst	Base	Median	%Fail		
IJS	-20.02	0.94	13.9%	-3.83	3.54	2.2%	3.14	5.38	6.75	0%	-55.05	11Y.5M
VNQ	-26.58	-1.64	19.7%	-3.59	3.05	4.3%	1.31	4.37	6.98	0%	-69.76	12Y.2M
CWB	-14.19	0.44	13.9%	-2.50	2.84	2.5%	2.76	3.91	5.11	0%	-45.00	11Y.5M
MTUM	-17.26	-5.53	23.4%	-3.05	2.60	2.2%	3.37	4.81	7.64	0%	-54.55	12Y.5M
TLT	-21.79	0.37	12.9%	-7.37	2.55	7.9%	-0.68	3.59	4.79	1.1%	-55.99	18Y.5M
EMB	-12.06	1.67	11.1%	-3.86	2.47	7.6%	0.67	3.63	8.01	0%	-35.97	13Y.3M
LQD	-11.76	0.32	12%	-3.07	2.18	7.6%	1.14	2.49	3.64	0%	-33.86	13Y.2M
BNDX	-9.52	0.78	10.5%	-3.24	2.03	8.3%	0.91	2.61	3.42	0%	-26.46	13Y.2M
HYG	-9.89	-1.09	21.9%	-2.13	1.90	5.8%	0.87	2.68	3.33	0%	-32.45	12Y.2M
VTV	-18.43	-4.60	22.8%	-5.42	1.48	4.7%	1.98	2.88	4.80	0%	-55.68	13Y.6M
VTI	-18.24	-4.37	20%	-5.40	1.18	6.9%	2.16	2.90	5.14	0%	-51.59	13Y.5M
BND	-10.69	0.09	14.5%	-3.61	0.84	8.3%	0.00	1.49	2.53	0.5%	-30.25	20Y.5M
TIP	-7.96	-0.43	20.3%	-2.39	0.10	13.7%	0.17	1.68	3.23	0%	-23.74	15Y.9M
IEI	-9.45	-0.57	23.7%	-3.52	0.10	13%	-0.85	1.21	2.67	7.7%	-26.99	21Y.1M
SCZ	-21.97	-5.36	35.4%	-4.39	-0.11	17%	-0.55	2.91	5.27	1.7%	-63.82	16Y.6M
VEA	-21.58	-5.93	31.7%	-4.84	-0.34	20.2%	-1.43	0.86	2.18	6.1%	-57.66	22Y.9M
SHY	-6.65	-1.40	47.4%	-2.90	-1.02	35.4%	-1.59	-0.29	0.65	29.8%	-23.76	25Y.8M
BIL	-4.61	-2.06	62.5%	-2.40	-1.62	66.4%	-1.84	-1.20	-0.68	71.8%	-25.55	30Y.0M*
EEM	-17.17	-6.03	44.6%	-9.04	-1.79	32.1%	-3.52	1.77	5.19	9.9%	-61.05	17Y.9M
GLD	-15.87	-8.89	42.5%	-8.11	-4.32	30.3%	1.46	3.82	6.62	0%	-45.57	13Y.3M

Order by **Baseline 7Y Return - Last 60 Years** (from 1963-12 to 2023-11)

Portfolio	3Y Rolling Annualized Return (%)			7Y Rolling Annualized Return (%)			15Y Rolling Annualized Return (%)				Max Draw-down (%)	Long Neg Period (Y.M)
	Worst	Base	%Fail	Worst	Base ▼	%Fail	Worst	Base	Median	%Fail		
IJS	-18.25	4.44	9.2%	-2.35	6.98	1.7%	5.15	8.94	14.42	0%	-54.13	8Y.1M
VNQ	-25.03	1.44	11.2%	-1.87	4.78	1.6%	3.84	8.22	10.82	0%	-68.30	11Y.1M
LQD	-6.71	2.00	7.6%	0.33	4.15	0%	3.30	5.03	7.09	0%	-23.27	6Y.3M
VTV	-16.62	1.09	12.4%	-3.00	4.15	1.6%	4.43	6.38	10.91	0%	-54.78	11Y.7M
VTI	-16.22	1.87	12.6%	-3.00	4.15	1.7%	4.37	6.49	10.48	0%	-50.84	11Y.7M
BND	-5.59	2.53	2.6%	-0.23	4.05	0.3%	2.36	4.28	7.03	0%	-17.28	7Y.6M
IEI	-4.27	2.12	2.9%	-0.11	3.38	0.3%	1.63	4.28	7.14	0%	-13.59	7Y.7M
TLT	-17.32	0.70	12.6%	-4.12	3.10	2.3%	1.81	5.52	8.25	0%	-47.74	12Y.1M
SHY	-1.26	1.29	2.3%	0.39	1.39	0%	0.87	2.34	6.67	0%	-8.52	3Y.11M
BIL	-0.10	0.60	9.3%	-0.05	0.68	3.5%	0.50	1.21	5.38	0%	-0.42	8Y.9M
GLD	-15.32	-6.07	32.9%	-6.75	-2.30	29.7%	-3.63	-1.12	7.05	19.6%	-61.78	27Y.5M

Order by **Baseline 7Y Return - Last 60 Years** (from 1963-12 to 2023-11) - **US Infl. Adjusted**

Portfolio	3Y Rolling Annualized Return (%)			7Y Rolling Annualized Return (%)			15Y Rolling Annualized Return (%)				Max Draw-down (%)	Long Neg Period (Y.M)
	Worst	Base	%Fail	Worst	Base ▼	%Fail	Worst	Base	Median	%Fail		
IJS	-20.02	0.29	14.6%	-8.11	3.86	5.5%	3.14	6.39	9.73	0%	-57.83	11Y.5M
VNQ	-26.58	-2.46	23.2%	-7.33	0.76	11.5%	0.14	4.35	7.44	0%	-69.76	14Y.11M
VTV	-18.43	-2.93	21%	-8.13	0.48	12.9%	-0.49	2.50	6.82	0.9%	-55.68	17Y.10M
VTI	-18.54	-2.55	20.6%	-8.51	0.01	14.9%	-1.47	2.39	6.97	2.2%	-54.53	18Y.1M
BND	-10.69	-1.75	25.1%	-4.53	-0.74	19.9%	-2.30	0.30	3.30	11.8%	-35.11	20Y.8M
IEI	-9.45	-1.86	29.6%	-4.53	-0.85	22%	-2.31	0.13	3.47	14.2%	-35.11	21Y.1M
SHY	-6.65	-1.57	36.2%	-3.25	-0.94	28.1%	-1.59	-0.10	2.29	16.8%	-23.89	25Y.8M
LQD	-14.61	-2.19	24.4%	-5.92	-1.09	24.2%	-3.58	1.18	3.95	12.9%	-45.79	21Y.3M
BIL	-4.61	-1.68	43.8%	-2.40	-1.35	43.3%	-1.84	-0.77	1.09	31.8%	-25.55	35Y.2M
TLT	-21.79	-3.83	26.6%	-7.37	-2.37	28.1%	-4.99	0.33	4.82	14.2%	-56.13	22Y.0M
GLD	-20.28	-9.47	51.1%	-11.38	-5.24	44.3%	-7.77	-4.24	3.96	33.1%	-82.57	43Y.11M*

Order by **Baseline 7Y Return** - **All data** (from 1871/1927 to 2023-11)

Portfolio	3Y Rolling Annualized Return (%)			7Y Rolling Annualized Return (%)			15Y Rolling Annualized Return (%)				Max Draw-down (%)	Long Neg Period (Y.M)
	Worst	Base	%Fail	Worst	Base ▼	%Fail	Worst	Base	Median	%Fail		
IJS	-49.09	1.17	13%	-7.75	5.98	4.3%	0.44	9.17	14.53	0%	-88.57	14Y.9M
VTV	-43.29	-0.19	15.3%	-8.41	3.75	5.9%	-1.07	6.25	10.63	1.1%	-84.40	15Y.7M
VTI	-43.81	-0.56	15.9%	-9.49	3.29	4.2%	-0.35	5.49	8.60	0.1%	-84.60	15Y.8M
BND	-5.59	2.15	1.6%	-0.23	2.57	0.1%	1.40	2.67	4.00	0%	-17.28	7Y.6M
IEI	-4.27	2.02	1.7%	-0.11	2.47	0.1%	1.37	2.65	3.94	0%	-13.59	7Y.7M
LQD	-6.71	1.93	3.6%	0.33	2.46	0%	1.32	2.65	4.03	0%	-23.27	6Y.3M
TLT	-17.32	1.45	7.9%	-4.12	2.10	2.8%	0.07	2.44	4.28	0%	-47.74	14Y.2M
SHY	-1.26	1.46	1.1%	0.39	1.52	0%	0.87	2.11	4.40	0%	-8.52	3Y.11M
VNQ	-25.90	-0.81	17.8%	-7.36	1.29	7.9%	-1.75	2.31	8.05	1.8%	-68.30	19Y.5M
BIL	-0.10	0.65	3.6%	-0.05	0.76	1.3%	0.29	1.18	4.72	0%	-0.42	8Y.9M
GLD	-15.32	-1.61	23.9%	-6.75	-1.32	22.2%	-3.63	-0.50	0.05	21.3%	-61.78	62Y.0M

Order by **Baseline 7Y Return** - **All data** (from 1871/1927 to 2023-11) - **US Infl. Adjusted**

Portfolio	3Y Rolling Annualized Return (%)			7Y Rolling Annualized Return (%)			15Y Rolling Annualized Return (%)				Max Draw-down (%)	Long Neg Period (Y.M)
	Worst	Base	%Fail	Worst	Base ▼	%Fail	Worst	Base	Median	%Fail		
IJS	-45.05	-1.91	17.5%	-8.11	3.63	6%	0.72	6.44	10.61	0%	-85.57	14Y.8M
VTI	-39.36	-2.49	20.7%	-8.51	0.77	12.6%	-2.10	2.40	6.93	2.5%	-80.55	26Y.4M
VTV	-38.79	-4.05	21.7%	-8.13	0.34	13.4%	-1.22	2.19	6.65	1.4%	-80.30	20Y.1M
VNQ	-26.58	-3.33	31%	-7.33	-0.56	22.1%	-3.71	0.18	3.85	13.2%	-69.76	48Y.0M
BND	-13.89	-2.23	26.6%	-7.81	-1.23	25.1%	-3.27	-0.65	2.01	21.8%	-48.08	51Y.10M
IEI	-13.90	-2.29	28.3%	-7.82	-1.26	26%	-3.29	-0.68	1.92	22.6%	-48.09	51Y.11M
LQD	-14.61	-2.39	26.9%	-7.93	-1.41	26.9%	-3.58	-0.79	2.27	25.9%	-56.56	84Y.5M
SHY	-12.29	-2.01	30.1%	-7.07	-1.41	25.7%	-3.27	-0.49	1.90	19.8%	-45.12	52Y.1M
BIL	-10.74	-1.91	33.8%	-6.82	-1.62	32.4%	-3.90	-0.88	1.22	24.4%	-48.08	92Y.5M
TLT	-21.79	-3.09	29.4%	-8.20	-2.33	31.4%	-4.99	-1.40	2.66	32.5%	-70.04	87Y.7M
GLD	-20.28	-5.84	58.4%	-11.38	-4.43	56.9%	-7.77	-3.77	-0.10	50.5%	-82.57	132Y.3M

Ranking: Baseline 15Y Return

Order by **Baseline 15Y Return - Last 30 Years** (from 1993-12 to 2023-11)

Portfolio	3Y Rolling Annualized Return (%)			7Y Rolling Annualized Return (%)			15Y Rolling Annualized Return (%)				Max Draw-down (%)	Long Neg Period (Y.M)
	Worst	Base	%Fail	Worst	Base	%Fail	Worst	Base ▼	Median	%Fail		
IJS	-18.25	3.65	10.8%	-1.42	6.00	0.7%	5.15	7.80	9.07	0%	-54.13	8Y.1M
MTUM	-15.43	-3.44	19.1%	-0.57	5.24	0.7%	5.61	7.13	10.08	0%	-53.85	10Y.6M
VNQ	-25.03	1.58	11.7%	-1.16	5.57	0.7%	3.84	6.51	9.52	0%	-68.30	7Y.8M
CWB	-12.29	2.82	10.2%	0.04	5.07	0%	5.15	6.36	7.44	0%	-43.81	8Y.6M
GLD	-15.02	-6.98	33.9%	-6.20	-2.30	24.2%	3.86	6.28	8.84	0%	-42.91	12Y.1M
TLT	-17.32	2.73	7.1%	-4.12	4.78	5.4%	1.81	5.76	7.02	0%	-47.74	12Y.1M
EMB	-7.65	3.53	7.4%	-0.47	4.25	0.7%	3.08	5.67	10.28	0%	-31.43	8Y.2M
VTV	-16.62	-2.60	17.5%	-3.00	4.01	1.4%	4.43	5.32	7.00	0%	-54.78	11Y.7M
VTI	-16.22	-1.94	16.9%	-2.98	3.78	2.2%	4.37	5.30	7.55	0%	-50.84	11Y.7M
SCZ	-20.24	-2.72	26.5%	-1.95	1.92	8.3%	1.82	5.17	7.62	0%	-63.26	9Y.4M
HYG	-7.69	1.64	5.5%	0.42	4.22	0%	3.43	4.97	5.62	0%	-30.85	5Y.10M
BNDX	-4.35	3.16	6.2%	0.18	3.98	0%	3.31	4.85	5.62	0%	-14.88	6Y.5M
LQD	-6.71	2.94	6.5%	0.33	4.15	0%	3.56	4.71	5.91	0%	-23.27	6Y.3M
EEM	-15.31	-4.00	33.9%	-6.71	-0.15	15.9%	-1.21	3.98	7.53	1.1%	-60.44	16Y.1M*
TIP	-2.68	1.49	6.2%	0.61	2.34	0%	2.51	3.78	5.31	0%	-14.76	6Y.5M
BND	-5.59	2.05	5.5%	-0.23	2.60	0.7%	2.36	3.62	4.64	0%	-17.28	7Y.6M
IEI	-4.27	1.24	6.2%	-0.11	1.77	0.7%	1.63	3.34	4.79	0%	-13.59	7Y.7M
VEA	-19.64	-3.37	22.8%	-2.53	1.87	4.7%	0.92	3.21	4.48	0%	-57.00	12Y.6M
SHY	-1.26	0.52	4.9%	0.39	0.72	0%	0.87	1.83	2.71	0%	-5.36	3Y.11M
BIL	-0.10	-0.03	19.7%	-0.05	0.16	7.9%	0.50	0.81	1.29	0%	-0.42	8Y.9M

Order by **Baseline 15Y Return - Last 30 Years** (from 1993-12 to 2023-11) - **US Infl. Adjusted**

Portfolio	3Y Rolling Annualized Return (%)			7Y Rolling Annualized Return (%)			15Y Rolling Annualized Return (%)				Max Draw-down (%)	Long Neg Period (Y.M)
	Worst	Base	%Fail	Worst	Base	%Fail	Worst	Base ▼	Median	%Fail		
IJS	-20.02	0.94	13.9%	-3.83	3.54	2.2%	3.14	5.38	6.75	0%	-55.05	11Y.5M
MTUM	-17.26	-5.53	23.4%	-3.05	2.60	2.2%	3.37	4.81	7.64	0%	-54.55	12Y.5M
VNQ	-26.58	-1.64	19.7%	-3.59	3.05	4.3%	1.31	4.37	6.98	0%	-69.76	12Y.2M
CWB	-14.19	0.44	13.9%	-2.50	2.84	2.5%	2.76	3.91	5.11	0%	-45.00	11Y.5M
GLD	-15.87	-8.89	42.5%	-8.11	-4.32	30.3%	1.46	3.82	6.62	0%	-45.57	13Y.3M
EMB	-12.06	1.67	11.1%	-3.86	2.47	7.6%	0.67	3.63	8.01	0%	-35.97	13Y.3M
TLT	-21.79	0.37	12.9%	-7.37	2.55	7.9%	-0.68	3.59	4.79	1.1%	-55.99	18Y.5M
SCZ	-21.97	-5.36	35.4%	-4.39	-0.11	17%	-0.55	2.91	5.27	1.7%	-63.82	16Y.6M
VTI	-18.24	-4.37	20%	-5.40	1.18	6.9%	2.16	2.90	5.14	0%	-51.59	13Y.5M
VTV	-18.43	-4.60	22.8%	-5.42	1.48	4.7%	1.98	2.88	4.80	0%	-55.68	13Y.6M
HYG	-9.89	-1.09	21.9%	-2.13	1.90	5.8%	0.87	2.68	3.33	0%	-32.45	12Y.2M
BNDX	-9.52	0.78	10.5%	-3.24	2.03	8.3%	0.91	2.61	3.42	0%	-26.46	13Y.2M
LQD	-11.76	0.32	12%	-3.07	2.18	7.6%	1.14	2.49	3.64	0%	-33.86	13Y.2M
EEM	-17.17	-6.03	44.6%	-9.04	-1.79	32.1%	-3.52	1.77	5.19	9.9%	-61.05	17Y.9M
TIP	-7.96	-0.43	20.3%	-2.39	0.10	13.7%	0.17	1.68	3.23	0%	-23.74	15Y.9M
BND	-10.69	0.09	14.5%	-3.61	0.84	8.3%	0.00	1.49	2.53	0.5%	-30.25	20Y.5M
IEI	-9.45	-0.57	23.7%	-3.52	0.10	13%	-0.85	1.21	2.67	7.7%	-26.99	21Y.1M
VEA	-21.58	-5.93	31.7%	-4.84	-0.34	20.2%	-1.43	0.86	2.18	6.1%	-57.66	22Y.9M
SHY	-6.65	-1.40	47.4%	-2.90	-1.02	35.4%	-1.59	-0.29	0.65	29.8%	-23.76	25Y.8M
BIL	-4.61	-2.06	62.5%	-2.40	-1.62	66.4%	-1.84	-1.20	-0.68	71.8%	-25.55	30Y.0M*

Order by **Baseline 15Y Return** - **Last 60 Years** (from 1963-12 to 2023-11)

Portfolio	3Y Rolling Annualized Return (%)			7Y Rolling Annualized Return (%)			15Y Rolling Annualized Return (%)				Max Draw-down (%)	Long Neg Period (Y.M)
	Worst	Base	%Fail	Worst	Base	%Fail	Worst	Base ▼	Median	%Fail		
IJS	-18.25	4.44	9.2%	-2.35	6.98	1.7%	5.15	8.94	14.42	0%	-54.13	8Y.1M
VNQ	-25.03	1.44	11.2%	-1.87	4.78	1.6%	3.84	8.22	10.82	0%	-68.30	11Y.1M
VTI	-16.22	1.87	12.6%	-3.00	4.15	1.7%	4.37	6.49	10.48	0%	-50.84	11Y.7M
VTV	-16.62	1.09	12.4%	-3.00	4.15	1.6%	4.43	6.38	10.91	0%	-54.78	11Y.7M
TLT	-17.32	0.70	12.6%	-4.12	3.10	2.3%	1.81	5.52	8.25	0%	-47.74	12Y.1M
LQD	-6.71	2.00	7.6%	0.33	4.15	0%	3.30	5.03	7.09	0%	-23.27	6Y.3M
BND	-5.59	2.53	2.6%	-0.23	4.05	0.3%	2.36	4.28	7.03	0%	-17.28	7Y.6M
IEI	-4.27	2.12	2.9%	-0.11	3.38	0.3%	1.63	4.28	7.14	0%	-13.59	7Y.7M
SHY	-1.26	1.29	2.3%	0.39	1.39	0%	0.87	2.34	6.67	0%	-8.52	3Y.11M
BIL	-0.10	0.60	9.3%	-0.05	0.68	3.5%	0.50	1.21	5.38	0%	-0.42	8Y.9M
GLD	-15.32	-6.07	32.9%	-6.75	-2.30	29.7%	-3.63	-1.12	7.05	19.6%	-61.78	27Y.5M

Order by **Baseline 15Y Return** - **Last 60 Years** (from 1963-12 to 2023-11) - **US Infl. Adjusted**

Portfolio	3Y Rolling Annualized Return (%)			7Y Rolling Annualized Return (%)			15Y Rolling Annualized Return (%)				Max Draw-down (%)	Long Neg Period (Y.M)
	Worst	Base	%Fail	Worst	Base	%Fail	Worst	Base ▼	Median	%Fail		
IJS	-20.02	0.29	14.6%	-8.11	3.86	5.5%	3.14	6.39	9.73	0%	-57.83	11Y.5M
VNQ	-26.58	-2.46	23.2%	-7.33	0.76	11.5%	0.14	4.35	7.44	0%	-69.76	14Y.11M
VTV	-18.43	-2.93	21%	-8.13	0.48	12.9%	-0.49	2.50	6.82	0.9%	-55.68	17Y.10M
VTI	-18.54	-2.55	20.6%	-8.51	0.01	14.9%	-1.47	2.39	6.97	2.2%	-54.53	18Y.1M
LQD	-14.61	-2.19	24.4%	-5.92	-1.09	24.2%	-3.58	1.18	3.95	12.9%	-45.79	21Y.3M
TLT	-21.79	-3.83	26.6%	-7.37	-2.37	28.1%	-4.99	0.33	4.82	14.2%	-56.13	22Y.0M
BND	-10.69	-1.75	25.1%	-4.53	-0.74	19.9%	-2.30	0.30	3.30	11.8%	-35.11	20Y.8M
IEI	-9.45	-1.86	29.6%	-4.53	-0.85	22%	-2.31	0.13	3.47	14.2%	-35.11	21Y.1M
SHY	-6.65	-1.57	36.2%	-3.25	-0.94	28.1%	-1.59	-0.10	2.29	16.8%	-23.89	25Y.8M
BIL	-4.61	-1.68	43.8%	-2.40	-1.35	43.3%	-1.84	-0.77	1.09	31.8%	-25.55	35Y.2M
GLD	-20.28	-9.47	51.1%	-11.38	-5.24	44.3%	-7.77	-4.24	3.96	33.1%	-82.57	43Y.11M*

Order by **Baseline 15Y Return - All data** (from 1871/1927 to 2023-11)

Portfolio	3Y Rolling Annualized Return (%)			7Y Rolling Annualized Return (%)			15Y Rolling Annualized Return (%)				Max Draw-down (%)	Long Neg Period (Y.M)
	Worst	Base	%Fail	Worst	Base	%Fail	Worst	Base ▼	Median	%Fail		
IJS	-49.09	1.17	13%	-7.75	5.98	4.3%	0.44	9.17	14.53	0%	-88.57	14Y.9M
VTV	-43.29	-0.19	15.3%	-8.41	3.75	5.9%	-1.07	6.25	10.63	1.1%	-84.40	15Y.7M
VTI	-43.81	-0.56	15.9%	-9.49	3.29	4.2%	-0.35	5.49	8.60	0.1%	-84.60	15Y.8M
BND	-5.59	2.15	1.6%	-0.23	2.57	0.1%	1.40	2.67	4.00	0%	-17.28	7Y.6M
IEI	-4.27	2.02	1.7%	-0.11	2.47	0.1%	1.37	2.65	3.94	0%	-13.59	7Y.7M
LQD	-6.71	1.93	3.6%	0.33	2.46	0%	1.32	2.65	4.03	0%	-23.27	6Y.3M
TLT	-17.32	1.45	7.9%	-4.12	2.10	2.8%	0.07	2.44	4.28	0%	-47.74	14Y.2M
VNQ	-25.90	-0.81	17.8%	-7.36	1.29	7.9%	-1.75	2.31	8.05	1.8%	-68.30	19Y.5M
SHY	-1.26	1.46	1.1%	0.39	1.52	0%	0.87	2.11	4.40	0%	-8.52	3Y.11M
BIL	-0.10	0.65	3.6%	-0.05	0.76	1.3%	0.29	1.18	4.72	0%	-0.42	8Y.9M
GLD	-15.32	-1.61	23.9%	-6.75	-1.32	22.2%	-3.63	-0.50	0.05	21.3%	-61.78	62Y.0M

Order by **Baseline 15Y Return - All data** (from 1871/1927 to 2023-11) - **US Infl. Adjusted**

Portfolio	3Y Rolling Annualized Return (%)			7Y Rolling Annualized Return (%)			15Y Rolling Annualized Return (%)				Max Draw-down (%)	Long Neg Period (Y.M)
	Worst	Base	%Fail	Worst	Base	%Fail	Worst	Base ▼	Median	%Fail		
IJS	-45.05	-1.91	17.5%	-8.11	3.63	6%	0.72	6.44	10.61	0%	-85.57	14Y.8M
VTI	-39.36	-2.49	20.7%	-8.51	0.77	12.6%	-2.10	2.40	6.93	2.5%	-80.55	26Y.4M
VTV	-38.79	-4.05	21.7%	-8.13	0.34	13.4%	-1.22	2.19	6.65	1.4%	-80.30	20Y.1M
VNQ	-26.58	-3.33	31%	-7.33	-0.56	22.1%	-3.71	0.18	3.85	13.2%	-69.76	48Y.0M
SHY	-12.29	-2.01	30.1%	-7.07	-1.41	25.7%	-3.27	-0.49	1.90	19.8%	-45.12	52Y.1M
BND	-13.89	-2.23	26.6%	-7.81	-1.23	25.1%	-3.27	-0.65	2.01	21.8%	-48.08	51Y.10M
IEI	-13.90	-2.29	28.3%	-7.82	-1.26	26%	-3.29	-0.68	1.92	22.6%	-48.09	51Y.11M
LQD	-14.61	-2.39	26.9%	-7.93	-1.41	26.9%	-3.58	-0.79	2.27	25.9%	-56.56	84Y.5M
BIL	-10.74	-1.91	33.8%	-6.82	-1.62	32.4%	-3.90	-0.88	1.22	24.4%	-48.08	92Y.5M
TLT	-21.79	-3.09	29.4%	-8.20	-2.33	31.4%	-4.99	-1.40	2.66	32.5%	-70.04	87Y.7M
GLD	-20.28	-5.84	58.4%	-11.38	-4.43	56.9%	-7.77	-3.77	-0.10	50.5%	-82.57	132Y.3M

Ranking: Median 15Y Return

Order by **Median 15Y Return** - **Last 30 Years** (from 1993-12 to 2023-11)

Portfolio	3Y Rolling Annualized Return (%)			7Y Rolling Annualized Return (%)			15Y Rolling Annualized Return (%)				Max Draw-down (%)	Long Neg Period (Y.M)
	Worst	Base	%Fail	Worst	Base	%Fail	Worst	Base	Median ▼	%Fail		
EMB	-7.65	3.53	7.4%	-0.47	4.25	0.7%	3.08	5.67	10.28	0%	-31.43	8Y.2M
MTUM	-15.43	-3.44	19.1%	-0.57	5.24	0.7%	5.61	7.13	10.08	0%	-53.85	10Y.6M
VNQ	-25.03	1.58	11.7%	-1.16	5.57	0.7%	3.84	6.51	9.52	0%	-68.30	7Y.8M
IJS	-18.25	3.65	10.8%	-1.42	6.00	0.7%	5.15	7.80	9.07	0%	-54.13	8Y.1M
GLD	-15.02	-6.98	33.9%	-6.20	-2.30	24.2%	3.86	6.28	8.84	0%	-42.91	12Y.1M
SCZ	-20.24	-2.72	26.5%	-1.95	1.92	8.3%	1.82	5.17	7.62	0%	-63.26	9Y.4M
VTI	-16.22	-1.94	16.9%	-2.98	3.78	2.2%	4.37	5.30	7.55	0%	-50.84	11Y.7M
EEM	-15.31	-4.00	33.9%	-6.71	-0.15	15.9%	-1.21	3.98	7.53	1.1%	-60.44	16Y.1M*
CWB	-12.29	2.82	10.2%	0.04	5.07	0%	5.15	6.36	7.44	0%	-43.81	8Y.6M
TLT	-17.32	2.73	7.1%	-4.12	4.78	5.4%	1.81	5.76	7.02	0%	-47.74	12Y.1M
VTV	-16.62	-2.60	17.5%	-3.00	4.01	1.4%	4.43	5.32	7.00	0%	-54.78	11Y.7M
LQD	-6.71	2.94	6.5%	0.33	4.15	0%	3.56	4.71	5.91	0%	-23.27	6Y.3M
HYG	-7.69	1.64	5.5%	0.42	4.22	0%	3.43	4.97	5.62	0%	-30.85	5Y.10M
BNDX	-4.35	3.16	6.2%	0.18	3.98	0%	3.31	4.85	5.62	0%	-14.88	6Y.5M
TIP	-2.68	1.49	6.2%	0.61	2.34	0%	2.51	3.78	5.31	0%	-14.76	6Y.5M
IEI	-4.27	1.24	6.2%	-0.11	1.77	0.7%	1.63	3.34	4.79	0%	-13.59	7Y.7M
BND	-5.59	2.05	5.5%	-0.23	2.60	0.7%	2.36	3.62	4.64	0%	-17.28	7Y.6M
VEA	-19.64	-3.37	22.8%	-2.53	1.87	4.7%	0.92	3.21	4.48	0%	-57.00	12Y.6M
SHY	-1.26	0.52	4.9%	0.39	0.72	0%	0.87	1.83	2.71	0%	-5.36	3Y.11M
BIL	-0.10	-0.03	19.7%	-0.05	0.16	7.9%	0.50	0.81	1.29	0%	-0.42	8Y.9M

Order by **Median 15Y Return** - **Last 30 Years** (from 1993-12 to 2023-11) - **US Infl. Adjusted**

Portfolio	3Y Rolling Annualized Return (%)			7Y Rolling Annualized Return (%)			15Y Rolling Annualized Return (%)				Max Draw-down (%)	Long Neg Period (Y.M)
	Worst	Base	%Fail	Worst	Base	%Fail	Worst	Base	Median ▼	%Fail		
EMB	-12.06	1.67	11.1%	-3.86	2.47	7.6%	0.67	3.63	8.01	0%	-35.97	13Y.3M
MTUM	-17.26	-5.53	23.4%	-3.05	2.60	2.2%	3.37	4.81	7.64	0%	-54.55	12Y.5M
VNQ	-26.58	-1.64	19.7%	-3.59	3.05	4.3%	1.31	4.37	6.98	0%	-69.76	12Y.2M
IJS	-20.02	0.94	13.9%	-3.83	3.54	2.2%	3.14	5.38	6.75	0%	-55.05	11Y.5M
GLD	-15.87	-8.89	42.5%	-8.11	-4.32	30.3%	1.46	3.82	6.62	0%	-45.57	13Y.3M
SCZ	-21.97	-5.36	35.4%	-4.39	-0.11	17%	-0.55	2.91	5.27	1.7%	-63.82	16Y.6M
EEM	-17.17	-6.03	44.6%	-9.04	-1.79	32.1%	-3.52	1.77	5.19	9.9%	-61.05	17Y.9M
VTI	-18.24	-4.37	20%	-5.40	1.18	6.9%	2.16	2.90	5.14	0%	-51.59	13Y.5M
CWB	-14.19	0.44	13.9%	-2.50	2.84	2.5%	2.76	3.91	5.11	0%	-45.00	11Y.5M
VTV	-18.43	-4.60	22.8%	-5.42	1.48	4.7%	1.98	2.88	4.80	0%	-55.68	13Y.6M
TLT	-21.79	0.37	12.9%	-7.37	2.55	7.9%	-0.68	3.59	4.79	1.1%	-55.99	18Y.5M
LQD	-11.76	0.32	12%	-3.07	2.18	7.6%	1.14	2.49	3.64	0%	-33.86	13Y.2M
BNDX	-9.52	0.78	10.5%	-3.24	2.03	8.3%	0.91	2.61	3.42	0%	-26.46	13Y.2M
HYG	-9.89	-1.09	21.9%	-2.13	1.90	5.8%	0.87	2.68	3.33	0%	-32.45	12Y.2M
TIP	-7.96	-0.43	20.3%	-2.39	0.10	13.7%	0.17	1.68	3.23	0%	-23.74	15Y.9M
IEI	-9.45	-0.57	23.7%	-3.52	0.10	13%	-0.85	1.21	2.67	7.7%	-26.99	21Y.1M
BND	-10.69	0.09	14.5%	-3.61	0.84	8.3%	0.00	1.49	2.53	0.5%	-30.25	20Y.5M
VEA	-21.58	-5.93	31.7%	-4.84	-0.34	20.2%	-1.43	0.86	2.18	6.1%	-57.66	22Y.9M
SHY	-6.65	-1.40	47.4%	-2.90	-1.02	35.4%	-1.59	-0.29	0.65	29.8%	-23.76	25Y.8M
BIL	-4.61	-2.06	62.5%	-2.40	-1.62	66.4%	-1.84	-1.20	-0.68	71.8%	-25.55	30Y.0M*

Order by **Median 15Y Return - Last 60 Years** (from 1963-12 to 2023-11)

Portfolio	3Y Rolling Annualized Return (%)			7Y Rolling Annualized Return (%)			15Y Rolling Annualized Return (%)				Max Draw-down (%)	Long Neg Period (Y.M)
	Worst	Base	%Fail	Worst	Base	%Fail	Worst	Base	Median	%Fail		
IJS	-18.25	4.44	9.2%	-2.35	6.98	1.7%	5.15	8.94	14.42	0%	-54.13	8Y.1M
VTV	-16.62	1.09	12.4%	-3.00	4.15	1.6%	4.43	6.38	10.91	0%	-54.78	11Y.7M
VNQ	-25.03	1.44	11.2%	-1.87	4.78	1.6%	3.84	8.22	10.82	0%	-68.30	11Y.1M
VTI	-16.22	1.87	12.6%	-3.00	4.15	1.7%	4.37	6.49	10.48	0%	-50.84	11Y.7M
TLT	-17.32	0.70	12.6%	-4.12	3.10	2.3%	1.81	5.52	8.25	0%	-47.74	12Y.1M
IEI	-4.27	2.12	2.9%	-0.11	3.38	0.3%	1.63	4.28	7.14	0%	-13.59	7Y.7M
LQD	-6.71	2.00	7.6%	0.33	4.15	0%	3.30	5.03	7.09	0%	-23.27	6Y.3M
GLD	-15.32	-6.07	32.9%	-6.75	-2.30	29.7%	-3.63	-1.12	7.05	19.6%	-61.78	27Y.5M
BND	-5.59	2.53	2.6%	-0.23	4.05	0.3%	2.36	4.28	7.03	0%	-17.28	7Y.6M
SHY	-1.26	1.29	2.3%	0.39	1.39	0%	0.87	2.34	6.67	0%	-8.52	3Y.11M
BIL	-0.10	0.60	9.3%	-0.05	0.68	3.5%	0.50	1.21	5.38	0%	-0.42	8Y.9M

Order by **Median 15Y Return - Last 60 Years** (from 1963-12 to 2023-11) - **US Infl. Adjusted**

Portfolio	3Y Rolling Annualized Return (%)			7Y Rolling Annualized Return (%)			15Y Rolling Annualized Return (%)				Max Draw-down (%)	Long Neg Period (Y.M)
	Worst	Base	%Fail	Worst	Base	%Fail	Worst	Base	Median ▼	%Fail		
IJS	-20.02	0.29	14.6%	-8.11	3.86	5.5%	3.14	6.39	9.73	0%	-57.83	11Y.5M
VNQ	-26.58	-2.46	23.2%	-7.33	0.76	11.5%	0.14	4.35	7.44	0%	-69.76	14Y.11M
VTI	-18.54	-2.55	20.6%	-8.51	0.01	14.9%	-1.47	2.39	6.97	2.2%	-54.53	18Y.1M
VTV	-18.43	-2.93	21%	-8.13	0.48	12.9%	-0.49	2.50	6.82	0.9%	-55.68	17Y.10M
TLT	-21.79	-3.83	26.6%	-7.37	-2.37	28.1%	-4.99	0.33	4.82	14.2%	-56.13	22Y.0M
GLD	-20.28	-9.47	51.1%	-11.38	-5.24	44.3%	-7.77	-4.24	3.96	33.1%	-82.57	43Y.11M*
LQD	-14.61	-2.19	24.4%	-5.92	-1.09	24.2%	-3.58	1.18	3.95	12.9%	-45.79	21Y.3M
IEI	-9.45	-1.86	29.6%	-4.53	-0.85	22%	-2.31	0.13	3.47	14.2%	-35.11	21Y.1M
BND	-10.69	-1.75	25.1%	-4.53	-0.74	19.9%	-2.30	0.30	3.30	11.8%	-35.11	20Y.8M
SHY	-6.65	-1.57	36.2%	-3.25	-0.94	28.1%	-1.59	-0.10	2.29	16.8%	-23.89	25Y.8M
BIL	-4.61	-1.68	43.8%	-2.40	-1.35	43.3%	-1.84	-0.77	1.09	31.8%	-25.55	35Y.2M

Order by **Median 15Y Return** - **All data** (from 1871/1927 to 2023-11)

Portfolio	3Y Rolling Annualized Return (%)			7Y Rolling Annualized Return (%)			15Y Rolling Annualized Return (%)				Max Draw-down (%)	Long Neg Period (Y.M)
	Worst	Base	%Fail	Worst	Base	%Fail	Worst	Base	Median ▼	%Fail		
IJS	-49.09	1.17	13%	-7.75	5.98	4.3%	0.44	9.17	14.53	0%	-88.57	14Y.9M
VTV	-43.29	-0.19	15.3%	-8.41	3.75	5.9%	-1.07	6.25	10.63	1.1%	-84.40	15Y.7M
VTI	-43.81	-0.56	15.9%	-9.49	3.29	4.2%	-0.35	5.49	8.60	0.1%	-84.60	15Y.8M
VNQ	-25.90	-0.81	17.8%	-7.36	1.29	7.9%	-1.75	2.31	8.05	1.8%	-68.30	19Y.5M
BIL	-0.10	0.65	3.6%	-0.05	0.76	1.3%	0.29	1.18	4.72	0%	-0.42	8Y.9M
SHY	-1.26	1.46	1.1%	0.39	1.52	0%	0.87	2.11	4.40	0%	-8.52	3Y.11M
TLT	-17.32	1.45	7.9%	-4.12	2.10	2.8%	0.07	2.44	4.28	0%	-47.74	14Y.2M
LQD	-6.71	1.93	3.6%	0.33	2.46	0%	1.32	2.65	4.03	0%	-23.27	6Y.3M
BND	-5.59	2.15	1.6%	-0.23	2.57	0.1%	1.40	2.67	4.00	0%	-17.28	7Y.6M
IEI	-4.27	2.02	1.7%	-0.11	2.47	0.1%	1.37	2.65	3.94	0%	-13.59	7Y.7M
GLD	-15.32	-1.61	23.9%	-6.75	-1.32	22.2%	-3.63	-0.50	0.05	21.3%	-61.78	62Y.0M

Order by **Median 15Y Return** - **All data** (from 1871/1927 to 2023-11) - **US Infl. Adjusted**

Portfolio	3Y Rolling Annualized Return (%)			7Y Rolling Annualized Return (%)			15Y Rolling Annualized Return (%)				Max Draw-down (%)	Long Neg Period (Y.M)
	Worst	Base	%Fail	Worst	Base	%Fail	Worst	Base	Median ▼	%Fail		
IJS	-45.05	-1.91	17.5%	-8.11	3.63	6%	0.72	6.44	10.61	0%	-85.57	14Y.8M
VTI	-39.36	-2.49	20.7%	-8.51	0.77	12.6%	-2.10	2.40	6.93	2.5%	-80.55	26Y.4M
VTV	-38.79	-4.05	21.7%	-8.13	0.34	13.4%	-1.22	2.19	6.65	1.4%	-80.30	20Y.1M
VNQ	-26.58	-3.33	31%	-7.33	-0.56	22.1%	-3.71	0.18	3.85	13.2%	-69.76	48Y.0M
TLT	-21.79	-3.09	29.4%	-8.20	-2.33	31.4%	-4.99	-1.40	2.66	32.5%	-70.04	87Y.7M
LQD	-14.61	-2.39	26.9%	-7.93	-1.41	26.9%	-3.58	-0.79	2.27	25.9%	-56.56	84Y.5M
BND	-13.89	-2.23	26.6%	-7.81	-1.23	25.1%	-3.27	-0.65	2.01	21.8%	-48.08	51Y.10M
IEI	-13.90	-2.29	28.3%	-7.82	-1.26	26%	-3.29	-0.68	1.92	22.6%	-48.09	51Y.11M
SHY	-12.29	-2.01	30.1%	-7.07	-1.41	25.7%	-3.27	-0.49	1.90	19.8%	-45.12	52Y.1M
BIL	-10.74	-1.91	33.8%	-6.82	-1.62	32.4%	-3.90	-0.88	1.22	24.4%	-48.08	92Y.5M
GLD	-20.28	-5.84	58.4%	-11.38	-4.43	56.9%	-7.77	-3.77	-0.10	50.5%	-82.57	132Y.3M

Considerations

The world of investments is often steeped in myths and common beliefs that can lead to surprising financial choices.

For example, "investing in a diversified stock asset over the long term is always a safe and profitable strategy".

We do not doubt the validity of this strategy, but always remember, when retrospectively looking at only the return, you are actually overlooking the entire journey that led there.

You have ignored all the negative aspects of the journey, which often lead investors to abandon their strategy.

Let's look, for example, at the Longest Negative Period of various assets, considering the last 30 years. What have been the most efficient asset classes according to this metric?

The asset SHY (short-term treasuries) is in the first position, with 3 years and 11 months. Would you have ever thought? An investment in short-term US Treasury bonds has, in the worst case, required waiting for about 4 years to have a positive return. The maximum drawdown was -5.36%.

And if we want to further reduce the risk and go into cash assets (BIL), we have an incredible Longest Negative Period of 8 years and 9 months, despite a maximum drawdown of only -0.42%.

Even the sectoral real estate stock (VNQ) had a shorter maximum negative period (7 years and 8 months), although the drawdown in this case was a substantial -68.3%.

The quintessential investment in the US stock market (VTI) has given a maximum negative period of 11 years and 7 months. We are beyond the classic 10 years, which everyone refers to as the 'psychological' threshold for long-term investment.

These are numbers that make you reflect and can lead to pessimism. Are we sure we can withstand such long and deep drawdowns?

And we haven't shown you the most striking data yet. Considering all the historical data at our disposal, have you noticed the longest negative period for gold (GLD)? 62 years.

Yet practically all the most famous Lazy Portfolios have an allocation to gold... How is that possible?

You can already guess why, since we have already talked about the concept of correlation. When assets work together, they can sometimes balance each other so harmoniously that the resulting portfolio has much more interesting metrics.

It's the magic of diversification, which continues to be a key principle for building resilient and enduring portfolios.

Lazy Portfolios with 2 equally weighted Assets

In these types of portfolios, each asset carries a 50% weight.

These portfolios are straightforward to implement and maintain because, during each rebalancing, you simply need to reallocate the assets to the same weight.

Always remember that on the *LazyPortfolioEtf.com* website, you can also simulate non-equally weighted asset allocations by entering the percentage weights you prefer.

Ranking: Baseline 3Y Return

Order by **Baseline 3Y Return - Last 30 Years** (from 1993-12 to 2023-11)

Portfolio	3Y Rolling Annualized Return (%)			7Y Rolling Annualized Return (%)			15Y Rolling Annualized Return (%)				Max Draw-down (%)	Long Neg Period (Y.M)
	Worst	Base ▼	%Fail	Worst	Base	%Fail	Worst	Base	Median	%Fail		
TLT-CWB	-8.59	5.50	4%	2.34	7.15	0%	6.22	7.58	8.45	0%	-31.98	4Y.4M
IJS-TLT	-3.99	4.82	3.4%	1.55	7.57	0%	6.53	8.05	9.25	0%	-29.71	6Y.0M
EMB-CWB	-6.22	4.74	3.4%	4.33	6.49	0%	5.28	7.17	8.99	0%	-32.02	4Y.9M
VNQ-CWB	-18.04	4.66	8%	0.30	5.76	0%	4.92	7.56	8.65	0%	-55.16	6Y.11M
BNDX-CWB	-4.74	4.57	4.3%	2.38	5.84	0%	5.55	6.35	7.01	0%	-24.72	4Y.11M
CWB-LQD	-5.53	4.55	4%	2.08	5.97	0%	5.53	6.36	7.03	0%	-27.13	5Y.1M
IJS-BNDX	-7.89	4.46	5.2%	2.06	5.74	0%	5.66	6.80	7.84	0%	-29.49	5Y.2M
IJS-TIP	-7.24	4.36	4.6%	3.03	6.01	0%	5.12	6.40	7.96	0%	-27.87	5Y.1M
IEI-CWB	-2.55	4.35	2.8%	4.15	5.61	0%	5.14	5.89	6.78	0%	-19.06	3Y.7M
IJS-IEI	-4.77	4.33	2.5%	3.40	5.71	0%	5.30	6.27	7.62	0%	-22.74	4Y.5M
IJS-BND	-6.33	4.30	4.3%	2.44	5.57	0%	5.28	6.40	7.41	0%	-26.74	5Y.0M
IJS-CWB	-15.06	4.28	8.9%	-0.23	6.07	0.7%	5.87	7.31	8.51	0%	-48.15	8Y.1M
BND-CWB	-3.15	4.24	3.4%	2.96	5.64	0%	5.10	5.88	6.56	0%	-20.75	4Y.3M
IJS-EMB	-9.59	4.22	6.8%	3.06	6.60	0%	5.48	7.01	10.02	0%	-35.42	5Y.1M
IJS-SHY	-5.98	4.22	5.8%	2.15	4.72	0%	4.38	5.48	6.51	0%	-25.95	5Y.1M
MTUM-GLD	-4.23	4.17	4.6%	5.99	7.51	0%	7.33	8.83	10.18	0%	-27.55	3Y.11M
TIP-CWB	-4.04	4.16	3.1%	3.43	5.72	0%	5.29	5.91	7.16	0%	-24.88	4Y.9M
IJS-LQD	-8.39	4.15	5.5%	1.90	5.99	0%	5.67	7.02	7.89	0%	-31.41	5Y.3M
VTI-EMB	-7.69	4.14	3.4%	3.07	7.02	0%	5.97	7.94	8.90	0%	-33.48	5Y.2M
VTV-EMB	-8.46	3.94	6.5%	3.08	6.25	0%	5.23	7.02	8.71	0%	-35.58	5Y.2M
SHY-CWB	-2.69	3.68	2.5%	2.95	4.66	0%	4.48	4.99	5.72	0%	-18.56	4Y.3M

Order by **Baseline 3Y Return - Last 30 Years** (from 1993-12 to 2023-11) - **US Infl. Adjusted**

Portfolio	3Y Rolling Annualized Return (%)			7Y Rolling Annualized Return (%)			15Y Rolling Annualized Return (%)				Max Draw-down (%)	Long Neg Period (Y.M)
	Worst	Base ▼	%Fail	Worst	Base	%Fail	Worst	Base	Median	%Fail		
TLT-CWB	-13.56	3.01	8%	-1.13	4.64	1.1%	3.73	5.40	6.05	0%	-41.85	8Y.11M
EMB-CWB	-8.71	2.65	9.2%	0.79	4.14	0%	2.83	5.04	6.61	0%	-34.42	6Y.4M
IEI-CWB	-7.84	2.51	7.1%	1.02	3.40	0%	2.69	3.73	4.43	0%	-28.44	5Y.9M
TIP-CWB	-7.31	2.29	6.5%	0.80	3.49	0%	2.84	3.74	4.78	0%	-27.46	5Y.9M
IJS-TLT	-9.13	2.28	10.2%	-1.89	5.02	1.4%	4.05	5.95	6.81	0%	-36.99	9Y.4M
BNDX-CWB	-7.85	2.11	9.8%	-0.22	3.10	0.4%	3.09	4.10	4.69	0%	-28.47	8Y.3M
VNQ-CWB	-19.82	2.05	10.5%	-2.16	3.36	1.4%	2.37	5.19	6.36	0%	-57.15	11Y.6M
BND-CWB	-8.41	1.92	8.3%	0.34	3.04	0%	2.65	3.68	4.27	0%	-30.02	7Y.10M
IJS-CWB	-16.90	1.81	11.7%	-2.72	3.64	2.5%	3.56	5.04	6.15	0%	-49.19	11Y.5M
EMB-LQD	-11.26	1.53	8.6%	-3.41	2.63	7.2%	0.92	3.43	6.01	0%	-34.45	13Y.3M
BNDX-EMB	-10.17	1.50	8.9%	-3.52	2.53	7.9%	1.01	3.23	6.03	0%	-30.58	13Y.3M
EMB-TLT	-16.33	1.49	7.1%	-5.47	2.91	7.6%	1.13	4.31	7.07	0%	-44.64	14Y.10M
MTUM-GLD	-6.54	1.48	10.8%	3.48	5.22	0%	4.85	6.40	7.83	0%	-29.19	4Y.8M
CWB-LQD	-8.95	1.46	9.8%	-0.51	3.30	0.7%	3.04	4.12	4.75	0%	-31.91	8Y.3M
IJS-TIP	-9.25	1.41	10.5%	0.44	3.30	0%	3.03	4.13	5.60	0%	-29.32	6Y.11M
SHY-CWB	-6.40	1.37	7.7%	0.34	2.32	0%	2.05	2.86	3.38	0%	-24.94	7Y.10M
TLT-HYG	-13.69	1.30	9.2%	-3.96	2.90	7.2%	1.92	3.97	4.69	0%	-38.89	12Y.2M
EMB-HYG	-9.17	1.24	10.5%	-2.37	2.64	7.2%	1.21	3.59	5.86	0%	-29.35	11Y.8M
VTI-GLD	-6.95	1.19	12.3%	-0.08	3.01	0.4%	3.86	5.65	6.43	0%	-27.75	7Y.2M
BNDX-TLT	-15.58	1.09	11.4%	-5.11	2.64	7.9%	0.88	3.50	4.41	0%	-42.51	14Y.10M
BNDX-HYG	-7.64	1.08	11.1%	-2.06	2.01	7.9%	1.44	2.81	3.54	0%	-24.04	11Y.3M

Order by **Baseline 3Y Return - Last 60 Years** (from 1963-12 to 2023-11)

Portfolio	3Y Rolling Annualized Return (%)			7Y Rolling Annualized Return (%)			15Y Rolling Annualized Return (%)				Max Draw-down (%)	Long Neg Period (Y.M)
	Worst	Base ▼	%Fail	Worst	Base	%Fail	Worst	Base	Median	%Fail		
IJS-BND	-6.33	4.98	3.7%	2.16	6.26	0%	5.28	7.23	11.06	0%	-26.74	6Y.4M
IJS-IEI	-4.77	4.94	2.8%	2.15	6.40	0%	5.30	7.42	11.24	0%	-22.74	6Y.4M
IJS-LQD	-8.39	4.84	4.8%	0.94	6.43	0%	5.67	7.74	11.24	0%	-31.41	6Y.8M
IJS-TLT	-4.94	4.83	3.4%	0.94	7.72	0%	6.53	8.95	11.36	0%	-29.71	6Y.6M
IJS-SHY	-5.98	4.63	3.9%	2.15	5.46	0%	4.38	6.33	10.83	0%	-25.95	6Y.1M
IJS-BIL	-7.10	4.47	5.1%	1.19	4.98	0%	3.82	5.64	10.27	0%	-28.87	6Y.1M
VTI-IEI	-3.88	4.10	2.9%	1.34	5.61	0%	5.49	6.48	9.08	0%	-22.24	5Y.10M
VTI-SHY	-4.22	4.08	5.1%	1.35	4.84	0%	4.39	5.82	8.52	0%	-24.21	5Y.10M
IJS-VNQ	-21.37	3.97	8.9%	-1.59	6.48	1.1%	5.43	9.04	12.08	0%	-60.63	7Y.8M
IJS-GLD	-2.36	3.87	2.3%	2.55	6.67	0%	5.37	7.80	10.32	0%	-26.49	3Y.9M
VTI-BND	-4.38	3.78	4.5%	1.35	5.44	0%	5.29	6.33	8.88	0%	-24.96	5Y.10M
VTV-SHY	-4.75	3.63	5.3%	1.42	4.67	0%	4.26	5.31	8.95	0%	-26.45	5Y.10M
VTI-LQD	-6.45	3.63	6.7%	0.18	5.46	0%	5.00	6.49	9.15	0%	-29.35	6Y.5M
VTV-IEI	-3.49	3.61	2.5%	1.36	5.39	0%	5.02	6.19	9.50	0%	-23.72	5Y.10M
VTI-BIL	-6.48	3.56	6.6%	0.48	4.17	0%	3.51	5.24	7.91	0%	-26.70	9Y.3M
VTI-TLT	-5.35	3.50	5.8%	0.03	5.38	0%	4.38	7.50	9.70	0%	-27.37	6Y.5M
VTV-BND	-5.10	3.42	4.5%	1.37	5.14	0%	5.00	6.08	9.35	0%	-27.21	5Y.10M
VTI-VNQ	-19.67	3.41	8.9%	-2.13	5.91	1.1%	4.94	8.26	10.75	0%	-58.60	9Y.8M
VTI-GLD	-4.65	3.39	4.4%	2.35	5.68	0%	3.85	6.90	9.09	0%	-33.29	5Y.1M
VTI-IJS	-16.60	3.35	10.2%	-2.10	6.62	1.6%	6.05	8.30	12.39	0%	-51.92	9Y.9M
VTV-BIL	-5.91	3.23	6.6%	0.55	4.10	0%	3.46	4.69	8.14	0%	-28.88	8Y.6M

Order by **Baseline 3Y Return - Last 60 Years** (from 1963-12 to 2023-11) - **US Infl. Adjusted**

Portfolio	3Y Rolling Annualized Return (%)			7Y Rolling Annualized Return (%)			15Y Rolling Annualized Return (%)				Max Draw-down (%)	Long Neg Period (Y.M)
	Worst	Base ▼	%Fail	Worst	Base	%Fail	Worst	Base	Median	%Fail		
IJS-SHY	-10.61	0.86	12.9%	-3.50	2.35	4.4%	2.19	3.85	6.57	0%	-34.03	9Y.4M
IJS-IEI	-11.00	0.81	13.1%	-3.88	2.91	4.2%	2.43	4.23	6.94	0%	-34.81	11Y.7M
IJS-GLD	-6.91	0.78	12%	1.05	3.67	0%	2.23	4.79	7.49	0%	-33.07	5Y.7M
IJS-BIL	-10.07	0.75	13.3%	-3.60	2.18	4.7%	1.84	3.38	5.84	0%	-33.22	9Y.4M
IJS-BND	-11.00	0.49	13.3%	-3.87	2.82	4.6%	2.43	4.23	6.89	0%	-34.79	11Y.7M
IJS-LQD	-13.35	0.34	14.2%	-5.02	2.81	4.7%	1.76	4.33	6.84	0%	-39.93	13Y.1M
IJS-TLT	-11.68	0.03	14.6%	-4.80	2.81	5%	1.33	4.71	7.71	0%	-39.25	13Y.4M
IJS-VNQ	-23.08	-0.19	15.3%	-7.40	3.13	6.1%	2.87	5.51	8.48	0%	-62.26	11Y.7M
VTI-IJS	-18.59	-0.23	15.5%	-7.82	2.57	6.6%	1.90	4.62	8.18	0%	-54.31	11Y.9M
VTI-VNQ	-21.41	-0.25	16.5%	-7.69	1.65	11.5%	0.05	4.49	7.02	0%	-60.17	15Y.3M
VNQ-SHY	-10.82	-0.39	17.1%	-3.88	0.74	9.1%	0.28	2.80	5.29	0%	-39.05	13Y.0M
VNQ-BIL	-12.06	-0.48	18.5%	-3.56	0.54	9.3%	0.37	2.35	4.50	0%	-41.49	13Y.0M
VTV-VNQ	-22.30	-0.52	17.1%	-7.53	0.97	9.4%	0.36	4.42	7.19	0%	-62.22	14Y.7M
VTV-GLD	-7.59	-0.57	17.7%	-1.30	2.95	2.7%	0.93	4.06	5.98	0%	-38.00	8Y.0M
VTV-SHY	-8.77	-0.73	19.1%	-4.07	0.75	9%	-0.38	2.37	4.42	0.5%	-30.27	16Y.8M
VTI-SHY	-10.46	-0.80	19.4%	-4.11	0.98	11.6%	-0.39	2.47	4.26	1.7%	-34.75	16Y.9M
VTI-BIL	-9.32	-0.81	19.4%	-3.78	0.39	12.9%	-0.32	1.65	3.72	0.5%	-31.71	16Y.7M
VTI-GLD	-6.95	-0.86	18.1%	-0.47	2.60	0.9%	0.59	3.61	5.79	0%	-41.20	12Y.7M
VTV-IEI	-8.85	-0.86	21.6%	-4.40	0.46	10.2%	-1.00	3.26	4.97	6.8%	-31.05	18Y.6M
IJS-VTV	-19.19	-0.93	16.1%	-7.46	2.64	5.8%	2.41	4.73	8.60	0%	-55.29	11Y.8M
VTI-IEI	-10.54	-1.01	20.7%	-4.41	1.13	11.6%	-1.03	2.87	5.05	6.1%	-34.69	18Y.5M

Order by **Baseline 3Y Return** - **All data** (from 1871/1927 to 2023-11)

Portfolio	3Y Rolling Annualized Return (%)			7Y Rolling Annualized Return (%)			15Y Rolling Annualized Return (%)				Max Draw-down (%)	Long Neg Period (Y.M)
	Worst	Base ▼	%Fail	Worst	Base	%Fail	Worst	Base	Median	%Fail		
IJS-IEI	-23.26	3.46	7.4%	0.89	6.04	0%	4.01	7.69	10.18	0%	-58.38	6Y.4M
IJS-SHY	-23.14	3.42	8.4%	0.62	5.31	0%	3.44	6.87	10.28	0%	-58.12	8Y.7M
IJS-BND	-23.25	3.36	7.9%	0.91	6.03	0%	4.02	7.55	10.19	0%	-58.36	6Y.4M
IJS-TLT	-24.33	3.34	7.5%	0.59	6.71	0%	4.14	8.32	9.90	0%	-60.20	6Y.6M
IJS-LQD	-23.39	3.19	8.2%	0.88	6.19	0%	4.11	7.76	10.02	0%	-58.59	6Y.8M
IJS-BIL	-24.05	3.11	9.6%	-0.33	4.86	0.1%	2.75	6.17	9.74	0%	-59.54	12Y.8M
VTV-IEI	-19.94	2.74	6.9%	-0.56	4.60	0.2%	2.45	5.87	7.95	0%	-53.22	12Y.8M
VTV-BND	-19.93	2.53	8.1%	-0.55	4.54	0.2%	2.46	5.83	7.90	0%	-53.20	12Y.8M
VTI-SHY	-20.30	2.48	6.7%	-1.17	4.31	0.2%	2.12	5.26	6.63	0%	-53.35	12Y.9M
IJS-GLD	-25.48	2.48	7.5%	1.45	5.77	0%	3.56	7.64	9.84	0%	-61.69	6Y.4M
VTV-LQD	-20.06	2.45	9.2%	-0.56	4.47	0.2%	2.57	5.93	7.96	0%	-53.44	10Y.9M
VTI-IEI	-20.40	2.36	5.7%	-1.33	4.11	0.2%	2.39	5.11	6.74	0%	-53.59	8Y.10M
VTI-BIL	-21.24	2.33	7.4%	-1.40	4.02	0.6%	1.28	5.06	6.59	0%	-54.90	13Y.4M
VTV-GLD	-22.14	2.29	7.5%	0.57	4.61	0%	2.21	5.82	8.26	0%	-56.74	12Y.8M
SHY-LQD	-3.75	2.24	1.2%	0.60	2.52	0%	1.43	2.74	4.02	0%	-14.35	4Y.10M
VTV-SHY	-19.83	2.17	9.3%	-0.87	4.21	0.3%	1.71	5.27	7.79	0%	-52.96	13Y.1M
VTI-TLT	-21.43	2.17	6.7%	-1.43	4.05	0.3%	2.55	5.08	7.07	0%	-55.49	8Y.11M
VTI-BND	-20.39	2.17	6.3%	-1.32	4.11	0.2%	2.39	5.11	6.72	0%	-53.58	8Y.9M
TLT-SHY	-8.96	2.14	2.8%	-1.45	2.48	0.5%	1.08	2.51	4.28	0%	-27.72	11Y.5M
BND-IEI	-4.92	2.10	1.7%	-0.16	2.52	0.1%	1.38	2.66	3.98	0%	-15.43	7Y.6M
BND-SHY	-3.24	2.08	1.2%	0.25	2.24	0%	1.41	2.67	4.05	0%	-11.35	6Y.3M

Order by **Baseline 3Y Return** - **All data** (from 1871/1927 to 2023-11) - **US Infl. Adjusted**

Portfolio	3Y Rolling Annualized Return (%)			7Y Rolling Annualized Return (%)			15Y Rolling Annualized Return (%)				Max Draw-down (%)	Long Neg Period (Y.M)
	Worst	Base ▼	%Fail	Worst	Base	%Fail	Worst	Base	Median	%Fail		
IJS-IEI	-17.17	0.01	14.9%	-3.88	3.23	2.9%	2.43	4.31	6.62	0%	-47.45	11Y.7M
IJS-BND	-17.16	-0.02	15%	-3.87	3.23	3%	2.43	4.33	6.57	0%	-47.42	11Y.7M
IJS-SHY	-17.04	-0.17	15.3%	-3.50	2.68	3.2%	2.19	3.99	6.54	0%	-47.11	9Y.4M
IJS-GLD	-19.57	-0.28	16.1%	-1.46	3.52	1.6%	2.23	4.47	6.85	0%	-51.62	8Y.3M
IJS-LQD	-17.31	-0.40	15.7%	-5.02	3.27	3.2%	1.76	4.39	6.67	0%	-47.71	13Y.1M
IJS-BIL	-18.03	-0.43	16.4%	-3.60	2.29	4.3%	1.84	3.58	6.16	0%	-48.91	9Y.4M
IJS-TLT	-18.33	-0.48	16.1%	-4.80	3.40	3.4%	1.33	4.42	6.98	0%	-49.74	13Y.4M
VTI-BIL	-14.99	-0.60	17%	-5.35	0.80	11.6%	-1.13	1.69	4.63	1.5%	-43.05	19Y.6M
VTI-SHY	-13.98	-0.61	16.9%	-6.05	1.27	11%	-1.68	1.96	4.80	2%	-43.27	21Y.6M
VTI-IEI	-14.08	-0.68	17.4%	-6.45	1.29	9.8%	-2.22	1.94	4.90	3.6%	-45.15	22Y.3M
IJS-VNQ	-31.96	-0.86	17%	-7.40	3.04	4.8%	0.07	4.98	7.98	0%	-72.62	15Y.5M
VTV-GLD	-15.96	-0.86	19.1%	-2.37	2.04	5.6%	0.41	2.72	5.15	0%	-45.38	13Y.8M
VTI-BND	-14.07	-0.87	17.7%	-6.44	1.28	10%	-2.21	1.95	4.90	3.6%	-45.14	22Y.3M
VTI-GLD	-16.51	-1.02	19.2%	-7.58	1.15	8.3%	-3.50	1.80	4.69	6.2%	-49.52	30Y.2M
VTV-SHY	-13.47	-1.05	19.8%	-4.07	0.79	9.2%	-0.38	1.80	4.03	0.3%	-40.60	16Y.8M
VTV-IEI	-13.59	-1.07	20.5%	-4.40	0.79	8.4%	-1.00	1.97	4.58	3.8%	-40.93	18Y.6M
VTI-LQD	-14.22	-1.11	18.6%	-6.51	1.11	10.3%	-2.31	1.91	4.98	4.3%	-45.30	22Y.7M
VTI-VNQ	-29.37	-1.22	18.3%	-7.69	1.58	10.1%	-1.44	2.51	6.38	1%	-69.34	19Y.5M
VNQ-SHY	-10.82	-1.24	24.8%	-3.88	-0.21	17.2%	-1.27	0.15	1.92	12.5%	-39.05	48Y.3M
VTI-TLT	-15.20	-1.35	18.1%	-6.67	0.94	10.6%	-2.50	1.95	5.43	5.3%	-45.41	22Y.7M
VNQ-BND	-11.03	-1.40	25.9%	-4.27	-0.18	17.8%	-1.45	0.19	2.34	9.8%	-39.79	48Y.3M

Ranking: Maximum Drawdown

Order by **Maximum Drawdown - Last 30 Years** (from 1993-12 to 2023-11)

Portfolio	3Y Rolling Annualized Return (%)			7Y Rolling Annualized Return (%)			15Y Rolling Annualized Return (%)				Max Draw-down (%) ▼	Long Neg Period (Y.M)
	Worst	Base	%Fail	Worst	Base	%Fail	Worst	Base	Median	%Fail		
SHY-BIL	-0.20	0.28	2.5%	0.28	0.56	0%	0.70	1.37	2.00	0%	-2.40	3Y.3M
IEI-BIL	-1.29	0.73	5.2%	0.50	1.09	0%	1.19	2.18	3.08	0%	-6.58	4Y.2M
TIP-BIL	-1.19	0.87	5.2%	0.50	1.48	0%	1.59	2.47	3.37	0%	-7.09	6Y.0M
BNDX-BIL	-1.83	1.88	5.8%	0.82	2.24	0%	1.97	2.86	3.66	0%	-7.28	4Y.4M
BND-BIL	-1.86	1.16	5.2%	0.65	1.44	0%	1.51	2.36	3.00	0%	-8.42	4Y.4M
SHY-IEI	-2.65	0.92	5.2%	0.26	1.29	0%	1.26	2.60	3.77	0%	-9.51	6Y.4M
SHY-TIP	-1.81	0.90	6.8%	0.58	1.49	0%	1.76	2.84	4.07	0%	-9.64	5Y.11M
BNDX-SHY	-2.67	2.06	5.8%	0.42	2.48	0%	2.14	3.39	4.37	0%	-10.08	4Y.7M
BND-SHY	-3.24	1.37	5.2%	0.25	1.67	0%	1.66	2.73	3.69	0%	-11.35	6Y.3M
LQD-BIL	-2.34	1.89	4.9%	1.04	2.44	0%	2.15	2.92	3.65	0%	-11.42	4Y.4M
IEI-TIP	-3.44	1.18	6.5%	0.48	1.97	0%	2.25	3.59	5.09	0%	-12.85	4Y.5M
SHY-HYG	-1.24	1.92	5.2%	1.62	2.80	0%	2.70	3.74	4.43	0%	-12.86	3Y.10M
IEI-HYG	-2.19	2.59	4.9%	1.27	3.33	0%	3.35	4.57	5.44	0%	-13.46	4Y.4M
BNDX-IEI	-4.30	2.36	6.2%	0.04	2.96	0%	2.64	4.20	5.45	0%	-13.85	7Y.3M
BNDX-TIP	-3.48	2.32	4.9%	0.64	2.82	0%	2.95	4.40	5.67	0%	-13.95	4Y.6M
SHY-LQD	-3.75	2.09	5.2%	0.60	2.64	0%	2.41	3.28	4.35	0%	-14.35	4Y.10M
HYG-BIL	-1.72	1.67	2.5%	1.64	2.53	0%	2.36	3.24	3.78	0%	-14.48	4Y.4M
BND-TIP	-4.12	1.68	6.5%	0.41	2.26	0%	2.50	3.71	5.00	0%	-15.08	4Y.7M
BND-HYG	-2.86	2.85	6.2%	1.20	3.68	0%	3.36	4.65	5.33	0%	-15.15	4Y.7M
EMB-BIL	-3.33	2.21	5.8%	0.58	2.47	0%	1.96	3.34	5.88	0%	-15.27	6Y.4M
BND-IEI	-4.92	1.64	5.8%	-0.16	2.22	0.7%	2.06	3.49	4.72	0%	-15.43	7Y.6M

Order by **Maximum Drawdown - Last 30 Years** (from 1993-12 to 2023-11) - **US Infl. Adjusted**

Portfolio	3Y Rolling Annualized Return (%)			7Y Rolling Annualized Return (%)			15Y Rolling Annualized Return (%)				Max Draw-down (%) ▼	Long Neg Period (Y.M)
	Worst	Base	%Fail	Worst	Base	%Fail	Worst	Base	Median	%Fail		
HYG-BIL	-5.33	-0.02	15.4%	-1.45	0.67	9.8%	-0.02	1.19	1.57	0.5%	-17.20	15Y.9M
TIP-BIL	-5.83	-0.82	28.6%	-2.16	-0.59	23.1%	-0.76	0.36	1.30	9.9%	-18.46	21Y.3M
BNDX-BIL	-6.60	-0.05	16%	-2.61	0.63	9.8%	-0.39	0.81	1.60	7.2%	-19.10	20Y.10M
SHY-HYG	-5.90	0.43	12.9%	-1.82	1.08	7.9%	0.31	1.60	2.24	0%	-19.73	13Y.6M
IEI-BIL	-6.67	-1.05	35.7%	-2.81	-0.62	29.6%	-1.27	0.06	1.03	13.8%	-20.35	25Y.1M
SHY-TIP	-7.14	-0.81	27.4%	-2.56	-0.38	19.1%	-0.60	0.70	2.00	8.3%	-20.66	21Y.1M
BND-BIL	-7.17	-0.65	27.7%	-2.75	-0.26	21.7%	-0.85	0.23	0.95	12.2%	-21.06	25Y.1M
TIP-HYG	-6.73	0.51	11.7%	-1.63	1.46	5.8%	1.16	2.50	3.52	0%	-21.89	12Y.3M
BNDX-SHY	-7.90	0.03	14.2%	-3.01	0.80	9%	-0.23	1.24	2.29	1.7%	-22.40	16Y.11M
CWB-BIL	-5.96	0.55	12.9%	-0.56	1.64	2.2%	1.68	2.26	2.74	0%	-22.72	9Y.0M
LQD-BIL	-7.62	-0.10	15.7%	-2.39	0.67	9%	-0.24	0.80	1.60	2.8%	-22.72	20Y.6M
VTI-IEI	-4.87	-0.05	15.4%	0.01	2.66	0%	3.31	3.78	4.56	0%	-22.95	10Y.1M
SHY-IEI	-7.94	-0.95	31.4%	-3.16	-0.45	22%	-1.21	0.49	1.70	10.5%	-23.05	22Y.2M
IEI-HYG	-7.48	0.73	9.8%	-2.18	1.62	7.6%	0.94	2.42	3.23	0%	-23.10	13Y.1M
BNDX-HYG	-7.64	1.08	11.1%	-2.06	2.01	7.9%	1.44	2.81	3.54	0%	-24.04	11Y.3M
EMB-BIL	-7.94	0.37	12.6%	-2.85	0.76	9%	-0.43	1.28	3.76	6.1%	-24.13	17Y.0M
SHY-BIL	-5.56	-1.59	52.3%	-2.64	-1.25	44.8%	-1.67	-0.65	-0.03	50.8%	-24.31	28Y.4M
BND-SHY	-8.48	-0.55	24.6%	-3.15	-0.06	16.3%	-0.78	0.61	1.63	9.9%	-24.36	22Y.3M
IJS-GLD	-3.71	1.07	8.6%	1.05	3.54	0%	4.36	5.75	7.37	0%	-24.56	5Y.6M
IEI-TIP	-8.67	-0.56	19.7%	-2.94	0.11	14.8%	-0.12	1.45	2.99	1.7%	-24.76	15Y.11M
BND-HYG	-8.11	0.78	9.8%	-2.23	1.77	7.6%	0.96	2.44	3.09	0%	-24.87	13Y.0M

Order by **Maximum Drawdown** - **Last 60 Years** (from 1963-12 to 2023-11)

Portfolio	3Y Rolling Annualized Return (%)			7Y Rolling Annualized Return (%)			15Y Rolling Annualized Return (%)				Max Draw-down (%) ▼	Long Neg Period (Y.M)
	Worst	Base	%Fail	Worst	Base	%Fail	Worst	Base	Median	%Fail		
SHY-BIL	-0.20	0.74	1.2%	0.28	1.02	0%	0.70	1.76	6.07	0%	-3.75	3Y.3M
IEI-BIL	-1.29	1.89	2.5%	0.50	1.84	0%	1.19	2.76	6.21	0%	-6.58	4Y.2M
BND-BIL	-1.86	2.28	2.5%	0.65	2.28	0%	1.51	2.73	6.09	0%	-8.42	4Y.4M
SHY-IEI	-2.65	1.87	2.5%	0.26	2.26	0%	1.26	3.32	6.99	0%	-9.51	6Y.4M
BND-SHY	-3.24	2.14	2.5%	0.25	2.78	0%	1.66	3.30	6.81	0%	-11.35	6Y.3M
LQD-BIL	-2.34	2.89	2.3%	1.04	3.36	0%	2.15	3.47	6.29	0%	-11.42	4Y.4M
SHY-LQD	-3.75	2.59	2.5%	0.60	3.88	0%	2.41	4.04	7.10	0%	-14.35	4Y.10M
BND-IEI	-4.92	2.33	2.8%	-0.16	3.67	0.3%	2.06	4.26	7.08	0%	-15.43	7Y.6M
IEI-LQD	-5.45	2.39	3.8%	0.17	4.08	0%	2.89	4.67	7.08	0%	-18.25	7Y.3M
BND-LQD	-6.13	2.41	3.9%	0.07	4.16	0%	3.02	4.74	6.94	0%	-20.18	7Y.3M
VTI-IEI	-3.88	4.10	2.9%	1.34	5.61	0%	5.49	6.48	9.08	0%	-22.24	5Y.10M
IJS-IEI	-4.77	4.94	2.8%	2.15	6.40	0%	5.30	7.42	11.24	0%	-22.74	6Y.4M
SHY-GLD	-7.15	0.70	11.1%	-2.77	2.03	4.1%	2.24	3.43	6.49	0%	-23.13	11Y.2M
VTV-TLT	-3.72	2.57	3.8%	0.08	5.87	0%	4.28	7.36	9.91	0%	-23.60	7Y.5M
VTV-IEI	-3.49	3.61	2.5%	1.36	5.39	0%	5.02	6.19	9.50	0%	-23.72	5Y.10M
BIL-GLD	-7.40	0.12	13.9%	-2.87	1.21	4.6%	1.22	2.56	5.72	0%	-23.89	11Y.2M
VTI-SHY	-4.22	4.08	5.1%	1.35	4.84	0%	4.39	5.82	8.52	0%	-24.21	5Y.10M
TLT-BIL	-7.55	2.42	3.1%	-0.98	3.83	0.8%	1.68	4.40	6.56	0%	-24.31	8Y.11M
VTI-BND	-4.38	3.78	4.5%	1.35	5.44	0%	5.29	6.33	8.88	0%	-24.96	5Y.10M
BND-GLD	-6.85	0.93	9.2%	-2.02	2.65	2.3%	2.84	4.17	7.20	0%	-25.70	11Y.2M
IEI-GLD	-6.94	0.85	9.6%	-2.42	2.71	2.8%	2.99	4.28	7.34	0%	-25.70	11Y.2M

Order by **Maximum Drawdown** - **Last 60 Years** (from 1963-12 to 2023-11) - **US Infl. Adjusted**

Portfolio	3Y Rolling Annualized Return (%)			7Y Rolling Annualized Return (%)			15Y Rolling Annualized Return (%)				Max Draw-down (%) ▼	Long Neg Period (Y.M)
	Worst	Base	%Fail	Worst	Base	%Fail	Worst	Base	Median	%Fail		
IEI-BIL	-6.67	-1.38	33.7%	-3.16	-0.71	27.6%	-1.27	0.06	2.18	14.2%	-22.87	25Y.1M
BND-BIL	-7.17	-1.23	29.9%	-3.16	-0.56	24.2%	-1.26	0.09	2.02	13.7%	-22.87	25Y.1M
SHY-BIL	-5.56	-1.61	38.8%	-2.64	-1.16	34.1%	-1.67	-0.38	1.67	24.4%	-24.31	28Y.4M
LQD-BIL	-7.62	-1.16	23.1%	-3.77	-0.82	18.8%	-1.84	0.24	2.26	12%	-28.72	20Y.6M
SHY-IEI	-7.94	-1.60	30.7%	-3.88	-0.76	23.1%	-1.52	0.26	2.87	12.8%	-29.48	22Y.2M
BND-SHY	-8.48	-1.46	27.5%	-3.88	-0.52	20.6%	-1.51	0.29	2.71	12.6%	-29.48	22Y.3M
VTV-SHY	-8.77	-0.73	19.1%	-4.07	0.75	9%	-0.38	2.37	4.42	0.5%	-30.27	16Y.8M
VTV-BIL	-7.95	-1.01	19.9%	-3.75	0.52	9.4%	-0.07	1.69	3.83	0.4%	-30.31	15Y.5M
VTV-BND	-8.85	-1.41	22.6%	-4.39	0.43	10.5%	-1.00	3.11	4.91	6.7%	-31.02	18Y.6M
VTV-IEI	-8.85	-0.86	21.6%	-4.40	0.46	10.2%	-1.00	3.26	4.97	6.8%	-31.05	18Y.6M
VTI-BIL	-9.32	-0.81	19.4%	-3.78	0.39	12.9%	-0.32	1.65	3.72	0.5%	-31.71	16Y.7M
IJS-GLD	-6.91	0.78	12%	1.05	3.67	0%	2.23	4.79	7.49	0%	-33.07	5Y.7M
IJS-BIL	-10.07	0.75	13.3%	-3.60	2.18	4.7%	1.84	3.38	5.84	0%	-33.22	9Y.4M
SHY-GLD	-8.09	-2.79	40.2%	-4.25	-0.67	25.9%	-1.05	0.40	3.21	10.7%	-33.57	25Y.9M
IJS-SHY	-10.61	0.86	12.9%	-3.50	2.35	4.4%	2.19	3.85	6.57	0%	-34.03	9Y.4M
VTI-IEI	-10.54	-1.01	20.7%	-4.41	1.13	11.6%	-1.03	2.87	5.05	6.1%	-34.69	18Y.5M
VTI-BND	-10.54	-1.31	21.6%	-4.41	0.96	12.2%	-1.02	2.87	5.04	6.1%	-34.69	18Y.5M
VTI-SHY	-10.46	-0.80	19.4%	-4.11	0.98	11.6%	-0.39	2.47	4.26	1.7%	-34.75	16Y.9M
IJS-BND	-11.00	0.49	13.3%	-3.87	2.82	4.6%	2.43	4.23	6.89	0%	-34.79	11Y.7M
IJS-IEI	-11.00	0.81	13.1%	-3.88	2.91	4.2%	2.43	4.23	6.94	0%	-34.81	11Y.7M
SHY-LQD	-9.42	-1.39	23.1%	-4.51	-0.65	18.2%	-2.08	0.41	2.98	11.1%	-34.96	19Y.11M

Order by **Maximum Drawdown - All data** (from 1871/1927 to 2023-11)

Portfolio	3Y Rolling Annualized Return (%)			7Y Rolling Annualized Return (%)			15Y Rolling Annualized Return (%)				Max Draw-down (%) ▼	Long Neg Period (Y.M)
	Worst	Base	%Fail	Worst	Base	%Fail	Worst	Base	Median	%Fail		
SHY-BIL	-0.20	1.07	0.4%	0.28	1.04	0%	0.70	1.63	4.53	0%	-3.75	3Y.3M
IEI-BIL	-1.29	1.71	0.9%	0.50	1.66	0%	1.19	2.25	4.16	0%	-6.58	4Y.2M
BND-BIL	-1.86	1.77	0.9%	0.65	1.79	0%	1.30	2.28	4.16	0%	-8.42	4Y.4M
SHY-IEI	-2.65	2.03	1.2%	0.26	2.16	0%	1.26	2.60	4.05	0%	-9.51	6Y.4M
BND-SHY	-3.24	2.08	1.2%	0.25	2.24	0%	1.41	2.67	4.05	0%	-11.35	6Y.3M
LQD-BIL	-2.34	2.04	0.9%	0.99	2.19	0%	1.33	2.40	4.07	0%	-11.42	4Y.4M
SHY-LQD	-3.75	2.24	1.2%	0.60	2.52	0%	1.43	2.74	4.02	0%	-14.35	4Y.10M
BND-IEI	-4.92	2.10	1.7%	-0.16	2.52	0.1%	1.38	2.66	3.98	0%	-15.43	7Y.6M
IEI-LQD	-5.45	2.06	2.1%	0.17	2.52	0%	1.35	2.69	4.01	0%	-18.25	7Y.3M
BND-LQD	-6.13	2.08	2.1%	0.07	2.55	0%	1.36	2.70	4.03	0%	-20.18	7Y.3M
SHY-GLD	-7.15	0.81	8.4%	-2.77	1.34	4.5%	0.47	1.82	2.49	0%	-23.13	12Y.2M
BIL-GLD	-7.40	0.49	9.9%	-2.87	0.99	4.2%	0.30	1.48	2.54	0%	-23.89	12Y.0M
TLT-BIL	-7.55	2.03	1.6%	-0.98	2.16	0.3%	1.05	2.13	4.36	0%	-24.31	8Y.11M
IEI-GLD	-6.94	0.94	7.8%	-2.42	1.38	4.4%	0.35	1.48	2.27	0%	-25.70	12Y.11M
BND-GLD	-6.85	0.97	7.6%	-2.02	1.41	4%	0.36	1.49	2.29	0%	-25.70	12Y.11M
TLT-SHY	-8.96	2.14	2.8%	-1.45	2.48	0.5%	1.08	2.51	4.28	0%	-27.72	11Y.5M
LQD-GLD	-6.52	0.94	7.6%	-1.08	1.32	3.9%	0.32	1.38	2.22	0%	-28.85	13Y.0M
TLT-GLD	-8.67	0.74	8.8%	-1.29	1.21	5.5%	-0.18	1.35	2.70	0.5%	-30.76	23Y.5M
TLT-IEI	-10.67	1.77	4.2%	-1.93	2.36	0.6%	0.92	2.61	4.15	0%	-31.85	11Y.5M
BND-TLT	-11.39	1.80	4.2%	-2.05	2.38	0.5%	0.94	2.62	4.16	0%	-33.78	11Y.5M
VNQ-IEI	-10.37	1.12	9%	-1.44	2.21	0.9%	1.14	2.69	6.35	0%	-34.02	13Y.1M

Order by **Maximum Drawdown - All data** (from 1871/1927 to 2023-11) - **US Infl. Adjusted**

Portfolio	3Y Rolling Annualized Return (%)			7Y Rolling Annualized Return (%)			15Y Rolling Annualized Return (%)				Max Draw-down (%) ▼	Long Neg Period (Y.M)
	Worst	Base	%Fail	Worst	Base	%Fail	Worst	Base	Median	%Fail		
VNQ-IEI	-10.40	-1.41	26.1%	-4.27	-0.19	18.2%	-1.46	0.18	2.32	10.1%	-36.35	48Y.3M
VNQ-SHY	-10.82	-1.24	24.8%	-3.88	-0.21	17.2%	-1.27	0.15	1.92	12.5%	-39.05	48Y.3M
VNQ-BND	-11.03	-1.40	25.9%	-4.27	-0.18	17.8%	-1.45	0.19	2.34	9.8%	-39.79	48Y.3M
VTV-SHY	-13.47	-1.05	19.8%	-4.07	0.79	9.2%	-0.38	1.80	4.03	0.3%	-40.60	16Y.8M
VTV-BND	-13.57	-1.44	21.1%	-4.39	0.71	8.6%	-1.00	1.99	4.48	3.7%	-40.91	18Y.6M
VTV-IEI	-13.59	-1.07	20.5%	-4.40	0.79	8.4%	-1.00	1.97	4.58	3.8%	-40.93	18Y.6M
VTV-LQD	-13.72	-1.92	22%	-5.45	0.70	9.7%	-1.45	1.97	4.78	4.6%	-41.21	20Y.8M
VNQ-BIL	-12.06	-1.52	28%	-3.56	-0.45	19.9%	-1.75	-0.16	1.58	17.8%	-41.49	49Y.2M
VNQ-GLD	-7.20	-2.47	37.5%	-3.27	-1.00	32.6%	-2.14	-0.72	2.79	27.9%	-41.97	42Y.2M
VTV-BIL	-14.44	-1.66	21%	-3.75	0.56	9.9%	-0.07	1.55	3.58	0.2%	-42.49	18Y.6M
VNQ-TLT	-12.75	-2.29	30.5%	-5.39	-0.61	25.3%	-2.28	-0.36	2.36	23.3%	-42.87	50Y.7M
VTI-BIL	-14.99	-0.60	17%	-5.35	0.80	11.6%	-1.13	1.69	4.63	1.5%	-43.05	19Y.6M
VTI-SHY	-13.98	-0.61	16.9%	-6.05	1.27	11%	-1.68	1.96	4.80	2%	-43.27	21Y.6M
VTV-TLT	-14.76	-1.71	22.8%	-5.61	0.52	12.1%	-2.05	1.94	5.31	5.3%	-43.44	22Y.2M
BND-BIL	-12.31	-1.76	28.3%	-6.78	-1.30	24.6%	-2.95	-0.64	1.53	19.6%	-43.51	53Y.0M
IEI-BIL	-12.32	-1.79	29.9%	-6.79	-1.33	26%	-2.96	-0.71	1.56	19.8%	-43.52	54Y.4M
VNQ-LQD	-13.09	-1.60	28%	-5.15	-0.23	18.5%	-1.94	0.05	2.37	13%	-43.91	49Y.1M
SHY-BIL	-11.52	-1.95	31.3%	-6.44	-1.49	28.8%	-3.43	-0.55	1.59	22%	-44.20	56Y.1M
VTI-BND	-14.07	-0.87	17.7%	-6.44	1.28	10%	-2.21	1.95	4.90	3.6%	-45.14	22Y.3M
VTI-IEI	-14.08	-0.68	17.4%	-6.45	1.29	9.8%	-2.22	1.94	4.90	3.6%	-45.15	22Y.3M
VTI-LQD	-14.22	-1.11	18.6%	-6.51	1.11	10.3%	-2.31	1.91	4.98	4.3%	-45.30	22Y.7M

Ranking: Longest Negative Period

Order by **Longest Negative Period - Last 30 Years** (from 1993-12 to 2023-11)

Portfolio	3Y Rolling Annualized Return (%)			7Y Rolling Annualized Return (%)			15Y Rolling Annualized Return (%)				Max Draw-down (%)	Long Neg Period (Y.M) ▲
	Worst	Base	%Fail	Worst	Base	%Fail	Worst	Base	Median	%Fail		
SHY-BIL	-0.20	0.28	2.5%	0.28	0.56	0%	0.70	1.37	2.00	0%	-2.40	3Y.3M
IJS-GLD	-1.26	3.34	2.8%	2.55	5.67	0%	6.84	8.28	9.88	0%	-23.76	3Y.6M
IEI-CWB	-2.55	4.35	2.8%	4.15	5.61	0%	5.14	5.89	6.78	0%	-19.06	3Y.7M
MTUM-IEI	-2.60	1.94	5.5%	3.89	6.12	0%	5.95	6.67	7.88	0%	-23.30	3Y.9M
SHY-HYG	-1.24	1.92	5.2%	1.62	2.80	0%	2.70	3.74	4.43	0%	-12.86	3Y.10M
MTUM-GLD	-4.23	4.17	4.6%	5.99	7.51	0%	7.33	8.83	10.18	0%	-27.55	3Y.11M
VTI-TLT	-4.50	3.07	5.8%	3.77	6.03	0%	6.97	7.62	8.35	0%	-27.37	4Y.2M
MTUM-SHY	-3.87	1.17	10.8%	2.68	5.07	0%	5.04	5.68	6.97	0%	-25.91	4Y.2M
MTUM-BND	-4.21	1.05	9.2%	2.93	5.92	0%	5.92	6.52	7.92	0%	-26.65	4Y.2M
IEI-BIL	-1.29	0.73	5.2%	0.50	1.09	0%	1.19	2.18	3.08	0%	-6.58	4Y.3M
BND-CWB	-3.15	4.24	3.4%	2.96	5.64	0%	5.10	5.88	6.56	0%	-20.75	4Y.3M
SHY-CWB	-2.69	3.68	2.5%	2.95	4.66	0%	4.48	4.99	5.72	0%	-18.56	4Y.3M
VTI-IEI	-2.77	2.96	3.1%	2.56	5.52	0%	5.55	6.18	6.92	0%	-21.38	4Y.3M
TLT-CWB	-8.59	5.50	4%	2.34	7.15	0%	6.22	7.58	8.45	0%	-31.98	4Y.4M
MTUM-EMB	-7.57	3.42	5.8%	4.38	7.08	0%	6.11	8.78	9.84	0%	-35.06	4Y.4M
VTV-IEI	-3.49	3.17	2.5%	2.64	5.45	0%	5.02	5.89	6.38	0%	-23.72	4Y.4M
IEI-HYG	-2.19	2.59	4.9%	1.27	3.33	0%	3.35	4.57	5.44	0%	-13.46	4Y.4M
VTV-TLT	-3.09	2.47	3.1%	2.91	6.29	0%	6.25	7.25	8.07	0%	-23.60	4Y.4M
MTUM-TIP	-5.33	2.15	6.5%	3.49	6.33	0%	6.12	6.96	8.02	0%	-29.16	4Y.4M
LQD-BIL	-2.34	1.89	4.9%	1.04	2.44	0%	2.15	2.92	3.65	0%	-11.42	4Y.4M
BNDX-BIL	-1.83	1.88	5.8%	0.82	2.24	0%	1.97	2.86	3.66	0%	-7.28	4Y.4M

Order by **Longest Negative Period - Last 30 Years** (from 1993-12 to 2023-11) - **US Infl. Adjusted**

Portfolio	3Y Rolling Annualized Return (%)			7Y Rolling Annualized Return (%)			15Y Rolling Annualized Return (%)				Max Draw-down (%)	Long Neg Period (Y.M) ▲
	Worst	Base	%Fail	Worst	Base	%Fail	Worst	Base	Median	%Fail		
MTUM-GLD	-6.54	1.48	10.8%	3.48	5.22	0%	4.85	6.40	7.83	0%	-29.19	4Y.8M
IJS-GLD	-3.71	1.07	8.6%	1.05	3.54	0%	4.36	5.75	7.37	0%	-24.56	5Y.6M
IEI-CWB	-7.84	2.51	7.1%	1.02	3.40	0%	2.69	3.73	4.43	0%	-28.44	5Y.9M
TIP-CWB	-7.31	2.29	6.5%	0.80	3.49	0%	2.84	3.74	4.78	0%	-27.46	5Y.9M
VTI-EMB	-9.69	0.84	13.2%	0.50	4.57	0%	3.50	5.76	6.57	0%	-34.51	5Y.10M
VTV-EMB	-10.45	0.95	13.2%	0.51	3.86	0%	2.78	4.91	6.38	0%	-36.73	6Y.3M
MTUM-EMB	-9.57	0.12	14.5%	1.40	4.75	0%	3.64	6.64	7.52	0%	-36.06	6Y.3M
EMB-CWB	-8.71	2.65	9.2%	0.79	4.14	0%	2.83	5.04	6.61	0%	-34.42	6Y.4M
IJS-TIP	-9.25	1.41	10.5%	0.44	3.30	0%	3.03	4.13	5.60	0%	-29.32	6Y.11M
IJS-SCZ	-20.62	0.16	14.5%	0.37	2.78	0%	2.24	4.46	6.42	0%	-59.00	6Y.11M
CWB-GLD	-4.74	0.24	13.5%	0.01	2.05	0%	3.47	5.15	6.58	0%	-30.63	7Y.1M
VTI-GLD	-6.95	1.19	12.3%	-0.08	3.01	0.4%	3.86	5.65	6.43	0%	-27.75	7Y.2M
IJS-SHY	-8.02	0.67	12.9%	-0.35	2.20	0.7%	2.19	3.22	4.28	0%	-27.43	7Y.2M
IJS-IEI	-6.83	1.06	12.3%	-0.02	3.20	0.4%	2.85	3.98	5.27	0%	-25.40	7Y.3M
VTV-GLD	-5.35	1.01	11.1%	-0.47	2.99	0.7%	3.80	5.37	6.26	0%	-27.61	7Y.3M
IJS-EMB	-11.55	0.79	13.2%	-0.25	4.35	0.7%	3.02	4.78	7.62	0%	-36.71	7Y.3M
IJS-BNDX	-9.88	0.64	13.2%	-0.44	3.29	0.7%	3.29	4.44	5.46	0%	-30.90	7Y.3M
IJS-BND	-8.36	0.53	12.6%	-0.12	3.17	1.1%	2.83	4.05	5.15	0%	-28.20	7Y.3M
IJS-LQD	-10.37	0.56	12.3%	-0.64	3.40	0.7%	3.27	4.63	5.60	0%	-32.78	7Y.7M
MTUM-TLT	-13.66	0.24	13.2%	-0.40	4.17	0.7%	4.57	5.68	7.33	0%	-40.02	7Y.7M
SCZ-VNQ	-23.81	-1.27	20.3%	-0.30	2.21	0.7%	1.10	3.86	6.58	0%	-64.97	7Y.7M

Order by **Longest Negative Period - Last 60 Years** (from 1963-12 to 2023-11)

Portfolio	3Y Rolling Annualized Return (%)			7Y Rolling Annualized Return (%)			15Y Rolling Annualized Return (%)				Max Draw-down (%)	Long Neg Period (Y.M) ▲
	Worst	Base	%Fail	Worst	Base	%Fail	Worst	Base	Median	%Fail		
SHY-BIL	-0.20	0.74	1.2%	0.28	1.02	0%	0.70	1.76	6.07	0%	-3.75	3Y.3M
IJS-GLD	-2.36	3.87	2.3%	2.55	6.67	0%	5.37	7.80	10.32	0%	-26.49	3Y.9M
IEI-BIL	-1.29	1.89	2.5%	0.50	1.84	0%	1.19	2.76	6.21	0%	-6.58	4Y.2M
LQD-BIL	-2.34	2.89	2.3%	1.04	3.36	0%	2.15	3.47	6.29	0%	-11.42	4Y.4M
BND-BIL	-1.86	2.28	2.5%	0.65	2.28	0%	1.51	2.73	6.09	0%	-8.42	4Y.4M
SHY-LQD	-3.75	2.59	2.5%	0.60	3.88	0%	2.41	4.04	7.10	0%	-14.35	4Y.10M
VNQ-IEI	-7.46	2.73	6.1%	1.36	4.90	0%	4.44	7.01	9.32	0%	-33.27	5Y.0M
VTI-GLD	-4.65	3.39	4.4%	2.35	5.68	0%	3.85	6.90	9.09	0%	-33.29	5Y.1M
VNQ-SHY	-8.94	2.80	5.3%	1.77	4.74	0%	3.82	6.56	8.53	0%	-36.11	5Y.2M
VNQ-BND	-9.06	2.62	6.7%	1.32	4.93	0%	4.38	6.95	9.10	0%	-36.89	5Y.2M
VNQ-BIL	-10.20	2.82	4.5%	1.83	4.41	0%	3.47	6.08	7.97	0%	-38.67	5Y.4M
VTI-IEI	-3.88	4.10	2.9%	1.34	5.61	0%	5.49	6.48	9.08	0%	-22.24	5Y.10M
VTI-SHY	-4.22	4.08	5.1%	1.35	4.84	0%	4.39	5.82	8.52	0%	-24.21	5Y.10M
VTI-BND	-4.38	3.78	4.5%	1.35	5.44	0%	5.29	6.33	8.88	0%	-24.96	5Y.10M
VTV-SHY	-4.75	3.63	5.3%	1.42	4.67	0%	4.26	5.31	8.95	0%	-26.45	5Y.10M
VTV-IEI	-3.49	3.61	2.5%	1.36	5.39	0%	5.02	6.19	9.50	0%	-23.72	5Y.10M
VTV-BND	-5.10	3.42	4.5%	1.37	5.14	0%	5.00	6.08	9.35	0%	-27.21	5Y.10M
VNQ-LQD	-11.16	2.53	8%	0.44	5.10	0%	4.83	6.92	9.34	0%	-41.20	5Y.10M
IJS-SHY	-5.98	4.63	3.9%	2.15	5.46	0%	4.38	6.33	10.83	0%	-25.95	6Y.1M
IJS-BIL	-7.10	4.47	5.1%	1.19	4.98	0%	3.82	5.64	10.27	0%	-28.87	6Y.1M
VTV-GLD	-2.95	2.93	3.5%	1.95	5.79	0%	4.03	7.30	8.88	0%	-29.36	6Y.1M

Order by **Longest Negative Period - Last 60 Years** (from 1963-12 to 2023-11) - **US Infl. Adjusted**

Portfolio	3Y Rolling Annualized Return (%)			7Y Rolling Annualized Return (%)			15Y Rolling Annualized Return (%)				Max Draw-down (%)	Long Neg Period (Y.M) ▲
	Worst	Base	%Fail	Worst	Base	%Fail	Worst	Base	Median	%Fail		
IJS-GLD	-6.91	0.78	12%	1.05	3.67	0%	2.23	4.79	7.49	0%	-33.07	5Y.7M
VTV-GLD	-7.59	-0.57	17.7%	-1.30	2.95	2.7%	0.93	4.06	5.98	0%	-38.00	8Y.0M
IJS-SHY	-10.61	0.86	12.9%	-3.50	2.35	4.4%	2.19	3.85	6.57	0%	-34.03	9Y.4M
IJS-BIL	-10.07	0.75	13.3%	-3.60	2.18	4.7%	1.84	3.38	5.84	0%	-33.22	9Y.4M
IJS-IEI	-11.00	0.81	13.1%	-3.88	2.91	4.2%	2.43	4.23	6.94	0%	-34.81	11Y.7M
IJS-BND	-11.00	0.49	13.3%	-3.87	2.82	4.6%	2.43	4.23	6.89	0%	-34.79	11Y.7M
IJS-VNQ	-23.08	-0.19	15.3%	-7.40	3.13	6.1%	2.87	5.51	8.48	0%	-62.26	11Y.7M
IJS-VTV	-19.19	-0.93	16.1%	-7.46	2.64	5.8%	2.41	4.73	8.60	0%	-55.29	11Y.8M
VTI-IJS	-18.59	-0.23	15.5%	-7.82	2.57	6.0%	1.90	4.62	8.18	0%	-54.31	11Y.9M
VTI-GLD	-6.95	-0.86	18.1%	-0.47	2.60	0.9%	0.59	3.61	5.79	0%	-41.20	12Y.7M
VNQ-SHY	-10.82	-0.39	17.1%	-3.88	0.74	9.1%	0.28	2.80	5.29	0%	-39.05	13Y.0M
VNQ-BIL	-12.06	-0.48	18.5%	-3.56	0.54	9.3%	0.37	2.35	4.50	0%	-41.49	13Y.0M
IJS-LQD	-13.35	0.34	14.2%	-5.02	2.81	4.7%	1.76	4.33	6.84	0%	-39.93	13Y.1M
IJS-TLT	-11.68	0.03	14.6%	-4.80	2.81	5%	1.33	4.71	7.71	0%	-39.25	13Y.4M
VTV-VNQ	-22.30	-0.52	17.1%	-7.53	0.97	9.4%	0.36	4.42	7.19	0%	-62.22	14Y.7M
VNQ-GLD	-7.20	-1.93	26.6%	-1.65	1.07	8%	0.08	2.02	6.47	0%	-37.93	15Y.1M
VTI-VNQ	-21.41	-0.25	16.5%	-7.69	1.65	11.5%	0.05	4.49	7.02	0%	-60.17	15Y.3M
VTV-BIL	-7.95	-1.01	19.9%	-3.75	0.52	9.4%	-0.07	1.69	3.83	0.4%	-30.31	15Y.5M
VTI-BIL	-9.32	-0.81	19.4%	-3.78	0.39	12.9%	-0.32	1.65	3.72	0.5%	-31.71	16Y.7M
VTV-SHY	-8.77	-0.73	19.1%	-4.07	0.75	9%	-0.38	2.37	4.42	0.5%	-30.27	16Y.8M
VTI-SHY	-10.46	-0.80	19.4%	-4.11	0.98	11.6%	-0.39	2.47	4.26	1.7%	-34.75	16Y.9M

Order by **Longest Negative Period** - **All data** (from 1871/1927 to 2023-11)

Portfolio	3Y Rolling Annualized Return (%)			7Y Rolling Annualized Return (%)			15Y Rolling Annualized Return (%)				Max Draw-down (%)	Long Neg Period (Y.M) ▲
	Worst	Base	%Fail	Worst	Base	%Fail	Worst	Base	Median	%Fail		
SHY-BIL	-0.20	1.07	0.4%	0.28	1.04	0%	0.70	1.63	4.53	0%	-3.75	3Y.3M
IEI-BIL	-1.29	1.71	0.9%	0.50	1.66	0%	1.19	2.25	4.16	0%	-6.58	4Y.2M
LQD-BIL	-2.34	2.04	0.9%	0.99	2.19	0%	1.33	2.40	4.07	0%	-11.42	4Y.4M
BND-BIL	-1.86	1.77	0.9%	0.65	1.79	0%	1.30	2.28	4.16	0%	-8.42	4Y.4M
SHY-LQD	-3.75	2.24	1.2%	0.60	2.52	0%	1.43	2.74	4.02	0%	-14.35	4Y.10M
BND-SHY	-3.24	2.08	1.2%	0.25	2.24	0%	1.41	2.67	4.05	0%	-11.35	6Y.3M
IJS-IEI	-23.26	3.46	7.4%	0.89	6.04	0%	4.01	7.69	10.18	0%	-58.38	6Y.4M
IJS-BND	-23.25	3.36	7.9%	0.91	6.03	0%	4.02	7.55	10.19	0%	-58.36	6Y.4M
IJS-GLD	-25.48	2.48	7.5%	1.45	5.77	0%	3.56	7.64	9.84	0%	-61.69	6Y.4M
SHY-IEI	-2.65	2.03	1.2%	0.26	2.16	0%	1.26	2.60	4.05	0%	-9.51	6Y.4M
IJS-TLT	-24.33	3.34	7.5%	0.59	6.71	0%	4.14	8.32	9.90	0%	-60.20	6Y.6M
IJS-LQD	-23.39	3.19	8.2%	0.88	6.19	0%	4.11	7.76	10.02	0%	-58.59	6Y.8M
BND-LQD	-6.13	2.08	2.1%	0.07	2.55	0%	1.36	2.70	4.03	0%	-20.18	7Y.3M
IEI-LQD	-5.45	2.06	2.1%	0.17	2.52	0%	1.35	2.69	4.01	0%	-18.25	7Y.3M
BND-IEI	-4.92	2.10	1.7%	-0.16	2.52	0.1%	1.38	2.66	3.98	0%	-15.43	7Y.6M
IJS-SHY	-23.14	3.42	8.4%	0.62	5.31	0%	3.44	6.87	10.28	0%	-58.12	8Y.7M
VTI-BND	-20.39	2.17	6.3%	-1.32	4.11	0.2%	2.39	5.11	6.72	0%	-53.58	8Y.9M
VTI-LQD	-20.52	2.00	7.5%	-1.40	4.01	0.2%	2.26	5.02	6.73	0%	-53.81	8Y.9M
VTI-IEI	-20.40	2.36	5.7%	-1.33	4.11	0.2%	2.39	5.11	6.74	0%	-53.59	8Y.10M
VTI-TLT	-21.43	2.17	6.7%	-1.43	4.05	0.3%	2.55	5.08	7.07	0%	-55.49	8Y.11M
TLT-BIL	-7.55	2.03	1.6%	-0.98	2.16	0.3%	1.05	2.13	4.36	0%	-24.31	8Y.11M

Order by **Longest Negative Period** - **All data** (from 1871/1927 to 2023-11) - **US Infl. Adjusted**

Portfolio	3Y Rolling Annualized Return (%)			7Y Rolling Annualized Return (%)			15Y Rolling Annualized Return (%)				Max Draw-down (%)	Long Neg Period (Y.M) ▲
	Worst	Base	%Fail	Worst	Base	%Fail	Worst	Base	Median	%Fail		
IJS-GLD	-19.57	-0.28	16.1%	-1.46	3.52	1.6%	2.23	4.47	6.85	0%	-51.62	8Y.3M
IJS-SHY	-17.04	-0.17	15.3%	-3.50	2.68	3.2%	2.19	3.99	6.54	0%	-47.11	9Y.4M
IJS-BIL	-18.03	-0.43	16.4%	-3.60	2.29	4.3%	1.84	3.58	6.16	0%	-48.91	9Y.4M
IJS-IEI	-17.17	0.01	14.9%	-3.88	3.23	2.9%	2.43	4.31	6.62	0%	-47.45	11Y.7M
IJS-BND	-17.16	-0.02	15%	-3.87	3.23	3%	2.43	4.33	6.57	0%	-47.42	11Y.7M
IJS-LQD	-17.31	-0.40	15.7%	-5.02	3.27	3.2%	1.76	4.39	6.67	0%	-47.71	13Y.1M
IJS-TLT	-18.33	-0.48	16.1%	-4.80	3.40	3.4%	1.33	4.42	6.98	0%	-49.74	13Y.4M
VTV-GLD	-15.96	-0.86	19.1%	-2.37	2.04	5.6%	0.41	2.72	5.15	0%	-45.38	13Y.8M
VTI-IJS	-42.15	-2.53	18.1%	-7.82	2.67	7.3%	1.04	4.62	8.75	0%	-83.15	14Y.5M
IJS-VTV	-41.85	-2.29	18.5%	-7.46	2.65	7.2%	0.66	4.65	8.95	0%	-83.01	14Y.8M
IJS-VNQ	-31.96	-0.86	17%	-7.40	3.04	4.8%	0.07	4.98	7.98	0%	-72.62	15Y.5M
VTV-SHY	-13.47	-1.05	19.8%	-4.07	0.79	9.2%	-0.38	1.80	4.03	0.3%	-40.60	16Y.8M
VTV-IEI	-13.59	-1.07	20.5%	-4.40	0.79	8.4%	-1.00	1.97	4.58	3.8%	-40.93	18Y.6M
VTV-BND	-13.57	-1.44	21.1%	-4.39	0.71	8.6%	-1.00	1.99	4.48	3.7%	-40.91	18Y.6M
VTV-BIL	-14.44	-1.66	21%	-3.75	0.56	9.9%	-0.07	1.55	3.58	0.2%	-42.49	18Y.6M
VTI-VNQ	-29.37	-1.22	18.3%	-7.69	1.58	10.1%	-1.44	2.51	6.38	1%	-69.34	19Y.5M
VTI-BIL	-14.99	-0.60	17%	-5.35	0.80	11.6%	-1.13	1.69	4.63	1.5%	-43.05	19Y.6M
VTV-VNQ	-28.76	-1.64	19.2%	-7.53	0.89	10%	-1.53	2.24	6.33	1.8%	-68.76	19Y.6M
VTI-VTV	-39.00	-3.56	21.5%	-8.26	0.77	11.9%	-0.94	2.28	6.77	1.5%	-80.36	19Y.11M
VTV-LQD	-13.72	-1.92	22%	-5.45	0.70	9.7%	-1.45	1.97	4.78	4.6%	-41.21	20Y.8M
VTI-SHY	-13.98	-0.61	16.9%	-6.05	1.27	11%	-1.68	1.96	4.80	2%	-43.27	21Y.6M

Ranking: Baseline 7Y Return

Order by **Baseline 7Y Return - Last 30 Years** (from 1993-12 to 2023-11)

Portfolio	3Y Rolling Annualized Return (%)			7Y Rolling Annualized Return (%)			15Y Rolling Annualized Return (%)				Max Draw-down (%)	Long Neg Period (Y.M)
	Worst	Base	%Fail	Worst	Base ▼	%Fail	Worst	Base	Median	%Fail		
IJS-TLT	-3.99	4.82	3.4%	1.55	7.57	0%	6.53	8.05	9.25	0%	-29.71	6Y.0M
MTUM-GLD	-4.23	4.17	4.6%	5.99	7.51	0%	7.33	8.83	10.18	0%	-27.55	3Y.11M
TLT-CWB	-8.59	5.50	4%	2.34	7.15	0%	6.22	7.58	8.45	0%	-31.98	4Y.4M
MTUM-EMB	-7.57	3.42	5.8%	4.38	7.08	0%	6.11	8.78	9.84	0%	-35.06	4Y.4M
VTI-EMB	-7.69	4.14	3.4%	3.07	7.02	0%	5.97	7.94	8.90	0%	-33.48	5Y.2M
MTUM-TLT	-8.69	2.38	5.5%	3.10	6.92	0%	7.06	8.13	9.77	0%	-33.28	5Y.2M
IJS-EMB	-9.59	4.22	6.8%	3.06	6.60	0%	5.48	7.01	10.02	0%	-35.42	5Y.1M
VNQ-TLT	-7.76	3.13	9.5%	-0.60	6.57	0.7%	5.03	7.53	9.61	0%	-36.95	8Y.9M
EMB-CWB	-6.22	4.74	3.4%	4.33	6.49	0%	5.28	7.17	8.99	0%	-32.02	4Y.9M
MTUM-VNQ	-19.57	2.24	9.2%	-0.24	6.42	0.7%	6.95	8.95	9.82	0%	-59.01	8Y.10M
MTUM-TIP	-5.33	2.15	6.5%	3.49	6.33	0%	6.12	6.96	8.02	0%	-29.16	4Y.4M
VTV-TLT	-3.09	2.47	3.1%	2.91	6.29	0%	6.25	7.25	8.07	0%	-23.60	4Y.4M
MTUM-EEM	-14.43	-0.06	15.4%	2.24	6.28	0%	4.13	7.30	9.13	0%	-57.25	9Y.2M
IJS-MTUM	-16.55	2.29	13.2%	-0.71	6.27	0.7%	7.25	8.43	9.67	0%	-52.24	9Y.2M
VTV-EMB	-8.46	3.94	6.5%	3.08	6.25	0%	5.23	7.02	8.71	0%	-35.58	5Y.2M
MTUM-LQD	-6.29	0.86	9.5%	2.43	6.19	0%	6.36	7.07	8.37	0%	-30.96	5Y.0M
MTUM-BNDX	-5.92	0.86	9.2%	2.53	6.14	0%	6.39	6.93	8.29	0%	-29.61	4Y.4M
MTUM-IEI	-2.60	1.94	5.5%	3.89	6.12	0%	5.95	6.67	7.88	0%	-23.30	3Y.9M
VNQ-EMB	-12.45	3.22	9.5%	1.09	6.10	0%	4.54	6.61	10.63	0%	-43.90	5Y.2M
VTI-VNQ	-19.67	2.94	9.2%	-1.51	6.08	0.7%	4.94	7.84	8.79	0%	-58.60	9Y.8M
IJS-CWB	-15.06	4.28	8.9%	-0.23	6.07	0.7%	5.87	7.31	8.51	0%	-48.15	8Y.1M

Order by **Baseline 7Y Return - Last 30 Years** (from 1993-12 to 2023-11) - **US Infl. Adjusted**

Portfolio	3Y Rolling Annualized Return (%)			7Y Rolling Annualized Return (%)			15Y Rolling Annualized Return (%)				Max Draw-down (%)	Long Neg Period (Y.M)
	Worst	Base	%Fail	Worst	Base ▼	%Fail	Worst	Base	Median	%Fail		
MTUM-GLD	-6.54	1.48	10.8%	3.48	5.22	0%	4.85	6.40	7.83	0%	-29.19	4Y.8M
IJS-TLT	-9.13	2.28	10.2%	-1.89	5.02	1.4%	4.05	5.95	6.81	0%	-36.99	9Y.4M
MTUM-EMB	-9.57	0.12	14.5%	1.40	4.75	0%	3.64	6.64	7.52	0%	-36.06	6Y.3M
TLT-CWB	-13.56	3.01	8%	-1.13	4.64	1.1%	3.73	5.40	6.05	0%	-41.85	8Y.11M
VNQ-TLT	-12.75	0.72	12.9%	-3.99	4.63	5.1%	2.67	5.25	7.07	0%	-42.87	11Y.6M
VTI-EMB	-9.69	0.84	13.2%	0.50	4.57	0%	3.50	5.76	6.57	0%	-34.51	5Y.10M
IJS-EMB	-11.55	0.79	13.2%	-0.25	4.35	0.7%	3.02	4.78	7.62	0%	-36.71	7Y.3M
VNQ-EMB	-14.35	1.08	12.6%	-2.36	4.24	4.3%	2.09	4.53	8.24	0%	-46.49	10Y.6M
MTUM-TLT	-13.66	0.24	13.2%	-0.40	4.17	0.7%	4.57	5.68	7.33	0%	-40.02	7Y.7M
EMB-CWB	-8.71	2.65	9.2%	0.79	4.14	0%	2.83	5.24	6.61	0%	-34.42	6Y.4M
IJS-MTUM	-18.36	-0.34	16.3%	-3.19	3.91	1.8%	5.11	6.04	7.27	0%	-53.03	10Y.11M
MTUM-EEM	-16.49	-2.58	20.9%	0.39	3.88	0%	1.69	4.95	6.69	0%	-57.91	9Y.10M
VTV-EMB	-10.45	0.95	13.2%	0.51	3.86	0%	2.78	4.91	6.38	0%	-36.73	6Y.3M
SCZ-EMB	-11.57	-0.34	16%	-1.78	3.75	5.4%	0.68	4.46	8.38	0%	-42.34	10Y.0M
MTUM-VNQ	-21.31	-0.51	16.6%	-2.73	3.74	1.1%	4.46	6.49	7.42	0%	-59.64	10Y.8M
MTUM-TIP	-7.38	-0.81	18.2%	0.91	3.71	0%	3.65	4.63	5.81	0%	-29.89	8Y.11M
IJS-CWB	-16.90	1.81	11.7%	-2.72	3.64	2.5%	3.56	5.04	6.15	0%	-49.19	11Y.5M
VTI-VNQ	-21.41	0.11	14.5%	-3.96	3.57	2.5%	2.39	5.32	6.42	0%	-60.17	11Y.9M
IJS-GLD	-3.71	1.07	8.6%	1.05	3.54	0%	4.36	5.75	7.37	0%	-24.56	5Y.6M
TIP-CWB	-7.31	2.29	6.5%	0.80	3.49	0%	2.84	3.74	4.78	0%	-27.46	5Y.9M
MTUM-LQD	-8.46	-1.55	19.7%	-0.13	3.48	0.4%	3.89	4.73	6.04	0%	-32.02	9Y.10M

Order by **Baseline 7Y Return - Last 60 Years** (from 1963-12 to 2023-11)

Portfolio	3Y Rolling Annualized Return (%)			7Y Rolling Annualized Return (%)			15Y Rolling Annualized Return (%)				Max Draw-down (%)	Long Neg Period (Y.M)
	Worst	Base	%Fail	Worst	Base ▼	%Fail	Worst	Base	Median	%Fail		
IJS-TLT	-4.94	4.83	3.4%	0.94	7.72	0%	6.53	8.95	11.36	0%	-29.71	6Y.6M
IJS-GLD	-2.36	3.87	2.3%	2.55	6.67	0%	5.37	7.80	10.32	0%	-26.49	3Y.9M
VTI-IJS	-16.60	3.35	10.2%	-2.10	6.62	1.6%	6.05	8.30	12.39	0%	-51.92	9Y.9M
IJS-VNQ	-21.37	3.97	8.9%	-1.59	6.48	1.1%	5.43	9.04	12.08	0%	-60.63	7Y.8M
IJS-LQD	-8.39	4.84	4.8%	0.94	6.43	0%	5.67	7.74	11.24	0%	-31.41	6Y.8M
IJS-IEI	-4.77	4.94	2.8%	2.15	6.40	0%	5.30	7.42	11.24	0%	-22.74	6Y.4M
IJS-BND	-6.33	4.98	3.7%	2.16	6.26	0%	5.28	7.23	11.06	0%	-26.74	6Y.4M
IJS-VTV	-17.40	2.52	10.7%	-2.09	6.05	1.3%	5.74	8.13	12.63	0%	-54.38	10Y.11M
VTI-VNQ	-19.67	3.41	8.9%	-2.13	5.91	1.1%	4.94	8.26	10.75	0%	-58.60	9Y.8M
VTV-TLT	-3.72	2.57	3.8%	0.08	5.87	0%	4.28	7.36	9.91	0%	-23.60	7Y.5M
VTV-GLD	-2.95	2.93	3.5%	1.95	5.79	0%	4.03	7.30	8.88	0%	-29.36	6Y.1M
VTI-GLD	-4.65	3.39	4.4%	2.35	5.68	0%	3.85	6.90	9.09	0%	-33.29	5Y.1M
VNQ-TLT	-7.76	1.98	9.1%	-0.60	5.63	0.3%	4.74	7.91	10.22	0%	-36.95	8Y.9M
VTI-IEI	-3.88	4.10	2.9%	1.34	5.61	0%	5.49	6.48	9.08	0%	-22.24	5Y.10M
IJS-SHY	-5.98	4.63	3.9%	2.15	5.46	0%	4.38	6.33	10.83	0%	-25.95	6Y.1M
VTI-LQD	-6.45	3.63	6.7%	0.18	5.46	0%	5.00	6.49	9.15	0%	-29.35	6Y.5M
VTI-BND	-4.38	3.78	4.5%	1.35	5.44	0%	5.29	6.33	8.88	0%	-24.96	5Y.10M
VTV-IEI	-3.49	3.61	2.5%	1.36	5.39	0%	5.02	6.19	9.50	0%	-23.72	5Y.10M
VTI-TLT	-5.35	3.50	5.8%	0.03	5.38	0%	4.38	7.50	9.70	0%	-27.37	6Y.5M
VTV-LQD	-7.19	3.22	6.4%	0.24	5.22	0%	4.92	6.34	9.56	0%	-31.53	6Y.5M
VTV-BND	-5.10	3.42	4.5%	1.37	5.14	0%	5.00	6.08	9.35	0%	-27.21	5Y.10M

Order by **Baseline 7Y Return - Last 60 Years** (from 1963-12 to 2023-11) - **US Infl. Adjusted**

Portfolio	3Y Rolling Annualized Return (%)			7Y Rolling Annualized Return (%)			15Y Rolling Annualized Return (%)				Max Draw-down (%)	Long Neg Period (Y.M)
	Worst	Base	%Fail	Worst	Base ▼	%Fail	Worst	Base	Median	%Fail		
IJS-GLD	-6.91	0.78	12%	1.05	3.67	0%	2.23	4.79	7.49	0%	-33.07	5Y.7M
IJS-VNQ	-23.08	-0.19	15.3%	-7.40	3.13	6.1%	2.87	5.51	8.48	0%	-62.26	11Y.7M
VTV-GLD	-7.59	-0.57	17.7%	-1.30	2.95	2.7%	0.93	4.06	5.98	0%	-38.00	8Y.0M
IJS-IEI	-11.00	0.81	13.1%	-3.88	2.91	4.2%	2.43	4.23	6.94	0%	-34.81	11Y.7M
IJS-BND	-11.00	0.49	13.3%	-3.87	2.82	4.6%	2.43	4.23	6.89	0%	-34.79	11Y.7M
IJS-LQD	-13.35	0.34	14.2%	-5.02	2.81	4.7%	1.76	4.33	6.84	0%	-39.93	13Y.1M
IJS-TLT	-11.68	0.03	14.6%	-4.80	2.81	5%	1.33	4.71	7.71	0%	-39.25	13Y.4M
IJS-VTV	-19.19	-0.93	16.1%	-7.46	2.64	5.8%	2.41	4.73	8.60	0%	-55.29	11Y.8M
VTI-GLD	-6.95	-0.86	18.1%	-0.47	2.60	0.9%	0.59	3.61	5.79	0%	-41.20	12Y.7M
VTI-IJS	-18.59	-0.23	15.5%	-7.82	2.57	6.6%	1.90	4.62	8.18	0%	-54.31	11Y.9M
IJS-SHY	-10.61	0.86	12.9%	-3.50	2.35	4.4%	2.19	3.85	6.57	0%	-34.03	9Y.4M
IJS-BIL	-10.07	0.75	13.3%	-3.60	2.18	4.7%	1.84	3.38	5.84	0%	-33.22	9Y.4M
VTI-VNQ	-21.41	-0.25	16.5%	-7.69	1.65	11.5%	0.05	4.49	7.02	0%	-60.17	15Y.3M
VTI-IEI	-10.54	-1.01	20.7%	-4.41	1.13	11.6%	-1.03	2.87	5.05	6.1%	-34.69	18Y.5M
VNQ-GLD	-7.20	-1.93	26.6%	-1.65	1.07	8%	0.08	2.02	6.47	0%	-37.93	15Y.1M
VTI-SHY	-10.46	-0.80	19.4%	-4.11	0.98	11.6%	-0.39	2.47	4.26	1.7%	-34.75	16Y.9M
VTV-VNQ	-22.30	-0.52	17.1%	-7.53	0.97	9.4%	0.36	4.42	7.19	0%	-62.22	14Y.7M
VTI-BND	-10.54	-1.31	21.6%	-4.41	0.96	12.2%	-1.02	2.87	5.04	6.1%	-34.69	18Y.5M
VTV-SHY	-8.77	-0.73	19.1%	-4.07	0.75	9%	-0.38	2.37	4.42	0.5%	-30.27	16Y.8M
VNQ-SHY	-10.82	-0.39	17.1%	-3.88	0.74	9.1%	0.28	2.80	5.29	0%	-39.05	13Y.0M
VTI-VTV	-17.67	-2.62	20.3%	-8.26	0.63	11.9%	-0.94	2.52	6.71	2%	-53.37	18Y.0M

Order by **Baseline 7Y Return - All data** (from 1871/1927 to 2023-11)

Portfolio	3Y Rolling Annualized Return (%)			7Y Rolling Annualized Return (%)			15Y Rolling Annualized Return (%)				Max Draw-down (%)	Long Neg Period (Y.M)
	Worst	Base	%Fail	Worst	Base ▼	%Fail	Worst	Base	Median	%Fail		
IJS-TLT	-24.33	3.34	7.5%	0.59	6.71	0%	4.14	8.32	9.90	0%	-60.20	6Y.6M
IJS-LQD	-23.39	3.19	8.2%	0.88	6.19	0%	4.11	7.76	10.02	0%	-58.59	6Y.8M
IJS-IEI	-23.26	3.46	7.4%	0.89	6.04	0%	4.01	7.69	10.18	0%	-58.38	6Y.4M
IJS-BND	-23.25	3.36	7.9%	0.91	6.03	0%	4.02	7.55	10.19	0%	-58.36	6Y.4M
IJS-GLD	-25.48	2.48	7.5%	1.45	5.77	0%	3.56	7.64	9.84	0%	-61.69	6Y.4M
VTI-IJS	-46.41	0.86	13.9%	-7.15	5.74	4.1%	0.75	8.49	12.73	0%	-86.65	14Y.8M
IJS-VNQ	-36.96	1.75	12.5%	-4.86	5.51	2.8%	1.70	8.44	11.07	0%	-78.32	14Y.4M
IJS-VTV	-46.12	0.51	14.3%	-7.72	5.37	4%	0.39	8.18	12.74	0%	-86.54	14Y.9M
IJS-SHY	-23.14	3.42	8.4%	0.62	5.31	0%	3.44	6.87	10.28	0%	-58.12	8Y.7M
IJS-BIL	-24.05	3.11	9.6%	-0.33	4.86	0.1%	2.75	6.17	9.74	0%	-59.54	12Y.8M
VTI-VNQ	-34.57	1.65	12.6%	-5.56	4.74	3.3%	-0.19	6.65	9.35	0.1%	-75.75	15Y.3M
VTV-GLD	-22.14	2.29	7.5%	0.57	4.61	0%	2.21	5.82	8.26	0%	-56.74	12Y.8M
VTV-IEI	-19.94	2.74	6.9%	-0.56	4.60	0.2%	2.45	5.87	7.95	0%	-53.22	12Y.8M
VTV-BND	-19.93	2.53	8.1%	-0.55	4.54	0.2%	2.46	5.83	7.90	0%	-53.20	12Y.8M
VTV-LQD	-20.06	2.45	9.2%	-0.56	4.47	0.2%	2.57	5.93	7.96	0%	-53.44	10Y.9M
VTV-TLT	-21.03	2.04	7.5%	-0.86	4.44	0.4%	2.58	5.42	8.18	0%	-55.21	10Y.9M
VTI-SHY	-20.30	2.48	6.7%	-1.17	4.31	0.2%	2.12	5.26	6.63	0%	-53.35	12Y.9M
VTV-SHY	-19.83	2.17	9.3%	-0.87	4.21	0.3%	1.71	5.27	7.79	0%	-52.96	13Y.1M
VTI-VTV	-43.48	-0.28	15.3%	-7.64	4.15	5.2%	-0.66	6.42	10.64	0.3%	-84.44	15Y.7M
VTV-VNQ	-33.99	1.27	12.7%	-6.21	4.13	3.8%	-0.54	6.22	9.27	0.2%	-75.26	15Y.7M
VTI-IEI	-20.40	2.36	5.7%	-1.33	4.11	0.2%	2.39	5.11	6.74	0%	-53.59	8Y.10M

Order by **Baseline 7Y Return - All data** (from 1871/1927 to 2023-11) - **US Infl. Adjusted**

Portfolio	3Y Rolling Annualized Return (%)			7Y Rolling Annualized Return (%)			15Y Rolling Annualized Return (%)				Max Draw-down (%)	Long Neg Period (Y.M)
	Worst	Base	%Fail	Worst	Base ▼	%Fail	Worst	Base	Median	%Fail		
IJS-GLD	-19.57	-0.28	16.1%	-1.46	3.52	1.6%	2.23	4.47	6.85	0%	-51.62	8Y.3M
IJS-TLT	-18.33	-0.48	16.1%	-4.80	3.40	3.4%	1.33	4.42	6.98	0%	-49.74	13Y.4M
IJS-LQD	-17.31	-0.40	15.7%	-5.02	3.27	3.2%	1.76	4.39	6.67	0%	-47.71	13Y.1M
IJS-IEI	-17.17	0.01	14.9%	-3.88	3.23	2.9%	2.43	4.31	6.62	0%	-47.45	11Y.7M
IJS-BND	-17.16	-0.02	15%	-3.87	3.23	3%	2.43	4.33	6.57	0%	-47.42	11Y.7M
IJS-VNQ	-31.96	-0.86	17%	-7.40	3.04	4.8%	0.07	4.98	7.98	0%	-72.62	15Y.5M
IJS-SHY	-17.04	-0.17	15.3%	-3.50	2.68	3.2%	2.19	3.99	6.54	0%	-47.11	9Y.4M
VTI-IJS	-42.15	-2.53	18.1%	-7.82	2.67	7.3%	1.04	4.62	8.75	0%	-83.15	14Y.5M
IJS-VTV	-41.85	-2.29	18.5%	-7.46	2.65	7.2%	0.66	4.65	8.95	0%	-83.01	14Y.8M
IJS-BIL	-18.03	-0.43	16.4%	-3.60	2.29	4.3%	1.84	3.58	6.16	0%	-48.91	9Y.4M
VTV-GLD	-15.96	-0.86	19.1%	-2.37	2.04	5.6%	0.41	2.72	5.15	0%	-45.38	13Y.8M
VTI-VNQ	-29.37	-1.22	18.3%	-7.69	1.58	10.1%	-1.44	2.51	6.38	1%	-69.34	19Y.5M
VTI-IEI	-14.08	-0.68	17.4%	-6.45	1.29	9.8%	-2.22	1.94	4.90	3.6%	-45.15	22Y.3M
VTI-BND	-14.07	-0.87	17.7%	-6.44	1.28	10%	-2.21	1.95	4.90	3.6%	-45.14	22Y.3M
VTI-SHY	-13.98	-0.61	16.9%	-6.05	1.27	11%	-1.68	1.96	4.80	2%	-43.27	21Y.6M
VTI-GLD	-16.51	-1.02	19.2%	-7.58	1.15	8.3%	-3.50	1.80	4.69	6.2%	-49.52	30Y.2M
VTI-LQD	-14.22	-1.11	18.6%	-6.51	1.11	10.3%	-2.31	1.91	4.98	4.3%	-45.30	22Y.7M
VTI-TLT	-15.20	-1.35	18.1%	-6.67	0.94	10.6%	-2.50	1.95	5.43	5.3%	-45.41	22Y.7M
VTV-VNQ	-28.76	-1.64	19.2%	-7.53	0.89	10%	-1.53	2.24	6.33	1.8%	-68.76	19Y.6M
VTI-BIL	-14.99	-0.60	17%	-5.35	0.80	11.6%	-1.13	1.69	4.63	1.5%	-43.05	19Y.6M
VTV-IEI	-13.59	-1.07	20.5%	-4.40	0.79	8.4%	-1.00	1.97	4.58	3.8%	-40.93	18Y.6M

124

Ranking: Baseline 15Y Return

Order by **Baseline 15Y Return** - **Last 30 Years** (from 1993-12 to 2023-11)

Portfolio	3Y Rolling Annualized Return (%)			7Y Rolling Annualized Return (%)			15Y Rolling Annualized Return (%)				Max Draw-down (%)	Long Neg Period (Y.M)
	Worst	Base	%Fail	Worst	Base	%Fail	Worst	Base ▼	Median	%Fail		
MTUM-VNQ	-19.57	2.24	9.2%	-0.24	6.42	0.7%	6.95	8.95	9.82	0%	-59.01	8Y.10M
MTUM-GLD	-4.23	4.17	4.6%	5.99	7.51	0%	7.33	8.83	10.18	0%	-27.55	3Y.11M
MTUM-EMB	-7.57	3.42	5.8%	4.38	7.08	0%	6.11	8.78	9.84	0%	-35.06	4Y.4M
IJS-MTUM	-16.55	2.29	13.2%	-0.71	6.27	0.7%	7.25	8.43	9.67	0%	-52.24	9Y.2M
IJS-GLD	-1.26	3.34	2.8%	2.55	5.67	0%	6.84	8.28	9.88	0%	-23.76	3Y.6M
MTUM-TLT	-8.69	2.38	5.5%	3.10	6.92	0%	7.06	8.13	9.77	0%	-33.28	5Y.2M
VTI-GLD	-4.65	3.62	6.2%	2.35	5.19	0%	6.44	8.11	8.96	0%	-26.09	5Y.0M
IJS-TLT	-3.99	4.82	3.4%	1.55	7.57	0%	6.53	8.05	9.25	0%	-29.71	6Y.0M
MTUM-SCZ	-17.68	0.09	14.5%	3.06	5.38	0%	5.13	8.02	9.10	0%	-58.64	5Y.9M
VTI-EMB	-7.69	4.14	3.4%	3.07	7.02	0%	5.97	7.94	8.90	0%	-33.48	5Y.2M
VTV-GLD	-2.95	3.19	3.7%	1.95	5.15	0%	6.39	7.86	8.60	0%	-25.94	5Y.2M
VTI-VNQ	-19.67	2.94	9.2%	-1.51	6.08	0.7%	4.94	7.84	8.79	0%	-58.60	9Y.8M
IJS-VNQ	-21.37	3.52	10.2%	-1.09	5.70	0.7%	5.43	7.62	9.47	0%	-60.63	7Y.8M
VTI-TLT	-4.50	3.07	5.8%	3.77	6.03	0%	6.97	7.62	8.35	0%	-27.37	4Y.2M
CWB-GLD	-2.75	2.02	4.9%	2.36	4.12	0%	6.10	7.60	8.94	0%	-29.04	4Y.9M
TLT-CWB	-8.59	5.50	4%	2.34	7.15	0%	6.22	7.58	8.45	0%	-31.98	4Y.4M
VNQ-CWB	-18.04	4.66	8%	0.30	5.76	0%	4.92	7.56	8.65	0%	-55.16	6Y.11M
VNQ-TLT	-7.76	3.13	9.5%	-0.60	6.57	0.7%	5.03	7.53	9.61	0%	-36.95	8Y.9M
VTI-IJS	-16.60	1.99	12.6%	-2.04	5.81	1.1%	6.05	7.46	8.55	0%	-51.92	9Y.9M
IJS-CWB	-15.06	4.28	8.9%	-0.23	6.07	0.7%	5.87	7.31	8.51	0%	-48.15	8Y.1M
MTUM-CWB	-13.64	0.44	14.2%	0.12	5.72	0%	5.86	7.31	8.89	0%	-47.92	9Y.3M

Order by **Baseline 15Y Return** - **Last 30 Years** (from 1993-12 to 2023-11) - **US Infl. Adjusted**

Portfolio	3Y Rolling Annualized Return (%)			7Y Rolling Annualized Return (%)			15Y Rolling Annualized Return (%)				Max Draw-down (%)	Long Neg Period (Y.M)
	Worst	Base	%Fail	Worst	Base	%Fail	Worst	Base ▼	Median	%Fail		
MTUM-EMB	-9.57	0.12	14.5%	1.40	4.75	0%	3.64	6.64	7.52	0%	-36.06	6Y.3M
MTUM-VNQ	-21.31	-0.51	16.6%	-2.73	3.74	1.1%	4.46	6.49	7.42	0%	-59.64	10Y.8M
MTUM-GLD	-6.54	1.48	10.8%	3.48	5.22	0%	4.85	6.40	7.83	0%	-29.19	4Y.8M
IJS-MTUM	-18.36	-0.34	16.3%	-3.19	3.91	1.8%	5.11	6.04	7.27	0%	-53.03	10Y.11M
IJS-TLT	-9.13	2.28	10.2%	-1.89	5.02	1.4%	4.05	5.95	6.81	0%	-36.99	9Y.4M
VTI-EMB	-9.69	0.84	13.2%	0.50	4.57	0%	3.50	5.76	6.57	0%	-34.51	5Y.10M
IJS-GLD	-3.71	1.07	8.6%	1.05	3.54	0%	4.36	5.75	7.37	0%	-24.56	5Y.6M
MTUM-TLT	-13.66	0.24	13.2%	-0.40	4.17	0.7%	4.57	5.68	7.33	0%	-40.02	7Y.7M
VTI-GLD	-6.95	1.19	12.3%	-0.08	3.01	0.4%	3.86	5.65	6.43	0%	-27.75	7Y.2M
MTUM-SCZ	-19.46	-2.27	20.6%	0.66	3.02	0%	2.68	5.57	6.73	0%	-59.27	10Y.10M
TLT-CWB	-13.56	3.01	8%	-1.13	4.64	1.1%	3.73	5.40	6.05	0%	-41.85	8Y.11M
VTV-GLD	-5.35	1.01	11.1%	-0.47	2.99	0.7%	3.80	5.37	6.26	0%	-27.61	7Y.3M
VTI-VNQ	-21.41	0.11	14.5%	-3.96	3.57	2.5%	2.39	5.32	6.42	0%	-60.17	11Y.9M
IJS-VNQ	-23.08	0.65	13.5%	-3.51	3.35	2.2%	2.87	5.25	7.00	0%	-62.26	11Y.7M
VNQ-TLT	-12.75	0.72	12.9%	-3.99	4.63	5.1%	2.67	5.25	7.07	0%	-42.87	11Y.6M
VNQ-CWB	-19.82	2.05	10.5%	-2.16	3.36	1.4%	2.37	5.19	6.36	0%	-57.15	11Y.6M
CWB-GLD	-4.74	0.24	13.5%	0.01	2.05	0%	3.47	5.15	6.58	0%	-30.63	7Y.1M
VTI-TLT	-9.66	0.34	13.2%	0.25	3.17	0%	4.47	5.15	5.89	0%	-33.99	8Y.6M
EMB-CWB	-8.71	2.65	9.2%	0.79	4.14	0%	2.83	5.04	6.61	0%	-34.42	6Y.4M
VTI-IJS	-18.41	-0.26	15.7%	-4.48	3.10	2.9%	3.47	5.04	6.07	0%	-52.88	11Y.8M
IJS-CWB	-16.90	1.81	11.7%	-2.72	3.64	2.5%	3.56	5.04	6.15	0%	-49.19	11Y.5M

Order by **Baseline 15Y Return - Last 60 Years** (from 1963-12 to 2023-11)

Portfolio	3Y Rolling Annualized Return (%)			7Y Rolling Annualized Return (%)			15Y Rolling Annualized Return (%)				Max Draw-down (%)	Long Neg Period (Y.M)
	Worst	Base	%Fail	Worst	Base	%Fail	Worst	Base ▼	Median	%Fail		
IJS-VNQ	-21.37	3.97	8.9%	-1.59	6.48	1.1%	5.43	9.04	12.08	0%	-60.63	7Y.8M
IJS-TLT	-4.94	4.83	3.4%	0.94	7.72	0%	6.53	8.95	11.36	0%	-29.71	6Y.6M
VTI-IJS	-16.60	3.35	10.2%	-2.10	6.62	1.6%	6.05	8.30	12.39	0%	-51.92	9Y.9M
VTI-VNQ	-19.67	3.41	8.9%	-2.13	5.91	1.1%	4.94	8.26	10.75	0%	-58.60	9Y.8M
IJS-VTV	-17.40	2.52	10.7%	-2.09	6.05	1.3%	5.74	8.13	12.63	0%	-54.38	10Y.11M
VNQ-TLT	-7.76	1.98	9.1%	-0.60	5.63	0.3%	4.74	7.91	10.22	0%	-36.95	8Y.9M
IJS-GLD	-2.36	3.87	2.3%	2.55	6.67	0%	5.37	7.80	10.32	0%	-26.49	3Y.9M
VTV-VNQ	-20.58	3.15	8.8%	-1.97	5.06	1.3%	4.67	7.79	10.95	0%	-60.85	10Y.3M
IJS-LQD	-8.39	4.84	4.8%	0.94	6.43	0%	5.67	7.74	11.24	0%	-31.41	6Y.8M
VTI-TLT	-5.35	3.50	5.8%	0.03	5.38	0%	4.38	7.50	9.70	0%	-27.37	6Y.5M
IJS-IEI	-4.77	4.94	2.8%	2.15	6.40	0%	5.30	7.42	11.24	0%	-22.74	6Y.4M
VTV-TLT	-3.72	2.57	3.8%	0.08	5.87	0%	4.28	7.36	9.91	0%	-23.60	7Y.5M
VTV-GLD	-2.95	2.93	3.5%	1.95	5.79	0%	4.03	7.30	8.88	0%	-29.36	6Y.1M
IJS-BND	-6.33	4.98	3.7%	2.16	6.26	0%	5.28	7.23	11.06	0%	-26.74	6Y.4M
VNQ-IEI	-7.46	2.73	6.1%	1.36	4.90	0%	4.44	7.01	9.32	0%	-33.27	5Y.0M
VNQ-BND	-9.06	2.62	6.7%	1.32	4.93	0%	4.38	6.95	9.10	0%	-36.89	5Y.2M
VNQ-LQD	-11.16	2.53	8%	0.44	5.10	0%	4.83	6.92	9.34	0%	-41.20	5Y.10M
VTI-GLD	-4.65	3.39	4.4%	2.35	5.68	0%	3.85	6.90	9.09	0%	-33.29	5Y.1M
VNQ-SHY	-8.94	2.80	5.3%	1.77	4.74	0%	3.82	6.56	8.53	0%	-36.11	5Y.2M
VTI-VTV	-15.85	1.51	12.3%	-2.97	4.53	1.7%	4.68	6.52	10.62	0%	-52.41	11Y.7M
VTI-LQD	-6.45	3.63	6.7%	0.18	5.46	0%	5.00	6.49	9.15	0%	-29.35	6Y.5M

Order by **Baseline 15Y Return - Last 60 Years** (from 1963-12 to 2023-11) - **US Infl. Adjusted**

Portfolio	3Y Rolling Annualized Return (%)			7Y Rolling Annualized Return (%)			15Y Rolling Annualized Return (%)				Max Draw-down (%)	Long Neg Period (Y.M)
	Worst	Base	%Fail	Worst	Base	%Fail	Worst	Base ▼	Median	%Fail		
IJS-VNQ	-23.08	-0.19	15.3%	-7.40	3.13	6.1%	2.87	5.51	8.48	0%	-62.26	11Y.7M
IJS-GLD	-6.91	0.78	12%	1.05	3.67	0%	2.23	4.79	7.49	0%	-33.07	5Y.7M
IJS-VTV	-19.19	-0.93	16.1%	-7.46	2.64	5.8%	2.41	4.73	8.60	0%	-55.29	11Y.8M
IJS-TLT	-11.68	0.03	14.6%	-4.80	2.81	5%	1.33	4.71	7.71	0%	-39.25	13Y.4M
VTI-IJS	-18.59	-0.23	15.5%	-7.82	2.57	6.6%	1.90	4.62	8.18	0%	-54.31	11Y.9M
VTI-VNQ	-21.41	-0.25	16.5%	-7.69	1.65	11.5%	0.05	4.49	7.02	0%	-60.17	15Y.3M
VTV-VNQ	-22.30	-0.52	17.1%	-7.53	0.97	9.4%	0.36	4.42	7.19	0%	-62.22	14Y.7M
IJS-LQD	-13.35	0.34	14.2%	-5.02	2.81	4.7%	1.76	4.33	6.84	0%	-39.93	13Y.1M
IJS-BND	-11.00	0.49	13.3%	-3.87	2.82	4.6%	2.43	4.23	6.89	0%	-34.79	11Y.7M
IJS-IEI	-11.00	0.81	13.1%	-3.88	2.91	4.2%	2.43	4.23	6.94	0%	-34.81	11Y.7M
VTV-GLD	-7.59	-0.57	17.7%	-1.30	2.95	2.7%	0.93	4.06	5.98	0%	-38.00	8Y.0M
IJS-SHY	-10.61	0.86	12.9%	-3.50	2.35	4.4%	2.19	3.85	6.57	0%	-34.03	9Y.4M
VTV-TLT	-10.16	-2.04	25.4%	-5.61	-0.40	17.1%	-2.05	3.75	6.23	8.9%	-35.68	19Y.4M
VTI-GLD	-6.95	-0.86	18.1%	-0.47	2.60	0.9%	0.59	3.61	5.79	0%	-41.20	12Y.7M
VTV-LQD	-11.04	-2.03	24.4%	-5.45	0.15	13.5%	-1.45	3.42	5.12	8.1%	-36.06	18Y.8M
VNQ-TLT	-12.75	-2.30	24.2%	-5.39	-0.18	17%	-1.39	3.41	6.92	8.3%	-42.87	18Y.10M
IJS-BIL	-10.07	0.75	13.3%	-3.60	2.18	4.7%	1.84	3.38	5.84	0%	-33.22	9Y.4M
VTV-IEI	-8.85	-0.86	21.6%	-4.40	0.46	10.2%	-1.00	3.26	4.97	6.8%	-31.05	18Y.6M
VNQ-LQD	-13.09	-1.27	22.2%	-5.15	0.21	13%	-0.78	3.22	6.09	5.4%	-43.91	18Y.8M
VTV-BND	-8.85	-1.41	22.6%	-4.39	0.43	10.5%	-1.00	3.11	4.91	6.7%	-31.02	18Y.6M
VNQ-BND	-11.03	-1.05	18.8%	-4.27	0.38	11.3%	-0.33	2.91	5.78	0.4%	-39.79	17Y.10M

Order by **Baseline 15Y Return** - **All data** (from 1871/1927 to 2023-11)

Portfolio	3Y Rolling Annualized Return (%)			7Y Rolling Annualized Return (%)			15Y Rolling Annualized Return (%)				Max Draw-down (%)	Long Neg Period (Y.M)
	Worst	Base	%Fail	Worst	Base	%Fail	Worst	Base ▼	Median	%Fail		
VTI-IJS	-46.41	0.86	13.9%	-7.15	5.74	4.1%	0.75	8.49	12.73	0%	-86.65	14Y.8M
IJS-VNQ	-36.96	1.75	12.5%	-4.86	5.51	2.8%	1.70	8.44	11.07	0%	-78.32	14Y.4M
IJS-TLT	-24.33	3.34	7.5%	0.59	6.71	0%	4.14	8.32	9.90	0%	-60.20	6Y.6M
IJS-VTV	-46.12	0.51	14.3%	-7.72	5.37	4%	0.39	8.18	12.74	0%	-86.54	14Y.9M
IJS-LQD	-23.39	3.19	8.2%	0.88	6.19	0%	4.11	7.76	10.02	0%	-58.59	6Y.8M
IJS-IEI	-23.26	3.46	7.4%	0.89	6.04	0%	4.01	7.69	10.18	0%	-58.38	6Y.4M
IJS-GLD	-25.48	2.48	7.5%	1.45	5.77	0%	3.56	7.64	9.84	0%	-61.69	6Y.4M
IJS-BND	-23.25	3.36	7.9%	0.91	6.03	0%	4.02	7.55	10.19	0%	-58.36	6Y.4M
IJS-SHY	-23.14	3.42	8.4%	0.62	5.31	0%	3.44	6.87	10.28	0%	-58.12	8Y.7M
VTI-VNQ	-34.57	1.65	12.6%	-5.56	4.74	3.3%	-0.19	6.65	9.35	0.1%	-75.75	15Y.3M
VTI-VTV	-43.48	-0.28	15.3%	-7.64	4.15	5.2%	-0.66	6.42	10.64	0.3%	-84.44	15Y.7M
VTV-VNQ	-33.99	1.27	12.7%	-6.21	4.13	3.8%	-0.54	6.22	9.27	0.2%	-75.26	15Y.7M
IJS-BIL	-24.05	3.11	9.6%	-0.33	4.86	0.1%	2.75	6.17	9.74	0%	-59.54	12Y.8M
VTV-LQD	-20.06	2.45	9.2%	-0.56	4.47	0.2%	2.57	5.93	7.96	0%	-53.44	10Y.9M
VTV-IEI	-19.94	2.74	6.9%	-0.56	4.60	0.2%	2.45	5.87	7.95	0%	-53.22	12Y.8M
VTV-BND	-19.93	2.53	8.1%	-0.55	4.54	0.2%	2.46	5.83	7.90	0%	-53.20	12Y.8M
VTV-GLD	-22.14	2.29	7.5%	0.57	4.61	0%	2.21	5.82	8.26	0%	-56.74	12Y.8M
VTV-TLT	-21.03	2.04	7.5%	-0.86	4.44	0.4%	2.58	5.42	8.18	0%	-55.21	10Y.9M
VTV-SHY	-19.83	2.17	9.3%	-0.87	4.21	0.3%	1.71	5.27	7.79	0%	-52.96	13Y.1M
VTI-SHY	-20.30	2.48	6.7%	-1.17	4.31	0.2%	2.12	5.26	6.63	0%	-53.35	12Y.9M
VTI-BND	-20.39	2.17	6.3%	-1.32	4.11	0.2%	2.39	5.11	6.72	0%	-53.58	8Y.9M

Order by **Baseline 15Y Return** - **All data** (from 1871/1927 to 2023-11) - **US Infl. Adjusted**

Portfolio	3Y Rolling Annualized Return (%)			7Y Rolling Annualized Return (%)			15Y Rolling Annualized Return (%)				Max Draw-down (%)	Long Neg Period (Y.M)
	Worst	Base	%Fail	Worst	Base	%Fail	Worst	Base ▼	Median	%Fail		
IJS-VNQ	-31.96	-0.86	17%	-7.40	3.04	4.8%	0.07	4.98	7.98	0%	-72.62	15Y.5M
IJS-VTV	-41.85	-2.29	18.5%	-7.46	2.65	7.2%	0.66	4.65	8.95	0%	-83.01	14Y.8M
VTI-IJS	-42.15	-2.53	18.1%	-7.82	2.67	7.3%	1.04	4.62	8.75	0%	-83.15	14Y.5M
IJS-GLD	-19.57	-0.28	16.1%	-1.46	3.52	1.6%	2.23	4.47	6.85	0%	-51.62	8Y.3M
IJS-TLT	-18.33	-0.48	16.1%	-4.80	3.40	3.4%	1.33	4.42	6.98	0%	-49.74	13Y.4M
IJS-LQD	-17.31	-0.40	15.7%	-5.02	3.27	3.2%	1.76	4.39	6.67	0%	-47.71	13Y.1M
IJS-BND	-17.16	-0.02	15%	-3.87	3.23	3%	2.43	4.33	6.57	0%	-47.42	11Y.7M
IJS-IEI	-17.17	0.01	14.9%	-3.88	3.23	2.9%	2.43	4.31	6.62	0%	-47.45	11Y.7M
IJS-SHY	-17.04	-0.17	15.3%	-3.50	2.68	3.2%	2.19	3.99	6.54	0%	-47.11	9Y.4M
IJS-BIL	-18.03	-0.43	16.4%	-3.60	2.29	4.3%	1.84	3.58	6.16	0%	-48.91	9Y.4M
VTV-GLD	-15.96	-0.86	19.1%	-2.37	2.04	5.6%	0.41	2.72	5.15	0%	-45.38	13Y.8M
VTI-VNQ	-29.37	-1.22	18.3%	-7.69	1.58	10.1%	-1.44	2.51	6.38	1%	-69.34	19Y.5M
VTI-VTV	-39.00	-3.56	21.5%	-8.26	0.77	11.9%	-0.94	2.28	6.77	1.5%	-80.36	19Y.11M
VTV-VNQ	-28.76	-1.64	19.2%	-7.53	0.89	10%	-1.53	2.24	6.33	1.8%	-68.76	19Y.6M
VTV-BND	-13.57	-1.44	21.1%	-4.39	0.71	8.6%	-1.00	1.99	4.48	3.7%	-40.91	18Y.6M
VTV-IEI	-13.59	-1.07	20.5%	-4.40	0.79	8.4%	-1.00	1.97	4.58	3.8%	-40.93	18Y.6M
VTV-LQD	-13.72	-1.92	22%	-5.45	0.70	9.7%	-1.45	1.97	4.78	4.6%	-41.21	20Y.8M
VTI-SHY	-13.98	-0.61	16.9%	-6.05	1.27	11%	-1.68	1.96	4.80	2%	-43.27	21Y.6M
VTI-BND	-14.07	-0.87	17.7%	-6.44	1.28	10%	-2.21	1.95	4.90	3.6%	-45.14	22Y.3M
VTI-TLT	-15.20	-1.35	18.1%	-6.67	0.94	10.6%	-2.50	1.95	5.43	5.3%	-45.41	22Y.7M
VTV-TLT	-14.76	-1.71	22.8%	-5.61	0.52	12.1%	-2.05	1.94	5.31	5.3%	-43.44	22Y.2M

Ranking: Median 15Y Return

Order by **Median 15Y Return** - **Last 30 Years** (from 1993-12 to 2023-11)

Portfolio	3Y Rolling Annualized Return (%)			7Y Rolling Annualized Return (%)			15Y Rolling Annualized Return (%)				Max Draw-down (%)	Long Neg Period (Y.M)
	Worst	Base	%Fail	Worst	Base	%Fail	Worst	Base	Median ▼	%Fail		
SCZ-EMB	-9.62	1.61	9.8%	1.66	5.81	0%	3.09	6.47	10.72	0%	-40.94	6Y.3M
VNQ-EMB	-12.45	3.22	9.5%	1.09	6.10	0%	4.54	6.61	10.63	0%	-43.90	5Y.2M
MTUM-GLD	-4.23	4.17	4.6%	5.99	7.51	0%	7.33	8.83	10.18	0%	-27.55	3Y.11M
VNQ-GLD	-4.27	1.25	12%	1.52	4.14	0%	5.62	7.28	10.17	0%	-32.62	5Y.8M
EEM-EMB	-6.29	1.62	11.1%	0.68	3.51	0%	1.51	6.00	10.13	0%	-41.52	9Y.10M
EMB-GLD	-7.36	0.84	12%	-1.13	3.25	1.1%	3.92	6.51	10.02	0%	-25.22	10Y.1M
IJS-EMB	-9.59	4.22	6.8%	3.06	6.60	0%	5.48	7.01	10.02	0%	-35.42	5Y.1M
EEM-TLT	-11.07	2.25	9.2%	-0.91	3.86	0.7%	2.64	7.14	9.90	0%	-34.84	10Y.10M
IJS-GLD	-1.26	3.34	2.8%	2.55	5.67	0%	6.84	8.28	9.88	0%	-23.76	3Y.6M
MTUM-EMB	-7.57	3.42	5.8%	4.38	7.08	0%	6.11	8.78	9.84	0%	-35.06	4Y.4M
MTUM-VNQ	-19.57	2.24	9.2%	-0.24	6.42	0.7%	6.95	8.95	9.82	0%	-59.01	8Y.10M
MTUM-TLT	-8.69	2.38	5.5%	3.10	6.92	0%	7.06	8.13	9.77	0%	-33.28	5Y.2M
IJS-MTUM	-16.55	2.29	13.2%	-0.71	6.27	0.7%	7.25	8.43	9.67	0%	-52.24	9Y.2M
EEM-VNQ	-17.29	0.63	12.3%	1.90	4.52	0%	2.50	5.90	9.61	0%	-61.82	5Y.10M
VNQ-TLT	-7.76	3.13	9.5%	-0.60	6.57	0.7%	5.03	7.53	9.61	0%	-36.95	8Y.9M
IJS-VNQ	-21.37	3.52	10.2%	-1.09	5.70	0.7%	5.43	7.62	9.47	0%	-60.63	7Y.8M
EMB-TLT	-11.54	3.58	6.2%	-2.15	4.72	3.6%	3.55	6.41	9.33	0%	-34.26	11Y.3M
EEM-GLD	-12.24	-3.74	30.8%	-4.59	-0.43	17%	2.36	6.04	9.26	0%	-40.74	11Y.6M
IJS-TLT	-3.99	4.82	3.4%	1.55	7.57	0%	6.53	8.05	9.25	0%	-29.71	6Y.0M
SCZ-TLT	-8.83	2.98	6.8%	-0.16	4.88	0.4%	4.19	7.29	9.19	0%	-33.97	7Y.4M
IJS-EEM	-14.08	1.51	11.1%	1.48	5.56	0%	3.79	6.50	9.16	0%	-55.48	6Y.4M

Order by **Median 15Y Return** - **Last 30 Years** (from 1993-12 to 2023-11) - **US Infl. Adjusted**

Portfolio	3Y Rolling Annualized Return (%)			7Y Rolling Annualized Return (%)			15Y Rolling Annualized Return (%)				Max Draw-down (%)	Long Neg Period (Y.M)
	Worst	Base	%Fail	Worst	Base	%Fail	Worst	Base	Median ▼	%Fail		
SCZ-EMB	-11.57	-0.34	16%	-1.78	3.75	5.4%	0.68	4.46	8.38	0%	-42.34	10Y.0M
VNQ-EMB	-14.35	1.08	12.6%	-2.36	4.24	4.3%	2.09	4.53	8.24	0%	-46.49	10Y.6M
MTUM-GLD	-6.54	1.48	10.8%	3.48	5.22	0%	4.85	6.40	7.83	0%	-29.19	4Y.8M
EEM-EMB	-10.76	-0.57	18.5%	-2.51	1.85	7.2%	-0.86	3.98	7.74	1.1%	-42.56	16Y.1M
EMB-GLD	-8.44	-1.42	23.1%	-2.64	0.56	10.8%	1.52	4.37	7.69	0%	-31.18	13Y.0M
VNQ-GLD	-6.25	-1.48	21.9%	-1.02	1.90	2.5%	3.15	4.91	7.63	0%	-32.33	8Y.0M
IJS-EMB	-11.55	0.79	13.2%	-0.25	4.35	0.7%	3.02	4.78	7.62	0%	-36.71	7Y.3M
EEM-TLT	-15.88	-0.02	15.1%	-4.27	1.67	7.2%	0.24	4.79	7.57	0%	-44.83	16Y.0M
MTUM-EMB	-9.57	0.12	14.5%	1.40	4.75	0%	3.64	6.64	7.52	0%	-36.06	6Y.3M
MTUM-VNQ	-21.31	-0.51	16.6%	-2.73	3.74	1.1%	4.46	6.49	7.42	0%	-59.64	10Y.8M
IJS-GLD	-3.71	1.07	8.6%	1.05	3.54	0%	4.36	5.75	7.37	0%	-24.56	5Y.6M
MTUM-TLT	-13.66	0.24	13.2%	-0.40	4.17	0.7%	4.57	5.68	7.33	0%	-40.02	7Y.7M
IJS-MTUM	-18.36	-0.34	16.3%	-3.19	3.91	1.8%	5.11	6.04	7.27	0%	-53.03	10Y.11M
EEM-VNQ	-19.08	-1.76	23.4%	-0.80	2.01	0.7%	0.10	3.61	7.25	0%	-62.41	16Y.0M
VNQ-TLT	-12.75	0.72	12.9%	-3.99	4.63	5.1%	2.67	5.25	7.07	0%	-42.87	11Y.6M
EMB-TLT	-16.33	1.49	7.1%	-5.47	2.91	7.6%	1.13	4.31	7.07	0%	-44.64	14Y.10M
IJS-VNQ	-23.08	0.65	13.5%	-3.51	3.35	2.2%	2.87	5.25	7.00	0%	-62.26	11Y.7M
EEM-GLD	-14.16	-5.71	43.1%	-6.97	-1.98	27.4%	-0.03	3.65	6.90	0.5%	-46.98	15Y.0M
IJS-TLT	-9.13	2.28	10.2%	-1.89	5.02	1.4%	4.05	5.95	6.81	0%	-36.99	9Y.4M
SCZ-GLD	-11.52	-4.28	30.5%	-5.68	0.91	12.3%	1.74	4.10	6.79	0%	-35.46	11Y.5M
MTUM-SCZ	-19.46	-2.27	20.6%	0.66	3.02	0%	2.68	5.57	6.73	0%	-59.27	9Y.10M

Order by **Median 15Y Return** - **Last 60 Years** (from 1963-12 to 2023-11)

Portfolio	3Y Rolling Annualized Return (%)			7Y Rolling Annualized Return (%)			15Y Rolling Annualized Return (%)				Max Draw-down (%)	Long Neg Period (Y.M)
	Worst	Base	%Fail	Worst	Base	%Fail	Worst	Base	Median ▼	%Fail		
IJS-VTV	-17.40	2.52	10.7%	-2.09	6.05	1.3%	5.74	8.13	12.63	0%	-54.38	10Y.11M
VTI-IJS	-16.60	3.35	10.2%	-2.10	6.62	1.6%	6.05	8.30	12.39	0%	-51.92	9Y.9M
IJS-VNQ	-21.37	3.97	8.9%	-1.59	6.48	1.1%	5.43	9.04	12.08	0%	-60.63	7Y.8M
IJS-TLT	-4.94	4.83	3.4%	0.94	7.72	0%	6.53	8.95	11.36	0%	-29.71	6Y.6M
IJS-IEI	-4.77	4.94	2.8%	2.15	6.40	0%	5.30	7.42	11.24	0%	-22.74	6Y.4M
IJS-LQD	-8.39	4.84	4.8%	0.94	6.43	0%	5.67	7.74	11.24	0%	-31.41	6Y.8M
IJS-BND	-6.33	4.98	3.7%	2.16	6.26	0%	5.28	7.23	11.06	0%	-26.74	6Y.4M
VTV-VNQ	-20.58	3.15	8.8%	-1.97	5.06	1.3%	4.67	7.79	10.95	0%	-60.85	10Y.3M
IJS-SHY	-5.98	4.63	3.9%	2.15	5.46	0%	4.38	6.33	10.83	0%	-25.95	6Y.1M
VTI-VNQ	-19.67	3.41	8.9%	-2.13	5.91	1.1%	4.94	8.26	10.75	0%	-58.60	9Y.8M
VTI-VTV	-15.85	1.51	12.3%	-2.97	4.53	1.7%	4.68	6.52	10.62	0%	-52.41	11Y.7M
IJS-GLD	-2.36	3.87	2.3%	2.55	6.67	0%	5.37	7.80	10.32	0%	-26.49	3Y.9M
IJS-BIL	-7.10	4.47	5.1%	1.19	4.98	0%	3.82	5.64	10.27	0%	-28.67	6Y.1M
VNQ-TLT	-7.76	1.98	9.1%	-0.60	5.63	0.3%	4.74	7.91	10.22	0%	-36.95	8Y.9M
VNQ-GLD	-4.27	1.44	9.2%	0.87	3.95	0%	3.31	5.68	10.22	0%	-32.62	6Y.5M
VTV-TLT	-3.72	2.57	3%	0.08	5.87	0%	4.28	7.36	9.91	0%	-23.60	7Y.5M
VTI-TLT	-5.35	3.50	5.8%	0.03	5.38	0%	4.38	7.50	9.70	0%	-27.37	6Y.5M
VTV-LQD	-7.19	3.22	6.4%	0.24	5.22	0%	4.92	6.34	9.56	0%	-31.53	6Y.5M
VTV-IEI	-3.49	3.61	2.5%	1.36	5.39	0%	5.02	6.19	9.50	0%	-23.72	5Y.10M
VTV-BND	-5.10	3.42	4.5%	1.37	5.14	0%	5.00	6.08	9.35	0%	-27.21	5Y.10M
VNQ-LQD	-11.16	2.53	8%	0.44	5.10	0%	4.83	6.92	9.34	0%	-41.20	5Y.10M

Order by **Median 15Y Return** - **Last 60 Years** (from 1963-12 to 2023-11) - **US Infl. Adjusted**

Portfolio	3Y Rolling Annualized Return (%)			7Y Rolling Annualized Return (%)			15Y Rolling Annualized Return (%)				Max Draw-down (%)	Long Neg Period (Y.M)
	Worst	Base	%Fail	Worst	Base	%Fail	Worst	Base	Median ▼	%Fail		
IJS-VTV	-19.19	-0.93	16.1%	-7.46	2.64	5.8%	2.41	4.73	8.60	0%	-55.29	11Y.8M
IJS-VNQ	-23.08	-0.19	15.3%	-7.40	3.13	6.1%	2.87	5.51	8.48	0%	-62.26	11Y.7M
VTI-IJS	-18.59	-0.23	15.5%	-7.82	2.57	6.6%	1.90	4.62	8.18	0%	-54.31	11Y.9M
IJS-TLT	-11.68	0.03	14.6%	-4.80	2.81	5%	1.33	4.71	7.71	0%	-39.25	13Y.4M
IJS-GLD	-6.91	0.78	12%	1.05	3.67	0%	2.23	4.79	7.49	0%	-33.07	5Y.7M
VTV-VNQ	-22.30	-0.52	17.1%	-7.53	0.97	9.4%	0.36	4.42	7.19	0%	-62.22	14Y.7M
VTI-VNQ	-21.41	-0.25	16.5%	-7.69	1.65	11.5%	0.05	4.49	7.02	0%	-60.17	15Y.3M
IJS-IEI	-11.00	0.81	13.1%	-3.88	2.91	4.2%	2.43	4.23	6.94	0%	-34.81	11Y.7M
VNQ-TLT	-12.75	-2.30	24.2%	-5.39	-0.18	17%	-1.39	3.41	6.92	8.3%	-42.87	18Y.10M
IJS-BND	-11.00	0.49	13.3%	-3.87	2.82	4.6%	2.43	4.23	6.89	0%	-34.79	11Y.7M
IJS-LQD	-13.35	0.34	14.2%	-5.02	2.81	4.7%	1.76	4.33	6.84	0%	-39.93	13Y.1M
VTI-VTV	-17.67	-2.62	20.3%	-8.26	0.63	11.9%	-0.94	2.52	6.71	2%	-53.37	18Y.0M
IJS-SHY	-10.61	0.86	12.9%	-3.50	2.35	4.4%	2.19	3.85	6.57	0%	-34.03	9Y.4M
VNQ-GLD	-7.20	-1.93	26.6%	-1.65	1.07	8%	0.08	2.02	6.47	0%	-37.93	15Y.1M
VTI-TLT	-11.90	-2.00	22%	-5.65	0.30	13.5%	-2.12	2.73	6.25	10.4%	-38.41	19Y.8M
VTV-TLT	-10.16	-2.04	25.4%	-5.61	-0.40	17.1%	-2.05	3.75	6.23	8.9%	-35.68	19Y.4M
VNQ-LQD	-13.09	-1.27	22.2%	-5.15	0.21	13%	-0.78	3.22	6.09	5.4%	-43.91	18Y.8M
VTV-GLD	-7.59	-0.57	17.7%	-1.30	2.95	2.7%	0.93	4.06	5.98	0%	-38.00	8Y.0M
VNQ-IEI	-10.40	-1.05	19.1%	-4.27	0.36	11.5%	-0.34	2.86	5.96	0.4%	-36.35	17Y.10M
IJS-BIL	-10.07	0.75	13.3%	-3.60	2.18	4.7%	1.84	3.38	5.84	0%	-33.22	9Y.4M
VTI-GLD	-6.95	-0.86	18.1%	-0.47	2.60	0.9%	0.59	3.61	5.79	0%	-41.20	12Y.7M

129

Order by **Median 15Y Return - All data** (from 1871/1927 to 2023-11)

Portfolio	3Y Rolling Annualized Return (%)			7Y Rolling Annualized Return (%)			15Y Rolling Annualized Return (%)				Max Draw-down (%)	Long Neg Period (Y.M)
	Worst	Base	%Fail	Worst	Base	%Fail	Worst	Base	Median ▼	%Fail		
IJS-VTV	-46.12	0.51	14.3%	-7.72	5.37	4%	0.39	8.18	12.74	0%	-86.54	14Y.9M
VTI-IJS	-46.41	0.86	13.9%	-7.15	5.74	4.1%	0.75	8.49	12.73	0%	-86.65	14Y.8M
IJS-VNQ	-36.96	1.75	12.5%	-4.86	5.51	2.8%	1.70	8.44	11.07	0%	-78.32	14Y.4M
VTI-VTV	-43.48	-0.28	15.3%	-7.64	4.15	5.2%	-0.66	6.42	10.64	0.3%	-84.44	15Y.7M
IJS-SHY	-23.14	3.42	8.4%	0.62	5.31	0%	3.44	6.87	10.28	0%	-58.12	8Y.7M
IJS-BND	-23.25	3.36	7.9%	0.91	6.03	0%	4.02	7.55	10.19	0%	-58.36	6Y.4M
IJS-IEI	-23.26	3.46	7.4%	0.89	6.04	0%	4.01	7.69	10.18	0%	-58.38	6Y.4M
IJS-LQD	-23.39	3.19	8.2%	0.88	6.19	0%	4.11	7.76	10.02	0%	-58.59	6Y.8M
IJS-TLT	-24.33	3.34	7.5%	0.59	6.71	0%	4.14	8.32	9.90	0%	-60.20	6Y.6M
IJS-GLD	-25.48	2.48	7.5%	1.45	5.77	0%	3.56	7.64	9.84	0%	-61.69	6Y.4M
IJS-BIL	-24.05	3.11	9.6%	-0.33	4.86	0.1%	2.75	6.17	9.74	0%	-59.54	12Y.8M
VTI-VNQ	-34.57	1.65	12.6%	-5.56	4.74	3.3%	-0.19	6.65	9.35	0.1%	-75.75	15Y.3M
VTV-VNQ	-33.99	1.27	12.7%	-6.21	4.13	3.8%	-0.54	6.22	9.27	0.2%	-75.26	15Y.7M
VTV-GLD	-22.14	2.29	7.5%	0.57	4.61	0%	2.21	5.82	8.26	0%	-56.74	12Y.8M
VTV-TLT	-21.03	2.04	7.5%	0.86	4.44	0.4%	2.58	5.42	8.18	0%	-55.21	10Y.9M
VTV-LQD	-20.06	2.45	9.2%	-0.56	4.47	0.2%	2.57	5.93	7.96	0%	-53.44	10Y.9M
VTV-IEI	-19.94	2.74	6.9%	-0.56	4.60	0.2%	2.45	5.87	7.95	0%	-53.22	12Y.8M
VTV-BND	-19.93	2.53	8.1%	-0.55	4.54	0.2%	2.46	5.83	7.90	0%	-53.20	12Y.8M
VTV-SHY	-19.83	2.17	9.3%	-0.87	4.21	0.3%	1.71	5.27	7.79	0%	-52.96	13Y.1M
VTV-BIL	-20.73	1.68	10.9%	-1.81	3.69	1.9%	0.88	4.72	7.65	0%	-54.46	13Y.6M
VTI-TLT	-21.43	2.17	6.7%	-1.43	4.05	0.3%	2.55	5.08	7.07	0%	-55.49	8Y.11M

Order by **Median 15Y Return - All data** (from 1871/1927 to 2023-11) - **US Infl. Adjusted**

Portfolio	3Y Rolling Annualized Return (%)			7Y Rolling Annualized Return (%)			15Y Rolling Annualized Return (%)				Max Draw-down (%)	Long Neg Period (Y.M)
	Worst	Base	%Fail	Worst	Base	%Fail	Worst	Base	Median ▼	%Fail		
IJS-VTV	-41.85	-2.29	18.5%	-7.46	2.65	7.2%	0.66	4.65	8.95	0%	-83.01	14Y.8M
VTI-IJS	-42.15	-2.53	18.1%	-7.82	2.67	7.3%	1.04	4.62	8.75	0%	-83.15	14Y.5M
IJS-VNQ	-31.96	-0.86	17%	-7.40	3.04	4.8%	0.07	4.98	7.98	0%	-72.62	15Y.5M
IJS-TLT	-18.33	-0.48	16.1%	-4.80	3.40	3.4%	1.33	4.42	6.98	0%	-49.74	13Y.4M
IJS-GLD	-19.57	-0.28	16.1%	-1.46	3.52	1.6%	2.23	4.47	6.85	0%	-51.62	8Y.3M
VTI-VTV	-39.00	-3.56	21.5%	-8.26	0.77	11.9%	-0.94	2.28	6.77	1.5%	-80.36	19Y.11M
IJS-LQD	-17.31	-0.40	15.7%	-5.02	3.27	3.2%	1.76	4.39	6.67	0%	-47.71	13Y.1M
IJS-IEI	-17.17	0.01	14.9%	-3.88	3.23	2.9%	2.43	4.31	6.62	0%	-47.45	11Y.7M
IJS-BND	-17.16	-0.02	15%	-3.87	3.23	3%	2.43	4.33	6.57	0%	-47.42	11Y.7M
IJS-SHY	-17.04	-0.17	15.3%	-3.50	2.68	3.2%	2.19	3.99	6.54	0%	-47.11	9Y.4M
VTI-VNQ	-29.37	-1.22	18.3%	-7.69	1.58	10.1%	-1.44	2.51	6.38	1%	-69.34	19Y.5M
VTV-VNQ	-28.76	-1.64	19.2%	-7.53	0.89	10%	-1.53	2.24	6.33	1.8%	-68.76	19Y.6M
IJS-BIL	-18.03	-0.43	16.4%	-3.60	2.29	4.3%	1.84	3.58	6.16	0%	-48.91	9Y.4M
VTI-TLT	-15.20	-1.35	18.1%	-6.67	0.94	10.6%	-2.50	1.95	5.43	5.3%	-45.41	22Y.7M
VTV-TLT	-14.76	-1.71	22.8%	-5.61	0.52	12.1%	-2.05	1.94	5.31	5.3%	-43.44	22Y.2M
VTV-GLD	-15.96	-0.86	19.1%	-2.37	2.04	5.6%	0.41	2.72	5.15	0%	-45.38	13Y.8M
VTI-LQD	-14.22	-1.11	18.6%	-6.51	1.11	10.3%	-2.31	1.91	4.98	4.3%	-45.30	22Y.7M
VTI-IEI	-14.08	-0.68	17.4%	-6.45	1.29	9.8%	-2.22	1.94	4.90	3.6%	-45.15	22Y.3M
VTI-BND	-14.07	-0.87	17.7%	-6.44	1.28	10%	-2.21	1.95	4.90	3.6%	-45.14	22Y.3M
VTI-SHY	-13.98	-0.61	16.9%	-6.05	1.27	11%	-1.68	1.96	4.80	2%	-43.27	21Y.6M
VTV-LQD	-13.72	-1.92	22%	-5.45	0.70	9.7%	-1.45	1.97	4.78	4.6%	-41.21	20Y.8M

Lazy Portfolios with 3 equally weighted Assets

The portfolios in this scenario start to become more efficient.

They can include 3 different asset classes (stocks-bonds-gold) and remain relatively simple to manage.

Verify whether, with the budget at your disposal, you find it convenient to handle 3 assets at once, especially during rebalancing or when introducing new liquidity.

You can overcome this by using ETFs with a low share price. For example, if you need to invest $500 and use ETFs with a share price of $350, you may struggle to set the correct weights. Since it's not possible to invest in fractional shares, you would need to either buy one share ($350) or two shares ($700).

By using ETFs with more "affordable" share prices, you can get much closer to the desired amount. If, for instance, one share of the ETF is priced at $27, you can buy 18 shares ($486) or 19 shares ($513), always aiming to invest $500.

Ranking: Baseline 3Y Return

Order by **Baseline 3Y Return** - **Last 30 Years** (from 1993-12 to 2023-11)

Portfolio	3Y Rolling Annualized Return (%)			7Y Rolling Annualized Return (%)			15Y Rolling Annualized Return (%)				Max Draw-down (%)	Long Neg Period (Y.M)
	Worst	Base ▼	%Fail	Worst	Base	%Fail	Worst	Base	Median	%Fail		
IJS-IEI-CWB	-6.90	5.45	3.7%	2.71	6.40	0%	5.86	6.93	7.76	0%	-28.97	5Y.1M
IJS-TLT-CWB	-6.03	5.45	3.4%	3.70	7.34	0%	6.96	8.18	8.99	0%	-26.77	4Y.5M
MTUM-EMB-TLT	-7.59	5.32	5.5%	2.02	7.97	0%	5.88	8.57	9.55	0%	-28.75	5Y.9M
IJS-CWB-LQD	-9.37	5.26	5.8%	1.65	6.30	0%	5.98	7.17	7.98	0%	-34.59	5Y.4M
IJS-EMB-CWB	-10.18	5.25	5.8%	2.91	6.65	0%	6.08	7.62	9.05	0%	-37.19	5Y.3M
IJS-BNDX-CWB	-9.12	5.23	5.5%	1.75	6.36	0%	5.95	7.12	7.86	0%	-33.57	5Y.3M
BNDX-TLT-CWB	-6.89	5.22	4.9%	1.86	6.25	0%	5.47	6.83	7.68	0%	-25.53	4Y.5M
IJS-BND-CWB	-7.99	5.14	4.6%	2.02	6.18	0%	5.76	6.89	7.65	0%	-31.59	5Y.2M
IJS-TIP-CWB	-8.66	5.14	5.5%	2.42	6.31	0%	5.61	6.90	7.92	0%	-32.46	5Y.3M
VTI-EMB-TLT	-4.78	5.13	5.2%	2.43	7.36	0%	5.74	7.90	9.01	0%	-26.55	4Y.4M
VTI-VNQ-EMB	-13.11	5.08	7.4%	2.15	6.75	0%	5.87	7.64	9.53	0%	-45.35	5Y.5M
EMB-TLT-CWB	-7.46	5.07	5.2%	1.54	6.59	0%	5.24	7.37	9.07	0%	-28.31	4Y.7M
TLT-CWB-LQD	-7.80	5.02	4.9%	1.75	6.25	0%	5.37	6.75	7.71	0%	-28.38	4Y.6M
IJS-SHY-CWB	-7.77	4.95	5.5%	1.87	5.60	0%	5.14	6.29	7.05	0%	-31.13	5Y.3M
MTUM-EMB-GLD	-2.12	4.93	1.5%	4.91	6.98	0%	6.07	8.62	10.04	0%	-26.56	3Y.3M
IJS-VNQ-CWB	-18.06	4.92	8.3%	-0.24	5.88	0.7%	5.57	7.70	8.84	0%	-54.74	7Y.8M
VNQ-EMB-CWB	-12.04	4.89	7.1%	3.36	6.44	0%	5.51	7.33	9.53	0%	-42.54	5Y.3M
VTV-EMB-TLT	-3.86	4.85	4.9%	1.84	7.02	0%	5.31	7.44	8.88	0%	-23.11	4Y.7M
BND-TLT-CWB	-7.34	4.85	4.6%	1.62	5.93	0%	5.04	6.57	7.33	0%	-26.76	4Y.5M
VTI-EMB-IEI	-2.22	4.79	2.2%	3.81	6.44	0%	5.02	6.72	7.83	0%	-20.10	3Y.8M
VTV-EMB-CWB	-9.50	4.75	7.1%	2.37	6.24	0%	5.89	7.46	8.31	0%	-37.36	5Y.3M

Order by **Baseline 3Y Return** - **Last 30 Years** (from 1993-12 to 2023-11) - **US Infl. Adjusted**

Portfolio	3Y Rolling Annualized Return (%)			7Y Rolling Annualized Return (%)			15Y Rolling Annualized Return (%)				Max Draw-down (%)	Long Neg Period (Y.M)
	Worst	Base ▼	%Fail	Worst	Base	%Fail	Worst	Base	Median	%Fail		
EMB-TLT-CWB	-12.46	3.28	8%	-1.90	4.80	2.9%	2.78	5.16	6.75	0%	-39.01	9Y.5M
MTUM-EMB-GLD	-7.44	3.23	6.8%	1.34	5.08	0%	3.59	6.51	7.73	0%	-28.58	5Y.9M
VTI-EMB-TLT	-9.93	3.00	7.7%	-1.04	5.36	1.1%	3.27	5.68	6.64	0%	-32.26	8Y.11M
MTUM-EMB-TLT	-12.61	2.87	7.7%	-1.46	5.70	1.8%	3.41	6.41	7.14	0%	-37.50	8Y.11M
BNDX-TLT-CWB	-11.93	2.86	8.3%	-1.59	4.00	2.9%	3.00	4.50	5.34	0%	-36.87	9Y.2M
BNDX-EMB-CWB	-8.60	2.76	9.2%	-0.39	4.15	0.7%	2.43	4.45	5.77	0%	-30.55	7Y.4M
VTV-EMB-TLT	-9.06	2.74	8%	-1.61	4.79	2.5%	2.86	5.31	6.52	0%	-29.88	9Y.2M
TLT-TIP-CWB	-11.47	2.67	7.1%	-1.42	3.75	1.8%	2.80	4.36	5.31	0%	-36.12	9Y.5M
BND-TLT-CWB	-12.35	2.65	8%	-1.82	3.68	2.9%	2.58	4.26	5.02	0%	-37.86	9Y.8M
VTI-EMB-GLD	-4.34	2.63	7.4%	1.77	4.15	0%	3.41	5.97	7.15	0%	-27.25	5Y.1M
TLT-IEI-CWB	-11.88	2.61	6.2%	-1.73	3.86	3.3%	2.60	4.19	5.02	0%	-36.65	9Y.8M
BND-EMB-CWB	-8.98	2.60	8.6%	-0.60	3.78	0.7%	2.08	4.05	5.46	0%	-30.93	8Y.8M
VTI-EMB-IEI	-5.54	2.57	7.7%	0.27	4.12	0%	2.58	4.52	5.58	0%	-26.09	6Y.8M
EMB-IEI-CWB	-8.60	2.57	8.3%	-0.53	3.70	0.7%	2.12	3.99	5.51	0%	-29.93	8Y.8M
VTV-EMB-GLD	-3.62	2.55	7.4%	1.16	3.88	0%	3.07	5.40	7.09	0%	-27.15	5Y.8M
TLT-CWB-LQD	-12.79	2.55	8.6%	-1.69	3.86	2.5%	2.91	4.46	5.30	0%	-39.22	9Y.5M
IJS-TIP-CWB	-10.64	2.52	9.5%	-0.14	3.73	0.4%	3.59	4.68	5.65	0%	-33.82	8Y.1M
EMB-CWB-LQD	-9.34	2.51	9.5%	-0.46	4.08	0.7%	2.39	4.34	5.84	0%	-32.88	7Y.7M
IJS-EMB-TLT	-9.55	2.45	8%	-2.46	5.08	4%	3.05	5.41	7.44	0%	-34.38	9Y.8M
MTUM-TLT-GLD	-11.02	2.43	7.7%	0.21	5.05	0%	4.06	6.46	7.34	0%	-31.37	7Y.3M
IJS-IEI-CWB	-8.92	2.41	9.2%	0.14	3.63	0%	3.56	4.65	5.45	0%	-30.39	6Y.11M

Order by **Baseline 3Y Return** - **Last 60 Years** (from 1963-12 to 2023-11)

Portfolio	3Y Rolling Annualized Return (%)			7Y Rolling Annualized Return (%)			15Y Rolling Annualized Return (%)				Max Draw-down (%)	Long Neg Period (Y.M)
	Worst	Base ▼	%Fail	Worst	Base	%Fail	Worst	Base	Median	%Fail		
VTI-IJS-GLD	-4.97	5.40	2.3%	4.54	8.18	0%	6.67	8.85	10.62	0%	-31.57	4Y.11M
IJS-VTV-GLD	-5.47	4.97	2.3%	4.17	7.86	0%	6.75	8.62	10.82	0%	-32.93	5Y.0M
IJS-TLT-LQD	-4.79	4.76	3.2%	1.20	6.81	0%	5.63	7.74	10.25	0%	-26.67	6Y.1M
IJS-TLT-GLD	-1.86	4.74	0.6%	2.90	6.90	0%	6.28	8.48	10.06	0%	-19.87	3Y.9M
IJS-VNQ-IEI	-11.03	4.68	5.8%	1.05	6.35	0%	5.52	8.45	10.88	0%	-39.93	6Y.6M
IJS-TLT-IEI	-3.88	4.67	2.2%	1.15	6.48	0%	5.08	7.73	10.14	0%	-23.47	5Y.11M
IJS-BND-TLT	-4.38	4.67	2.6%	1.06	6.68	0%	5.23	7.67	10.08	0%	-25.09	6Y.1M
IJS-IEI-LQD	-2.83	4.65	2%	2.48	6.07	0%	4.83	7.02	10.11	0%	-17.55	4Y.3M
IJS-BND-LQD	-3.86	4.64	2.3%	2.44	6.09	0%	4.82	6.93	10.06	0%	-19.08	4Y.5M
IJS-VNQ-BND	-12.11	4.64	6%	1.05	6.37	0%	5.47	8.28	10.79	0%	-42.21	6Y.6M
IJS-VNQ-SHY	-11.86	4.58	6.3%	1.25	5.93	0%	5.07	7.73	10.60	0%	-41.76	6Y.4M
IJS-VNQ-LQD	-13.51	4.55	6.7%	0.24	6.58	0%	5.74	8.42	10.92	0%	-44.90	6Y.8M
IJS-TLT-SHY	-2.67	4.54	1.9%	1.46	6.22	0%	4.80	7.18	9.99	0%	-21.02	5Y.5M
VTI-IJS-IEI	-7.89	4.49	5.4%	0.62	6.71	0%	6.32	7.68	11.07	0%	-32.26	6Y.7M
VTI-IJS-LQD	-10.36	4.49	6.6%	-0.16	6.67	0.2%	6.26	7.91	11.02	0%	-37.60	7Y.1M
VTI-IJS-TLT	-7.23	4.47	5.3%	-0.25	7.25	0.2%	7.31	8.66	11.18	0%	-31.32	7Y.1M
IJS-VNQ-GLD	-8.73	4.43	2.8%	3.22	7.07	0%	6.51	8.25	11.00	0%	-37.64	4Y.4M
IJS-TLT-BIL	-1.67	4.41	1.3%	1.78	5.91	0%	4.70	6.73	9.50	0%	-18.73	5Y.2M
IJS-LQD-GLD	-0.12	4.40	0.2%	3.09	6.74	0%	5.88	7.75	9.38	0%	-20.10	3Y.0M
VTI-IJS-BND	-8.97	4.40	6%	0.63	6.56	0%	6.23	7.62	10.94	0%	-34.68	6Y.7M
IJS-BND-IEI	-1.47	4.37	0.7%	2.34	5.75	0%	4.48	6.58	10.09	0%	-15.37	3Y.11M

Order by **Baseline 3Y Return** - **Last 60 Years** (from 1963-12 to 2023-11) - **US Infl. Adjusted**

Portfolio	3Y Rolling Annualized Return (%)			7Y Rolling Annualized Return (%)			15Y Rolling Annualized Return (%)				Max Draw-down (%)	Long Neg Period (Y.M)
	Worst	Base ▼	%Fail	Worst	Base	%Fail	Worst	Base	Median	%Fail		
IJS-VTV-GLD	-7.52	1.88	9.9%	1.43	4.70	0%	3.57	6.01	7.37	0%	-34.29	6Y.4M
VTI-IJS-GLD	-7.03	1.83	8.8%	1.50	4.76	0%	3.50	6.07	7.38	0%	-33.09	6Y.4M
IJS-TLT-GLD	-7.17	1.64	9.6%	-0.61	3.77	0.3%	3.59	5.52	6.88	0%	-27.87	8Y.9M
IJS-IEI-GLD	-3.36	1.57	8.8%	0.55	3.41	0%	3.10	4.87	6.44	0%	-24.42	6Y.2M
IJS-BND-GLD	-3.32	1.54	9.2%	0.52	3.45	0%	3.10	4.78	6.33	0%	-24.40	6Y.2M
IJS-SHY-GLD	-3.45	1.36	8.3%	0.80	3.22	0%	2.69	4.34	5.90	0%	-23.25	5Y.9M
IJS-LQD-GLD	-3.68	1.31	9.6%	0.71	3.63	0%	3.32	5.00	6.54	0%	-26.02	5Y.11M
IJS-BIL-GLD	-3.91	1.05	8.9%	0.63	2.81	0%	2.19	3.78	5.36	0%	-21.98	5Y.3M
IJS-VNQ-GLD	-10.62	0.93	12.1%	1.40	3.99	0%	3.34	5.31	8.00	0%	-38.59	5Y.11M
IJS-SHY-IEI	-8.17	0.68	11.7%	-2.58	2.02	4.9%	1.58	2.97	5.43	0%	-26.15	11Y.10M
VTI-IJS-SHY	-12.91	0.62	14.2%	-4.89	2.40	5.3%	1.67	3.79	6.27	0%	-40.15	11Y.9M
VTI-IJS-IEI	-13.17	0.59	13.7%	-5.09	2.77	5.3%	1.24	4.33	6.54	0%	-40.61	12Y.11M
IJS-BND-SHY	-8.17	0.55	12.6%	-2.57	2.01	4.6%	1.59	3.03	5.38	0%	-26.15	11Y.10M
IJS-IEI-BIL	-7.82	0.54	13%	-2.51	1.83	4.6%	1.40	2.80	5.12	0%	-24.55	11Y.7M
VTI-VNQ-GLD	-9.05	0.53	12.1%	0.11	3.76	0%	2.53	4.87	6.79	0%	-38.25	6Y.11M
VTI-VTV-GLD	-8.87	0.50	13.1%	-0.08	3.66	0.2%	2.55	5.00	6.40	0%	-33.91	9Y.2M
VTI-SHY-GLD	-4.24	0.49	12.6%	0.90	2.81	0%	1.87	3.70	4.81	0%	-27.06	6Y.8M
VTV-SHY-GLD	-5.12	0.49	11.8%	-0.20	2.69	0.9%	2.00	3.77	4.84	0%	-25.03	7Y.3M
IJS-VTV-IEI	-11.71	0.44	14%	-5.03	2.58	4.6%	1.53	4.16	6.89	0%	-40.26	11Y.10M
IJS-SHY-BIL	-7.56	0.42	13.9%	-2.28	1.40	4.4%	0.96	2.50	4.95	0%	-23.98	9Y.11M
IJS-VNQ-SHY	-13.77	0.39	13.1%	-4.66	2.65	5.2%	2.58	4.06	6.67	0%	-44.00	11Y.1M

Order by **Baseline 3Y Return - All data** (from 1871/1927 to 2023-11)

Portfolio	3Y Rolling Annualized Return (%)			7Y Rolling Annualized Return (%)			15Y Rolling Annualized Return (%)				Max Draw-down (%)	Long Neg Period (Y.M)
	Worst	Base ▼	%Fail	Worst	Base	%Fail	Worst	Base	Median	%Fail		
IJS-TLT-IEI	-14.82	3.66	5.4%	1.15	5.80	0%	4.47	6.76	8.09	0%	-41.85	6Y.3M
VTI-IJS-GLD	-31.68	3.61	8%	-1.21	7.03	0.3%	2.78	8.60	10.46	0%	-71.16	13Y.1M
IJS-BND-TLT	-14.81	3.59	5.7%	1.06	5.75	0%	4.48	6.77	8.09	0%	-41.84	6Y.3M
IJS-VTV-GLD	-31.37	3.52	7.8%	-1.56	6.92	0.7%	2.54	8.39	10.43	0%	-70.94	13Y.1M
IJS-TLT-SHY	-14.73	3.51	5.4%	1.46	5.58	0%	4.09	6.55	7.98	0%	-41.63	6Y.3M
IJS-BND-IEI	-14.10	3.50	4.6%	2.34	5.47	0%	4.36	6.61	8.10	0%	-40.28	6Y.3M
IJS-BND-SHY	-14.02	3.47	5.1%	2.55	5.02	0%	3.97	6.19	8.07	0%	-40.07	6Y.3M
IJS-SHY-IEI	-14.03	3.47	4.9%	2.54	5.01	0%	3.97	6.21	8.08	0%	-40.08	6Y.3M
IJS-BND-BIL	-14.67	3.45	5.7%	1.92	4.66	0%	3.52	5.76	7.88	0%	-41.36	6Y.3M
IJS-IEI-BIL	-14.68	3.42	5.4%	1.91	4.71	0%	3.51	5.81	7.88	0%	-41.38	6Y.3M
IJS-LQD-BIL	-14.76	3.38	5.9%	1.91	4.84	0%	3.58	5.99	7.89	0%	-41.55	6Y.3M
IJS-TLT-BIL	-15.37	3.37	5.5%	1.77	5.39	0%	3.64	6.39	7.72	0%	-42.88	6Y.3M
IJS-IEI-LQD	-14.19	3.36	5.4%	2.48	5.68	0%	4.42	6.69	8.10	0%	-40.48	6Y.3M
IJS-TLT-GLD	-16.34	3.34	4.8%	2.70	5.47	0%	4.31	6.33	8.85	0%	-44.73	6Y.0M
IJC-TLT-LQD	-14.91	3.33	6%	1.20	5.74	0%	4.54	6.80	8.19	0%	42.03	6Y.3M
IJS-BND-LQD	-14.18	3.30	5.6%	2.44	5.67	0%	4.43	6.69	8.06	0%	-40.46	6Y.3M
IJS-SHY-LQD	-14.11	3.30	5.5%	2.54	5.20	0%	4.04	6.37	8.06	0%	-40.26	6Y.3M
IJS-BND-GLD	-15.64	3.25	4.5%	2.70	5.35	0%	4.19	6.38	8.36	0%	-43.25	6Y.0M
IJS-IEI-GLD	-15.65	3.21	4.5%	2.69	5.30	0%	4.18	6.38	8.44	0%	-43.26	6Y.0M
IJS-LQD-GLD	-15.73	3.21	4.4%	2.81	5.46	0%	4.25	6.49	8.49	0%	-43.44	6Y.0M
IJS-SHY-BIL	-14.61	3.19	6.7%	1.71	4.17	0%	3.12	5.21	7.93	0%	-41.19	6Y.3M

Order by **Baseline 3Y Return - All data** (from 1871/1927 to 2023-11) - **US Infl. Adjusted**

Portfolio	3Y Rolling Annualized Return (%)			7Y Rolling Annualized Return (%)			15Y Rolling Annualized Return (%)				Max Draw-down (%)	Long Neg Period (Y.M)
	Worst	Base ▼	%Fail	Worst	Base	%Fail	Worst	Base	Median	%Fail		
VTI-IJS-GLD	-26.27	0.71	13.6%	-1.50	4.48	1.3%	2.89	5.33	7.25	0%	-63.58	12Y.9M
IJS-IEI-GLD	-9.27	0.60	13%	-2.33	2.91	1.8%	1.22	3.61	5.45	0%	-28.36	8Y.9M
IJS-VTV-GLD	-25.93	0.52	13.9%	-1.57	4.17	1.4%	2.78	5.21	7.17	0%	-63.30	13Y.0M
IJS-BND-GLD	-9.26	0.48	13.3%	-2.32	2.97	1.8%	1.23	3.67	5.43	0%	-28.34	8Y.9M
IJS-TLT-GLD	-9.71	0.42	13.6%	-2.54	2.97	1.8%	1.33	3.54	5.85	0%	-30.21	8Y.9M
IJS-SHY-GLD	-9.32	0.42	13.1%	-2.38	2.62	3.3%	0.89	3.49	5.26	0%	-28.12	12Y.7M
IJS-LQD-GLD	-9.29	0.39	13.7%	-2.32	3.07	1.5%	1.29	3.68	5.59	0%	-28.57	8Y.9M
IJS-BND-SHY	-9.58	0.35	13.9%	-2.57	1.97	4%	1.37	2.94	4.69	0%	-28.04	11Y.10M
IJS-SHY-IEI	-9.59	0.34	13.4%	-2.58	1.96	4.2%	1.36	2.93	4.79	0%	-28.06	11Y.10M
IJS-BND-IEI	-9.62	0.25	14.2%	-2.75	2.12	4.3%	1.17	2.99	5.04	0%	-28.20	13Y.3M
IJS-BIL-GLD	-9.59	0.25	13.7%	-2.23	2.39	3.5%	0.69	3.17	4.91	0%	-29.71	12Y.9M
IJS-VNQ-BND	-17.53	0.05	14.8%	-4.89	2.83	3.8%	0.56	3.67	5.98	0%	-49.35	13Y.9M
IJS-IEI-BIL	-9.70	0.04	14.7%	-2.51	1.82	4.3%	1.16	2.72	4.41	0%	-28.19	12Y.4M
IJS-BND-BIL	-9.69	0.03	14.9%	-2.50	1.82	4.3%	1.17	2.76	4.37	0%	-28.17	12Y.4M
IJS-VNQ-IEI	-17.54	0.02	14.7%	-4.89	2.89	3.8%	0.56	3.66	6.01	0%	-49.36	13Y.9M
IJS-SHY-LQD	-9.69	0.00	15%	-3.17	1.95	4.3%	1.30	2.92	4.80	0%	-29.59	13Y.3M
VTV-IEI-GLD	-8.60	-0.05	15.3%	-2.14	1.39	8.6%	-0.30	2.27	4.25	0.6%	-27.31	17Y.2M
VTV-BND-GLD	-8.59	-0.08	15.7%	-2.13	1.39	8.6%	-0.29	2.28	4.20	0.6%	-27.31	17Y.2M
IJS-LQD-BIL	-9.72	-0.12	15.3%	-3.23	1.82	4.3%	1.23	2.80	4.41	0%	-28.33	12Y.10M
IJS-VNQ-GLD	-19.17	-0.13	15.3%	-1.31	3.21	2%	2.11	4.01	6.04	0%	-52.13	9Y.3M
VTV-LQD-GLD	-8.60	-0.13	15.8%	-2.13	1.44	8.5%	-0.22	2.27	4.25	0.6%	-29.36	17Y.0M

Ranking: Maximum Drawdown

Order by **Maximum Drawdown - Last 30 Years** (from 1993-12 to 2023-11)

Portfolio	3Y Rolling Annualized Return (%)			7Y Rolling Annualized Return (%)			15Y Rolling Annualized Return (%)				Max Draw-down (%) ▼	Long Neg Period (Y.M)
	Worst	Base	%Fail	Worst	Base	%Fail	Worst	Base	Median	%Fail		
SHY-IEI-BIL	-1.27	0.68	5.2%	0.47	0.94	0%	1.09	2.07	2.97	0%	-6.17	4Y.2M
SHY-TIP-BIL	-0.66	0.76	6.2%	0.48	1.19	0%	1.36	2.27	3.16	0%	-6.24	4Y.3M
BNDX-SHY-BIL	-1.52	1.43	5.8%	0.71	1.76	0%	1.62	2.56	3.36	0%	-6.60	4Y.3M
BND-SHY-BIL	-1.56	0.92	5.2%	0.58	1.18	0%	1.30	2.18	2.91	0%	-7.40	4Y.4M
SHY-HYG-BIL	-0.64	1.44	1.8%	1.34	2.07	0%	2.01	2.84	3.37	0%	-8.32	3Y.5M
IEI-TIP-BIL	-1.69	0.95	6.2%	0.67	1.50	0%	1.71	2.78	3.87	0%	-8.39	4Y.2M
IEI-HYG-BIL	-1.21	1.88	4.6%	1.34	2.41	0%	2.45	3.38	4.05	0%	-8.81	3Y.10M
BNDX-TIP-BIL	-1.67	1.73	4.9%	0.93	2.08	0%	2.19	3.33	4.25	0%	-9.11	4Y.2M
BNDX-IEI-BIL	-2.25	1.77	5.8%	0.52	2.11	0%	1.96	3.11	4.08	0%	-9.14	4Y.6M
SHY-LQD-BIL	-1.87	1.50	5.2%	0.92	1.86	0%	1.81	2.58	3.34	0%	-9.40	4Y.4M
BND-TIP-BIL	-2.09	1.16	6.5%	0.82	1.71	0%	1.88	2.87	3.80	0%	-9.56	4Y.2M
BND-HYG-BIL	-1.49	1.99	4.6%	1.33	2.66	0%	2.48	3.49	4.04	0%	-9.93	4Y.2M
BND-IEI-BIL	-2.66	1.23	5.2%	0.42	1.58	0%	1.64	2.71	3.61	0%	-10.16	4Y.7M
SHY-IEI-TIP	-2.61	0.97	6.2%	0.55	1.62	0%	1.81	3.01	4.33	0%	-10.30	4Y.4M
BND-BNDX-BIL	-2.67	2.01	5.8%	0.52	2.40	0%	2.13	3.22	4.00	0%	-10.35	4Y.7M
EMB-SHY-BIL	-2.46	1.72	6.2%	0.60	1.93	0%	1.71	2.89	4.83	0%	-10.58	6Y.2M
SHY-IEI-HYG	-1.76	2.01	5.2%	1.07	2.54	0%	2.61	3.69	4.49	0%	-10.70	4Y.4M
BNDX-SHY-TIP	-2.60	1.76	4.9%	0.65	2.22	0%	2.29	3.57	4.72	0%	-10.98	4Y.5M
BNDX-SHY-IEI	-3.17	1.90	5.8%	0.24	2.24	0%	2.07	3.42	4.54	0%	-11.03	6Y.3M
BNDX-SHY-HYG	-2.23	2.59	5.5%	1.16	3.20	0%	3.05	4.13	4.82	0%	-11.33	4Y.4M
BND-SHY-TIP	-3.02	1.29	6.2%	0.53	1.86	0%	1.99	3.09	4.27	0%	-11.40	4Y.5M

Order by **Maximum Drawdown - Last 30 Years** (from 1993-12 to 2023-11) - **US Infl. Adjusted**

Portfolio	3Y Rolling Annualized Return (%)			7Y Rolling Annualized Return (%)			15Y Rolling Annualized Return (%)				Max Draw-down (%) ▼	Long Neg Period (Y.M)
	Worst	Base	%Fail	Worst	Base	%Fail	Worst	Base	Median	%Fail		
VTV-SHY-IEI	-3.45	0.67	9.2%	-0.02	2.08	0.4%	1.41	2.68	3.01	0%	-16.60	7Y.7M
VTV-IEI-BIL	-3.20	-0.23	15.7%	0.16	1.65	0%	1.19	2.23	2.62	0%	-16.79	8Y.2M
SHY-HYG-BIL	-5.32	-0.04	15.4%	-1.88	0.32	9.4%	-0.36	0.71	1.28	6.1%	-17.06	19Y.11M
VTI-SHY-BIL	-4.06	-0.69	18.8%	-0.68	1.24	1.1%	1.31	1.72	2.34	0%	-17.12	10Y.2M
VTV-BND-SHY	-3.80	0.20	12.6%	-0.07	1.91	0.7%	1.43	2.61	3.00	0%	-17.56	8Y.2M
VTI-IEI-BIL	-3.03	0.07	14.5%	0.09	1.64	0%	1.75	2.39	2.93	0%	-17.66	9Y.2M
MTUM-SHY-BIL	-5.09	-1.14	20.6%	0.21	1.52	0%	1.42	2.05	3.01	0%	-18.26	9Y.4M
IJS-SHY-BIL	-4.87	-0.14	16.3%	-0.48	1.32	1.8%	0.96	1.78	2.74	0%	-18.29	9Y.11M
TIP-HYG-BIL	-5.65	0.27	13.5%	-1.72	0.65	7.6%	0.25	1.39	2.14	0%	-18.39	13Y.10M
VTV-SHY-GLD	-2.27	0.80	9.2%	1.03	2.46	0%	2.49	3.89	4.69	0%	-18.55	5Y.6M
VTV-IEI-TIP	-3.98	1.43	7.7%	0.07	2.86	0%	2.01	3.33	3.90	0%	-18.56	7Y.3M
VTV-SHY-BIL	-4.01	-0.77	19.1%	-0.61	0.99	0.7%	0.75	1.58	1.96	0%	-18.71	10Y.2M
VTI-BND-BIL	-3.78	-0.36	16.9%	-0.51	1.52	1.1%	1.75	2.30	2.88	0%	-18.72	10Y.2M
SHY-TIP-BIL	-6.03	-0.94	34.2%	-2.37	-0.68	27.4%	-0.98	0.17	1.10	11.6%	-18.88	22Y.7M
VTV-SHY-TIP	-4.11	0.76	11.7%	0.33	2.20	0%	1.58	2.77	3.26	0%	-18.89	6Y.8M
VTV-BNDX-IEI	-4.61	1.14	9.5%	-0.15	2.72	0.7%	2.19	3.54	3.99	0%	-18.93	7Y.7M
VTI-SHY-GLD	-2.89	0.64	10.8%	1.33	2.73	0%	2.88	4.19	4.88	0%	-18.95	5Y.0M
VTV-IEI-GLD	-3.29	1.22	7.4%	1.28	2.79	0%	2.91	4.38	5.34	0%	-19.01	5Y.0M
VTV-BIL-GLD	-3.10	0.60	10.8%	0.32	2.19	0%	2.27	3.48	4.21	0%	-19.02	6Y.4M
VTI-TIP-BIL	-4.41	0.00	15.1%	-0.07	2.08	0.4%	1.90	2.64	3.07	0%	-19.02	9Y.2M
VTI-BIL-GLD	-4.29	0.35	12.6%	0.62	2.32	0%	2.68	3.78	4.45	0%	-19.12	5Y.9M

Order by **Maximum Drawdown - Last 60 Years** (from 1963-12 to 2023-11)

Portfolio	3Y Rolling Annualized Return (%)			7Y Rolling Annualized Return (%)			15Y Rolling Annualized Return (%)				Max Draw-down (%) ▼	Long Neg Period (Y.M)
	Worst	Base	%Fail	Worst	Base	%Fail	Worst	Base	Median	%Fail		
SHY-IEI-BIL	-1.27	1.70	2.5%	0.47	1.66	0%	1.09	2.61	6.33	0%	-6.17	4Y.2M
BND-SHY-BIL	-1.56	2.01	2.5%	0.58	1.96	0%	1.30	2.60	6.32	0%	-7.40	4Y.4M
SHY-LQD-BIL	-1.87	2.62	2.5%	0.92	2.74	0%	1.81	3.08	6.30	0%	-9.40	4Y.4M
BND-IEI-BIL	-2.66	2.25	2.5%	0.42	2.63	0%	1.64	3.25	6.51	0%	-10.16	4Y.7M
IEI-LQD-BIL	-2.99	2.79	2.5%	0.66	3.49	0%	2.14	3.75	6.79	0%	-12.04	4Y.5M
BND-SHY-IEI	-3.59	2.23	2.5%	0.14	2.92	0%	1.68	3.64	7.10	0%	-12.10	6Y.4M
BND-LQD-BIL	-3.42	2.87	2.5%	0.62	3.68	0%	2.25	3.75	6.66	0%	-13.32	4Y.7M
VTI-SHY-IEI	-1.28	3.90	0.4%	2.80	5.13	0%	4.39	5.45	8.16	0%	-13.54	3Y.6M
LQD-BIL-GLD	-4.32	1.94	4.4%	-0.59	3.24	0.6%	2.96	4.64	6.22	0%	-13.75	7Y.6M
VTV-SHY-IEI	-0.31	3.77	0.4%	2.79	4.70	0%	3.83	5.20	8.47	0%	-13.83	3Y.6M
IJS-SHY-IEI	-1.23	3.95	0.7%	2.67	5.19	0%	4.04	5.95	9.77	0%	-13.83	3Y.9M
VTI-IEI-BIL	-0.59	3.78	0.4%	2.65	4.75	0%	4.17	5.08	7.87	0%	-13.84	3Y.6M
SHY-IEI-LQD	-3.92	2.51	2.5%	0.37	3.85	0%	2.24	4.12	7.09	0%	-13.98	6Y.3M
BND-BIL-GLD	-4.55	1.73	5.3%	-1.24	2.97	1.6%	2.48	4.32	5.90	0%	-14.21	7Y.11M
VTV-BND-IEI	-0.97	3.84	0.9%	2.54	5.09	0%	4.28	5.71	8.65	0%	-14.43	3Y.6M
VTV-TLT-BIL	-1.23	3.14	1.3%	2.18	4.97	0%	4.48	5.82	8.28	0%	-14.62	4Y.2M
VTI-BND-SHY	-1.28	4.01	0.7%	2.59	4.99	0%	4.40	5.44	8.12	0%	-14.63	3Y.7M
IJS-IEI-BIL	-1.96	4.08	0.7%	2.93	4.85	0%	3.82	5.64	9.33	0%	-14.64	3Y.8M
IEI-BIL-GLD	-4.61	1.61	5.6%	-1.52	2.82	2.3%	2.31	4.39	5.97	0%	-14.76	8Y.3M
BND-SHY-GLD	-4.38	1.77	5.3%	-1.17	3.21	1.6%	2.59	4.87	6.46	0%	-14.98	7Y.9M
SHY-IEI-GLD	-4.45	1.63	5.6%	-1.46	3.05	2%	2.42	4.89	6.57	0%	-14.98	7Y.11M

Order by **Maximum Drawdown - Last 60 Years** (from 1963-12 to 2023-11) - **US Infl. Adjusted**

Portfolio	3Y Rolling Annualized Return (%)			7Y Rolling Annualized Return (%)			15Y Rolling Annualized Return (%)				Max Draw-down (%) ▼	Long Neg Period (Y.M)
	Worst	Base	%Fail	Worst	Base	%Fail	Worst	Base	Median	%Fail		
VTV-IEI-BIL	-6.21	-0.70	20.6%	-2.85	0.49	10.2%	-0.69	1.75	3.68	6.1%	-21.63	18Y.0M
VTV-BND-BIL	-6.21	-0.98	22.2%	-2.84	0.48	10.5%	-0.69	1.83	3.56	6.1%	-21.63	17Y.11M
VTV-SHY-BIL	-6.16	-0.76	20.3%	-2.64	0.63	9.7%	-0.29	1.51	3.37	0.7%	-21.73	16Y.8M
IJS-BIL-GLD	-3.91	1.05	8.9%	0.63	2.81	0%	2.19	3.78	5.36	0%	-21.98	5Y.3M
BND-SHY-BIL	-6.90	-1.26	31.1%	-3.19	-0.62	25.8%	-1.12	0.10	2.08	13.1%	-23.15	25Y.2M
SHY-IEI-BIL	-6.66	-1.43	34.7%	-3.19	-0.77	27.5%	-1.38	0.05	2.17	14.1%	-23.15	25Y.2M*
IJS-SHY-GLD	-3.45	1.36	8.3%	0.80	3.22	0%	2.69	4.34	5.90	0%	-23.25	5Y.9M
BND-BIL-GLD	-6.88	-1.29	31.2%	-2.74	0.19	13%	0.11	1.38	2.93	0%	-23.84	15Y.7M
IEI-BIL-GLD	-6.57	-1.37	32%	-3.02	0.19	13.7%	-0.06	1.42	2.96	0.2%	-23.84	15Y.7M
VTV-BND-IEI	-7.09	-1.01	19%	-3.27	0.19	12.2%	-1.32	2.39	4.28	8.3%	-23.87	18Y.8M
VTV-BND-SHY	-7.04	-0.82	19.1%	-3.05	0.52	10.8%	-0.90	2.03	3.94	6.3%	-23.97	18Y.2M
VTV-SHY-IEI	-7.04	-0.65	17.5%	-3.05	0.52	10.8%	-0.90	1.92	4.08	6.3%	-23.97	18Y.2M
IJS-SHY-BIL	-7.56	0.42	13.9%	-2.28	1.40	4.4%	0.96	2.50	4.95	0%	-23.98	9Y.11M
SHY-BIL-GLD	-5.73	-1.51	34.2%	-3.25	-0.04	15.5%	-0.39	0.88	2.59	0.5%	-24.02	19Y.7M
IJS-BND-GLD	-3.32	1.54	9.2%	0.52	3.45	0%	3.10	4.78	6.33	0%	-24.40	6Y.2M
VTV-BIL-GLD	-4.59	0.13	13.9%	-0.35	2.35	1.1%	1.31	3.19	4.38	0%	-24.41	7Y.5M
IJS-IEI-GLD	-3.36	1.57	8.8%	0.55	3.41	0%	3.10	4.87	6.44	0%	-24.42	6Y.2M
IJS-BND-BIL	-7.82	0.32	13.3%	-2.50	1.82	4.6%	1.41	2.84	5.09	0%	-24.53	11Y.7M
IJS-IEI-BIL	-7.82	0.54	13%	-2.51	1.83	4.6%	1.40	2.80	5.12	0%	-24.55	11Y.7M
VNQ-BIL-GLD	-4.00	-0.76	22.9%	-0.52	1.11	3.1%	0.80	2.21	4.82	0%	-24.59	12Y.11M
VNQ-SHY-IEI	-8.05	-0.51	18.4%	-3.04	0.38	11.8%	-0.46	1.98	4.81	1.3%	-24.65	17Y.10M

Order by **Maximum Drawdown - All data** (from 1871/1927 to 2023-11)

Portfolio	3Y Rolling Annualized Return (%)			7Y Rolling Annualized Return (%)			15Y Rolling Annualized Return (%)				Max Drawdown (%) ▼	Long Neg Period (Y.M)
	Worst	Base	%Fail	Worst	Base	%Fail	Worst	Base	Median	%Fail		
SHY-IEI-BIL	-1.27	1.67	0.9%	0.47	1.61	0%	1.09	2.17	4.25	0%	-6.17	4Y.2M
BND-SHY-BIL	-1.56	1.71	0.9%	0.58	1.68	0%	1.18	2.25	4.25	0%	-7.40	4Y.4M
SHY-LQD-BIL	-1.87	1.91	0.9%	0.87	1.96	0%	1.24	2.35	4.19	0%	-9.40	4Y.4M
BND-IEI-BIL	-2.66	2.01	1%	0.42	2.10	0%	1.38	2.49	4.01	0%	-10.16	4Y.7M
IEI-LQD-BIL	-2.99	2.17	1%	0.66	2.27	0%	1.40	2.53	3.97	0%	-12.04	4Y.5M
BND-SHY-IEI	-3.59	2.14	1.4%	0.14	2.42	0%	1.46	2.65	4.00	0%	-12.10	6Y.4M
BND-LQD-BIL	-3.42	2.24	1%	0.62	2.31	0%	1.40	2.57	3.97	0%	-13.32	4Y.7M
LQD-BIL-GLD	-4.32	1.52	2.4%	-0.59	1.71	0.2%	0.84	2.04	3.13	0%	-13.75	7Y.6M
SHY-IEI-LQD	-3.92	2.22	1.4%	0.37	2.55	0%	1.45	2.63	3.98	0%	-13.98	6Y.3M
BND-BIL-GLD	-4.55	1.44	2.8%	-1.24	1.63	0.6%	0.87	2.11	3.11	0%	-14.21	7Y.11M
IEI-BIL-GLD	-4.61	1.40	2.9%	-1.52	1.61	0.9%	0.86	2.11	3.10	0%	-14.76	8Y.3M
BND-SHY-GLD	-4.38	1.55	3.4%	-1.17	1.86	0.6%	0.95	2.10	3.20	0%	-14.98	7Y.9M
SHY-IEI-GLD	-4.45	1.53	3.6%	-1.46	1.85	0.7%	0.94	2.10	3.18	0%	-14.98	8Y.0M
BND-SHY-LQD	-4.36	2.27	1.4%	0.33	2.60	0%	1.46	2.66	4.00	0%	-15.26	6Y.3M
SHY-BIL-LQD-GLD	-4.77	1.16	4.1%	-1.76	1.31	1.3%	0.59	2.21	3.23	0%	-16.09	11Y.2M
SHY-LQD-GLD	-4.15	1.59	3.2%	-0.52	1.91	0.2%	0.96	2.11	3.20	0%	-16.71	7Y.4M
TLT-SHY-BIL	-5.33	2.00	1.4%	-0.42	2.07	0.2%	1.23	2.26	4.30	0%	-17.63	8Y.9M
BND-IEI-GLD	-4.23	1.43	3.2%	-0.94	1.86	0.6%	0.89	1.93	3.02	0%	-17.77	7Y.11M
BND-IEI-LQD	-5.50	2.08	2%	0.04	2.54	0%	1.36	2.71	4.00	0%	-17.86	7Y.4M
BND-LQD-GLD	-4.09	1.43	3.3%	-0.09	1.82	0.2%	0.87	1.89	2.99	0%	-19.78	7Y.11M
IEI-LQD-GLD	-4.01	1.42	3.3%	-0.30	1.81	0.4%	0.86	1.89	2.98	0%	-19.78	7Y.11M

Order by **Maximum Drawdown - All data** (from 1871/1927 to 2023-11) - **US Infl. Adjusted**

Portfolio	3Y Rolling Annualized Return (%)			7Y Rolling Annualized Return (%)			15Y Rolling Annualized Return (%)				Max Drawdown (%) ▼	Long Neg Period (Y.M)
	Worst	Base	%Fail	Worst	Base	%Fail	Worst	Base	Median	%Fail		
VTV-BIL-GLD	-8.81	-0.54	18.2%	-2.46	0.67	9%	-0.83	2.01	3.81	4.6%	-24.54	18Y.1M
VNQ-SHY-IEI	-8.05	-1.26	26.2%	-3.04	-0.60	20.9%	-1.34	-0.20	1.91	19.2%	-24.75	49Y.2M
VTV-SHY-GLD	-8.67	-0.18	16.8%	-2.19	0.97	8.6%	-0.63	2.26	4.07	3.2%	-25.03	17Y.9M
VTV-SHY-BIL	-9.06	-1.07	21.8%	-2.64	0.14	13.8%	-0.69	1.00	2.80	4%	-25.88	18Y.0M
VNQ-BND-SHY	-8.05	-1.25	26.1%	-3.03	-0.59	20.9%	-1.33	-0.19	1.92	18.9%	-25.89	49Y.2M
VTV-SHY-IEI	-8.86	-0.84	19.2%	-3.05	0.26	13.2%	-0.90	1.20	3.25	4%	-25.97	18Y.8M
VTV-BND-SHY	-8.87	-0.77	18.2%	-3.05	0.27	13.2%	-0.90	1.19	3.25	4%	-25.99	18Y.8M
VTV-BND-BIL	-8.99	-1.08	21.9%	-2.84	0.22	13.2%	-0.69	1.07	2.95	4.7%	-26.21	17Y.11M
VTV-IEI-BIL	-9.00	-0.90	20.9%	-2.85	0.21	13.1%	-0.69	1.06	2.95	4.8%	-26.23	18Y.0M
VTV-LQD-BIL	-9.00	-1.43	22.5%	-3.51	0.15	13.7%	-0.96	0.98	3.07	4.9%	-26.31	19Y.10M
VTV-BND-IEI	-8.80	-0.95	18.4%	-3.27	0.18	12.6%	-1.32	1.14	3.68	4.7%	-26.32	20Y.7M
VTV-TLT-BIL	-8.98	-1.28	22.7%	-3.63	-0.20	16.9%	-1.37	0.83	3.55	5.5%	-26.65	20Y.10M
VTV-TLT-SHY	-8.85	-1.16	19.9%	-3.84	-0.07	15.9%	-1.59	0.94	3.91	5.1%	-26.68	21Y.3M
VNQ-BND-IEI	-8.33	-1.41	27.5%	-3.30	-0.43	22.1%	-1.00	-0.24	2.25	21.5%	-27.24	49Y.2M
VTV-IEI-GLD	-8.60	-0.05	15.3%	-2.14	1.39	8.6%	-0.30	2.27	4.25	0.6%	-27.31	17Y.2M
VTV-SHY-LQD	-8.87	-1.16	20.1%	-3.73	0.24	13.2%	-1.17	1.09	3.42	4.4%	-27.54	20Y.6M
VTV-IEI-LQD	-8.81	-1.06	19.5%	-3.95	0.12	13.1%	-1.60	1.05	3.92	4.9%	-27.63	21Y.4M
VTV-BND-LQD	-8.80	-1.09	19.7%	-3.94	0.12	13.1%	-1.59	1.05	3.90	4.9%	-27.63	21Y.4M
IJS-SHY-BIL	-9.72	-0.14	15.7%	-2.28	1.38	5.9%	0.84	2.46	4.21	0%	-28.03	12Y.9M
IJS-BND-SHY	-9.58	0.35	13.9%	-2.57	1.97	4%	1.37	2.94	4.69	0%	-28.04	11Y.10M

Ranking: Longest Negative Period

Order by **Longest Negative Period - Last 30 Years** (from 1993-12 to 2023-11)

Portfolio	3Y Rolling Annualized Return (%)			7Y Rolling Annualized Return (%)			15Y Rolling Annualized Return (%)				Max Draw-down (%)	Long Neg Period (Y.M) ▲
	Worst	Base	%Fail	Worst	Base	%Fail	Worst	Base	Median	%Fail		
VTV-BND-GLD	0.10	3.55	0%	3.57	5.23	0%	5.36	6.79	7.58	0%	-18.59	2Y.6M
VTV-IEI-GLD	0.10	3.58	0%	3.34	5.24	0%	5.36	6.81	7.71	0%	-16.56	2Y.9M
VTI-IEI-GLD	0.21	3.39	0%	3.47	5.44	0%	5.75	7.19	7.86	0%	-16.66	2Y.9M
VTI-SHY-IEI	0.15	3.45	0%	3.19	4.87	0%	4.39	5.10	5.49	0%	-13.30	2Y.10M
VTV-BNDX-GLD	0.69	3.97	0%	3.71	5.45	0%	5.69	6.96	7.89	0%	-20.54	2Y.11M
IJS-BNDX-GLD	0.25	3.85	0%	3.05	5.42	0%	5.90	7.25	8.77	0%	-18.47	2Y.11M
VTI-BNDX-GLD	0.16	3.75	0%	4.02	5.67	0%	6.10	7.32	8.07	0%	-20.64	2Y.11M
VTV-LQD-GLD	0.31	3.64	0%	3.84	5.47	0%	5.69	7.06	7.92	0%	-22.18	2Y.11M
VTV-EMB-GLD	-0.27	4.61	0.3%	3.44	6.17	0%	5.53	7.52	9.43	0%	-25.48	3Y.0M
VTI-EMB-GLD	-0.16	4.41	0.3%	3.99	6.55	0%	5.89	8.18	9.47	0%	-25.58	3Y.0M
IJS-LQD-GLD	-0.12	3.72	0.3%	3.09	5.55	0%	5.88	7.38	8.76	0%	-20.10	3Y.0M
VTI-BND-GLD	-0.10	3.20	0.3%	3.69	5.43	0%	5.73	7.07	7.80	0%	-18.69	3Y.0M
VTV-SHY-IEI	-0.31	3.45	0.3%	3.26	4.57	0%	3.83	4.80	5.30	0%	-13.83	3Y.1M
VTI-LQD-GLD	0.20	3.41	0%	4.16	5.74	0%	6.05	7.37	8.13	0%	-22.28	3Y.1M
VTV-BND-IEI	-0.55	3.68	0.3%	3.16	5.22	0%	4.28	5.41	5.88	0%	-14.43	3Y.2M
IEI-CWB-BIL	-0.90	3.34	0.6%	3.43	4.10	0%	3.73	4.37	5.14	0%	-12.65	3Y.2M
SHY-CWB-BIL	-0.55	2.85	0.3%	2.94	3.46	0%	3.29	3.79	4.48	0%	-12.00	3Y.2M
MTUM-EMB-GLD	-2.12	4.93	1.5%	4.91	6.98	0%	6.07	8.62	10.04	0%	-26.56	3Y.3M
MTUM-BNDX-GLD	-1.68	4.06	1.2%	5.18	6.89	0%	6.09	8.01	8.79	0%	-21.60	3Y.3M
MTUM-TIP-GLD	-1.20	3.87	0.9%	4.39	6.36	0%	5.84	7.92	8.66	0%	-22.11	3Y.3M
VTI-BND-IEI	-0.12	3.80	0.6%	3.37	5.24	0%	4.82	5.68	6.10	0%	-16.62	3Y.3M

Order by **Longest Negative Period - Last 30 Years** (from 1993-12 to 2023-11) - **US Infl. Adjusted**

Portfolio	3Y Rolling Annualized Return (%)			7Y Rolling Annualized Return (%)			15Y Rolling Annualized Return (%)				Max Draw-down (%)	Long Neg Period (Y.M) ▲
	Worst	Base	%Fail	Worst	Base	%Fail	Worst	Base	Median	%Fail		
MTUM-CWB-GLD	-6.04	1.96	9.8%	3.85	5.58	0%	4.82	5.99	7.01	0%	-31.65	4Y.6M
VTI-TIP-GLD	-3.49	1.05	8.3%	1.74	3.24	0%	3.42	4.98	5.71	0%	-22.92	4Y.6M
MTUM-TIP-GLD	-6.57	1.81	6.2%	1.85	4.36	0%	3.39	5.67	6.37	0%	-23.87	4Y.8M
VTV-TIP-GLD	-2.80	1.35	6.2%	1.63	2.89	0%	3.03	4.63	5.51	0%	-22.83	4Y.8M
MTUM-SHY-GLD	-0.01	1.32	8.6%	1.77	3.89	0%	2.92	4.75	5.63	0%	-22.09	4Y.8M
VTI-BNDX-GLD	-3.93	1.06	11.4%	1.55	3.23	0%	3.62	4.79	5.65	0%	-22.42	4Y.8M
BNDX-CWB-GLD	-6.16	0.96	10.8%	1.27	2.45	0%	3.04	4.67	5.70	0%	-26.56	4Y.8M
MTUM-BIL-GLD	-5.12	0.83	10.8%	2.07	3.55	0%	2.81	4.27	5.24	0%	-20.40	4Y.8M
MTUM-HYG-GLD	-5.63	0.55	13.5%	2.37	4.33	0%	3.85	5.32	6.42	0%	-27.20	4Y.8M
MTUM-IEI-GLD	-7.04	2.05	7.1%	1.49	4.35	0%	3.26	5.45	6.24	0%	-24.35	4Y.9M
CWB-LQD-GLD	-6.82	0.80	10.2%	1.07	2.52	0%	3.00	4.52	5.79	0%	-29.12	4Y.9M
MTUM-VNQ-GLD	-8.95	1.45	9.8%	2.47	5.72	0%	4.50	6.39	7.90	0%	-39.24	4Y.11M
VTV-BNDX-GLD	-3.25	1.26	7.7%	1.25	3.12	0%	3.23	4.56	5.49	0%	-22.33	4Y.11M
VTI-IEI-GLD	-3.94	1.23	9.5%	1.85	3.03	0%	3.28	4.81	5.53	0%	-20.90	4Y.11M
IJS-MTUM-GLD	-6.95	1.84	9.5%	3.21	6.16	0%	5.06	6.68	7.66	0%	-33.70	5Y.0M
IJS-TIP-GLD	-2.42	1.55	6.8%	0.77	3.13	0%	3.22	4.83	6.44	0%	-22.74	5Y.0M
VTV-IEI-GLD	-3.29	1.22	7.4%	1.28	2.79	0%	2.91	4.38	5.34	0%	-19.01	5Y.0M
IJS-BIL-GLD	-1.76	1.05	6.8%	0.63	2.37	0%	2.47	3.85	5.09	0%	-19.35	5Y.0M
VTV-LQD-GLD	-3.86	0.90	9.5%	1.37	3.15	0%	3.23	4.65	5.53	0%	-23.94	5Y.0M
VTI-BND-GLD	-4.30	0.87	11.1%	1.66	2.97	0%	3.25	4.72	5.41	0%	-21.72	5Y.0M
VTI-SHY-GLD	-2.89	0.64	10.8%	1.33	2.73	0%	2.88	4.19	4.88	0%	-18.95	5Y.0M

Order by **Longest Negative Period** - **Last 60 Years** (from 1963-12 to 2023-11)

Portfolio	3Y Rolling Annualized Return (%)			7Y Rolling Annualized Return (%)			15Y Rolling Annualized Return (%)				Max Draw-down (%)	Long Neg Period (Y.M) ▲
	Worst	Base	%Fail	Worst	Base	%Fail	Worst	Base	Median	%Fail		
IJS-LQD-GLD	-0.12	4.40	0.2%	3.09	6.74	0%	5.88	7.75	9.38	0%	-20.10	3Y.0M
IJS-IEI-GLD	-0.18	4.21	0.2%	2.80	6.28	0%	5.56	7.44	9.21	0%	-18.24	3Y.3M
VTI-SHY-GLD	-0.44	4.12	0.4%	3.27	5.67	0%	5.03	6.63	7.68	0%	-17.24	3Y.3M
VTI-LQD-GLD	-0.25	4.09	0.3%	3.97	6.27	0%	5.53	7.39	8.53	0%	-22.28	3Y.3M
VTI-BND-GLD	-0.10	4.06	0.3%	3.69	6.03	0%	5.35	7.15	8.21	0%	-18.73	3Y.3M
VTI-IEI-GLD	-0.10	4.03	0.2%	3.47	6.06	0%	5.50	7.23	8.32	0%	-18.73	3Y.3M
VTV-SHY-GLD	-0.16	3.67	0.4%	3.10	5.32	0%	4.93	6.50	7.73	0%	-16.68	3Y.3M
IJS-BND-GLD	-0.12	4.28	0.2%	2.87	6.40	0%	5.56	7.44	9.08	0%	-18.23	3Y.4M
IJS-SHY-GLD	-0.61	3.92	0.4%	2.37	5.79	0%	5.13	6.94	8.60	0%	-17.52	3Y.4M
IJS-BIL-GLD	-0.83	3.86	0.4%	2.13	5.56	0%	4.91	6.52	8.07	0%	-15.93	3Y.4M
VNQ-LQD-GLD	-2.07	2.44	3.2%	2.42	5.09	0%	5.04	6.67	9.16	0%	-24.33	3Y.5M
VTI-BND-IEI	-1.34	4.17	0.7%	2.58	5.41	0%	4.82	6.00	8.32	0%	-16.62	3Y.6M
VTI-SHY-IEI	-1.28	3.90	0.4%	2.80	5.13	0%	4.39	5.45	8.16	0%	-13.54	3Y.6M
VTV-BND-IEI	-0.97	3.84	0.9%	2.54	5.09	0%	4.28	5.71	8.65	0%	-14.43	3Y.6M
VTI-IEI-BIL	-0.59	3.78	0.4%	2.65	4.75	0%	4.17	5.08	7.87	0%	-13.84	3Y.6M
VTV-SHY-IEI	-0.31	3.77	0.4%	2.79	4.70	0%	3.83	5.20	8.47	0%	-13.83	3Y.6M
VTV-IEI-BIL	-1.05	3.49	0.3%	2.72	4.44	0%	3.60	4.80	8.04	0%	-15.50	3Y.6M
VTV-BIL-GLD	-0.65	3.33	0.7%	2.76	4.86	0%	4.42	6.00	7.19	0%	-17.15	3Y.6M
VTI-BND-SHY	-1.28	4.01	0.7%	2.59	4.99	0%	4.40	5.44	8.12	0%	-14.63	3Y.7M
VNQ-BND-GLD	-1.16	2.30	2.2%	1.92	4.80	0%	4.72	6.42	8.87	0%	-21.58	3Y.7M
IJS-IEI-BIL	-1.96	4.08	0.7%	2.93	4.85	0%	3.82	5.64	9.33	0%	-14.64	3Y.8M

Order by **Longest Negative Period** - **Last 60 Years** (from 1963-12 to 2023-11) - **US Infl. Adjusted**

Portfolio	3Y Rolling Annualized Return (%)			7Y Rolling Annualized Return (%)			15Y Rolling Annualized Return (%)				Max Draw-down (%)	Long Neg Period (Y.M) ▲
	Worst	Base	%Fail	Worst	Base	%Fail	Worst	Base	Median	%Fail		
IJS-BIL-GLD	-3.91	1.05	8.9%	0.63	2.81	0%	2.19	3.78	5.36	0%	-21.98	5Y.3M
IJS-SHY-GLD	-3.45	1.36	8.3%	0.80	3.22	0%	2.69	4.34	5.90	0%	-23.25	5Y.9M
IJS-LQD-GLD	-3.68	1.31	9.6%	0.71	3.63	0%	3.32	5.00	6.54	0%	-26.02	5Y.11M
IJS-VNQ-GLD	-10.62	0.93	12.1%	1.40	3.99	0%	3.34	5.31	8.00	0%	-38.59	5Y.11M
IJS-IEI-GLD	-3.36	1.57	8.8%	0.55	3.41	0%	3.10	4.87	6.44	0%	-24.42	6Y.2M
IJS-BND-GLD	-3.32	1.54	9.2%	0.52	3.45	0%	3.10	4.78	6.33	0%	-24.40	6Y.2M
IJS-VTV-GLD	-7.52	1.88	9.9%	1.43	4.70	0%	3.57	6.01	7.37	0%	-34.29	6Y.4M
VTI-IJS-GLD	-7.03	1.83	8.8%	1.50	4.76	0%	3.50	6.07	7.38	0%	-33.09	6Y.4M
VTI-BIL-GLD	-4.29	0.04	14.6%	0.22	2.42	0%	1.20	3.13	4.30	0%	-26.62	6Y.7M
VTI-SHY-GLD	-4.24	0.49	12.6%	0.90	2.81	0%	1.87	3.70	4.81	0%	-27.06	6Y.8M
VTI-VNQ-GLD	-9.05	0.53	12.1%	0.11	3.76	0%	2.53	4.87	6.79	0%	-38.25	6Y.11M
VTI-IEI-GLD	-5.06	0.38	12.3%	0.40	3.13	0%	2.32	4.05	5.15	0%	-29.29	6Y.11M
VTI-BND-GLD	-5.05	0.35	13%	0.41	3.11	0%	2.18	3.94	5.10	0%	-29.29	6Y.11M
VTI-LQD-GLD	-5.20	0.29	13.4%	0.30	3.31	0%	2.35	4.09	5.29	0%	-31.30	6Y.11M
VTV-SHY-GLD	-5.12	0.49	11.8%	-0.20	2.69	0.9%	2.00	3.77	4.84	0%	-25.03	7Y.3M
VTV-BIL-GLD	-4.59	0.13	13.9%	-0.35	2.35	1.1%	1.31	3.19	4.38	0%	-24.41	7Y.5M
VTV-IEI-GLD	-5.95	0.34	11.5%	-0.65	2.99	1.9%	2.45	4.07	5.32	0%	-27.31	7Y.9M
VTV-BND-GLD	-5.94	0.28	12.4%	-0.64	3.05	1.9%	2.31	3.99	5.25	0%	-27.31	7Y.9M
VTV-LQD-GLD	-6.10	0.27	12.9%	-0.74	3.22	2%	2.49	4.15	5.47	0%	-29.36	7Y.10M
VTV-VNQ-GLD	-9.59	0.30	13.6%	-1.15	3.73	2.2%	2.59	4.90	6.85	0%	-39.54	8Y.0M
VTV-TLT-GLD	-7.31	0.08	14%	-1.44	3.35	2.8%	2.76	4.26	5.89	0%	-29.91	8Y.1M

139

Order by **Longest Negative Period - All data** (from 1871/1927 to 2023-11)

Portfolio	3Y Rolling Annualized Return (%)			7Y Rolling Annualized Return (%)			15Y Rolling Annualized Return (%)				Max Draw-down (%)	Long Neg Period (Y.M) ▲
	Worst	Base	%Fail	Worst	Base	%Fail	Worst	Base	Median	%Fail		
SHY-IEI-BIL	-1.27	1.67	0.9%	0.47	1.61	0%	1.09	2.17	4.25	0%	-6.17	4Y.2M
SHY-LQD-BIL	-1.87	1.91	0.9%	0.87	1.96	0%	1.24	2.35	4.19	0%	-9.40	4Y.4M
BND-SHY-BIL	-1.56	1.71	0.9%	0.58	1.68	0%	1.18	2.25	4.25	0%	-7.40	4Y.4M
IEI-LQD-BIL	-2.99	2.17	1%	0.66	2.27	0%	1.40	2.53	3.97	0%	-12.04	4Y.5M
BND-LQD-BIL	-3.42	2.24	1%	0.62	2.31	0%	1.40	2.57	3.97	0%	-13.32	4Y.7M
BND-IEI-BIL	-2.66	2.01	1%	0.42	2.10	0%	1.38	2.49	4.01	0%	-10.16	4Y.9M
VNQ-BND-IEI	-5.25	1.54	4.2%	0.51	2.39	0%	1.85	2.80	5.72	0%	-21.47	5Y.9M
VNQ-IEI-LQD	-5.34	1.45	5.5%	0.62	2.41	0%	1.77	2.79	5.96	0%	-24.24	5Y.9M
VNQ-BND-LQD	-5.57	1.44	5.7%	0.63	2.42	0%	1.78	2.79	6.01	0%	-26.37	5Y.9M
IJS-TLT-GLD	-16.34	3.34	4.8%	2.70	5.47	0%	4.31	6.33	8.85	0%	-44.73	6Y.0M
IJS-BND-GLD	-15.64	3.25	4.5%	2.70	5.35	0%	4.19	6.38	8.36	0%	-43.25	6Y.0M
IJS-IEI-GLD	-15.65	3.21	4.5%	2.69	5.30	0%	4.18	6.38	8.44	0%	-43.26	6Y.0M
IJS-LQD-GLD	-15.73	3.21	4.4%	2.81	5.46	0%	4.25	6.49	8.49	0%	-43.44	6Y.0M
VTV-IEI-GLD	-13.35	3.15	4.2%	1.49	4.49	0%	3.12	5.17	7.32	0%	-38.99	6Y.0M
VTV-LQD-CLD	13.43	3.09	3.9%	1.49	4.50	0%	3.21	5.21	7.49	0%	-39.16	6Y.0M
VTV-BND-GLD	-13.34	3.08	4.2%	1.50	4.47	0%	3.13	5.18	7.24	0%	-38.97	6Y.0M
IJS-SHY-GLD	-15.58	3.08	5.6%	2.18	5.13	0%	3.79	6.28	8.03	0%	-43.07	6Y.1M
VTV-BND-IEI	-11.81	3.05	3.6%	1.47	4.42	0%	3.19	5.23	6.51	0%	-35.90	6Y.1M
VTV-SHY-IEI	-11.74	3.12	3.9%	1.26	4.35	0%	2.68	4.90	6.53	0%	-35.70	6Y.2M
VTV-IEI-LQD	-11.90	2.96	3.9%	1.46	4.39	0%	3.27	5.27	6.56	0%	-36.10	6Y.2M
VTV-BND-SHY	-11.74	2.96	4%	1.26	4.34	0%	2.69	4.91	6.48	0%	-35.68	6Y.2M

Order by **Longest Negative Period - All data** (from 1871/1927 to 2023-11) - **US Infl. Adjusted**

Portfolio	3Y Rolling Annualized Return (%)			7Y Rolling Annualized Return (%)			15Y Rolling Annualized Return (%)				Max Draw-down (%)	Long Neg Period (Y.M) ▲
	Worst	Base	%Fail	Worst	Base	%Fail	Worst	Base	Median	%Fail		
IJS-IEI-GLD	-9.27	0.60	13%	-2.33	2.91	1.8%	1.22	3.61	5.45	0%	-28.36	8Y.9M
IJS-BND-GLD	-9.26	0.48	13.3%	-2.32	2.97	1.8%	1.23	3.67	5.43	0%	-28.34	8Y.9M
IJS-TLT-GLD	-9.71	0.42	13.6%	-2.54	2.97	1.8%	1.33	3.54	5.85	0%	-30.21	8Y.9M
IJS-LQD-GLD	-9.29	0.39	13.7%	-2.32	3.07	1.5%	1.29	3.68	5.59	0%	-28.57	8Y.9M
IJS-VNQ-GLD	-19.17	-0.13	15.3%	-1.31	3.21	2%	2.11	4.01	6.04	0%	-52.13	9Y.3M
IJS-BND-SHY	-9.58	0.35	13.9%	-2.57	1.97	4%	1.37	2.94	4.69	0%	-28.04	11Y.10M
IJS-SHY-IEI	-9.59	0.34	13.4%	-2.58	1.96	4.2%	1.36	2.93	4.79	0%	-28.06	11Y.10M
IJS-IEI-BIL	-9.70	0.04	14.7%	-2.51	1.82	4.3%	1.16	2.72	4.41	0%	-28.19	12Y.4M
IJS-BND-BIL	-9.69	0.03	14.9%	-2.50	1.82	4.3%	1.17	2.76	4.37	0%	-28.17	12Y.4M
IJS-SHY-GLD	-9.32	0.42	13.1%	-2.38	2.62	3.3%	0.89	3.49	5.26	0%	-28.12	12Y.7M
VTI-IJS-GLD	-26.27	0.71	13.6%	-1.50	4.48	1.3%	2.89	5.33	7.25	0%	-63.58	12Y.9M
IJS-BIL-GLD	-9.59	0.25	13.7%	-2.23	2.39	3.5%	0.69	3.17	4.91	0%	-29.71	12Y.9M
IJS-SHY-BIL	-9.72	-0.14	15.7%	-2.28	1.38	5.9%	0.84	2.46	4.21	0%	-28.03	12Y.9M
IJS-VTV-IEI	-24.42	-0.19	16%	-5.03	2.92	3.2%	1.53	3.88	6.75	0%	-61.15	12Y.9M
IJS-VTV-BND	-24.41	-0.49	16.4%	-5.03	2.90	3.3%	1.53	3.87	6.75	0%	-61.14	12Y.9M
IJS-LQD-BIL	-9.72	-0.12	15.3%	-3.23	1.82	4.3%	1.23	2.80	4.41	0%	-28.33	12Y.10M
VTI-IJS-BND	-24.72	-0.77	16%	-5.09	3.19	3.8%	1.24	4.02	6.70	0%	-61.39	12Y.10M
VTI-IJS-IEI	-24.73	-0.36	15.6%	-5.09	3.28	3.6%	1.24	4.05	6.70	0%	-61.41	12Y.11M
IJS-VTV-GLD	-25.93	0.52	13.9%	-1.57	4.17	1.4%	2.78	5.21	7.17	0%	-63.30	13Y.0M
VTI-IJS-SHY	-24.65	-0.42	16.2%	-4.89	2.84	4.1%	1.67	3.81	6.59	0%	-61.23	13Y.0M
IJS-VNQ-SHY	-17.50	-0.13	15.1%	-4.66	2.65	4.5%	0.70	3.56	5.85	0%	-49.23	13Y.1M

Ranking: Baseline 7Y Return

Order by **Baseline 7Y Return - Last 30 Years** (from 1993-12 to 2023-11)

Portfolio	3Y Rolling Annualized Return (%)			7Y Rolling Annualized Return (%)			15Y Rolling Annualized Return (%)				Max Draw-down (%)	Long Neg Period (Y.M)
	Worst	Base	%Fail	Worst	Base ▼	%Fail	Worst	Base	Median	%Fail		
IJS-MTUM-GLD	-4.89	4.43	3.1%	5.80	8.54	0%	7.56	9.27	10.03	0%	-32.67	3Y.7M
MTUM-EMB-TLT	-7.59	5.32	5.5%	2.02	7.97	0%	5.88	8.57	9.55	0%	-28.75	5Y.9M
MTUM-VNQ-TLT	-8.70	4.37	9.2%	3.09	7.88	0%	6.83	9.21	9.92	0%	-36.68	4Y.11M
MTUM-VNQ-GLD	-7.03	4.62	3.7%	6.09	7.87	0%	6.99	9.01	10.37	0%	-38.30	3Y.9M
MTUM-EEM-TLT	-7.24	3.80	9.2%	2.80	7.77	0%	5.04	8.55	9.90	0%	-34.03	5Y.10M
MTUM-CWB-GLD	-3.72	4.60	4.3%	6.38	7.72	0%	7.32	8.31	9.45	0%	-29.26	3Y.5M
VTI-VNQ-TLT	-8.90	4.32	7.4%	3.00	7.63	0%	6.72	8.43	9.22	0%	-35.77	5Y.1M
MTUM-SCZ-TLT	-6.79	1.60	9.2%	3.32	7.58	0%	5.91	8.79	9.82	0%	-35.31	5Y.9M
IJS-MTUM-TLT	-6.93	3.32	5.8%	3.42	7.52	0%	7.42	8.85	9.61	0%	-30.84	4Y.4M
VTV-MTUM-GLD	-6.29	2.37	7.1%	5.39	7.44	0%	7.35	8.17	9.32	0%	-33.82	4Y.5M
VTI-IJS-GLD	-4.97	3.87	3.4%	4.54	7.41	0%	6.86	8.53	9.26	0%	-31.57	4Y.11M
VTI-EMB-TLT	-4.78	5.13	5.2%	2.43	7.36	0%	5.74	7.90	9.01	0%	-26.55	4Y.4M
MTUM-TLT-CWB	-5.72	2.50	5.5%	4.08	7.36	0%	7.28	8.25	9.21	0%	-29.85	4Y.2M
VTI-SCZ-TLT	-6.90	2.13	7.4%	3.76	7.35	0%	5.83	8.06	8.96	0%	-34.32	4Y.3M
MTUM-TLT-GLD	-5.91	4.55	2.8%	3.75	7.35	0%	6.53	8.89	9.65	0%	-22.67	4Y.1M
IJS-TLT-CWB	-6.03	5.45	3.4%	3.70	7.34	0%	6.96	8.18	8.99	0%	-26.77	4Y.5M
IJS-VNQ-TLT	-10.35	3.76	7.4%	1.96	7.33	0%	6.40	7.85	9.80	0%	-37.77	5Y.3M
VTV-VNQ-TLT	-9.52	4.42	7.4%	2.91	7.25	0%	6.21	7.91	8.89	0%	-37.59	5Y.2M
IJS-SCZ-TLT	-8.21	3.71	5.8%	2.30	7.25	0%	5.57	7.79	9.57	0%	-34.88	5Y.11M
VTI-MTUM-GLD	-8.13	3.25	7.4%	5.33	7.24	0%	7.26	8.25	9.47	0%	-32.55	4Y.5M
IJS-VTV-GLD	-5.47	4.06	2.2%	4.17	7.22	0%	6.76	8.23	8.99	0%	-32.93	5Y.0M

Order by **Baseline 7Y Return - Last 30 Years** (from 1993-12 to 2023-11) - **US Infl. Adjusted**

Portfolio	3Y Rolling Annualized Return (%)			7Y Rolling Annualized Return (%)			15Y Rolling Annualized Return (%)				Max Draw-down (%)	Long Neg Period (Y.M)
	Worst	Base	%Fail	Worst	Base ▼	%Fail	Worst	Base	Median	%Fail		
IJS-MTUM-GLD	-6.95	1.84	9.5%	3.21	6.16	0%	5.06	6.68	7.66	0%	-33.70	5Y.0M
MTUM-VNQ-GLD	-8.95	1.45	9.8%	2.47	5.72	0%	4.50	6.39	7.90	0%	-39.24	4Y.11M
MTUM-EEM-TLT	-12.26	1.64	13.2%	-0.68	5.71	0.7%	2.58	6.36	7.55	0%	-38.66	8Y.11M
MTUM-EMB-TLT	-12.61	2.87	7.7%	-1.46	5.70	1.8%	3.41	6.41	7.14	0%	-37.50	8Y.11M
MTUM-CWB-GLD	-6.04	1.96	9.8%	3.85	5.58	0%	4.82	5.99	7.01	0%	-31.65	4Y.6M
MTUM-VNQ-TLT	-10.68	1.86	12.6%	-0.42	5.50	0.7%	4.35	6.71	7.59	0%	-38.50	8Y.9M
VTI-EMB-TLT	-9.93	3.00	7.7%	-1.04	5.36	1.1%	3.27	5.68	6.64	0%	-32.26	8Y.11M
MTUM-SCZ-TLT	-10.85	-1.10	16.6%	-0.18	5.28	0.7%	3.44	6.25	7.41	0%	-37.79	7Y.5M
VTI-IJS-GLD	-7.03	1.57	8.3%	2.05	5.13	0%	4.26	6.03	6.87	0%	-32.62	5Y.8M
VTI-VNQ-TLT	-10.87	1.45	11.7%	-0.07	5.11	0.4%	4.13	5.91	6.81	0%	-37.87	8Y.9M
IJS-EMB-TLT	-9.55	2.45	8%	-2.46	5.08	4%	3.05	5.41	7.44	0%	-34.38	9Y.8M
MTUM-EMB-GLD	-7.44	3.23	6.8%	1.34	5.08	0%	3.59	6.51	7.73	0%	-28.58	5Y.9M
IJS-VNQ-TLT	-12.29	1.39	12%	-1.49	5.08	1.8%	3.92	5.75	7.26	0%	-40.40	9Y.0M
MTUM-TLT-GLD	-11.02	2.43	7.7%	0.21	5.05	0%	4.06	6.46	7.34	0%	-31.37	7Y.3M
VNQ-TLT-CWB	-9.84	2.19	11.4%	-0.70	5.02	0.7%	3.82	5.57	6.81	0%	-37.69	8Y.9M
VTV-MTUM-GLD	-8.55	-0.25	15.4%	2.76	4.91	0%	4.85	5.72	6.83	0%	-34.84	5Y.2M
VTI-SCZ-TLT	-8.92	-0.62	16.3%	0.25	4.90	0%	3.35	5.61	6.61	0%	-35.32	7Y.3M
IJS-CWB-GLD	-6.03	2.28	5.2%	2.15	4.84	0%	4.25	5.84	6.89	0%	-29.11	5Y.6M
IJS-MTUM-TLT	-8.95	0.17	14.2%	0.84	4.84	0%	4.92	6.42	7.35	0%	-35.07	6Y.5M
EMB-TLT-CWB	-12.46	3.28	8%	-1.90	4.80	2.9%	2.78	5.16	6.75	0%	-39.01	9Y.5M
VTV-EMB-TLT	-9.06	2.74	8%	-1.61	4.79	2.5%	2.86	5.31	6.52	0%	-29.88	9Y.2M

Order by **Baseline 7Y Return - Last 60 Years** (from 1963-12 to 2023-11)

Portfolio	3Y Rolling Annualized Return (%)			7Y Rolling Annualized Return (%)			15Y Rolling Annualized Return (%)				Max Draw-down (%)	Long Neg Period (Y.M)
	Worst	Base	%Fail	Worst	Base ▼	%Fail	Worst	Base	Median	%Fail		
VTI-IJS-GLD	-4.97	5.40	2.3%	4.54	8.18	0%	6.67	8.85	10.62	0%	-31.57	4Y.11M
IJS-VTV-GLD	-5.47	4.97	2.3%	4.17	7.86	0%	6.75	8.62	10.82	0%	-32.93	5Y.0M
VTI-VTV-GLD	-6.61	4.36	4.5%	3.24	7.31	0%	5.70	7.89	9.84	0%	-32.70	5Y.5M
VTI-IJS-TLT	-7.23	4.47	5.3%	-0.25	7.25	0.2%	7.31	8.66	11.18	0%	-31.32	7Y.1M
IJS-VNQ-TLT	-10.35	4.33	6.4%	0.20	7.15	0%	6.40	9.07	11.29	0%	-37.77	6Y.8M
VTI-VNQ-GLD	-7.13	4.26	2.6%	3.86	7.10	0%	5.67	8.19	9.94	0%	-37.29	4Y.8M
IJS-VNQ-GLD	-8.73	4.43	2.8%	3.22	7.07	0%	6.51	8.25	11.00	0%	-37.64	4Y.4M
IJS-TLT-GLD	-1.86	4.74	0.6%	2.90	6.90	0%	6.28	8.48	10.06	0%	-19.87	3Y.9M
IJS-VTV-TLT	-7.65	4.22	5.3%	-0.18	6.89	0.2%	6.79	8.49	11.43	0%	-31.90	7Y.1M
IJS-TLT-LQD	-4.79	4.76	3.2%	1.20	6.81	0%	5.63	7.74	10.25	0%	-26.67	6Y.1M
VTI-IJS-VNQ	-19.16	4.28	8.3%	-1.71	6.77	1.3%	5.58	8.90	11.94	0%	-57.10	8Y.7M
VTV-VNQ-GLD	-7.68	3.79	3.1%	2.79	6.75	0%	5.74	8.09	9.97	0%	-38.60	6Y.1M
IJS-LQD-GLD	-0.12	4.40	0.2%	3.09	6.74	0%	5.88	7.75	9.38	0%	-20.10	3Y.0M
VTI-IJS-IEI	-7.89	4.49	5.4%	0.62	6.71	0%	6.32	7.68	11.07	0%	-32.26	6Y.7M
IJS-BND-TLT	-4.38	4.67	2.6%	1.06	6.68	0%	5.23	7.67	10.08	0%	-25.09	6Y.1M
VTI-IJS-LQD	-10.36	4.49	6.6%	-0.16	6.67	0.2%	6.26	7.91	11.02	0%	-37.60	7Y.1M
IJS-VNQ-LQD	-13.51	4.55	6.7%	0.24	6.58	0%	5.74	8.42	10.92	0%	-44.90	6Y.8M
VTI-IJS-BND	-8.97	4.40	6%	0.63	6.56	0%	6.23	7.62	10.94	0%	-34.68	6Y.7M
IJS-TLT-IEI	-3.88	4.67	2.2%	1.15	6.48	0%	5.08	7.73	10.14	0%	-23.47	5Y.11M
VTI-TLT-GLD	-2.75	4.12	1.8%	3.17	6.45	0%	5.83	7.88	9.27	0%	-21.42	4Y.9M
IJS-BND-GLD	-0.12	4.28	0.2%	2.87	6.40	0%	5.56	7.44	9.08	0%	-18.23	3Y.4M

Order by **Baseline 7Y Return - Last 60 Years** (from 1963-12 to 2023-11) - **US Infl. Adjusted**

Portfolio	3Y Rolling Annualized Return (%)			7Y Rolling Annualized Return (%)			15Y Rolling Annualized Return (%)				Max Draw-down (%)	Long Neg Period (Y.M)
	Worst	Base	%Fail	Worst	Base ▼	%Fail	Worst	Base	Median	%Fail		
VTI-IJS-GLD	-7.03	1.83	8.8%	1.50	4.76	0%	3.50	6.07	7.38	0%	-33.09	6Y.4M
IJS-VTV-GLD	-7.52	1.88	9.9%	1.43	4.70	0%	3.57	6.01	7.37	0%	-34.29	6Y.4M
IJS-VNQ-GLD	-10.62	0.93	12.1%	1.40	3.99	0%	3.34	5.31	8.00	0%	-38.59	5Y.11M
IJS-TLT-GLD	-7.17	1.64	9.6%	-0.61	3.77	0.3%	3.59	5.52	6.88	0%	-27.87	8Y.9M
VTI-VNQ-GLD	-9.05	0.53	12.1%	0.11	3.76	0%	2.53	4.87	6.79	0%	-38.25	6Y.11M
VTV-VNQ-GLD	-9.59	0.30	13.6%	-1.15	3.73	2.2%	2.59	4.90	6.85	0%	-39.54	8Y.0M
VTI-VTV-GLD	-8.87	0.50	13.1%	-0.08	3.66	0.2%	2.55	5.00	6.40	0%	-33.91	9Y.2M
IJS-LQD-GLD	-3.68	1.31	9.6%	0.71	3.63	0%	3.32	5.00	6.54	0%	-26.02	5Y.11M
IJS-BND-GLD	-3.32	1.54	9.2%	0.52	3.45	0%	3.10	4.78	6.33	0%	-24.40	6Y.2M
IJS-IEI-GLD	-3.36	1.57	8.8%	0.55	3.41	0%	3.10	4.87	6.44	0%	-24.42	6Y.2M
VTV-TLT-GLD	-7.31	0.08	14%	-1.44	3.35	2.8%	2.76	4.26	5.89	0%	-29.91	8Y.1M
VTI-LQD-GLD	-5.20	0.29	13.4%	0.30	3.31	0%	2.35	4.09	5.29	0%	-31.30	6Y.11M
VTI-TLT-GLD	-8.04	0.24	13.9%	-0.47	3.29	1.3%	2.64	4.25	5.55	0%	-31.83	8Y.4M
VTV-LQD-GLD	-6.10	0.27	12.9%	-0.74	3.22	2%	2.49	4.15	5.47	0%	-29.36	7Y.10M
IJS-SHY-GLD	-3.45	1.36	8.3%	0.80	3.22	0%	2.69	4.34	5.90	0%	-23.25	5Y.9M
VTI-IEI-GLD	-5.06	0.38	12.3%	0.40	3.13	0%	2.32	4.05	5.15	0%	-29.29	6Y.11M
VTI-BND-GLD	-5.05	0.35	13%	0.41	3.11	0%	2.18	3.94	5.10	0%	-29.29	6Y.11M
VTV-BND-GLD	-5.94	0.28	12.4%	-0.64	3.05	1.9%	2.31	3.99	5.25	0%	-27.31	7Y.9M
VTV-IEI-GLD	-5.95	0.34	11.5%	-0.65	2.99	1.9%	2.45	4.07	5.32	0%	-27.31	7Y.9M
IJS-VNQ-IEI	-13.02	0.26	13.1%	-4.89	2.83	5.3%	2.16	4.37	7.17	0%	-42.28	11Y.2M
IJS-BIL-GLD	-3.91	1.05	8.9%	0.63	2.81	0%	2.19	3.78	5.36	0%	-21.98	5Y.3M

Order by **Baseline 7Y Return** - **All data** (from 1871/1927 to 2023-11)

Portfolio	3Y Rolling Annualized Return (%)			7Y Rolling Annualized Return (%)			15Y Rolling Annualized Return (%)				Max Draw-down (%)	Long Neg Period (Y.M)
	Worst	Base	%Fail	Worst	Base ▼	%Fail	Worst	Base	Median	%Fail		
VTI-IJS-GLD	-31.68	3.61	8%	-1.21	7.03	0.3%	2.78	8.60	10.46	0%	-71.16	13Y.1M
IJS-VTV-GLD	-31.37	3.52	7.8%	-1.56	6.92	0.7%	2.54	8.39	10.43	0%	-70.94	13Y.1M
VTI-IJS-TLT	-30.95	2.77	9.5%	-1.80	6.72	1.1%	3.14	8.33	10.44	0%	-70.39	12Y.10M
IJS-VTV-TLT	-30.69	2.74	9.6%	-2.21	6.25	1.2%	2.87	8.10	10.47	0%	-70.22	13Y.0M
VTI-IJS-IEI	-30.26	2.87	9.7%	-1.57	6.25	0.7%	3.07	7.71	10.62	0%	-69.44	12Y.10M
VTI-IJS-LQD	-30.34	2.75	10.4%	-1.58	6.13	0.7%	3.14	7.81	10.54	0%	-69.55	12Y.10M
VTI-IJS-BND	-30.25	2.64	10%	-1.56	6.11	0.7%	3.08	7.65	10.59	0%	-69.43	12Y.10M
IJS-VTV-IEI	-29.97	2.62	9.8%	-1.97	5.83	1%	2.80	7.46	10.63	0%	-69.24	13Y.1M
IJS-TLT-IEI	-14.82	3.66	5.4%	1.15	5.80	0%	4.47	6.76	8.09	0%	-41.85	6Y.3M
IJS-VTV-LQD	-30.05	2.45	10%	-1.98	5.79	1.1%	2.87	7.63	10.56	0%	-69.35	13Y.0M
IJS-VNQ-GLD	-25.11	2.85	7.3%	-0.41	5.78	0.1%	2.71	6.85	9.28	0%	-62.09	12Y.10M
VTI-IJS-VNQ	-39.20	1.77	12.2%	-5.45	5.76	2.9%	1.35	8.41	11.27	0%	-80.53	14Y.4M
IJS-VTV-BND	-29.96	2.45	10.1%	-1.97	5.75	1%	2.81	7.40	10.61	0%	-69.23	13Y.0M
IJS-BND-TLT	-14.81	3.59	5.7%	1.06	5.75	0%	4.48	6.77	8.09	0%	-41.84	6Y.3M
IJS-TLT-LQD	-14.91	3.33	6%	1.20	5.74	0%	4.54	6.80	8.19	0%	-42.03	6Y.3M
IJS-IEI-LQD	-14.19	3.36	5.4%	2.48	5.68	0%	4.42	6.69	8.10	0%	-40.48	6Y.3M
IJS-BND-LQD	-14.18	3.30	5.6%	2.44	5.67	0%	4.43	6.69	8.06	0%	-40.46	6Y.3M
VTI-IJS-SHY	-30.18	2.55	10.2%	-1.75	5.59	0.7%	2.70	7.11	10.58	0%	-69.30	13Y.1M
IJS-VNQ-IEI	-23.60	2.79	9%	-1.01	5.59	0.3%	2.87	7.13	9.25	0%	-59.90	12Y.8M
IJS-TLT-SHY	-14.73	3.51	5.4%	1.46	5.58	0%	4.09	6.55	7.98	0%	-41.63	6Y.3M
IJS-VNQ-LQD	-23.67	2.71	9.4%	-1.02	5.57	0.3%	2.94	7.19	9.31	0%	-60.02	12Y.8M

Order by **Baseline 7Y Return** - **All data** (from 1871/1927 to 2023-11) - **US Infl. Adjusted**

Portfolio	3Y Rolling Annualized Return (%)			7Y Rolling Annualized Return (%)			15Y Rolling Annualized Return (%)				Max Draw-down (%)	Long Neg Period (Y.M)
	Worst	Base	%Fail	Worst	Base ▼	%Fail	Worst	Base	Median	%Fail		
VTI-IJS-GLD	-26.27	0.71	13.6%	-1.50	4.48	1.3%	2.89	5.33	7.25	0%	-63.58	12Y.9M
IJS-VTV-GLD	-25.93	0.52	13.9%	-1.57	4.17	1.4%	2.78	5.21	7.17	0%	-63.30	13Y.0M
VTI-IJS-IEI	-24.73	-0.36	15.6%	-5.09	3.28	3.6%	1.24	4.05	6.70	0%	-61.41	12Y.11M
IJS-VNQ-GLD	-19.17	-0.13	15.3%	-1.31	3.21	2%	2.11	4.01	6.04	0%	-52.13	9Y.3M
VTI-IJS-TLT	-25.48	-0.64	17%	-5.92	3.21	3.7%	0.51	3.89	7.01	0%	-62.61	14Y.2M
VTI-IJS-BND	-24.72	-0.77	16%	-5.09	3.19	3.8%	1.24	4.02	6.70	0%	-61.39	12Y.10M
VTI-IJS-LQD	-24.82	-0.99	16.6%	-5.86	3.14	4.6%	0.78	4.00	6.73	0%	-61.54	13Y.11M
IJS-LQD-GLD	-9.29	0.39	13.7%	-2.32	3.07	1.5%	1.29	3.68	5.59	0%	-28.57	8Y.9M
VTI-VTV-GLD	-23.94	-0.24	15.8%	-2.43	3.04	2.9%	1.42	3.98	5.97	0%	-60.27	13Y.4M
IJS-BND-GLD	-9.26	0.48	13.3%	-2.32	2.97	1.8%	1.23	3.67	5.43	0%	-28.34	8Y.9M
IJS-TLT-GLD	-9.71	0.42	13.6%	-2.54	2.97	1.8%	1.33	3.54	5.85	0%	-30.21	8Y.9M
IJS-VTV-IEI	-24.42	-0.19	16%	-5.03	2.92	3.2%	1.53	3.88	6.75	0%	-61.15	12Y.9M
IJS-IEI-GLD	-9.27	0.60	13%	-2.33	2.91	1.8%	1.22	3.61	5.45	0%	-28.36	8Y.9M
IJS-VTV-BND	-24.41	-0.49	16.4%	-5.03	2.90	3.3%	1.53	3.87	6.75	0%	-61.14	12Y.9M
IJS-VNQ-LQD	-24.50	-0.67	16.7%	-5.76	2.89	3.3%	1.07	3.86	6.74	0%	-61.29	13Y.8M
IJS-VNQ-IEI	-17.54	0.02	14.7%	-4.89	2.89	3.8%	0.56	3.66	6.01	0%	-49.36	13Y.9M
VTI-IJS-VNQ	-34.38	-0.67	17.1%	-7.48	2.85	5.3%	0.23	4.41	7.79	0%	-75.41	14Y.3M
VTI-IJS-SHY	-24.65	-0.42	16.2%	-4.89	2.84	4.1%	1.67	3.81	6.59	0%	-61.23	13Y.0M
IJS-VNQ-BND	-17.53	0.05	14.8%	-4.89	2.83	3.8%	0.56	3.67	5.98	0%	-49.35	13Y.9M
IJS-VTV-TLT	-25.19	-0.82	16.9%	-5.85	2.83	3.3%	0.80	3.78	6.98	0%	-62.40	13Y.11M
IJS-VNQ-LQD	-17.62	-0.22	15.6%	-5.68	2.75	3.8%	0.16	3.67	6.01	0%	-49.52	13Y.11M

Ranking: Baseline 15Y Return

Order by **Baseline 15Y Return - Last 30 Years** (from 1993-12 to 2023-11)

Portfolio	3Y Rolling Annualized Return (%)			7Y Rolling Annualized Return (%)			15Y Rolling Annualized Return (%)				Max Draw-down (%)	Long Neg Period (Y.M)
	Worst	Base	%Fail	Worst	Base	%Fail	Worst	Base ▼	Median	%Fail		
IJS-MTUM-GLD	-4.89	4.43	3.1%	5.80	8.54	0%	7.56	9.27	10.03	0%	-32.67	3Y.7M
MTUM-VNQ-TLT	-8.70	4.37	9.2%	3.09	7.88	0%	6.83	9.21	9.92	0%	-36.68	4Y.11M
MTUM-VNQ-GLD	-7.03	4.62	3.7%	6.09	7.87	0%	6.99	9.01	10.37	0%	-38.30	3Y.9M
MTUM-TLT-GLD	-5.91	4.55	2.8%	3.75	7.35	0%	6.53	8.89	9.65	0%	-22.67	4Y.1M
IJS-MTUM-TLT	-6.93	3.32	5.8%	3.42	7.52	0%	7.42	8.85	9.61	0%	-30.84	4Y.4M
MTUM-SCZ-TLT	-6.79	1.60	9.2%	3.32	7.58	0%	5.91	8.79	9.82	0%	-35.31	5Y.9M
IJS-MTUM-VNQ	-19.05	4.07	8.9%	-0.51	6.34	0.7%	7.10	8.73	9.76	0%	-57.12	8Y.2M
MTUM-EMB-GLD	-2.12	4.93	1.5%	4.91	6.98	0%	6.07	8.62	10.04	0%	-26.56	3Y.3M
MTUM-EMB-TLT	-7.59	5.32	5.5%	2.02	7.97	0%	5.88	8.57	9.55	0%	-28.75	5Y.9M
MTUM-EEM-TLT	-7.24	3.80	9.2%	2.80	7.77	0%	5.04	8.55	9.90	0%	-34.03	5Y.10M
VTI-IJS-GLD	-4.97	3.87	3.4%	4.54	7.41	0%	6.86	8.53	9.26	0%	-31.57	4Y.11M
IJS-MTUM-EMB	-11.10	4.42	7.7%	2.63	6.98	0%	6.59	8.47	9.79	0%	-40.72	5Y.2M
VTI-VNQ-TLT	-8.90	4.32	7.4%	3.00	7.63	0%	6.72	8.43	9.22	0%	-35.77	5Y.1M
MTUM-VNQ-EMB	-12.97	4.22	9.2%	3.04	6.85	0%	6.02	8.39	10.32	0%	-45.98	5Y.3M
MTUM-VNQ-CWB	-16.94	2.42	9.5%	0.20	5.91	0%	6.81	8.34	9.10	0%	-53.56	8Y.7M
MTUM-CWB-GLD	-3.72	4.60	4.3%	6.38	7.72	0%	7.32	8.31	9.45	0%	-29.26	3Y.5M
MTUM-EMB-CWB	-8.95	3.64	7.4%	3.24	6.88	0%	6.42	8.31	9.40	0%	-37.02	5Y.1M
MTUM-EEM-CWB	-7.43	2.72	8%	2.93	5.57	0%	4.87	8.30	9.83	0%	-36.61	5Y.2M
MTUM-TLT-CWB	-5.72	2.50	5.5%	4.08	7.36	0%	7.28	8.25	9.21	0%	-29.85	4Y.2M
VTI-MTUM-GLD	-8.13	3.25	7.4%	5.33	7.24	0%	7.26	8.25	9.47	0%	-32.55	4Y.5M
IJS-CWB-GLD	-3.95	4.39	1.8%	4.11	7.08	0%	6.84	8.24	9.23	0%	-27.81	3Y.5M

Order by **Baseline 15Y Return - Last 30 Years** (from 1993-12 to 2023-11) - **US Infl. Adjusted**

Portfolio	3Y Rolling Annualized Return (%)			7Y Rolling Annualized Return (%)			15Y Rolling Annualized Return (%)				Max Draw-down (%)	Long Neg Period (Y.M)
	Worst	Base	%Fail	Worst	Base	%Fail	Worst	Base ▼	Median	%Fail		
MTUM-VNQ-TLT	-10.68	1.86	12.6%	-0.42	5.50	0.7%	4.35	6.71	7.59	0%	-38.50	8Y.9M
IJS-MTUM-GLD	-6.95	1.84	9.5%	3.21	6.16	0%	5.06	6.68	7.66	0%	-33.70	5Y.0M
MTUM-EMB-GLD	-7.44	3.23	6.8%	1.34	5.08	0%	3.59	6.51	7.73	0%	-28.58	5Y.9M
MTUM-TLT-GLD	-11.02	2.43	7.7%	0.21	5.05	0%	4.06	6.46	7.34	0%	-31.37	7Y.3M
IJS-MTUM-TLT	-8.95	0.17	14.2%	0.84	4.84	0%	4.92	6.42	7.35	0%	-35.07	6Y.5M
MTUM-EMB-TLT	-12.61	2.87	7.7%	-1.46	5.70	1.8%	3.41	6.41	7.14	0%	-37.50	8Y.11M
MTUM-VNQ-GLD	-8.95	1.45	9.8%	2.47	5.72	0%	4.50	6.39	7.90	0%	-39.24	4Y.11M
MTUM-VNQ-EMB	-14.85	2.07	13.2%	0.47	4.40	0%	3.55	6.38	7.94	0%	-46.81	6Y.5M
MTUM-EEM-TLT	-12.26	1.64	13.2%	-0.68	5.71	0.7%	2.58	6.36	7.55	0%	-38.66	8Y.11M
IJS-MTUM-EMB	-13.02	1.05	13.2%	0.07	4.42	0%	4.11	6.34	7.48	0%	-41.63	6Y.11M
IJS-MTUM-VNQ	-20.81	1.15	12.6%	-2.99	3.82	1.8%	4.60	6.30	7.40	0%	-57.98	10Y.11M
MTUM-SCZ-TLT	-10.85	-1.10	16.6%	-0.18	5.28	0.7%	3.44	6.25	7.41	0%	-37.79	7Y.5M
VTI-IJS-GLD	-7.03	1.57	8.3%	2.05	5.13	0%	4.26	6.03	6.87	0%	-32.62	5Y.8M
MTUM-SCZ-EMB	-13.27	-0.30	15.4%	1.04	3.89	0%	2.50	6.02	7.75	0%	-46.06	6Y.6M
MTUM-EMB-CWB	-10.92	0.05	14.8%	0.67	4.37	0%	3.94	6.02	6.92	0%	-37.98	5Y.9M
MTUM-EEM-EMB	-10.11	0.62	13.5%	0.54	4.63	0%	1.75	6.00	7.51	0%	-44.95	6Y.7M
MTUM-CWB-GLD	-6.04	1.96	9.8%	3.85	5.58	0%	4.82	5.99	7.01	0%	-31.65	4Y.1M
VTI-EMB-GLD	-4.34	2.63	7.4%	1.77	4.15	0%	3.41	5.97	7.15	0%	-27.25	5Y.1M
MTUM-VNQ-LQD	-13.97	1.20	13.2%	-0.69	4.03	0.7%	3.74	5.92	6.57	0%	-44.43	8Y.11M
VTI-VNQ-TLT	-10.87	1.45	11.7%	-0.07	5.11	0.4%	4.13	5.91	6.81	0%	-37.87	8Y.9M
VTI-MTUM-EMB	-11.94	-1.25	18.2%	-0.50	4.50	0.4%	4.35	5.90	7.07	0%	-41.40	9Y.4M

Order by **Baseline 15Y Return** - **Last 60 Years** (from 1963-12 to 2023-11)

Portfolio	3Y Rolling Annualized Return (%)			7Y Rolling Annualized Return (%)			15Y Rolling Annualized Return (%)				Max Draw-down (%)	Long Neg Period (Y.M)
	Worst	Base	%Fail	Worst	Base	%Fail	Worst	Base ▼	Median	%Fail		
IJS-VNQ-TLT	-10.35	4.33	6.4%	0.20	7.15	0%	6.40	9.07	11.29	0%	-37.77	6Y.8M
VTI-IJS-VNQ	-19.16	4.28	8.3%	-1.71	6.77	1.3%	5.58	8.90	11.94	0%	-57.10	8Y.7M
VTI-IJS-GLD	-4.97	5.40	2.3%	4.54	8.18	0%	6.67	8.85	10.62	0%	-31.57	4Y.11M
VTI-IJS-TLT	-7.23	4.47	5.3%	-0.25	7.25	0.2%	7.31	8.66	11.18	0%	-31.32	7Y.1M
IJS-VTV-GLD	-5.47	4.97	2.3%	4.17	7.86	0%	6.75	8.62	10.82	0%	-32.93	5Y.0M
IJS-VTV-VNQ	-19.75	3.73	8%	-1.57	6.35	0.9%	5.39	8.56	12.07	0%	-58.66	8Y.6M
VTI-VNQ-TLT	-8.90	3.72	7.2%	-0.48	5.93	0.3%	5.47	8.54	10.18	0%	-35.77	7Y.6M
IJS-VTV-TLT	-7.65	4.22	5.3%	-0.18	6.89	0.2%	6.79	8.49	11.43	0%	-31.90	7Y.1M
IJS-TLT-GLD	-1.86	4.74	0.6%	2.90	6.90	0%	6.28	8.48	10.06	0%	-19.87	3Y.9M
IJS-VNQ-IEI	-11.03	4.68	5.8%	1.05	6.35	0%	5.52	8.45	10.88	0%	-39.93	6Y.6M
IJS-VNQ-LQD	-13.51	4.55	6.7%	0.24	6.58	0%	5.74	8.42	10.92	0%	-44.90	6Y.8M
IJS-VNQ-BND	-12.11	4.64	6%	1.05	6.37	0%	5.47	8.28	10.79	0%	-42.21	6Y.6M
IJS-VNQ-GLD	-8.73	4.43	2.8%	3.22	7.07	0%	6.51	8.25	11.00	0%	-37.64	4Y.4M
VTI-VNQ-GLD	-7.13	4.26	2.6%	3.86	7.10	0%	5.67	8.19	9.94	0%	-37.29	4Y.8M
VTV-VNQ-GLD	-7.68	3.79	3.1%	2.79	6.75	0%	5.74	8.09	9.97	0%	-38.60	6Y.1M
VTV-VNQ-TLT	-9.52	3.00	7.3%	-0.43	6.24	0.3%	5.30	7.97	10.24	0%	-37.59	7Y.8M
VTI-IJS-LQD	-10.36	4.49	6.6%	-0.16	6.67	0.2%	6.26	7.91	11.02	0%	-37.60	7Y.1M
VTI-VTV-GLD	-6.61	4.36	4.5%	3.24	7.31	0%	5.70	7.89	9.84	0%	-32.70	5Y.5M
VTI-TLT-GLD	-2.75	4.12	1.8%	3.17	6.45	0%	5.83	7.88	9.27	0%	-21.42	4Y.9M
VTV-TLT-GLD	-2.35	3.83	2.2%	2.17	6.25	0%	5.95	7.87	9.18	0%	-18.03	6Y.3M
IJS-LQD-GLD	-0.12	4.40	0.2%	3.09	6.74	0%	5.88	7.75	9.38	0%	-20.10	3Y.0M

Order by **Baseline 15Y Return** - **Last 60 Years** (from 1963-12 to 2023-11) - **US Infl. Adjusted**

Portfolio	3Y Rolling Annualized Return (%)			7Y Rolling Annualized Return (%)			15Y Rolling Annualized Return (%)				Max Draw-down (%)	Long Neg Period (Y.M)
	Worst	Base	%Fail	Worst	Base	%Fail	Worst	Base ▼	Median	%Fail		
VTI-IJS-GLD	-7.03	1.83	8.8%	1.50	4.76	0%	3.50	6.07	7.38	0%	-33.09	6Y.4M
IJS-VTV-GLD	-7.52	1.88	9.9%	1.43	4.70	0%	3.57	6.01	7.37	0%	-34.29	6Y.4M
IJS-TLT-GLD	-7.17	1.64	9.6%	-0.61	3.77	0.3%	3.59	5.52	6.88	0%	-27.87	8Y.9M
IJS-VNQ-GLD	-10.62	0.93	12.1%	1.40	3.99	0%	3.34	5.31	8.00	0%	-38.59	5Y.11M
VTI-IJS-TLT	-13.66	-0.29	16.1%	-5.92	2.52	6.1%	0.51	5.23	7.22	0%	-43.50	14Y.2M
IJS-VTV-TLT	-12.45	-0.25	15.8%	-5.85	2.42	5%	0.80	5.08	7.37	0%	-43.11	13Y.11M
VTI-IJS-VNQ	-20.91	0.29	14.3%	-7.48	2.79	6.3%	1.85	5.03	7.97	0%	-57.97	11Y.9M
IJS-LQD-GLD	-3.68	1.31	9.6%	0.71	3.63	0%	3.32	5.00	6.54	0%	-26.02	5Y.11M
VTI-VTV-GLD	-8.87	0.50	13.1%	-0.08	3.66	0.2%	2.55	5.00	6.40	0%	-33.91	9Y.2M
IJS-VTV-VNQ	-21.49	0.05	14.6%	-7.20	2.57	6.4%	2.18	4.98	8.15	0%	-59.49	11Y.8M
VTV-VNQ-GLD	-9.59	0.30	13.6%	-1.15	3.73	2.2%	2.59	4.90	6.85	0%	-39.54	8Y.0M
IJS-IEI-GLD	-3.36	1.57	8.8%	0.55	3.41	0%	3.10	4.87	6.44	0%	-24.42	6Y.2M
VTI-VNQ-GLD	-9.05	0.53	12.1%	0.11	3.76	0%	2.53	4.87	6.79	0%	-38.25	6Y.11M
IJS-VNQ-TLT	-13.48	-0.03	15%	-5.49	2.47	6.1%	1.43	4.79	7.91	0%	-40.40	11Y.9M
IJS-BND-GLD	-3.32	1.54	9.2%	0.52	3.45	0%	3.10	4.78	6.33	0%	-24.40	6Y.2M
VTV-VNQ-TLT	-11.81	-1.48	20%		0.34	12.9%	-0.92	4.46	6.92	5.4%	-39.96	18Y.8M
IJS-VNQ-LQD	-15.38	0.06	14.7%	-5.68	2.64	5.7%	1.71	4.43	7.27	0%	-47.11	11Y.7M
VTI-IJS-LQD	-14.80	-0.10	15.3%	-5.86	2.55	7.2%	0.78	4.39	6.69	0%	-43.69	13Y.11M
IJS-VNQ-IEI	-13.02	0.26	13.1%	-4.89	2.83	5.3%	2.16	4.37	7.17	0%	-42.28	11Y.2M
IJS-VNQ-BND	-14.01	0.33	13.4%	-4.89	2.77	5.3%	2.16	4.36	7.09	0%	-44.47	11Y.2M
IJS-SHY-GLD	-3.45	1.36	8.3%	0.80	3.22	0%	2.69	4.34	5.90	0%	-23.25	5Y.9M

Order by **Baseline 15Y Return - All data** (from 1871/1927 to 2023-11)

Portfolio	3Y Rolling Annualized Return (%)			7Y Rolling Annualized Return (%)			15Y Rolling Annualized Return (%)				Max Draw-down (%)	Long Neg Period (Y.M)
	Worst	Base	%Fail	Worst	Base	%Fail	Worst	Base ▼	Median	%Fail		
VTI-IJS-GLD	-31.68	3.61	8%	-1.21	7.03	0.3%	2.78	8.60	10.46	0%	-71.16	13Y.1M
VTI-IJS-VNQ	-39.20	1.77	12.2%	-5.45	5.76	2.9%	1.35	8.41	11.27	0%	-80.53	14Y.4M
IJS-VTV-GLD	-31.37	3.52	7.8%	-1.56	6.92	0.7%	2.54	8.39	10.43	0%	-70.94	13Y.1M
VTI-IJS-TLT	-30.95	2.77	9.5%	-1.80	6.72	1.1%	3.14	8.33	10.44	0%	-70.39	12Y.10M
IJS-VTV-TLT	-30.69	2.74	9.6%	-2.21	6.25	1.2%	2.87	8.10	10.47	0%	-70.22	13Y.0M
IJS-VTV-VNQ	-38.86	1.67	12%	-5.82	5.46	2.7%	1.15	8.08	11.33	0%	-80.31	14Y.4M
VTI-IJS-VTV	-45.31	0.37	14.3%	-7.42	5.31	4.1%	0.53	7.91	12.04	0%	-85.89	14Y.9M
VTI-IJS-LQD	-30.34	2.75	10.4%	-1.58	6.13	0.7%	3.14	7.81	10.54	0%	-69.55	12Y.10M
VTI-IJS-IEI	-30.26	2.87	9.7%	-1.57	6.25	0.7%	3.07	7.71	10.62	0%	-69.44	12Y.10M
VTI-IJS-BND	-30.25	2.64	10%	-1.56	6.11	0.7%	3.08	7.65	10.59	0%	-69.43	12Y.10M
IJS-VTV-LQD	-30.05	2.45	10%	-1.98	5.79	1.1%	2.87	7.63	10.56	0%	-69.35	13Y.0M
IJS-VTV-IEI	-29.97	2.62	9.8%	-1.97	5.83	1%	2.80	7.46	10.63	0%	-69.24	13Y.1M
IJS-VTV-BND	-29.96	2.45	10.1%	-1.97	5.75	1%	2.81	7.40	10.61	0%	-69.23	13Y.0M
VTI-VTV-GLD	-29.53	2.54	9.4%	-1.75	5.56	0.7%	1.57	7.29	9.26	0%	-68.54	13Y.5M
IJS-VNQ-LQD	-23.67	2.71	9.4%	-1.02	5.57	0.3%	2.94	7.19	9.31	0%	-60.02	12Y.8M
IJS-VNQ-BND	-23.59	2.72	9.1%	-1.00	5.51	0.3%	2.88	7.14	9.19	0%	-59.89	12Y.8M
IJS-VNQ-IEI	-23.60	2.79	9%	-1.01	5.59	0.3%	2.87	7.13	9.25	0%	-59.90	12Y.8M
VTI-IJS-SHY	-30.18	2.55	10.2%	-1.75	5.59	0.7%	2.70	7.11	10.58	0%	-69.30	13Y.1M
IJS-VNQ-TLT	-24.21	2.77	9.2%	-1.17	5.51	0.3%	2.98	7.06	9.64	0%	-60.93	12Y.8M
IJS-VNQ-SHY	-23.56	2.69	9.2%	-1.21	5.10	0.3%	2.48	6.99	8.92	0%	-59.80	13Y.1M
VTI-VTV-VNQ	-37.22	1.00	13.8%	-6.20	4.88	3.5%	-0.26	6.89	10.04	0.1%	-78.65	15Y.3M

Order by **Baseline 15Y Return - All data** (from 1871/1927 to 2023-11) - **US Infl. Adjusted**

Portfolio	3Y Rolling Annualized Return (%)			7Y Rolling Annualized Return (%)			15Y Rolling Annualized Return (%)				Max Draw-down (%)	Long Neg Period (Y.M)
	Worst	Base	%Fail	Worst	Base	%Fail	Worst	Base ▼	Median	%Fail		
VTI-IJS-GLD	-26.27	0.71	13.6%	-1.50	4.48	1.3%	2.89	5.33	7.25	0%	-63.58	12Y.9M
IJS-VTV-GLD	-25.93	0.52	13.9%	-1.57	4.17	1.4%	2.78	5.21	7.17	0%	-63.30	13Y.0M
VTI-IJS-VNQ	-34.38	-0.67	17.1%	-7.48	2.85	5.3%	0.23	4.41	7.79	0%	-75.41	14Y.3M
IJS-VTV-VNQ	-34.02	-0.91	16.9%	-7.20	2.61	5.5%	0.21	4.41	7.86	0%	-75.13	14Y.3M
VTI-IJS-IEI	-24.73	-0.36	15.6%	-5.09	3.28	3.6%	1.24	4.05	6.70	0%	-61.41	12Y.11M
VTI-IJS-BND	-24.72	-0.77	16%	-5.09	3.19	3.8%	1.24	4.02	6.70	0%	-61.39	12Y.10M
IJS-VNQ-GLD	-19.17	-0.13	15.3%	-1.31	3.21	2%	2.11	4.01	6.04	0%	-52.13	9Y.3M
VTI-IJS-LQD	-24.82	-0.99	16.6%	-5.86	3.14	4.6%	0.78	4.00	6.73	0%	-61.54	13Y.11M
VTI-VTV-GLD	-23.94	-0.24	15.8%	-2.43	3.04	2.9%	1.42	3.98	5.97	0%	-60.27	13Y.4M
VTI-IJS-TLT	-25.48	-0.64	17%	-5.92	3.21	3.7%	0.51	3.89	7.01	0%	-62.61	14Y.2M
IJS-VTV-IEI	-24.42	-0.19	16%	-5.03	2.92	3.2%	1.53	3.88	6.75	0%	-61.15	12Y.9M
IJS-VTV-BND	-24.41	-0.49	16.4%	-5.03	2.90	3.3%	1.53	3.87	6.75	0%	-61.14	12Y.9M
IJS-VTV-LQD	-24.50	-0.67	16.7%	-5.76	2.89	3.3%	1.07	3.86	6.74	0%	-61.29	13Y.8M
VTI-IJS-VTV	-40.98	-2.58	18.9%	-7.75	2.21	8.1%	0.38	3.83	8.10	0%	-82.18	14Y.8M
VTI-IJS-SHY	-24.65	-0.42	16.2%	-4.89	2.84	4.1%	1.67	3.81	6.59	0%	-61.23	13Y.0M
IJS-VTV-TLT	-25.19	-0.82	16.9%	-5.85	2.83	3.3%	0.80	3.78	6.98	0%	-62.40	13Y.11M
IJS-VTV-SHY	-24.33	-0.61	16.3%	-4.82	2.67	3.8%	1.96	3.74	6.67	0%	-60.97	13Y.1M
IJS-LQD-GLD	-9.29	0.39	13.7%	-2.32	3.07	1.5%	1.29	3.68	5.59	0%	-28.57	8Y.9M
IJS-VNQ-LQD	-17.62	-0.22	15.6%	-5.68	2.75	3.8%	0.16	3.67	6.01	0%	-49.52	13Y.11M
IJS-VNQ-BND	-17.53	0.05	14.8%	-4.89	2.83	3.8%	0.56	3.67	5.98	0%	-49.35	13Y.9M
IJS-BND-GLD	-9.26	0.48	13.3%	-2.32	2.97	1.8%	1.23	3.67	5.43	0%	-28.34	8Y.9M

Ranking: Median 15Y Return

Order by **Median 15Y Return** - **Last 30 Years** (from 1993-12 to 2023-11)

Portfolio	3Y Rolling Annualized Return (%)			7Y Rolling Annualized Return (%)			15Y Rolling Annualized Return (%)				Max Draw-down (%)	Long Neg Period (Y.M)
	Worst	Base	%Fail	Worst	Base	%Fail	Worst	Base	Median ▼	%Fail		
SCZ-VNQ-EMB	-14.50	2.67	10.2%	2.11	5.97	0%	4.01	6.65	10.68	0%	-49.86	5Y.2M
SCZ-EMB-GLD	-2.67	1.46	7.1%	2.16	4.28	0%	3.93	7.02	10.61	0%	-30.32	4Y.10M
SCZ-EMB-TLT	-7.70	4.73	6.8%	-0.17	6.29	0.7%	3.87	7.19	10.56	0%	-30.85	7Y.4M
EEM-VNQ-EMB	-11.07	2.31	6.5%	1.73	5.26	0%	3.03	6.65	10.47	0%	-48.25	6Y.0M
VNQ-EMB-GLD	-2.35	2.17	4.6%	2.21	4.97	0%	4.85	7.13	10.46	0%	-27.11	3Y.9M
EEM-VNQ-TLT	-6.53	3.53	5.8%	0.54	5.62	0%	3.88	7.47	10.43	0%	-39.05	7Y.3M
MTUM-VNQ-GLD	-7.03	4.62	3.7%	6.09	7.87	0%	6.99	9.01	10.37	0%	-38.30	3Y.9M
IJS-EMB-GLD	-0.55	4.26	1.8%	2.41	5.83	0%	5.71	7.78	10.37	0%	-23.57	3Y.4M
MTUM-VNQ-EMB	-12.97	4.22	9.2%	3.04	6.85	0%	6.02	8.39	10.32	0%	-45.98	5Y.3M
IJS-SCZ-EMB	-12.51	3.54	8.9%	3.21	5.98	0%	4.58	6.77	10.30	0%	-44.94	5Y.1M
MTUM-SCZ-EMB	-11.35	2.35	9.8%	4.58	6.22	0%	4.94	8.10	10.23	0%	-45.22	5Y.0M
EEM-EMB-TLT	-9.23	4.03	7.7%	-0.67	4.25	0.7%	2.83	7.02	10.22	0%	-31.98	9Y.2M
IJS-EEM-EMB	-9.11	3.08	4.3%	1.88	6.26	0%	3.90	6.74	10.20	0%	-43.21	5Y.10M
VNQ-EMB-TLT	-6.83	3.71	6.8%	-0.46	6.20	0.7%	4.67	7.11	10.19	0%	-31.29	7Y.5M
EEM-EMB-GLD	-7.46	-0.18	15.7%	0.13	2.89	0%	2.76	6.51	10.17	0%	-33.38	9Y.10M
EEM-VNQ-GLD	-4.88	0.50	13.5%	0.57	3.39	0%	3.73	6.62	10.16	0%	-40.89	7Y.10M
IJS-VNQ-EMB	-14.37	3.96	7.7%	2.59	6.35	0%	5.55	7.11	10.14	0%	-47.23	5Y.5M
SCZ-EEM-EMB	-9.57	1.31	8.9%	1.69	4.68	0%	1.88	6.31	10.11	0%	-47.64	6Y.3M
IJS-VNQ-GLD	-8.73	3.55	4.9%	3.22	6.71	0%	6.52	7.94	10.08	0%	-37.64	4Y.4M
IJS-EEM-TLT	-4.67	4.20	3.1%	1.84	6.52	0%	4.80	7.81	10.04	0%	-33.46	6Y.1M
MTUM-EMB-GLD	-2.12	4.93	1.5%	4.91	6.98	0%	6.07	8.62	10.04	0%	-26.56	3Y.3M

Order by **Median 15Y Return** - **Last 30 Years** (from 1993-12 to 2023-11) - **US Infl. Adjusted**

Portfolio	3Y Rolling Annualized Return (%)			7Y Rolling Annualized Return (%)			15Y Rolling Annualized Return (%)				Max Draw-down (%)	Long Neg Period (Y.M)
	Worst	Base	%Fail	Worst	Base	%Fail	Worst	Base	Median ▼	%Fail		
VNQ-EMB-GLD	-6.18	-0.16	15.7%	-1.02	2.49	1.8%	2.40	5.02	8.16	0%	-27.52	10Y.0M
SCZ-VNQ-EMB	-16.35	0.04	14.5%	-1.37	3.79	2.9%	1.57	4.60	8.09	0%	-50.89	9Y.4M
EEM-VNQ-EMB	-12.99	0.20	14.5%	-1.74	3.44	2.9%	0.62	4.55	8.07	0%	-49.04	10Y.10M
SCZ-EMB-GLD	-7.11	-1.11	18.5%	-0.70	1.95	1.1%	1.50	4.86	8.06	0%	-32.71	11Y.6M
SCZ-EMB-TLT	-12.69	2.37	8.6%	-3.55	4.53	7.2%	1.44	5.13	8.04	0%	-38.63	11Y.8M
IJS-EMB-GLD	-3.96	2.05	8.9%	0.40	3.66	0%	3.25	5.54	8.00	0%	-26.93	6Y.3M
MTUM-VNQ-EMB	-14.85	2.07	13.2%	0.47	4.40	0%	3.55	6.38	7.94	0%	-46.81	6Y.5M
EEM-EMB-TLT	-14.14	1.83	9.5%	-4.04	2.56	7.2%	0.42	4.89	7.94	0%	-41.09	14Y.1M
EEM-VNQ-TLT	-11.48	1.38	8.3%	-2.87	3.71	4%	1.45	5.01	7.94	0%	-39.99	11Y.9M
MTUM-VNQ-GLD	-8.95	1.45	9.5%	2.47	5.72	0%	4.50	6.39	7.90	0%	-39.24	4Y.1M
EEM-EMB-GLD	-8.37	-2.47	25.9%	-1.39	0.58	8.7%	0.35	4.51	7.84	0%	-34.56	13Y.2M
EEM-VNQ-GLD	-6.94	-2.14	24.6%	-1.94	1.19	5.8%	1.31	4.36	7.78	0%	-41.79	11Y.6M
IJS-SCZ-EMB	-14.41	0.09	14.8%	-0.05	3.77	0.4%	2.14	4.62	7.77	0%	-46.05	7Y.7M
IJS-EEM-EMB	-11.08	0.92	11.7%	-0.50	4.24	0.7%	1.47	4.72	7.75	0%	-44.08	9Y.5M
MTUM-SCZ-EMB	-13.27	-0.30	15.4%	1.04	3.89	0%	2.50	6.02	7.75	0%	-46.06	6Y.0M
MTUM-EMB-GLD	-7.44	3.23	6.8%	1.34	5.08	0%	3.59	6.51	7.73	0%	-28.58	5Y.9M
SCZ-EEM-EMB	-11.53	-0.79	20%	-1.64	2.37	2.9%	-0.50	4.09	7.68	1.1%	-48.44	16Y.0M
IJS-MTUM-GLD	-6.95	1.84	9.5%	3.21	6.16	0%	5.06	6.68	7.66	0%	-33.70	5Y.0M
VNQ-EMB-TLT	-11.87	1.49	11.4%	-3.85	4.28	5.4%	2.22	4.98	7.65	0%	-37.74	11Y.9M
IJS-VNQ-EMB	-16.23	0.69	13.9%	-0.41	4.05	0.7%	3.09	4.86	7.59	0%	-48.80	7Y.7M
MTUM-VNQ-TLT	-10.68	1.86	12.6%	-0.42	5.50	0.7%	4.35	6.71	7.59	0%	-38.50	8Y.9M

Order by **Median 15Y Return** - **Last 60 Years** (from 1963-12 to 2023-11)

Portfolio	3Y Rolling Annualized Return (%)			7Y Rolling Annualized Return (%)			15Y Rolling Annualized Return (%)				Max Draw-down (%)	Long Neg Period (Y.M)
	Worst	Base	%Fail	Worst	Base	%Fail	Worst	Base	Median ▼	%Fail		
IJS-VTV-VNQ	-19.75	3.73	8%	-1.57	6.35	0.9%	5.39	8.56	12.07	0%	-58.66	8Y.6M
VTI-IJS-VNQ	-19.16	4.28	8.3%	-1.71	6.77	1.3%	5.58	8.90	11.94	0%	-57.10	8Y.7M
VTI-IJS-VTV	-16.60	2.81	11%	-2.35	5.97	1.4%	5.63	7.75	11.81	0%	-52.88	10Y.11M
IJS-VTV-TLT	-7.65	4.22	5.3%	-0.18	6.89	0.2%	6.79	8.49	11.43	0%	-31.90	7Y.1M
IJS-VNQ-TLT	-10.35	4.33	6.4%	0.20	7.15	0%	6.40	9.07	11.29	0%	-37.77	6Y.8M
IJS-VTV-IEI	-8.40	4.15	5.4%	0.69	6.31	0%	5.82	7.40	11.28	0%	-34.39	6Y.6M
IJS-VTV-BND	-9.49	3.99	5.8%	0.69	6.10	0%	5.73	7.35	11.20	0%	-36.83	6Y.6M
VTI-IJS-TLT	-7.23	4.47	5.3%	-0.25	7.25	0.2%	7.31	8.66	11.18	0%	-31.32	7Y.1M
IJS-VTV-LQD	-10.88	4.19	6%	-0.08	6.31	0.2%	5.94	7.66	11.10	0%	-39.68	7Y.0M
VTI-IJS-IEI	-7.89	4.49	5.4%	0.62	6.71	0%	6.32	7.68	11.07	0%	-32.26	6Y.7M
VTI-IJS-LQD	-10.36	4.49	6.6%	-0.16	6.67	0.2%	6.26	7.91	11.02	0%	-37.60	7Y.1M
IJS-VTV-SHY	-9.25	4.01	6%	0.72	5.73	0%	5.11	6.74	11.01	0%	-36.36	6Y.6M
IJS-VNQ-GLD	-8.73	4.43	2.8%	3.22	7.07	0%	6.51	8.25	11.00	0%	-37.64	4Y.4M
VTI-IJS-BND	-8.97	4.40	6%	0.63	6.56	0%	6.23	7.62	10.94	0%	-34.68	6Y.7M
IJS-VNQ-LQD	-13.51	4.55	6.7%	0.24	6.50	0%	5.74	8.42	10.92	0%	-44.90	6Y.8M
IJS-VNQ-IEI	-11.03	4.68	5.8%	1.05	6.35	0%	5.52	8.45	10.88	0%	-39.93	6Y.6M
VTI-VTV-VNQ	-18.65	3.21	10.8%	-2.22	5.44	1.1%	4.93	7.74	10.83	0%	-57.34	10Y.11M
IJS-VTV-GLD	-5.47	4.97	2.3%	4.17	7.86	0%	6.75	8.62	10.82	0%	-32.93	5Y.0M
VTI-IJS-SHY	-8.74	4.33	6%	0.71	6.18	0%	5.61	6.98	10.82	0%	-34.21	6Y.6M
IJS-VNQ-BND	-12.11	4.64	6%	1.05	6.37	0%	5.47	8.28	10.79	0%	-42.21	6Y.6M
VTI-IJS-GLD	-4.97	5.40	2.3%	4.54	8.18	0%	6.67	8.85	10.62	0%	-31.57	4Y.11M

Order by **Median 15Y Return** - **Last 60 Years** (from 1963-12 to 2023-11) - **US Infl. Adjusted**

Portfolio	3Y Rolling Annualized Return (%)			7Y Rolling Annualized Return (%)			15Y Rolling Annualized Return (%)				Max Draw-down (%)	Long Neg Period (Y.M)
	Worst	Base	%Fail	Worst	Base	%Fail	Worst	Base	Median ▼	%Fail		
IJS-VTV-VNQ	-21.49	0.05	14.6%	-7.20	2.57	6.4%	2.18	4.98	8.15	0%	-59.49	11Y.4M
IJS-VNQ-GLD	-10.62	0.93	12.1%	1.40	3.99	0%	3.34	5.31	8.00	0%	-38.59	5Y.11M
VTI-IJS-VNQ	-20.91	0.29	14.3%	-7.48	2.79	6.3%	1.85	5.03	7.97	0%	-57.97	11Y.7M
IJS-VNQ-TLT	-13.48	-0.03	15%	-5.49	2.47	6.1%	1.43	4.79	7.91	0%	-40.40	11Y.9M
VTI-IJS-VTV	-18.40	-0.57	16.6%	-7.75	2.08	6.9%	1.16	3.91	7.67	0%	-53.82	13Y.8M
VTI-IJS-GLD	-7.03	1.83	8.8%	1.50	4.76	0%	3.50	6.07	7.38	0%	-33.09	6Y.4M
IJS-VTV-GLD	-7.52	1.88	9.9%	1.43	4.70	0%	3.57	6.01	7.37	0%	-34.29	6Y.4M
IJS-VTV-TLT	-12.45	-0.25	15.8%	-5.85	2.42	5%	0.80	5.08	7.37	0%	-43.11	13Y.11M
IJS-VNQ-LQD	-15.38	0.06	14.7%	-5.68	2.64	5.7%	1.71	4.43	7.27	0%	-47.11	11Y.7M
VTI-IJS-TLT	-13.66	-0.29	16.1%	-5.92	2.52	6.1%	0.51	5.23	7.22	0%	-43.50	14Y.2M
IJS-VNQ-IEI	-13.02	0.26	13.1%	-4.89	2.83	5.3%	2.16	4.37	7.17	0%	-42.28	11Y.2M
IJS-VNQ-BND	-14.01	0.33	13.4%	-4.89	2.77	5.3%	2.16	4.36	7.09	0%	-44.47	11Y.2M
VTI-VNQ-TLT	-13.01	-0.81	16.9%	-6.13	0.75	10.8%	-0.88	4.16	7.03	4.3%	-40.04	18Y.8M
VTV-VNQ-TLT	-11.81	-1.48	20%	-6.09	0.34	12.9%	-0.92	4.46	6.92	5.4%	-39.96	18Y.8M
IJS-VTV-IEI	-11.71	0.44	14%	-5.03	2.58	4.6%	1.53	4.16	6.89	0%	-40.26	11Y.10M
IJS-VTV-LQD	-13.32	-0.14	15.3%	-5.76	2.41	5%	1.07	4.20	6.88	0%	-43.29	13Y.8M
IJS-TLT-GLD	-7.17	1.64	9.6%	-0.61	3.77	0.3%	3.59	5.52	6.88	0%	-27.87	8Y.9M
VTV-VNQ-GLD	-9.59	0.30	13.6%	-1.15	3.73	2.2%	2.59	4.90	6.85	0%	-39.54	8Y.0M
IJS-VTV-BND	-11.71	0.06	14.7%	-5.03	2.47	4.9%	1.53	3.98	6.82	0%	-40.24	11Y.10M
VTI-VTV-VNQ	-20.42	-1.01	17.5%	-7.78	1.22	10.4%	-0.08	4.11	6.82	0.2%	-58.20	15Y.3M
VTI-VNQ-GLD	-9.05	0.53	12.1%	0.11	3.76	0%	2.53	4.87	6.79	0%	-38.25	6Y.11M

Order by **Median 15Y Return - All data** (from 1871/1927 to 2023-11)

Portfolio	3Y Rolling Annualized Return (%)			7Y Rolling Annualized Return (%)			15Y Rolling Annualized Return (%)				Max Draw-down (%)	Long Neg Period (Y.M)
	Worst	Base	%Fail	Worst	Base	%Fail	Worst	Base	Median ▼	%Fail		
VTI-IJS-VTV	-45.31	0.37	14.3%	-7.42	5.31	4.1%	0.53	7.91	12.04	0%	-85.89	14Y.9M
IJS-VTV-VNQ	-38.86	1.67	12%	-5.82	5.46	2.7%	1.15	8.08	11.33	0%	-80.31	14Y.4M
VTI-IJS-VNQ	-39.20	1.77	12.2%	-5.45	5.76	2.9%	1.35	8.41	11.27	0%	-80.53	14Y.4M
IJS-VTV-IEI	-29.97	2.62	9.8%	-1.97	5.83	1%	2.80	7.46	10.63	0%	-69.24	13Y.1M
VTI-IJS-IEI	-30.26	2.87	9.7%	-1.57	6.25	0.7%	3.07	7.71	10.62	0%	-69.44	12Y.10M
IJS-VTV-BND	-29.96	2.45	10.1%	-1.97	5.75	1%	2.81	7.40	10.61	0%	-69.23	13Y.0M
VTI-IJS-BND	-30.25	2.64	10%	-1.56	6.11	0.7%	3.08	7.65	10.59	0%	-69.43	12Y.10M
VTI-IJS-SHY	-30.18	2.55	10.2%	-1.75	5.59	0.7%	2.70	7.11	10.58	0%	-69.30	13Y.1M
IJS-VTV-SHY	-29.89	2.22	10.1%	-2.15	5.25	1.1%	2.43	6.84	10.56	0%	-69.09	13Y.3M
IJS-VTV-LQD	-30.05	2.45	10%	-1.98	5.79	1.1%	2.87	7.63	10.56	0%	-69.35	13Y.0M
VTI-IJS-LQD	-30.34	2.75	10.4%	-1.58	6.13	0.7%	3.14	7.81	10.54	0%	-69.55	12Y.10M
IJS-VTV-TLT	-30.69	2.74	9.6%	-2.21	6.25	1.2%	2.87	8.10	10.47	0%	-70.22	13Y.0M
VTI-IJS-GLD	-31.68	3.61	8%	-1.21	7.03	0.3%	2.78	8.60	10.46	0%	-71.16	13Y.1M
VTI-IJS-TLT	-30.95	2.77	9.5%	-1.80	6.72	1.1%	3.14	8.33	10.44	0%	-70.39	12Y.10M
IJS-VTV-GLD	-31.37	3.52	7.8%	-1.56	6.92	0.7%	2.54	8.39	10.43	0%	-70.94	13Y.1M
IJS-VTV-BIL	-30.45	1.94	10.6%	-2.78	4.75	1.8%	1.97	6.41	10.27	0%	-69.79	13Y.5M
VTI-IJS-BIL	-30.76	2.22	10.9%	-2.39	5.09	1.4%	2.24	6.70	10.22	0%	-70.02	13Y.5M
VTI-VTV-VNQ	-37.22	1.00	13.8%	-6.20	4.88	3.5%	-0.26	6.89	10.04	0.1%	-78.65	15Y.3M
IJS-VNQ-TLT	-24.21	2.77	9.2%	-1.17	5.51	0.3%	2.98	7.06	9.64	0%	-60.93	12Y.8M
VTI-VTV-TLT	-28.82	1.53	11.1%	-2.59	4.97	2%	1.85	6.42	9.38	0%	-67.74	13Y.4M
IJS-VNQ-LQD	-23.67	2.71	9.4%	-1.02	5.57	0.3%	2.94	7.19	9.31	0%	-60.02	12Y.8M

Order by **Median 15Y Return - All data** (from 1871/1927 to 2023-11) - **US Infl. Adjusted**

Portfolio	3Y Rolling Annualized Return (%)			7Y Rolling Annualized Return (%)			15Y Rolling Annualized Return (%)				Max Draw-down (%)	Long Neg Period (Y.M)
	Worst	Base	%Fail	Worst	Base	%Fail	Worst	Base	Median ▼	%Fail		
VTI-IJS-VTV	-40.98	-2.58	18.9%	-7.75	2.21	8.1%	0.38	3.83	8.10	0%	-82.18	14Y.9M
IJS-VTV-VNQ	-34.02	-0.91	16.9%	-7.20	2.61	5.5%	0.21	4.41	7.86	0%	-75.13	14Y.3M
VTI-IJS-VNQ	-34.38	-0.67	17.1%	-7.48	2.85	5.3%	0.23	4.41	7.79	0%	-75.41	14Y.3M
VTI-IJS-GLD	-26.27	0.71	13.6%	-1.50	4.48	1.3%	2.89	5.33	7.25	0%	-63.58	12Y.9M
IJS-VTV-GLD	-25.93	0.52	13.9%	-1.57	4.17	1.4%	2.78	5.21	7.17	0%	-63.30	13Y.0M
VTI-IJS-TLT	-25.48	-0.64	17%	-5.92	3.21	3.7%	0.51	3.89	7.01	0%	-62.61	14Y.2M
IJS-VTV-TLT	-25.19	-0.82	16.9%	-5.85	2.83	3.3%	0.80	3.78	6.98	0%	-62.40	13Y.11M
IJS-VTV-IEI	-24.42	-0.19	16%	-5.03	2.92	3.2%	1.53	3.88	6.75	0%	-61.15	12Y.9M
IJS-VTV-BND	-24.41	-0.49	16.4%	-5.03	2.90	3.3%	1.53	3.87	6.75	0%	-61.14	12Y.9M
IJS-VTV-LQD	-24.50	-0.67	16.7%	-5.76	2.89	3.3%	1.07	3.86	6.74	0%	-61.29	13Y.8M
VTI-IJS-LQD	-24.82	-0.99	16.6%	-5.86	3.14	4.6%	0.78	4.00	6.73	0%	-61.54	13Y.11M
VTI-IJS-IEI	-24.73	-0.36	15.6%	-5.09	3.28	3.6%	1.24	4.05	6.70	0%	-61.41	12Y.11M
VTI-IJS-BND	-24.72	-0.77	16%	-5.09	3.19	3.8%	1.24	4.02	6.70	0%	-61.39	12Y.10M
IJS-VTV-SHY	-24.33	-0.61	16.3%	-4.82	2.67	3.8%	1.96	3.74	6.67	0%	-60.97	13Y.1M
VTI-IJS-SHY	-24.65	-0.42	16.2%	-4.89	2.84	4.1%	1.67	3.81	6.59	0%	-61.23	13Y.0M
VTI-VTV-VNQ	-32.24	-2.15	18.9%	-7.78	1.25	9.7%	-0.81	2.62	6.57	0.8%	-73.05	16Y.2M
IJS-VTV-BIL	-24.93	-1.06	17.4%	-4.66	2.43	4.4%	1.85	3.50	6.36	0%	-61.85	13Y.4M
VTI-IJS-BIL	-25.27	-1.05	16.7%	-4.86	2.43	4.7%	1.72	3.60	6.29	0%	-62.14	13Y.3M
IJS-VNQ-TLT	-18.20	-0.19	15.8%	-5.49	2.68	4%	0.11	3.56	6.18	0%	-50.66	14Y.0M
IJS-VNQ-GLD	-19.17	-0.13	15.3%	-1.31	3.21	2%	2.11	4.01	6.04	0%	-52.13	9Y.3M
IJS-VNQ-LQD	-17.62	-0.22	15.6%	-5.68	2.75	3.8%	0.16	3.67	6.01	0%	-49.52	13Y.11M

Lazy Portfolios with 4 equally weighted Assets

If your budget allows, you can consider portfolios with 4 assets. In the case of equally weighted assets, each will account for 25% of the total.

Diversification becomes more intriguing in these instances, and we can discover various combinations of portfolios that almost suit different types of goals and time horizons well.

Ranking: Baseline 3Y Return

Order by **Baseline 3Y Return - Last 30 Years** (from 1993-12 to 2023-11)

Portfolio	3Y Rolling Annualized Return (%)			7Y Rolling Annualized Return (%)			15Y Rolling Annualized Return (%)				Max Draw-down (%)	Long Neg Period (Y.M)
	Worst	Base ▼	%Fail	Worst	Base	%Fail	Worst	Base	Median	%Fail		
MTUM-EMB-TLT-GLD	-5.80	5.65	4.3%	2.74	6.59	0%	5.74	8.46	9.84	0%	-23.20	4Y.2M
IJS-EMB-TLT-CWB	-4.83	5.58	3.4%	3.04	7.44	0%	6.09	7.84	9.27	0%	-24.94	4Y.3M
MTUM-BNDX-EMB-TLT	-6.67	5.43	5.8%	1.64	7.24	0%	5.40	7.73	8.66	0%	-24.50	5Y.2M
MTUM-EMB-TLT-IEI	-6.66	5.41	5.2%	1.58	7.02	0%	5.09	7.38	8.41	0%	-24.34	5Y.2M
MTUM-BND-EMB-TLT	-6.99	5.37	5.2%	1.52	6.98	0%	5.08	7.42	8.36	0%	-25.55	5Y.10M
MTUM-VNQ-EMB-GLD	-5.15	5.28	2.8%	4.49	7.22	0%	6.13	8.57	10.47	0%	-32.69	3Y.8M
VTV-VNQ-EMB-CWB	-13.12	5.27	7.7%	1.85	6.22	0%	5.87	7.57	8.79	0%	-45.72	5Y.5M
IJS-MTUM-VNQ-GLD	-9.69	5.26	5.5%	4.37	8.19	0%	7.14	9.00	10.14	0%	-41.66	4Y.5M
IJS-TLT-IEI-CWB	-3.02	5.24	2.2%	3.19	6.85	0%	5.98	7.19	8.05	0%	-22.81	3Y.10M
MTUM-EMB-TLT-LQD	-7.31	5.23	5.8%	1.62	7.16	0%	5.34	7.65	8.69	0%	-26.76	5Y.10M
IJS-MTUM-EMB-GLD	-3.81	5.18	1.2%	5.16	8.03	0%	6.57	8.83	10.19	0%	-28.14	3Y.5M
IJS-MTUM-TLT-GLD	-1.31	5.18	1.5%	4.78	8.28	0%	7.15	9.12	9.86	0%	-21.70	3Y.4M
IJS-VNQ-CWB-LQD	-12.95	5.17	7.1%	1.34	6.13	0%	5.88	7.40	8.47	0%	-43.85	5Y.7M
IJS-BNDX-TLT-CWB	-3.98	5.17	3.1%	3.29	6.89	0%	6.23	7.47	8.26	0%	-22.96	4Y.3M
MTUM-VNQ-TLT-GLD	-3.65	5.16	2.5%	3.63	7.66	0%	6.60	8.82	10.07	0%	-25.25	3Y.9M
IJS-TLT-CWB-GLD	-1.12	5.16	1.2%	4.58	6.80	0%	6.75	8.26	9.31	0%	-20.66	3Y.3M
IJS-TLT-CWB-LQD	-4.25	5.15	3.1%	3.21	6.83	0%	6.19	7.44	8.28	0%	-25.24	4Y.3M
VTI-VNQ-EMB-CWB	-12.72	5.14	7.1%	1.86	6.60	0%	6.20	7.89	8.93	0%	-44.32	5Y.5M
VTI-EMB-TLT-IEI	-4.54	5.14	4.6%	1.89	6.31	0%	4.97	6.82	8.03	0%	-22.55	4Y.4M
IJS-TLT-TIP-CWB	-3.67	5.12	2.8%	3.41	6.82	0%	6.08	7.22	8.20	0%	-23.62	4Y.2M
MTUM-EMB-TLT-TIP	-6.33	5.11	5.2%	1.84	6.98	0%	5.23	7.41	8.56	0%	-25.13	4Y.7M

Order by **Baseline 3Y Return - Last 30 Years** (from 1993-12 to 2023-11) - **US Infl. Adjusted**

Portfolio	3Y Rolling Annualized Return (%)			7Y Rolling Annualized Return (%)			15Y Rolling Annualized Return (%)				Max Draw-down (%)	Long Neg Period (Y.M)
	Worst	Base ▼	%Fail	Worst	Base	%Fail	Worst	Base	Median	%Fail		
MTUM-EMB-TLT-GLD	-10.92	3.82	5.8%	-0.77	4.77	1.1%	3.27	6.28	7.42	0%	-31.87	7Y.8M
MTUM-BNDX-EMB-TLT	-11.74	3.35	7.7%	-1.82	5.17	4.3%	2.94	5.51	6.38	0%	-34.76	9Y.2M
MTUM-BNDX-EMB-GLD	-7.90	3.28	6.5%	0.25	4.41	0%	3.06	5.71	6.76	0%	-27.70	6Y.3M
MTUM-EMB-LQD-GLD	-8.37	3.27	6.8%	0.28	4.49	0%	3.02	5.71	6.81	0%	-29.48	6Y.3M
MTUM-EMB-TLT-IEI	-11.73	3.19	6.8%	-1.88	4.80	4.3%	2.63	5.17	6.12	0%	-34.60	9Y.2M
MTUM-EMB-TLT-LQD	-12.33	3.12	8%	-1.82	5.06	3.3%	2.87	5.44	6.39	0%	-36.57	9Y.2M
MTUM-BND-EMB-TLT	-12.02	3.12	6.8%	-1.92	4.90	4.3%	2.62	5.21	6.07	0%	-35.53	9Y.2M
MTUM-VNQ-EMB-GLD	-7.20	3.10	9.8%	0.92	5.24	0%	3.65	6.41	8.12	0%	-33.62	5Y.10M
MTUM-EMB-TLT-TIP	-11.42	3.06	7.4%	-1.63	4.85	2.5%	2.78	5.23	6.31	0%	-34.21	9Y.2M
BNDX-EMB-TLT-CWB	-11.61	3.06	8%	-2.10	4.18	5.1%	2.45	4.62	6.01	0%	-35.95	10Y.6M
IJS-TLT-CWB-GLD	-6.47	3.01	5.5%	1.01	4.68	0%	4.25	5.82	6.90	0%	-28.13	5Y.11M
MTUM-BND-EMB-GLD	-8.17	3.00	5.8%	0.15	4.12	0%	2.78	5.49	6.56	0%	-27.99	6Y.4M
IJS-EMB-TLT-CWB	-8.72	2.99	9.2%	-0.45	4.98	0.7%	3.62	5.66	6.84	0%	-33.39	7Y.4M
MTUM-EMB-CWB-GLD	-6.35	2.98	6.8%	2.46	5.50	0%	3.93	6.42	7.28	0%	-30.51	4Y.8M
MTUM-EMB-TIP-GLD	-7.55	2.96	7.4%	0.44	3.82	0%	2.90	5.40	6.78	0%	-26.70	6Y.2M
MTUM-EEM-EMB-TLT	-11.83	2.94	9.2%	-1.39	5.49	1.4%	2.17	6.25	7.67	0%	-37.27	9Y.3M
VTI-EMB-TLT-IEI	-9.70	2.94	6.8%	-1.56	4.28	4.7%	2.52	4.62	5.72	0%	-30.39	9Y.4M
MTUM-EMB-IEI-GLD	-7.91	2.90	5.5%	0.18	3.91	0%	2.79	5.46	6.62	0%	-27.23	6Y.4M
MTUM-TLT-CWB-GLD	-9.10	2.90	8%	1.59	5.33	0%	4.43	6.20	7.09	0%	-30.67	5Y.9M
SCZ-EMB-TLT-CWB	-10.85	2.89	9.2%	-1.32	5.07	1.4%	2.39	5.43	7.38	0%	-36.53	9Y.4M
VTI-BNDX-EMB-TLT	-9.74	2.89	8%	-1.51	4.55	4.3%	2.82	5.00	5.93	0%	-30.58	9Y.2M

Order by **Baseline 3Y Return - Last 60 Years** (from 1963-12 to 2023-11)

Portfolio	3Y Rolling Annualized Return (%)			7Y Rolling Annualized Return (%)			15Y Rolling Annualized Return (%)				Max Draw-down (%)	Long Neg Period (Y.M)
	Worst	Base ▼	%Fail	Worst	Base	%Fail	Worst	Base	Median	%Fail		
VTI-IJS-TLT-GLD	-0.79	5.72	0.6%	5.09	7.77	0%	7.06	8.97	10.45	0%	-21.63	3Y.3M
VTI-IJS-VNQ-GLD	-9.78	5.72	3.2%	3.75	8.03	0%	6.38	9.02	10.93	0%	-40.95	4Y.11M
VTI-IJS-VTV-GLD	-7.82	5.70	4.5%	3.16	7.87	0%	6.44	8.54	11.23	0%	-37.61	5Y.1M
IJS-VTV-TLT-GLD	-1.18	5.50	1.3%	4.63	7.56	0%	6.68	8.76	10.50	0%	-22.65	3Y.3M
VTI-IJS-IEI-GLD	-1.41	5.29	0.4%	4.47	7.45	0%	6.39	8.26	9.99	0%	-21.51	3Y.2M
VTI-IJS-LQD-GLD	-3.27	5.26	0.6%	4.67	7.61	0%	6.59	8.41	10.12	0%	-25.16	3Y.7M
IJS-VTV-VNQ-GLD	-10.19	5.26	3.8%	3.67	7.70	0%	6.27	8.79	11.06	0%	-41.91	4Y.11M
VTI-IJS-BND-GLD	-2.22	5.20	0.6%	4.51	7.36	0%	6.37	8.19	9.89	0%	-22.91	3Y.3M
IJS-VTV-LQD-GLD	-3.64	5.17	1.2%	4.24	7.30	0%	6.21	8.20	10.17	0%	-26.27	3Y.7M
VTI-IJS-SHY-GLD	-2.05	5.14	0.6%	4.14	7.11	0%	6.06	7.76	9.54	0%	-22.53	3Y.2M
VTI-IJS-VNQ-IEI	-11.86	5.09	6.7%	0.15	6.64	0%	6.24	8.16	11.09	0%	-42.23	6Y.8M
VTI-IJS-VNQ-SHY	-12.51	5.05	6.7%	0.30	6.36	0%	5.90	7.70	10.84	0%	-43.60	6Y.10M
VTI-IJS-VNQ-TLT	-11.21	5.05	6.1%	-0.50	7.27	0.3%	6.81	8.82	11.12	0%	-40.38	7Y.5M
IJS-VTV-BND-GLD	-2.59	5.02	0.7%	4.09	7.07	0%	5.98	7.97	9.99	0%	-24.05	3Y.3M
VTI-IJS-VNQ-DND	12.69	5.02	6.7%	0.15	6.63	0%	6.06	8.15	11.04	0%	-43.93	6Y.8M
VTI-IJS-BIL-GLD	-2.66	4.97	0.9%	3.95	6.85	0%	5.89	7.40	9.14	0%	-23.77	3Y.3M
IJS-VTV-IEI-GLD	-1.78	4.96	0.6%	4.05	7.07	0%	6.00	8.01	10.07	0%	-22.46	3Y.2M
IJS-VTV-VNQ-IEI	-12.29	4.92	6.9%	0.20	6.21	0%	5.84	7.97	11.19	0%	-43.73	6Y.8M
VTI-IJS-TLT-IEI	-4.40	4.91	2.3%	1.18	6.87	0%	6.25	7.81	10.40	0%	-22.92	6Y.3M
VTI-IJS-VNQ-LQD	-13.74	4.88	7%	-0.43	6.68	0.3%	5.91	8.27	11.07	0%	-45.92	7Y.4M
IJS-VTV-SHY-GLD	-2.41	4.86	0.6%	3.71	6.77	0%	5.66	7.51	9.65	0%	-23.66	3Y.3M

Order by **Baseline 3Y Return - Last 60 Years** (from 1963-12 to 2023-11) - **US Infl. Adjusted**

Portfolio	3Y Rolling Annualized Return (%)			7Y Rolling Annualized Return (%)			15Y Rolling Annualized Return (%)				Max Draw-down (%)	Long Neg Period (Y.M)
	Worst	Base ▼	%Fail	Worst	Base	%Fail	Worst	Base	Median	%Fail		
IJS-VTV-IEI-GLD	-5.07	2.04	6.9%	0.95	4.03	0%	3.53	5.40	6.41	0%	-28.29	6Y.4M
VTI-IJS-IEI-GLD	-4.44	2.00	6.6%	1.00	4.27	0%	3.91	5.51	6.39	0%	-27.36	6Y.4M
IJS-VTV-TLT-GLD	-5.96	2.00	7.7%	0.35	4.15	0%	4.05	5.61	6.95	0%	-29.43	6Y.6M
IJS-VTV-SHY-GLD	-4.56	1.94	6.9%	1.12	3.86	0%	3.20	5.08	6.23	0%	-27.45	6Y.4M
IJS-VTV-BND-GLD	-5.06	1.93	7.7%	0.95	3.98	0%	3.52	5.38	6.33	0%	-28.28	6Y.4M
VTI-IJS-TLT-GLD	-5.32	1.92	7.7%	0.39	4.30	0%	3.86	5.60	7.09	0%	-28.50	6Y.5M
VTI-IJS-SHY-GLD	-4.17	1.92	6.9%	1.16	4.13	0%	3.59	5.21	6.16	0%	-26.53	6Y.4M
VTI-IJS-BND-GLD	-4.43	1.85	7.3%	1.00	4.19	0%	3.89	5.48	6.32	0%	-27.35	6Y.4M
IJS-VTV-LQD-GLD	-5.73	1.80	8.2%	0.45	4.09	0%	3.74	5.46	6.46	0%	-28.42	6Y.5M
IJS-BND-TLT-GLD	-8.02	1.80	7.7%	-1.32	3.48	0.8%	2.91	4.75	6.07	0%	-27.25	9Y.4M
IJS-TLT-SHY-GLD	-6.85	1.75	7.5%	-1.09	3.36	0.6%	2.64	4.76	5.77	0%	-24.72	9Y.2M
VTI-IJS-LQD-GLD	-5.36	1.72	7.9%	0.49	4.31	0%	4.07	5.53	6.49	0%	-27.49	6Y.5M
IJS-BND-IEI-GLD	-4.86	1.70	7.3%	-0.46	3.25	0.3%	2.39	4.54	5.64	0%	-22.69	8Y.9M
IJS-TLT-BIL-GLD	-6.16	1.69	8%	-0.87	3.20	0.5%	2.50	4.49	5.43	0%	-23.03	8Y.10M
VTI-IJS-BIL-GLD	-4.74	1.66	7.3%	1.30	3.94	0%	3.17	4.83	5.86	0%	-25.18	6Y.1M
IJS-BND-LQD-GLD	-5.44	1.64	8%	-0.33	3.32	0.3%	2.65	4.64	5.71	0%	-24.52	7Y.8M
IJS-VTV-BIL-GLD	-5.10	1.63	8.5%	1.26	3.73	0%	3.04	4.74	5.93	0%	-26.10	6Y.1M
IJS-IEI-LQD-GLD	-5.12	1.63	7.7%	-0.31	3.32	0.3%	2.66	4.68	5.78	0%	-23.97	7Y.8M
IJS-TLT-IEI-GLD	-7.69	1.63	7.7%	-1.29	3.46	0.9%	2.85	4.81	6.13	0%	-26.48	9Y.4M
IJS-SHY-LQD-GLD	-4.28	1.61	8%	-0.11	3.26	0.2%	2.37	4.39	5.46	0%	-22.55	7Y.8M
IJS-BND-SHY-GLD	-4.03	1.56	7.2%	-0.27	3.11	0.2%	2.10	4.15	5.27	0%	-21.27	7Y.8M

Order by **Baseline 3Y Return** - **All data** (from 1871/1927 to 2023-11)

Portfolio	3Y Rolling Annualized Return (%)			7Y Rolling Annualized Return (%)			15Y Rolling Annualized Return (%)				Max Draw-down (%)	Long Neg Period (Y.M)
	Worst	Base ▼	%Fail	Worst	Base	%Fail	Worst	Base	Median	%Fail		
VTI-IJS-IEI-GLD	-22.93	4.28	6%	1.05	6.45	0%	3.59	7.65	9.07	0%	-57.76	8Y.7M
VTI-IJS-TLT-GLD	-23.44	4.21	5.9%	0.92	6.49	0%	3.67	7.73	9.33	0%	-58.64	8Y.7M
VTI-IJS-BND-GLD	-22.93	4.14	6.1%	1.06	6.43	0%	3.59	7.64	9.04	0%	-57.75	8Y.7M
VTI-IJS-LQD-GLD	-23.00	4.09	6%	1.05	6.58	0%	3.64	7.70	9.07	0%	-57.86	8Y.7M
IJS-VTV-TLT-GLD	-23.20	4.07	6.3%	0.63	6.26	0%	3.46	7.65	9.23	0%	-58.45	8Y.7M
IJS-VTV-IEI-GLD	-22.68	4.04	6%	0.76	6.29	0%	3.38	7.51	9.02	0%	-57.54	8Y.7M
IJS-VTV-LQD-GLD	-22.74	3.98	6.4%	0.76	6.37	0%	3.43	7.63	9.01	0%	-57.65	8Y.7M
IJS-VTV-BND-GLD	-22.67	3.98	6%	0.77	6.31	0%	3.39	7.50	8.97	0%	-57.53	8Y.7M
IJS-VTV-SHY-GLD	-22.62	3.92	6.1%	0.61	6.12	0%	3.09	7.21	8.89	0%	-57.42	8Y.9M
VTI-IJS-SHY-GLD	-22.88	3.91	6.1%	0.91	6.30	0%	3.30	7.41	8.94	0%	-57.64	8Y.9M
VTI-IJS-VNQ-GLD	-29.85	3.82	8.1%	-1.83	6.76	0.5%	2.35	8.15	9.85	0%	-69.16	13Y.3M
IJS-VTV-VNQ-GLD	-29.57	3.60	8.5%	-2.11	6.49	0.7%	2.20	7.93	9.78	0%	-68.92	13Y.4M
VTI-IJS-SHY-IEI	-21.76	3.58	7.2%	0.47	5.61	0%	3.44	6.66	9.03	0%	-55.89	8Y.9M
IJS-VTV-BIL-GLD	-23.08	3.58	6.7%	0.14	5.92	0%	2.74	6.96	8.67	0%	-58.13	12Y.8M
VTI-IJS-BND-IEI	-21.81	3.56	6.6%	0.62	5.93	0%	3.73	7.02	9.02	0%	-56.01	8Y.7M
VTI-IJS-IEI-LQD	-21.88	3.55	7.3%	0.61	5.99	0%	3.78	7.17	8.95	0%	-56.12	8Y.7M
VTI-IJS-TLT-IEI	-22.34	3.55	6.5%	0.47	6.11	0%	3.80	7.47	8.95	0%	-56.94	8Y.7M
IJS-BND-TLT-IEI	-9.95	3.53	4.5%	0.84	5.23	0%	4.43	5.86	7.21	0%	-30.46	5Y.11M
VTI-IJS-BIL-GLD	-23.35	3.52	6.5%	0.42	6.06	0%	2.95	7.15	8.77	0%	-58.36	8Y.9M
VTI-VTV-IEI-GLD	-21.26	3.49	6.8%	0.43	5.48	0%	2.56	6.64	8.19	0%	-55.18	8Y.10M
IJS-BND-TLT-GLD	-11.12	3.49	4.1%	2.17	4.93	0%	4.40	5.45	8.06	0%	-32.97	6Y.0M

Order by **Baseline 3Y Return** - **All data** (from 1871/1927 to 2023-11) - **US Infl. Adjusted**

Portfolio	3Y Rolling Annualized Return (%)			7Y Rolling Annualized Return (%)			15Y Rolling Annualized Return (%)				Max Draw-down (%)	Long Neg Period (Y.M)
	Worst	Base ▼	%Fail	Worst	Base	%Fail	Worst	Base	Median	%Fail		
IJS-VTV-IEI-GLD	-16.54	1.30	11.4%	-1.03	3.48	1.4%	1.86	4.41	6.04	0%	-46.38	7Y.11M
VTI-IJS-IEI-GLD	-16.82	1.23	11.2%	-0.96	3.70	1.3%	1.89	4.53	6.11	0%	-46.66	7Y.11M
VTI-IJS-SHY-GLD	-16.77	1.16	11.6%	-1.33	3.57	1.8%	1.65	4.39	5.86	0%	-46.51	12Y.5M
IJS-VTV-TLT-GLD	-17.11	1.10	11.9%	-1.00	3.55	0.9%	1.94	4.29	6.31	0%	-47.53	8Y.0M
VTI-IJS-BND-GLD	-16.81	1.10	11.6%	-0.96	3.64	1.3%	1.90	4.50	6.08	0%	-46.65	7Y.11M
IJS-VTV-BND-GLD	-16.54	1.09	11.9%	-1.02	3.47	1.4%	1.87	4.41	6.01	0%	-46.37	7Y.11M
IJS-VTV-LQD-GLD	-16.61	1.07	12.2%	-0.95	3.46	1.3%	1.91	4.41	6.06	0%	-46.52	7Y.11M
IJS-VTV-SHY-GLD	-16.49	1.01	11.7%	-1.40	3.43	1.8%	1.61	4.27	5.81	0%	-46.23	12Y.5M
VTI-IJS-LQD-GLD	-16.89	0.99	12%	-0.89	3.67	1.1%	1.94	4.50	6.16	0%	-46.79	7Y.11M
VTI-IJS-TLT-GLD	-17.37	0.92	11.9%	-1.05	3.67	1%	1.97	4.43	6.33	0%	-47.77	8Y.1M
VTI-IJS-BIL-GLD	-17.27	0.77	12.2%	-1.59	3.43	2.5%	1.49	4.23	5.59	0%	-47.42	12Y.8M
IJS-BND-IEI-GLD	-8.94	0.70	11.3%	-2.78	2.18	2.6%	0.51	2.51	4.84	0%	-25.64	12Y.7M
IJS-BND-LQD-GLD	-8.95	0.70	11.4%	-2.78	2.26	2.4%	0.56	2.56	4.92	0%	-25.69	12Y.6M
IJS-IEI-LQD-GLD	-8.96	0.70	11.3%	-2.79	2.22	2.4%	0.55	2.55	4.91	0%	-25.70	12Y.6M
IJS-VTV-BIL-GLD	-16.98	0.70	12.9%	-1.66	3.17	2.5%	1.46	4.08	5.52	0%	-47.13	12Y.8M
IJS-SHY-IEI-GLD	-8.92	0.67	11.8%	-2.82	1.95	3.9%	0.26	2.46	4.72	0%	-25.50	12Y.11M
IJS-TLT-SHY-GLD	-8.97	0.63	11.9%	-2.98	2.11	3.3%	0.34	2.38	4.85	0%	-25.71	12Y.8M
IJS-BND-SHY-GLD	-8.91	0.60	11.7%	-2.82	2.05	3.9%	0.26	2.48	4.70	0%	-25.49	12Y.11M
IJS-BND-TLT-GLD	-8.99	0.58	11.7%	-2.94	2.14	2.6%	0.59	2.40	5.04	0%	-27.25	12Y.1M
IJS-TLT-LQD-GLD	-9.01	0.57	12.1%	-2.94	2.18	2.5%	0.64	2.41	5.05	0%	-28.13	12Y.1M
IJS-TLT-IEI-GLD	-8.99	0.55	11.7%	-2.95	2.13	2.7%	0.59	2.39	5.05	0%	-26.48	12Y.1M

Ranking: Maximum Drawdown

Order by **Maximum Drawdown** - **Last 30 Years** (from 1993-12 to 2023-11)

Portfolio	3Y Rolling Annualized Return (%)			7Y Rolling Annualized Return (%)			15Y Rolling Annualized Return (%)				Max Draw-down (%) ▼	Long Neg Period (Y.M)
	Worst	Base	%Fail	Worst	Base	%Fail	Worst	Base	Median	%Fail		
SHY-IEI-TIP-BIL	-1.53	0.83	6.2%	0.61	1.30	0%	1.50	2.54	3.59	0%	-7.60	4Y.2M
SHY-IEI-HYG-BIL	-1.06	1.56	4.9%	1.13	2.01	0%	2.10	3.01	3.69	0%	-7.91	3Y.10M
BNDX-SHY-TIP-BIL	-1.51	1.43	4.9%	0.86	1.82	0%	1.87	2.97	3.88	0%	-8.11	4Y.2M
BNDX-SHY-IEI-BIL	-1.94	1.51	5.8%	0.55	1.79	0%	1.69	2.79	3.73	0%	-8.17	4Y.5M
BNDX-SHY-HYG-BIL	-1.52	2.01	4.9%	1.24	2.55	0%	2.44	3.35	3.97	0%	-8.38	4Y.2M
BND-SHY-TIP-BIL	-1.79	1.02	6.2%	0.78	1.47	0%	1.64	2.61	3.55	0%	-8.42	4Y.2M
SHY-TIP-HYG-BIL	-0.41	1.52	3.7%	1.47	2.01	0%	2.26	3.12	3.83	0%	-8.54	3Y.3M
BND-SHY-HYG-BIL	-1.27	1.76	4.9%	1.17	2.22	0%	2.17	3.10	3.66	0%	-8.74	4Y.2M
BND-SHY-IEI-BIL	-2.23	1.07	5.2%	0.47	1.38	0%	1.45	2.49	3.39	0%	-8.97	4Y.5M
BND-BNDX-SHY-BIL	-2.24	1.68	5.5%	0.55	1.98	0%	1.83	2.88	3.69	0%	-9.11	4Y.6M
BNDX-SHY-BIL-GLD	-2.80	0.91	8.6%	-0.26	1.90	0.4%	2.34	3.84	5.17	0%	-9.35	7Y.3M
VTI-SHY-IEI-BIL	1.02	3.02	0%	3.06	4.03	0%	3.47	4.13	4.55	0%	-9.83	2Y.7M
BNDX-IEI-TIP-BIL	-2.32	1.60	4.9%	0.68	2.07	0%	2.13	3.35	4.41	0%	-9.88	4Y.5M
IEI-TIP-HYG-BIL	-1.26	1.82	4%	1.29	2.21	0%	2.53	3.53	4.37	0%	-9.99	3Y.10M
VTV-SHY-IEI-BIL	0.68	2.87	0%	2.95	3.65	0%	3.03	3.84	4.33	0%	-10.02	2Y.7M
BNDX-IEI-HYG-BIL	-1.96	2.28	5.2%	1.06	2.81	0%	2.71	3.80	4.52	0%	-10.12	4Y.4M
SHY-TIP-LQD-BIL	-2.04	1.47	5.2%	0.97	1.93	0%	2.01	2.88	3.85	0%	-10.16	4Y.2M
BND-IEI-TIP-BIL	-2.63	1.20	5.5%	0.59	1.70	0%	1.89	2.99	4.06	0%	-10.22	4Y.5M
IJS-SHY-IEI-BIL	-0.03	2.90	0.3%	2.42	3.77	0%	3.20	3.83	4.95	0%	-10.36	3Y.0M
SHY-IEI-LQD-BIL	-2.47	1.52	5.2%	0.67	1.89	0%	1.83	2.78	3.72	0%	-10.37	4Y.5M
SHY-HYG-LQD-BIL	-1.51	1.99	4.6%	1.36	2.68	0%	2.47	3.38	4.01	0%	-10.44	4Y.2M

Order by **Maximum Drawdown** - **Last 30 Years** (from 1993-12 to 2023-11) - **US Infl. Adjusted**

Portfolio	3Y Rolling Annualized Return (%)			7Y Rolling Annualized Return (%)			15Y Rolling Annualized Return (%)				Max Draw-down (%) ▼	Long Neg Period (Y.M)
	Worst	Base	%Fail	Worst	Base	%Fail	Worst	Base	Median	%Fail		
VTV-SHY-TIP-BIL	-3.14	0.50	11.7%	-0.21	1.57	1.1%	0.78	1.85	2.32	0%	-14.38	8Y.11M
VTV-SHY-IEI-BIL	-3.58	0.69	9.5%	-0.48	1.46	4.3%	0.63	1.76	2.12	0%	-14.61	9Y.2M
VTV-BNDX-SHY-BIL	-4.04	0.20	13.2%	-0.41	1.48	3.6%	0.91	2.04	2.40	0%	-14.88	8Y.11M
VTV-SHY-BIL-GLD	-2.64	0.75	8.3%	0.66	1.76	0%	1.47	2.83	3.48	0%	-14.99	6Y.2M
VTV-BND-SHY-BIL	-3.79	0.32	11.7%	-0.51	1.33	4%	0.65	1.75	2.12	0%	-15.14	9Y.2M
VTV-IEI-TIP-BIL	-3.82	1.00	7.7%	-0.39	2.09	1.4%	1.10	2.24	2.81	0%	-15.85	8Y.11M
VTV-BNDX-TIP-BIL	-3.84	0.83	10.8%	-0.31	2.10	1.1%	1.37	2.62	3.02	0%	-16.14	8Y.10M
VNQ-SHY-BIL-GLD *	-4.44	-0.52	20.3%	-0.92	0.93	4.7%	1.07	2.66	4.28	0%	-16.25	12Y.6M
VTV-BNDX-IEI-BIL	-4.45	0.89	9.2%	-0.59	1.97	4.3%	1.24	2.49	2.90	0%	-16.34	8Y.11M
VTV-SHY-LQD-BIL	-4.04	0.08	13.9%	-0.34	1.41	1.4%	0.93	2.07	2.42	0%	-16.44	8Y.11M
VTV-IEI-BIL-GLD	-3.40	1.08	7.1%	0.49	1.99	0%	1.77	3.25	3.96	0%	-16.44	6Y.2M
VTI-SHY-IEI-BIL	-3.83	0.87	7.7%	0.02	1.59	0%	1.06	1.98	2.29	0%	-16.46	8Y.8M
VTV-BND-TIP-BIL	-4.11	0.70	9.5%	-0.43	1.95	1.4%	1.11	2.31	2.76	0%	-16.49	8Y.11M
VTI-SHY-BIL-GLD	-3.06	0.63	10.5%	0.93	1.91	0%	1.77	3.10	3.62	0%	-16.54	4Y.11M
VTV-BND-IEI-BIL	-4.49	0.92	8%	-0.70	1.83	4.3%	0.98	2.20	2.60	0%	-16.60	9Y.2M
VTI-SHY-TIP-BIL	-3.46	0.86	8%	0.34	1.80	0%	1.19	2.09	2.47	0%	-16.69	7Y.7M
VTV-BND-BNDX-BIL	-4.66	0.60	11.7%	-0.59	1.91	3.3%	1.25	2.50	2.86	0%	-16.93	8Y.11M
VTI-BNDX-SHY-BIL	-3.83	0.44	11.7%	-0.08	1.57	0.4%	1.34	2.22	2.60	0%	-16.95	9Y.2M
VTV-BND-BIL-GLD	-3.64	0.95	8.3%	0.48	1.98	0%	1.78	3.27	3.90	0%	-16.97	6Y.2M
VTV-BNDX-BIL-GLD	-3.36	1.10	7.7%	0.56	2.20	0%	2.05	3.30	4.17	0%	-17.19	6Y.2M
VTI-BND-SHY-BIL	-4.13	0.43	9.8%	0.05	1.46	0%	1.07	1.96	2.32	0%	-17.24	8Y.8M

Order by **Maximum Drawdown** - **Last 60 Years** (from 1963-12 to 2023-11)

Portfolio	3Y Rolling Annualized Return (%)			7Y Rolling Annualized Return (%)			15Y Rolling Annualized Return (%)				Max Draw-down (%) ▼	Long Neg Period (Y.M)
	Worst	Base	%Fail	Worst	Base	%Fail	Worst	Base	Median	%Fail		
BND-SHY-IEI-BIL	-2.23	2.10	2.5%	0.47	2.32	0%	1.45	3.03	6.46	0%	-8.97	4Y.5M
VTI-SHY-IEI-BIL	0.64	3.43	0%	3.06	4.32	0%	3.47	4.47	7.50	0%	-9.83	2Y.9M
VTV-SHY-IEI-BIL	0.68	3.40	0%	2.95	3.96	0%	3.03	4.22	7.59	0%	-10.02	2Y.7M
IJS-SHY-IEI-BIL	-0.03	3.50	0.2%	2.42	4.23	0%	3.20	4.79	8.69	0%	-10.36	3Y.0M
SHY-IEI-LQD-BIL	-2.47	2.49	2.5%	0.67	2.91	0%	1.83	3.38	6.64	0%	-10.37	4Y.5M
VTV-BND-IEI-BIL	0.50	3.65	0%	2.78	4.38	0%	3.38	4.72	7.91	0%	-10.45	2Y.11M
BND-SHY-BIL-GLD	-3.29	2.24	4.7%	-0.82	2.83	1.3%	2.11	4.55	5.76	0%	-10.52	7Y.9M
VTI-BND-SHY-BIL	0.24	3.42	0%	2.61	4.28	0%	3.48	4.47	7.40	0%	-10.83	2Y.10M
SHY-IEI-BIL-GLD	-3.34	2.17	5.1%	-1.03	2.63	1.6%	1.97	4.58	5.84	0%	-10.92	7Y.11M
VTV-BND-SHY-IEI	0.03	3.70	0%	2.57	4.60	0%	3.55	5.03	8.15	0%	-11.02	3Y.5M
IJS-BND-SHY-BIL	-0.80	3.66	0.3%	2.39	4.28	0%	3.22	4.80	8.61	0%	-11.27	3Y.2M
BND-SHY-LQD-BIL	-2.79	2.66	2.5%	0.65	3.13	0%	1.97	3.39	6.55	0%	-11.33	4Y.5M
IJS-BND-IEI-BIL	-0.20	3.84	0.2%	2.19	4.75	0%	3.55	5.27	8.82	0%	-11.42	3Y.1M
SHY-LQD-BIL-GLD	-3.12	2.27	4.1%	-0.32	3.25	0.5%	2.47	4.75	5.94	0%	-11.53	7Y.4M
IJS-SHY-BIL-GLD	-0.46	3.82	0.4%	2.02	4.85	0%	4.05	6.21	7.42	0%	-11.79	3Y.4M
VTV-BND-SHY-BIL	-0.10	3.32	0.2%	2.67	4.00	0%	3.05	4.21	7.49	0%	-11.81	3Y.0M
VTV-TLT-SHY-BIL	-1.11	3.61	0.9%	2.17	4.65	0%	3.70	5.14	7.86	0%	-12.10	4Y.1M
VTV-IEI-BIL-GLD	0.05	3.61	0%	2.58	4.73	0%	4.20	6.04	7.29	0%	-12.28	2Y.9M
BND-IEI-BIL-GLD	-3.17	2.20	4.7%	-0.64	3.20	0.9%	2.35	4.89	6.20	0%	-12.32	7Y.8M
VTI-BND-IEI-BIL	0.48	3.66	0%	3.20	4.76	0%	3.81	4.95	7.76	0%	-12.33	3Y.2M
VTV-SHY-BIL-GLD	-0.14	3.52	0.2%	2.39	4.52	0%	3.89	5.62	6.94	0%	-12.35	3Y.3M

Order by **Maximum Drawdown** - **Last 60 Years** (from 1963-12 to 2023-11) - **US Infl. Adjusted**

Portfolio	3Y Rolling Annualized Return (%)			7Y Rolling Annualized Return (%)			15Y Rolling Annualized Return (%)				Max Draw-down (%) ▼	Long Neg Period (Y.M)
	Worst	Base	%Fail	Worst	Base	%Fail	Worst	Base	Median	%Fail		
VTV-SHY-BIL-GLD	-3.57	0.69	9.6%	0.20	2.06	0%	1.47	3.08	3.85	0%	-17.54	6Y.11M
VNQ-SHY-BIL-GLD	-4.44	-0.25	17.7%	-0.92	1.15	2.2%	1.07	2.58	4.20	0%	-17.78	12Y.6M
IJS-SHY-BIL-GLD	-2.22	1.16	8.2%	0.13	2.70	0%	1.63	3.44	4.63	0%	-18.05	8Y.7M
VTI-SHY-BIL-GLD	-3.06	0.62	10.5%	0.93	2.16	0%	1.77	3.07	3.84	0%	-19.13	6Y.6M
VTV-SHY-IEI-BIL	-5.55	-0.53	18.1%	-2.26	0.33	12.9%	-0.73	1.22	3.39	6.3%	-19.30	17Y.11M
VTV-BND-SHY-BIL	-5.55	-0.67	19.1%	-2.26	0.33	12.7%	-0.72	1.26	3.28	6.3%	-19.30	17Y.11M
VTV-BND-IEI-BIL	-5.59	-0.88	18.1%	-2.53	0.18	13%	-1.03	1.44	3.52	8%	-19.34	18Y.8M
VTV-IEI-BIL-GLD	-4.19	0.77	9.6%	-0.13	2.27	0.8%	1.77	3.40	4.19	0%	-19.37	7Y.2M
VTV-BND-BIL-GLD	-4.18	0.73	10.1%	-0.12	2.27	0.8%	1.78	3.31	4.13	0%	-19.37	7Y.2M
IJS-IEI-BIL-GLD	-3.03	1.36	7.7%	-0.05	2.84	0.2%	1.94	3.87	5.01	0%	-19.47	8Y.7M
VNQ-BND-BIL-GLD	-5.46	-0.16	17.7%	-1.12	1.51	2.5%	1.35	2.91	4.46	0%	-19.61	12Y.2M
VNQ-IEI-BIL-GLD	-5.21	-0.22	18.1%	-1.10	1.44	3%	1.36	2.94	4.50	0%	-19.61	12Y.3M
VNQ-SHY-IEI-BIL	-6.53	-0.39	18%	-2.25	0.20	13.5%	-0.40	1.55	3.87	1.5%	-19.65	17Y.10M
VTV-BND-SHY-GLD	-4.85	1.04	9.1%	-0.23	2.52	0.5%	1.93	3.60	4.46	0%	-19.87	7Y.3M
VTV-SHY-IEI-GLD	-4.86	1.04	9.3%	-0.24	2.53	0.6%	1.87	3.60	4.50	0%	-19.87	7Y.3M
IJS-BND-BIL-GLD	-3.34	1.44	8%	-0.06	2.90	0.2%	1.95	3.85	4.94	0%	-20.00	7Y.8M
VNQ-BND-SHY-BIL	-6.53	-0.42	17.7%	-2.25	0.22	13.2%	-0.40	1.55	3.83	1.5%	-20.02	17Y.10M
VNQ-SHY-IEI-GLD	-5.88	-0.07	16.2%	-1.31	1.74	3%	1.51	3.24	4.81	0%	-20.11	12Y.5M
VNQ-BND-SHY-GLD	-6.14	-0.03	15.3%	-1.33	1.77	2.5%	1.50	3.23	4.77	0%	-20.20	12Y.3M
IJS-SHY-IEI-GLD	-3.71	1.44	7.3%	-0.25	3.06	0.2%	2.10	4.15	5.36	0%	-20.74	8Y.7M
VTI-IEI-BIL-GLD	-3.84	0.65	10.2%	0.69	2.42	0%	2.07	3.37	4.13	0%	-20.93	6Y.8M

Order by **Maximum Drawdown - All data** (from 1871/1927 to 2023-11)

Portfolio	3Y Rolling Annualized Return (%)			7Y Rolling Annualized Return (%)			15Y Rolling Annualized Return (%)				Max Draw-down (%) ▼	Long Neg Period (Y.M)
	Worst	Base	%Fail	Worst	Base	%Fail	Worst	Base	Median	%Fail		
BND-SHY-IEI-BIL	-2.23	1.92	1%	0.47	1.94	0%	1.36	2.44	4.09	0%	-8.97	4Y.5M
SHY-IEI-LQD-BIL	-2.47	2.03	1%	0.67	2.10	0%	1.37	2.50	4.09	0%	-10.37	4Y.5M
BND-SHY-BIL-GLD	-3.29	1.51	2.3%	-0.82	1.59	0.5%	0.93	2.38	3.43	0%	-10.52	7Y.9M
SHY-IEI-BIL-GLD	-3.34	1.48	2.4%	-1.03	1.59	0.6%	0.92	2.33	3.42	0%	-10.92	7Y.11M
BND-SHY-LQD-BIL	-2.79	2.10	1%	0.65	2.18	0%	1.37	2.51	4.09	0%	-11.33	4Y.5M
SHY-LQD-BIL-GLD	-3.12	1.61	2.1%	-0.32	1.80	0.2%	0.97	2.40	3.40	0%	-11.53	7Y.4M
BND-IEI-BIL-GLD	-3.17	1.72	2.3%	-0.64	1.87	0.3%	1.05	2.20	3.38	0%	-12.32	7Y.8M
BND-IEI-LQD-BIL	-3.63	2.26	1.1%	0.44	2.43	0%	1.43	2.55	3.93	0%	-13.30	4Y.10M
IEI-LQD-BIL-GLD	-3.00	1.79	2.2%	-0.14	1.98	0.1%	1.05	2.16	3.39	0%	-13.55	7Y.3M
BND-SHY-IEI-GLD	-3.05	1.71	2.8%	-0.59	2.04	0.2%	1.10	2.28	3.43	0%	-13.74	7Y.8M
BND-LQD-BIL-GLD	-2.95	1.83	2.3%	0.07	2.01	0%	1.06	2.16	3.39	0%	-14.46	7Y.2M
BND-SHY-IEI-LQD	-4.34	2.23	1.4%	0.22	2.61	0%	1.44	2.62	3.97	0%	-14.76	6Y.4M
SHY-IEI-LQD-GLD	-3.06	1.74	2.7%	-0.10	2.07	0.1%	1.08	2.27	3.46	0%	-14.98	7Y.3M
BND-SHY-LQD-GLD	-3.32	1.79	2.8%	0.12	2.09	0%	1.09	2.28	3.47	0%	-15.90	6Y.9M
VNQ-BND-IEI-BIL	-3.19	1.70	2.2%	0.58	2.25	0%	1.79	2.60	5.16	0%	-16.17	5Y.7M
VNQ-SHY-IEI-BIL	-3.17	1.66	2.2%	0.06	2.18	0%	1.39	2.59	4.90	0%	-16.25	7Y.1M
TLT-SHY-IEI-BIL	-5.06	2.17	1.5%	-0.34	2.23	0.2%	1.29	2.40	4.19	0%	-16.45	8Y.9M
VNQ-BND-IEI-GLD	-3.92	1.32	2.6%	0.71	1.85	0%	1.19	2.51	6.51	0%	-16.46	5Y.2M
VNQ-BND-SHY-IEI	-2.66	1.78	2.2%	0.88	2.42	0%	2.06	2.75	5.20	0%	-16.52	4Y.9M
VNQ-BND-SHY-GLD	-3.89	1.38	2.3%	0.41	1.85	0%	1.23	2.43	6.14	0%	-16.54	5Y.6M
VNQ-SHY-IEI-GLD	-3.90	1.37	2.2%	0.40	1.84	0%	1.23	2.42	6.17	0%	-16.55	5Y.6M

Order by **Maximum Drawdown - All data** (from 1871/1927 to 2023-11) - **US Infl. Adjusted**

Portfolio	3Y Rolling Annualized Return (%)			7Y Rolling Annualized Return (%)			15Y Rolling Annualized Return (%)				Max Draw-down (%) ▼	Long Neg Period (Y.M)
	Worst	Base	%Fail	Worst	Base	%Fail	Worst	Base	Median	%Fail		
VTV-BND-SHY-GLD	-8.18	0.10	14.2%	-2.76	0.62	11.3%	-0.93	1.49	3.64	5.9%	-23.74	20Y.3M
VTV-SHY-IEI-GLD	-8.19	0.13	14.4%	-2.77	0.65	11.5%	-0.93	1.49	3.64	5.9%	-23.76	20Y.3M
VTV-SHY-LQD-GLD	-8.19	0.16	13.8%	-2.73	0.67	11.6%	-0.88	1.48	3.65	5.6%	-23.81	20Y.2M
VTV-BND-BIL-GLD	-8.29	-0.04	15.2%	-2.95	0.52	11.9%	-1.08	1.43	3.40	7.1%	-23.83	20Y.6M
VTV-IEI-BIL-GLD	-8.29	0.03	14.9%	-2.95	0.52	11.9%	-1.08	1.42	3.45	7.1%	-23.84	20Y.6M
VTV-LQD-BIL-GLD	-8.29	-0.08	15.3%	-2.91	0.52	12.1%	-1.03	1.42	3.44	6.8%	-23.90	20Y.5M
VTV-BND-IEI-GLD	-8.17	0.07	14.2%	-2.66	0.83	11.1%	-0.68	1.46	3.79	3.3%	-23.90	17Y.9M
VTV-BND-LQD-GLD	-8.19	0.09	14.2%	-2.65	0.97	11.2%	-0.62	1.45	3.84	3.1%	-23.95	17Y.9M
VTV-IEI-LQD-GLD	-8.19	0.09	14.4%	-2.66	0.94	11.2%	-0.63	1.44	3.84	3.2%	-23.96	17Y.9M
VTV-TLT-SHY-GLD	-8.20	-0.03	15.1%	-2.85	0.66	12.4%	-0.84	1.28	3.66	4.9%	-23.97	18Y.0M
VTV-TLT-BIL-GLD	-8.28	-0.11	16.3%	-2.88	0.51	13%	-0.99	1.20	3.39	6.1%	-24.06	20Y.3M
VTV-TLT-IEI-GLD	-8.23	-0.13	15.8%	-2.82	0.71	11.6%	-0.59	1.22	3.86	2.8%	-24.39	17Y.9M
VTV-BND-TLT-GLD	-8.22	-0.12	15.9%	-2.81	0.72	11.4%	-0.59	1.23	3.84	2.6%	-24.80	17Y.9M
VNQ-BND-SHY-IEI	-7.11	-1.44	27.9%	-3.43	-0.74	24.4%	-1.48	-0.40	1.88	24.4%	-25.18	49Y.5M
VTV-BND-SHY-BIL	-8.68	-0.87	19.5%	-3.26	-0.44	18.2%	-0.98	0.66	2.52	9.8%	-25.30	20Y.3M
VTV-SHY-IEI-BIL	-8.69	-0.87	18.9%	-3.27	-0.45	18.4%	-0.99	0.66	2.53	9.8%	-25.31	20Y.3M
VTV-SHY-BIL-GLD	-8.34	-0.15	15.5%	-3.13	0.54	12.4%	-1.33	1.41	3.28	8.4%	-25.35	21Y.2M
VTV-SHY-LQD-BIL	-8.70	-1.08	20.3%	-3.23	-0.43	17.6%	-0.93	0.63	2.61	9.8%	-25.37	20Y.2M
VTV-BND-SHY-IEI	-8.72	-0.95	18.1%	-2.99	-0.27	18.2%	-1.19	0.78	3.04	7.1%	-25.37	20Y.8M
IJS-SHY-BIL-GLD	-8.97	0.33	13.4%	-2.75	1.58	5.2%	-0.14	2.26	4.22	0.4%	-25.44	17Y.2M
VTV-BND-IEI-BIL	-8.71	-0.99	18.3%	-3.09	-0.34	17.9%	-1.03	0.75	2.73	8.8%	-25.46	20Y.5M

Ranking: Longest Negative Period

Order by **Longest Negative Period - Last 30 Years** (from 1993-12 to 2023-11)

Portfolio	3Y Rolling Annualized Return (%)			7Y Rolling Annualized Return (%)			15Y Rolling Annualized Return (%)				Max Draw-down (%)	Long Neg Period (Y.M) ▲
	Worst	Base	%Fail	Worst	Base	%Fail	Worst	Base	Median	%Fail		
VTV-BNDX-BIL-GLD	0.51	3.36	0%	3.25	4.48	0%	4.48	5.71	6.45	0%	-15.28	2Y.4M
VTV-BNDX-SHY-GLD	0.67	3.57	0%	3.40	4.67	0%	4.60	5.97	6.82	0%	-14.93	2Y.5M
VTV-BND-SHY-GLD	0.22	3.32	0%	2.81	4.51	0%	4.37	5.74	6.54	0%	-13.43	2Y.6M
VTV-LQD-BIL-GLD	0.22	3.32	0%	3.16	4.60	0%	4.49	5.82	6.48	0%	-16.50	2Y.6M
VTV-BND-BIL-GLD	0.06	3.04	0%	2.77	4.37	0%	4.21	5.48	6.20	0%	-13.78	2Y.6M
VTI-IEI-BIL-GLD	0.13	2.99	0%	2.69	4.62	0%	4.52	5.79	6.36	0%	-12.35	2Y.6M
VTI-BNDX-BIL-GLD	0.60	3.26	0%	3.45	4.79	0%	4.80	6.03	6.56	0%	-15.36	2Y.7M
VTI-SHY-IEI-BIL	1.02	3.02	0%	3.06	4.03	0%	3.47	4.13	4.55	0%	-9.83	2Y.7M
VTI-BND-BIL-GLD	0.14	2.95	0%	2.86	4.56	0%	4.51	5.82	6.31	0%	-13.85	2Y.7M
VTV-SHY-IEI-BIL	0.68	2.87	0%	2.95	3.65	0%	3.03	3.84	4.33	0%	-10.02	2Y.7M
VTV-BNDX-TIP-GLD	0.07	3.87	0%	3.36	5.17	0%	4.99	6.48	7.46	0%	-18.23	2Y.9M
VTI-BNDX-SHY-GLD	0.76	3.49	0%	3.49	4.94	0%	4.92	6.30	6.89	0%	-15.01	2Y.9M
VTV-SHY-IEI-GLD	0.21	3.34	0%	2.62	4.47	0%	4.28	5.69	6.62	0%	-11.95	2Y.9M
VTI-SHY-IEI-GLD	0.29	3.20	0%	2.72	4.77	0%	4.60	6.02	6.67	0%	-12.36	2Y.9M
VTV-IEI-BIL-GLD	0.05	3.08	0%	2.58	4.34	0%	4.20	5.42	6.27	0%	-12.28	2Y.9M
VTV-BNDX-IEI-GLD	0.67	3.84	0%	3.55	4.90	0%	4.87	6.39	7.31	0%	-14.86	2Y.10M
IJS-BNDX-IEI-GLD	0.76	3.79	0%	3.04	4.72	0%	5.13	6.56	7.96	0%	-14.48	2Y.10M
IJS-BNDX-SHY-GLD	0.44	3.62	0%	2.72	4.57	0%	4.81	6.13	7.45	0%	-13.40	2Y.10M
VTV-SHY-LQD-GLD	0.38	3.53	0%	3.19	4.87	0%	4.65	6.06	6.84	0%	-16.14	2Y.10M
IJS-SHY-LQD-GLD	0.07	3.49	0%	2.78	4.79	0%	4.81	6.14	7.47	0%	-14.60	2Y.10M
IJS-BNDX-BIL-GLD	0.28	3.49	0%	2.54	4.44	0%	4.65	5.91	7.20	0%	-13.73	2Y.10M

Order by **Longest Negative Period - Last 30 Years** (from 1993-12 to 2023-11) - **US Infl. Adjusted**

Portfolio	3Y Rolling Annualized Return (%)			7Y Rolling Annualized Return (%)			15Y Rolling Annualized Return (%)				Max Draw-down (%)	Long Neg Period (Y.M) ▲
	Worst	Base	%Fail	Worst	Base	%Fail	Worst	Base	Median	%Fail		
MTUM-SHY-CWB-GLD	-5.21	2.06	7.7%	2.82	4.41	0%	3.55	4.91	5.70	0%	-24.29	3Y.10M
IJS-IEI-CWB-GLD	-3.54	2.45	3.4%	1.95	3.95	0%	3.60	5.10	6.07	0%	-24.69	3Y.11M
MTUM-TIP-CWB-GLD	-5.68	2.24	6.8%	2.85	4.87	0%	3.93	5.52	6.34	0%	-26.36	3Y.11M
MTUM-IEI-CWB-GLD	-6.01	2.47	7.7%	2.59	4.80	0%	3.87	5.44	6.21	0%	-25.98	4Y.1M
MTUM-BNDX-CWB-GLD	-6.01	2.27	9.8%	2.67	5.02	0%	4.07	5.49	6.34	0%	-26.46	4Y.2M
MTUM-BND-CWB-GLD	-6.29	2.20	8.9%	2.56	4.78	0%	3.84	5.33	6.13	0%	-26.75	4Y.2M
MTUM-CWB-BIL-GLD	-4.51	1.62	9.5%	3.06	4.17	0%	3.39	4.53	5.38	0%	-24.22	4Y.2M
IJS-BND-CWB-GLD	-3.83	2.50	4.9%	1.92	4.03	0%	3.58	5.12	5.99	0%	-25.24	4Y.3M
IJS-TIP-CWB-GLD	-4.11	2.47	4.6%	2.00	4.03	0%	3.67	5.18	6.20	0%	-24.57	4Y.3M
IJS-SHY-CWB-GLD	-3.45	2.21	3.7%	2.07	3.75	0%	3.28	4.69	5.56	0%	-23.27	4Y.3M
MTUM-VNQ-TIP-GLD	-6.02	2.63	8.9%	1.30	4.81	0%	3.67	5.74	7.01	0%	-30.48	4Y.4M
IJS-BNDX-VNQ-GLD	-4.44	2.47	5.2%	2.03	4.19	0%	3.81	5.12	6.22	0%	-24.98	4Y.4M
MTUM-VNQ-SHY-GLD	-5.48	1.99	8.6%	1.28	4.45	0%	3.29	5.29	6.36	0%	-29.12	4Y.4M
VTI-VNQ-IEI-GLD	-4.83	1.73	7.7%	1.34	3.91	0%	3.43	5.00	6.24	0%	-26.99	4Y.4M
VNQ-BNDX-CWB-GLD	-5.78	1.35	8.9%	0.96	3.48	0%	3.29	4.77	6.35	0%	-27.25	4Y.4M
MTUM-VNQ-BIL-GLD	-6.11	1.31	9.5%	1.50	4.17	0%	3.14	5.05	6.00	0%	-30.29	4Y.4M
VNQ-IEI-CWB-GLD	-4.95	1.29	7.1%	0.89	3.37	0%	3.07	4.72	6.35	0%	-24.02	4Y.4M
VNQ-TIP-CWB-GLD	-5.37	1.20	7.1%	1.13	3.35	0%	3.15	4.86	6.47	0%	-26.80	4Y.4M
VNQ-BND-CWB-GLD	-5.23	1.13	7.7%	0.85	3.37	0%	3.03	4.67	6.22	0%	-25.79	4Y.4M
VTI-MTUM-TIP-GLD	-5.25	1.08	11.1%	3.11	4.76	0%	4.27	5.37	6.38	0%	-25.81	4Y.4M
VNQ-SHY-CWB-GLD	-4.85	0.95	7.4%	1.10	3.11	0%	2.78	4.28	5.84	0%	-25.42	4Y.4M

Order by **Longest Negative Period - Last 60 Years** (from 1963-12 to 2023-11)

Portfolio	3Y Rolling Annualized Return (%)			7Y Rolling Annualized Return (%)			15Y Rolling Annualized Return (%)				Max Draw-down (%)	Long Neg Period (Y.M) ▲
	Worst	Base	%Fail	Worst	Base	%Fail	Worst	Base	Median	%Fail		
VTI-IEI-BIL-GLD	0.13	3.77	0%	2.69	5.12	0%	4.52	6.16	7.29	0%	-12.35	2Y.6M
VTV-LQD-BIL-GLD	0.22	3.71	0%	3.16	5.22	0%	4.49	6.24	7.39	0%	-16.50	2Y.6M
VTV-BND-BIL-GLD	0.06	3.64	0%	2.77	4.81	0%	4.21	5.98	7.26	0%	-13.78	2Y.6M
VTI-BND-BIL-GLD	0.14	3.87	0%	2.86	5.17	0%	4.51	6.13	7.16	0%	-13.85	2Y.7M
VTV-SHY-IEI-BIL	0.68	3.40	0%	2.95	3.96	0%	3.03	4.22	7.59	0%	-10.02	2Y.7M
VTI-SHY-IEI-GLD	0.29	3.91	0%	2.72	5.43	0%	4.60	6.51	7.66	0%	-12.36	2Y.9M
VTV-IEI-BIL-GLD	0.05	3.61	0%	2.58	4.73	0%	4.20	6.04	7.29	0%	-12.28	2Y.9M
VTI-SHY-IEI-BIL	0.64	3.43	0%	3.06	4.32	0%	3.47	4.47	7.50	0%	-9.83	2Y.9M
IJS-SHY-LQD-GLD	0.07	4.28	0%	2.78	5.84	0%	4.81	7.07	8.40	0%	-14.60	2Y.10M
VTI-LQD-BIL-GLD	0.30	3.88	0%	3.24	5.48	0%	4.78	6.37	7.28	0%	-16.57	2Y.10M
VTI-BND-SHY-BIL	0.24	3.42	0%	2.61	4.28	0%	3.48	4.47	7.40	0%	-10.83	2Y.10M
IJS-BND-SHY-GLD	0.07	4.08	0%	2.58	5.61	0%	4.54	6.87	8.19	0%	-13.70	2Y.11M
VTV-BND-IEI-BIL	0.50	3.65	0%	2.78	4.38	0%	3.38	4.72	7.91	0%	-10.45	2Y.11M
IJS-LQD-BIL-GLD	-0.09	4.25	0.2%	2.60	5.61	0%	4.65	6.69	7.94	0%	-14.94	3Y.0M
IJS-SHY-IEI-BIL	-0.03	3.50	0.2%	2.42	4.23	0%	3.20	4.79	8.69	0%	-10.36	3Y.0M
VTV-BND-SHY-BIL	-0.10	3.32	0.2%	2.67	4.00	0%	3.05	4.21	7.49	0%	-11.81	3Y.0M
VTI-BND-SHY-GLD	0.30	3.94	0%	2.89	5.48	0%	4.67	6.46	7.55	0%	-13.51	3Y.1M
IJS-BND-IEI-BIL	-0.20	3.84	0.2%	2.19	4.75	0%	3.55	5.27	8.82	0%	-11.42	3Y.1M
VTI-IJS-IEI-GLD	-1.41	5.29	0.4%	4.47	7.45	0%	6.39	8.26	9.99	0%	-21.51	3Y.2M
VTI-IJS-SHY-GLD	-2.05	5.14	0.6%	4.14	7.11	0%	6.06	7.76	9.54	0%	-22.53	3Y.2M
IJS-VTV-IEI-GLD	-1.78	4.96	0.6%	4.05	7.07	0%	6.00	8.01	10.07	0%	-22.46	3Y.2M

Order by **Longest Negative Period - Last 60 Years** (from 1963-12 to 2023-11) - **US Infl. Adjusted**

Portfolio	3Y Rolling Annualized Return (%)			7Y Rolling Annualized Return (%)			15Y Rolling Annualized Return (%)				Max Draw-down (%)	Long Neg Period (Y.M) ▲
	Worst	Base	%Fail	Worst	Base	%Fail	Worst	Base	Median	%Fail		
IJS-VNQ-BIL-GLD	-7.47	0.86	9.6%	0.68	3.27	0%	2.80	4.46	6.29	0%	-29.83	5Y.5M
VTI-IJS-BIL-GLD	-4.74	1.66	7.3%	1.30	3.94	0%	3.17	4.83	5.86	0%	-25.18	6Y.1M
IJS-VTV-BIL-GLD	-5.10	1.63	8.5%	1.26	3.73	0%	3.04	4.74	5.93	0%	-26.10	6Y.1M
IJS-VNQ-SHY-GLD	-6.85	1.05	9.3%	0.46	3.44	0%	2.97	4.84	6.62	0%	-28.68	6Y.2M
IJS-VTV-IEI-GLD	-5.07	2.04	6.9%	0.95	4.03	0%	3.53	5.40	6.41	0%	-28.29	6Y.4M
VTI-IJS-IEI-GLD	-4.44	2.00	6.6%	1.00	4.27	0%	3.91	5.51	6.39	0%	-27.36	6Y.4M
IJS-VTV-SHY-GLD	-4.56	1.94	6.9%	1.12	3.86	0%	3.20	5.08	6.23	0%	-27.45	6Y.4M
IJS-VTV-BND-GLD	-5.06	1.93	7.7%	0.95	3.98	0%	3.52	5.38	6.33	0%	-28.28	6Y.4M
VTI-IJS-SHY-GLD	-4.17	1.92	6.9%	1.16	4.13	0%	3.59	5.21	6.16	0%	-26.53	6Y.4M
VTI-IJS-BND-GLD	-4.43	1.85	7.3%	1.00	4.19	0%	3.89	5.48	6.32	0%	-27.35	6Y.4M
VTI-IJS-TLT-GLD	-5.32	1.92	7.7%	0.39	4.30	0%	3.86	5.60	7.09	0%	-28.50	6Y.5M
IJS-VTV-LQD-GLD	-5.73	1.80	8.2%	0.45	4.09	0%	3.74	5.46	6.46	0%	-28.42	6Y.5M
VTI-IJS-LQD-GLD	-5.36	1.72	7.9%	0.49	4.31	0%	4.07	5.53	6.49	0%	-27.49	6Y.5M
IJS-VTV-TLT-GLD	-5.96	2.00	7.7%	0.35	4.15	0%	4.05	5.61	6.95	0%	-29.43	6Y.6M
VTI-SHY-BIL-GLD	-3.06	0.62	10.5%	0.93	2.16	0%	1.77	3.07	3.84	0%	-19.13	6Y.6M
VTI-VTV-BIL-GLD	-6.43	0.71	10.7%	0.34	3.09	0%	2.46	4.01	5.02	0%	-25.79	6Y.8M
VTI-LQD-BIL-GLD	-4.28	0.69	10.8%	0.62	2.62	0%	2.28	3.37	4.28	0%	-22.52	6Y.8M
VTI-IEI-BIL-GLD	-3.84	0.65	10.2%	0.69	2.42	0%	2.07	3.37	4.13	0%	-20.93	6Y.8M
VTI-BND-BIL-GLD	-4.10	0.63	10.7%	0.70	2.39	0%	2.07	3.31	4.09	0%	-20.93	6Y.8M
VTI-VTV-SHY-GLD	-5.76	1.11	9.9%	0.46	3.42	0%	3.01	4.37	5.34	0%	-25.38	6Y.9M
VTI-BND-SHY-GLD	-4.77	1.01	8.9%	0.65	2.66	0%	2.22	3.58	4.41	0%	-21.42	6Y.9M

Order by **Longest Negative Period** - **All data** (from 1871/1927 to 2023-11)

Portfolio	3Y Rolling Annualized Return (%)			7Y Rolling Annualized Return (%)			15Y Rolling Annualized Return (%)				Max Draw-down (%)	Long Neg Period (Y.M) ▲
	Worst	Base	%Fail	Worst	Base	%Fail	Worst	Base	Median	%Fail		
BND-SHY-LQD-BIL	-2.79	2.10	1%	0.65	2.18	0%	1.37	2.51	4.09	0%	-11.33	4Y.5M
SHY-IEI-LQD-BIL	-2.47	2.03	1%	0.67	2.10	0%	1.37	2.50	4.09	0%	-10.37	4Y.5M
BND-SHY-IEI-BIL	-2.23	1.92	1%	0.47	1.94	0%	1.36	2.44	4.09	0%	-8.97	4Y.5M
VNQ-BND-IEI-LQD	-3.25	1.79	3%	0.87	2.49	0%	1.93	2.86	5.55	0%	-19.88	4Y.7M
VNQ-BND-SHY-IEI	-2.66	1.78	2.2%	0.88	2.42	0%	2.06	2.75	5.20	0%	-16.52	4Y.9M
VNQ-SHY-IEI-LQD	-2.73	1.73	2.5%	1.00	2.43	0%	2.04	2.77	5.34	0%	-17.70	4Y.9M
VNQ-BND-SHY-LQD	-2.72	1.71	2.8%	1.01	2.44	0%	2.04	2.77	5.35	0%	-18.85	4Y.9M
BND-IEI-LQD-BIL	-3.63	2.26	1.1%	0.44	2.43	0%	1.43	2.55	3.93	0%	-13.30	4Y.10M
VNQ-BND-LQD-GLD	-3.98	1.35	2.9%	0.73	1.91	0%	1.18	2.50	6.66	0%	-18.83	5Y.1M
VNQ-IEI-LQD-GLD	-3.99	1.34	2.7%	0.72	1.90	0%	1.17	2.50	6.65	0%	-17.70	5Y.1M
VNQ-BND-IEI-GLD	-3.92	1.32	2.6%	0.71	1.85	0%	1.19	2.51	6.51	0%	-16.46	5Y.2M
VNQ-SHY-LQD-GLD	-3.96	1.36	2.2%	0.53	1.85	0%	1.22	2.45	6.29	0%	-17.78	5Y.4M
VNQ-TLT-SHY-GLD	-4.38	1.15	3.4%	0.57	1.69	0%	0.99	2.31	6.72	0%	-19.18	5Y.4M
VTI-BND-SHY-IEI	-7.89	3.20	1.6%	1.55	4.02	0%	3.01	4.44	5.44	0%	-25.52	5Y.6M
VTI-SHY-IEI-LQD	-7.96	3.11	1.7%	1.51	3.98	0%	2.95	4.42	5.48	0%	-25.69	5Y.6M
VTI-BND-SHY-LQD	-7.95	3.11	1.8%	1.52	3.99	0%	2.95	4.43	5.47	0%	-25.68	5Y.6M
VTV-BND-IEI-LQD	-7.74	3.11	3%	2.01	4.24	0%	3.55	4.80	5.82	0%	-25.62	5Y.6M
VTV-SHY-IEI-LQD	-7.69	3.10	2.6%	2.09	4.14	0%	3.17	4.67	5.70	0%	-25.46	5Y.6M
VTV-BND-TLT-IEI	-8.22	3.05	4.1%	1.44	4.02	0%	3.43	4.74	5.90	0%	-26.83	5Y.6M
VTV-BND-SHY-LQD	-7.69	3.02	2.9%	2.10	4.13	0%	3.17	4.67	5.70	0%	-25.44	5Y.6M
VNQ-BND-SHY-GLD	-3.89	1.38	2.3%	0.41	1.85	0%	1.23	2.43	6.14	0%	-16.54	5Y.6M

Order by **Longest Negative Period** - **All data** (from 1871/1927 to 2023-11) - **US Infl. Adjusted**

Portfolio	3Y Rolling Annualized Return (%)			7Y Rolling Annualized Return (%)			15Y Rolling Annualized Return (%)				Max Draw-down (%)	Long Neg Period (Y.M) ▲
	Worst	Base	%Fail	Worst	Base	%Fail	Worst	Base	Median	%Fail		
IJS-VTV-IEI-GLD	-16.54	1.30	11.4%	-1.03	3.48	1.4%	1.86	4.41	6.04	0%	-46.38	7Y.11M
VTI-IJS-IEI-GLD	-16.82	1.23	11.2%	-0.96	3.70	1.3%	1.89	4.53	6.11	0%	-46.66	7Y.11M
VTI-IJS-BND-GLD	-16.81	1.10	11.6%	-0.96	3.64	1.3%	1.90	4.50	6.08	0%	-46.65	7Y.11M
IJS-VTV-BND-GLD	-16.54	1.09	11.9%	-1.02	3.47	1.4%	1.87	4.41	6.01	0%	-46.37	7Y.11M
IJS-VTV-LQD-GLD	-16.61	1.07	12.2%	-0.95	3.46	1.3%	1.91	4.41	6.06	0%	-46.52	7Y.11M
VTI-IJS-LQD-GLD	-16.89	0.99	12%	-0.89	3.67	1.1%	1.94	4.50	6.16	0%	-46.79	7Y.11M
IJS-VTV-TLT-GLD	-17.11	1.10	11.9%	-1.00	3.55	0.9%	1.94	4.29	6.31	0%	-47.53	8Y.0M
VTI-IJS-TLT-GLD	-17.37	0.92	11.9%	-1.05	3.67	1%	1.97	4.43	6.33	0%	-47.77	8Y.1M
IJS-VNQ-TLT-GLD	-11.85	0.24	14.1%	-1.92	2.61	2.2%	1.28	3.14	5.47	0%	-36.71	8Y.10M
IJS-VNQ-LQD-GLD	-11.41	0.24	13.6%	-1.76	2.70	2.1%	1.25	3.23	5.29	0%	-35.68	9Y.0M
IJS-VNQ-BND-GLD	-11.34	0.31	13.1%	-1.76	2.68	2.3%	1.20	3.25	5.21	0%	-35.52	9Y.2M
IJS-VNQ-IEI-GLD	-11.34	0.31	13.1%	-1.77	2.68	2.3%	1.19	3.24	5.25	0%	-35.54	9Y.2M
IJS-VNQ-SHY-GLD	-11.31	0.25	13.1%	-1.81	2.65	3.2%	0.95	3.22	5.03	0%	-35.42	9Y.6M
IJS-VNQ-SHY-IEI	-10.35	0.20	14.3%	-3.58	2.03	4.6%	0.81	2.70	4.71	0%	-32.81	11Y.8M
IJS-VNQ-BND-SHY	-10.35	0.15	14.3%	-3.58	2.04	4.6%	0.82	2.71	4.66	0%	-33.42	11Y.8M
IJS-VNQ-IEI-BIL	-10.58	0.07	14.5%	-3.61	1.94	5.4%	0.71	2.61	4.51	0%	-33.93	11Y.8M
IJS-VNQ-BND-BIL	-10.57	0.00	14.9%	-3.61	1.94	5.6%	0.71	2.62	4.47	0%	-34.73	11Y.8M
IJS-BND-TLT-GLD	-8.99	0.58	11.7%	-2.94	2.14	2.6%	0.59	2.40	5.04	0%	-27.25	12Y.1M
IJS-TLT-LQD-GLD	-9.01	0.57	12.1%	-2.94	2.18	2.5%	0.64	2.41	5.05	0%	-28.13	12Y.1M
IJS-TLT-IEI-GLD	-8.99	0.55	11.7%	-2.95	2.13	2.7%	0.59	2.39	5.05	0%	-26.48	12Y.1M
IJS-VTV-IEI-BIL	-15.78	-0.14	15.3%	-3.62	2.14	4.1%	1.31	3.06	5.19	0%	-44.96	12Y.4M

Ranking: Baseline 7Y Return

Order by **Baseline 7Y Return - Last 30 Years** (from 1993-12 to 2023-11)

Portfolio	3Y Rolling Annualized Return (%) Worst	Base	%Fail	7Y Rolling Annualized Return (%) Worst	Base ▼	%Fail	15Y Rolling Annualized Return (%) Worst	Base	Median	%Fail	Max Drawdown (%)	Long Neg Period (Y.M)
IJS-MTUM-TLT-GLD	-1.31	5.18	1.5%	4.78	8.28	0%	7.15	9.12	9.86	0%	-21.70	3Y.4M
VTI-IJS-MTUM-GLD	-7.41	3.89	8%	3.82	8.22	0%	7.71	8.65	9.52	0%	-37.45	4Y.4M
IJS-MTUM-VNQ-GLD	-9.69	5.26	5.5%	4.37	8.19	0%	7.14	9.00	10.14	0%	-41.66	4Y.5M
VTI-MTUM-VNQ-GLD	-8.81	3.64	8%	4.16	8.19	0%	7.19	8.75	9.62	0%	-41.52	4Y.4M
IJS-MTUM-CWB-GLD	-6.62	4.99	3.7%	4.65	8.16	0%	7.44	8.69	9.49	0%	-34.79	4Y.3M
IJS-MTUM-EMB-GLD	-3.81	5.18	1.2%	5.16	8.03	0%	6.57	8.83	10.19	0%	-28.14	3Y.5M
IJS-MTUM-EEM-TLT	-7.11	2.98	4.6%	3.97	8.02	0%	5.95	8.78	9.87	0%	-38.54	4Y.2M
VTI-MTUM-EMB-GLD	-2.93	4.33	2.8%	6.21	7.98	0%	6.76	8.73	9.60	0%	-27.92	3Y.3M
IJS-VTV-MTUM-GLD	-7.76	4.17	9.5%	3.80	7.97	0%	7.38	8.57	9.32	0%	-38.39	4Y.4M
MTUM-VNQ-CWB-GLD	-7.99	4.90	4.3%	4.99	7.87	0%	7.03	8.71	9.70	0%	-38.97	4Y.4M
IJS-MTUM-LQD-GLD	-3.17	4.86	1.2%	5.61	7.84	0%	6.70	8.42	9.16	0%	-25.99	3Y.5M
VTV-MTUM-VNQ-GLD	-9.19	3.94	8%	4.10	7.81	0%	6.98	8.55	9.42	0%	-42.43	4Y.5M
IJS-MTUM-BNDX-GLD	-2.95	4.94	1.2%	5.65	7.75	0%	6.71	8.39	9.12	0%	-25.48	3Y.5M
VTV-MTUM-EMB-GLD	-3.27	4.19	1.2%	5.94	7.73	0%	6.41	8.53	9.49	0%	-28.97	3Y.5M
IJS-MTUM-EMB-TLT	-5.48	4.72	3.7%	3.35	7.72	0%	6.45	8.60	9.85	0%	-26.90	4Y.4M
MTUM-SCZ-EMB-TLT	-5.65	4.05	6.8%	2.45	7.71	0%	5.32	8.40	10.28	0%	-30.36	5Y.10M
MTUM-EEM-VNQ-TLT	-8.49	3.12	5.8%	2.99	7.69	0%	5.33	8.71	10.24	0%	-42.55	4Y.7M
VTI-MTUM-EMB-TLT	-4.48	2.87	4.6%	4.28	7.68	0%	6.64	8.58	9.34	0%	-26.91	4Y.2M
MTUM-TLT-CWB-GLD	-3.88	4.98	1.8%	5.17	7.68	0%	6.93	8.61	9.47	0%	-23.67	3Y.5M
VTI-IJS-VNQ-GLD	-9.78	4.95	5.5%	3.75	7.67	0%	6.38	8.47	9.42	0%	-40.95	4Y.11M
MTUM-VNQ-TLT-GLD	-3.65	5.16	2.5%	3.63	7.66	0%	6.60	8.82	10.07	0%	-25.25	3Y.9M

Order by **Baseline 7Y Return - Last 30 Years** (from 1993-12 to 2023-11) - **US Infl. Adjusted**

Portfolio	3Y Rolling Annualized Return (%) Worst	Base	%Fail	7Y Rolling Annualized Return (%) Worst	Base ▼	%Fail	15Y Rolling Annualized Return (%) Worst	Base	Median	%Fail	Max Drawdown (%)	Long Neg Period (Y.M)
VTI-MTUM-EMB-GLD	-5.03	1.89	9.8%	3.01	5.98	0%	4.27	6.42	7.31	0%	-29.73	4Y.8M
IJS-MTUM-EMB-GLD	-5.89	2.69	6.5%	2.01	5.98	0%	4.09	6.68	7.82	0%	-29.24	5Y.9M
IJS-MTUM-TLT-GLD	-6.67	2.63	6.2%	1.21	5.81	0%	4.65	6.74	7.50	0%	-27.58	6Y.0M
IJS-MTUM-VNQ-GLD	-11.60	2.01	9.2%	1.82	5.76	0%	4.65	6.50	7.74	0%	-42.56	5Y.4M
VTV-MTUM-EMB-GLD	-5.36	1.56	9.8%	2.58	5.71	0%	3.94	6.31	7.10	0%	-30.06	4Y.9M
IJS-MTUM-CWB-GLD	-8.64	2.12	11.1%	2.09	5.70	0%	4.94	6.28	7.13	0%	-35.79	5Y.2M
IJS-MTUM-EEM-TLT	-9.12	0.48	13.5%	0.45	5.70	0%	3.48	6.32	7.43	0%	-39.49	6Y.8M
VTI-IJS-MTUM-GLD	-9.41	0.91	13.2%	1.23	5.67	0%	5.09	6.19	7.15	0%	-38.41	9Y.2M
MTUM-VNQ-TLT-GLD	-8.88	2.82	7.7%	0.09	5.64	0%	4.11	6.28	7.70	0%	-30.22	7Y.4M
IJS-MTUM-BNDX-GLD	-5.06	2.04	7.4%	2.22	5.61	0%	4.23	6.00	6.79	0%	-26.38	4Y.9M
IJS-MTUM-LQD-GLD	-5.27	2.11	7.1%	2.24	5.60	0%	4.21	6.08	6.83	0%	-27.13	4Y.10M
MTUM-VNQ-EMB-TLT	-10.11	2.37	11.7%	-1.22	5.57	1.4%	3.54	6.39	7.73	0%	-35.68	8Y.10M
VTI-MTUM-VNQ-GLD	-10.78	0.38	14.5%	1.58	5.54	0%	4.59	6.29	7.35	0%	-42.41	5Y.4M
IJS-VTV-MTUM-GLD	-9.76	1.14	12.6%	1.25	5.53	0%	4.89	6.11	6.92	0%	-39.34	5Y.3M
MTUM-EMB-CWB-GLD	-6.35	2.98	6.8%	2.46	5.50	0%	3.93	6.42	7.28	0%	-30.51	4Y.8M
MTUM-EEM-EMB-TLT	-11.83	2.94	9.2%	-1.39	5.49	1.4%	2.17	6.25	7.67	0%	-37.27	9Y.3M
MTUM-EEM-VNQ-TLT	-10.47	0.69	13.2%	-0.50	5.45	0.7%	2.86	6.17	7.77	0%	-43.43	8Y.9M
MTUM-SCZ-EMB-TLT	-10.75	1.83	11.7%	-1.02	5.40	1.1%	2.87	6.38	7.83	0%	-35.82	8Y.9M
VTI-IJS-EMB-GLD	-5.98	2.52	5.2%	2.29	5.38	0%	3.98	6.16	7.26	0%	-28.43	4Y.11M
VTI-SCZ-EMB-TLT	-8.75	1.79	10.8%	-0.72	5.37	0.7%	2.76	5.76	7.32	0%	-33.77	8Y.9M

Order by **Baseline 7Y Return - Last 60 Years** (from 1963-12 to 2023-11)

Portfolio	3Y Rolling Annualized Return (%)			7Y Rolling Annualized Return (%)			15Y Rolling Annualized Return (%)				Max Draw-down (%)	Long Neg Period (Y.M)
	Worst	Base	%Fail	Worst	Base ▼	%Fail	Worst	Base	Median	%Fail		
VTI-IJS-VNQ-GLD	-9.78	5.72	3.2%	3.75	8.03	0%	6.38	9.02	10.93	0%	-40.95	4Y.11M
VTI-IJS-VTV-GLD	-7.82	5.70	4.5%	3.16	7.87	0%	6.44	8.54	11.23	0%	-37.61	5Y.1M
VTI-IJS-TLT-GLD	-0.79	5.72	0.6%	5.09	7.77	0%	7.06	8.97	10.45	0%	-21.63	3Y.3M
IJS-VTV-VNQ-GLD	-10.19	5.26	3.8%	3.67	7.70	0%	6.27	8.79	11.06	0%	-41.91	4Y.11M
VTI-IJS-LQD-GLD	-3.27	5.26	0.6%	4.67	7.61	0%	6.59	8.41	10.12	0%	-25.16	3Y.7M
IJS-VTV-TLT-GLD	-1.18	5.50	1.3%	4.63	7.56	0%	6.68	8.76	10.50	0%	-22.65	3Y.3M
VTI-IJS-IEI-GLD	-1.41	5.29	0.4%	4.47	7.45	0%	6.39	8.26	9.99	0%	-21.51	3Y.2M
VTI-VTV-VNQ-GLD	-9.26	4.61	4.4%	3.48	7.41	0%	5.90	8.53	10.53	0%	-41.70	5Y.5M
VTI-IJS-BND-GLD	-2.22	5.20	0.6%	4.51	7.36	0%	6.37	8.19	9.89	0%	-22.91	3Y.3M
IJS-VTV-LQD-GLD	-3.64	5.17	1.2%	4.24	7.30	0%	6.21	8.20	10.17	0%	-26.27	3Y.7M
VTI-IJS-VNQ-TLT	-11.21	5.05	6.1%	-0.50	7.27	0.3%	6.81	8.82	11.12	0%	-40.38	7Y.5M
IJS-VNQ-TLT-GLD	-3.16	4.76	1.2%	2.88	7.14	0%	6.35	8.64	10.71	0%	-24.90	4Y.0M
VTI-IJS-SHY-GLD	-2.05	5.14	0.6%	4.14	7.11	0%	6.06	7.76	9.54	0%	-22.53	3Y.2M
VTI-VTV-TLT-GLD	-2.42	4.49	2.2%	3.45	7.11	0%	6.91	8.28	9.55	0%	-20.38	5Y.5M
IJS-VTV-IEI-GLD	-1.78	4.96	0.6%	4.05	7.07	0%	6.00	8.01	10.07	0%	-22.46	3Y.2M
IJS-VTV-BND-GLD	-2.59	5.02	0.7%	4.09	7.07	0%	5.98	7.97	9.99	0%	-24.05	3Y.3M
VTI-VNQ-TLT-GLD	-2.10	4.35	1.5%	3.19	7.04	0%	6.45	8.56	9.89	0%	-24.29	5Y.2M
VTI-VNQ-LQD-GLD	-4.69	4.36	1.6%	3.79	6.92	0%	6.09	8.10	9.38	0%	-29.74	3Y.8M
IJS-VNQ-LQD-GLD	-5.97	4.64	1.2%	3.46	6.91	0%	5.94	8.04	10.24	0%	-30.10	4Y.3M
VTI-VTV-LQD-GLD	-2.70	4.38	2.6%	4.05	6.89	0%	6.15	7.73	9.24	0%	-25.98	4Y.9M
VTI-IJS-TLT-IEI	-4.40	4.91	2.3%	1.18	6.87	0%	6.25	7.81	10.40	0%	-22.92	6Y.3M

Order by **Baseline 7Y Return - Last 60 Years** (from 1963-12 to 2023-11) - **US Infl. Adjusted**

Portfolio	3Y Rolling Annualized Return (%)			7Y Rolling Annualized Return (%)			15Y Rolling Annualized Return (%)				Max Draw-down (%)	Long Neg Period (Y.M)
	Worst	Base	%Fail	Worst	Base ▼	%Fail	Worst	Base	Median	%Fail		
VTI-IJS-VNQ-GLD	-11.68	1.33	9.6%	-0.46	4.53	0.2%	3.80	6.09	7.37	0%	-41.86	7Y.5M
VTI-IJS-VTV-GLD	-9.82	1.43	11%	-0.83	4.51	0.2%	3.86	5.89	7.08	0%	-38.57	9Y.2M
IJS-VTV-VNQ-GLD	-12.09	1.50	10.1%	-0.48	4.36	0.2%	3.68	5.99	7.44	0%	-42.80	7Y.5M
VTI-IJS-LQD-GLD	-5.36	1.72	7.9%	0.49	4.31	0%	4.07	5.53	6.49	0%	-27.49	6Y.5M
VTI-IJS-TLT-GLD	-5.32	1.92	7.7%	0.39	4.30	0%	3.86	5.60	7.09	0%	-28.50	6Y.5M
VTI-IJS-IEI-GLD	-4.44	2.00	6.6%	1.00	4.27	0%	3.91	5.51	6.39	0%	-27.36	6Y.4M
VTI-IJS-BND-GLD	-4.43	1.85	7.3%	1.00	4.19	0%	3.89	5.48	6.32	0%	-27.35	6Y.4M
VTI-IJS-SHY-GLD	-4.17	1.92	6.9%	1.16	4.13	0%	3.59	5.21	6.16	0%	-26.53	6Y.4M
IJS-VTV-LQD-GLD	-5.73	1.80	8.2%	0.45	4.09	0%	3.74	5.46	6.46	0%	-28.42	6Y.5M
IJS-VTV-IEI-GLD	-5.07	2.04	6.9%	0.95	4.03	0%	3.53	5.40	6.41	0%	-28.29	6Y.4M
VTI-VTV-VNQ-GLD	-11.23	0.66	12.4%	-0.94	3.98	0.6%	3.25	5.38	6.71	0%	-42.59	10Y.2M
IJS-VTV-BND-GLD	-5.06	1.93	7.7%	0.95	3.98	0%	3.52	5.38	6.33	0%	-28.28	6Y.4M
VTI-IJS-BIL-GLD	-4.74	1.66	7.3%	1.30	3.94	0%	3.17	4.83	5.86	0%	-25.18	6Y.1M
IJS-VTV-SHY-GLD	-4.56	1.94	6.9%	1.12	3.86	0%	3.20	5.08	6.23	0%	-27.45	6Y.4M
IJS-VNQ-TLT-GLD	-6.01	1.04	10.5%	-0.62	3.77	0.3%	3.87	5.48	7.24	0%	-29.22	8Y.9M
IJS-VTV-BIL-GLD	-5.10	1.63	8.5%	1.26	3.73	0%	3.04	4.74	5.93	0%	-26.10	6Y.1M
IJS-VNQ-LQD-GLD	-7.91	0.78	10.8%	0.37	3.71	0%	3.48	5.21	6.87	0%	-31.17	7Y.3M
IJS-VNQ-BND-GLD	-6.89	1.03	9.9%	0.24	3.61	0%	3.26	5.16	6.78	0%	-29.05	7Y.3M
IJS-VNQ-IEI-GLD	-6.04	1.01	9.8%	0.27	3.58	0%	3.29	5.19	6.86	0%	-27.37	7Y.3M
IJS-TLT-LQD-GLD	-8.30	1.50	8.3%	-1.19	3.54	0.6%	3.16	4.77	6.26	0%	-28.13	9Y.2M

Order by **Baseline 7Y Return - All data** (from 1871/1927 to 2023-11)

Portfolio	3Y Rolling Annualized Return (%)			7Y Rolling Annualized Return (%)			15Y Rolling Annualized Return (%)				Max Draw-down (%)	Long Neg Period (Y.M)
	Worst	Base	%Fail	Worst	Base ▼	%Fail	Worst	Base	Median	%Fail		
VTI-IJS-VTV-GLD	-34.52	2.95	9.3%	-2.86	7.05	1.6%	2.15	8.39	10.86	0%	-74.99	13Y.6M
VTI-IJS-VNQ-GLD	-29.85	3.82	8.1%	-1.83	6.76	0.5%	2.35	8.15	9.85	0%	-69.16	13Y.3M
VTI-IJS-LQD-GLD	-23.00	4.09	6%	1.05	6.58	0%	3.64	7.70	9.07	0%	-57.86	8Y.7M
IJS-VTV-VNQ-GLD	-29.57	3.60	8.5%	-2.11	6.49	0.7%	2.20	7.93	9.78	0%	-68.92	13Y.4M
VTI-IJS-TLT-GLD	-23.44	4.21	5.9%	0.92	6.49	0%	3.67	7.73	9.33	0%	-58.64	8Y.7M
VTI-IJS-IEI-GLD	-22.93	4.28	6%	1.05	6.45	0%	3.59	7.65	9.07	0%	-57.76	8Y.7M
VTI-IJS-BND-GLD	-22.93	4.14	6.1%	1.06	6.43	0%	3.59	7.64	9.04	0%	-57.75	8Y.7M
IJS-VTV-LQD-GLD	-22.74	3.98	6.4%	0.76	6.37	0%	3.43	7.63	9.01	0%	-57.65	8Y.7M
IJS-VTV-BND-GLD	-22.67	3.98	6%	0.77	6.31	0%	3.39	7.50	8.97	0%	-57.53	8Y.7M
VTI-IJS-SHY-GLD	-22.88	3.91	6.1%	0.91	6.30	0%	3.30	7.41	8.94	0%	-57.64	8Y.9M
IJS-VTV-IEI-GLD	-22.68	4.04	6%	0.76	6.29	0%	3.38	7.51	9.02	0%	-57.54	8Y.7M
IJS-VTV-TLT-GLD	-23.20	4.07	6.3%	0.63	6.26	0%	3.46	7.65	9.23	0%	-58.45	8Y.7M
VTI-IJS-VTV-TLT	-34.01	1.98	12.2%	-3.34	6.25	2.3%	2.39	7.96	10.61	0%	-74.51	13Y.5M
VTI-IJS-VNQ-TLT	-29.21	2.70	9.9%	-2.37	6.16	0.9%	2.61	7.89	9.71	0%	-68.45	13Y.3M
VTI-IJS-TLT-LQD	22.40	3.38	7.3%	0.46	6.16	0%	3.85	7.47	9.00	0%	-57.05	8Y.7M
VTI-IJS-BND-TLT	-22.34	3.47	6.5%	0.47	6.16	0%	3.81	7.45	8.94	0%	-56.65	8Y.7M
IJS-VTV-SHY-GLD	-22.62	3.92	6.1%	0.61	6.12	0%	3.09	7.21	8.89	0%	-57.42	8Y.9M
VTI-IJS-TLT-IEI	-22.34	3.55	6.5%	0.47	6.11	0%	3.80	7.47	8.95	0%	-56.94	8Y.7M
VTI-IJS-TLT-SHY	-22.28	3.40	6.7%	0.33	6.09	0%	3.52	7.21	8.83	0%	-56.81	8Y.9M
VTI-IJS-VNQ-IEI	-28.75	2.79	10.3%	-2.24	6.07	0.7%	2.54	7.76	9.61	0%	-67.78	13Y.3M
VTI-IJS-BIL-GLD	-23.35	3.52	6.5%	0.42	6.06	0%	2.95	7.15	8.77	0%	-58.36	8Y.9M

Order by **Baseline 7Y Return - All data** (from 1871/1927 to 2023-11) - **US Infl. Adjusted**

Portfolio	3Y Rolling Annualized Return (%)			7Y Rolling Annualized Return (%)			15Y Rolling Annualized Return (%)				Max Draw-down (%)	Long Neg Period (Y.M)
	Worst	Base	%Fail	Worst	Base ▼	%Fail	Worst	Base	Median	%Fail		
VTI-IJS-VTV-GLD	-29.33	0.08	14.8%	-1.90	3.88	1.5%	2.01	5.25	7.05	0%	-68.42	13Y.4M
VTI-IJS-VNQ-GLD	-24.29	0.40	13.7%	-1.60	3.82	1.8%	2.20	4.63	6.85	0%	-61.06	13Y.3M
VTI-IJS-IEI-GLD	-16.82	1.23	11.2%	-0.96	3.70	1.3%	1.89	4.53	6.11	0%	-46.66	7Y.11M
VTI-IJS-LQD-GLD	-16.89	0.99	12%	-0.89	3.67	1.1%	1.94	4.50	6.16	0%	-46.79	7Y.11M
VTI-IJS-TLT-GLD	-17.37	0.92	11.9%	-1.05	3.67	1%	1.97	4.43	6.33	0%	-47.77	8Y.1M
IJS-VTV-VNQ-GLD	-23.98	0.37	13.7%	-1.67	3.65	1.8%	2.04	4.49	6.80	0%	-60.75	13Y.4M
VTI-IJS-BND-GLD	-16.81	1.10	11.6%	-0.96	3.64	1.3%	1.90	4.50	6.08	0%	-46.65	7Y.11M
VTI-IJS-SHY-GLD	-16.77	1.16	11.6%	-1.33	3.57	1.8%	1.65	4.39	5.86	0%	-46.51	12Y.5M
IJS-VTV-TLT-GLD	-17.11	1.10	11.9%	-1.00	3.55	0.9%	1.94	4.29	6.31	0%	-47.53	8Y.0M
IJS-VTV-IEI-GLD	-16.54	1.30	11.4%	-1.03	3.48	1.4%	1.86	4.41	6.04	0%	-46.38	7Y.11M
IJS-VTV-BND-GLD	-16.54	1.09	11.9%	-1.02	3.47	1.4%	1.87	4.41	6.01	0%	-46.37	7Y.11M
IJS-VTV-LQD-GLD	-16.61	1.07	12.2%	-0.95	3.46	1.3%	1.91	4.41	6.06	0%	-46.52	7Y.11M
VTI-IJS-BIL-GLD	-17.27	0.77	12.2%	-1.59	3.43	2.5%	1.49	4.23	5.59	0%	-47.42	12Y.8M
IJS-VTV-SHY-GLD	-16.49	1.01	11.7%	-1.40	3.43	1.8%	1.61	4.27	5.81	0%	-46.23	12Y.5M
IJS-VTV-BIL-GLD	-16.98	0.70	12.9%	-1.66	3.17	2.5%	1.46	4.08	5.52	0%	-47.13	12Y.8M
VTI-IJS-VNQ-BND	-23.09	-0.01	15%	-5.54	2.92	3.9%	0.61	3.69	6.48	0%	-59.31	13Y.9M
VTI-IJS-VNQ-IEI	-23.10	0.02	14.9%	-5.54	2.91	3.8%	0.60	3.69	6.56	0%	-59.32	13Y.9M
VTI-IJS-VNQ-LQD	-23.16	-0.36	15.6%	-6.14	2.87	4.6%	0.29	3.64	6.62	0%	-59.42	13Y.11M
VTI-IJS-VNQ-SHY	-23.07	-0.02	15.1%	-5.40	2.75	4.3%	0.71	3.57	6.25	0%	-59.23	13Y.4M
VTI-VTV-VNQ-GLD	-22.57	-0.06	15%	-2.40	2.73	3.1%	0.89	3.31	5.95	0%	-58.51	13Y.5M
VTI-IJS-VNQ-TLT	-23.60	-0.55	16%	-6.16	2.70	4.2%	0.27	3.54	7.01	0%	-60.16	13Y.11M

Ranking: Baseline 15Y Return

Order by **Baseline 15Y Return - Last 30 Years** (from 1993-12 to 2023-11)

Portfolio	3Y Rolling Annualized Return (%)			7Y Rolling Annualized Return (%)			15Y Rolling Annualized Return (%)				Max Draw-down (%)	Long Neg Period (Y.M)
	Worst	Base	%Fail	Worst	Base	%Fail	Worst	Base ▼	Median	%Fail		
IJS-MTUM-TLT-GLD	-1.31	5.18	1.5%	4.78	8.28	0%	7.15	9.12	9.86	0%	-21.70	3Y.4M
IJS-MTUM-VNQ-GLD	-9.69	5.26	5.5%	4.37	8.19	0%	7.14	9.00	10.14	0%	-41.66	4Y.5M
IJS-MTUM-VNQ-TLT	-11.07	4.48	7.7%	2.73	7.43	0%	7.07	8.85	9.93	0%	-40.46	5Y.2M
IJS-MTUM-EMB-GLD	-3.81	5.18	1.2%	5.16	8.03	0%	6.57	8.83	10.19	0%	-28.14	3Y.5M
MTUM-VNQ-TLT-GLD	-3.65	5.16	2.5%	3.63	7.66	0%	6.60	8.82	10.07	0%	-25.25	3Y.9M
MTUM-VNQ-TLT-CWB	-9.26	3.85	7.4%	3.29	7.36	0%	7.01	8.78	9.51	0%	-37.32	5Y.1M
IJS-MTUM-EEM-TLT	-7.11	2.98	4.6%	3.97	8.02	0%	5.95	8.78	9.87	0%	-38.54	4Y.2M
VTI-MTUM-VNQ-GLD	-8.81	3.64	8%	4.16	8.19	0%	7.19	8.75	9.62	0%	-41.52	4Y.4M
VTI-MTUM-EMB-GLD	-2.93	4.33	2.8%	6.21	7.98	0%	6.76	8.73	9.60	0%	-27.92	3Y.3M
MTUM-VNQ-CWB-GLD	-7.99	4.90	4.3%	4.99	7.87	0%	7.03	8.71	9.70	0%	-38.97	4Y.4M
MTUM-EEM-VNQ-TLT	-8.49	3.12	5.8%	2.99	7.69	0%	5.33	8.71	10.24	0%	-42.55	4Y.7M
IJS-MTUM-CWB-GLD	-6.62	4.99	3.7%	4.65	8.16	0%	7.44	8.69	9.49	0%	-34.79	4Y.3M
IJS-MTUM-SCZ-TLT	-9.65	3.18	8.6%	4.34	7.31	0%	6.36	8.68	9.81	0%	-39.50	4Y.11M
VTI-IJS-MTUM-GLD	-7.41	3.89	8%	3.82	8.22	0%	7.71	8.65	9.52	0%	-37.45	4Y.4M
VTI-MTUM-VNQ-TLT	-10.10	2.33	9.5%	2.37	7.51	0%	7.26	8.63	9.49	0%	-40.05	5Y.2M
MTUM-TLT-CWB-GLD	-3.88	4.98	1.8%	5.17	7.68	0%	6.93	8.61	9.47	0%	-23.67	3Y.5M
IJS-MTUM-EMB-TLT	-5.48	4.72	3.7%	3.35	7.72	0%	6.45	8.60	9.85	0%	-26.90	4Y.4M
MTUM-EMB-CWB-GLD	-2.15	4.87	3.1%	5.79	7.51	0%	6.41	8.59	9.55	0%	-28.11	3Y.3M
VTI-MTUM-EMB-TLT	-4.48	2.87	4.6%	4.28	7.68	0%	6.64	8.58	9.34	0%	-26.91	4Y.2M
IJS-VTV-MTUM-GLD	-7.76	4.17	9.5%	3.80	7.97	0%	7.38	8.57	9.32	0%	-38.39	4Y.4M
MTUM-VNQ-EMB-GLD	-5.15	5.28	2.8%	4.49	7.22	0%	6.13	8.57	10.47	0%	-32.69	3Y.8M

Order by **Baseline 15Y Return - Last 30 Years** (from 1993-12 to 2023-11) - **US Infl. Adjusted**

Portfolio	3Y Rolling Annualized Return (%)			7Y Rolling Annualized Return (%)			15Y Rolling Annualized Return (%)				Max Draw-down (%)	Long Neg Period (Y.M)
	Worst	Base	%Fail	Worst	Base	%Fail	Worst	Base ▼	Median	%Fail		
IJS-MTUM-TLT-GLD	-6.67	2.63	6.2%	1.21	5.81	0%	4.65	6.74	7.50	0%	-27.58	6Y.0M
IJS-MTUM-EMB-GLD	-5.89	2.69	6.5%	2.01	5.98	0%	4.09	6.68	7.82	0%	-29.24	5Y.9M
IJS-MTUM-VNQ-TLT	-13.00	1.75	12.9%	0.17	4.97	0%	4.57	6.64	7.52	0%	-41.47	7Y.3M
IJS-MTUM-VNQ-GLD	-11.60	2.01	9.2%	1.82	5.76	0%	4.65	6.50	7.74	0%	-42.56	5Y.4M
IJS-MTUM-EMB-TLT	-8.40	1.65	10.8%	-0.15	5.20	0.7%	3.97	6.47	7.45	0%	-33.26	7Y.4M
MTUM-VNQ-TLT-CWB	-11.22	0.64	12.6%	0.72	4.88	0%	4.52	6.44	7.16	0%	-38.28	6Y.3M
VTI-MTUM-VNQ-EMB	-15.32	0.18	14.8%	-0.91	4.24	0.7%	4.09	6.44	7.15	0%	-47.93	9Y.2M
VTI-MTUM-EMB-GLD	-5.03	1.89	9.8%	3.01	5.98	0%	4.27	6.42	7.31	0%	-29.73	4Y.8M
MTUM-EMB-CWB-GLD	-6.35	2.98	6.8%	2.46	5.50	0%	3.93	6.42	7.28	0%	-30.51	4Y.8M
MTUM-VNQ-CWB-GLD	-7.20	3.10	9.8%	0.92	5.24	0%	3.65	6.41	8.12	0%	-33.62	5Y.10M
IJS-MTUM-SCZ-TLT	-11.61	-0.62	15.7%	0.80	4.86	0%	3.88	6.40	7.42	0%	-40.43	6Y.7M
MTUM-VNQ-EMB-TLT	-10.11	2.37	11.7%	-1.22	5.57	1.4%	3.54	6.39	7.73	0%	-35.68	8Y.10M
MTUM-SCZ-EMB-TLT	-10.75	1.83	11.7%	-1.02	5.40	1.1%	2.87	6.38	7.83	0%	-35.82	8Y.9M
MTUM-VNQ-CWB-GLD	-9.99	1.65	9.8%	2.42	5.61	0%	4.54	6.33	7.38	0%	-39.91	5Y.3M
IJS-MTUM-EEM-TLT	-9.12	0.48	13.5%	0.45	5.70	0%	3.48	6.32	7.43	0%	-39.49	6Y.8M
VTV-MTUM-EMB-GLD	-5.36	1.56	9.8%	2.58	5.71	0%	3.94	6.31	7.10	0%	-30.06	4Y.9M
VTI-MTUM-VNQ-GLD	-10.78	0.38	14.5%	1.58	5.54	0%	4.59	6.29	7.35	0%	-42.41	5Y.4M
MTUM-VNQ-TLT-GLD	-8.88	2.82	7.7%	0.09	5.64	0%	4.11	6.28	7.70	0%	-30.22	7Y.4M
MTUM-MTUM-TLT-GLD	-10.92	3.82	5.8%	-0.77	4.77	1.1%	3.27	6.28	7.42	0%	-31.87	7Y.8M
IJS-MTUM-CWB-GLD	-8.64	2.12	11.1%	2.09	5.70	0%	4.94	6.28	7.13	0%	-35.79	5Y.2M
MTUM-EEM-EMB-TLT	-11.83	2.94	9.2%	-1.39	5.49	1.4%	2.17	6.25	7.67	0%	-37.27	9Y.3M

163

Order by **Baseline 15Y Return - Last 60 Years** (from 1963-12 to 2023-11)

Portfolio	3Y Rolling Annualized Return (%)			7Y Rolling Annualized Return (%)			15Y Rolling Annualized Return (%)				Max Draw-down (%)	Long Neg Period (Y.M)
	Worst	Base	%Fail	Worst	Base	%Fail	Worst	Base ▼	Median	%Fail		
VTI-IJS-VNQ-GLD	-9.78	5.72	3.2%	3.75	8.03	0%	6.38	9.02	10.93	0%	-40.95	4Y.11M
VTI-IJS-TLT-GLD	-0.79	5.72	0.6%	5.09	7.77	0%	7.06	8.97	10.45	0%	-21.63	3Y.3M
VTI-IJS-VNQ-TLT	-11.21	5.05	6.1%	-0.50	7.27	0.3%	6.81	8.82	11.12	0%	-40.38	7Y.5M
IJS-VTV-VNQ-GLD	-10.19	5.26	3.8%	3.67	7.70	0%	6.27	8.79	11.06	0%	-41.91	4Y.11M
IJS-VTV-TLT-GLD	-1.18	5.50	1.3%	4.63	7.56	0%	6.68	8.76	10.50	0%	-22.65	3Y.3M
IJS-VTV-VNQ-TLT	-11.67	4.68	6.7%	-0.44	6.68	0.2%	6.56	8.65	11.28	0%	-41.99	7Y.5M
IJS-VNQ-TLT-GLD	-3.16	4.76	1.2%	2.88	7.14	0%	6.35	8.64	10.71	0%	-24.90	4Y.0M
VTI-VNQ-TLT-GLD	-2.10	4.35	1.5%	3.19	7.04	0%	6.45	8.56	9.89	0%	-24.29	5Y.2M
VTI-IJS-VTV-GLD	-7.82	5.70	4.5%	3.16	7.87	0%	6.44	8.54	11.23	0%	-37.61	5Y.1M
VTI-VTV-VNQ-GLD	-9.26	4.61	4.4%	3.48	7.41	0%	5.90	8.53	10.53	0%	-41.70	5Y.5M
VTI-IJS-LQD-GLD	-3.27	5.26	0.6%	4.67	7.61	0%	6.59	8.41	10.12	0%	-25.16	3Y.7M
VTI-IJS-VTV-VNQ	-18.52	3.71	9.6%	-1.89	6.22	1.1%	5.43	8.31	11.73	0%	-56.51	9Y.9M
VTV-VNQ-TLT-GLD	-2.52	3.89	1.9%	2.45	6.83	0%	6.19	8.29	9.93	0%	-25.26	6Y.3M
VTI-VTV-TLT-GLD	-2.42	4.49	2.2%	3.45	7.11	0%	6.91	8.28	9.55	0%	-20.38	5Y.5M
VTI-IJS-VNQ-LQD	-13.74	4.88	7%	-0.43	6.68	0.3%	5.91	8.27	11.07	0%	-45.92	7Y.4M
VTI-IJS-IEI-GLD	-1.41	5.29	0.4%	4.47	7.45	0%	6.39	8.26	9.99	0%	-21.51	3Y.2M
VTI-IJS-VTV-TLT	-9.25	4.00	8.3%	-0.81	6.73	0.3%	6.86	8.23	11.17	0%	-36.27	7Y.5M
IJS-VTV-LQD-GLD	-3.64	5.17	1.2%	4.24	7.30	0%	6.21	8.20	10.17	0%	-26.27	3Y.7M
VTI-IJS-BND-GLD	-2.22	5.20	0.6%	4.51	7.36	0%	6.37	8.19	9.89	0%	-22.91	3Y.3M
VTI-IJS-VNQ-IEI	-11.86	5.09	6.7%	0.15	6.64	0%	6.24	8.16	11.09	0%	-42.23	6Y.8M
VTI-IJS-VNQ-BND	-12.69	5.02	6.7%	0.15	6.63	0%	6.06	8.15	11.04	0%	-43.93	6Y.8M

Order by **Baseline 15Y Return - Last 60 Years** (from 1963-12 to 2023-11) - **US Infl. Adjusted**

Portfolio	3Y Rolling Annualized Return (%)			7Y Rolling Annualized Return (%)			15Y Rolling Annualized Return (%)				Max Draw-down (%)	Long Neg Period (Y.M)
	Worst	Base	%Fail	Worst	Base	%Fail	Worst	Base ▼	Median	%Fail		
VTI-IJS-VNQ-GLD	-11.68	1.33	9.6%	-0.46	4.53	0.2%	3.80	6.09	7.37	0%	-41.86	7Y.5M
IJS-VTV-VNQ-GLD	-12.09	1.50	10.1%	-0.48	4.36	0.2%	3.68	5.99	7.44	0%	-42.80	7Y.5M
VTI-IJS-VTV-GLD	-9.82	1.43	11%	-0.83	4.51	0.2%	3.86	5.89	7.08	0%	-38.57	9Y.2M
IJS-VTV-TLT-GLD	-5.96	2.00	7.7%	0.35	4.15	0%	4.05	5.61	6.95	0%	-29.43	6Y.6M
VTI-IJS-TLT-GLD	-5.32	1.92	7.7%	0.39	4.30	0%	3.86	5.60	7.09	0%	-28.50	6Y.5M
VTI-IJS-LQD-GLD	-5.36	1.72	7.9%	0.49	4.31	0%	4.07	5.53	6.49	0%	-27.49	6Y.5M
VTI-IJS-IEI-GLD	-4.44	2.00	6.6%	1.00	4.27	0%	3.91	5.51	6.39	0%	-27.36	6Y.4M
IJS-VNQ-TLT-GLD	-6.01	1.04	10.5%	-0.62	3.77	0.3%	3.87	5.48	7.24	0%	-29.22	8Y.9M
VTI-IJS-BND-GLD	-4.43	1.85	7.3%	1.00	4.19	0%	3.89	5.48	6.32	0%	-27.35	6Y.4M
IJS-VTV-LQD-GLD	-5.73	1.80	8.2%	0.45	4.09	0%	3.74	5.46	6.46	0%	-28.42	6Y.5M
IJS-VTV-IEI-GLD	-5.07	2.04	6.9%	0.95	4.03	0%	3.53	5.40	6.41	0%	-28.29	6Y.4M
VTI-VTV-VNQ-GLD	-11.23	0.66	12.4%	-0.94	3.98	0.6%	3.25	5.38	6.71	0%	-42.59	10Y.2M
IJS-VTV-BND-GLD	-5.06	1.93	7.7%	0.95	3.98	0%	3.52	5.38	6.33	0%	-28.28	6Y.4M
VTI-IJS-SHY-GLD	-4.17	1.92	6.9%	1.16	4.13	0%	3.59	5.21	6.16	0%	-26.53	6Y.4M
IJS-VNQ-LQD-GLD	-7.91	0.78	10.8%	0.37	3.71	0%	3.48	5.21	6.87	0%	-31.17	7Y.3M
IJS-VNQ-IEI-GLD	-6.04	1.01	9.8%	0.27	3.58	0%	3.29	5.19	6.86	0%	-27.37	7Y.3M
IJS-VNQ-BND-GLD	-6.89	1.03	9.9%	0.24	3.61	0%	3.26	5.16	6.78	0%	-29.05	7Y.3M
VTI-IJS-VNQ-TLT	-14.53	0.06	14.9%	-6.16	2.33	6.1%	0.79	5.15	7.49	0%	-42.74	13Y.8M
IJS-VTV-SHY-GLD	-4.56	1.94	6.9%	1.12	3.86	0%	3.20	5.08	6.23	0%	-27.45	6Y.4M
IJS-VTV-VNQ-TLT	-13.59	-0.11	15%	-6.10	2.18	5.7%	1.01	4.97	7.63	0%	-43.41	12Y.10M
IJS-VNQ-SHY-GLD	-6.85	1.05	9.3%	0.46	3.44	0%	2.97	4.84	6.62	0%	-28.68	6Y.2M

Order by **Baseline 15Y Return - All data** (from 1871/1927 to 2023-11)

Portfolio	3Y Rolling Annualized Return (%)			7Y Rolling Annualized Return (%)			15Y Rolling Annualized Return (%)				Max Draw-down (%)	Long Neg Period (Y.M)
	Worst	Base	%Fail	Worst	Base	%Fail	Worst	Base ▼	Median	%Fail		
VTI-IJS-VTV-GLD	-34.52	2.95	9.3%	-2.86	7.05	1.6%	2.15	8.39	10.86	0%	-74.99	13Y.6M
VTI-IJS-VNQ-GLD	-29.85	3.82	8.1%	-1.83	6.76	0.5%	2.35	8.15	9.85	0%	-69.16	13Y.3M
VTI-IJS-VTV-VNQ	-40.10	1.38	13%	-6.07	5.55	2.8%	0.82	8.09	11.40	0%	-81.44	14Y.6M
VTI-IJS-VTV-TLT	-34.01	1.98	12.2%	-3.34	6.25	2.3%	2.39	7.96	10.61	0%	-74.51	13Y.5M
IJS-VTV-VNQ-GLD	-29.57	3.60	8.5%	-2.11	6.49	0.7%	2.20	7.93	9.78	0%	-68.92	13Y.4M
VTI-IJS-VNQ-TLT	-29.21	2.70	9.9%	-2.37	6.16	0.9%	2.61	7.89	9.71	0%	-68.45	13Y.3M
VTI-IJS-VNQ-LQD	-28.81	2.86	10.4%	-2.24	6.02	0.8%	2.60	7.76	9.58	0%	-67.86	13Y.3M
VTI-IJS-VNQ-IEI	-28.75	2.79	10.3%	-2.24	6.07	0.7%	2.54	7.76	9.61	0%	-67.78	13Y.3M
VTI-IJS-TLT-GLD	-23.44	4.21	5.9%	0.92	6.49	0%	3.67	7.73	9.33	0%	-58.64	8Y.7M
VTI-IJS-LQD-GLD	-23.00	4.09	6%	1.05	6.58	0%	3.64	7.70	9.07	0%	-57.86	8Y.7M
VTI-IJS-VNQ-BND	-28.74	2.80	10.3%	-2.23	5.98	0.7%	2.55	7.69	9.61	0%	-67.78	13Y.3M
IJS-VTV-VNQ-TLT	-28.96	2.73	10.3%	-2.68	5.93	1%	2.44	7.68	9.65	0%	-68.24	13Y.3M
IJS-VTV-TLT-GLD	-23.20	4.07	6.3%	0.63	6.26	0%	3.46	7.65	9.23	0%	-58.45	8Y.7M
VTI-IJS-IEI-GLD	-22.93	4.28	6%	1.05	6.45	0%	3.59	7.65	9.07	0%	-57.76	8Y.7M
VTI-IJS-BND-GLD	-22.93	4.14	6.1%	1.06	6.43	0%	3.59	7.64	9.04	0%	-57.75	8Y.7M
IJS-VTV-LQD-GLD	-22.74	3.98	6.4%	0.76	6.37	0%	3.43	7.63	9.01	0%	-57.65	8Y.7M
VTI-IJS-VTV-IEI	-33.49	1.95	11.8%	-3.16	5.80	1.9%	2.35	7.55	10.64	0%	-73.86	13Y.5M
IJS-VTV-VNQ-LQD	-28.54	2.65	10.7%	-2.55	5.65	0.9%	2.43	7.55	9.56	0%	-67.63	13Y.3M
VTI-IJS-VTV-LQD	-33.55	1.95	12.1%	-3.17	5.71	2.2%	2.40	7.52	10.59	0%	-73.94	13Y.5M
IJS-VTV-IEI-GLD	-22.68	4.04	6%	0.76	6.29	0%	3.38	7.51	9.02	0%	-57.54	8Y.7M
IJS-VTV-BND-GLD	-22.67	3.98	6%	0.77	6.31	0%	3.39	7.50	8.97	0%	-57.53	8Y.7M

Order by **Baseline 15Y Return - All data** (from 1871/1927 to 2023-11) - **US Infl. Adjusted**

Portfolio	3Y Rolling Annualized Return (%)			7Y Rolling Annualized Return (%)			15Y Rolling Annualized Return (%)				Max Draw-down (%)	Long Neg Period (Y.M)
	Worst	Base	%Fail	Worst	Base	%Fail	Worst	Base ▼	Median	%Fail		
VTI-IJS-VTV-GLD	-29.33	0.08	14.8%	-1.90	3.88	1.5%	2.01	5.25	7.05	0%	-68.42	13Y.4M
VTI-IJS-VNQ-GLD	-24.29	0.40	13.7%	-1.60	3.82	1.8%	2.20	4.63	6.85	0%	-61.06	13Y.3M
VTI-IJS-IEI-GLD	-16.82	1.23	11.2%	-0.96	3.70	1.3%	1.89	4.53	6.11	0%	-46.66	7Y.11M
VTI-IJS-BND-GLD	-16.81	1.10	11.6%	-0.96	3.64	1.3%	1.90	4.50	6.08	0%	-46.65	7Y.11M
VTI-IJS-LQD-GLD	-16.89	0.99	12%	-0.89	3.67	1.1%	1.94	4.50	6.16	0%	-46.79	7Y.11M
IJS-VTV-VNQ-GLD	-23.98	0.37	13.7%	-1.67	3.65	1.8%	2.04	4.49	6.80	0%	-60.75	13Y.4M
VTI-IJS-TLT-GLD	-17.37	0.92	11.9%	-1.05	3.67	1%	1.97	4.43	6.33	0%	-47.77	8Y.1M
IJS-VTV-BND-GLD	-16.54	1.09	11.9%	-1.02	3.47	1.4%	1.87	4.41	6.01	0%	-46.37	7Y.11M
IJS-VTV-LQD-GLD	-16.61	1.07	12.2%	-0.95	3.46	1.3%	1.91	4.41	6.06	0%	-46.52	7Y.11M
IJS-VTV-IEI-GLD	-16.54	1.30	11.4%	-1.03	3.48	1.4%	1.86	4.41	6.04	0%	-46.38	7Y.11M
VTI-IJS-SHY-GLD	-16.77	1.16	11.6%	-1.33	3.57	1.8%	1.65	4.39	5.86	0%	-46.51	12Y.5M
IJS-VTV-TLT-GLD	-17.11	1.10	11.9%	-1.00	3.55	0.9%	1.94	4.29	6.31	0%	-47.53	8Y.0M
IJS-VTV-SHY-GLD	-16.49	1.01	11.7%	-1.40	3.43	1.8%	1.61	4.27	5.81	0%	-46.23	12Y.5M
VTI-IJS-BIL-GLD	-17.27	0.77	12.2%	-1.59	3.43	2.5%	1.49	4.23	5.59	0%	-47.42	12Y.8M
IJS-VTV-BIL-GLD	-16.98	0.70	12.9%	-1.66	3.17	2.5%	1.46	4.08	5.52	0%	-47.13	12Y.8M
VTI-IJS-VTV-VNQ	-35.34	-1.56	18.4%	-7.46	2.47	6.7%	0.29	3.98	7.67	0%	-76.56	14Y.6M
VTI-IJS-VNQ-BND	-23.09	-0.01	15%	-5.54	2.92	3.9%	0.61	3.69	6.48	0%	-59.31	13Y.9M
VTI-IJS-VNQ-IEI	-23.10	0.02	14.9%	-5.54	2.91	3.8%	0.60	3.69	6.56	0%	-59.32	13Y.9M
IJS-VTV-VNQ-BND	-22.80	0.01	14.9%	-5.49	2.62	4%	0.55	3.67	6.44	0%	-59.01	13Y.9M
IJS-VTV-VNQ-IEI	-22.81	0.02	14.9%	-5.49	2.62	4%	0.55	3.66	6.53	0%	-59.02	13Y.10M
VTI-IJS-VNQ-LQD	-23.16	-0.36	15.6%	-6.14	2.87	4.6%	0.29	3.64	6.62	0%	-59.42	13Y.11M

Ranking: Median 15Y Return

Order by **Median 15Y Return - Last 30 Years** (from 1993-12 to 2023-11)

Portfolio	3Y Rolling Annualized Return (%)			7Y Rolling Annualized Return (%)			15Y Rolling Annualized Return (%)				Max Draw-down (%)	Long Neg Period (Y.M)
	Worst	Base	%Fail	Worst	Base	%Fail	Worst	Base	Median ▼	%Fail		
SCZ-VNQ-EMB-GLD	-6.23	2.22	3.4%	2.80	5.44	0%	4.50	7.20	10.65	0%	-35.64	3Y.9M
SCZ-VNQ-EMB-TLT	-7.80	3.90	7.7%	0.68	6.76	0%	4.47	7.31	10.60	0%	-34.51	6Y.4M
EEM-VNQ-EMB-GLD	-3.61	1.92	6.2%	1.59	4.38	0%	3.68	7.01	10.57	0%	-34.66	4Y.9M
IJS-VNQ-EMB-GLD	-6.22	3.61	2.8%	2.94	6.34	0%	5.81	7.72	10.53	0%	-32.27	4Y.2M
SCZ-EEM-EMB-TLT	-6.87	3.55	6.2%	0.41	5.46	0%	3.00	7.16	10.53	0%	-32.80	6Y.6M
IJS-SCZ-EMB-GLD	-4.83	3.40	1.8%	2.79	6.26	0%	5.10	7.61	10.48	0%	-31.31	3Y.6M
MTUM-VNQ-EMB-GLD	-5.15	5.28	2.8%	4.49	7.22	0%	6.13	8.57	10.47	0%	-32.69	3Y.8M
MTUM-SCZ-VNQ-EMB	-14.51	3.85	9.5%	4.17	6.29	0%	5.17	7.88	10.44	0%	-50.42	5Y.3M
EEM-VNQ-EMB-TLT	-6.13	4.04	5.8%	0.36	5.46	0%	3.73	7.23	10.44	0%	-33.42	7Y.3M
MTUM-SCZ-EMB-GLD	-3.88	3.92	3.1%	4.70	7.03	0%	5.35	8.41	10.41	0%	-32.21	3Y.5M
SCZ-EEM-EMB-GLD	-5.31	0.82	10.8%	1.41	3.57	0%	2.88	6.82	10.39	0%	-36.49	5Y.5M
SCZ-EEM-VNQ-EMB	-13.19	1.78	10.2%	2.21	5.34	0%	2.92	6.54	10.38	0%	-52.06	5Y.11M
IJS-EEM-EMB-GLD	-2.82	3.06	3.7%	1.66	5.21	0%	4.34	7.41	10.33	0%	-30.35	4Y.9M
IJS-EEM-VNQ-EMB	-12.86	3.31	7.1%	2.56	6.43	0%	4.40	6.87	10.33	0%	-49.01	5Y.1M
IJS-EEM-EMB-TLT	-4.33	4.83	4.3%	1.32	6.15	0%	4.42	7.42	10.32	0%	-29.00	6Y.3M
IJS-SCZ-EMB-TLT	-6.43	3.87	4.3%	1.67	7.43	0%	5.06	7.47	10.31	0%	-30.06	6Y.1M
SCZ-EMB-TLT-GLD	-5.60	2.92	4.6%	1.19	4.46	0%	4.22	7.28	10.31	0%	-25.89	5Y.3M
MTUM-SCZ-EMB-TLT	-5.65	4.05	6.8%	2.45	7.71	0%	5.32	8.40	10.28	0%	-30.36	5Y.10M
IJS-SCZ-VNQ-EMB	-15.44	3.58	8.9%	3.32	6.05	0%	4.86	6.82	10.28	0%	-50.95	5Y.4M
MTUM-EEM-VNQ-EMB	-12.03	3.41	8.6%	3.90	6.60	0%	4.64	7.93	10.28	0%	-49.53	5Y.0M
EEM-VNQ-TLT-GLD	-4.26	1.75	7.1%	1.75	3.99	0%	4.24	7.32	10.25	0%	-26.86	5Y.1M

Order by **Median 15Y Return - Last 30 Years** (from 1993-12 to 2023-11) - **US Infl. Adjusted**

Portfolio	3Y Rolling Annualized Return (%)			7Y Rolling Annualized Return (%)			15Y Rolling Annualized Return (%)				Max Draw-down (%)	Long Neg Period (Y.M)
	Worst	Base	%Fail	Worst	Base	%Fail	Worst	Base	Median ▼	%Fail		
EEM-VNQ-EMB-GLD	-6.86	-0.62	19.4%	-0.92	2.05	1.1%	1.26	4.86	8.18	0%	-35.66	11Y.6M
SCZ-VNQ-EMB-TLT	-10.17	1.84	12.3%	-2.75	4.82	5.1%	2.03	5.17	8.16	0%	-36.60	10Y.6M
EEM-VNQ-EMB-TLT	-11.21	1.92	8%	-3.04	3.84	5.1%	1.30	5.13	8.16	0%	-36.48	11Y.10M
MTUM-VNQ-EMB-GLD	-7.20	3.10	9.8%	0.92	5.24	0%	3.65	6.41	8.12	0%	-33.62	5Y.10M
SCZ-EEM-EMB-TLT	-11.91	1.60	9.5%	-2.99	3.63	6.9%	0.59	5.10	8.11	0%	-38.33	13Y.0M
SCZ-VNQ-EMB-GLD	-8.26	-0.20	16.6%	-0.62	3.34	0.7%	2.05	5.02	8.11	0%	-36.63	7Y.9M
IJS-VNQ-EMB-GLD	-8.25	1.31	10.5%	0.14	4.47	0%	3.34	5.67	8.02	0%	-33.20	7Y.3M
MTUM-SCZ-EMB-GLD	-6.74	1.85	8.9%	1.13	5.25	0%	2.89	6.21	8.01	0%	-34.60	6Y.2M
IJS-EEM-EMB-GLD	-4.82	0.86	12.3%	0.13	3.00	0%	1.90	5.18	7.98	0%	-32.56	9Y.9M
MTUM-SCZ-VNQ-EMB	-16.37	1.60	13.9%	0.66	3.87	0%	2.72	5.87	7.98	0%	-51.18	6Y.6M
IJS-SCZ-EMB-GLD	-6.89	1.07	10.2%	0.46	4.17	0%	2.65	5.48	7.95	0%	-32.70	6Y.6M
MTUM-EEM-VNQ-EMB	-13.94	0.74	14.8%	0.36	4.53	0%	2.20	5.88	7.94	0%	-50.30	7Y.3M
IJS-EEM-EMB-TLT	-9.51	2.72	8.3%	-2.11	4.47	3.3%	1.98	5.44	7.93	0%	-35.33	10Y.10M
SCZ-EEM-VNQ-EMB	-15.07	-0.75	17.9%	-1.25	3.14	1.4%	0.51	4.37	7.93	0%	-52.80	9Y.7M
SCZ-EEM-EMB-GLD	-7.64	-1.51	22.5%	-1.12	1.23	4.7%	0.47	4.39	7.90	0%	-38.73	12Y.6M
IJS-SCZ-EMB-TLT	-8.48	1.53	12%	-1.77	5.24	2.9%	2.61	5.44	7.90	0%	-34.32	9Y.8M
EEM-VNQ-TLT-GLD	-9.46	-0.48	17.2%	-1.72	1.83	2.2%	1.80	4.85	7.85	0%	-30.59	12Y.2M
SCZ-EMB-TLT-GLD	-10.73	0.62	10.5%	-2.27	2.56	4.3%	1.78	5.24	7.85	0%	-34.43	12Y.2M
MTUM-SCZ-EMB-TLT	-10.75	1.83	11.7%	-1.02	5.40	1.1%	2.87	6.38	7.83	0%	-35.82	8Y.9M
IJS-MTUM-EMB-GLD	-5.89	2.69	6.5%	2.01	5.98	0%	4.09	6.68	7.82	0%	-29.24	5Y.9M
MTUM-EEM-EMB-GLD	-7.65	1.40	11.4%	0.78	3.99	0%	2.11	5.99	7.82	0%	-34.51	6Y.3M

Order by **Median 15Y Return** - **Last 60 Years** (from 1963-12 to 2023-11)

Portfolio	3Y Rolling Annualized Return (%)			7Y Rolling Annualized Return (%)			15Y Rolling Annualized Return (%)				Max Draw-down (%)	Long Neg Period (Y.M)
	Worst	Base	%Fail	Worst	Base	%Fail	Worst	Base	Median ▼	%Fail		
VTI-IJS-VTV-VNQ	-18.52	3.71	9.6%	-1.89	6.22	1.1%	5.43	8.31	11.73	0%	-56.51	9Y.9M
IJS-VTV-VNQ-TLT	-11.67	4.68	6.7%	-0.44	6.68	0.2%	6.56	8.65	11.28	0%	-41.99	7Y.5M
VTI-IJS-VTV-GLD	-7.82	5.70	4.5%	3.16	7.87	0%	6.44	8.54	11.23	0%	-37.61	5Y.1M
IJS-VTV-VNQ-IEI	-12.29	4.92	6.9%	0.20	6.21	0%	5.84	7.97	11.19	0%	-43.73	6Y.8M
VTI-IJS-VTV-TLT	-9.25	4.00	8.3%	-0.81	6.73	0.3%	6.86	8.23	11.17	0%	-36.27	7Y.5M
IJS-VTV-VNQ-LQD	-14.18	4.75	7.3%	-0.37	6.28	0.3%	5.78	8.08	11.15	0%	-47.35	7Y.4M
IJS-VTV-VNQ-BND	-13.12	4.63	6.9%	0.21	6.25	0%	5.80	7.91	11.12	0%	-45.39	6Y.8M
VTI-IJS-VNQ-TLT	-11.21	5.05	6.1%	-0.50	7.27	0.3%	6.81	8.82	11.12	0%	-40.38	7Y.5M
VTI-IJS-VNQ-IEI	-11.86	5.09	6.7%	0.15	6.64	0%	6.24	8.16	11.09	0%	-42.23	6Y.8M
VTI-IJS-VNQ-LQD	-13.74	4.88	7%	-0.43	6.68	0.3%	5.91	8.27	11.07	0%	-45.92	7Y.4M
IJS-VTV-VNQ-GLD	-10.19	5.26	3.8%	3.67	7.70	0%	6.27	8.79	11.06	0%	-41.91	4Y.11M
VTI-IJS-VNQ-BND	-12.69	5.02	6.7%	0.15	6.63	0%	6.06	8.15	11.04	0%	-43.93	6Y.8M
VTI-IJS-VTV-IEI	-9.94	4.10	7.9%	-0.15	6.32	0.2%	6.06	7.55	11.02	0%	-38.30	8Y.1M
VTI-IJS-VTV-LQD	-11.82	4.00	8.3%	-0.74	6.24	0.6%	5.96	7.57	10.97	0%	-42.17	8Y.6M
IJS-VTV-VNQ-SHY	-12.94	4.59	6.7%	0.36	5.99	0%	5.49	7.47	10.94	0%	-45.07	6Y.11M
VTI-IJS-VNQ-GLD	-9.78	5.72	3.2%	3.75	8.03	0%	6.38	9.02	10.93	0%	-40.95	4Y.11M
VTI-IJS-VTV-BND	-10.77	3.88	8%	-0.14	6.17	0.3%	5.91	7.43	10.89	0%	-40.09	8Y.6M
VTI-IJS-VTV-SHY	-10.60	3.76	7.7%	-0.11	5.87	0.2%	5.47	7.08	10.86	0%	-39.76	8Y.6M
VTI-IJS-VNQ-SHY	-12.51	5.05	6.7%	0.30	6.36	0%	5.90	7.70	10.84	0%	-43.60	6Y.10M
IJS-VNQ-TLT-GLD	-3.16	4.76	1.2%	2.88	7.14	0%	6.35	8.64	10.71	0%	-24.90	4Y.0M
IJS-VTV-VNQ-BIL	-13.53	4.21	6.6%	0.10	5.71	0%	5.30	7.13	10.69	0%	-46.29	6Y.11M

Order by **Median 15Y Return** - **Last 60 Years** (from 1963-12 to 2023-11) - **US Infl. Adjusted**

Portfolio	3Y Rolling Annualized Return (%)			7Y Rolling Annualized Return (%)			15Y Rolling Annualized Return (%)				Max Draw-down (%)	Long Neg Period (Y.M)
	Worst	Base	%Fail	Worst	Base	%Fail	Worst	Base	Median ▼	%Fail		
VTI-IJS-VTV-VNQ	-20.29	-0.37	16.1%	-7.46	2.29	7.2%	1.31	4.55	7.80	0%	-57.38	11Y.9M
IJS-VTV-VNQ-TLT	-13.59	-0.11	15%	-6.10	2.18	5.7%	1.01	4.97	7.63	0%	-43.41	12Y.10M
VTI-IJS-VNQ-TLT	-14.53	0.06	14.9%	-6.16	2.33	6.1%	0.79	5.15	7.49	0%	-42.74	13Y.8M
IJS-VTV-VNQ-GLD	-12.09	1.50	10.1%	-0.48	4.36	0.2%	3.68	5.99	7.44	0%	-42.80	7Y.5M
VTI-IJS-VNQ-GLD	-11.68	1.33	9.6%	-0.46	4.53	0.2%	3.80	6.09	7.37	0%	-41.86	7Y.5M
IJS-VNQ-TLT-GLD	-6.01	1.04	10.5%	-0.62	3.77	0.3%	3.87	5.48	7.24	0%	-29.22	8Y.9M
IJS-VTV-VNQ-LQD	-16.04	0.28	14.2%	-6.03	2.33	5.8%	1.21	4.50	7.17	0%	-48.55	11Y.9M
VTI-IJS-VTV-TLT	-13.86	-0.56	17.4%	-6.44	2.22	6.9%	0.29	4.73	7.09	0%	-45.32	14Y.3M
VTI-IJS-TLT-GLD	-5.32	1.92	7.7%	0.39	4.30	0%	3.86	5.60	7.09	0%	-28.50	6Y.5M
IJS-VTV-VNQ-IEI	-14.19	0.63	13.1%	-5.49	2.47	5.3%	1.55	4.38	7.09	0%	-44.97	11Y.7M
VTI-IJS-VTV-GLD	-9.82	1.43	11%	-0.83	4.51	0.2%	3.86	5.89	7.08	0%	-38.57	9Y.2M
IJS-VTV-VNQ-BND	-15.00	0.50	13.1%	-5.49	2.47	5.3%	1.56	4.41	7.04	0%	-46.60	11Y.7M
VTI-IJS-VNQ-LQD	-15.61	0.34	14.3%	-6.14	2.41	6.4%	0.99	4.64	6.96	0%	-47.23	12Y.10M
IJS-VTV-TLT-GLD	-5.96	2.00	7.7%	0.35	4.15	0%	4.05	5.61	6.95	0%	-29.43	6Y.6M
VTI-IJS-VNQ-IEI	-14.17	0.70	13.1%	-5.54	2.59	5.2%	1.33	4.54	6.95	0%	-43.59	11Y.7M
IJS-VNQ-TLT-LQD	-12.05	-0.47	16.4%	-4.84	1.85	6.6%	0.47	4.03	6.91	0%	-35.07	14Y.6M
IJS-VTV-VNQ-SHY	-14.82	0.55	13.4%	-5.34	2.48	5.3%	1.88	4.20	6.89	0%	-46.26	11Y.4M
VTI-IJS-VNQ-BND	-14.58	0.52	13.3%	-5.54	2.56	5.3%	1.34	4.55	6.88	0%	-45.25	11Y.7M
IJS-VNQ-LQD-GLD	-7.91	0.78	10.8%	0.37	3.71	0%	3.48	5.21	6.87	0%	-31.17	7Y.3M
VTI-VTV-VNQ-TLT	-13.36	-1.05	18.5%	-6.58	0.75	10.7%	-0.73	4.44	6.86	2.4%	-41.71	18Y.5M
IJS-VNQ-IEI-GLD	-6.04	1.01	9.8%	0.27	3.58	0%	3.29	5.19	6.86	0%	-27.37	7Y.3M

167

Order by **Median 15Y Return - All data** (from 1871/1927 to 2023-11)

Portfolio	3Y Rolling Annualized Return (%)			7Y Rolling Annualized Return (%)			15Y Rolling Annualized Return (%)				Max Draw-down (%)	Long Neg Period (Y.M)
	Worst	Base	%Fail	Worst	Base	%Fail	Worst	Base	Median ▼	%Fail		
VTI-IJS-VTV-VNQ	-40.10	1.38	13%	-6.07	5.55	2.8%	0.82	8.09	11.40	0%	-81.44	14Y.6M
VTI-IJS-VTV-GLD	-34.52	2.95	9.3%	-2.86	7.05	1.6%	2.15	8.39	10.86	0%	-74.99	13Y.6M
VTI-IJS-VTV-SHY	-33.43	1.72	11.9%	-3.29	5.29	2.3%	2.04	7.16	10.65	0%	-73.77	13Y.7M
VTI-IJS-VTV-BND	-33.48	1.92	11.9%	-3.15	5.75	2%	2.35	7.50	10.65	0%	-73.86	13Y.5M
VTI-IJS-VTV-IEI	-33.49	1.95	11.8%	-3.16	5.80	1.9%	2.35	7.55	10.64	0%	-73.86	13Y.5M
VTI-IJS-VTV-TLT	-34.01	1.98	12.2%	-3.34	6.25	2.3%	2.39	7.96	10.61	0%	-74.51	13Y.5M
VTI-IJS-VTV-LQD	-33.55	1.95	12.1%	-3.17	5.71	2.2%	2.40	7.52	10.59	0%	-73.94	13Y.5M
VTI-IJS-VTV-BIL	-33.84	1.57	12.4%	-3.76	4.96	2.9%	1.63	6.86	10.41	0%	-74.23	13Y.10M
VTI-IJS-VNQ-GLD	-29.85	3.82	8.1%	-1.83	6.76	0.5%	2.35	8.15	9.85	0%	-69.16	13Y.3M
IJS-VTV-VNQ-GLD	-29.57	3.60	8.5%	-2.11	6.49	0.7%	2.20	7.93	9.78	0%	-68.92	13Y.4M
VTI-IJS-VNQ-TLT	-29.21	2.70	9.9%	-2.37	6.16	0.9%	2.61	7.89	9.71	0%	-68.45	13Y.3M
IJS-VTV-VNQ-TLT	-28.96	2.73	10.3%	-2.68	5.93	1%	2.44	7.68	9.65	0%	-68.24	13Y.3M
VTI-IJS-VNQ-IEI	-28.75	2.79	10.3%	-2.24	6.07	0.7%	2.54	7.76	9.61	0%	-67.78	13Y.3M
VTI-IJS-VNQ-BND	-28.74	2.80	10.3%	-2.23	5.98	0.7%	2.55	7.69	9.61	0%	-67.78	13Y.3M
IJS-VTV-VNQ-GLIY	-28.45	2.35	10.6%	-2.69	5.22	1.4%	2.01	7.22	9.59	0%	-67.47	13Y.5M
IJS-VTV-VNQ-IEI	-28.48	2.61	10.7%	-2.54	5.66	0.8%	2.37	7.47	9.58	0%	-67.55	13Y.4M
VTI-IJS-VNQ-LQD	-28.81	2.86	10.4%	-2.24	6.02	0.8%	2.60	7.76	9.58	0%	-67.86	13Y.3M
IJS-VTV-VNQ-BND	-28.47	2.59	10.7%	-2.54	5.58	0.8%	2.37	7.43	9.57	0%	-67.54	13Y.4M
IJS-VTV-VNQ-LQD	-28.54	2.65	10.7%	-2.55	5.65	0.9%	2.43	7.55	9.56	0%	-67.63	13Y.3M
VTI-IJS-VNQ-SHY	-28.72	2.58	10.6%	-2.38	5.65	0.9%	2.18	7.44	9.55	0%	-67.71	13Y.5M
VTI-IJS-VNQ-BIL	-29.17	2.33	10.7%	-2.87	5.27	1.7%	1.76	7.20	9.42	0%	-68.29	13Y.7M

Order by **Median 15Y Return - All data** (from 1871/1927 to 2023-11) - **US Infl. Adjusted**

Portfolio	3Y Rolling Annualized Return (%)			7Y Rolling Annualized Return (%)			15Y Rolling Annualized Return (%)				Max Draw-down (%)	Long Neg Period (Y.M)
	Worst	Base	%Fail	Worst	Base	%Fail	Worst	Base	Median ▼	%Fail		
VTI-IJS-VTV-VNQ	-35.34	-1.56	18.4%	-7.46	2.47	6.7%	0.29	3.98	7.67	0%	-76.56	14Y.6M
VTI-IJS-VTV-TLT	-28.78	-1.48	18.3%	-6.44	2.67	4.7%	0.29	3.54	7.06	0%	-67.81	14Y.3M
VTI-IJS-VTV-GLD	-29.33	0.08	14.8%	-1.90	3.88	1.5%	2.01	5.25	7.05	0%	-68.42	13Y.4M
VTI-IJS-VNQ-TLT	-23.60	-0.55	16%	-6.16	2.70	4.2%	0.27	3.54	7.01	0%	-60.16	13Y.11M
IJS-VTV-VNQ-TLT	-23.32	-0.34	16%	-6.10	2.41	4%	0.21	3.61	6.91	0%	-59.89	15Y.2M
VTI-IJS-VTV-LQD	-28.28	-1.29	17.7%	-6.38	2.58	5.1%	0.49	3.61	6.87	0%	-67.09	14Y.2M
VTI-IJS-VNQ-GLD	-24.29	0.40	13.7%	-1.60	3.82	1.8%	2.20	4.63	6.85	0%	-61.06	13Y.3M
VTI-IJS-VTV-IEI	-28.21	-0.91	17%	-5.82	2.69	4.7%	0.84	3.63	6.81	0%	-67.00	13Y.11M
VTI-IJS-VTV-BND	-28.21	-1.13	17.4%	-5.82	2.64	4.9%	0.84	3.61	6.81	0%	-66.99	13Y.11M
IJS-VTV-VNQ-GLD	-23.98	0.37	13.7%	-1.67	3.65	1.8%	2.04	4.49	6.80	0%	-60.75	13Y.4M
VTI-IJS-VTV-SHY	-28.15	-1.14	17%	-5.66	2.48	5.5%	1.16	3.46	6.68	0%	-66.88	13Y.8M
VTI-IJS-VNQ-LQD	-23.16	-0.36	15.6%	-6.14	2.87	4.6%	0.29	3.64	6.62	0%	-59.42	13Y.11M
VTI-IJS-VNQ-IEI	-23.10	0.02	14.9%	-5.54	2.91	3.8%	0.60	3.69	6.56	0%	-59.32	13Y.9M
IJS-VTV-VNQ-LQD	-22.87	-0.16	15.5%	-6.03	2.55	4.2%	0.25	3.62	6.55	0%	-59.12	13Y.11M
IJS-VTV-VNQ-IEI	-22.81	0.02	14.9%	-5.49	2.62	4%	0.55	3.66	6.53	0%	-59.02	13Y.10M
VTI-IJS-VNQ-BND	-23.09	-0.01	15%	-5.54	2.92	3.9%	0.61	3.69	6.48	0%	-59.31	13Y.9M
VTI-IJS-VTV-BIL	-28.59	-1.52	17.4%	-5.48	2.15	5.4%	1.20	3.34	6.46	0%	-67.46	13Y.8M
IJS-VTV-VNQ-BND	-22.80	0.01	14.9%	-5.49	2.62	4%	0.55	3.67	6.44	0%	-59.01	13Y.9M
VTI-IJS-TLT-GLD	-17.37	0.92	11.9%	-1.05	3.67	1%	1.97	4.43	6.33	0%	-47.77	8Y.1M
IJS-VTV-TLT-GLD	-17.11	1.10	11.9%	-1.00	3.55	0.9%	1.94	4.29	6.31	0%	-47.53	8Y.0M
VTI-IJS-VNQ-SHY	-23.07	-0.02	15.1%	-5.40	2.75	4.3%	0.71	3.57	6.25	0%	-59.23	13Y.4M

Lazy Portfolios with 5 equally weighted Assets

By choosing 5 equally weighted assets, each of them will account for 20%. In theory, simulations could continue, but adding new assets might not bring substantial added value when considering the portfolio management challenges.

It's worth noting that Lazy Portfolios, which should form the core part of your overall portfolio, prioritize simplicity as their strong suit.

However, this doesn't rule out the possibility that, for a reasonable portion of your wealth (the satellite portion), you can opt for numerous other ETFs that invest in specific or niche sectors. While it may not adhere strictly to Lazy or Passive Investing, it could still be reasonable, especially if you have a higher overall budget.

Ranking: Baseline 3Y Return

Order by **Baseline 3Y Return - Last 30 Years** (from 1993-12 to 2023-11)

Portfolio	3Y Rolling Annualized Return (%)			7Y Rolling Annualized Return (%)			15Y Rolling Annualized Return (%)				Max Draw-down (%)	Long Neg Period (Y.M)
	Worst	Base ▼	%Fail	Worst	Base	%Fail	Worst	Base	Median	%Fail		
IJS-MTUM-EMB-TLT-GLD	-2.10	5.98	1.8%	3.75	7.59	0%	6.39	8.74	10.09	0%	-22.31	3Y.9M
VTI-IJS-EMB-TLT-GLD	-0.87	5.63	0.9%	4.00	7.13	0%	6.32	8.36	9.58	0%	-21.87	3Y.3M
IJS-MTUM-VNQ-TIP-GLD	-6.82	5.62	3.4%	4.99	7.49	0%	6.46	8.19	9.53	0%	-34.12	4Y.3M
IJS-MTUM-VNQ-EMB-GLD	-7.79	5.61	3.7%	5.04	7.79	0%	6.45	8.55	10.40	0%	-36.58	4Y.3M
MTUM-EMB-TLT-CWB-GLD	-4.17	5.61	1.8%	4.09	7.23	0%	6.20	8.49	9.50	0%	-23.90	3Y.9M
IJS-MTUM-TLT-IEI-GLD	-1.83	5.54	1.2%	3.87	7.28	0%	6.29	8.24	8.93	0%	-19.48	3Y.5M
IJS-MTUM-BNDX-TLT-GLD	-1.82	5.50	1.5%	3.92	7.52	0%	6.51	8.36	9.10	0%	-19.89	3Y.9M
IJS-MTUM-VNQ-IEI-GLD	-5.75	5.47	3.1%	5.20	7.51	0%	6.42	8.23	9.42	0%	-32.02	4Y.2M
IJS-MTUM-VNQ-TLT-GLD	-5.22	5.46	2.5%	4.41	8.16	0%	6.96	8.96	10.11	0%	-30.50	3Y.9M
IJS-MTUM-EMB-CWB-GLD	-5.36	5.45	2.5%	5.55	7.95	0%	6.70	8.60	9.61	0%	-30.72	3Y.8M
IJS-MTUM-TLT-TIP-GLD	-1.57	5.42	1.2%	4.07	7.32	0%	6.37	8.24	9.11	0%	-20.25	3Y.4M
MTUM-BNDX-EMB-TLT-GLD	-5.46	5.42	4.6%	2.28	6.03	0%	5.37	7.77	9.09	0%	-21.21	4Y.3M
IJS-MTUM-VNQ-TLT-TIP	-8.06	5.40	6.5%	3.60	7.20	0%	6.38	8.05	9.20	0%	-33.09	5Y.0M
IJS-MTUM-BND-TLT-GLD	-2.08	5.36	1.5%	3.84	7.37	0%	6.29	8.18	8.87	0%	-20.28	3Y.9M
IJS-MTUM-TLT-LQD-GLD	-2.33	5.33	1.8%	3.94	7.59	0%	6.48	8.37	9.11	0%	-21.63	3Y.9M
MTUM-VNQ-EMB-IEI-CWB	-8.16	5.33	6.8%	3.74	6.47	0%	5.79	7.72	8.94	0%	-34.60	5Y.0M
IJS-MTUM-VNQ-LQD-GLD	-7.26	5.32	3.4%	4.58	7.76	0%	6.56	8.40	9.53	0%	-34.99	4Y.4M
VTV-EMB-TLT-CWB-GLD	-1.67	5.31	1.2%	4.07	6.38	0%	5.91	7.91	9.02	0%	-21.50	3Y.4M
IJS-MTUM-VNQ-EMB-CWB	-13.75	5.30	7.7%	1.81	6.55	0%	6.54	8.27	9.48	0%	-46.36	5Y.5M
IJS-MTUM-VNQ-BND-GLD	-6.42	5.29	3.4%	4.82	7.50	0%	6.40	8.23	9.31	0%	-33.35	4Y.3M
IJS-MTUM-VNQ-EMB-TLT	-9.05	5.29	7.1%	3.30	7.45	0%	6.37	8.38	10.10	0%	-35.67	5Y.0M

Order by **Baseline 3Y Return - Last 30 Years** (from 1993-12 to 2023-11) - **US Infl. Adjusted**

Portfolio	3Y Rolling Annualized Return (%)			7Y Rolling Annualized Return (%)			15Y Rolling Annualized Return (%)				Max Draw-down (%)	Long Neg Period (Y.M)
	Worst	Base ▼	%Fail	Worst	Base	%Fail	Worst	Base	Median	%Fail		
MTUM-EMB-TLT-CWB-GLD	-9.37	3.71	6.5%	0.54	5.42	0%	3.71	6.27	7.24	0%	-31.67	6Y.3M
IJS-MTUM-EMB-TLT-GLD	-7.42	3.69	6.8%	0.21	5.89	0%	3.92	6.48	7.61	0%	-28.19	7Y.3M
MTUM-BNDX-EMB-TLT-GLD	-10.60	3.58	5.8%	-1.21	4.42	1.8%	2.90	5.63	6.69	0%	-30.52	8Y.9M
MTUM-EMB-TLT-LQD-GLD	-10.98	3.51	5.8%	-1.19	4.40	1.8%	2.85	5.58	6.71	0%	-31.94	8Y.9M
MTUM-VNQ-BNDX-EMB-GLD	-6.67	3.43	8.6%	0.15	4.95	0%	3.23	5.72	7.27	0%	-27.85	7Y.3M
IJS-MTUM-VNQ-EMB-GLD	-9.79	3.31	10.5%	1.49	5.63	0%	3.98	6.53	7.98	0%	-37.56	5Y.11M
IJS-MTUM-EMB-IEI-GLD	-4.90	3.29	7.1%	0.96	5.16	0%	3.42	5.65	6.99	0%	-25.79	6Y.1M
MTUM-EMB-TLT-IEI-CWB	-10.24	3.28	7.7%	-0.40	4.88	0.7%	3.21	5.39	6.24	0%	-33.67	7Y.7M
MTUM-EMB-TLT-TIP-CWB	-10.00	3.28	8%	-0.21	4.87	0.7%	3.29	5.40	6.40	0%	-33.35	7Y.4M
MTUM-VNQ-EMB-TLT-GLD	-9.18	3.28	7.7%	-0.67	5.23	0.7%	3.45	6.34	7.78	0%	-29.59	8Y.9M
MTUM-EEM-BNDX-EMB-TLT	-11.30	3.27	8%	-1.63	5.00	2.9%	2.05	5.67	6.94	0%	-35.14	9Y.5M
MTUM-SCZ-EMB-TLT-GLD	-9.72	3.26	7.1%	-0.50	5.41	0.7%	2.91	6.28	7.92	0%	-32.23	7Y.4M
VTI-IJS-EMB-TLT-GLD	-5.76	3.26	6.5%	0.45	5.16	0%	3.85	6.06	7.21	0%	-27.07	6Y.3M
MTUM-EEM-BND-EMB-TLT	-11.55	3.26	8%	-1.77	4.74	3.3%	1.82	5.51	6.74	0%	-35.76	10Y.6M
MTUM-EMB-TLT-IEI-GLD	-10.59	3.25	5.8%	-1.27	3.91	1.8%	2.66	5.32	6.53	0%	-30.33	8Y.9M
VTI-EMB-TLT-CWB-GLD	-7.55	3.25	6.2%	0.82	4.78	0%	3.61	5.82	6.86	0%	-29.62	5Y.10M
MTUM-BND-TLT-GLD	-10.81	3.25	5.8%	-1.29	4.06	1.8%	2.65	5.35	6.50	0%	-31.09	8Y.10M
MTUM-BNDX-EMB-LQD-GLD	-8.56	3.25	7.1%	-0.39	4.05	0.7%	2.70	5.17	6.22	0%	-28.60	7Y.8M
IJS-MTUM-EMB-TIP-GLD	-4.63	3.24	7.1%	1.16	5.07	0%	3.48	5.80	7.09	0%	-25.72	6Y.0M
MTUM-BNDX-EMB-TLT-CWB	-10.27	3.21	8.3%	-0.32	4.76	0.7%	3.41	5.60	6.41	0%	-33.81	7Y.4M
MTUM-VNQ-EMB-LQD-GLD	-7.07	3.20	8.3%	0.16	4.85	0%	3.20	5.82	7.34	0%	-28.48	7Y.3M

Order by **Baseline 3Y Return** - **Last 60 Years** (from 1963-12 to 2023-11)

Portfolio	3Y Rolling Annualized Return (%)			7Y Rolling Annualized Return (%)			15Y Rolling Annualized Return (%)				Max Draw-down (%)	Long Neg Period (Y.M)
	Worst	Base ▼	%Fail	Worst	Base	%Fail	Worst	Base	Median	%Fail		
VTI-IJS-VTV-TLT-GLD	-3.78	5.70	1.6%	4.70	7.79	0%	7.09	8.80	10.64	0%	-26.81	3Y.8M
VTI-IJS-VNQ-LQD-GLD	-7.35	5.69	1.9%	4.07	7.56	0%	6.35	8.68	10.54	0%	-34.40	4Y.5M
VTI-IJS-VNQ-BND-GLD	-6.51	5.66	1.5%	4.30	7.40	0%	6.30	8.49	10.42	0%	-32.74	4Y.4M
VTI-IJS-VNQ-TLT-GLD	-5.33	5.63	1.2%	4.63	7.76	0%	6.87	9.05	10.77	0%	-29.90	4Y.2M
VTI-IJS-VNQ-IEI-GLD	-5.85	5.59	1.3%	4.50	7.36	0%	6.32	8.50	10.44	0%	-31.41	4Y.3M
VTI-IJS-VTV-VNQ-GLD	-11.08	5.58	4.5%	2.53	7.65	0%	6.14	8.85	11.51	0%	-43.67	5Y.2M
VTI-IJS-TLT-LQD-GLD	-0.61	5.54	0.4%	4.18	7.33	0%	6.41	8.51	9.84	0%	-21.13	3Y.3M
VTI-IJS-VNQ-SHY-GLD	-6.43	5.51	1.8%	4.18	7.18	0%	6.06	8.17	10.15	0%	-32.46	4Y.4M
VTI-IJS-VTV-BND-GLD	-4.98	5.50	2.3%	3.75	7.44	0%	6.49	8.04	10.37	0%	-29.81	4Y.4M
VTI-IJS-VTV-IEI-GLD	-4.32	5.49	1.6%	4.16	7.48	0%	6.52	8.07	10.42	0%	-28.44	4Y.2M
VTI-IJS-TLT-IEI-GLD	-0.07	5.49	0.2%	4.11	7.33	0%	6.22	8.37	9.80	0%	-18.99	3Y.3M
VTI-IJS-BND-TLT-GLD	-0.36	5.47	0.3%	4.08	7.21	0%	6.22	8.35	9.76	0%	-19.78	3Y.3M
VTI-IJS-VTV-LQD-GLD	-5.83	5.46	2.2%	3.54	7.59	0%	6.41	8.23	10.47	0%	-31.51	4Y.4M
IJS-VTV-VNQ-IEI-GLD	-6.18	5.38	1.8%	4.16	7.14	0%	6.01	8.44	10.49	0%	-32.28	4Y.3M
IJS-VTV-VNQ-TLT-GLD	-5.67	5.38	1.9%	4.25	7.52	0%	6.57	8.92	10.83	0%	-30.82	4Y.2M
IJS-VTV-VNQ-BND-GLD	-6.84	5.38	2%	4.18	7.15	0%	5.99	8.38	10.47	0%	-33.59	4Y.4M
IJS-VTV-VNQ-LQD-GLD	-7.68	5.36	2.2%	4.01	7.33	0%	6.16	8.54	10.56	0%	-35.24	4Y.5M
VTI-IJS-VTV-SHY-GLD	-4.85	5.34	1.9%	3.66	7.21	0%	6.25	7.67	10.22	0%	-29.52	4Y.3M
VTI-IJS-VNQ-BIL-GLD	-6.95	5.32	2%	3.78	7.01	0%	5.92	7.87	9.76	0%	-33.38	4Y.4M
IJS-VTV-TLT-LQD-GLD	-0.70	5.32	0.9%	3.82	7.11	0%	6.11	8.33	9.87	0%	-19.07	3Y.3M
IJS-VTV-BND-TLT-GLD	-0.30	5.29	0.3%	3.71	6.99	0%	5.91	8.15	9.78	0%	-18.37	3Y.3M

Order by **Baseline 3Y Return** - **Last 60 Years** (from 1963-12 to 2023-11) - **US Infl. Adjusted**

Portfolio	3Y Rolling Annualized Return (%)			7Y Rolling Annualized Return (%)			15Y Rolling Annualized Return (%)				Max Draw-down (%)	Long Neg Period (Y.M)
	Worst	Base ▼	%Fail	Worst	Base	%Fail	Worst	Base	Median	%Fail		
IJS-VTV-TLT-IEI-GLD	-5.25	2.22	7.7%	0.13	3.84	0%	3.08	4.86	6.34	0%	-25.53	7Y.3M
IJS-VTV-BND-TLT-GLD	-5.30	2.18	7.7%	0.13	3.81	0%	3.08	4.86	6.28	0%	-25.52	7Y.3M
IJS-VTV-BND-IEI-GLD	-4.53	2.10	6.4%	0.60	3.65	0%	2.93	4.83	5.80	0%	-24.58	6Y.5M
VTI-IJS-TLT-IEI-GLD	-5.47	2.09	7.5%	0.17	3.84	0%	2.94	4.79	6.38	0%	-24.77	6Y.5M
IJS-VTV-SHY-IEI-GLD	-4.04	2.08	5.7%	0.74	3.50	0%	2.67	4.63	5.53	0%	-23.90	6Y.5M
IJS-VTV-TLT-SHY-GLD	-4.76	2.08	7.3%	0.26	3.69	0%	3.21	4.88	5.97	0%	-24.84	6Y.5M
VTI-IJS-BND-TLT-GLD	-5.75	2.05	7.7%	0.17	3.81	0%	2.94	4.80	6.36	0%	-25.02	6Y.5M
VTI-IJS-SHY-IEI-GLD	-3.54	2.05	5.7%	0.77	3.69	0%	2.99	4.75	5.56	0%	-23.15	6Y.5M
VTI-IJS-TLT-SHY-GLD	-4.79	2.02	7.2%	0.30	3.81	0%	3.20	4.83	6.03	0%	-24.09	6Y.5M
VTI-IJS-BND-IEI-GLD	-4.02	2.00	6.4%	0.64	3.79	0%	3.23	4.86	5.82	0%	-23.82	6Y.5M
IJS-VTV-BND-SHY-GLD	-4.04	1.99	6.3%	0.74	3.51	0%	2.67	4.62	5.46	0%	-23.90	6Y.5M
IJS-VTV-TLT-LQD-GLD	-5.51	1.98	8.2%	-0.27	3.82	0.2%	2.87	4.79	6.45	0%	-25.64	7Y.5M
VTI-IJS-BND-SHY-GLD	-3.54	1.94	6%	0.78	3.64	0%	2.98	4.72	5.48	0%	-23.15	6Y.5M
IJS-VTV-IEI-LQD-GLD	-4.62	1.92	7.5%	0.21	3.77	0%	3.12	4.83	5.91	0%	-24.70	6Y.5M
VTI-IJS-IEI-LQD-GLD	-4.11	1.90	7.5%	0.25	3.89	0%	3.15	4.84	5.96	0%	-23.94	6Y.5M
VTI-IJS-TLT-LQD-GLD	-5.99	1.89	8.6%	-0.23	3.80	0.2%	2.72	4.79	6.52	0%	-26.17	7Y.2M
IJS-VTV-BND-LQD-GLD	-4.62	1.88	7.6%	0.21	3.71	0%	3.11	4.82	5.83	0%	-24.70	6Y.5M
IJS-VTV-TLT-BIL-GLD	-4.44	1.87	7.3%	0.38	3.53	0%	3.09	4.70	5.68	0%	-23.73	6Y.5M
VTI-IJS-TLT-BIL-GLD	-4.22	1.85	7.3%	0.42	3.64	0%	3.22	4.68	5.73	0%	-22.97	6Y.5M
VTI-IJS-IEI-BIL-GLD	-3.22	1.84	5.7%	0.89	3.50	0%	2.86	4.52	5.29	0%	-22.03	6Y.4M
IJS-VTV-SHY-LQD-GLD	-4.13	1.83	6.7%	0.34	3.66	0%	2.87	4.70	5.56	0%	-24.01	6Y.5M

Order by **Baseline 3Y Return - All data** (from 1871/1927 to 2023-11)

Portfolio	3Y Rolling Annualized Return (%)			7Y Rolling Annualized Return (%)			15Y Rolling Annualized Return (%)				Max Draw-down (%)	Long Neg Period (Y.M)
	Worst	Base ▼	%Fail	Worst	Base	%Fail	Worst	Base	Median	%Fail		
VTI-IJS-TLT-IEI-GLD	-17.96	4.28	4.4%	2.08	5.97	0%	3.97	6.88	8.56	0%	-48.43	6Y.3M
VTI-IJS-TLT-LQD-GLD	-18.01	4.22	4.6%	2.08	6.02	0%	4.01	6.94	8.63	0%	-48.52	6Y.3M
VTI-IJS-BND-TLT-GLD	-17.95	4.19	4.5%	2.09	5.98	0%	3.97	6.89	8.51	0%	-48.42	6Y.3M
VTI-IJS-IEI-LQD-GLD	-17.60	4.18	4.7%	2.17	6.05	0%	3.94	6.85	8.30	0%	-47.69	6Y.2M
IJS-VTV-TLT-IEI-GLD	-17.75	4.16	4.4%	1.83	5.77	0%	3.79	6.77	8.50	0%	-48.25	6Y.3M
VTI-IJS-BND-IEI-GLD	-17.54	4.14	4.5%	2.18	5.93	0%	3.90	6.81	8.27	0%	-47.59	6Y.2M
IJS-VTV-BND-IEI-GLD	-17.33	4.14	4.4%	1.93	5.77	0%	3.72	6.73	8.19	0%	-47.40	6Y.3M
VTI-IJS-BND-LQD-GLD	-17.59	4.14	4.8%	2.18	6.04	0%	3.94	6.85	8.27	0%	-47.69	6Y.2M
VTI-IJS-TLT-SHY-GLD	-17.91	4.12	4.4%	1.97	5.90	0%	3.74	6.72	8.30	0%	-48.31	6Y.2M
IJS-VTV-IEI-LQD-GLD	-17.39	4.12	4.4%	1.92	5.86	0%	3.76	6.77	8.27	0%	-47.50	6Y.3M
IJS-VTV-BND-LQD-GLD	-17.38	4.10	4.4%	1.93	5.86	0%	3.77	6.78	8.23	0%	-47.49	6Y.3M
VTI-IJS-SHY-LQD-GLD	-17.56	4.07	4.9%	2.06	5.91	0%	3.70	6.76	8.15	0%	-47.58	6Y.2M
IJS-VTV-BND-TLT-GLD	-17.75	4.06	4.4%	1.83	5.79	0%	3.80	6.78	8.46	0%	-48.24	6Y.3M
VTI-IJS-SHY-IEI-GLD	-17.51	4.06	4.8%	2.06	5.75	0%	3.66	6.74	8.13	0%	-47.49	6Y.2M
VTI-IJS-VNQ-SHY-GLD	-23.18	4.05	6.5%	-0.22	6.26	0.1%	2.68	7.14	8.76	0%	-58.75	12Y.9M
VTI-IJS-VNQ-IEI-GLD	-23.20	4.04	6.3%	-0.10	6.29	0.1%	2.98	7.22	9.02	0%	-58.82	12Y.8M
IJS-VTV-TLT-SHY-GLD	-17.71	4.04	4.5%	1.71	5.71	0%	3.56	6.63	8.23	0%	-48.13	6Y.3M
IJS-VTV-TLT-LQD-GLD	-17.81	4.03	4.8%	1.82	5.89	0%	3.83	6.84	8.56	0%	-48.35	6Y.3M
IJS-VTV-VNQ-IEI-GLD	-22.97	4.01	6.3%	-0.34	6.06	0.1%	2.84	7.15	8.98	0%	-58.60	12Y.8M
IJS-VTV-SHY-IEI-GLD	-17.29	3.98	4.9%	1.81	5.56	0%	3.49	6.57	8.09	0%	-47.29	6Y.3M
IJS-VTV-VNQ-BND-GLD	-22.97	3.97	6.5%	-0.33	6.02	0.1%	2.85	7.16	8.94	0%	-58.59	12Y.8M

Order by **Baseline 3Y Return - All data** (from 1871/1927 to 2023-11) - **US Infl. Adjusted**

Portfolio	3Y Rolling Annualized Return (%)			7Y Rolling Annualized Return (%)			15Y Rolling Annualized Return (%)				Max Draw-down (%)	Long Neg Period (Y.M)
	Worst	Base ▼	%Fail	Worst	Base	%Fail	Worst	Base	Median	%Fail		
IJS-VTV-BND-IEI-GLD	-10.77	1.20	10.5%	-1.49	2.78	1.6%	1.19	3.79	5.22	0%	-33.57	12Y.5M
IJS-VTV-SHY-IEI-GLD	-10.73	1.17	10.6%	-1.52	2.74	2.3%	0.99	3.79	5.09	0%	-33.44	12Y.8M
IJS-VTV-TLT-IEI-GLD	-11.23	1.12	11.4%	-1.62	2.64	1.5%	1.26	3.59	5.50	0%	-34.65	11Y.10M
IJS-VTV-IEI-LQD-GLD	-10.83	1.12	11%	-1.49	2.73	1.5%	1.23	3.77	5.30	0%	-33.71	12Y.5M
IJS-VTV-TLT-SHY-GLD	-11.18	1.11	11.4%	-1.65	2.65	1.8%	1.06	3.68	5.29	0%	-34.50	12Y.7M
IJS-VTV-BND-LQD-GLD	-10.83	1.10	11.1%	-1.49	2.70	1.5%	1.24	3.77	5.28	0%	-33.70	12Y.5M
IJS-VTV-BND-TLT-GLD	-11.22	1.10	11.3%	-1.62	2.66	1.5%	1.26	3.59	5.51	0%	-34.64	11Y.10M
IJS-VTV-BND-SHY-GLD	-10.72	1.05	10.8%	-1.52	2.75	2.3%	1.00	3.79	5.06	0%	-33.43	12Y.8M
IJS-VTV-IEI-BIL-GLD	-11.14	1.03	11.3%	-1.44	2.62	2.7%	0.87	3.63	4.90	0%	-34.31	12Y.10M
VTI-IJS-BND-IEI-GLD	-11.00	1.01	10.5%	-1.53	2.98	1.5%	1.22	3.90	5.34	0%	-33.82	12Y.5M
IJS-VTV-SHY-LQD-GLD	-10.78	1.01	11.1%	-1.52	2.73	2.1%	1.04	3.81	5.12	0%	-33.57	12Y.8M
VTI-IJS-SHY-IEI-GLD	-10.96	0.99	10.3%	-1.56	2.95	2.1%	1.02	3.89	5.14	0%	-33.69	12Y.8M
VTI-IJS-IEI-LQD-GLD	-11.06	0.98	11.1%	-1.53	2.95	1.5%	1.26	3.89	5.41	0%	-33.95	12Y.4M
VTI-IJS-TLT-SHY-GLD	-11.40	0.97	11.3%	-1.69	2.87	1.8%	1.09	3.80	5.39	0%	-34.73	12Y.7M
VTI-IJS-BND-LQD-GLD	-11.06	0.96	11.3%	-1.53	2.97	1.5%	1.27	3.90	5.39	0%	-33.94	12Y.4M
IJS-VTV-TLT-LQD-GLD	-11.29	0.95	11.5%	-1.62	2.67	1.6%	1.30	3.54	5.52	0%	-34.77	11Y.10M
VTI-IJS-BND-SHY-GLD	-10.96	0.94	10.5%	-1.56	2.94	2.1%	1.03	3.90	5.11	0%	-33.68	12Y.8M
VTI-IJS-TLT-IEI-GLD	-11.45	0.91	11.1%	-1.66	2.81	1.5%	1.29	3.68	5.53	0%	-34.87	11Y.10M
VTI-IJS-IEI-BIL-GLD	-11.38	0.89	10.7%	-1.48	2.85	2.5%	0.90	3.73	4.95	0%	-34.57	12Y.8M
VTI-IJS-SHY-LQD-GLD	-11.02	0.88	10.9%	-1.56	2.93	2.1%	1.07	3.89	5.19	0%	-33.81	12Y.8M
IJS-VTV-TLT-BIL-GLD	-11.58	0.88	11.8%	-1.56	2.62	2.4%	0.94	3.59	5.11	0%	-35.35	12Y.8M

Ranking: Maximum Drawdown

Order by **Maximum Drawdown - Last 30 Years** (from 1993-12 to 2023-11)

Portfolio	3Y Rolling Annualized Return (%)			7Y Rolling Annualized Return (%)			15Y Rolling Annualized Return (%)				Max Draw-down (%) ▼	Long Neg Period (Y.M)
	Worst	Base	%Fail	Worst	Base	%Fail	Worst	Base	Median	%Fail		
SHY-IEI-HYG-BIL-GLD	-2.35	1.23	7.4%	0.31	2.21	0%	2.58	4.02	5.14	0%	-8.66	6Y.1M
VTV-BND-SHY-IEI-BIL	0.32	2.95	0%	2.37	3.61	0%	2.96	3.89	4.35	0%	-8.70	2Y.11M
VTV-BNDX-SHY-IEI-BIL	0.12	3.09	0%	2.47	3.82	0%	3.19	4.10	4.60	0%	-8.90	2Y.11M
BNDX-SHY-IEI-TIP-BIL	-2.05	1.41	4.9%	0.67	1.81	0%	1.88	3.06	4.08	0%	-8.95	4Y.4M
SHY-IEI-TIP-HYG-BIL	-1.19	1.55	4.6%	1.16	1.90	0%	2.21	3.21	4.02	0%	-8.97	3Y.10M
BNDX-SHY-IEI-HYG-BIL	-1.69	1.97	5.2%	0.98	2.42	0%	2.36	3.43	4.15	0%	-9.14	4Y.4M
BND-SHY-IEI-TIP-BIL	-2.29	1.06	4.9%	0.61	1.52	0%	1.69	2.75	3.80	0%	-9.24	4Y.4M
BNDX-SHY-TIP-BIL-GLD	-2.69	1.12	8.3%	0.07	1.98	0%	2.39	3.96	5.27	0%	-9.26	6Y.10M
VTV-SHY-IEI-TIP-BIL	1.01	2.80	0%	2.63	3.51	0%	3.07	3.90	4.48	0%	-9.27	2Y.8M
BNDX-SHY-TIP-HYG-BIL	-1.20	1.93	4.6%	1.22	2.40	0%	2.48	3.51	4.26	0%	-9.37	4Y.4M
BND-SHY-IEI-HYG-BIL	-1.80	1.73	5.2%	0.92	2.13	0%	2.18	3.17	3.88	0%	-9.41	4Y.4M
VTV-SHY-IEI-BIL-GLD	0.15	2.84	0%	2.15	3.66	0%	3.56	4.75	5.60	0%	-9.42	2Y.9M
BND-BNDX-SHY-TIP-BIL	-2.30	1.55	4.9%	0.67	1.97	0%	1.99	3.11	4.04	0%	-9.61	4Y.5M
BND-SHY-TIP-HYG-BIL	-1.45	1.69	4.6%	1.16	2.07	0%	2.31	3.24	3.99	0%	-9.70	4Y.2M
BND-SHY-TIP-BIL-GLD	-3.09	0.87	8.9%	-0.38	1.81	1.8%	2.21	3.71	5.00	0%	-9.72	7Y.6M
VTI-SHY-IEI-BIL-GLD	0.22	2.94	0%	2.24	3.91	0%	3.82	5.01	5.68	0%	-9.77	2Y.6M
VTV-BND-BNDX-SHY-BIL	-0.06	2.96	0.3%	2.47	3.93	0%	3.20	4.15	4.57	0%	-9.77	3Y.0M
BND-BNDX-SHY-HYG-BIL	-1.85	2.08	5.2%	0.97	2.58	0%	2.45	3.46	4.11	0%	-9.79	4Y.4M
BND-SHY-HYG-BIL-GLD	-2.26	1.34	6.5%	0.48	2.33	0%	2.68	4.06	5.09	0%	-9.82	5Y.3M
SHY-IEI-TIP-BIL-GLD	-3.13	0.77	8.6%	-0.55	1.73	2.9%	2.11	3.67	5.04	0%	-9.85	7Y.8M
IJS-SHY-IEI-TIP-BIL	0.63	2.86	0%	2.15	3.40	0%	3.21	3.92	4.95	0%	-9.88	2Y.11M

Order by **Maximum Drawdown - Last 30 Years** (from 1993-12 to 2023-11) - **US Infl. Adjusted**

Portfolio	3Y Rolling Annualized Return (%)			7Y Rolling Annualized Return (%)			15Y Rolling Annualized Return (%)				Max Draw-down (%) ▼	Long Neg Period (Y.M)
	Worst	Base	%Fail	Worst	Base	%Fail	Worst	Base	Median	%Fail		
VTV-SHY-IEI-TIP-BIL	-4.29	1.03	6.5%	-0.85	1.73	5.4%	0.67	1.80	2.35	0%	-15.44	10Y.7M
VTV-BNDX-SHY-TIP-BIL	-4.28	0.98	8.6%	-0.79	1.83	4.7%	0.90	2.06	2.55	0%	-15.70	9Y.10M
VTV-SHY-TIP-BIL-GLD	-3.69	1.01	7.7%	0.07	1.43	0%	1.27	2.71	3.50	0%	-15.74	9Y.8M
VTV-SHY-IEI-BIL-GLD	-4.01	0.96	7.1%	-0.16	1.43	0.4%	1.16	2.57	3.37	0%	-15.95	10Y.0M
VTV-SHY-IEI-HYG-BIL	-4.18	0.52	10.5%	-0.56	1.67	4%	0.85	2.02	2.45	0%	-15.99	9Y.10M
VTV-BND-SHY-TIP-BIL	-4.54	0.86	7.7%	-0.87	1.73	4.7%	0.69	1.83	2.35	0%	-16.07	10Y.6M
VTV-SHY-HYG-BIL-GLD	-3.10	0.47	10.2%	0.36	1.88	0%	1.50	2.88	3.46	0%	-16.23	7Y.8M
VTV-BNDX-SHY-IEI-BIL	-4.61	1.10	7.4%	-1.02	1.75	6.5%	0.78	1.97	2.42	0%	-16.24	10Y.0M
VTV-BNDX-SHY-BIL-GLD	-3.98	1.34	6.5%	-0.10	1.89	0.4%	1.42	2.87	3.54	0%	-16.31	7Y.9M
VTV-BND-SHY-HYG-BIL	-4.34	0.24	13.2%	-0.58	1.59	4%	0.86	2.05	2.42	0%	-16.44	9Y.5M
VTV-BND-SHY-BIL-GLD	-4.20	1.00	7.1%	-0.17	1.59	0.4%	1.21	2.64	3.34	0%	-16.54	9Y.8M
VTV-BND-SHY-IEI-BIL	-4.85	1.02	6.8%	-1.09	1.66	6.5%	0.57	1.77	2.21	0%	-16.55	10Y.7M
VTV-BND-BNDX-SHY-BIL	-4.85	0.97	8.9%	-1.03	1.66	6.1%	0.80	2.02	2.41	0%	-16.86	9Y.11M
VTV-IEI-TIP-BIL-GLD	-4.30	1.20	7.7%	-0.08	1.60	0.4%	1.48	3.02	3.88	0%	-16.91	9Y.8M
VTV-IEI-TIP-HYG-BIL	-4.12	1.01	9.5%	-0.49	2.17	1.8%	1.21	2.49	2.97	0%	-16.93	9Y.4M
VNQ-BNDX-SHY-BIL-GLD	-5.41	0.22	12.3%	-1.37	1.06	4.7%	1.12	2.69	4.11	0%	-17.00	12Y.5M
VNQ-SHY-IEI-BIL-GLD	-5.43	-0.16	15.7%	-1.43	0.76	6.5%	0.89	2.49	3.93	0%	-17.08	13Y.0M
VTV-BNDX-IEI-TIP-BIL	-4.93	1.32	7.7%	-0.94	2.18	4.7%	1.15	2.42	2.96	0%	-17.10	9Y.8M
VTV-SHY-TIP-HYG-BIL	-3.99	0.45	11.7%	-0.33	1.79	1.4%	0.95	2.17	2.59	0%	-17.13	9Y.8M
VTV-BNDX-TIP-BIL-GLD	-4.28	1.55	7.4%	-0.01	2.02	0.4%	1.73	3.28	4.05	0%	-17.17	7Y.8M
VTV-SHY-TIP-LQD-BIL	-4.72	0.90	8.3%	-0.74	1.74	4%	0.91	2.05	2.60	0%	-17.18	9Y.8M

Order by **Maximum Drawdown - Last 60 Years** (from 1963-12 to 2023-11)

Portfolio	3Y Rolling Annualized Return (%)			7Y Rolling Annualized Return (%)			15Y Rolling Annualized Return (%)				Max Draw-down (%) ▼	Long Neg Period (Y.M)
	Worst	Base	%Fail	Worst	Base	%Fail	Worst	Base	Median	%Fail		
VTV-BND-SHY-IEI-BIL	0.32	3.40	0%	2.37	3.97	0%	2.96	4.26	7.58	0%	-8.70	2Y.11M
VTV-SHY-IEI-BIL-GLD	0.15	3.49	0%	2.15	4.27	0%	3.56	5.50	7.00	0%	-9.42	2Y.9M
VTI-SHY-IEI-BIL-GLD	0.22	3.79	0%	2.24	4.80	0%	3.82	5.60	6.88	0%	-9.77	2Y.6M
VTV-SHY-IEI-LQD-BIL	0.11	3.39	0%	2.52	4.24	0%	3.20	4.55	7.75	0%	-10.05	2Y.11M
IJS-BND-SHY-IEI-BIL	0.15	3.55	0%	1.91	4.34	0%	3.10	4.74	8.36	0%	-10.17	2Y.11M
VTV-BND-IEI-BIL-GLD	0.31	3.60	0%	2.43	4.60	0%	3.86	5.88	7.21	0%	-10.55	2Y.10M
VTV-BND-SHY-BIL-GLD	0.16	3.50	0%	2.31	4.34	0%	3.63	5.48	6.92	0%	-10.60	2Y.5M
VTI-BND-SHY-BIL-GLD	0.22	3.78	0%	2.38	4.87	0%	3.88	5.61	6.83	0%	-10.65	2Y.9M
IJS-SHY-IEI-BIL-GLD	0.01	3.86	0%	2.18	4.62	0%	3.77	6.00	7.42	0%	-10.71	3Y.3M
IJS-BND-SHY-BIL-GLD	0.05	3.87	0%	2.24	4.72	0%	3.78	5.97	7.35	0%	-10.71	2Y.11M
VTV-BND-SHY-IEI-GLD	0.10	3.73	0%	2.45	4.69	0%	3.93	6.13	7.50	0%	-10.72	3Y.3M
VTI-BND-SHY-IEI-BIL	0.22	3.73	0%	2.71	4.32	0%	3.31	4.47	7.51	0%	-10.77	3Y.2M
VTV-BND-SHY-LQD-BIL	-0.06	3.50	0.2%	2.49	4.25	0%	3.21	4.52	7.67	0%	-10.84	3Y.3M
BND-SHY-IEI-BIL-GLD	-2.44	2.38	4.7%	-0.42	2.90	0.6%	2.07	4.54	6.16	0%	-10.96	7Y.4M
IJS-SHY-IEI-LQD-BIL	-0.06	3.66	0.2%	2.04	4.53	0%	3.33	5.02	8.48	0%	-11.45	3Y.10M
VTV-TLT-SHY-BIL-GLD	-0.99	3.59	0.6%	2.59	4.97	0%	4.08	6.18	7.30	0%	-11.58	3Y.5M
IJS-SHY-LQD-BIL-GLD	0.05	3.97	0%	2.41	5.09	0%	4.01	6.20	7.50	0%	-11.61	2Y.10M
BND-SHY-IEI-LQD-BIL	-3.09	2.58	2.5%	0.50	3.17	0%	1.95	3.56	6.80	0%	-11.72	4Y.7M
VNQ-SHY-IEI-BIL-GLD	-0.53	2.69	0.7%	1.20	4.02	0%	3.31	5.68	7.19	0%	-11.73	3Y.5M
IJS-BND-IEI-BIL-GLD	0.30	3.97	0%	2.50	5.15	0%	4.02	6.36	7.68	0%	-11.75	2Y.10M
VTI-BND-IEI-BIL-GLD	0.29	3.82	0%	2.49	5.05	0%	4.12	5.99	7.14	0%	-11.77	3Y.2M

Order by **Maximum Drawdown - Last 60 Years** (from 1963-12 to 2023-11) - **US Infl. Adjusted**

Portfolio	3Y Rolling Annualized Return (%)			7Y Rolling Annualized Return (%)			15Y Rolling Annualized Return (%)				Max Draw-down (%) ▼	Long Neg Period (Y.M)
	Worst	Base	%Fail	Worst	Base	%Fail	Worst	Base	Median	%Fail		
VTV-SHY-IEI-BIL-GLD	-4.01	0.89	8.3%	-0.16	2.05	0.2%	1.16	2.95	3.73	0%	-15.95	10Y.0M
VTV-BND-SHY-BIL-GLD	-4.20	0.94	8.2%	-0.17	2.10	0.2%	1.21	2.94	3.67	0%	-16.54	9Y.8M
VNQ-SHY-IEI-BIL-GLD	-5.43	0.12	14.2%	-1.43	1.66	3.1%	0.89	2.78	4.02	0%	-17.08	13Y.0M
VNQ-BND-SHY-BIL-GLD	-5.63	0.15	13.7%	-1.43	1.71	2.5%	0.89	2.78	4.02	0%	-17.75	12Y.11M
VTV-SHY-LQD-BIL-GLD	-4.32	1.01	8.3%	-0.03	2.24	0.2%	1.43	3.04	3.81	0%	-17.76	7Y.9M
VTV-BND-IEI-BIL-GLD	-4.81	0.95	8.9%	-0.31	2.18	0.6%	1.45	3.12	3.98	0%	-17.93	8Y.9M
VTI-SHY-IEI-BIL-GLD	-4.34	0.86	8.5%	0.26	2.17	0%	1.42	3.03	3.69	0%	-17.94	7Y.9M
IJS-SHY-IEI-BIL-GLD	-3.68	1.11	6.6%	-0.59	2.57	0.8%	1.34	3.47	4.49	0%	-18.40	10Y.9M
VTI-BND-SHY-BIL-GLD	-4.54	0.91	8.6%	0.25	2.18	0%	1.45	2.99	3.65	0%	-18.56	7Y.9M
VNQ-SHY-LQD-BIL-GLD	-5.77	0.13	13.3%	-1.30	1.78	2.2%	1.11	2.84	4.13	0%	-18.67	12Y.5M
IJS-BND-SHY-BIL-GLD	-3.92	1.20	6.6%	-0.59	2.61	0.6%	1.35	3.45	4.44	0%	-18.81	10Y.8M
VTV-BND-SHY-IEI-GLD	-5.34	1.02	8.9%	-0.47	2.17	1.1%	1.52	3.30	4.31	0%	-18.95	9Y.8M
VTV-IEI-LQD-BIL-GLD	-4.94	0.90	9.1%	-0.24	2.28	0.9%	1.67	3.22	4.17	0%	-19.15	7Y.9M
VNQ-BND-IEI-BIL-GLD	-6.25	0.01	14.7%	-1.58	1.83	3.1%	1.12	2.90	4.19	0%	-19.37	12Y.9M
VTV-BND-LQD-BIL-GLD	-5.13	0.86	9.1%	-0.23	2.29	0.9%	1.67	3.20	4.13	0%	-19.76	7Y.9M
VTI-LQD-BIL-GLD	-4.69	0.99	8.3%	0.38	2.27	0%	1.67	3.09	3.84	0%	-19.78	7Y.9M
VTV-BND-SHY-IEI-BIL	-5.48	-0.64	17.8%	-2.63	-0.02	15.2%	-0.99	1.05	3.28	7.8%	-19.81	18Y.7M
IJS-SHY-LQD-BIL-GLD	-4.11	1.37	6.6%	-0.46	2.73	0.3%	1.57	3.55	4.53	0%	-19.83	9Y.8M
VTI-BND-IEI-BIL-GLD	-5.16	0.94	8.6%	0.10	2.22	0%	1.69	3.13	3.97	0%	-19.93	7Y.9M
IJS-BND-IEI-BIL-GLD	-4.58	1.30	6.9%	-0.74	2.70	0.8%	1.59	3.69	4.68	0%	-19.96	10Y.9M
IJS-BND-SHY-IEI-BIL	-5.90	0.27	13.7%	-1.88	1.15	8.8%	0.55	1.94	4.08	0%	-19.97	13Y.8M

Order by **Maximum Drawdown - All data** (from 1871/1927 to 2023-11)

Portfolio	3Y Rolling Annualized Return (%)			7Y Rolling Annualized Return (%)			15Y Rolling Annualized Return (%)				Max Draw-down (%) ▼	Long Neg Period (Y.M)
	Worst	Base	%Fail	Worst	Base	%Fail	Worst	Base	Median	%Fail		
BND-SHY-IEI-BIL-GLD	-2.44	1.70	2.3%	-0.42	1.85	0.2%	1.09	2.37	3.53	0%	-10.96	7Y.4M
BND-SHY-IEI-LQD-BIL	-3.09	2.14	1.1%	0.50	2.28	0%	1.41	2.58	4.00	0%	-11.72	4Y.7M
SHY-IEI-LQD-BIL-GLD	-2.31	1.77	2.2%	-0.02	1.95	0.1%	1.10	2.44	3.52	0%	-11.94	7Y.3M
BND-SHY-LQD-BIL-GLD	-2.31	1.78	2.2%	0.15	1.96	0%	1.11	2.46	3.52	0%	-12.68	6Y.3M
VNQ-BND-IEI-BIL-GLD	-2.54	1.49	1.6%	0.82	1.87	0%	1.35	2.30	5.91	0%	-13.01	5Y.2M
VNQ-BND-SHY-IEI-BIL	-1.53	1.80	1.7%	0.74	2.27	0%	1.94	2.55	4.80	0%	-13.18	4Y.9M
VNQ-BND-SHY-BIL-GLD	-2.52	1.51	1.6%	0.35	1.85	0%	1.38	2.24	5.72	0%	-13.19	5Y.6M
VNQ-SHY-IEI-BIL-GLD	-2.52	1.50	1.5%	0.34	1.83	0%	1.38	2.23	5.76	0%	-13.19	5Y.6M
VNQ-BND-SHY-IEI-GLD	-2.11	1.55	1.8%	0.86	1.99	0%	1.40	2.38	6.18	0%	-13.83	5Y.1M
VNQ-IEI-LQD-BIL-GLD	-2.60	1.52	1.7%	0.85	1.91	0%	1.33	2.30	6.00	0%	-14.02	4Y.11M
VNQ-SHY-IEI-LQD-BIL	-1.58	1.74	1.9%	0.84	2.30	0%	1.99	2.55	5.03	0%	-14.14	4Y.9M
VNQ-SHY-LQD-BIL-GLD	-2.57	1.52	1.6%	0.44	1.91	0%	1.37	2.26	5.72	0%	-14.23	5Y.4M
BND-IEI-LQD-BIL-GLD	-2.95	1.91	2.4%	0.29	2.11	0%	1.13	2.30	3.55	0%	-14.29	6Y.3M
VNQ-BND-LQD-BIL-GLD	-2.59	1.53	1.5%	0.86	1.92	0%	1.34	2.31	6.00	0%	-14.92	4Y.11M
VNQ-BND-IEI-LQD-BIL	-2.13	1.82	1.9%	1.05	2.39	0%	2.00	2.61	5.07	0%	-15.04	4Y.6M
VNQ-BND-SHY-LQD-BIL	-1.58	1.75	1.9%	0.85	2.31	0%	1.99	2.55	5.03	0%	-15.08	4Y.9M
VNQ-SHY-IEI-LQD-GLD	-2.17	1.58	1.5%	0.87	2.03	0%	1.39	2.40	6.23	0%	-15.09	5Y.1M
VNQ-TLT-SHY-BIL-GLD	-2.91	1.35	2.4%	0.62	1.74	0%	1.19	2.16	6.08	0%	-15.20	5Y.2M
BND-SHY-IEI-LQD-GLD	-3.50	1.83	2.7%	0.33	2.19	0%	1.15	2.36	3.60	0%	-15.44	6Y.5M
VNQ-BND-SHY-LQD-GLD	-2.16	1.58	1.6%	0.88	2.04	0%	1.39	2.40	6.25	0%	-15.99	5Y.1M
TLT-SHY-IEI-BIL-GLD	-4.20	1.81	2.6%	-0.03	1.97	0.1%	1.02	2.15	3.64	0%	-16.36	7Y.0M

Order by **Maximum Drawdown - All data** (from 1871/1927 to 2023-11) - **US Infl. Adjusted**

Portfolio	3Y Rolling Annualized Return (%)			7Y Rolling Annualized Return (%)			15Y Rolling Annualized Return (%)				Max Draw-down (%) ▼	Long Neg Period (Y.M)
	Worst	Base	%Fail	Worst	Base	%Fail	Worst	Base	Median	%Fail		
VTI-VNQ-SHY-IEI-GLD	-7.57	0.18	13.2%	-2.24	1.12	7.7%	-0.51	1.64	3.70	2%	-21.26	17Y.7M
VTV-VNQ-SHY-IEI-GLD	-7.56	0.21	14%	-2.20	0.93	8.4%	-0.56	1.56	3.58	2.5%	-21.81	20Y.2M
VTI-VNQ-IEI-BIL-GLD	-7.65	0.06	14.4%	-2.15	1.07	8.2%	-0.63	1.54	3.48	3.3%	-21.85	18Y.10M
VTV-VNQ-BND-IEI-GLD	-7.51	0.15	14.2%	-2.17	1.05	8.3%	-0.35	1.52	3.69	0.9%	-22.13	16Y.11M
VTV-VNQ-TLT-BIL-GLD	-7.62	-0.17	16.1%	-2.24	0.83	9.5%	-0.60	1.33	3.49	2.6%	-22.21	20Y.2M
VTI-VNQ-BND-SHY-GLD	-7.56	0.17	13.6%	-2.23	1.13	7.7%	-0.51	1.64	3.65	2%	-22.29	17Y.7M
VTI-VNQ-BND-IEI-GLD	-7.52	0.23	13.6%	-2.20	1.14	7.3%	-0.31	1.61	3.82	0.8%	-22.73	16Y.11M
VTV-VNQ-IEI-BIL-GLD	-7.64	0.03	14.4%	-2.11	0.82	8.8%	-0.68	1.50	3.43	3.6%	-22.78	20Y.3M
VTI-VNQ-SHY-BIL-GLD	-7.69	0.00	14.8%	-2.30	1.04	8.6%	-0.83	1.60	3.37	4.7%	-23.15	20Y.5M
VTV-VNQ-BND-SHY-GLD	-7.56	0.09	14%	-2.19	0.93	8.4%	-0.55	1.57	3.58	2.5%	-23.22	20Y.2M
VTI-VNQ-BND-BIL-GLD	-7.64	0.06	14.4%	-2.14	1.07	8.1%	-0.63	1.55	3.48	3.1%	-23.27	18Y.5M
IJS-VNQ-BND-SHY-GLD	-7.94	0.35	12.8%	-2.28	2.09	3.6%	0.42	2.48	4.50	0%	-23.39	12Y.7M
IJS-VNQ-SHY-IEI-GLD	-7.94	0.40	12.6%	-2.29	2.08	3.6%	0.41	2.48	4.51	0%	-23.40	12Y.8M
IJS-VNQ-BND-IEI-GLD	-7.89	0.47	12.2%	-2.25	2.07	2.7%	0.61	2.52	4.70	0%	-23.51	12Y.4M
VTI-VNQ-TLT-BIL-GLD	-7.63	-0.01	15%	-2.27	0.95	8%	-0.56	1.38	3.56	2.3%	-23.54	17Y.8M
IJS-VNQ-IEI-LQD-GLD	-7.90	0.31	13.1%	-2.26	2.03	2.7%	0.65	2.49	4.72	0%	-23.65	8Y.10M
VTV-VNQ-SHY-BIL-GLD	-7.69	-0.09	15.7%	-2.39	0.78	9.6%	-0.88	1.50	3.31	5%	-23.91	20Y.9M
VTV-VNQ-IEI-LQD-GLD	-7.52	0.06	14.6%	-2.17	1.02	8.5%	-0.31	1.54	3.75	0.9%	-23.93	16Y.11M
VTV-BND-SHY-IEI-GLD	-8.11	0.27	14%	-3.30	0.39	12.3%	-1.12	0.94	3.44	7.9%	-23.95	21Y.0M
VTV-BND-SHY-LQD-GLD	-8.13	0.22	13.9%	-3.27	0.46	12.2%	-1.08	0.94	3.47	7.7%	-23.99	21Y.0M

175

Ranking: Longest Negative Period

Order by **Longest Negative Period** - **Last 30 Years** (from 1993-12 to 2023-11)

Portfolio	3Y Rolling Annualized Return (%)			7Y Rolling Annualized Return (%)			15Y Rolling Annualized Return (%)				Max Draw-down (%)	Long Neg Period (Y.M) ▲
	Worst	Base	%Fail	Worst	Base	%Fail	Worst	Base	Median	%Fail		
VTV-BNDX-SHY-BIL-GLD	0.53	3.17	0%	2.77	3.97	0%	3.82	4.98	5.79	0%	-11.82	2Y.5M
VTV-SHY-LQD-BIL-GLD	0.29	3.17	0%	2.63	4.09	0%	3.86	5.08	5.80	0%	-12.77	2Y.5M
VTV-BND-SHY-BIL-GLD	0.16	2.93	0%	2.31	3.76	0%	3.63	4.80	5.59	0%	-10.60	2Y.5M
VTV-SHY-IEI-HYG-GLD	0.42	3.26	0%	3.10	4.39	0%	4.31	5.68	6.51	0%	-13.68	2Y.6M
VTI-BNDX-SHY-BIL-GLD	0.59	3.02	0%	2.86	4.21	0%	4.08	5.32	5.84	0%	-11.88	2Y.6M
VTI-IEI-HYG-BIL-GLD	0.36	2.95	0%	3.16	4.64	0%	4.46	5.72	6.26	0%	-14.01	2Y.6M
VTI-SHY-IEI-BIL-GLD	0.22	2.94	0%	2.24	3.91	0%	3.82	5.01	5.68	0%	-9.77	2Y.6M
IJS-BNDX-SHY-BIL-GLD	0.35	3.25	0%	2.35	3.75	0%	4.00	5.12	6.30	0%	-10.59	2Y.8M
VTV-SHY-IEI-TIP-BIL	1.01	2.80	0%	2.63	3.51	0%	3.07	3.90	4.48	0%	-9.27	2Y.8M
VTV-BNDX-TIP-BIL-GLD	0.04	3.33	0%	2.85	4.27	0%	4.14	5.43	6.31	0%	-14.49	2Y.9M
VTV-BNDX-IEI-BIL-GLD	0.68	3.32	0%	2.90	4.04	0%	4.04	5.33	6.19	0%	-11.77	2Y.9M
VTV-IEI-HYG-BIL-GLD	0.29	3.07	0%	2.96	4.37	0%	4.18	5.48	6.21	0%	-13.95	2Y.9M
VTI-BND-SHY-BIL-GLD	0.22	2.85	0%	2.38	4.06	0%	3.88	5.04	5.68	0%	-10.65	2Y.9M
VTV-SHY-IEI-BIL-GLD	0.15	2.84	0%	2.15	3.66	0%	3.56	4.75	5.60	0%	-9.42	2Y.9M
VTV-IEI-TIP-CWB-GLD	0.67	4.48	0%	4.01	5.81	0%	5.40	6.68	7.48	0%	-18.57	2Y.10M
IJS-SHY-IEI-CWB-GLD	0.69	4.46	0%	3.48	5.39	0%	5.19	6.41	7.42	0%	-14.86	2Y.10M
VTV-SHY-IEI-CWB-GLD	1.21	4.19	0%	4.03	5.41	0%	5.07	6.29	6.94	0%	-15.91	2Y.10M
VTI-SHY-TIP-CWB-GLD	0.41	4.15	0%	4.04	5.75	0%	5.41	6.41	7.25	0%	-18.71	2Y.10M
VTI-SHY-IEI-CWB-GLD	1.38	4.15	0%	4.09	5.63	0%	5.31	6.39	7.12	0%	-15.96	2Y.10M
VTI-VTV-BND-IEI-GLD	0.06	4.02	0%	4.84	5.93	0%	5.57	6.82	7.30	0%	-17.50	2Y.10M
VTV-IEI-CWB-BIL-GLD	0.74	4.00	0%	3.91	5.20	0%	4.93	6.07	6.67	0%	-16.19	2Y.10M

Order by **Longest Negative Period** - **Last 30 Years** (from 1993-12 to 2023-11) - **US Infl. Adjusted**

Portfolio	3Y Rolling Annualized Return (%)			7Y Rolling Annualized Return (%)			15Y Rolling Annualized Return (%)				Max Draw-down (%)	Long Neg Period (Y.M) ▲
	Worst	Base	%Fail	Worst	Base	%Fail	Worst	Base	Median	%Fail		
VTI-SHY-IEI-CWB-GLD	-4.13	1.83	5.2%	1.86	3.20	0%	2.85	4.14	4.75	0%	-21.87	3Y.10M
VTI-IEI-TIP-CWB-GLD	-4.50	2.20	6.2%	1.89	3.56	0%	3.18	4.54	5.31	0%	-22.79	3Y.11M
VTI-BND-SHY-CWB-GLD	-4.34	1.98	7.1%	1.84	3.13	0%	2.83	4.05	4.70	0%	-22.49	3Y.11M
VTV-IEI-TIP-CWB-GLD	-4.02	2.28	4.9%	1.55	3.42	0%	2.94	4.41	5.23	0%	-21.22	4Y.0M
MTUM-SHY-CWB-BIL-GLD	-4.82	1.63	8.6%	1.95	3.42	0%	2.59	3.91	4.53	0%	-21.74	4Y.1M
VTI-BNDX-IEI-CWB-GLD	-4.77	2.33	7.1%	1.74	3.56	0%	3.29	4.67	5.28	0%	-23.62	4Y.2M
MTUM-SHY-TIP-CWB-GLD	-5.72	2.26	6.2%	1.81	3.93	0%	3.04	4.64	5.33	0%	-23.63	4Y.2M
VTI-BND-IEI-CWB-GLD	-4.99	2.18	5.5%	1.66	3.39	0%	3.07	4.50	5.10	0%	-23.86	4Y.2M
VTI-BNDX-SHY-CWB-GLD	-4.12	2.08	7.4%	1.91	3.35	0%	3.05	4.24	4.88	0%	-22.26	4Y.2M
MTUM-IEI-CWB-BIL-GLD	-5.46	2.07	7.7%	1.78	3.74	0%	2.84	4.32	4.94	0%	-23.09	4Y.2M
VTV-SHY-TIP-CWB-GLD	-3.38	2.03	4.6%	1.72	3.20	0%	2.69	4.09	4.82	0%	-20.48	4Y.2M
MTUM-TIP-CWB-BIL-GLD	-5.17	1.85	7.1%	1.99	3.79	0%	2.91	4.45	5.04	0%	-22.61	4Y.2M
VTI-MTUM-TIP-BIL-GLD	-4.01	0.94	11.1%	2.42	3.85	0%	3.18	4.28	5.12	0%	-20.76	4Y.3M
VTI-TLT-CWB-BIL-GLD	-6.05	1.84	6.8%	1.30	3.47	0%	3.20	4.52	5.15	0%	-24.68	4Y.4M
VTI-VNQ-SHY-BIL-GLD	-4.11	1.35	8%	0.90	2.95	0%	2.23	3.76	4.61	0%	-22.96	4Y.4M
VNQ-TIP-CWB-BIL-GLD	-4.32	1.18	8.3%	0.60	2.56	0%	2.28	3.83	5.15	0%	-21.65	4Y.4M
VNQ-SHY-TIP-CWB-GLD	-4.89	1.16	7.7%	0.41	2.64	0%	2.40	4.03	5.44	0%	-21.52	4Y.4M
VNQ-SHY-CWB-BIL-GLD	-3.95	1.02	8%	0.55	2.36	0%	1.96	3.50	4.69	0%	-20.54	4Y.4M
VTI-IEI-CWB-BIL-GLD	-3.57	1.68	7.1%	2.04	2.99	0%	2.73	3.83	4.49	0%	-20.84	4Y.5M
VTI-MTUM-TLT-CWB-GLD	-6.62	1.41	11.4%	2.89	5.07	0%	4.85	5.92	6.78	0%	-28.67	4Y.5M
VTV-MTUM-TLT-CWB-GLD	-6.08	1.22	11.1%	2.61	5.16	0%	4.60	5.90	6.66	0%	-26.53	4Y.5M

Order by **Longest Negative Period** - **Last 60 Years** (from 1963-12 to 2023-11)

Portfolio	3Y Rolling Annualized Return (%)			7Y Rolling Annualized Return (%)			15Y Rolling Annualized Return (%)				Max Draw-down (%)	Long Neg Period (Y.M) ▲
	Worst	Base	%Fail	Worst	Base	%Fail	Worst	Base	Median	%Fail		
VTV-SHY-LQD-BIL-GLD	0.29	3.67	0%	2.63	4.62	0%	3.86	5.72	7.00	0%	-12.77	2Y.5M
VTV-BND-SHY-BIL-GLD	0.16	3.50	0%	2.31	4.34	0%	3.63	5.48	6.92	0%	-10.60	2Y.5M
VTI-SHY-IEI-BIL-GLD	0.22	3.79	0%	2.24	4.80	0%	3.82	5.60	6.88	0%	-9.77	2Y.6M
VTI-BND-SHY-BIL-GLD	0.22	3.78	0%	2.38	4.87	0%	3.88	5.61	6.83	0%	-10.65	2Y.9M
VTV-SHY-IEI-BIL-GLD	0.15	3.49	0%	2.15	4.27	0%	3.56	5.50	7.00	0%	-9.42	2Y.9M
IJS-BND-IEI-BIL-GLD	0.30	3.97	0%	2.50	5.15	0%	4.02	6.36	7.68	0%	-11.75	2Y.10M
IJS-SHY-LQD-BIL-GLD	0.05	3.97	0%	2.41	5.09	0%	4.01	6.20	7.50	0%	-11.61	2Y.10M
VTI-SHY-LQD-BIL-GLD	0.36	3.90	0%	2.69	5.04	0%	4.11	5.81	6.90	0%	-12.83	2Y.10M
VTV-IEI-LQD-BIL-GLD	0.45	3.73	0%	2.74	4.93	0%	4.11	6.11	7.30	0%	-12.72	2Y.10M
VTV-BND-IEI-BIL-GLD	0.31	3.60	0%	2.43	4.60	0%	3.86	5.88	7.21	0%	-10.55	2Y.10M
VTI-IJS-SHY-IEI-GLD	0.12	5.13	0%	3.95	6.62	0%	5.44	7.36	9.20	0%	-16.78	2Y.11M
VTI-IJS-TLT-BIL-GLD	0.15	5.02	0%	4.48	6.91	0%	5.86	7.75	9.22	0%	-16.77	2Y.11M
IJS-IEI-LQD-BIL-GLD	0.30	4.05	0%	2.67	5.47	0%	4.25	6.58	7.84	0%	-12.87	2Y.11M
IJS-BND-SHY-BIL-GLD	0.05	3.87	0%	2.24	4.72	0%	3.78	5.97	7.35	0%	-10.71	2Y.11M
IJS-BND-SHY-IEI-BIL	0.15	3.55	0%	1.91	4.34	0%	3.10	4.74	8.36	0%	-10.17	2Y.11M
VTV-BND-SHY-IEI-BIL	0.32	3.40	0%	2.37	3.97	0%	2.96	4.26	7.58	0%	-8.70	2Y.11M
VTV-SHY-IEI-LQD-BIL	0.11	3.39	0%	2.52	4.24	0%	3.20	4.55	7.75	0%	-10.05	2Y.11M
VTI-IJS-IEI-LQD-GLD	-0.85	5.18	0.3%	4.40	7.15	0%	5.89	7.90	9.55	0%	-18.54	3Y.1M
VTI-IJS-BND-IEI-GLD	-0.02	5.17	0.2%	4.25	6.87	0%	5.69	7.69	9.44	0%	-16.88	3Y.1M
VTI-IJS-BND-SHY-GLD	-0.52	5.08	0.3%	3.99	6.62	0%	5.44	7.28	9.12	0%	-17.48	3Y.1M
IJS-VTV-TLT-BIL-GLD	-0.15	4.92	0.2%	4.07	6.56	0%	5.54	7.53	9.29	0%	-16.40	3Y.1M

Order by **Longest Negative Period** - **Last 60 Years** (from 1963-12 to 2023-11) - **US Infl. Adjusted**

Portfolio	3Y Rolling Annualized Return (%)			7Y Rolling Annualized Return (%)			15Y Rolling Annualized Return (%)				Max Draw-down (%)	Long Neg Period (Y.M) ▲
	Worst	Base	%Fail	Worst	Base	%Fail	Worst	Base	Median	%Fail		
VTI-IJS-IEI-BIL-GLD	-3.22	1.84	5.7%	0.89	3.50	0%	2.86	4.52	5.29	0%	-22.03	6Y.4M
IJS-VTV-IEI-BIL-GLD	-3.72	1.80	6.1%	0.85	3.33	0%	2.54	4.40	5.29	0%	-22.78	6Y.4M
IJS-VTV-BND-BIL-GLD	-3.72	1.75	6.4%	0.85	3.35	0%	2.54	4.38	5.22	0%	-22.78	6Y.4M
IJS-VTV-SHY-BIL-GLD	-3.36	1.70	6.4%	0.98	3.18	0%	2.28	4.13	5.18	0%	-22.10	6Y.4M
VTI-IJS-BND-BIL-GLD	-3.22	1.68	6.6%	0.89	3.46	0%	2.86	4.48	5.25	0%	-22.02	6Y.4M
VTI-IJS-SHY-BIL-GLD	-2.99	1.64	6.3%	1.01	3.41	0%	2.60	4.28	5.13	0%	-21.35	6Y.4M
IJS-VTV-BND-IEI-GLD	-4.53	2.10	6.4%	0.60	3.65	0%	2.93	4.83	5.80	0%	-24.58	6Y.5M
VTI-IJS-TLT-IEI-GLD	-5.47	2.09	7.5%	0.17	3.84	0%	2.94	4.79	6.38	0%	-24.77	6Y.5M
IJS-VTV-SHY-IEI-GLD	-4.04	2.08	5.7%	0.74	3.50	0%	2.67	4.63	5.53	0%	-23.90	6Y.5M
IJS-VTV-TLT-SHY-GLD	-4.76	2.08	7.3%	0.26	3.69	0%	3.21	4.88	5.97	0%	-24.84	6Y.5M
VTI-IJS-BND-TLT-GLD	-5.75	2.05	7.7%	0.17	3.81	0%	2.94	4.80	6.36	0%	-25.02	6Y.5M
VTI-IJS-SHY-IEI-GLD	-3.54	2.05	5.7%	0.77	3.69	0%	2.99	4.75	5.56	0%	-23.15	6Y.5M
VTI-IJS-TLT-SHY-GLD	-4.79	2.02	7.2%	0.30	3.81	0%	3.20	4.83	6.03	0%	-24.09	6Y.5M
VTI-IJS-BND-IEI-GLD	-4.02	2.00	6.4%	0.64	3.79	0%	3.23	4.86	5.82	0%	-23.82	6Y.5M
IJS-VTV-BND-SHY-GLD	-4.04	1.99	6.3%	0.74	3.51	0%	2.67	4.62	5.46	0%	-23.90	6Y.5M
VTI-IJS-BND-SHY-GLD	-3.54	1.94	6%	0.78	3.64	0%	2.98	4.72	5.48	0%	-23.15	6Y.5M
IJS-VTV-IEI-LQD-GLD	-4.62	1.92	7.5%	0.21	3.77	0%	3.12	4.83	5.91	0%	-24.70	6Y.5M
VTI-IJS-IEI-LQD-GLD	-4.11	1.90	7.5%	0.25	3.89	0%	3.15	4.84	5.96	0%	-23.94	6Y.5M
IJS-VTV-BND-LQD-GLD	-4.62	1.88	7.6%	0.21	3.71	0%	3.11	4.82	5.83	0%	-24.70	6Y.5M
IJS-VTV-TLT-BIL-GLD	-4.44	1.87	7.3%	0.38	3.53	0%	3.09	4.70	5.68	0%	-23.73	6Y.5M
VTI-IJS-TLT-BIL-GLD	-4.22	1.85	7.3%	0.42	3.64	0%	3.22	4.68	5.73	0%	-22.97	6Y.5M

Order by **Longest Negative Period** - All data (from 1871/1927 to 2023-11)

Portfolio	3Y Rolling Annualized Return (%)			7Y Rolling Annualized Return (%)			15Y Rolling Annualized Return (%)				Max Draw-down (%)	Long Neg Period (Y.M)
	Worst	Base	%Fail	Worst	Base	%Fail	Worst	Base	Median	%Fail		
VNQ-BND-IEI-LQD-BIL	-2.13	1.82	1.9%	1.05	2.39	0%	2.00	2.61	5.07	0%	-15.04	4Y.6M
VNQ-BND-IEI-LQD-GLD	-2.46	1.62	2.2%	0.85	2.10	0%	1.36	2.41	6.49	0%	-17.26	4Y.6M
BND-SHY-IEI-LQD-BIL	-3.09	2.14	1.1%	0.50	2.28	0%	1.41	2.58	4.00	0%	-11.72	4Y.7M
VNQ-BND-SHY-IEI-LQD	-2.71	1.88	2%	0.87	2.51	0%	2.05	2.76	5.16	0%	-16.46	4Y.7M
VNQ-BND-SHY-IEI-BIL	-1.53	1.80	1.7%	0.74	2.27	0%	1.94	2.55	4.80	0%	-13.18	4Y.9M
VNQ-BND-SHY-LQD-BIL	-1.58	1.75	1.9%	0.85	2.31	0%	1.99	2.55	5.03	0%	-15.08	4Y.9M
VNQ-SHY-IEI-LQD-BIL	-1.58	1.74	1.9%	0.84	2.30	0%	1.99	2.55	5.03	0%	-14.14	4Y.9M
VNQ-TLT-LQD-BIL-GLD	-3.57	1.38	2.2%	0.74	1.81	0%	1.14	2.20	6.46	0%	-18.64	4Y.9M
VNQ-BND-TLT-BIL-GLD	-3.41	1.36	2.4%	0.79	1.80	0%	1.15	2.21	6.37	0%	-17.37	4Y.9M
VNQ-TLT-IEI-BIL-GLD	-3.18	1.35	2.4%	0.78	1.78	0%	1.15	2.20	6.38	0%	-16.47	4Y.9M
VNQ-BND-LQD-BIL-GLD	-2.59	1.53	1.5%	0.86	1.92	0%	1.34	2.31	6.00	0%	-14.92	4Y.11M
VNQ-IEI-LQD-BIL-GLD	-2.60	1.52	1.7%	0.85	1.91	0%	1.33	2.30	6.00	0%	-14.02	4Y.11M
VTI-BND-SHY-IEI-LQD	-5.40	3.08	1.7%	1.97	3.89	0%	2.95	4.19	5.13	0%	-18.94	5Y.1M
VNQ-BND-SHY-LQD-GLD	-2.16	1.58	1.6%	0.88	2.04	0%	1.39	2.40	6.25	0%	-15.99	5Y.1M
VNQ-SHY-IEI-LQD-GLD	-2.17	1.58	1.6%	0.87	2.03	0%	1.39	2.40	6.23	0%	-15.09	5Y.1M
VNQ-BND-SHY-IEI-GLD	-2.11	1.55	1.8%	0.86	1.99	0%	1.40	2.38	6.18	0%	-13.83	5Y.1M
VTI-TLT-SHY-IEI-BIL	-6.13	3.32	1.9%	1.90	3.94	0%	2.95	4.27	5.11	0%	-20.60	5Y.2M
VTI-BND-TLT-SHY-BIL	-6.13	3.32	1.9%	1.90	3.95	0%	2.96	4.28	5.12	0%	-20.59	5Y.2M
VTI-TLT-SHY-LQD-BIL	-6.19	3.24	2%	1.97	3.93	0%	3.01	4.28	5.13	0%	-20.73	5Y.2M
VTI-BND-SHY-LQD-BIL	-5.77	3.24	1.4%	1.82	3.92	0%	2.93	4.24	5.05	0%	-19.60	5Y.2M
VTI-SHY-IEI-LQD-BIL	-5.77	3.22	1.3%	1.81	3.90	0%	2.92	4.24	5.06	0%	-19.62	5Y.2M

Order by **Longest Negative Period** - All data (from 1871/1927 to 2023-11) - **US Infl. Adjusted**

Portfolio	3Y Rolling Annualized Return (%)			7Y Rolling Annualized Return (%)			15Y Rolling Annualized Return (%)				Max Draw-down (%)	Long Neg Period (Y.M)
	Worst	Base	%Fail	Worst	Base	%Fail	Worst	Base	Median	%Fail		
VTI-IJS-VNQ-BND-GLD	-17.11	0.65	12.7%	-1.23	3.20	1.5%	1.78	3.87	5.85	0%	-47.99	8Y.10M
VTI-IJS-VNQ-LQD-GLD	-17.16	0.49	13.3%	-1.17	3.23	1.8%	1.82	3.84	5.84	0%	-48.09	8Y.10M
IJS-VNQ-IEI-LQD-GLD	-7.90	0.31	13.1%	-2.26	2.03	2.7%	0.65	2.49	4.72	0%	-23.65	8Y.10M
IJS-VNQ-BND-LQD-GLD	-7.89	0.31	13.1%	-2.25	2.03	2.7%	0.66	2.50	4.72	0%	-24.73	8Y.10M
VTI-IJS-VNQ-IEI-GLD	-17.11	0.67	12.7%	-1.23	3.22	1.5%	1.78	3.87	5.86	0%	-48.00	8Y.11M
VTI-IJS-VNQ-TLT-GLD	-17.52	0.46	13.4%	-1.09	3.15	1.7%	1.85	3.78	5.79	0%	-48.81	8Y.11M
VTI-IJS-VTV-TLT-GLD	-21.68	0.59	13.4%	-1.25	3.65	1.2%	2.31	4.31	6.59	0%	-56.27	9Y.0M
IJS-VTV-VNQ-LQD-GLD	-16.91	0.53	13%	-1.23	3.10	1.6%	1.79	3.81	5.82	0%	-47.81	9Y.0M
IJS-VTV-VNQ-TLT-GLD	-17.28	0.52	13.3%	-1.15	3.07	1.7%	1.81	3.76	5.82	0%	-48.55	9Y.0M
IJS-VTV-VNQ-IEI-GLD	-16.86	0.74	12.8%	-1.30	3.06	1.8%	1.74	3.79	5.81	0%	-47.72	9Y.2M
VTI-IJS-VNQ-SHY-GLD	-17.08	0.68	13.4%	-1.53	3.19	2.2%	1.58	3.83	5.76	0%	-47.91	9Y.2M
IJS-VTV-VNQ-BND-GLD	-16.86	0.67	12.8%	-1.30	3.06	1.8%	1.75	3.79	5.81	0%	-47.71	9Y.2M
IJS-VTV-VNQ-SHY-GLD	-16.83	0.64	13.2%	-1.60	3.04	2.3%	1.54	3.72	5.71	0%	-47.62	9Y.5M
VTI-IJS-VTV-IEI-GLD	-21.23	0.54	13%	-1.35	3.67	1.2%	2.24	4.49	6.20	0%	-55.48	11Y.0M
VTI-IJS-VTV-BND-GLD	-21.23	0.51	13.3%	-1.35	3.60	1.1%	2.24	4.48	6.18	0%	-55.47	11Y.0M
VTI-IJS-VTV-LQD-GLD	-21.29	0.47	13.8%	-1.29	3.66	1.4%	2.28	4.40	6.31	0%	-55.57	11Y.0M
IJS-VNQ-TLT-IEI-GLD	-7.88	0.30	13%	-2.39	1.95	2.8%	0.68	2.39	4.77	0%	-27.16	11Y.6M
IJS-VNQ-BND-TLT-GLD	-7.87	0.27	13%	-2.38	1.95	2.8%	0.68	2.39	4.78	0%	-28.06	11Y.6M
IJS-VNQ-TLT-LQD-GLD	-7.88	0.14	13.6%	-2.38	1.91	2.7%	0.72	2.38	4.79	0%	-28.95	11Y.6M
VTI-IJS-TLT-LQD-GLD	-11.51	0.72	11.7%	-1.66	2.84	1.5%	1.33	3.63	5.55	0%	-35.00	11Y.9M
IJS-VTV-TLT-IEI-GLD	-11.23	1.12	11.4%	-1.62	2.64	1.5%	1.26	3.59	5.50	0%	-34.65	11Y.10M

Ranking: Baseline 7Y Return

Order by **Baseline 7Y Return - Last 30 Years** (from 1993-12 to 2023-11)

Portfolio	3Y Rolling Annualized Return (%)			7Y Rolling Annualized Return (%)			15Y Rolling Annualized Return (%)				Max Draw-down (%)	Long Neg Period (Y.M)
	Worst	Base	%Fail	Worst	Base ▼	%Fail	Worst	Base	Median	%Fail		
VTI-IJS-MTUM-TLT-GLD	-3.39	4.08	2.2%	5.30	8.37	0%	7.46	8.79	9.54	0%	-26.55	3Y.7M
IJS-VTV-MTUM-TLT-GLD	-3.69	4.17	1.5%	5.32	8.24	0%	7.17	8.64	9.35	0%	-27.46	3Y.7M
VTI-IJS-MTUM-EMB-GLD	-5.99	4.91	2.8%	4.83	8.23	0%	6.94	8.86	9.61	0%	-32.97	4Y.3M
IJS-MTUM-VNQ-TLT-GLD	-5.22	5.46	2.5%	4.41	8.16	0%	6.96	8.96	10.11	0%	-30.50	3Y.9M
IJS-MTUM-TLT-CWB-GLD	-2.75	5.04	2.2%	5.75	8.16	0%	7.22	8.72	9.57	0%	-24.09	3Y.5M
VTI-MTUM-EMB-CWB-GLD	-4.69	4.52	3.1%	5.18	8.04	0%	6.83	8.40	9.36	0%	-30.61	3Y.8M
VTI-IJS-MTUM-VNQ-GLD	-10.70	5.06	7.7%	3.09	8.03	0%	7.21	8.87	9.59	0%	-43.51	5Y.1M
VTI-MTUM-VNQ-TLT-GLD	-4.44	3.69	2.5%	5.23	8.00	0%	7.12	8.96	9.70	0%	-30.18	3Y.8M
VTI-VTV-MTUM-EMB-GLD	-5.59	3.82	5.5%	4.49	7.98	0%	6.82	8.37	9.15	0%	-33.63	4Y.2M
VTI-IJS-MTUM-LQD-GLD	-5.47	4.10	3.7%	4.06	7.96	0%	7.04	8.21	8.92	0%	-31.32	4Y.3M
IJS-VTV-MTUM-EMB-GLD	-6.28	5.17	2.5%	4.85	7.96	0%	6.66	8.58	9.54	0%	-33.78	4Y.3M
IJS-MTUM-EMB-CWB-GLD	-5.36	5.45	2.5%	5.55	7.95	0%	6.70	8.60	9.61	0%	-30.72	3Y.8M
IJS-MTUM-VNQ-CWB-GLD	-10.04	5.24	6.2%	3.75	7.93	0%	7.14	8.69	9.66	0%	-41.50	4Y.11M
VTI-IJS-MTUM-BNDX-GLD	-5.31	4.07	4.3%	4.12	7.92	0%	7.06	8.19	8.87	0%	-30.78	4Y.3M
IJS-MTUM-EEM-EMB-TLT	-5.80	4.38	3.7%	3.14	7.90	0%	5.47	8.38	10.16	0%	-34.06	5Y.9M
IJS-MTUM-SCZ-TLT-GLD	-4.10	4.22	2.2%	4.64	7.90	0%	6.40	8.65	10.00	0%	-29.73	3Y.6M
VTI-MTUM-VNQ-EMB-GLD	-7.08	4.81	4%	5.13	7.89	0%	6.61	8.83	9.89	0%	-36.39	4Y.3M
VTI-IJS-MTUM-TIP-GLD	-5.06	4.46	2.8%	4.51	7.87	0%	6.94	8.16	8.87	0%	-30.46	4Y.2M
VTI-MTUM-EEM-EMB-TLT	-5.08	3.64	5.5%	3.99	7.87	0%	5.51	8.62	9.57	0%	-33.82	4Y.2M
VTI-MTUM-EMB-TLT-GLD	-2.80	5.08	1.5%	4.55	7.85	0%	6.51	8.74	9.48	0%	-23.23	3Y.5M
VTV-MTUM-VNQ-TLT-GLD	-4.76	3.81	2.8%	4.90	7.85	0%	6.83	8.83	9.49	0%	-31.07	3Y.8M

Order by **Baseline 7Y Return - Last 30 Years** (from 1993-12 to 2023-11) - **US Infl. Adjusted**

Portfolio	3Y Rolling Annualized Return (%)			7Y Rolling Annualized Return (%)			15Y Rolling Annualized Return (%)				Max Draw-down (%)	Long Neg Period (Y.M)
	Worst	Base	%Fail	Worst	Base ▼	%Fail	Worst	Base	Median	%Fail		
IJS-MTUM-VNQ-TLT-GLD	-7.28	2.73	9.2%	0.85	6.09	0%	4.47	6.52	7.66	0%	-31.57	6Y.2M
IJS-MTUM-TLT-CWB-GLD	-6.21	2.44	6.8%	2.15	5.89	0%	4.73	6.45	7.18	0%	-27.95	5Y.9M
IJS-MTUM-EMB-TLT-GLD	-7.42	3.69	6.8%	0.21	5.89	0%	3.92	6.48	7.61	0%	-28.19	7Y.3M
VTI-MTUM-EMB-TLT-GLD	-8.08	3.04	8.3%	0.98	5.89	0%	4.02	6.51	7.23	0%	-28.84	5Y.11M
VTI-IJS-MTUM-EMB-GLD	-8.03	1.23	10.5%	2.22	5.85	0%	4.45	6.50	7.27	0%	-34.00	5Y.2M
VTI-MTUM-VNQ-TLT-GLD	-6.51	0.88	11.4%	1.64	5.83	0%	4.62	6.34	7.31	0%	-31.25	4Y.11M
IJS-MTUM-EEM-EMB-TLT	-8.60	1.90	8.9%	-0.36	5.83	0.7%	3.01	6.34	7.70	0%	-35.07	8Y.8M
IJS-MTUM-SCZ-TLT-GLD	-6.30	1.39	9.2%	1.07	5.82	0%	3.92	6.19	7.49	0%	-30.81	6Y.3M
VTV-MTUM-EMB-TLT-GLD	-7.60	2.88	7.1%	0.67	5.81	0%	3.79	6.32	7.04	0%	-26.81	6Y.2M
VTI-MTUM-EEM-EMB-TLT	-8.85	1.29	11.4%	0.47	5.75	0%	3.04	6.22	7.18	0%	-34.83	6Y.7M
MTUM-VNQ-TLT-CWB-GLD	-7.68	2.61	8%	1.26	5.71	0%	4.34	6.33	7.38	0%	-29.78	5Y.9M
VTV-MTUM-VNQ-TLT-GLD	-6.82	1.04	10.2%	1.32	5.67	0%	4.35	6.28	7.18	0%	-32.13	5Y.9M
IJS-MTUM-EMB-CWB-GLD	-7.41	2.26	6.8%	2.82	5.65	0%	4.22	6.47	7.29	0%	-31.78	5Y.2M
VTI-MTUM-EMB-CWB-GLD	-6.75	1.35	9.5%	2.56	5.64	0%	4.34	6.11	6.94	0%	-32.11	5Y.2M
IJS-MTUM-VNQ-EMB-GLD	-9.79	3.31	10.5%	1.49	5.63	0%	3.98	6.53	7.98	0%	-37.56	5Y.11M
IJS-VTV-MTUM-TLT-GLD	-5.78	1.05	9.5%	2.21	5.59	0%	4.68	6.21	6.98	0%	-28.57	5Y.9M
IJS-VTV-MTUM-EMB-GLD	-8.31	1.35	10.5%	2.23	5.58	0%	4.18	6.38	7.14	0%	-34.80	5Y.2M
VTI-IJS-EEM-EMB-TLT	-7.90	1.94	8.3%	-0.13	5.56	0.4%	2.88	5.81	7.29	0%	-34.48	8Y.8M
MTUM-EEM-EMB-TLT-CWB	-10.51	2.46	8.9%	-0.04	5.55	0.4%	2.73	6.19	7.24	0%	-35.85	7Y.3M
VTI-IJS-MTUM-TLT-GLD	-5.48	1.07	9.8%	2.55	5.55	0%	4.96	6.30	7.11	0%	-27.68	4Y.11M
VTI-MTUM-VNQ-EMB-GLD	-9.09	1.44	10.5%	2.31	5.53	0%	4.13	6.49	7.46	0%	-37.37	5Y.3M

Order by **Baseline 7Y Return - Last 60 Years** (from 1963-12 to 2023-11)

Portfolio	3Y Rolling Annualized Return (%)			7Y Rolling Annualized Return (%)			15Y Rolling Annualized Return (%)				Max Draw-down (%)	Long Neg Period (Y.M)
	Worst	Base	%Fail	Worst	Base ▼	%Fail	Worst	Base	Median	%Fail		
VTI-IJS-VTV-TLT-GLD	-3.78	5.70	1.6%	4.70	7.79	0%	7.09	8.80	10.64	0%	-26.81	3Y.8M
VTI-IJS-VNQ-TLT-GLD	-5.33	5.63	1.2%	4.63	7.76	0%	6.87	9.05	10.77	0%	-29.90	4Y.2M
VTI-IJS-VTV-VNQ-GLD	-11.08	5.58	4.5%	2.53	7.65	0%	6.14	8.85	11.51	0%	-43.67	5Y.2M
VTI-IJS-VTV-LQD-GLD	-5.83	5.46	2.2%	3.54	7.59	0%	6.41	8.23	10.47	0%	-31.51	4Y.4M
VTI-IJS-VNQ-LQD-GLD	-7.35	5.69	1.9%	4.07	7.56	0%	6.35	8.68	10.54	0%	-34.40	4Y.5M
IJS-VTV-VNQ-TLT-GLD	-5.67	5.38	1.9%	4.25	7.52	0%	6.57	8.92	10.83	0%	-30.82	4Y.2M
VTI-IJS-VTV-IEI-GLD	-4.32	5.49	1.6%	4.16	7.48	0%	6.52	8.07	10.42	0%	-28.44	4Y.2M
VTI-IJS-VTV-BND-GLD	-4.98	5.50	2.3%	3.75	7.44	0%	6.49	8.04	10.37	0%	-29.81	4Y.3M
VTI-IJS-VNQ-BND-GLD	-6.51	5.66	1.5%	4.30	7.40	0%	6.30	8.49	10.42	0%	-32.74	4Y.4M
VTI-IJS-VNQ-IEI-GLD	-5.85	5.59	1.3%	4.50	7.36	0%	6.32	8.50	10.44	0%	-31.41	4Y.3M
VTI-IJS-TLT-LQD-GLD	-0.61	5.54	0.4%	4.18	7.33	0%	6.41	8.51	9.84	0%	-21.13	3Y.3M
IJS-VTV-VNQ-LQD-GLD	-7.68	5.36	2.2%	4.01	7.33	0%	6.16	8.54	10.56	0%	-35.24	4Y.5M
VTI-IJS-TLT-IEI-GLD	-0.07	5.49	0.2%	4.11	7.33	0%	6.22	8.37	9.80	0%	-18.99	3Y.3M
VTI-VTV-VNQ-TLT-GLD	-4.86	4.42	2%	3.43	7.32	0%	6.69	8.72	10.22	0%	-30.46	5Y.8M
VTI-IJJ-DND-TLT-GLD	-0.36	5.47	0.3%	1.08	7.21	0%	6.22	8.35	9.76	0%	-19.78	3Y.3M
VTI-IJS-VTV-SHY-GLD	-4.85	5.34	1.9%	3.66	7.21	0%	6.25	7.67	10.22	0%	-29.52	4Y.3M
VTI-IJS-VNQ-SHY-GLD	-6.43	5.51	1.6%	4.18	7.18	0%	6.06	8.17	10.15	0%	-32.46	4Y.4M
IJS-VTV-VNQ-BND-GLD	-6.84	5.38	2%	4.18	7.15	0%	5.99	8.38	10.47	0%	-33.59	4Y.4M
VTI-IJS-IEI-LQD-GLD	-0.85	5.18	0.3%	4.40	7.15	0%	5.89	7.90	9.55	0%	-18.54	3Y.1M
IJS-VTV-VNQ-IEI-GLD	-6.18	5.38	1.8%	4.16	7.14	0%	6.01	8.44	10.49	0%	-32.28	4Y.3M
IJS-VTV-TLT-LQD-GLD	-0.70	5.32	0.9%	3.82	7.11	0%	6.11	8.33	9.87	0%	-19.07	3Y.3M

Order by **Baseline 7Y Return - Last 60 Years** (from 1963-12 to 2023-11) - **US Infl. Adjusted**

Portfolio	3Y Rolling Annualized Return (%)			7Y Rolling Annualized Return (%)			15Y Rolling Annualized Return (%)				Max Draw-down (%)	Long Neg Period (Y.M)
	Worst	Base	%Fail	Worst	Base ▼	%Fail	Worst	Base	Median	%Fail		
VTI-IJS-VTV-VNQ-GLD	-13.01	1.13	11.7%	-1.95	4.41	1.4%	3.56	5.85	7.23	0%	-44.54	9Y.8M
VTI-IJS-VNQ-TLT-GLD	-7.38	1.35	10.7%	-1.00	4.26	0.6%	3.50	5.48	7.30	0%	-30.97	8Y.11M
VTI-IJS-VNQ-LQD-GLD	-9.36	1.12	10.2%	-0.92	4.22	0.8%	3.70	5.41	6.86	0%	-35.41	7Y.6M
VTI-IJS-VNQ-BND-GLD	-8.54	1.43	9.3%	-0.51	4.22	0.2%	3.82	5.41	6.73	0%	-33.78	7Y.5M
VTI-IJS-VNQ-IEI-GLD	-7.89	1.49	9.3%	-0.52	4.15	0.2%	3.85	5.43	6.82	0%	-32.47	7Y.5M
VTI-IJS-VNQ-SHY-GLD	-8.40	1.52	9.9%	-0.39	4.11	0.2%	3.59	5.34	6.46	0%	-33.50	7Y.5M
VTI-IJS-VTV-LQD-GLD	-7.87	1.24	10.8%	-1.18	4.07	0.6%	3.30	5.22	6.51	0%	-32.56	8Y.11M
VTI-IJS-VTV-SHY-GLD	-6.91	1.53	9.9%	-0.63	4.06	0.2%	3.77	5.13	6.10	0%	-30.60	7Y.5M
VTI-IJS-VTV-BND-GLD	-7.04	1.54	9.8%	-0.76	4.05	0.2%	3.53	5.20	6.36	0%	-30.89	7Y.6M
VTI-IJS-VTV-IEI-GLD	-6.40	1.59	9.3%	-0.76	4.03	0.2%	3.53	5.26	6.41	0%	-29.83	7Y.6M
IJS-VTV-VNQ-TLT-GLD	-7.71	1.39	10.4%	-1.02	4.02	0.3%	3.65	5.44	7.28	0%	-31.88	9Y.0M
VTI-IJS-VTV-TLT-GLD	-6.35	1.42	9.8%	-1.25	4.02	0.5%	3.10	5.42	7.02	0%	-30.73	9Y.0M
IJS-VTV-VNQ-LQD-GLD	-9.68	1.20	9.9%	-0.94	4.01	0.5%	3.68	5.36	6.86	0%	-36.24	8Y.11M
IJS-VTV-VNQ-IEI-GLD	-8.21	1.63	9.5%	-0.54	3.92	0.3%	3.55	5.39	6.80	0%	-33.32	7Y.6M
VTI-IJS-IEI-LQD-GLD	-4.11	1.90	7.5%	0.25	3.89	0%	3.15	4.84	5.96	0%	-23.94	6Y.5M
IJS-VTV-VNQ-BND-GLD	-8.86	1.60	9.5%	-0.54	3.89	0.2%	3.52	5.40	6.71	0%	-34.61	7Y.6M
IJS-VTV-TLT-IEI-GLD	-5.25	2.22	7.7%	0.13	3.84	0%	3.08	4.86	6.34	0%	-25.53	7Y.3M
VTI-IJS-TLT-IEI-GLD	-5.47	2.09	7.5%	0.17	3.84	0%	2.94	4.79	6.38	0%	-24.77	6Y.5M
VTI-IJS-VNQ-BIL-GLD	-8.87	1.34	9.6%	-0.28	3.83	0.2%	3.45	5.07	6.16	0%	-34.40	7Y.2M
VTI-IJS-BND-LQD-GLD	-4.11	1.79	7.9%	0.25	3.83	0%	3.16	4.82	5.91	0%	-24.14	6Y.5M
VTI-IJS-VTV-BIL-GLD	-7.37	1.51	10.7%	-0.51	3.83	0.2%	3.49	4.86	5.86	0%	-31.54	7Y.5M

Order by **Baseline 7Y Return** - **All data** (from 1871/1927 to 2023-11)

Portfolio	3Y Rolling Annualized Return (%)			7Y Rolling Annualized Return (%)			15Y Rolling Annualized Return (%)				Max Draw-down (%)	Long Neg Period (Y.M)
	Worst	Base	%Fail	Worst	Base ▼	%Fail	Worst	Base	Median	%Fail		
VTI-IJS-VTV-VNQ-GLD	-32.46	3.32	9.2%	-2.97	6.70	1.4%	1.79	8.21	10.09	0%	-72.73	13Y.7M
VTI-IJS-VTV-IEI-GLD	-27.02	3.73	7.1%	-0.66	6.67	0.2%	2.98	7.78	9.63	0%	-64.74	12Y.9M
VTI-IJS-VTV-BND-GLD	-27.02	3.73	7.5%	-0.66	6.64	0.2%	2.99	7.75	9.62	0%	-64.74	12Y.9M
VTI-IJS-VTV-LQD-GLD	-27.07	3.71	7.5%	-0.67	6.60	0.2%	3.02	7.81	9.64	0%	-64.81	12Y.9M
VTI-IJS-VTV-TLT-GLD	-27.44	3.74	7.1%	-0.78	6.55	0.2%	3.04	8.13	9.63	0%	-65.37	12Y.9M
VTI-IJS-VTV-SHY-GLD	-26.98	3.70	7.5%	-0.78	6.54	0.2%	2.75	7.55	9.52	0%	-64.66	13Y.0M
VTI-IJS-VTV-BIL-GLD	-27.33	3.37	8.2%	-1.16	6.30	0.4%	2.41	7.25	9.37	0%	-65.14	13Y.1M
VTI-IJS-VNQ-IEI-GLD	-23.20	4.04	6.3%	-0.10	6.29	0.1%	2.98	7.22	9.02	0%	-58.82	12Y.8M
VTI-IJS-VNQ-BND-GLD	-23.20	3.95	6.4%	-0.09	6.28	0.1%	2.99	7.22	8.95	0%	-58.81	12Y.8M
VTI-IJS-VNQ-LQD-GLD	-23.25	3.97	6.6%	-0.10	6.28	0.1%	3.03	7.26	9.05	0%	-58.89	12Y.8M
VTI-IJS-VNQ-SHY-GLD	-23.18	4.05	6.5%	-0.22	6.26	0.1%	2.68	7.14	8.76	0%	-58.75	12Y.9M
VTI-IJS-VTV-VNQ-TLT	-31.99	2.48	11.4%	-3.42	6.20	2.1%	1.98	7.82	10.07	0%	-72.25	13Y.5M
VTI-IJS-VNQ-BIL-GLD	-23.56	3.78	7%	-0.61	6.15	0.2%	2.35	7.01	8.50	0%	-59.32	13Y.1M
VTI-IJS-VNQ-TLT-GLD	-23.58	3.90	6.1%	-0.19	6.10	0.1%	3.05	7.17	9.38	0%	-59.46	12Y.8M
IJS-VTV-VNQ-IEI-GLD	-22.97	4.01	6.3%	-0.34	6.06	0.1%	2.84	7.15	8.98	0%	-58.60	12Y.8M
VTI-IJS-IEI-LQD-GLD	-17.60	4.18	4.7%	2.17	6.05	0%	3.94	6.85	8.30	0%	-47.69	6Y.2M
IJS-VTV-VNQ-LQD-GLD	-23.02	3.94	6.5%	-0.34	6.04	0.1%	2.89	7.17	9.02	0%	-58.67	12Y.8M
VTI-IJS-VTV-TLT-LQD	-26.63	2.70	8.9%	-1.14	6.04	0.6%	3.19	7.37	9.52	0%	-64.29	12Y.8M
VTI-IJS-BND-LQD-GLD	-17.59	4.14	4.8%	2.18	6.04	0%	3.94	6.85	8.27	0%	-47.69	6Y.2M
VTI-IJS-TLT-LQD-GLD	-18.01	4.22	4.6%	2.08	6.02	0%	4.01	6.94	8.63	0%	-48.52	6Y.3M
IJS-VTV-VNQ-BND-GLD	-22.97	3.97	6.5%	-0.33	6.02	0.1%	2.85	7.16	8.94	0%	-58.59	12Y.8M

Order by **Baseline 7Y Return** - **All data** (from 1871/1927 to 2023-11) - **US Infl. Adjusted**

Portfolio	3Y Rolling Annualized Return (%)			7Y Rolling Annualized Return (%)			15Y Rolling Annualized Return (%)				Max Draw-down (%)	Long Neg Period (Y.M)
	Worst	Base	%Fail	Worst	Base ▼	%Fail	Worst	Base	Median	%Fail		
VTI-IJS-VTV-IEI-GLD	-21.23	0.54	13%	-1.35	3.67	1.2%	2.24	4.49	6.20	0%	-55.48	11Y.0M
VTI-IJS-VTV-LQD-GLD	-21.29	0.47	13.8%	-1.29	3.66	1.4%	2.28	4.40	6.31	0%	-55.57	11Y.0M
VTI-IJS-VTV-TLT-GLD	-21.68	0.59	13.4%	-1.25	3.65	1.2%	2.31	4.31	6.59	0%	-56.27	9Y.0M
VTI-IJS-VTV-VNQ-GLD	-27.10	0.01	14.9%	-1.95	3.64	2.5%	1.64	4.63	6.84	0%	-65.56	13Y.4M
VTI-IJS-VTV-BND-GLD	-21.23	0.51	13.3%	-1.35	3.60	1.1%	2.24	4.48	6.18	0%	-55.47	11Y.0M
VTI-IJS-VTV-SHY-GLD	-21.19	0.49	13.6%	-1.65	3.52	1.6%	2.04	4.47	5.95	0%	-55.37	12Y.8M
VTI-IJS-VTV-BIL-GLD	-21.57	0.24	14.4%	-1.86	3.31	1.8%	1.92	4.33	5.73	0%	-55.98	13Y.0M
VTI-IJS-VNQ-LQD-GLD	-17.16	0.49	13.3%	-1.17	3.23	1.8%	1.82	3.84	5.84	0%	-48.09	8Y.10M
VTI-IJS-VNQ-IEI-GLD	-17.11	0.67	12.7%	-1.23	3.22	1.5%	1.78	3.87	5.86	0%	-48.00	8Y.11M
VTI-IJS-VNQ-BND-GLD	-17.11	0.65	12.7%	-1.23	3.20	1.5%	1.78	3.87	5.85	0%	-47.99	8Y.10M
VTI-IJS-VNQ-SHY-GLD	-17.08	0.68	13.4%	-1.53	3.19	2.2%	1.58	3.83	5.76	0%	-47.91	9Y.2M
VTI-IJS-VNQ-TLT-GLD	-17.52	0.46	13.4%	-1.09	3.15	1.7%	1.85	3.78	5.79	0%	-48.81	8Y.11M
IJS-VTV-VNQ-LQD-GLD	-16.91	0.53	13%	-1.23	3.10	1.6%	1.79	3.81	5.82	0%	-47.81	9Y.0M
IJS-VTV-VNQ-TLT-GLD	-17.28	0.52	13.3%	-1.15	3.07	1.7%	1.81	3.76	5.82	0%	-48.55	9Y.0M
VTI-IJS-VNQ-BIL-GLD	-17.49	0.33	13.6%	-1.74	3.06	2.3%	1.46	3.74	5.59	0%	-48.64	12Y.8M
IJS-VTV-VNQ-IEI-GLD	-16.86	0.74	12.8%	-1.30	3.06	1.8%	1.74	3.79	5.81	0%	-47.72	9Y.2M
IJS-VTV-VNQ-BND-GLD	-16.86	0.67	12.8%	-1.30	3.06	1.8%	1.75	3.79	5.81	0%	-47.71	9Y.2M
IJS-VTV-VNQ-SHY-GLD	-16.83	0.64	13.2%	-1.60	3.04	2.3%	1.54	3.72	5.71	0%	-47.62	9Y.5M
VTI-IJS-BND-IEI-GLD	-11.00	1.01	10.5%	-1.53	2.98	1.5%	1.22	3.90	5.34	0%	-33.82	12Y.5M
VTI-IJS-BND-LQD-GLD	-11.06	0.96	11.3%	-1.53	2.97	1.5%	1.27	3.90	5.39	0%	-33.94	12Y.4M
VTI-IJS-SHY-IEI-GLD	-10.96	0.99	10.3%	-1.56	2.95	2.1%	1.02	3.89	5.14	0%	-33.69	12Y.8M

Ranking: Baseline 15Y Return

Order by **Baseline 15Y Return** - **Last 30 Years** (from 1993-12 to 2023-11)

Portfolio	3Y Rolling Annualized Return (%)			7Y Rolling Annualized Return (%)			15Y Rolling Annualized Return (%)				Max Draw-down (%)	Long Neg Period (Y.M)
	Worst	Base	%Fail	Worst	Base	%Fail	Worst	Base ▼	Median	%Fail		
VTI-MTUM-VNQ-TLT-GLD	-4.44	3.69	2.5%	5.23	8.00	0%	7.12	8.96	9.70	0%	-30.18	3Y.8M
IJS-MTUM-VNQ-TLT-GLD	-5.22	5.46	2.5%	4.41	8.16	0%	6.96	8.96	10.11	0%	-30.50	3Y.9M
VTI-IJS-MTUM-VNQ-GLD	-10.70	5.06	7.7%	3.09	8.03	0%	7.21	8.87	9.59	0%	-43.51	5Y.1M
VTI-IJS-MTUM-EMB-GLD	-5.99	4.91	2.8%	4.83	8.23	0%	6.94	8.86	9.61	0%	-32.97	4Y.3M
VTI-MTUM-VNQ-EMB-GLD	-7.08	4.81	4%	5.13	7.89	0%	6.61	8.83	9.89	0%	-36.39	4Y.3M
VTV-MTUM-VNQ-TLT-GLD	-4.76	3.81	2.8%	4.90	7.85	0%	6.83	8.83	9.49	0%	-31.07	3Y.8M
MTUM-VNQ-TLT-CWB-GLD	-3.79	5.14	2.5%	4.83	7.82	0%	6.84	8.81	9.73	0%	-27.80	3Y.7M
VTI-IJS-MTUM-TLT-GLD	-3.39	4.08	2.2%	5.30	8.37	0%	7.46	8.79	9.54	0%	-26.55	3Y.7M
VTI-MTUM-VNQ-EMB-TLT	-8.25	4.39	7.1%	3.62	7.56	0%	6.54	8.77	9.59	0%	-35.32	5Y.0M
IJS-MTUM-EEM-TLT-GLD	-2.03	4.61	2.8%	4.36	7.18	0%	5.90	8.76	10.07	0%	-28.97	3Y.4M
VTI-MTUM-EMB-TLT-GLD	-2.80	5.08	1.5%	4.55	7.85	0%	6.51	8.74	9.48	0%	-23.23	3Y.5M
IJS-MTUM-EMB-TLT-GLD	-2.10	5.98	1.8%	3.75	7.59	0%	6.39	8.74	10.09	0%	-22.31	3Y.9M
IJS-MTUM-VNQ-TLT-CWB	-11.06	4.77	7.4%	2.44	7.21	0%	7.14	8.74	9.53	0%	-40.26	5Y.2M
VTI-MTUM-SCZ-TLT-GLD	-3.37	3.11	4.9%	5.43	7.80	0%	6.54	8.73	9.49	0%	-29.50	3Y.6M
IJS-MTUM-TLT-CWB-GLD	-2.75	5.04	2.2%	5.75	8.16	0%	7.22	8.72	9.57	0%	-24.09	3Y.5M
VTI-IJS-MTUM-VNQ-TLT	-11.74	3.66	8%	1.70	7.33	0%	7.32	8.70	9.47	0%	-42.38	5Y.4M
MTUM-VNQ-EMB-CWB-GLD	-6.43	5.28	3.1%	5.55	7.44	0%	6.37	8.69	9.89	0%	-34.21	4Y.2M
IJS-MTUM-VNQ-CWB-GLD	-10.04	5.24	6.2%	3.75	7.93	0%	7.14	8.69	9.66	0%	-41.50	4Y.11M
VTI-MTUM-SCZ-EMB-TLT	-7.14	2.47	6.2%	4.29	7.41	0%	5.96	8.69	9.53	0%	-34.58	4Y.3M
VTI-IJS-MTUM-EMB-TLT	-7.19	3.31	4.6%	3.31	7.41	0%	6.88	8.68	9.39	0%	-31.82	4Y.5M
IJS-VTV-MTUM-VNQ-GLD	-11.01	4.99	8%	3.04	7.85	0%	7.07	8.65	9.48	0%	-44.23	5Y.2M

Order by **Baseline 15Y Return** - **Last 30 Years** (from 1993-12 to 2023-11) - **US Infl. Adjusted**

Portfolio	3Y Rolling Annualized Return (%)			7Y Rolling Annualized Return (%)			15Y Rolling Annualized Return (%)				Max Draw-down (%)	Long Neg Period (Y.M)
	Worst	Base	%Fail	Worst	Base	%Fail	Worst	Base ▼	Median	%Fail		
VTI-MTUM-VNQ-EMB-TLT	-10.24	1.31	12.3%	0.59	5.16	0%	4.06	6.61	7.23	0%	-36.31	7Y.3M
IJS-MTUM-VNQ-EMB-GLD	-9.79	3.31	10.5%	1.49	5.63	0%	3.98	6.53	7.98	0%	-37.56	5Y.11M
IJS-MTUM-VNQ-TLT-GLD	-7.28	2.73	9.2%	0.85	6.09	0%	4.47	6.52	7.66	0%	-31.57	6Y.2M
VTI-MTUM-EMB-TLT-GLD	-8.08	3.04	8.3%	0.98	5.89	0%	4.02	6.51	7.23	0%	-28.84	5Y.11M
VTI-IJS-MTUM-EMB-GLD	-8.03	1.23	10.5%	2.22	5.85	0%	4.45	6.50	7.27	0%	-34.00	5Y.2M
VTI-MTUM-VNQ-EMB-GLD	-9.09	1.44	10.5%	2.31	5.53	0%	4.13	6.49	7.46	0%	-37.37	5Y.3M
IJS-MTUM-EMB-TLT-GLD	-7.42	3.69	6.8%	0.21	5.89	0%	3.92	6.48	7.61	0%	-28.19	7Y.3M
IJS-MTUM-EMB-CWB-GLD	-7.41	2.26	6.8%	2.82	5.65	0%	4.22	6.47	7.29	0%	-31.78	5Y.2M
VTI-MTUM-SCZ-EMB-TLT	-9.15	-0.38	16%	0.76	5.12	0%	3.50	6.46	7.18	0%	-35.58	6Y.6M
MTUM-VNQ-EMB-TLT-CWB	-9.59	1.87	12%	0.22	5.07	0%	3.85	6.46	7.30	0%	-34.55	7Y.3M
IJS-MTUM-TLT-CWB-GLD	-6.21	2.44	6.8%	2.15	5.89	0%	4.73	6.45	7.18	0%	-27.95	5Y.9M
VTI-IJS-MTUM-EMB-TLT	-9.20	0.59	13.5%	0.74	4.82	0%	4.39	6.39	7.06	0%	-32.87	6Y.3M
IJS-MTUM-VNQ-EMB-TLT	-11.02	1.53	12%	-0.21	5.17	0.7%	3.90	6.39	7.75	0%	-36.66	7Y.4M
IJS-VTV-MTUM-EMB-GLD	-8.31	1.35	10.5%	2.23	5.58	0%	4.18	6.38	7.14	0%	-34.80	5Y.2M
IJS-MTUM-EMB-TLT-CWB	-8.57	1.57	11.1%	0.99	4.90	0%	4.18	6.38	7.17	0%	-32.71	6Y.5M
VTV-MTUM-VNQ-EMB-TLT	-10.56	1.60	12.9%	0.28	4.88	0%	3.78	6.35	7.14	0%	-37.17	7Y.3M
VTI-IJS-MTUM-VNQ-GLD	-12.63	1.15	12.6%	0.57	5.44	0%	4.60	6.34	7.26	0%	-44.37	8Y.6M
VTI-MTUM-VNQ-TLT-GLD	-6.51	0.88	11.4%	1.64	5.83	0%	4.62	6.34	7.31	0%	-31.25	4Y.11M
IJS-MTUM-EEM-EMB-TLT	-8.60	1.90	8.9%	-0.36	5.83	0%	3.01	6.34	7.70	0%	-35.07	8Y.8M
MTUM-VNQ-EMB-TLT-GLD	-9.18	3.28	7.7%	-0.67	5.23	0.7%	3.45	6.34	7.78	0%	-29.59	8Y.9M
MTUM-VNQ-TLT-CWB-GLD	-7.68	2.61	8%	1.26	5.71	0%	4.34	6.33	7.38	0%	-29.78	5Y.9M

Order by **Baseline 15Y Return - Last 60 Years** (from 1963-12 to 2023-11)

Portfolio	3Y Rolling Annualized Return (%)			7Y Rolling Annualized Return (%)			15Y Rolling Annualized Return (%)				Max Draw-down (%)	Long Neg Period (Y.M)
	Worst	Base	%Fail	Worst	Base	%Fail	Worst	Base ▼	Median	%Fail		
VTI-IJS-VNQ-TLT-GLD	-5.33	5.63	1.2%	4.63	7.76	0%	6.87	9.05	10.77	0%	-29.90	4Y.2M
IJS-VTV-VNQ-TLT-GLD	-5.67	5.38	1.9%	4.25	7.52	0%	6.57	8.92	10.83	0%	-30.82	4Y.2M
VTI-IJS-VTV-VNQ-GLD	-11.08	5.58	4.5%	2.53	7.65	0%	6.14	8.85	11.51	0%	-43.67	5Y.2M
VTI-IJS-VTV-TLT-GLD	-3.78	5.70	1.6%	4.70	7.79	0%	7.09	8.80	10.64	0%	-26.81	3Y.8M
VTI-VTV-VNQ-TLT-GLD	-4.86	4.42	2%	3.43	7.32	0%	6.69	8.72	10.22	0%	-30.46	5Y.8M
VTI-IJS-VNQ-LQD-GLD	-7.35	5.69	1.9%	4.07	7.56	0%	6.35	8.68	10.54	0%	-34.40	4Y.5M
IJS-VTV-VNQ-LQD-GLD	-7.68	5.36	2.2%	4.01	7.33	0%	6.16	8.54	10.56	0%	-35.24	4Y.5M
VTI-IJS-TLT-LQD-GLD	-0.61	5.54	0.4%	4.18	7.33	0%	6.41	8.51	9.84	0%	-21.13	3Y.3M
VTI-IJS-VNQ-IEI-GLD	-5.85	5.59	1.3%	4.50	7.36	0%	6.32	8.50	10.44	0%	-31.41	4Y.3M
VTI-IJS-VTV-VNQ-TLT	-12.18	4.27	7.6%	-0.89	6.76	0.5%	6.48	8.50	11.08	0%	-43.32	7Y.5M
VTI-IJS-VNQ-BND-GLD	-6.51	5.66	1.5%	4.30	7.40	0%	6.30	8.49	10.42	0%	-32.74	4Y.4M
IJS-VTV-VNQ-IEI-GLD	-6.18	5.38	1.8%	4.16	7.14	0%	6.01	8.44	10.49	0%	-32.28	4Y.3M
IJS-VTV-VNQ-BND-GLD	-6.84	5.38	2%	4.18	7.15	0%	5.99	8.38	10.47	0%	-33.59	4Y.4M
VTI-IJS-TLT-IEI-GLD	-0.07	5.49	0.2%	4.11	7.33	0%	6.22	8.37	9.80	0%	-18.99	3Y.3M
VTI-IJS-BND-TLT-GLD	-0.36	5.47	0.3%	4.08	7.21	0%	6.22	8.35	9.76	0%	-19.78	3Y.3M
IJS-VTV-TLT-LQD-GLD	-0.70	5.32	0.9%	3.82	7.11	0%	6.11	8.33	9.87	0%	-19.07	3Y.3M
VTI-IJS-VTV-LQD-GLD	-5.83	5.46	2.2%	3.54	7.59	0%	6.41	8.23	10.47	0%	-31.51	4Y.4M
IJS-VTV-TLT-IEI-GLD	-0.30	5.29	0.3%	3.73	6.96	0%	5.91	8.22	9.84	0%	-18.38	3Y.3M
VTI-VTV-VNQ-LQD-GLD	-6.93	4.54	2.8%	3.84	7.08	0%	5.99	8.22	10.00	0%	-35.00	5Y.2M
VTI-IJS-VNQ-TLT-IEI	-7.20	5.07	4.8%	0.67	6.82	0%	6.23	8.20	10.49	0%	-30.54	6Y.4M
IJS-VNQ-TLT-LQD-GLD	-2.26	4.67	1.3%	2.43	6.87	0%	5.82	8.18	10.09	0%	-22.03	4Y.2M

Order by **Baseline 15Y Return - Last 60 Years** (from 1963-12 to 2023-11) - **US Infl. Adjusted**

Portfolio	3Y Rolling Annualized Return (%)			7Y Rolling Annualized Return (%)			15Y Rolling Annualized Return (%)				Max Draw-down (%)	Long Neg Period (Y.M)
	Worst	Base	%Fail	Worst	Base	%Fail	Worst	Base ▼	Median	%Fail		
VTI-IJS-VTV-VNQ-GLD	-13.01	1.13	11.7%	-1.95	4.41	1.4%	3.56	5.85	7.23	0%	-44.54	9Y.8M
VTI-IJS-VNQ-TLT-GLD	-7.38	1.35	10.7%	-1.00	4.26	0.6%	3.50	5.48	7.30	0%	-30.97	8Y.11M
IJS-VTV-VNQ-TLT-GLD	-7.71	1.39	10.4%	-1.02	4.02	0.3%	3.65	5.44	7.28	0%	-31.88	9Y.0M
VTI-IJS-VNQ-IEI-GLD	-7.89	1.49	9.3%	-0.52	4.15	0.2%	3.85	5.43	6.82	0%	-32.47	7Y.5M
VTI-IJS-VTV-TLT-GLD	-6.35	1.42	9.8%	-1.25	4.02	0.5%	3.10	5.42	7.02	0%	-30.73	9Y.0M
VTI-IJS-VNQ-LQD-GLD	-9.36	1.12	10.2%	-0.92	4.22	0.8%	3.70	5.41	6.86	0%	-35.41	7Y.6M
VTI-IJS-VNQ-BND-GLD	-8.54	1.43	9.3%	-0.51	4.22	0.2%	3.82	5.41	6.73	0%	-33.78	7Y.6M
IJS-VTV-VNQ-BND-GLD	-8.86	1.60	9.5%	-0.54	3.89	0.3%	3.52	5.40	6.71	0%	-34.61	7Y.6M
IJS-VTV-VNQ-IEI-GLD	-8.21	1.63	9.5%	-0.54	3.92	0.3%	3.55	5.39	6.80	0%	-33.32	7Y.6M
IJS-VTV-VNQ-LQD-GLD	-9.68	1.20	9.9%	-0.94	4.01	0.5%	3.68	5.36	6.86	0%	-36.24	8Y.11M
VTI-IJS-VNQ-SHY-GLD	-8.40	1.52	9.9%	-0.39	4.11	0.2%	3.59	5.34	6.46	0%	-33.50	7Y.5M
VTI-IJS-VTV-IEI-GLD	-6.40	1.59	9.3%	-0.76	4.03	0.2%	3.53	5.26	6.41	0%	-29.83	7Y.6M
VTI-IJS-VTV-LQD-GLD	-7.87	1.24	10.8%	-1.18	4.07	0.6%	3.30	5.22	6.51	0%	-32.56	8Y.11M
VTI-IJS-VTV-VNQ-TLT	-14.29	-0.17	15.6%	-6.52	2.19	6.4%	0.56	5.21	7.27	0%	-44.45	13Y.11M
VTI-IJS-VTV-BND-GLD	-7.04	1.54	9.8%	-0.76	4.05	0.2%	3.53	5.20	6.36	0%	-30.89	7Y.6M
IJS-VTV-VNQ-SHY-GLD	-8.71	1.56	9.2%	-0.41	3.82	0.2%	3.28	5.16	6.47	0%	-34.33	7Y.5M
VTI-IJS-VTV-SHY-GLD	-6.91	1.53	9.9%	-0.63	4.06	0.2%	3.77	5.13	6.10	0%	-30.60	7Y.5M
VTI-IJS-VNQ-BIL-GLD	-8.87	1.34	9.6%	-0.28	3.83	0.2%	3.45	5.07	6.16	0%	-34.40	7Y.2M
IJS-VTV-VNQ-BIL-GLD	-9.18	1.45	9.5%	-0.30	3.70	0.2%	3.15	4.93	6.21	0%	-35.23	7Y.5M
IJS-VTV-TLT-SHY-GLD	-4.76	2.08	7.3%	0.26	3.69	0%	3.21	4.88	5.97	0%	-24.84	6Y.5M
VTI-IJS-BND-IEI-GLD	-4.02	2.00	6.4%	0.64	3.79	0%	3.23	4.86	5.82	0%	-23.82	6Y.5M

Order by Baseline 15Y Return - All data (from 1871/1927 to 2023-11)

Portfolio	3Y Rolling Annualized Return (%)			7Y Rolling Annualized Return (%)			15Y Rolling Annualized Return (%)				Max Draw-down (%)	Long Neg Period (Y.M)
	Worst	Base	%Fail	Worst	Base	%Fail	Worst	Base ▼	Median	%Fail		
VTI-IJS-VTV-VNQ-GLD	-32.46	3.32	9.2%	-2.97	6.70	1.4%	1.79	8.21	10.09	0%	-72.73	13Y.7M
VTI-IJS-VTV-TLT-GLD	-27.44	3.74	7.1%	-0.78	6.55	0.2%	3.04	8.13	9.63	0%	-65.37	12Y.9M
VTI-IJS-VTV-VNQ-TLT	-31.99	2.48	11.4%	-3.42	6.20	2.1%	1.98	7.82	10.07	0%	-72.25	13Y.5M
VTI-IJS-VTV-LQD-GLD	-27.07	3.71	7.5%	-0.67	6.60	0.2%	3.02	7.81	9.64	0%	-64.81	12Y.9M
VTI-IJS-VTV-IEI-GLD	-27.02	3.73	7.1%	-0.66	6.67	0.2%	2.98	7.78	9.63	0%	-64.74	12Y.9M
VTI-IJS-VTV-BND-GLD	-27.02	3.73	7.5%	-0.66	6.64	0.2%	2.99	7.75	9.62	0%	-64.74	12Y.9M
VTI-IJS-VTV-VNQ-IEI	-31.60	2.46	11.2%	-3.29	5.82	1.8%	1.94	7.64	10.06	0%	-71.75	13Y.5M
VTI-IJS-VTV-VNQ-BND	-31.60	2.46	11.1%	-3.29	5.71	1.8%	1.94	7.61	10.06	0%	-71.74	13Y.5M
VTI-IJS-VTV-VNQ-LQD	-31.65	2.26	11.5%	-3.30	5.80	2.2%	1.98	7.59	10.06	0%	-71.80	13Y.5M
VTI-IJS-VTV-SHY-GLD	-26.98	3.70	7.5%	-0.78	6.54	0.2%	2.75	7.55	9.52	0%	-64.66	13Y.0M
VTI-IJS-VTV-TLT-IEI	-26.58	2.78	8.3%	-1.13	6.00	0.5%	3.15	7.43	9.52	0%	-64.21	12Y.8M
VTI-IJS-VTV-VNQ-SHY	-31.58	2.27	11.2%	-3.41	5.47	2%	1.65	7.42	10.06	0%	-71.69	13Y.8M
VTI-IJS-VTV-BND-TLT	-26.58	2.76	8.5%	-1.13	6.00	0.4%	3.15	7.41	9.51	0%	-64.21	12Y.8M
VTI-IJS-VTV-TLT-LQD	-26.63	2.70	8.9%	-1.14	6.04	0.6%	3.19	7.37	9.52	0%	-64.29	12Y.8M
VTI-IJS-VTV-TLT-3HY	-26.53	2.65	8.7%	1.24	5.86	0.6%	2.92	7.27	9.48	0%	-64.11	12Y.10M
VTI-IJS-VNQ-LQD-GLD	-23.25	3.97	6.6%	-0.10	6.28	0.1%	3.03	7.26	9.05	0%	-58.89	12Y.8M
VTI-IJS-VTV-BIL-GLD	-27.33	3.37	8.2%	-1.16	6.30	0.4%	2.41	7.25	9.37	0%	-65.14	13Y.1M
VTI-IJS-VNQ-BND-GLD	-23.20	3.95	6.4%	-0.09	6.28	0.1%	2.99	7.22	8.95	0%	-58.81	12Y.8M
VTI-IJS-VNQ-IEI-GLD	-23.20	4.04	6.3%	-0.10	6.29	0.1%	2.98	7.22	9.02	0%	-58.82	12Y.8M
VTI-IJS-VTV-VNQ-BIL	-31.92	2.03	11.5%	-3.79	5.21	2.4%	1.32	7.21	9.94	0%	-72.09	13Y.10M
VTI-IJS-VNQ-TLT-LQD	-22.73	3.04	8.7%	-0.62	5.61	0.2%	3.20	7.20	8.85	0%	-58.19	10Y.9M

Order by Baseline 15Y Return - All data (from 1871/1927 to 2023-11) - US Infl. Adjusted

Portfolio	3Y Rolling Annualized Return (%)			7Y Rolling Annualized Return (%)			15Y Rolling Annualized Return (%)				Max Draw-down (%)	Long Neg Period (Y.M)
	Worst	Base	%Fail	Worst	Base	%Fail	Worst	Base ▼	Median	%Fail		
VTI-IJS-VTV-VNQ-GLD	-27.10	0.01	14.9%	-1.95	3.64	2.5%	1.64	4.63	6.84	0%	-65.56	13Y.4M
VTI-IJS-VTV-IEI-GLD	-21.23	0.54	13%	-1.35	3.67	1.2%	2.24	4.49	6.20	0%	-55.48	11Y.0M
VTI-IJS-VTV-BND-GLD	-21.23	0.51	13.3%	-1.35	3.60	1.1%	2.24	4.48	6.18	0%	-55.47	11Y.0M
VTI-IJS-VTV-SHY-GLD	-21.19	0.49	13.6%	-1.65	3.52	1.6%	2.04	4.47	5.95	0%	-55.37	12Y.8M
VTI-IJS-VTV-LQD-GLD	-21.29	0.47	13.8%	-1.29	3.66	1.4%	2.28	4.40	6.31	0%	-55.57	11Y.0M
VTI-IJS-VTV-BIL-GLD	-21.57	0.24	14.4%	-1.86	3.31	1.8%	1.92	4.33	5.73	0%	-55.98	13Y.0M
VTI-IJS-VTV-TLT-GLD	-21.68	0.59	13.4%	-1.25	3.65	1.2%	2.31	4.31	6.59	0%	-56.27	9Y.0M
VTI-IJS-BND-IEI-GLD	-11.00	1.01	10.5%	-1.53	2.98	1.5%	1.22	3.90	5.34	0%	-33.82	12Y.5M
VTI-IJS-BND-LQD-GLD	-11.06	0.96	11.3%	-1.53	2.97	1.5%	1.27	3.90	5.39	0%	-33.94	12Y.4M
VTI-IJS-BND-SHY-GLD	-10.96	0.94	10.5%	-1.56	2.94	2.1%	1.03	3.90	5.11	0%	-33.68	12Y.8M
VTI-IJS-SHY-IEI-GLD	-10.96	0.99	10.3%	-1.56	2.95	2.1%	1.02	3.89	5.14	0%	-33.69	12Y.8M
VTI-IJS-IEI-LQD-GLD	-11.06	0.98	11.1%	-1.53	2.95	1.5%	1.26	3.89	5.41	0%	-33.95	12Y.4M
VTI-IJS-SHY-LQD-GLD	-11.02	0.88	10.9%	-1.56	2.93	2.1%	1.07	3.89	5.19	0%	-33.81	12Y.8M
VTI-IJS-VNQ-BND-GLD	-17.11	0.65	12.7%	-1.23	3.20	1.5%	1.78	3.87	5.85	0%	-47.99	8Y.10M
VTI-IJS-VNQ-IEI-GLD	-17.11	0.67	12.7%	-1.23	3.22	1.5%	1.78	3.87	5.86	0%	-48.00	8Y.11M
VTI-IJS-VNQ-LQD-GLD	-17.16	0.49	13.3%	-1.17	3.23	1.8%	1.82	3.84	5.84	0%	-48.09	8Y.10M
VTI-IJS-VNQ-SHY-GLD	-17.08	0.68	13.4%	-1.53	3.19	2.2%	1.58	3.83	5.76	0%	-47.91	9Y.2M
IJS-VTV-VNQ-LQD-GLD	-16.91	0.53	13%	-1.23	3.10	1.6%	1.79	3.81	5.82	0%	-47.81	9Y.0M
IJS-VTV-SHY-LQD-GLD	-10.78	1.01	11.1%	-1.52	2.73	2.1%	1.04	3.81	5.12	0%	-33.57	12Y.8M
VTI-IJS-TLT-SHY-GLD	-11.40	0.97	11.3%	-1.69	2.87	1.8%	1.09	3.80	5.39	0%	-34.73	12Y.7M
IJS-VTV-BND-IEI-GLD	-10.77	1.20	10.5%	-1.49	2.78	1.6%	1.19	3.79	5.22	0%	-33.57	12Y.5M

184

Ranking: Median 15Y Return

Order by **Median 15Y Return - Last 30 Years** (from 1993-12 to 2023-11)

Portfolio	3Y Rolling Annualized Return (%)			7Y Rolling Annualized Return (%)			15Y Rolling Annualized Return (%)				Max Draw-down (%)	Long Neg Period (Y.M)
	Worst	Base	%Fail	Worst	Base	%Fail	Worst	Base	Median ▼	%Fail		
MTUM-SCZ-VNQ-EMB-GLD	-7.88	4.85	4.9%	4.40	7.20	0%	5.51	8.21	10.66	0%	-39.35	4Y.3M
SCZ-EEM-VNQ-EMB-TLT	-7.71	3.24	6.5%	1.02	6.17	0%	3.64	7.25	10.65	0%	-39.71	6Y.3M
SCZ-VNQ-EMB-TLT-GLD	-3.76	3.23	5.2%	1.58	5.42	0%	4.68	7.46	10.50	0%	-25.31	4Y.4M
MTUM-SCZ-VNQ-EMB-TLT	-8.98	4.83	8.9%	2.62	7.46	0%	5.48	8.27	10.50	0%	-38.24	4Y.7M
SCZ-EEM-VNQ-EMB-GLD	-6.74	1.70	5.5%	2.13	4.67	0%	3.55	6.99	10.49	0%	-40.90	5Y.2M
SCZ-EEM-EMB-TLT-GLD	-5.11	2.07	7.1%	1.46	4.08	0%	3.47	7.23	10.48	0%	-28.28	5Y.10M
IJS-SCZ-VNQ-EMB-GLD	-8.67	3.23	4.9%	3.16	6.67	0%	5.27	7.53	10.46	0%	-38.95	4Y.4M
MTUM-EEM-VNQ-EMB-GLD	-5.85	3.90	3.4%	4.00	6.48	0%	4.90	8.14	10.45	0%	-38.62	3Y.7M
IJS-EEM-VNQ-EMB-GLD	-6.57	3.27	2.5%	2.26	5.83	0%	4.71	7.50	10.43	0%	-38.16	3Y.8M
IJS-EEM-VNQ-EMB-TLT	-7.72	4.21	4%	1.69	6.72	0%	4.76	7.55	10.42	0%	-37.18	6Y.0M
IJS-MTUM-VNQ-EMB-GLD	-7.79	5.61	3.7%	5.04	7.79	0%	6.45	8.55	10.40	0%	-36.58	4Y.3M
IJS-SCZ-EEM-EMB-TLT	-6.59	3.67	4.3%	1.79	6.68	0%	4.17	7.42	10.39	0%	-36.41	6Y.2M
IJS-SCZ-EEM-EMB-GLD	-5.59	2.70	4%	2.10	5.28	0%	4.06	7.30	10.39	0%	-37.67	4Y.9M
IJS-SCZ-EMB-TLT-GLD	-2.14	4.37	2.8%	2.49	6.17	0%	5.21	7.80	10.38	0%	-23.62	4Y.8M
IJS-MTUM-SCZ-EMB-GLD	-6.77	4.66	3.4%	4.86	7.64	0%	5.84	8.41	10.37	0%	-36.03	4Y.2M
MTUM-EEM-VNQ-EMB-TLT	-6.88	4.51	5.8%	2.36	7.30	0%	4.95	8.23	10.36	0%	-37.43	5Y.9M
MTUM-SCZ-EEM-EMB-TLT	-5.84	3.75	6.5%	2.39	7.31	0%	4.32	8.15	10.35	0%	-36.78	6Y.0M
MTUM-EEM-VNQ-TLT-GLD	-3.49	4.41	3.4%	3.45	6.70	0%	5.38	8.39	10.35	0%	-32.47	4Y.2M
MTUM-SCZ-EMB-TLT-GLD	-4.53	5.08	4%	3.01	7.06	0%	5.38	8.35	10.34	0%	-25.46	4Y.2M
EEM-VNQ-EMB-TLT-GLD	-4.47	2.89	6.2%	1.33	4.32	0%	4.03	7.31	10.32	0%	-25.31	4Y.10M
IJS-SCZ-VNQ-EMB-TLT	-9.88	3.68	7.7%	1.94	7.13	0%	5.24	7.47	10.31	0%	-38.30	5Y.10M

Order by **Median 15Y Return - Last 30 Years** (from 1993-12 to 2023-11) - **US Infl. Adjusted**

Portfolio	3Y Rolling Annualized Return (%)			7Y Rolling Annualized Return (%)			15Y Rolling Annualized Return (%)				Max Draw-down (%)	Long Neg Period (Y.M)
	Worst	Base	%Fail	Worst	Base	%Fail	Worst	Base	Median ▼	%Fail		
MTUM-SCZ-VNQ-EMB-GLD	-9.88	2.53	11.7%	0.84	5.30	0%	3.04	5.91	8.16	0%	-40.28	10Y.3M
SCZ-EEM-VNQ-EMB-TLT	-9.99	1.26	10.2%	-2.40	4.13	4.3%	1.22	4.92	8.14	0%	-40.64	10Y.10M
MTUM-EEM-VNQ-EMB-GLD	-7.89	1.69	8.9%	0.59	4.60	0%	2.44	5.89	8.06	0%	-39.56	6Y.3M
EEM-VNQ-EMB-TLT-GLD	-9.66	0.78	11.4%	-2.13	2.33	4%	1.60	5.21	8.05	0%	-31.33	12Y.3M
IJS-EEM-VNQ-EMB-GLD	-8.60	0.86	11.7%	0.01	3.80	0%	2.26	5.23	8.04	0%	-39.11	7Y.8M
SCZ-VNQ-EMB-TLT-GLD	-8.99	1.18	9.5%	-1.88	3.56	2.9%	2.23	5.28	8.03	0%	-30.68	10Y.6M
SCZ-EEM-VNQ-EMB-GLD	-8.76	-0.64	18.8%	-0.65	2.67	0.7%	1.13	4.76	8.03	0%	-41.81	9Y.10M
MTUM-SCZ-VNQ-EMB-TLT	-10.95	2.17	12.9%	-0.88	5.13	1.1%	3.02	6.02	8.03	0%	-39.19	8Y.9M
MTUM-EEM-VNQ-EMB-TLT	-9.95	2.27	9.5%	-1.12	5.47	1.1%	2.49	6.10	7.99	0%	-38.39	9Y.2M
IJS-MTUM-VNQ-EMB-GLD	-9.79	3.31	10.5%	1.49	5.63	0%	3.98	6.53	7.98	0%	-37.56	9Y.3M
IJS-SCZ-EEM-EMB-TLT	-8.73	1.50	9.2%	-1.66	4.75	2.2%	1.73	5.13	7.97	0%	-37.38	10Y.0M
IJS-SCZ-VNQ-EMB-GLD	-10.64	0.44	12%	0.24	4.59	0%	2.82	5.24	7.97	0%	-39.89	7Y.3M
IJS-EEM-VNQ-EMB-TLT	-9.72	2.07	9.8%	-1.76	4.97	2.5%	2.31	5.34	7.95	0%	-38.15	9Y.6M
IJS-EEM-EMB-TLT-GLD	-8.32	1.87	8%	-1.27	3.10	1.1%	2.14	5.65	7.94	0%	-30.73	11Y.1M
SCZ-EEM-EMB-TLT-GLD	-10.25	-0.11	15.4%	-2.00	1.99	3.6%	1.05	5.00	7.93	0%	-35.67	12Y.6M
IJS-MTUM-SCZ-EMB-GLD	-8.78	1.54	10.8%	1.71	5.49	0%	3.38	6.26	7.93	0%	-37.01	6Y.0M
MTUM-SCZ-EMB-TLT-GLD	-9.72	3.26	7.1%	-0.50	5.41	0.7%	2.91	6.28	7.92	0%	-32.23	7Y.4M
MTUM-EEM-VNQ-TLT-GLD	-8.73	2.13	8.6%	-0.07	4.65	0.4%	2.91	5.76	7.91	0%	-33.51	7Y.4M
MTUM-SCZ-EEM-EMB-TLT	-10.51	1.43	10.8%	-1.08	5.29	1.1%	1.88	5.77	7.90	0%	-37.75	9Y.2M
IJS-SCZ-EEM-EMB-GLD	-7.63	0.55	12.6%	0.20	3.00	0%	1.62	5.09	7.90	0%	-38.62	8Y.7M
IJS-SCZ-EMB-TLT-GLD	-7.43	2.17	7.1%	-1.01	4.29	1.1%	2.75	5.58	7.86	0%	-30.31	8Y.9M

Order by **Median 15Y Return - Last 60 Years** (from 1963-12 to 2023-11)

Portfolio	3Y Rolling Annualized Return (%)			7Y Rolling Annualized Return (%)			15Y Rolling Annualized Return (%)				Max Draw-down (%)	Long Neg Period (Y.M)
	Worst	Base	%Fail	Worst	Base	%Fail	Worst	Base	Median ▼	%Fail		
VTI-IJS-VTV-VNQ-GLD	-11.08	5.58	4.5%	2.53	7.65	0%	6.14	8.85	11.51	0%	-43.67	5Y.2M
VTI-IJS-VTV-VNQ-IEI	-12.75	4.19	7.2%	-0.36	6.48	0.2%	6.08	7.96	11.16	0%	-44.83	7Y.2M
VTI-IJS-VTV-VNQ-BND	-13.42	4.08	7.2%	-0.36	6.36	0.2%	5.87	7.93	11.09	0%	-46.17	8Y.1M
VTI-IJS-VTV-VNQ-TLT	-12.18	4.27	7.6%	-0.89	6.76	0.5%	6.48	8.50	11.08	0%	-43.32	7Y.5M
VTI-IJS-VTV-VNQ-LQD	-14.27	4.11	7.7%	-0.84	6.37	0.8%	5.74	8.09	11.01	0%	-47.72	8Y.1M
VTI-IJS-VTV-VNQ-SHY	-13.28	4.09	7.2%	-0.24	6.22	0.3%	5.74	7.64	10.99	0%	-45.92	8Y.1M
IJS-VTV-VNQ-TLT-GLD	-5.67	5.38	1.9%	4.25	7.52	0%	6.57	8.92	10.83	0%	-30.82	4Y.2M
VTI-IJS-VNQ-TLT-GLD	-5.33	5.63	1.2%	4.63	7.76	0%	6.87	9.05	10.77	0%	-29.90	4Y.2M
VTI-IJS-VTV-VNQ-BIL	-13.76	3.86	7.5%	-0.39	5.94	0.5%	5.42	7.38	10.70	0%	-46.90	8Y.6M
IJS-VTV-VNQ-TLT-IEI	-7.55	4.59	5%	0.70	6.35	0%	5.91	8.05	10.64	0%	-31.85	6Y.4M
VTI-IJS-VTV-TLT-GLD	-3.78	5.70	1.6%	4.70	7.79	0%	7.09	8.80	10.64	0%	-26.81	3Y.8M
IJS-VTV-VNQ-BND-TLT	-8.18	4.57	5.4%	0.70	6.35	0%	5.89	8.02	10.63	0%	-33.32	6Y.4M
IJS-VTV-VNQ-IEI-LQD	-9.48	4.75	5.6%	0.76	6.14	0%	5.52	7.60	10.62	0%	-36.58	6Y.4M
IJS-VTV-VNQ-BND-IEI	-8.64	4.70	5%	1.21	5.99	0%	5.34	7.51	10.59	0%	-34.82	6Y.1M
IJS-VTV-VNQ-TLT-LQD	-0.02	4.66	6%	0.25	6.39	0%	6.07	8.04	10.56	0%	-35.11	6Y.6M
IJS-VTV-VNQ-LQD-GLD	-7.68	5.36	2.2%	4.01	7.33	0%	6.16	8.54	10.56	0%	-35.24	4Y.5M
VTI-IJS-VTV-TLT-IEI	-5.64	4.32	4.2%	0.46	6.58	0%	6.43	7.70	10.55	0%	-27.40	6Y.5M
IJS-VTV-VNQ-BND-LQD	-10.13	4.76	5.6%	0.76	6.05	0%	5.49	7.55	10.55	0%	-38.01	6Y.4M
VTI-IJS-VNQ-LQD-GLD	-7.35	5.69	1.9%	4.07	7.56	0%	6.35	8.68	10.54	0%	-34.40	4Y.5M
IJS-VTV-VNQ-TLT-SHY	-8.03	4.66	4.7%	0.83	6.29	0%	5.66	7.77	10.54	0%	-33.01	6Y.4M
VTI-IJS-VTV-TLT-LQD	-7.10	4.08	5.1%	0.00	6.51	0.2%	6.50	7.77	10.53	0%	-30.46	7Y.0M

Order by **Median 15Y Return - Last 60 Years** (from 1963-12 to 2023-11) - **US Infl. Adjusted**

Portfolio	3Y Rolling Annualized Return (%)			7Y Rolling Annualized Return (%)			15Y Rolling Annualized Return (%)				Max Draw-down (%)	Long Neg Period (Y.M)
	Worst	Base	%Fail	Worst	Base	%Fail	Worst	Base	Median ▼	%Fail		
VTI-IJS-VNQ-TLT-GLD	-7.38	1.35	10.7%	-1.00	4.26	0.6%	3.50	5.48	7.30	0%	-30.97	8Y.11M
IJS-VTV-VNQ-TLT-GLD	-7.71	1.39	10.4%	-1.02	4.02	0.3%	3.65	5.44	7.28	0%	-31.88	9Y.0M
VTI-IJS-VTV-VNQ-TLT	-14.29	-0.17	15.6%	-6.52	2.19	6.4%	0.56	5.21	7.27	0%	-44.45	13Y.11M
VTI-IJS-VTV-VNQ-GLD	-13.01	1.13	11.7%	-1.95	4.41	1.4%	3.56	5.85	7.23	0%	-44.54	9Y.8M
VTI-IJS-VTV-TLT-GLD	-6.35	1.42	9.8%	-1.25	4.02	0.5%	3.10	5.42	7.02	0%	-30.73	9Y.0M
VTI-IJS-VTV-VNQ-LQD	-16.13	-0.19	15.3%	-6.47	2.24	7.2%	0.72	4.51	6.96	0%	-48.77	13Y.8M
VTI-IJS-VTV-VNQ-IEI	-14.64	0.29	14.2%	-6.02	2.34	6.1%	1.00	4.55	6.89	0%	-45.94	11Y.10M
VTI-IJS-VTV-VNQ-BND	-15.30	0.21	14.3%	-6.02	2.31	6.3%	1.00	4.42	6.87	0%	-47.24	11Y.10M
IJS-VTV-VNQ-TLT-IEI	-11.32	0.20	14.7%	-5.02	1.82	5.3%	0.53	4.24	6.87	0%	-35.97	13Y.7M
VTI-IJS-VNQ-LQD-GLD	-9.36	1.12	10.2%	-0.92	4.22	0.8%	3.70	5.41	6.86	0%	-35.41	7Y.6M
IJS-VTV-VNQ-LQD-GLD	-9.68	1.20	9.9%	-0.94	4.01	0.5%	3.68	5.36	6.86	0%	-36.24	8Y.11M
IJS-VTV-VNQ-TLT-LQD	-12.27	-0.47	15.5%	-5.45	1.75	6%	0.34	4.49	6.85	0%	-37.89	14Y.5M
VTI-IJS-VNQ-IEI-GLD	-7.89	1.49	9.3%	-0.52	4.15	0.2%	3.85	5.43	6.82	0%	-32.47	7Y.5M
VTI-IJS-VNQ-TLT-LQD	-13.15	-0.34	16.1%	-5.48	1.89	6.9%	0.23	4.55	6.81	0%	-39.03	14Y.6M
IJS-VTV-VNQ-BND-TLT	-11.32	0.04	14.9%	-5.02	1.77	5.3%	0.53	4.26	6.81	0%	-35.96	13Y.7M
IJS-VTV-VNQ-IEI-GLD	-8.21	1.63	9.5%	-0.54	3.92	0.3%	3.55	5.39	6.80	0%	-33.32	7Y.6M
IJS-VNQ-TLT-LQD-GLD	-7.13	1.01	10.7%	-1.06	3.48	0.6%	3.20	4.72	6.79	0%	-28.95	8Y.10M
VTI-VTV-VNQ-TLT-GLD	-7.26	0.45	13%	-1.40	3.59	1.3%	2.21	4.80	6.75	0%	-31.52	10Y.9M
VTI-IJS-VNQ-BND-GLD	-8.54	1.43	9.3%	-0.51	4.22	0.2%	3.82	5.41	6.73	0%	-33.78	7Y.5M
VTI-IJS-VNQ-TLT-IEI	-12.19	0.15	14.6%	-5.05	1.95	6.1%	0.49	4.41	6.71	0%	-37.10	13Y.11M
IJS-VTV-VNQ-BND-GLD	-8.86	1.60	9.5%	-0.54	3.89	0.3%	3.52	5.40	6.71	0%	-34.61	7Y.6M

Order by **Median 15Y Return** - **All data** (from 1871/1927 to 2023-11)

Portfolio	3Y Rolling Annualized Return (%)			7Y Rolling Annualized Return (%)			15Y Rolling Annualized Return (%)				Max Draw-down (%)	Long Neg Period (Y.M)
	Worst	Base	%Fail	Worst	Base	%Fail	Worst	Base	Median ▼	%Fail		
VTI-IJS-VTV-VNQ-GLD	-32.46	3.32	9.2%	-2.97	6.70	1.4%	1.79	8.21	10.09	0%	-72.73	13Y.7M
VTI-IJS-VTV-VNQ-TLT	-31.99	2.48	11.4%	-3.42	6.20	2.1%	1.98	7.82	10.07	0%	-72.25	13Y.5M
VTI-IJS-VTV-VNQ-BND	-31.60	2.46	11.1%	-3.29	5.71	1.8%	1.94	7.61	10.06	0%	-71.74	13Y.5M
VTI-IJS-VTV-VNQ-LQD	-31.65	2.26	11.5%	-3.30	5.80	2.2%	1.98	7.59	10.06	0%	-71.80	13Y.5M
VTI-IJS-VTV-VNQ-IEI	-31.60	2.46	11.2%	-3.29	5.82	1.8%	1.94	7.64	10.06	0%	-71.75	13Y.5M
VTI-IJS-VTV-VNQ-SHY	-31.58	2.27	11.2%	-3.41	5.47	2%	1.65	7.42	10.06	0%	-71.69	13Y.8M
VTI-IJS-VTV-VNQ-BIL	-31.92	2.03	11.5%	-3.79	5.21	2.4%	1.32	7.21	9.94	0%	-72.09	13Y.10M
VTI-IJS-VTV-LQD-GLD	-27.07	3.71	7.5%	-0.67	6.60	0.2%	3.02	7.81	9.64	0%	-64.81	12Y.9M
VTI-IJS-VTV-IEI-GLD	-27.02	3.73	7.1%	-0.66	6.67	0.2%	2.98	7.78	9.63	0%	-64.74	12Y.9M
VTI-IJS-VTV-TLT-GLD	-27.44	3.74	7.1%	-0.78	6.55	0.2%	3.04	8.13	9.63	0%	-65.37	12Y.9M
VTI-IJS-VTV-BND-GLD	-27.02	3.73	7.5%	-0.66	6.64	0.2%	2.99	7.75	9.62	0%	-64.74	12Y.9M
VTI-IJS-VTV-IEI-LQD	-26.21	2.85	9.1%	-1.01	5.83	0.3%	3.14	7.16	9.60	0%	-63.63	12Y.8M
VTI-IJS-VTV-BND-SHY	-26.11	2.52	9.5%	-1.12	5.43	0.4%	2.88	6.77	9.59	0%	-63.46	12Y.10M
VTI-IJS-VTV-BND-IEI	-26.16	2.85	9%	-1.00	5.77	0.3%	3.10	7.12	9.59	0%	-63.55	12Y.8M
VTI-IJS-VTV-SHY-IEI	-26.12	2.64	9.2%	-1.12	5.54	0.4%	2.87	6.82	9.59	0%	-63.46	12Y.10M
VTI-IJS-VTV-SHY-LQD	-26.16	2.60	9.7%	-1.12	5.48	0.4%	2.91	6.94	9.58	0%	-63.54	12Y.10M
VTI-IJS-VTV-BND-LQD	-26.21	2.80	9.4%	-1.01	5.75	0.3%	3.14	7.13	9.57	0%	-63.63	12Y.8M
VTI-IJS-VTV-TLT-IEI	-26.58	2.78	8.3%	-1.13	6.00	0.5%	3.15	7.43	9.52	0%	-64.21	12Y.8M
VTI-IJS-VTV-SHY-GLD	-26.98	3.70	7.5%	-0.78	6.54	0.2%	2.75	7.55	9.52	0%	-64.66	13Y.0M
VTI-IJS-VTV-TLT-LQD	-26.63	2.70	8.9%	-1.14	6.04	0.6%	3.19	7.37	9.52	0%	-64.29	12Y.8M
VTI-IJS-VTV-BND-TLT	-26.58	2.76	8.5%	-1.13	6.00	0.4%	3.15	7.41	9.51	0%	-64.21	12Y.8M

Order by **Median 15Y Return** - **All data** (from 1871/1927 to 2023-11) - **US Infl. Adjusted**

Portfolio	3Y Rolling Annualized Return (%)			7Y Rolling Annualized Return (%)			15Y Rolling Annualized Return (%)				Max Draw-down (%)	Long Neg Period (Y.M)
	Worst	Base	%Fail	Worst	Base	%Fail	Worst	Base	Median ▼	%Fail		
VTI-IJS-VTV-VNQ-TLT	-26.59	-0.68	16.9%	-6.52	2.52	4.7%	0.30	3.37	6.94	0%	-64.95	13Y.11M
VTI-IJS-VTV-VNQ-GLD	-27.10	0.01	14.9%	-1.95	3.64	2.5%	1.64	4.63	6.84	0%	-65.56	13Y.4M
VTI-IJS-VTV-TLT-GLD	-21.68	0.59	13.4%	-1.25	3.65	1.2%	2.31	4.31	6.59	0%	-56.27	9Y.0M
VTI-IJS-VTV-VNQ-LQD	-26.23	-0.69	16.6%	-6.47	2.64	5.2%	0.32	3.42	6.55	0%	-64.40	13Y.11M
VTI-IJS-VTV-VNQ-BND	-26.17	-0.59	16%	-6.02	2.65	4.8%	0.58	3.50	6.51	0%	-64.32	13Y.9M
VTI-IJS-VTV-VNQ-IEI	-26.18	-0.39	15.9%	-6.02	2.67	4.7%	0.57	3.50	6.50	0%	-64.32	13Y.9M
VTI-IJS-VTV-VNQ-SHY	-26.15	-0.59	16.1%	-5.91	2.52	5%	0.66	3.51	6.38	0%	-64.25	13Y.7M
VTI-IJS-VTV-LQD-GLD	-21.29	0.47	13.8%	-1.29	3.66	1.4%	2.28	4.40	6.31	0%	-55.57	11Y.0M
VTI-IJS-VTV-IEI-GLD	-21.23	0.54	13%	-1.35	3.67	1.2%	2.24	4.49	6.20	0%	-55.48	11Y.0M
VTI-IJS-VTV-VNQ-BIL	-26.52	-0.77	17%	-5.76	2.29	5.4%	0.58	3.35	6.18	0%	-64.76	13Y.8M
VTI-IJS-VTV-BND-GLD	-21.23	0.51	13.3%	-1.35	3.60	1.1%	2.24	4.48	6.18	0%	-55.47	11Y.0M
VTI-IJS-VTV-TLT-LQD	-20.81	-0.93	18.9%	-5.68	2.35	4.8%	-0.17	3.45	6.16	0.1%	-54.90	16Y.0M
VTI-IJS-VTV-TLT-IEI	-20.76	-0.64	17.5%	-5.25	2.40	4.6%	0.10	3.43	6.06	0%	-54.81	14Y.10M
VTI-IJS-VTV-BND-TLT	-20.75	-0.78	18.1%	-5.24	2.40	4.7%	0.10	3.43	6.05	0%	-54.80	14Y.10M
VTI-IJS-VNQ-TLT-LQD	-16.60	-0.67	16.6%	-5.48	2.13	4.7%	0.23	3.04	6.01	0%	-47.21	14Y.6M
VTI-IJS-VTV-LQD-GLD	-16.55	-0.56	15.7%	-5.05	2.28	4.3%	0.48	3.05	5.98	0%	-47.11	13Y.11M
VTI-IJS-VNQ-BND-TLT	-16.55	-0.55	15.9%	-5.05	2.19	4.3%	0.48	3.01	5.97	0%	-47.10	13Y.11M
VTI-IJS-VTV-SHY-GLD	-21.19	0.49	13.6%	-1.65	3.52	1.6%	2.04	4.47	5.95	0%	-55.37	12Y.8M
IJS-VTV-VNQ-TLT-LQD	-16.37	-0.82	16.3%	-5.45	1.93	4.2%	0.18	3.02	5.93	0%	-46.96	15Y.2M
VTI-IJS-VTV-TLT-SHY	-20.70	-0.84	17%	-5.12	2.50	4.5%	0.36	3.25	5.93	0%	-54.68	14Y.2M
IJS-VTV-VNQ-TLT-IEI	-16.32	-0.53	15.8%	-5.02	2.00	3.8%	0.42	3.09	5.92	0%	-46.86	13Y.11M

187

Lazy Portfolios (1-5 Assets)

We have calculated all possible portfolio combinations, using 1 to 5 equally weighted assets:

- **Portfolios with 1 asset**: the entire portfolio is allocated to a single asset.
- **Portfolios with 2 assets**: each asset represents half of the portfolio.
- **Portfolios with 3 assets**: each asset represents one-third of the portfolio.
- **Portfolios with 4 assets**: each asset represents one-fourth of the portfolio.
- **Portfolios with 5 assets**: each asset represents one-fifth of the portfolio.

The following rankings are computed based on all these combinations, as you have seen before. If you have no preferences regarding the number of assets to use, here is a comprehensive overview, summarizing everything.

As you already know, portfolios with 2 or more assets involve an annual rebalancing, conducted at the beginning of each year, to restore the original weights.

Ranking: Baseline 3Y Return

Order by **Baseline 3Y Return - Last 30 Years** (from 1993-12 to 2023-11)

Portfolio	3Y Rolling Annualized Return (%)			7Y Rolling Annualized Return (%)			15Y Rolling Annualized Return (%)				Max Draw-down (%)	Long Neg Period (Y.M)
	Worst	Base ▼	%Fail	Worst	Base	%Fail	Worst	Base	Median	%Fail		
IJS-MTUM-EMB-TLT-GLD	-2.10	5.98	1.8%	3.75	7.59	0%	6.39	8.74	10.09	0%	-22.31	3Y.9M
MTUM-EMB-TLT-GLD	-5.80	5.65	4.3%	2.74	6.59	0%	5.74	8.46	9.84	0%	-23.20	4Y.2M
VTI-IJS-EMB-TLT-GLD	-0.87	5.63	0.9%	4.00	7.13	0%	6.32	8.36	9.58	0%	-21.87	3Y.3M
IJS-MTUM-VNQ-TIP-GLD	-6.82	5.62	3.4%	4.99	7.49	0%	6.46	8.19	9.53	0%	-34.12	4Y.3M
IJS-MTUM-VNQ-EMB-GLD	-7.79	5.61	3.7%	5.04	7.79	0%	6.45	8.55	10.40	0%	-36.58	4Y.3M
MTUM-EMB-TLT-CWB-GLD	-4.17	5.61	1.8%	4.09	7.23	0%	6.20	8.49	9.50	0%	-23.90	3Y.9M
IJS-EMB-TLT-CWB	-4.83	5.58	3.4%	3.04	7.44	0%	6.09	7.84	9.27	0%	-24.94	4Y.3M
IJS-MTUM-TLT-IEI-GLD	-1.83	5.54	1.2%	3.87	7.28	0%	6.29	8.24	8.93	0%	-19.48	3Y.5M
TLT-CWB	-8.59	5.50	4%	2.34	7.15	0%	6.22	7.58	8.45	0%	-31.98	4Y.4M
IJS-MTUM-BNDX-TLT-GLD	-1.82	5.50	1.5%	3.92	7.52	0%	6.51	8.36	9.10	0%	-19.89	3Y.9M
IJS-MTUM-VNQ-IEI-GLD	-5.75	5.47	3.1%	5.20	7.51	0%	6.42	8.23	9.42	0%	-32.02	4Y.2M
IJS-MTUM-VNQ-TLT-GLD	-5.22	5.46	2.5%	4.41	8.16	0%	6.96	8.96	10.11	0%	-30.50	3Y.9M
IJS-MTUM-EMB-CWB-GLD	-5.36	5.45	2.5%	5.55	7.95	0%	6.70	8.60	9.61	0%	-30.72	3Y.8M
IJS-IEI-CWB	-6.90	5.45	3.7%	2.71	6.40	0%	5.86	6.93	7.76	0%	-28.97	5Y.1M
IJS-TLT-CWB	-6.03	5.45	3.4%	3.70	7.34	0%	6.96	8.18	8.99	0%	-26.77	4Y.5M
MTUM-BNDX-EMB-TLT	-6.67	5.43	5.8%	1.64	7.24	0%	5.40	7.73	8.66	0%	-24.50	5Y.2M
IJS-MTUM-TLT-TIP-GLD	-1.57	5.42	1.2%	4.07	7.32	0%	6.37	8.24	9.11	0%	-20.25	3Y.4M
MTUM-BNDX-EMB-TLT-GLD	-5.46	5.42	4.6%	2.28	6.03	0%	5.37	7.77	9.09	0%	-21.21	4Y.3M
MTUM-EMB-TLT-IEI	-6.66	5.41	5.2%	1.58	7.02	0%	5.09	7.38	8.41	0%	-24.34	5Y.2M
IJS-MTUM-VNQ-TLT-TIP	-8.06	5.40	6.5%	3.60	7.20	0%	6.38	8.05	9.20	0%	-33.09	5Y.0M
MTUM-BND-EMB-TLT	-6.99	5.37	5.2%	1.52	6.98	0%	5.08	7.42	8.36	0%	-25.55	5Y.10M

Order by **Baseline 3Y Return - Last 30 Years** (from 1993-12 to 2023-11) - **US Infl. Adjusted**

Portfolio	3Y Rolling Annualized Return (%)			7Y Rolling Annualized Return (%)			15Y Rolling Annualized Return (%)				Max Draw-down (%)	Long Neg Period (Y.M)
	Worst	Base ▼	%Fail	Worst	Base	%Fail	Worst	Base	Median	%Fail		
MTUM-EMB-TLT-GLD	-10.92	3.82	5.8%	-0.77	4.77	1.1%	3.27	6.28	7.42	0%	-31.87	7Y.8M
MTUM-EMB-TLT-CWB-GLD	-9.37	3.71	6.5%	0.54	5.42	0%	3.71	6.27	7.24	0%	-31.67	6Y.3M
IJS-MTUM-EMB-TLT-GLD	-7.42	3.69	6.8%	0.21	5.89	0%	3.92	6.48	7.61	0%	-28.19	7Y.3M
MTUM-BNDX-EMB-TLT-GLD	-10.60	3.58	5.8%	-1.21	4.42	1.8%	2.90	5.63	6.69	0%	-30.52	8Y.9M
MTUM-EMB-TLT-LQD-GLD	-10.98	3.51	5.8%	-1.19	4.40	1.8%	2.85	5.58	6.71	0%	-31.94	8Y.9M
MTUM-VNQ-BNDX-EMB-GLD	-6.67	3.43	8.6%	0.15	4.95	0%	3.23	5.72	7.27	0%	-27.85	7Y.3M
MTUM-BNDX-EMB-TLT	-11.74	3.35	7.7%	-1.82	5.17	4.3%	2.94	5.51	6.38	0%	-34.76	9Y.2M
IJS-MTUM-VNQ-EMB-GLD	-9.79	3.31	10.5%	1.49	5.63	0%	3.98	6.53	7.98	0%	-37.56	5Y.11M
IJS-MTUM-EMB-IEI-GLD	-4.90	3.29	7.1%	0.96	5.16	0%	3.42	5.65	6.99	0%	-25.79	6Y.1M
MTUM-EMB-TLT-IEI-CWB	-10.24	3.28	7.7%	-0.40	4.88	0.7%	3.21	5.39	6.24	0%	-33.67	7Y.7M
EMB-TLT-CWB	-12.46	3.28	8%	-1.90	4.80	2.9%	2.78	5.16	6.75	0%	-39.01	9Y.5M
MTUM-BNDX-EMB-GLD	-7.90	3.28	6.5%	0.25	4.41	0%	3.06	5.71	6.76	0%	-27.70	6Y.3M
MTUM-EMB-TLT-TIP-CWB	-10.00	3.28	8%	-0.21	4.87	0.7%	3.29	5.40	6.40	0%	-33.35	7Y.4M
MTUM-VNQ-EMB-TLT-GLD	-9.18	3.28	7.7%	-0.67	5.23	0.7%	3.45	6.34	7.78	0%	-29.59	8Y.9M
MTUM-EEM-BNDX-EMB-TLT	-11.30	3.27	8%	-1.63	5.00	2.9%	2.05	5.67	6.94	0%	-35.14	9Y.5M
MTUM-EMB-LQD-GLD	-8.37	3.27	6.8%	0.28	4.49	0%	3.02	5.71	6.81	0%	-29.48	6Y.3M
MTUM-SCZ-EMB-TLT-GLD	-9.72	3.26	7.1%	-0.50	5.41	0.7%	2.91	6.28	7.92	0%	-32.23	7Y.4M
VTI-IJS-EMB-TLT-GLD	-5.76	3.26	6.5%	0.45	5.16	0%	3.85	6.06	7.21	0%	-27.07	6Y.3M
MTUM-EEM-BND-EMB-TLT	-11.55	3.26	8%	-1.77	4.74	3.3%	1.82	5.51	6.74	0%	-35.76	10Y.6M
MTUM-EMB-TLT-IEI-GLD	-10.59	3.25	5.8%	-1.27	3.91	1.8%	2.66	5.32	6.53	0%	-30.33	8Y.9M
VTI-EMB-TLT-CWB-GLD	-7.55	3.25	6.2%	0.82	4.78	0%	3.61	5.82	6.86	0%	-29.62	5Y.10M

Order by **Baseline 3Y Return - Last 60 Years** (from 1963-12 to 2023-11)

Portfolio	3Y Rolling Annualized Return (%)			7Y Rolling Annualized Return (%)			15Y Rolling Annualized Return (%)				Max Draw-down (%)	Long Neg Period (Y.M)
	Worst	Base ▼	%Fail	Worst	Base	%Fail	Worst	Base	Median	%Fail		
VTI-IJS-TLT-GLD	-0.79	5.72	0.6%	5.09	7.77	0%	7.06	8.97	10.45	0%	-21.63	3Y.3M
VTI-IJS-VNQ-GLD	-9.78	5.72	3.2%	3.75	8.03	0%	6.38	9.02	10.93	0%	-40.95	4Y.11M
VTI-IJS-VTV-TLT-GLD	-3.78	5.70	1.6%	4.70	7.79	0%	7.09	8.80	10.64	0%	-26.81	3Y.8M
VTI-IJS-VTV-GLD	-7.82	5.70	4.5%	3.16	7.87	0%	6.44	8.54	11.23	0%	-37.61	5Y.1M
VTI-IJS-VNQ-LQD-GLD	-7.35	5.69	1.9%	4.07	7.56	0%	6.35	8.68	10.54	0%	-34.40	4Y.5M
VTI-IJS-VNQ-BND-GLD	-6.51	5.66	1.5%	4.30	7.40	0%	6.30	8.49	10.42	0%	-32.74	4Y.4M
VTI-IJS-VNQ-TLT-GLD	-5.33	5.63	1.2%	4.63	7.76	0%	6.87	9.05	10.77	0%	-29.90	4Y.2M
VTI-IJS-VNQ-IEI-GLD	-5.85	5.59	1.3%	4.50	7.36	0%	6.32	8.50	10.44	0%	-31.41	4Y.3M
VTI-IJS-VTV-VNQ-GLD	-11.08	5.58	4.5%	2.53	7.65	0%	6.14	8.85	11.51	0%	-43.67	5Y.2M
VTI-IJS-TLT-LQD-GLD	-0.61	5.54	0.4%	4.18	7.33	0%	6.41	8.51	9.84	0%	-21.13	3Y.3M
VTI-IJS-VNQ-SHY-GLD	-6.43	5.51	1.6%	4.18	7.18	0%	6.06	8.17	10.15	0%	-32.46	4Y.4M
IJS-VTV-TLT-GLD	-1.18	5.50	1.3%	4.63	7.56	0%	6.68	8.76	10.50	0%	-22.65	3Y.3M
VTI-IJS-VTV-BND-GLD	-4.98	5.50	2.3%	3.75	7.44	0%	6.49	8.04	10.37	0%	-29.81	4Y.3M
VTI-IJS-VTV-IEI-GLD	-4.32	5.49	1.6%	4.16	7.48	0%	6.52	8.07	10.42	0%	-28.44	4Y.2M
VTI-IJS-TLT-IEI-GLD	-0.07	5.49	0.2%	4.11	7.33	0%	6.22	8.37	9.80	0%	18.99	3Y.3M
VTI-IJS-BND-TLT-GLD	-0.36	5.47	0.3%	4.08	7.21	0%	6.22	8.35	9.76	0%	-19.78	3Y.3M
VTI-IJS-VTV-LQD-GLD	-5.83	5.46	2.2%	3.54	7.59	0%	6.41	8.23	10.47	0%	-31.51	4Y.4M
VTI-IJS-GLD	-4.97	5.40	2.3%	4.54	8.18	0%	6.67	8.85	10.62	0%	-31.57	4Y.11M
IJS-VTV-VNQ-IEI-GLD	-6.18	5.38	1.8%	4.16	7.14	0%	6.01	8.44	10.49	0%	-32.28	4Y.4M
IJS-VTV-VNQ-TLT-GLD	-5.67	5.38	1.9%	4.25	7.52	0%	6.57	8.92	10.83	0%	-30.82	4Y.2M
IJS-VTV-VNQ-BND-GLD	-6.84	5.38	2%	4.18	7.15	0%	5.99	8.38	10.47	0%	-33.59	4Y.4M

Order by **Baseline 3Y Return - Last 60 Years** (from 1963-12 to 2023-11) - **US Infl. Adjusted**

Portfolio	3Y Rolling Annualized Return (%)			7Y Rolling Annualized Return (%)			15Y Rolling Annualized Return (%)				Max Draw-down (%)	Long Neg Period (Y.M)
	Worst	Base ▼	%Fail	Worst	Base	%Fail	Worst	Base	Median	%Fail		
IJS-VTV-TLT-IEI-GLD	-5.25	2.22	7.7%	0.13	3.84	0%	3.08	4.86	6.34	0%	-25.53	7Y.3M
IJS-VTV-BND-TLT-GLD	-5.30	2.18	7.7%	0.13	3.81	0%	3.08	4.86	6.28	0%	-25.52	7Y.3M
IJS-VTV-BND-IEI-GLD	-4.53	2.10	6.4%	0.60	3.65	0%	2.93	4.83	5.80	0%	-24.58	6Y.5M
VTI-IJS-TLT-IEI-GLD	-5.47	2.09	7.5%	0.17	3.84	0%	2.94	4.79	6.38	0%	-24.77	6Y.5M
IJS-VTV-SHY-IEI-GLD	-4.04	2.08	5.7%	0.74	3.50	0%	2.67	4.63	5.53	0%	-23.90	6Y.5M
IJS-VTV-TLT-SHY-GLD	-4.76	2.08	7.3%	0.26	3.69	0%	3.21	4.88	5.97	0%	-24.84	6Y.5M
VTI-IJS-BND-TLT-GLD	-5.75	2.05	7.7%	0.17	3.81	0%	2.94	4.80	6.36	0%	-25.02	6Y.5M
VTI-IJS-SHY-IEI-GLD	-3.54	2.05	5.7%	0.77	3.69	0%	2.99	4.75	5.56	0%	-23.15	6Y.5M
IJS-VTV-IEI-GLD	-5.07	2.04	6.9%	0.95	4.03	0%	3.53	5.40	6.41	0%	-28.29	6Y.4M
VTI-IJS-TLT-SHY-GLD	-4.79	2.02	7.2%	0.30	3.81	0%	3.20	4.83	6.03	0%	-24.09	6Y.5M
VTI-IJS-BND-IEI-GLD	-4.02	2.00	6.4%	0.64	3.79	0%	3.23	4.86	5.82	0%	-23.82	6Y.5M
VTI-IJS-IEI-GLD	-4.44	2.00	6.6%	1.00	4.27	0%	3.91	5.51	6.39	0%	-27.36	6Y.4M
IJS-VTV-TLT-GLD	-5.96	2.00	7.7%	0.35	4.15	0%	4.05	5.61	6.95	0%	-29.43	6Y.6M
IJS-VTV-BND-SHY-GLD	-4.04	1.99	6.3%	0.74	3.51	0%	2.67	4.62	5.46	0%	-23.90	6Y.5M
IJS-VTV-TLT-LQD-GLD	-5.51	1.98	8.2%	-0.27	3.82	0.2%	2.87	4.79	6.45	0%	-25.64	7Y.5M
IJS-VTV-SHY-GLD	-4.56	1.94	6.9%	1.12	3.86	0%	3.20	5.08	6.23	0%	-27.45	6Y.4M
VTI-IJS-BND-SHY-GLD	-3.54	1.94	6%	0.78	3.64	0%	2.98	4.72	5.48	0%	-23.15	6Y.4M
IJS-VTV-BND-GLD	-5.06	1.93	7.7%	0.95	3.98	0%	3.52	5.38	6.33	0%	-28.28	6Y.4M
VTI-IJS-TLT-GLD	-5.32	1.92	7.7%	0.39	4.30	0%	3.86	5.60	7.09	0%	-28.50	6Y.5M
VTI-IJS-SHY-GLD	-4.17	1.92	6.9%	1.16	4.13	0%	3.59	5.21	6.16	0%	-26.53	6Y.4M
IJS-VTV-IEI-LQD-GLD	-4.62	1.92	7.5%	0.21	3.77	0%	3.12	4.83	5.91	0%	-24.70	6Y.5M

Order by **Baseline 3Y Return** - **All data** (from 1871/1927 to 2023-11)

Portfolio	3Y Rolling Annualized Return (%)			7Y Rolling Annualized Return (%)			15Y Rolling Annualized Return (%)				Max Draw-down (%)	Long Neg Period (Y.M)
	Worst	Base ▼	%Fail	Worst	Base	%Fail	Worst	Base	Median	%Fail		
VTI-IJS-TLT-IEI-GLD	-17.96	4.28	4.4%	2.08	5.97	0%	3.97	6.88	8.56	0%	-48.43	6Y.3M
VTI-IJS-IEI-GLD	-22.93	4.28	6%	1.05	6.45	0%	3.59	7.65	9.07	0%	-57.76	8Y.7M
VTI-IJS-TLT-LQD-GLD	-18.01	4.22	4.6%	2.08	6.02	0%	4.01	6.94	8.63	0%	-48.52	6Y.3M
VTI-IJS-TLT-GLD	-23.44	4.21	5.9%	0.92	6.49	0%	3.67	7.73	9.33	0%	-58.64	8Y.7M
VTI-IJS-BND-TLT-GLD	-17.95	4.19	4.5%	2.09	5.98	0%	3.97	6.89	8.51	0%	-48.42	6Y.3M
VTI-IJS-IEI-LQD-GLD	-17.60	4.18	4.7%	2.17	6.05	0%	3.94	6.85	8.30	0%	-47.69	6Y.2M
IJS-VTV-TLT-IEI-GLD	-17.75	4.16	4.4%	1.83	5.77	0%	3.79	6.77	8.50	0%	-48.25	6Y.3M
VTI-IJS-BND-GLD	-22.93	4.14	6.1%	1.06	6.43	0%	3.59	7.64	9.04	0%	-57.75	8Y.7M
VTI-IJS-BND-IEI-GLD	-17.54	4.14	4.5%	2.18	5.93	0%	3.90	6.81	8.27	0%	-47.59	6Y.2M
IJS-VTV-BND-IEI-GLD	-17.33	4.14	4.4%	1.93	5.77	0%	3.72	6.73	8.19	0%	-47.40	6Y.3M
VTI-IJS-BND-LQD-GLD	-17.59	4.14	4.8%	2.18	6.04	0%	3.94	6.85	8.27	0%	-47.69	6Y.2M
VTI-IJS-TLT-SHY-GLD	-17.91	4.12	4.4%	1.97	5.90	0%	3.74	6.72	8.30	0%	-48.31	6Y.2M
IJS-VTV-IEI-LQD-GLD	-17.39	4.12	4.4%	1.92	5.86	0%	3.76	6.77	8.27	0%	-47.50	6Y.3M
IJS-VTV-BND-LQD-GLD	-17.38	4.10	4.4%	1.93	5.86	0%	3.77	6.78	8.23	0%	-47.49	6Y.3M
VTI-IJS-LQD-GLD	-23.00	4.09	6%	1.05	6.58	0%	3.64	7.70	9.07	0%	-57.86	8Y.7M
VTI-IJS-SHY-LQD-GLD	-17.56	4.07	4.9%	2.06	5.91	0%	3.70	6.76	8.15	0%	-47.58	6Y.2M
IJS-VTV-TLT-GLD	-23.20	4.07	6.3%	0.63	6.26	0%	3.46	7.65	9.23	0%	-58.45	8Y.7M
IJS-VTV-BND-TLT-GLD	-17.75	4.06	4.4%	1.83	5.79	0%	3.80	6.78	8.46	0%	-48.24	6Y.3M
VTI-IJS-SHY-IEI-GLD	-17.51	4.06	4.8%	2.06	5.75	0%	3.66	6.74	8.13	0%	-47.49	6Y.2M
VTI-IJS-VNQ-SHY-GLD	-23.18	4.05	6.5%	-0.22	6.26	0.1%	2.68	7.14	8.76	0%	-58.75	12Y.9M
IJS-VTV-IEI-GLD	-22.68	4.04	6%	0.76	6.29	0%	3.38	7.51	9.02	0%	-57.54	8Y.7M

Order by **Baseline 3Y Return** - **All data** (from 1871/1927 to 2023-11) - **US Infl. Adjusted**

Portfolio	3Y Rolling Annualized Return (%)			7Y Rolling Annualized Return (%)			15Y Rolling Annualized Return (%)				Max Draw-down (%)	Long Neg Period (Y.M)
	Worst	Base ▼	%Fail	Worst	Base	%Fail	Worst	Base	Median	%Fail		
IJS-VTV-IEI-GLD	-16.54	1.30	11.4%	-1.03	3.48	1.4%	1.86	4.41	6.04	0%	-46.38	7Y.11M
VTI-IJS-IEI-GLD	-16.82	1.23	11.2%	-0.96	3.70	1.3%	1.89	4.53	6.11	0%	-46.66	7Y.11M
IJS-VTV-BND-IEI-GLD	-10.77	1.20	10.5%	-1.49	2.78	1.6%	1.19	3.79	5.22	0%	-33.57	12Y.5M
IJS-VTV-SHY-IEI-GLD	-10.73	1.17	10.6%	-1.52	2.74	2.3%	0.99	3.79	5.09	0%	-33.44	12Y.8M
VTI-IJS-SHY-GLD	-16.77	1.16	11.6%	-1.33	3.57	1.8%	1.65	4.39	5.86	0%	-46.51	12Y.5M
IJS-VTV-IEI-LQD-GLD	-10.83	1.12	11%	-1.49	2.73	1.5%	1.23	3.77	5.30	0%	-33.71	12Y.5M
IJS-VTV-TLT-IEI-GLD	-11.23	1.12	11.4%	-1.62	2.64	1.5%	1.26	3.59	5.50	0%	-34.65	11Y.10M
IJS-VTV-TLT-SHY-GLD	-11.18	1.11	11.4%	-1.65	2.65	1.8%	1.06	3.68	5.29	0%	-34.50	12Y.7M
IJS-VTV-TLT-GLD	-17.11	1.10	11.9%	-1.00	3.55	0.9%	1.94	4.29	6.31	0%	-47.53	8Y.0M
VTI-IJS-BND-GLD	-16.81	1.10	11.6%	-0.96	3.64	1.3%	1.90	4.50	6.08	0%	-46.65	7Y.11M
IJS-VTV-BND-LQD-GLD	-10.83	1.10	11.1%	-1.49	2.70	1.5%	1.24	3.77	5.28	0%	-33.70	12Y.5M
IJS-VTV-BND-TLT-GLD	-11.22	1.10	11.3%	-1.62	2.66	1.5%	1.26	3.59	5.51	0%	-34.64	11Y.10M
IJS-VTV-BND-GLD	-16.54	1.09	11.9%	-1.02	3.47	1.4%	1.87	4.41	6.01	0%	-46.37	7Y.11M
IJS-VTV-LQD-GLD	-16.61	1.07	12.2%	-0.95	3.46	1.3%	1.91	4.41	6.06	0%	-46.52	7Y.11M
IJS-VTV-BND-SHY-GLD	-10.72	1.05	10.8%	-1.52	2.75	2.3%	1.00	3.79	5.06	0%	-33.43	12Y.8M
IJS-VTV-IEI-BIL-GLD	-11.14	1.03	11.3%	-1.44	2.62	2.7%	0.87	3.63	4.90	0%	-34.31	12Y.10M
VTI-IJS-BND-IEI-GLD	-11.00	1.01	10.5%	-1.53	2.98	1.5%	1.22	3.90	5.34	0%	-33.82	12Y.5M
IJS-VTV-SHY-LQD-GLD	-10.78	1.01	11.1%	-1.52	2.73	2.1%	1.04	3.81	5.12	0%	-33.57	12Y.8M
IJS-VTV-SHY-GLD	-16.49	1.01	11.7%	-1.40	3.43	1.8%	1.61	4.27	5.81	0%	-46.23	12Y.5M
VTI-IJS-SHY-IEI-GLD	-10.96	0.99	10.3%	-1.56	2.95	2.1%	1.02	3.89	5.14	0%	-33.69	12Y.8M
VTI-IJS-LQD-GLD	-16.89	0.99	12%	-0.89	3.67	1.1%	1.94	4.50	6.16	0%	-46.79	7Y.11M

Ranking: Maximum Drawdown

Order by **Maximum Drawdown - Last 30 Years** (from 1993-12 to 2023-11)

Portfolio	3Y Rolling Annualized Return (%)			7Y Rolling Annualized Return (%)			15Y Rolling Annualized Return (%)				Max Draw-down (%) ▼	Long Neg Period (Y.M)
	Worst	Base	%Fail	Worst	Base	%Fail	Worst	Base	Median	%Fail		
BIL	-0.10	-0.03	19.7%	-0.05	0.16	7.9%	0.50	0.81	1.29	0%	-0.42	8Y.9M
SHY-BIL	-0.20	0.28	2.5%	0.28	0.56	0%	0.70	1.37	2.00	0%	-2.40	3Y.3M
SHY	-1.26	0.52	4.9%	0.39	0.72	0%	0.87	1.83	2.71	0%	-5.36	3Y.11M
SHY-IEI-BIL	-1.27	0.68	5.2%	0.47	0.94	0%	1.09	2.07	2.97	0%	-6.17	4Y.2M
SHY-TIP-BIL	-0.66	0.76	6.2%	0.48	1.19	0%	1.36	2.27	3.16	0%	-6.24	4Y.3M
IEI-BIL	-1.29	0.73	5.2%	0.50	1.09	0%	1.19	2.18	3.08	0%	-6.58	4Y.2M
BNDX-SHY-BIL	-1.52	1.43	5.8%	0.71	1.76	0%	1.62	2.56	3.36	0%	-6.60	4Y.3M
TIP-BIL	-1.19	0.87	5.2%	0.50	1.48	0%	1.59	2.47	3.37	0%	-7.09	6Y.0M
BNDX-BIL	-1.83	1.88	5.8%	0.82	2.24	0%	1.97	2.86	3.66	0%	-7.28	4Y.4M
BND-SHY-BIL	-1.56	0.92	5.2%	0.58	1.18	0%	1.30	2.18	2.91	0%	-7.40	4Y.4M
SHY-IEI-TIP-BIL	-1.53	0.83	6.2%	0.61	1.30	0%	1.50	2.54	3.59	0%	-7.60	4Y.2M
SHY-IEI-HYG-BIL	-1.06	1.56	4.9%	1.13	2.01	0%	2.10	3.01	3.69	0%	-7.91	3Y.10M
BNDX-SHY-TIP-BIL	-1.51	1.43	4.9%	0.86	1.82	0%	1.87	2.97	3.88	0%	-8.11	4Y.2M
BNDX-SHY-IEI-BIL	-1.94	1.51	5.8%	0.55	1.79	0%	1.69	2.79	3.73	0%	-8.17	4Y.5M
SHY-HYG-BIL	-0.64	1.44	1.8%	1.34	2.07	0%	2.01	2.84	3.37	0%	-8.32	3Y.5M
BNDX-SHY-HYG-BIL	-1.52	2.01	4.9%	1.24	2.55	0%	2.44	3.35	3.97	0%	-8.38	4Y.2M
IEI-TIP-BIL	-1.69	0.95	6.2%	0.67	1.50	0%	1.71	2.78	3.87	0%	-8.39	4Y.2M
BND-SHY-TIP-BIL	-1.79	1.02	6.2%	0.78	1.47	0%	1.64	2.61	3.55	0%	-8.42	4Y.2M
BND-BIL	-1.86	1.16	5.2%	0.65	1.44	0%	1.51	2.36	3.00	0%	-8.42	4Y.4M
SHY-TIP-HYG-BIL	-0.41	1.52	3.7%	1.47	2.01	0%	2.26	3.12	3.83	0%	-8.54	3Y.3M
SHY-IEI-HYG-BIL-GLD	-2.35	1.23	7.4%	0.31	2.21	0%	2.58	4.02	5.14	0%	-8.66	6Y.1M

Order by **Maximum Drawdown - Last 30 Years** (from 1993-12 to 2023-11) - **US Infl. Adjusted**

Portfolio	3Y Rolling Annualized Return (%)			7Y Rolling Annualized Return (%)			15Y Rolling Annualized Return (%)				Max Draw-down (%) ▼	Long Neg Period (Y.M)
	Worst	Base	%Fail	Worst	Base	%Fail	Worst	Base	Median	%Fail		
VTV-SHY-TIP-BIL	-3.14	0.50	11.7%	-0.21	1.57	1.1%	0.78	1.85	2.32	0%	-14.38	8Y.11M
VTV-SHY-IEI-BIL	-3.58	0.69	9.5%	-0.48	1.46	4.3%	0.63	1.76	2.12	0%	-14.61	9Y.2M
VTV-BNDX-SHY-BIL	-4.04	0.20	13.2%	-0.41	1.48	3.6%	0.91	2.04	2.40	0%	-14.88	8Y.11M
VTV-SHY-BIL-GLD	-2.64	0.75	8.3%	0.66	1.76	0%	1.47	2.83	3.48	0%	-14.99	6Y.2M
VTV-BND-SHY-BIL	-3.79	0.32	11.7%	-0.51	1.33	4%	0.65	1.75	2.12	0%	-15.14	9Y.2M
VTV-SHY-IEI-TIP-BIL	-4.29	1.03	6.5%	-0.85	1.73	5.4%	0.67	1.80	2.35	0%	-15.44	10Y.7M
VTV-BNDX-SHY-TIP-BIL	-4.28	0.98	8.6%	-0.79	1.83	4.7%	0.90	2.06	2.55	0%	-15.70	9Y.10M
VTV-SHY-TIP-BIL-GLD	-3.69	1.01	7.7%	0.07	1.43	0%	1.27	2.71	3.50	0%	-15.74	9Y.8M
VTV-IEI-TIP-BIL	-3.82	1.00	7.7%	-0.39	2.09	1.4%	1.10	2.24	2.81	0%	-15.85	8Y.11M
VTV-SHY-IEI-BIL-GLD	-4.01	0.96	7.1%	-0.16	1.43	0.4%	1.16	2.57	3.37	0%	-15.95	10Y.0M
VTV-SHY-IEI-HYG-BIL	-4.18	0.52	10.5%	-0.56	1.67	4%	0.85	2.02	2.45	0%	-15.99	9Y.10M
VTV-BND-SHY-TIP-BIL	-4.54	0.86	7.7%	-0.87	1.73	4.7%	0.69	1.83	2.35	0%	-16.07	10Y.6M
VTV-BNDX-TIP-BIL	-3.84	0.83	10.8%	-0.31	2.10	1.1%	1.37	2.62	3.02	0%	-16.14	8Y.10M
VTV-SHY-HYG-BIL-GLD	-3.10	0.47	10.2%	0.36	1.88	0%	1.50	2.88	3.46	0%	-16.23	7Y.8M
VTV-BNDX-SHY-IEI-BIL	-4.61	1.10	7.4%	-1.02	1.75	6.5%	0.78	1.97	2.42	0%	-16.24	10Y.0M
VNQ-SHY-BIL-GLD	-4.44	-0.52	20.3%	-0.92	0.93	4.7%	1.07	2.66	4.28	0%	-16.25	12Y.6M
VTV-BNDX-SHY-BIL-GLD	-3.98	1.34	6.5%	-0.10	1.89	0.4%	1.42	2.87	3.54	0%	-16.31	7Y.9M
VTV-BNDX-IEI-BIL	-4.45	0.89	9.2%	-0.59	1.97	4.3%	1.24	2.49	2.90	0%	-16.34	8Y.11M
VTV-SHY-LQD-BIL	-4.04	0.08	13.9%	-0.34	1.41	1.4%	0.93	2.07	2.42	0%	-16.44	6Y.2M
VTV-BND-SHY-HYG-BIL	-4.34	0.24	13.2%	-0.58	1.59	4%	0.86	2.05	2.42	0%	-16.44	9Y.5M
VTV-IEI-BIL-GLD	-3.40	1.08	7.1%	0.49	1.99	0%	1.77	3.25	3.96	0%	-16.44	6Y.2M

Order by **Maximum Drawdown** - **Last 60 Years** (from 1963-12 to 2023-11)

Portfolio	3Y Rolling Annualized Return (%)			7Y Rolling Annualized Return (%)			15Y Rolling Annualized Return (%)				Max Draw-down (%) ▼	Long Neg Period (Y.M)
	Worst	Base	%Fail	Worst	Base	%Fail	Worst	Base	Median	%Fail		
BIL	-0.10	0.60	9.3%	-0.05	0.68	3.5%	0.50	1.21	5.38	0%	-0.42	8Y.9M
SHY-BIL	-0.20	0.74	1.2%	0.28	1.02	0%	0.70	1.76	6.07	0%	-3.75	3Y.3M
SHY-IEI-BIL	-1.27	1.70	2.5%	0.47	1.66	0%	1.09	2.61	6.33	0%	-6.17	4Y.2M
IEI-BIL	-1.29	1.89	2.5%	0.50	1.84	0%	1.19	2.76	6.21	0%	-6.58	4Y.2M
BND-SHY-BIL	-1.56	2.01	2.5%	0.58	1.96	0%	1.30	2.60	6.32	0%	-7.40	4Y.4M
BND-BIL	-1.86	2.28	2.5%	0.65	2.28	0%	1.51	2.73	6.09	0%	-8.42	4Y.4M
SHY	-1.26	1.29	2.3%	0.39	1.39	0%	0.87	2.34	6.67	0%	-8.52	3Y.11M
VTV-BND-SHY-IEI-BIL	0.32	3.40	0%	2.37	3.97	0%	2.96	4.26	7.58	0%	-8.70	2Y.11M
BND-SHY-IEI-BIL	-2.23	2.10	2.5%	0.47	2.32	0%	1.45	3.03	6.46	0%	-8.97	4Y.5M
SHY-LQD-BIL	-1.87	2.62	2.5%	0.92	2.74	0%	1.81	3.08	6.30	0%	-9.40	4Y.4M
VTV-SHY-IEI-BIL-GLD	0.15	3.49	0%	2.15	4.27	0%	3.56	5.50	7.00	0%	-9.42	2Y.9M
SHY-IEI	-2.65	1.87	2.5%	0.26	2.26	0%	1.26	3.32	6.99	0%	-9.51	6Y.4M
VTI-SHY-IEI-BIL-GLD	0.22	3.79	0%	2.24	4.80	0%	3.82	5.60	6.88	0%	-9.77	2Y.6M
VTI-SHY-IEI-BIL	0.64	3.43	0%	3.06	4.32	0%	3.47	4.47	7.50	0%	-9.83	2Y.9M
VTV-SHY-IEI-BIL	0.68	3.40	0%	2.95	3.96	0%	3.03	4.22	7.59	0%	-10.02	2Y.7M
VTV-SHY-IEI-LQD-BIL	0.11	3.39	0%	2.52	4.24	0%	3.20	4.55	7.75	0%	-10.05	2Y.11M
BND-IEI-BIL	-2.66	2.25	2.5%	0.42	2.63	0%	1.64	3.25	6.51	0%	-10.16	4Y.7M
IJS-BND-SHY-IEI-BIL	0.15	3.55	0%	1.91	4.34	0%	3.10	4.74	8.36	0%	-10.17	2Y.11M
IJS-SHY-IEI-BIL	-0.03	3.50	0.2%	2.42	4.23	0%	3.20	4.79	8.69	0%	-10.36	3Y.0M
SHY-IEI-LQD-BIL	-2.47	2.49	2.5%	0.67	2.91	0%	1.83	3.38	6.64	0%	-10.37	4Y.5M
VTV-BND-IEI-BIL	0.50	3.65	0%	2.78	4.38	0%	3.38	4.72	7.91	0%	-10.45	2Y.11M

Order by **Maximum Drawdown** - **Last 60 Years** (from 1963-12 to 2023-11) - **US Infl. Adjusted**

Portfolio	3Y Rolling Annualized Return (%)			7Y Rolling Annualized Return (%)			15Y Rolling Annualized Return (%)				Max Draw-down (%) ▼	Long Neg Period (Y.M)
	Worst	Base	%Fail	Worst	Base	%Fail	Worst	Base	Median	%Fail		
VTV-SHY-IEI-BIL-GLD	-4.01	0.89	8.3%	-0.16	2.05	0.2%	1.16	2.95	3.73	0%	-15.95	10Y.0M
VTV-BND-SHY-BIL-GLD	-4.20	0.94	8.2%	-0.17	2.10	0.2%	1.21	2.94	3.67	0%	-16.54	9Y.8M
VNQ-SHY-IEI-BIL-GLD	-5.43	0.12	14.2%	-1.43	1.66	3.1%	0.89	2.78	4.02	0%	-17.08	13Y.0M
VTV-SHY-BIL-GLD	-3.57	0.69	9.6%	0.20	2.06	0%	1.47	3.08	3.85	0%	-17.54	6Y.11M
VNQ-BND-SHY-BIL-GLD	-5.63	0.15	13.7%	-1.43	1.71	2.5%	0.89	2.78	4.02	0%	-17.75	12Y.11M
VTV-SHY-LQD-BIL-GLD	-4.32	1.01	8.3%	-0.03	2.24	0.2%	1.43	3.04	3.81	0%	-17.76	7Y.9M
VNQ-SHY-BIL-GLD	-4.44	-0.25	17.7%	-0.92	1.15	2.2%	1.07	2.58	4.20	0%	-17.78	12Y.6M
VTV-BND-IEI-BIL-GLD	-4.81	0.95	8.9%	-0.31	2.18	0.6%	1.45	3.12	3.98	0%	-17.93	8Y.9M
VTI-SHY-IEI-BIL-GLD	-4.34	0.86	8.5%	0.26	2.17	0%	1.42	3.03	3.69	0%	-17.94	7Y.9M
IJS-SHY-BIL-GLD	-2.22	1.16	8.2%	0.13	2.70	0%	1.63	3.44	4.63	0%	-18.05	8Y.7M
IJS-SHY-IEI-BIL-GLD	-3.68	1.11	6.6%	-0.59	2.57	0.8%	1.34	3.47	4.49	0%	-18.40	10Y.9M
VTI-BND-SHY-BIL-GLD	-4.54	0.91	8.6%	0.25	2.18	0%	1.45	2.99	3.65	0%	-18.56	7Y.9M
VNQ-SHY-LQD-BIL-GLD	-5.77	0.13	13.3%	-1.30	1.78	2.2%	1.11	2.84	4.13	0%	-18.67	12Y.5M
IJS-BND-SHY-BIL-GLD	-3.92	1.20	6.6%	-0.59	2.61	0.6%	1.35	3.45	4.44	0%	-18.81	10Y.8M
VTV-BND-SHY-IEI-GLD	-5.34	1.02	8.9%	-0.47	2.17	1.1%	1.52	3.30	4.31	0%	-18.95	9Y.8M
VTI-SHY-BIL-GLD	-3.06	0.62	10.5%	0.93	2.16	0%	1.77	3.07	3.84	0%	-19.13	6Y.6M
VTV-IEI-LQD-BIL-GLD	-4.94	0.90	9.1%	-0.24	2.28	0.9%	1.67	3.22	4.17	0%	-19.15	7Y.9M
VTV-BND-SHY-BIL	-5.55	-0.67	19.1%	-2.26	0.33	12.7%	-0.72	1.26	3.28	6.3%	-19.30	17Y.11M
VTV-SHY-IEI-BIL	-5.55	-0.53	18.1%	-2.26	0.33	12.9%	-0.73	1.22	3.39	6.3%	-19.30	17Y.11M
VTV-BND-IEI-BIL	-5.59	-0.88	18.1%	-2.53	0.18	13%	-1.03	1.44	3.52	8%	-19.34	18Y.8M
VTV-BND-BIL-GLD	-4.18	0.73	10.1%	-0.12	2.27	0.8%	1.78	3.31	4.13	0%	-19.37	7Y.2M

Portfolio	3Y Rolling Annualized Return (%)			7Y Rolling Annualized Return (%)			15Y Rolling Annualized Return (%)				Max Draw- down (%) ▼	Long Neg Period (Y.M)
	Worst	Base	%Fail	Worst	Base	%Fail	Worst	Base	Median	%Fail		
BIL	-0.10	0.65	3.6%	-0.05	0.76	1.3%	0.29	1.18	4.72	0%	-0.42	8Y.9M
SHY-BIL	-0.20	1.07	0.4%	0.28	1.04	0%	0.70	1.63	4.53	0%	-3.75	3Y.3M
SHY-IEI-BIL	-1.27	1.67	0.9%	0.47	1.61	0%	1.09	2.17	4.25	0%	-6.17	4Y.2M
IEI-BIL	-1.29	1.71	0.9%	0.50	1.66	0%	1.19	2.25	4.16	0%	-6.58	4Y.2M
BND-SHY-BIL	-1.56	1.71	0.9%	0.58	1.68	0%	1.18	2.25	4.25	0%	-7.40	4Y.4M
BND-BIL	-1.86	1.77	0.9%	0.65	1.79	0%	1.30	2.28	4.16	0%	-8.42	4Y.4M
SHY	-1.26	1.46	1.1%	0.39	1.52	0%	0.87	2.11	4.40	0%	-8.52	3Y.11M
BND-SHY-IEI-BIL	-2.23	1.92	1%	0.47	1.94	0%	1.36	2.44	4.09	0%	-8.97	4Y.5M
SHY-LQD-BIL	-1.87	1.91	0.9%	0.87	1.96	0%	1.24	2.35	4.19	0%	-9.40	4Y.4M
SHY-IEI	-2.65	2.03	1.2%	0.26	2.16	0%	1.26	2.60	4.05	0%	-9.51	6Y.4M
BND-IEI-BIL	-2.66	2.01	1%	0.42	2.10	0%	1.38	2.49	4.01	0%	-10.16	4Y.7M
SHY-IEI-LQD-BIL	-2.47	2.03	1%	0.67	2.10	0%	1.37	2.50	4.09	0%	-10.37	4Y.5M
BND-SHY-BIL-GLD	-3.29	1.51	2.3%	-0.82	1.59	0.5%	0.93	2.38	3.43	0%	-10.52	7Y.9M
SHY-IEI-BIL-GLD	-3.34	1.48	2.4%	-1.03	1.59	0.6%	0.92	2.33	3.42	0%	-10.92	7Y.11M
BND-SHY-IEI-DIL-GLD	-2.44	1.70	2.3%	-0.42	1.85	0.2%	1.09	2.37	3.53	0%	-10.96	7Y.4M
BND-SHY-LQD-BIL	-2.79	2.10	1%	0.65	2.18	0%	1.37	2.51	4.09	0%	-11.33	4Y.5M
BND-SHY	-3.24	2.08	1.2%	0.25	2.24	0%	1.41	2.67	4.05	0%	-11.35	6Y.3M
LQD-BIL	-2.34	2.04	0.9%	0.99	2.19	0%	1.33	2.40	4.07	0%	-11.42	4Y.4M
SHY-LQD-BIL-GLD	-3.12	1.61	2.1%	-0.32	1.80	0.2%	0.97	2.40	3.40	0%	-11.53	7Y.4M
BND-SHY-IEI-LQD-BIL	-3.09	2.14	1.1%	0.50	2.28	0%	1.41	2.58	4.00	0%	-11.72	4Y.7M
SHY-IEI-LQD-BIL-GLD	-2.31	1.77	2.2%	-0.02	1.95	0.1%	1.10	2.44	3.52	0%	-11.94	7Y.3M

Portfolio	3Y Rolling Annualized Return (%)			7Y Rolling Annualized Return (%)			15Y Rolling Annualized Return (%)				Max Draw- down (%) ▼	Long Neg Period (Y.M)
	Worst	Base	%Fail	Worst	Base	%Fail	Worst	Base	Median	%Fail		
VTI-VNQ-SHY-IEI-GLD	-7.57	0.18	13.2%	-2.24	1.12	7.7%	-0.51	1.64	3.70	2%	-21.26	17Y.7M
VTV-VNQ-SHY-IEI-GLD	-7.56	0.21	14%	-2.20	0.93	8.4%	-0.56	1.56	3.58	2.5%	-21.81	20Y.2M
VTI-VNQ-IEI-BIL-GLD	-7.65	0.06	14.4%	-2.15	1.07	8.2%	-0.63	1.54	3.48	3.3%	-21.85	18Y.10M
VTV-VNQ-BND-IEI-GLD	-7.51	0.15	14.2%	-2.17	1.05	8.3%	-0.35	1.52	3.69	0.9%	-22.13	16Y.11M
VTI-VNQ-TLT-BIL-GLD	-7.62	-0.17	16.1%	-2.24	0.83	9.5%	-0.60	1.33	3.49	2.6%	-22.21	20Y.2M
VTI-VNQ-BND-SHY-GLD	-7.56	0.17	13.6%	-2.23	1.13	7.7%	-0.51	1.64	3.65	2%	-22.29	17Y.7M
VTI-VNQ-BND-IEI-GLD	-7.52	0.23	13.6%	-2.20	1.14	7.3%	-0.31	1.61	3.82	0.8%	-22.73	16Y.11M
VTV-VNQ-IEI-BIL-GLD	-7.64	0.03	14.4%	-2.11	0.82	8.8%	-0.68	1.50	3.43	3.6%	-22.78	20Y.3M
VTI-VNQ-SHY-BIL-GLD	-7.69	0.00	14.8%	-2.30	1.04	8.6%	-0.83	1.60	3.37	4.7%	-23.15	20Y.5M
VTV-VNQ-BND-SHY-GLD	-7.56	0.09	14%	-2.19	0.93	8.4%	-0.55	1.57	3.58	2.5%	-23.22	20Y.2M
VTI-VNQ-BND-BIL-GLD	-7.64	0.06	14.4%	-2.14	1.07	8.1%	-0.63	1.55	3.48	3.1%	-23.27	18Y.5M
IJS-VNQ-BND-SHY-GLD	-7.94	0.35	12.8%	-2.28	2.09	3.6%	0.42	2.48	4.50	0%	-23.39	12Y.7M
IJS-VNQ-SHY-IEI-GLD	-7.94	0.40	12.6%	-2.29	2.08	3.6%	0.41	2.48	4.51	0%	-23.40	12Y.8M
VTV-VNQ-TLT-SHY-GLD	-7.54	-0.03	15.3%	-2.32	0.93	9.4%	-0.48	1.43	3.62	1.7%	-23.43	17Y.6M
IJS-VNQ-BND-IEI-GLD	-7.89	0.47	12.2%	-2.25	2.07	2.7%	0.61	2.52	4.70	0%	-23.51	12Y.4M
VTI-VNQ-TLT-BIL-GLD	-7.63	-0.01	15%	-2.27	0.95	8%	-0.56	1.38	3.56	2.3%	-23.54	17Y.8M
IJS-VNQ-IEI-LQD-GLD	-7.90	0.31	13.1%	-2.26	2.03	2.7%	0.65	2.49	4.72	0%	-23.65	8Y.10M
VTV-BND-SHY-GLD	-8.18	0.10	14.2%	-2.76	0.62	11.3%	-0.93	1.49	3.64	5.9%	-23.74	20Y.3M
VTV-SHY-IEI-GLD	-8.19	0.13	14.4%	-2.77	0.65	11.5%	-0.93	1.49	3.64	5.9%	-23.76	20Y.3M
VTV-SHY-LQD-GLD	-8.19	0.16	13.8%	-2.73	0.67	11.6%	-0.88	1.48	3.65	5.6%	-23.81	20Y.2M
VTV-BND-BIL-GLD	-8.29	-0.04	15.2%	-2.95	0.52	11.9%	-1.08	1.43	3.40	7.1%	-23.83	20Y.6M

Ranking: Longest Negative Period

Order by **Longest Negative Period** - **Last 30 Years** (from 1993-12 to 2023-11)

Portfolio	3Y Rolling Annualized Return (%)			7Y Rolling Annualized Return (%)			15Y Rolling Annualized Return (%)				Max Draw-down (%)	Long Neg Period (Y.M) ▲
	Worst	Base	%Fail	Worst	Base	%Fail	Worst	Base	Median	%Fail		
VTV-BNDX-BIL-GLD	0.51	3.36	0%	3.25	4.48	0%	4.48	5.71	6.45	0%	-15.28	2Y.4M
VTV-BNDX-SHY-GLD	0.67	3.57	0%	3.40	4.67	0%	4.60	5.97	6.82	0%	-14.93	2Y.5M
VTV-BNDX-SHY-BIL-GLD	0.53	3.17	0%	2.77	3.97	0%	3.82	4.98	5.79	0%	-11.82	2Y.5M
VTV-SHY-LQD-BIL-GLD	0.29	3.17	0%	2.63	4.09	0%	3.86	5.08	5.80	0%	-12.77	2Y.5M
VTV-BND-SHY-BIL-GLD	0.16	2.93	0%	2.31	3.76	0%	3.63	4.80	5.59	0%	-10.60	2Y.5M
VTV-BND-GLD	0.10	3.55	0%	3.57	5.23	0%	5.36	6.79	7.58	0%	-18.59	2Y.6M
VTV-BND-SHY-GLD	0.22	3.32	0%	2.81	4.51	0%	4.37	5.74	6.54	0%	-13.43	2Y.6M
VTV-LQD-BIL-GLD	0.22	3.32	0%	3.16	4.60	0%	4.49	5.82	6.48	0%	-16.50	2Y.6M
VTV-SHY-IEI-HYG-GLD	0.42	3.26	0%	3.10	4.39	0%	4.31	5.68	6.51	0%	-13.68	2Y.6M
VTV-BND-BIL-GLD	0.06	3.04	0%	2.77	4.37	0%	4.21	5.48	6.20	0%	-13.78	2Y.6M
VTI-BNDX-SHY-BIL-GLD	0.59	3.02	0%	2.86	4.21	0%	4.08	5.32	5.84	0%	-11.88	2Y.6M
VTI-IEI-BIL-GLD	0.13	2.99	0%	2.69	4.62	0%	4.52	5.79	6.36	0%	-12.35	2Y.6M
VTI-IEI-HYG-BIL-GLD	0.36	2.95	0%	3.16	4.64	0%	4.46	5.72	6.26	0%	-14.01	2Y.6M
VTI-SHY-IEI-BIL-GLD	0.22	2.94	0%	2.24	3.91	0%	3.82	5.01	5.68	0%	-9.77	2Y.6M
VTI-BNDX-BIL-GLD	0.60	3.26	0%	3.45	4.79	0%	4.80	6.03	6.56	0%	-15.36	2Y.7M
VTI-SHY-IEI-BIL	1.02	3.02	0%	3.06	4.03	0%	3.47	4.13	4.55	0%	-9.83	2Y.7M
VTI-BND-BIL-GLD	0.14	2.95	0%	2.86	4.56	0%	4.51	5.82	6.31	0%	-13.85	2Y.7M
VTV-SHY-IEI-BIL	0.68	2.87	0%	2.95	3.65	0%	3.03	3.84	4.33	0%	-10.02	2Y.7M
IJS-BNDX-SHY-BIL-GLD	0.35	3.25	0%	2.35	3.75	0%	4.00	5.12	6.30	0%	-10.59	2Y.8M
VTV-SHY-IEI-TIP-BIL	1.01	2.80	0%	2.63	3.51	0%	3.07	3.90	4.48	0%	-9.27	2Y.8M
VTV-BNDX-TIP-GLD	0.07	3.87	0%	3.36	5.17	0%	4.99	6.48	7.46	0%	-18.23	2Y.9M

Order by **Longest Negative Period** - **Last 30 Years** (from 1993-12 to 2023-11) - **US Infl. Adjusted**

Portfolio	3Y Rolling Annualized Return (%)			7Y Rolling Annualized Return (%)			15Y Rolling Annualized Return (%)				Max Draw-down (%)	Long Neg Period (Y.M) ▲
	Worst	Base	%Fail	Worst	Base	%Fail	Worst	Base	Median	%Fail		
MTUM-SHY-CWB-GLD	-5.21	2.06	7.7%	2.82	4.41	0%	3.55	4.91	5.70	0%	-24.29	3Y.10M
VTI-SHY-IEI-CWB-GLD	-4.13	1.83	5.2%	1.86	3.20	0%	2.85	4.14	4.75	0%	-21.87	3Y.10M
IJS-IEI-CWB-GLD	-3.54	2.45	3.4%	1.95	3.95	0%	3.60	5.10	6.07	0%	-24.69	3Y.10M
MTUM-TIP-CWB-GLD	-5.68	2.24	6.8%	2.85	4.87	0%	3.93	5.52	6.34	0%	-26.36	3Y.11M
VTI-IEI-TIP-CWB-GLD	-4.50	2.20	6.2%	1.89	3.56	0%	3.18	4.54	5.31	0%	-22.79	3Y.11M
VTI-BND-SHY-CWB-GLD	-4.34	1.98	7.1%	1.84	3.13	0%	2.83	4.05	4.70	0%	-22.49	3Y.11M
VTV-IEI-TIP-CWB-GLD	-4.02	2.28	4.9%	1.55	3.42	0%	2.94	4.41	5.23	0%	-21.22	4Y.0M
MTUM-IEI-CWB-GLD	-6.01	2.47	7.7%	2.59	4.80	0%	3.87	5.44	6.21	0%	-25.98	4Y.1M
MTUM-SHY-CWB-BIL-GLD	-4.82	1.63	8.6%	1.95	3.42	0%	2.59	3.91	4.53	0%	-21.74	4Y.1M
VTI-BNDX-IEI-CWB-GLD	-4.77	2.33	7.1%	1.74	3.56	0%	3.29	4.67	5.28	0%	-23.62	4Y.2M
MTUM-BNDX-CWB-GLD	-6.01	2.27	9.8%	2.67	5.02	0%	4.07	5.49	6.34	0%	-26.46	4Y.2M
MTUM-SHY-TIP-CWB-GLD	-5.72	2.26	6.2%	1.81	3.93	0%	3.04	4.64	5.33	0%	-23.63	4Y.2M
MTUM-BND-CWB-GLD	-6.29	2.20	8.9%	2.56	4.78	0%	3.84	5.33	6.13	0%	-26.75	4Y.2M
VTI-BND-IEI-CWB-GLD	-4.99	2.18	5.5%	1.66	3.39	0%	3.07	4.50	5.10	0%	-23.86	4Y.2M
VTI-BNDX-SHY-CWB-GLD	-4.12	2.08	7.4%	1.91	3.35	0%	3.05	4.24	4.88	0%	-22.29	4Y.2M
MTUM-IEI-CWB-BIL-GLD	-5.46	2.07	7.7%	1.78	3.74	0%	2.84	4.32	4.94	0%	-23.09	4Y.2M
VTV-SHY-TIP-CWB-GLD	-3.38	2.03	4.6%	1.72	3.20	0%	2.69	4.09	4.82	0%	-20.48	4Y.2M
MTUM-TIP-CWB-BIL-GLD	-5.17	1.85	7.1%	1.99	3.79	0%	2.91	4.45	5.04	0%	-22.61	4Y.2M
MTUM-CWB-BIL-GLD	-4.51	1.62	9.5%	3.06	4.17	0%	3.39	4.53	5.38	0%	-24.22	4Y.2M
IJS-BND-CWB-GLD	-3.83	2.50	4.9%	1.92	4.03	0%	3.58	5.12	5.99	0%	-25.24	4Y.3M
IJS-TIP-CWB-GLD	-4.11	2.47	4.6%	2.00	4.03	0%	3.67	5.18	6.20	0%	-24.57	4Y.3M

Order by **Longest Negative Period** - Last 60 Years (from 1963-12 to 2023-11)

Portfolio	3Y Rolling Annualized Return (%)			7Y Rolling Annualized Return (%)			15Y Rolling Annualized Return (%)				Max Draw-down (%)	Long Neg Period (Y.M) ▲
	Worst	Base	%Fail	Worst	Base	%Fail	Worst	Base	Median	%Fail		
VTV-SHY-LQD-BIL-GLD	0.29	3.67	0%	2.63	4.62	0%	3.86	5.72	7.00	0%	-12.77	2Y.5M
VTV-BND-SHY-BIL-GLD	0.16	3.50	0%	2.31	4.34	0%	3.63	5.48	6.92	0%	-10.60	2Y.5M
VTI-SHY-IEI-BIL-GLD	0.22	3.79	0%	2.24	4.80	0%	3.82	5.60	6.88	0%	-9.77	2Y.6M
VTI-IEI-BIL-GLD	0.13	3.77	0%	2.69	5.12	0%	4.52	6.16	7.29	0%	-12.35	2Y.6M
VTV-LQD-BIL-GLD	0.22	3.71	0%	3.16	5.22	0%	4.49	6.24	7.39	0%	-16.50	2Y.6M
VTV-BND-BIL-GLD	0.06	3.64	0%	2.77	4.81	0%	4.21	5.98	7.26	0%	-13.78	2Y.6M
VTI-BND-BIL-GLD	0.14	3.87	0%	2.86	5.17	0%	4.51	6.13	7.16	0%	-13.85	2Y.7M
VTV-SHY-IEI-BIL	0.68	3.40	0%	2.95	3.96	0%	3.03	4.22	7.59	0%	-10.02	2Y.7M
VTI-SHY-IEI-GLD	0.29	3.91	0%	2.72	5.43	0%	4.60	6.51	7.66	0%	-12.36	2Y.9M
VTI-BND-SHY-BIL-GLD	0.22	3.78	0%	2.38	4.87	0%	3.88	5.61	6.83	0%	-10.65	2Y.9M
VTV-IEI-BIL-GLD	0.05	3.61	0%	2.58	4.73	0%	4.20	6.04	7.29	0%	-12.28	2Y.9M
VTV-SHY-IEI-BIL-GLD	0.15	3.49	0%	2.15	4.27	0%	3.56	5.50	7.00	0%	-9.42	2Y.9M
VTI-SHY-IEI-BIL	0.64	3.43	0%	3.06	4.32	0%	3.47	4.47	7.50	0%	-9.83	2Y.9M
IJS-SHY-LQD-GLD	0.07	4.28	0%	2.78	5.84	0%	4.81	7.07	8.40	0%	-14.60	2Y.10M
IJS-BND-IEI-BIL-GLD	0.30	3.97	0%	2.50	5.15	0%	4.02	6.36	7.68	0%	-11.75	2Y.10M
IJS-SHY-LQD-BIL-GLD	0.05	3.97	0%	2.41	5.09	0%	4.01	6.20	7.50	0%	-11.61	2Y.10M
VTI-SHY-LQD-BIL-GLD	0.36	3.90	0%	2.69	5.04	0%	4.11	5.81	6.90	0%	-12.83	2Y.10M
VTI-LQD-BIL-GLD	0.30	3.88	0%	3.24	5.48	0%	4.78	6.37	7.28	0%	-16.57	2Y.10M
VTV-IEI-LQD-BIL-GLD	0.45	3.73	0%	2.74	4.93	0%	4.11	6.11	7.30	0%	-12.72	2Y.10M
VTV-BND-IEI-BIL-GLD	0.31	3.60	0%	2.43	4.60	0%	3.86	5.88	7.21	0%	-10.55	2Y.10M
VTI-BND-SHY-BIL	0.24	3.42	0%	2.61	4.28	0%	3.48	4.47	7.40	0%	-10.83	2Y.10M

Order by **Longest Negative Period** - Last 60 Years (from 1963-12 to 2023-11) - **US Infl. Adjusted**

Portfolio	3Y Rolling Annualized Return (%)			7Y Rolling Annualized Return (%)			15Y Rolling Annualized Return (%)				Max Draw-down (%)	Long Neg Period (Y.M) ▲
	Worst	Base	%Fail	Worst	Base	%Fail	Worst	Base	Median	%Fail		
IJS-BIL-GLD	-3.91	1.05	8.9%	0.63	2.81	0%	2.19	3.78	5.36	0%	-21.98	5Y.3M
IJS-VNQ-BIL-GLD	-7.47	0.86	9.6%	0.68	3.27	0%	2.80	4.46	6.29	0%	-29.83	5Y.5M
IJS-GLD	-6.91	0.78	12%	1.05	3.67	0%	2.23	4.79	7.49	0%	-33.07	5Y.7M
IJS-SHY-GLD	-3.45	1.36	8.3%	0.80	3.22	0%	2.69	4.34	5.90	0%	-23.25	5Y.9M
IJS-LQD-GLD	-3.68	1.31	9.6%	0.71	3.63	0%	3.32	5.00	6.54	0%	-26.02	5Y.11M
IJS-VNQ-GLD	-10.62	0.93	12.1%	1.40	3.99	0%	3.34	5.31	8.00	0%	-38.59	5Y.11M
VTI-IJS-BIL-GLD	-4.74	1.66	7.3%	1.30	3.94	0%	3.17	4.83	5.86	0%	-25.18	6Y.1M
IJS-VTV-BIL-GLD	-5.10	1.63	8.5%	1.26	3.73	0%	3.04	4.74	5.93	0%	-26.10	6Y.1M
IJS-IEI-GLD	-3.36	1.57	8.8%	0.55	3.41	0%	3.10	4.87	6.44	0%	-24.42	6Y.2M
IJS-BND-GLD	-3.32	1.54	9.2%	0.52	3.45	0%	3.10	4.78	6.33	0%	-24.40	6Y.2M
IJS-VNQ-SHY-GLD	-6.85	1.05	9.3%	0.46	3.44	0%	2.97	4.84	6.62	0%	-28.68	6Y.2M
IJS-VTV-IEI-GLD	-5.07	2.04	6.9%	0.95	4.03	0%	3.53	5.40	6.41	0%	-28.29	6Y.4M
VTI-IJS-IEI-GLD	-4.44	2.00	6.6%	1.00	4.27	0%	3.91	5.51	6.39	0%	-27.36	6Y.4M
IJS-VTV-SHY-GLD	-4.56	1.94	6.9%	1.12	3.86	0%	3.20	5.08	6.23	0%	-27.45	6Y.4M
IJS-VTV-BND-GLD	-5.06	1.93	7.7%	0.95	3.98	0%	3.52	5.38	6.33	0%	-28.28	6Y.4M
VTI-IJS-SHY-GLD	-4.17	1.92	6.9%	1.16	4.13	0%	3.59	5.21	6.16	0%	-26.53	6Y.4M
IJS-VTV-GLD	-7.52	1.88	9.9%	1.43	4.70	0%	3.57	6.01	7.37	0%	-34.29	6Y.4M
VTI-IJS-BND-GLD	-4.43	1.85	7.3%	1.00	4.19	0%	3.89	5.48	6.32	0%	-27.35	6Y.4M
VTI-IJS-IEI-BIL-GLD	-3.22	1.84	5.7%	0.89	3.50	0%	2.86	4.52	5.29	0%	-22.03	6Y.4M
VTI-IJS-GLD	-7.03	1.83	8.8%	1.50	4.76	0%	3.50	6.07	7.38	0%	-33.09	6Y.4M
IJS-VTV-IEI-BIL-GLD	-3.72	1.80	6.1%	0.85	3.33	0%	2.54	4.40	5.29	0%	-22.78	6Y.4M

Order by **Longest Negative Period** - **All data** (from 1871/1927 to 2023-11)

Portfolio	3Y Rolling Annualized Return (%)			7Y Rolling Annualized Return (%)			15Y Rolling Annualized Return (%)				Max Draw-down (%)	Long Neg Period (Y.M) ▲
	Worst	Base	%Fail	Worst	Base	%Fail	Worst	Base	Median	%Fail		
SHY-BIL	-0.20	1.07	0.4%	0.28	1.04	0%	0.70	1.63	4.53	0%	-3.75	3Y.3M
SHY	-1.26	1.46	1.1%	0.39	1.52	0%	0.87	2.11	4.40	0%	-8.52	3Y.11M
IEI-BIL	-1.29	1.71	0.9%	0.50	1.66	0%	1.19	2.25	4.16	0%	-6.58	4Y.2M
SHY-IEI-BIL	-1.27	1.67	0.9%	0.47	1.61	0%	1.09	2.17	4.25	0%	-6.17	4Y.2M
LQD-BIL	-2.34	2.04	0.9%	0.99	2.19	0%	1.33	2.40	4.07	0%	-11.42	4Y.4M
SHY-LQD-BIL	-1.87	1.91	0.9%	0.87	1.96	0%	1.24	2.35	4.19	0%	-9.40	4Y.4M
BND-BIL	-1.86	1.77	0.9%	0.65	1.79	0%	1.30	2.28	4.16	0%	-8.42	4Y.4M
BND-SHY-BIL	-1.56	1.71	0.9%	0.58	1.68	0%	1.18	2.25	4.25	0%	-7.40	4Y.4M
IEI-LQD-BIL	-2.99	2.17	1%	0.66	2.27	0%	1.40	2.53	3.97	0%	-12.04	4Y.5M
BND-SHY-LQD-BIL	-2.79	2.10	1%	0.65	2.18	0%	1.37	2.51	4.09	0%	-11.33	4Y.5M
SHY-IEI-LQD-BIL	-2.47	2.03	1%	0.67	2.10	0%	1.37	2.50	4.09	0%	-10.37	4Y.5M
BND-SHY-IEI-BIL	-2.23	1.92	1%	0.47	1.94	0%	1.36	2.44	4.09	0%	-8.97	4Y.5M
VNQ-BND-IEI-LQD-BIL	-2.13	1.82	1.9%	1.05	2.39	0%	2.00	2.61	5.07	0%	-15.04	4Y.6M
VNQ-BND-IEI-LQD-GLD	-2.46	1.62	2.2%	0.85	2.10	0%	1.36	2.41	6.49	0%	-17.26	4Y.6M
BND-LQD-BIL	-3.42	2.24	1%	0.62	2.31	0%	1.40	2.57	3.97	0%	-13.32	4Y.7M
BND-SHY-IEI-LQD-BIL	-3.09	2.14	1.1%	0.50	2.28	0%	1.41	2.58	4.00	0%	-11.72	4Y.7M
BND-IEI-BIL	-2.66	2.01	1%	0.42	2.10	0%	1.38	2.49	4.01	0%	-10.16	4Y.7M
VNQ-BND-SHY-IEI-LQD	-2.71	1.88	2%	0.87	2.51	0%	2.05	2.76	5.16	0%	-16.46	4Y.7M
VNQ-BND-IEI-LQD	-3.25	1.79	3%	0.87	2.49	0%	1.93	2.86	5.55	0%	-19.88	4Y.7M
VNQ-BND-SHY-IEI-BIL	-1.53	1.80	1.7%	0.74	2.27	0%	1.94	2.55	4.80	0%	-13.18	4Y.9M
VNQ-BND-SHY-IEI	-2.66	1.78	2.2%	0.88	2.42	0%	2.06	2.75	5.20	0%	-16.52	4Y.9M

Order by **Longest Negative Period** - **All data** (from 1871/1927 to 2023-11) - **US Infl. Adjusted**

Portfolio	3Y Rolling Annualized Return (%)			7Y Rolling Annualized Return (%)			15Y Rolling Annualized Return (%)				Max Draw-down (%)	Long Neg Period (Y.M) ▲
	Worst	Base	%Fail	Worst	Base	%Fail	Worst	Base	Median	%Fail		
IJS-VTV-IEI-GLD	-16.54	1.30	11.4%	-1.03	3.48	1.4%	1.86	4.41	6.04	0%	-46.38	7Y.11M
VTI-IJS-IEI-GLD	-16.82	1.23	11.2%	-0.96	3.70	1.3%	1.89	4.53	6.11	0%	-46.66	7Y.11M
VTI-IJS-BND-GLD	-16.81	1.10	11.6%	-0.96	3.64	1.3%	1.90	4.50	6.08	0%	-46.65	7Y.11M
IJS-VTV-BND-GLD	-16.54	1.09	11.9%	-1.02	3.47	1.4%	1.87	4.41	6.01	0%	-46.37	7Y.11M
IJS-VTV-LQD-GLD	-16.61	1.07	12.2%	-0.95	3.46	1.3%	1.91	4.41	6.06	0%	-46.52	7Y.11M
VTI-IJS-LQD-GLD	-16.89	0.99	12%	-0.89	3.67	1.1%	1.94	4.50	6.16	0%	-46.79	7Y.11M
IJS-VTV-TLT-GLD	-17.11	1.10	11.9%	-1.00	3.55	0.9%	1.94	4.29	6.31	0%	-47.53	8Y.0M
VTI-IJS-TLT-GLD	-17.37	0.92	11.9%	-1.05	3.67	1%	1.97	4.43	6.33	0%	-47.77	8Y.1M
IJS-GLD	-19.57	-0.28	16.1%	-1.46	3.52	1.6%	2.23	4.47	6.85	0%	-51.62	8Y.3M
IJS-IEI-GLD	-9.27	0.60	13%	-2.33	2.91	1.8%	1.22	3.61	5.45	0%	-28.36	8Y.9M
IJS-BND-GLD	-9.26	0.48	13.3%	-2.32	2.97	1.8%	1.23	3.67	5.43	0%	-28.34	8Y.9M
IJS-TLT-GLD	-9.71	0.42	13.6%	-2.54	2.97	1.8%	1.33	3.54	5.85	0%	-30.21	8Y.9M
IJS-LQD-GLD	-9.29	0.39	13.7%	-2.32	3.07	1.5%	1.29	3.68	5.59	0%	-28.57	8Y.9M
VTI-IJS-VNQ-BND-GLD	-17.11	0.65	12.7%	-1.23	3.20	1.5%	1.78	3.87	5.85	0%	-47.99	8Y.10M
VTI-IJS-VNQ-LQD-GLD	-17.16	0.49	13.3%	-1.17	3.23	1.8%	1.82	3.84	5.84	0%	-48.09	8Y.10M
IJS-VNQ-IEI-LQD-GLD	-7.90	0.31	13.1%	-2.26	2.03	2.7%	0.65	2.49	4.72	0%	-23.65	8Y.10M
IJS-VNQ-BND-LQD-GLD	-7.89	0.31	13.1%	-2.25	2.03	2.7%	0.66	2.50	4.72	0%	-24.73	8Y.10M
IJS-VNQ-TLT-GLD	-11.85	0.24	14.1%	-1.92	2.61	2.2%	1.28	3.14	5.47	0%	-36.71	8Y.10M
VTI-IJS-VNQ-IEI-GLD	-17.11	0.67	12.7%	-1.23	3.22	1.5%	1.78	3.87	5.86	0%	-48.00	8Y.11M
VTI-IJS-VNQ-TLT-GLD	-17.52	0.46	13.4%	-1.09	3.15	1.7%	1.85	3.78	5.79	0%	-48.81	8Y.11M
VTI-IJS-VTV-TLT-GLD	-21.68	0.59	13.4%	-1.25	3.65	1.2%	2.31	4.31	6.59	0%	-56.27	9Y.0M

197

Ranking: Baseline 7Y Return

Order by **Baseline 7Y Return - Last 30 Years** (from 1993-12 to 2023-11)

Portfolio	3Y Rolling Annualized Return (%)			7Y Rolling Annualized Return (%)			15Y Rolling Annualized Return (%)				Max Draw-down (%)	Long Neg Period (Y.M)
	Worst	Base	%Fail	Worst	Base ▼	%Fail	Worst	Base	Median	%Fail		
IJS-MTUM-GLD	-4.89	4.43	3.1%	5.80	8.54	0%	7.56	9.27	10.03	0%	-32.67	3Y.7M
VTI-IJS-MTUM-TLT-GLD	-3.39	4.08	2.2%	5.30	8.37	0%	7.46	8.79	9.54	0%	-26.55	3Y.7M
IJS-MTUM-TLT-GLD	-1.31	5.18	1.5%	4.78	8.28	0%	7.15	9.12	9.86	0%	-21.70	3Y.4M
IJS-VTV-MTUM-TLT-GLD	-3.69	4.17	1.5%	5.32	8.24	0%	7.17	8.64	9.35	0%	-27.46	3Y.7M
VTI-IJS-MTUM-EMB-GLD	-5.99	4.91	2.8%	4.83	8.23	0%	6.94	8.86	9.61	0%	-32.97	4Y.3M
VTI-IJS-MTUM-GLD	-7.41	3.89	8%	3.82	8.22	0%	7.71	8.65	9.52	0%	-37.45	4Y.4M
IJS-MTUM-VNQ-GLD	-9.69	5.26	5.5%	4.37	8.19	0%	7.14	9.00	10.14	0%	-41.66	4Y.5M
VTI-MTUM-VNQ-GLD	-8.81	3.64	8%	4.16	8.19	0%	7.19	8.75	9.62	0%	-41.52	4Y.4M
IJS-MTUM-VNQ-TLT-GLD	-5.22	5.46	2.5%	4.41	8.16	0%	6.96	8.96	10.11	0%	-30.50	3Y.9M
IJS-MTUM-TLT-CWB-GLD	-2.75	5.04	2.2%	5.75	8.16	0%	7.22	8.72	9.57	0%	-24.09	3Y.5M
IJS-MTUM-CWB-GLD	-6.62	4.99	3.7%	4.65	8.16	0%	7.44	8.69	9.49	0%	-34.79	4Y.3M
VTI-MTUM-EMB-CWB-GLD	-4.69	4.52	3.1%	5.18	8.04	0%	6.83	8.40	9.36	0%	-30.61	3Y.8M
IJS-MTUM-EMB-GLD	-3.81	5.18	1.2%	5.16	8.03	0%	6.57	8.83	10.19	0%	-28.14	3Y.5M
VTI-IJS-MTUM-VNQ-GLD	-10.70	5.06	7.7%	3.09	8.03	0%	7.21	8.87	9.59	0%	-43.51	5Y.1M
IJS-MTUM-EEM-TLT	-7.11	2.98	4.6%	3.97	8.02	0%	5.95	8.78	9.87	0%	-38.54	4Y.2M
VTI-MTUM-VNQ-TLT-GLD	-4.44	3.69	2.5%	5.23	8.00	0%	7.12	8.96	9.70	0%	-30.18	3Y.8M
VTI-MTUM-EMB-GLD	-2.93	4.33	2.8%	6.21	7.98	0%	6.76	8.73	9.60	0%	-27.92	3Y.3M
VTI-VTV-MTUM-EMB-GLD	-5.59	3.82	5.5%	4.49	7.98	0%	6.82	8.37	9.15	0%	-33.63	4Y.2M
MTUM-EMB-TLT	-7.59	5.32	5.5%	2.02	7.97	0%	5.88	8.57	9.55	0%	-28.75	5Y.9M
IJS-VTV-MTUM-GLD	-7.76	4.17	9.5%	3.80	7.97	0%	7.38	8.57	9.32	0%	-38.39	4Y.4M
VTI-IJS-MTUM-LQD-GLD	-5.47	4.10	3.7%	4.06	7.96	0%	7.04	8.21	8.92	0%	-31.32	4Y.3M

Order by **Baseline 7Y Return - Last 30 Years** (from 1993-12 to 2023-11) - **US Infl. Adjusted**

Portfolio	3Y Rolling Annualized Return (%)			7Y Rolling Annualized Return (%)			15Y Rolling Annualized Return (%)				Max Draw-down (%)	Long Neg Period (Y.M)
	Worst	Base	%Fail	Worst	Base ▼	%Fail	Worst	Base	Median	%Fail		
IJS-MTUM-GLD	-6.95	1.84	9.5%	3.21	6.16	0%	5.06	6.68	7.66	0%	-33.70	5Y.0M
IJS-MTUM-VNQ-TLT-GLD	-7.28	2.73	9.2%	0.85	6.09	0%	4.47	6.52	7.66	0%	-31.57	6Y.2M
VTI-MTUM-EMB-GLD	-5.03	1.89	9.8%	3.01	5.98	0%	4.27	6.42	7.31	0%	-29.73	4Y.8M
IJS-MTUM-EMB-GLD	-5.89	2.69	6.5%	2.01	5.98	0%	4.09	6.68	7.82	0%	-29.24	5Y.9M
IJS-MTUM-TLT-CWB-GLD	-6.21	2.44	6.8%	2.15	5.89	0%	4.73	6.45	7.18	0%	-27.95	5Y.9M
IJS-MTUM-EMB-TLT-GLD	-7.42	3.69	6.8%	0.21	5.89	0%	3.92	6.48	7.61	0%	-28.19	7Y.3M
VTI-MTUM-EMB-TLT-GLD	-8.08	3.04	8.3%	0.98	5.89	0%	4.02	6.51	7.23	0%	-28.84	5Y.11M
VTI-IJS-MTUM-EMB-GLD	-8.03	1.23	10.5%	2.22	5.85	0%	4.45	6.50	7.27	0%	-34.00	5Y.2M
VTI-MTUM-VNQ-TLT-GLD	-6.51	0.88	11.4%	1.64	5.83	0%	4.62	6.34	7.31	0%	-31.25	4Y.11M
IJS-MTUM-EEM-EMB-TLT	-8.60	1.90	8.9%	-0.36	5.83	0.7%	3.01	6.34	7.70	0%	-35.07	8Y.8M
IJS-MTUM-SCZ-TLT-GLD	-6.30	1.39	9.2%	1.07	5.82	0%	3.92	6.19	7.49	0%	-30.81	6Y.3M
VTV-MTUM-EMB-TLT-GLD	-7.60	2.88	7.1%	0.67	5.81	0%	3.79	6.32	7.04	0%	-26.81	6Y.2M
IJS-MTUM-TLT-GLD	-6.67	2.63	6.2%	1.21	5.81	0%	4.65	6.74	7.50	0%	-27.58	6Y.0M
IJS-MTUM-VNQ-GLD	-11.60	2.01	9.2%	1.82	5.76	0%	4.65	6.50	7.74	0%	-42.56	5Y.4M
VTI-MTUM-EEM-EMB-TLT	-8.85	1.29	11.4%	0.47	5.75	0%	3.04	6.22	7.18	0%	-34.83	6Y.7M
MTUM-VNQ-GLD	-8.95	1.45	9.8%	2.47	5.72	0%	4.50	6.39	7.90	0%	-39.24	4Y.11M
MTUM-VNQ-TLT-CWB-GLD	-7.68	2.61	8%	1.26	5.71	0%	4.34	6.33	7.38	0%	-29.78	5Y.9M
MTUM-EEM-TLT	-12.26	1.64	13.2%	-0.68	5.71	0.7%	2.58	6.36	7.55	0%	-38.66	8Y.11M
VTV-MTUM-EMB-GLD	-5.36	1.56	9.8%	2.58	5.71	0%	3.94	6.31	7.10	0%	-30.06	4Y.9M
IJS-MTUM-CWB-GLD	-8.64	2.12	11.1%	2.09	5.70	0%	4.94	6.28	7.13	0%	-35.79	5Y.4M
MTUM-EMB-TLT	-12.61	2.87	7.7%	-1.46	5.70	1.8%	3.41	6.41	7.14	0%	-37.50	8Y.11M

Order by **Baseline 7Y Return** - **Last 60 Years** (from 1963-12 to 2023-11)

Portfolio	3Y Rolling Annualized Return (%)			7Y Rolling Annualized Return (%)			15Y Rolling Annualized Return (%)				Max Draw-down (%)	Long Neg Period (Y.M)
	Worst	Base	%Fail	Worst	Base ▼	%Fail	Worst	Base	Median	%Fail		
VTI-IJS-GLD	-4.97	5.40	2.3%	4.54	8.18	0%	6.67	8.85	10.62	0%	-31.57	4Y.11M
VTI-IJS-VNQ-GLD	-9.78	5.72	3.2%	3.75	8.03	0%	6.38	9.02	10.93	0%	-40.95	4Y.11M
VTI-IJS-VTV-GLD	-7.82	5.70	4.5%	3.16	7.87	0%	6.44	8.54	11.23	0%	-37.61	5Y.1M
IJS-VTV-GLD	-5.47	4.97	2.3%	4.17	7.86	0%	6.75	8.62	10.82	0%	-32.93	5Y.0M
VTI-IJS-VTV-TLT-GLD	-3.78	5.70	1.6%	4.70	7.79	0%	7.09	8.80	10.64	0%	-26.81	3Y.8M
VTI-IJS-TLT-GLD	-0.79	5.72	0.6%	5.09	7.77	0%	7.06	8.97	10.45	0%	-21.63	3Y.3M
VTI-IJS-VNQ-TLT-GLD	-5.33	5.63	1.2%	4.63	7.76	0%	6.87	9.05	10.77	0%	-29.90	4Y.2M
IJS-TLT	-4.94	4.83	3.4%	0.94	7.72	0%	6.53	8.95	11.36	0%	-29.71	6Y.6M
IJS-VTV-VNQ-GLD	-10.19	5.26	3.8%	3.67	7.70	0%	6.27	8.79	11.06	0%	-41.91	4Y.11M
VTI-IJS-VTV-VNQ-GLD	-11.08	5.58	4.5%	2.53	7.65	0%	6.14	8.85	11.51	0%	-43.67	5Y.2M
VTI-IJS-LQD-GLD	-3.27	5.26	0.6%	4.67	7.61	0%	6.59	8.41	10.12	0%	-25.16	3Y.7M
VTI-IJS-VTV-LQD-GLD	-5.83	5.46	2.2%	3.54	7.59	0%	6.41	8.23	10.47	0%	-31.51	4Y.4M
IJS-VTV-TLT-GLD	-1.18	5.50	1.3%	4.63	7.56	0%	6.68	8.76	10.50	0%	-22.65	3Y.3M
VTI-IJS-VNQ-LQD-GLD	-7.35	5.69	1.9%	4.07	7.56	0%	6.35	8.68	10.54	0%	-34.40	4Y.5M
IJS-VTV-VNQ-TLT-GLD	-5.67	5.38	1.9%	4.25	7.52	0%	6.57	8.92	10.83	0%	-30.82	4Y.2M
VTI-IJS-VTV-IEI-GLD	-4.32	5.49	1.6%	4.16	7.48	0%	6.52	8.07	10.42	0%	-28.44	4Y.2M
VTI-IJS-IEI-GLD	-1.41	5.29	0.4%	4.47	7.45	0%	6.39	8.26	9.99	0%	-21.51	3Y.2M
VTI-IJS-VTV-BND-GLD	-4.98	5.50	2.3%	3.75	7.44	0%	6.49	8.04	10.37	0%	-29.81	4Y.3M
VTI-VTV-VNQ-GLD	-9.26	4.61	4.4%	3.48	7.41	0%	5.90	8.53	10.53	0%	-41.70	5Y.5M
VTI-IJS-VNQ-BND-GLD	-6.51	5.66	1.5%	4.30	7.40	0%	6.30	8.49	10.42	0%	-32.74	4Y.4M
VTI-IJS-BND-GLD	-2.22	5.20	0.6%	4.51	7.36	0%	6.37	8.19	9.89	0%	-22.91	3Y.3M

Order by **Baseline 7Y Return** - **Last 60 Years** (from 1963-12 to 2023-11) - **US Infl. Adjusted**

Portfolio	3Y Rolling Annualized Return (%)			7Y Rolling Annualized Return (%)			15Y Rolling Annualized Return (%)				Max Draw-down (%)	Long Neg Period (Y.M)
	Worst	Base	%Fail	Worst	Base ▼	%Fail	Worst	Base	Median	%Fail		
VTI-IJS-GLD	-7.03	1.83	8.8%	1.50	4.76	0%	3.50	6.07	7.38	0%	-33.09	6Y.4M
IJS-VTV-GLD	-7.52	1.88	9.9%	1.43	4.70	0%	3.57	6.01	7.37	0%	-34.29	6Y.4M
VTI-IJS-VNQ-GLD	-11.68	1.33	9.6%	-0.46	4.53	0.2%	3.80	6.09	7.37	0%	-41.86	7Y.5M
VTI-IJS-VTV-GLD	-9.82	1.43	11%	-0.83	4.51	0.2%	3.86	5.89	7.08	0%	-38.57	9Y.2M
VTI-IJS-VTV-VNQ-GLD	-13.01	1.13	11.7%	-1.95	4.41	1.4%	3.56	5.85	7.23	0%	-44.54	9Y.8M
IJS-VTV-VNQ-GLD	-12.09	1.50	10.1%	-0.48	4.36	0.2%	3.68	5.99	7.44	0%	-42.80	7Y.5M
VTI-IJS-LQD-GLD	-5.36	1.72	7.9%	0.49	4.31	0%	4.07	5.53	6.49	0%	-27.49	6Y.5M
VTI-IJS-TLT-GLD	-5.32	1.92	7.7%	0.39	4.30	0%	3.86	5.60	7.09	0%	-28.50	6Y.5M
VTI-IJS-IEI-GLD	-4.44	2.00	6.6%	1.00	4.27	0%	3.91	5.51	6.39	0%	-27.36	6Y.4M
VTI-IJS-VNQ-TLT-GLD	-7.38	1.35	10.7%	-1.00	4.26	0.6%	3.50	5.48	7.30	0%	-30.97	8Y.11M
VTI-IJS-VNQ-LQD-GLD	-9.36	1.12	10.2%	-0.92	4.22	0.8%	3.70	5.41	6.86	0%	-35.41	7Y.6M
VTI-IJS-VNQ-BND-GLD	-8.54	1.43	9.3%	-0.51	4.22	0.2%	3.82	5.41	6.73	0%	-33.78	7Y.5M
VTI-IJS-BND-GLD	-4.43	1.85	7.3%	1.00	4.19	0%	3.89	5.48	6.32	0%	-27.35	6Y.4M
VTI-IJS-VNQ-IEI-GLD	-7.89	1.49	9.3%	-0.52	4.15	0.2%	3.85	5.43	6.82	0%	-32.47	7Y.5M
IJS-VTV-TLT-GLD	-5.96	2.00	7.7%	0.35	4.15	0%	4.05	5.61	6.95	0%	-29.43	6Y.6M
VTI-IJS-SHY-GLD	-4.17	1.92	6.9%	1.16	4.13	0%	3.59	5.21	6.16	0%	-26.53	6Y.4M
VTI-IJS-VNQ-SHY-GLD	-8.40	1.52	9.9%	-0.39	4.11	0.2%	3.59	5.34	6.46	0%	-33.50	7Y.5M
IJS-VTV-LQD-GLD	-5.73	1.80	8.2%	0.45	4.09	0%	3.74	5.46	6.46	0%	-28.42	6Y.5M
VTI-IJS-VTV-LQD-GLD	-7.87	1.24	10.8%	-1.18	4.07	0.6%	3.30	5.22	6.51	0%	-32.56	8Y.11M
VTI-IJS-VTV-SHY-GLD	-6.91	1.53	9.9%	-0.63	4.06	0.2%	3.77	5.13	6.10	0%	-30.60	7Y.5M
VTI-IJS-VTV-BND-GLD	-7.04	1.54	9.8%	-0.76	4.05	0.2%	3.53	5.20	6.36	0%	-30.89	7Y.6M

Order by **Baseline 7Y Return** - **All data** (from 1871/1927 to 2023-11)

Portfolio	3Y Rolling Annualized Return (%)			7Y Rolling Annualized Return (%)			15Y Rolling Annualized Return (%)				Max Draw-down (%)	Long Neg Period (Y.M)
	Worst	Base	%Fail	Worst	Base ▼	%Fail	Worst	Base	Median	%Fail		
VTI-IJS-VTV-GLD	-34.52	2.95	9.3%	-2.86	7.05	1.6%	2.15	8.39	10.86	0%	-74.99	13Y.6M
VTI-IJS-GLD	-31.68	3.61	8%	-1.21	7.03	0.3%	2.78	8.60	10.46	0%	-71.16	13Y.1M
IJS-VTV-GLD	-31.37	3.52	7.8%	-1.56	6.92	0.7%	2.54	8.39	10.43	0%	-70.94	13Y.1M
VTI-IJS-VNQ-GLD	-29.85	3.82	8.1%	-1.83	6.76	0.5%	2.35	8.15	9.85	0%	-69.16	13Y.3M
VTI-IJS-TLT	-30.95	2.77	9.5%	-1.80	6.72	1.1%	3.14	8.33	10.44	0%	-70.39	12Y.10M
IJS-TLT	-24.33	3.34	7.5%	0.59	6.71	0%	4.14	8.32	9.90	0%	-60.20	6Y.6M
VTI-IJS-VTV-VNQ-GLD	-32.46	3.32	9.2%	-2.97	6.70	1.4%	1.79	8.21	10.09	0%	-72.73	13Y.7M
VTI-IJS-VTV-IEI-GLD	-27.02	3.73	7.1%	-0.66	6.67	0.2%	2.98	7.78	9.63	0%	-64.74	12Y.9M
VTI-IJS-VTV-BND-GLD	-27.02	3.73	7.5%	-0.66	6.64	0.2%	2.99	7.75	9.62	0%	-64.74	12Y.9M
VTI-IJS-VTV-LQD-GLD	-27.07	3.71	7.5%	-0.67	6.60	0.2%	3.02	7.81	9.64	0%	-64.81	12Y.9M
VTI-IJS-LQD-GLD	-23.00	4.09	6%	1.05	6.58	0%	3.64	7.70	9.07	0%	-57.86	8Y.7M
VTI-IJS-VTV-TLT-GLD	-27.44	3.74	7.1%	-0.78	6.55	0.2%	3.04	8.13	9.63	0%	-65.37	12Y.9M
VTI-IJS-VTV-SHY-GLD	-26.98	3.70	7.5%	-0.78	6.54	0.2%	2.75	7.55	9.52	0%	-64.66	13Y.0M
IJS-VTV-VNQ-GLD	-29.57	3.60	8.5%	-2.11	6.49	0.7%	2.20	7.93	9.78	0%	-68.92	13Y.4M
VTI-IJS-TLT-GLD	-23.44	4.21	6.9%	0.92	6.49	0%	3.67	7.73	9.33	0%	-58.64	8Y.7M
VTI-IJS-IEI-GLD	-22.93	4.28	6%	1.05	6.45	0%	3.59	7.65	9.07	0%	-57.76	8Y.7M
VTI-IJS-BND-GLD	-22.93	4.14	6.1%	1.06	6.43	0%	3.59	7.64	9.04	0%	-57.75	8Y.7M
IJS-VTV-LQD-GLD	-22.74	3.98	6.4%	0.76	6.37	0%	3.43	7.63	9.01	0%	-57.65	8Y.7M
IJS-VTV-BND-GLD	-22.67	3.98	6%	0.77	6.31	0%	3.39	7.50	8.97	0%	-57.53	8Y.7M
VTI-IJS-SHY-GLD	-22.88	3.91	6.1%	0.91	6.30	0%	3.30	7.41	8.94	0%	-57.64	8Y.9M
VTI-IJS-VTV-BIL-GLD	-27.33	3.37	8.2%	-1.16	6.30	0.4%	2.41	7.25	9.37	0%	-65.14	13Y.1M

Order by **Baseline 7Y Return** - **All data** (from 1871/1927 to 2023-11) - **US Infl. Adjusted**

Portfolio	3Y Rolling Annualized Return (%)			7Y Rolling Annualized Return (%)			15Y Rolling Annualized Return (%)				Max Draw-down (%)	Long Neg Period (Y.M)
	Worst	Base	%Fail	Worst	Base ▼	%Fail	Worst	Base	Median	%Fail		
VTI-IJS-GLD	-26.27	0.71	13.6%	-1.50	4.48	1.3%	2.89	5.33	7.25	0%	-63.58	12Y.9M
IJS-VTV-GLD	-25.93	0.52	13.9%	-1.57	4.17	1.4%	2.78	5.21	7.17	0%	-63.30	13Y.0M
VTI-IJS-VTV-GLD	-29.33	0.08	14.8%	-1.90	3.88	1.5%	2.01	5.25	7.05	0%	-68.42	13Y.4M
VTI-IJS-VNQ-GLD	-24.29	0.40	13.7%	-1.60	3.82	1.8%	2.20	4.63	6.85	0%	-61.06	13Y.3M
VTI-IJS-IEI-GLD	-16.82	1.23	11.2%	-0.96	3.70	1.3%	1.89	4.53	6.11	0%	-46.66	7Y.11M
VTI-IJS-VTV-IEI-GLD	-21.23	0.54	13%	-1.35	3.67	1.2%	2.24	4.49	6.20	0%	-55.48	11Y.0M
VTI-IJS-LQD-GLD	-16.89	0.99	12%	-0.89	3.67	1.1%	1.94	4.50	6.16	0%	-46.79	7Y.11M
VTI-IJS-TLT-GLD	-17.37	0.92	11.9%	-1.05	3.67	1%	1.97	4.43	6.33	0%	-47.77	8Y.1M
VTI-IJS-VTV-LQD-GLD	-21.29	0.47	13.8%	-1.29	3.66	1.4%	2.28	4.40	6.31	0%	-55.57	11Y.0M
VTI-IJS-VTV-TLT-GLD	-21.68	0.59	13.4%	-1.25	3.65	1.2%	2.31	4.31	6.59	0%	-56.27	9Y.0M
IJS-VTV-VNQ-GLD	-23.98	0.37	13.7%	-1.67	3.65	1.8%	2.04	4.49	6.80	0%	-60.75	13Y.4M
VTI-IJS-BND-GLD	-16.81	1.10	11.6%	-0.96	3.64	1.3%	1.90	4.50	6.08	0%	-46.65	7Y.11M
VTI-IJS-VTV-VNQ-GLD	-27.10	0.01	14.9%	-1.95	3.64	2.5%	1.64	4.63	6.84	0%	-65.58	13Y.4M
IJS	-45.05	-1.91	17.5%	-8.11	3.63	6%	0.72	6.44	10.61	0%	-85.57	14Y.8M
VTI-IJS-VTV-BND-GLD	-21.23	0.51	13.3%	-1.35	3.60	1.1%	2.24	4.48	6.18	0%	-55.47	11Y.0M
VTI-IJS-SHY-GLD	-16.77	1.16	11.6%	-1.33	3.57	1.8%	1.65	4.39	5.86	0%	-46.51	12Y.5M
IJS-VTV-TLT-GLD	-17.11	1.10	11.9%	-1.00	3.55	0.9%	1.94	4.29	6.31	0%	-47.53	8Y.0M
IJS-GLD	-19.57	-0.28	16.1%	-1.46	3.52	1.6%	2.23	4.47	6.85	0%	-51.62	8Y.3M
VTI-IJS-VTV-SHY-GLD	-21.19	0.49	13.6%	-1.65	3.52	1.6%	2.04	4.47	5.95	0%	-55.37	12Y.8M
IJS-VTV-IEI-GLD	-16.54	1.30	11.4%	-1.03	3.48	1.4%	1.86	4.41	6.04	0%	-46.38	7Y.11M
IJS-VTV-BND-GLD	-16.54	1.09	11.9%	-1.02	3.47	1.4%	1.87	4.41	6.01	0%	-46.37	7Y.11M

Ranking: Baseline 15Y Return

Order by **Baseline 15Y Return - Last 30 Years** (from 1993-12 to 2023-11)

Portfolio	3Y Rolling Annualized Return (%)			7Y Rolling Annualized Return (%)			15Y Rolling Annualized Return (%)				Max Draw-down (%)	Long Neg Period (Y.M)
	Worst	Base	%Fail	Worst	Base	%Fail	Worst	Base ▼	Median	%Fail		
IJS-MTUM-GLD	-4.89	4.43	3.1%	5.80	8.54	0%	7.56	9.27	10.03	0%	-32.67	3Y.7M
MTUM-VNQ-TLT	-8.70	4.37	9.2%	3.09	7.88	0%	6.83	9.21	9.92	0%	-36.68	4Y.11M
IJS-MTUM-TLT-GLD	-1.31	5.18	1.5%	4.78	8.28	0%	7.15	9.12	9.86	0%	-21.70	3Y.4M
MTUM-VNQ-GLD	-7.03	4.62	3.7%	6.09	7.87	0%	6.99	9.01	10.37	0%	-38.30	3Y.9M
IJS-MTUM-VNQ-GLD	-9.69	5.26	5.5%	4.37	8.19	0%	7.14	9.00	10.14	0%	-41.66	4Y.5M
VTI-MTUM-VNQ-TLT-GLD	-4.44	3.69	2.5%	5.23	8.00	0%	7.12	8.96	9.70	0%	-30.18	3Y.8M
IJS-MTUM-VNQ-TLT-GLD	-5.22	5.46	2.5%	4.41	8.16	0%	6.96	8.96	10.11	0%	-30.50	3Y.9M
MTUM-VNQ	-19.57	2.24	9.2%	-0.24	6.42	0.7%	6.95	8.95	9.82	0%	-59.01	8Y.10M
MTUM-TLT-GLD	-5.91	4.55	2.8%	3.75	7.35	0%	6.53	8.89	9.65	0%	-22.67	4Y.1M
VTI-IJS-MTUM-VNQ-GLD	-10.70	5.06	7.7%	3.09	8.03	0%	7.21	8.87	9.59	0%	-43.51	5Y.1M
VTI-IJS-MTUM-EMB-GLD	-5.99	4.91	2.8%	4.83	8.23	0%	6.94	8.86	9.61	0%	-32.97	4Y.3M
IJS-MTUM-VNQ-TLT	-11.07	4.48	7.7%	2.73	7.43	0%	7.07	8.85	9.93	0%	-40.46	5Y.2M
IJS-MTUM-TLT	-6.93	3.32	5.8%	3.42	7.52	0%	7.42	8.85	9.61	0%	-30.84	4Y.4M
IJS-MTUM-EMB-GLD	-3.81	5.18	1.2%	5.16	8.03	0%	6.57	8.83	10.19	0%	-28.14	3Y.5M
VTI-MTUM-VNQ-EMB-GLD	-7.08	4.81	4%	5.13	7.89	0%	6.61	8.83	9.89	0%	-36.39	4Y.3M
MTUM-GLD	-4.23	4.17	4.6%	5.99	7.51	0%	7.33	8.83	10.18	0%	-27.55	3Y.11M
VTV-MTUM-VNQ-TLT-GLD	-4.76	3.81	2.8%	4.90	7.85	0%	6.83	8.83	9.49	0%	-31.07	3Y.8M
MTUM-VNQ-TLT-GLD	-3.65	5.16	2.5%	3.63	7.66	0%	6.60	8.82	10.07	0%	-25.25	3Y.9M
MTUM-VNQ-TLT-CWB-GLD	-3.79	5.14	2.5%	4.83	7.82	0%	6.84	8.81	9.73	0%	-27.80	3Y.9M
VTI-IJS-MTUM-TLT-GLD	-3.39	4.08	2.2%	5.30	8.37	0%	7.46	8.79	9.54	0%	-26.55	3Y.7M
MTUM-SCZ-TLT	-6.79	1.60	9.2%	3.32	7.58	0%	5.91	8.79	9.82	0%	-35.31	5Y.9M

Order by **Baseline 15Y Return - Last 30 Years** (from 1993-12 to 2023-11) - **US Infl. Adjusted**

Portfolio	3Y Rolling Annualized Return (%)			7Y Rolling Annualized Return (%)			15Y Rolling Annualized Return (%)				Max Draw-down (%)	Long Neg Period (Y.M)
	Worst	Base	%Fail	Worst	Base	%Fail	Worst	Base ▼	Median	%Fail		
IJS-MTUM-TLT-GLD	-6.67	2.63	6.2%	1.21	5.81	0%	4.65	6.74	7.50	0%	-27.58	6Y.0M
MTUM-VNQ-TLT	-10.68	1.86	12.6%	-0.42	5.50	0.7%	4.35	6.71	7.59	0%	-38.50	8Y.9M
IJS-MTUM-EMB-GLD	-5.89	2.69	6.5%	2.01	5.98	0%	4.09	6.68	7.82	0%	-29.24	5Y.9M
IJS-MTUM-GLD	-6.95	1.84	9.5%	3.21	6.16	0%	5.06	6.68	7.66	0%	-33.70	5Y.0M
IJS-MTUM-VNQ-TLT	-13.00	1.75	12.9%	0.17	4.97	0%	4.57	6.64	7.52	0%	-41.47	7Y.3M
MTUM-EMB	-9.57	0.12	14.5%	1.40	4.75	0%	3.64	6.64	7.52	0%	-36.06	6Y.3M
VTI-MTUM-VNQ-EMB-TLT	-10.24	1.31	12.3%	0.59	5.16	0%	4.06	6.61	7.23	0%	-36.31	7Y.3M
IJS-MTUM-VNQ-EMB-GLD	-9.79	3.31	10.5%	1.49	5.63	0%	3.98	6.53	7.98	0%	-37.56	5Y.11M
IJS-MTUM-VNQ-TLT-GLD	-7.28	2.73	9.2%	0.85	6.09	0%	4.47	6.52	7.66	0%	-31.57	6Y.2M
VTI-MTUM-EMB-TLT-GLD	-8.08	3.04	8.3%	0.98	5.89	0%	4.02	6.51	7.23	0%	-28.84	5Y.11M
MTUM-EMB-GLD	-7.44	3.23	6.8%	1.34	5.08	0%	3.59	6.51	7.73	0%	-28.58	5Y.9M
VTI-IJS-MTUM-EMB-GLD	-8.03	1.23	10.5%	2.22	5.85	0%	4.45	6.50	7.27	0%	-34.00	5Y.2M
IJS-MTUM-VNQ-GLD	-11.60	2.01	9.2%	1.82	5.76	0%	4.65	6.50	7.74	0%	-42.56	5Y.4M
VTI-MTUM-VNQ-EMB-GLD	-9.09	1.44	10.5%	2.31	5.53	0%	4.13	6.49	7.46	0%	-37.37	5Y.3M
MTUM-VNQ	-21.31	-0.51	16.6%	-2.73	3.74	1.1%	4.46	6.49	7.42	0%	-59.64	10Y.8M
IJS-MTUM-EMB-TLT-GLD	-7.42	3.69	6.8%	0.21	5.89	0%	3.92	6.48	7.61	0%	-28.19	7Y.3M
IJS-MTUM-EMB-CWB-GLD	-7.41	2.26	6.8%	2.82	5.65	0%	4.22	6.47	7.29	0%	-31.78	5Y.2M
IJS-MTUM-EMB-TLT	-8.40	1.65	10.8%	-0.15	5.20	0.7%	3.97	6.47	7.45	0%	-33.26	7Y.4M
VTI-MTUM-SCZ-EMB-TLT	-9.15	-0.38	16%	0.76	5.12	0%	3.50	6.46	7.18	0%	-35.58	6Y.6M
MTUM-VNQ-EMB-TLT-CWB	-9.59	1.87	12%	0.22	5.07	0%	3.85	6.46	7.30	0%	-34.55	7Y.3M
MTUM-TLT-GLD	-11.02	2.43	7.7%	0.21	5.05	0%	4.06	6.46	7.34	0%	-31.37	7Y.3M

201

Order by **Baseline 15Y Return - Last 60 Years** (from 1963-12 to 2023-11)

Portfolio	3Y Rolling Annualized Return (%)			7Y Rolling Annualized Return (%)			15Y Rolling Annualized Return (%)				Max Draw-down (%)	Long Neg Period (Y.M)
	Worst	Base	%Fail	Worst	Base	%Fail	Worst	Base ▼	Median	%Fail		
IJS-VNQ-TLT	-10.35	4.33	6.4%	0.20	7.15	0%	6.40	9.07	11.29	0%	-37.77	6Y.8M
VTI-IJS-VNQ-TLT-GLD	-5.33	5.63	1.2%	4.63	7.76	0%	6.87	9.05	10.77	0%	-29.90	4Y.2M
IJS-VNQ	-21.37	3.97	8.9%	-1.59	6.48	1.1%	5.43	9.04	12.08	0%	-60.63	7Y.8M
VTI-IJS-VNQ-GLD	-9.78	5.72	3.2%	3.75	8.03	0%	6.38	9.02	10.93	0%	-40.95	4Y.11M
VTI-IJS-TLT-GLD	-0.79	5.72	0.6%	5.09	7.77	0%	7.06	8.97	10.45	0%	-21.63	3Y.3M
IJS-TLT	-4.94	4.83	3.4%	0.94	7.72	0%	6.53	8.95	11.36	0%	-29.71	6Y.6M
IJS	-18.25	4.44	9.2%	-2.35	6.98	1.7%	5.15	8.94	14.42	0%	-54.13	8Y.1M
IJS-VTV-VNQ-TLT-GLD	-5.67	5.38	1.9%	4.25	7.52	0%	6.57	8.92	10.83	0%	-30.82	4Y.2M
VTI-IJS-VNQ	-19.16	4.28	8.3%	-1.71	6.77	1.3%	5.58	8.90	11.94	0%	-57.10	8Y.7M
VTI-IJS-VTV-VNQ-GLD	-11.08	5.58	4.5%	2.53	7.65	0%	6.14	8.85	11.51	0%	-43.67	5Y.2M
VTI-IJS-GLD	-4.97	5.40	2.3%	4.54	8.18	0%	6.67	8.85	10.62	0%	-31.57	4Y.11M
VTI-IJS-VNQ-TLT	-11.21	5.05	6.1%	-0.50	7.27	0.3%	6.81	8.82	11.12	0%	-40.38	7Y.5M
VTI-IJS-VTV-TLT-GLD	-3.78	5.70	1.6%	4.70	7.79	0%	7.09	8.80	10.64	0%	-26.81	3Y.8M
IJS-VTV-VNQ-GLD	-10.19	5.26	3.8%	3.67	7.70	0%	6.27	8.79	11.06	0%	-41.91	4Y.11M
IJS-VTV-TLT-GLD	-1.18	5.50	1.3%	4.63	7.56	0%	6.68	8.76	10.50	0%	22.66	3Y.3M
VTI-IJS-VNQ-TLT-GLD	-4.86	4.42	2%	3.43	7.32	0%	6.69	8.72	10.22	0%	-30.46	5Y.8M
VTI-IJS-VNQ-LQD-GLD	-7.35	5.69	1.9%	4.07	7.56	0%	6.35	8.68	10.54	0%	-34.40	4Y.5M
VTI-IJS-TLT	-7.23	4.47	5.3%	-0.25	7.25	0.2%	7.31	8.66	11.18	0%	-31.32	7Y.1M
IJS-VTV-VNQ-TLT	-11.67	4.68	6.7%	-0.44	6.68	0.2%	6.56	8.65	11.28	0%	-41.99	7Y.5M
IJS-VNQ-TLT-GLD	-3.16	4.76	1.2%	2.88	7.14	0%	6.35	8.64	10.71	0%	-24.90	4Y.0M
IJS-VTV-GLD	-5.47	4.97	2.3%	4.17	7.86	0%	6.75	8.62	10.82	0%	-32.93	5Y.0M

Order by **Baseline 15Y Return - Last 60 Years** (from 1963-12 to 2023-11) - **US Infl. Adjusted**

Portfolio	3Y Rolling Annualized Return (%)			7Y Rolling Annualized Return (%)			15Y Rolling Annualized Return (%)				Max Draw-down (%)	Long Neg Period (Y.M)
	Worst	Base	%Fail	Worst	Base	%Fail	Worst	Base ▼	Median	%Fail		
IJS	-20.02	0.29	14.6%	-8.11	3.86	5.5%	3.14	6.39	9.73	0%	-57.83	11Y.5M
VTI-IJS-VNQ-GLD	-11.68	1.33	9.6%	-0.46	4.53	0.2%	3.80	6.09	7.37	0%	-41.86	7Y.5M
VTI-IJS-GLD	-7.03	1.83	8.8%	1.50	4.76	0%	3.50	6.07	7.38	0%	-33.09	6Y.4M
IJS-VTV-GLD	-7.52	1.88	9.9%	1.43	4.70	0%	3.57	6.01	7.37	0%	-34.29	6Y.4M
IJS-VTV-VNQ-GLD	-12.09	1.50	10.1%	-0.48	4.36	0.2%	3.68	5.99	7.44	0%	-42.80	7Y.5M
VTI-IJS-VTV-GLD	-9.82	1.43	11%	-0.83	4.51	0.2%	3.86	5.89	7.08	0%	-38.57	9Y.2M
VTI-IJS-VTV-VNQ-GLD	-13.01	1.13	11.7%	-1.95	4.41	1.4%	3.56	5.85	7.23	0%	-44.54	9Y.8M
IJS-VTV-TLT-GLD	-5.96	2.00	7.7%	0.35	4.15	0%	4.05	5.61	6.95	0%	-29.43	6Y.6M
VTI-IJS-TLT-GLD	-5.32	1.92	7.7%	0.39	4.30	0%	3.86	5.60	7.09	0%	-28.50	6Y.5M
VTI-IJS-LQD-GLD	-5.36	1.72	7.9%	0.49	4.31	0%	4.07	5.53	6.49	0%	-27.49	6Y.5M
IJS-TLT-GLD	-7.17	1.64	9.6%	-0.61	3.77	0.3%	3.59	5.52	6.88	0%	-27.87	8Y.9M
VTI-IJS-IEI-GLD	-4.44	2.00	6.6%	1.00	4.27	0%	3.91	5.51	6.39	0%	-27.36	6Y.4M
IJS-VNQ	-23.08	-0.19	15.3%	-7.40	3.13	6.1%	2.87	5.51	8.48	0%	-62.26	11Y.7M
IJS-VNQ-TLT-GLD	-6.01	1.04	10.5%	-0.62	3.77	0.3%	3.87	5.48	7.24	0%	-29.22	8Y.9M
VTI-IJS-BND-GLD	-4.43	1.85	7.3%	1.00	4.19	0%	3.89	5.48	6.32	0%	-27.35	6Y.4M
VTI-IJS-VNQ-TLT-GLD	-7.38	1.35	10.7%	-1.00	4.26	0.6%	3.50	5.48	7.30	0%	-30.97	8Y.11M
IJS-VTV-LQD-GLD	-5.73	1.80	8.2%	0.45	4.09	0%	3.74	5.46	6.46	0%	-28.42	6Y.5M
IJS-VTV-VNQ-TLT-GLD	-7.71	1.39	10.4%	-1.02	4.02	0.3%	3.65	5.44	7.28	0%	-31.88	9Y.0M
VTI-IJS-VNQ-IEI-GLD	-7.89	1.49	9.3%	-0.52	4.15	0.2%	3.85	5.43	6.82	0%	-32.47	7Y.5M
VTI-IJS-VTV-TLT-GLD	-6.35	1.42	9.8%	-1.25	4.02	0.5%	3.10	5.42	7.02	0%	-30.73	9Y.0M
VTI-IJS-VNQ-LQD-GLD	-9.36	1.12	10.2%	-0.92	4.22	0.8%	3.70	5.41	6.86	0%	-35.41	7Y.6M

Order by **Baseline 15Y Return** - **All data** (from 1871/1927 to 2023-11)

Portfolio	3Y Rolling Annualized Return (%)			7Y Rolling Annualized Return (%)			15Y Rolling Annualized Return (%)				Max Draw-down (%)	Long Neg Period (Y.M)
	Worst	Base	%Fail	Worst	Base	%Fail	Worst	Base ▼	Median	%Fail		
IJS	-49.09	1.17	13%	-7.75	5.98	4.3%	0.44	9.17	14.53	0%	-88.57	14Y.9M
VTI-IJS-GLD	-31.68	3.61	8%	-1.21	7.03	0.3%	2.78	8.60	10.46	0%	-71.16	13Y.1M
VTI-IJS	-46.41	0.86	13.9%	-7.15	5.74	4.1%	0.75	8.49	12.73	0%	-86.65	14Y.8M
IJS-VNQ	-36.96	1.75	12.5%	-4.86	5.51	2.8%	1.70	8.44	11.07	0%	-78.32	14Y.4M
VTI-IJS-VNQ	-39.20	1.77	12.2%	-5.45	5.76	2.9%	1.35	8.41	11.27	0%	-80.53	14Y.4M
IJS-VTV-GLD	-31.37	3.52	7.8%	-1.56	6.92	0.7%	2.54	8.39	10.43	0%	-70.94	13Y.1M
VTI-IJS-VTV-GLD	-34.52	2.95	9.3%	-2.86	7.05	1.6%	2.15	8.39	10.86	0%	-74.99	13Y.6M
VTI-IJS-TLT	-30.95	2.77	9.5%	-1.80	6.72	1.1%	3.14	8.33	10.44	0%	-70.39	12Y.10M
IJS-TLT	-24.33	3.34	7.5%	0.59	6.71	0%	4.14	8.32	9.90	0%	-60.20	6Y.6M
VTI-IJS-VTV-VNQ-GLD	-32.46	3.32	9.2%	-2.97	6.70	1.4%	1.79	8.21	10.09	0%	-72.73	13Y.7M
IJS-VTV	-46.12	0.51	14.3%	-7.72	5.37	4%	0.39	8.18	12.74	0%	-86.54	14Y.9M
VTI-IJS-VNQ-GLD	-29.85	3.82	8.1%	-1.83	6.76	0.5%	2.35	8.15	9.85	0%	-69.16	13Y.3M
VTI-IJS-VTV-TLT-GLD	-27.44	3.74	7.1%	-0.78	6.55	0.2%	3.04	8.13	9.63	0%	-65.37	12Y.9M
IJS-VTV-TLT	-30.69	2.74	9.6%	-2.21	6.25	1.2%	2.87	8.10	10.47	0%	-70.22	13Y.0M
VTI-IJS-VTV-VNQ	-40.10	1.38	13%	-6.07	5.55	2.8%	0.82	8.09	11.40	0%	-81.44	14Y.6M
IJS-VTV-VNQ	-38.86	1.67	12%	-5.82	5.46	2.7%	1.15	8.08	11.33	0%	-80.31	14Y.4M
VTI-IJS-VTV-TLT	-34.01	1.98	12.2%	-3.34	6.25	2.3%	2.39	7.96	10.61	0%	-74.51	13Y.5M
IJS-VTV-VNQ-GLD	-29.57	3.60	8.5%	-2.11	6.49	0.7%	2.20	7.93	9.78	0%	-68.92	13Y.4M
VTI-IJS-VTV	-45.31	0.37	14.3%	-7.42	5.31	4.1%	0.53	7.91	12.04	0%	-85.89	14Y.9M
VTI-IJS-VNQ-TLT	-29.21	2.70	9.9%	-2.37	6.16	0.9%	2.61	7.89	9.71	0%	-68.45	13Y.3M
VTI-IJS-VTV-VNQ-TLT	-31.99	2.48	11.4%	-3.42	6.20	2.1%	1.98	7.82	10.07	0%	-72.25	13Y.5M

Order by **Baseline 15Y Return** - **All data** (from 1871/1927 to 2023-11) - **US Infl. Adjusted**

Portfolio	3Y Rolling Annualized Return (%)			7Y Rolling Annualized Return (%)			15Y Rolling Annualized Return (%)				Max Draw-down (%)	Long Neg Period (Y.M)
	Worst	Base	%Fail	Worst	Base	%Fail	Worst	Base ▼	Median	%Fail		
IJS	-45.05	-1.91	17.5%	-8.11	3.63	6%	0.72	6.44	10.61	0%	-85.57	14Y.8M
VTI-IJS-GLD	-26.27	0.71	13.6%	-1.50	4.48	1.3%	2.89	5.33	7.25	0%	-63.58	12Y.9M
VTI-IJS-VTV-GLD	-29.33	0.08	14.8%	-1.90	3.88	1.5%	2.01	5.25	7.05	0%	-68.42	13Y.4M
IJS-VTV-GLD	-25.93	0.52	13.9%	-1.57	4.17	1.4%	2.78	5.21	7.17	0%	-63.30	13Y.0M
IJS-VNQ	-31.96	-0.86	17%	-7.40	3.04	4.8%	0.07	4.98	7.98	0%	-72.62	15Y.5M
IJS-VTV	-41.85	-2.29	18.5%	-7.46	2.65	7.2%	0.66	4.65	8.95	0%	-83.01	14Y.8M
VTI-IJS-VTV-VNQ-GLD	-27.10	0.01	14.9%	-1.95	3.64	2.5%	1.64	4.63	6.84	0%	-65.56	13Y.4M
VTI-IJS-VNQ-GLD	-24.29	0.40	13.7%	-1.60	3.82	1.8%	2.20	4.63	6.85	0%	-61.06	13Y.3M
VTI-IJS	-42.15	-2.53	18.1%	-7.82	2.67	7.3%	1.04	4.62	8.75	0%	-83.15	14Y.8M
VTI-IJS-IEI-GLD	-16.82	1.23	11.2%	-0.96	3.70	1.3%	1.89	4.53	6.11	0%	-46.66	7Y.11M
VTI-IJS-BND-GLD	-16.81	1.10	11.6%	-0.96	3.64	1.3%	1.90	4.50	6.08	0%	-46.65	7Y.11M
VTI-IJS-LQD-GLD	-16.89	0.99	12%	-0.89	3.67	1.1%	1.94	4.50	6.16	0%	-46.79	7Y.11M
IJS-VTV-VNQ-GLD	-23.98	0.37	13.7%	-1.67	3.65	1.8%	2.04	4.49	6.80	0%	-60.75	13Y.4M
VTI-IJS-VTV-IEI-GLD	-21.23	0.54	13%	-1.35	3.67	1.2%	2.24	4.49	6.20	0%	-55.48	11Y.0M
VTI-IJS-VTV-BND-GLD	-21.23	0.51	13.3%	-1.35	3.60	1.1%	2.24	4.48	6.18	0%	-55.47	11Y.0M
IJS-GLD	-19.57	-0.28	16.1%	-1.46	3.52	1.6%	2.23	4.47	6.85	0%	-51.62	8Y.3M
VTI-IJS-VTV-SHY-GLD	-21.19	0.49	13.6%	-1.65	3.52	1.6%	2.04	4.47	5.95	0%	-55.37	12Y.8M
VTI-IJS-TLT-GLD	-17.37	0.92	11.9%	-1.05	3.67	1%	1.97	4.43	6.33	0%	-47.77	8Y.1M
IJS-TLT	-18.33	-0.48	16.1%	-4.80	3.40	3.4%	1.33	4.42	6.98	0%	-49.74	13Y.4M
IJS-VTV-BND-GLD	-16.54	1.09	11.9%	-1.02	3.47	1.4%	1.87	4.41	6.01	0%	-46.37	7Y.11M
IJS-VTV-LQD-GLD	-16.61	1.07	12.2%	-0.95	3.46	1.3%	1.91	4.41	6.06	0%	-46.52	7Y.11M

Ranking: Median 15Y Return

Order by Median 15Y Return - Last 30 Years (from 1993-12 to 2023-11)

Portfolio	3Y Rolling Annualized Return (%)			7Y Rolling Annualized Return (%)			15Y Rolling Annualized Return (%)				Max Draw-down (%)	Long Neg Period (Y.M)
	Worst	Base	%Fail	Worst	Base	%Fail	Worst	Base	Median ▼	%Fail		
SCZ-EMB	-9.62	1.61	9.8%	1.66	5.81	0%	3.09	6.47	10.72	0%	-40.94	6Y.3M
SCZ-VNQ-EMB	-14.50	2.67	10.2%	2.11	5.97	0%	4.01	6.65	10.68	0%	-49.86	5Y.2M
MTUM-SCZ-VNQ-EMB-GLD	-7.88	4.85	4.9%	4.40	7.20	0%	5.51	8.21	10.66	0%	-39.35	4Y.3M
SCZ-VNQ-EMB-GLD	-6.23	2.22	3.4%	2.80	5.44	0%	4.50	7.20	10.65	0%	-35.64	3Y.9M
SCZ-EEM-VNQ-EMB-TLT	-7.71	3.24	6.5%	1.02	6.17	0%	3.64	7.25	10.65	0%	-39.71	6Y.9M
VNQ-EMB	-12.45	3.22	9.5%	1.09	6.10	0%	4.54	6.61	10.63	0%	-43.90	5Y.2M
SCZ-EMB-GLD	-2.67	1.46	7.1%	2.16	4.28	0%	3.93	7.02	10.61	0%	-30.32	4Y.10M
SCZ-VNQ-EMB-TLT	-7.80	3.90	7.7%	0.68	6.76	0%	4.47	7.31	10.60	0%	-34.51	6Y.4M
EEM-VNQ-EMB-GLD	-3.61	1.92	6.2%	1.59	4.38	0%	3.68	7.01	10.57	0%	-34.66	4Y.9M
SCZ-EMB-TLT	-7.70	4.73	6.8%	-0.17	6.29	0.7%	3.87	7.19	10.56	0%	-30.85	7Y.4M
IJS-VNQ-EMB-GLD	-6.22	3.61	2.8%	2.94	6.34	0%	5.81	7.72	10.53	0%	-32.27	4Y.2M
SCZ-EEM-EMB-TLT	-6.87	3.55	6.2%	0.41	5.46	0%	3.00	7.16	10.53	0%	-32.80	6Y.6M
SCZ-VNQ-EMB-TLT-GLD	-3.76	3.23	5.2%	1.58	5.42	0%	4.68	7.46	10.50	0%	-25.31	4Y.4M
MTUM-SCZ-VNQ-EMB-TLT	-8.98	4.83	8.9%	2.62	7.46	0%	5.48	8.27	10.50	0%	-38.24	4Y.7M
SCZ-EEM-VNQ-EMB-GLD	-6.74	1.70	5.5%	2.13	4.67	0%	3.55	6.99	10.49	0%	-40.90	5Y.2M
IJS-SCZ-EMB-GLD	-4.83	3.40	1.8%	2.79	6.26	0%	5.10	7.61	10.48	0%	-31.31	3Y.6M
SCZ-EEM-EMB-TLT-GLD	-5.11	2.07	7.1%	1.46	4.08	0%	3.47	7.23	10.48	0%	-28.28	5Y.10M
EEM-VNQ-EMB	-11.07	2.31	6.5%	1.73	5.26	0%	3.03	6.65	10.47	0%	-48.25	6Y.0M
MTUM-VNQ-EMB-GLD	-5.15	5.28	2.8%	4.49	7.22	0%	6.13	8.57	10.47	0%	-32.69	3Y.8M
IJS-SCZ-VNQ-EMB-GLD	-8.67	3.23	4.9%	3.16	6.67	0%	5.27	7.53	10.46	0%	-38.95	4Y.3M
VNQ-EMB-GLD	-2.35	2.17	4.6%	2.21	4.97	0%	4.85	7.13	10.46	0%	-27.11	3Y.9M

Order by Median 15Y Return - Last 30 Years (from 1993-12 to 2023-11) - US Infl. Adjusted

Portfolio	3Y Rolling Annualized Return (%)			7Y Rolling Annualized Return (%)			15Y Rolling Annualized Return (%)				Max Draw-down (%)	Long Neg Period (Y.M)
	Worst	Base	%Fail	Worst	Base	%Fail	Worst	Base	Median ▼	%Fail		
SCZ-EMB	-11.57	-0.34	16%	-1.78	3.75	5.4%	0.68	4.46	8.38	0%	-42.34	10Y.0M
VNQ-EMB	-14.35	1.08	12.6%	-2.36	4.24	4.3%	2.09	4.53	8.24	0%	-46.49	10Y.6M
EEM-VNQ-EMB-GLD	-6.86	-0.62	19.4%	-0.92	2.05	1.1%	1.26	4.86	8.18	0%	-35.66	11Y.6M
SCZ-VNQ-EMB-GLD	-10.17	1.84	12.3%	-2.75	4.82	5.1%	2.03	5.17	8.16	0%	-36.60	10Y.6M
EEM-VNQ-EMB-TLT	-11.21	1.92	8%	-3.04	3.84	5.1%	1.30	5.13	8.16	0%	-36.48	11Y.10M
MTUM-SCZ-VNQ-EMB-GLD	-9.88	2.53	11.7%	0.84	5.30	0%	3.04	5.91	8.16	0%	-40.28	6Y.3M
VNQ-EMB-GLD	-6.18	-0.16	15.7%	-1.02	2.49	1.8%	2.40	5.02	8.16	0%	-27.52	10Y.9M
SCZ-EEM-VNQ-EMB-TLT	-9.99	1.26	10.2%	-2.40	4.13	4.3%	1.22	4.92	8.14	0%	-40.64	10Y.10M
MTUM-VNQ-EMB-GLD	-7.20	3.10	9.8%	0.92	5.24	0%	3.65	6.41	8.12	0%	-33.62	5Y.10M
SCZ-EEM-EMB-TLT	-11.91	1.60	9.5%	-2.99	3.63	6.9%	0.59	5.10	8.11	0%	-38.33	13Y.0M
SCZ-VNQ-EMB-GLD	-8.26	-0.20	16.6%	-0.62	3.34	0.7%	2.05	5.02	8.11	0%	-36.63	7Y.9M
SCZ-VNQ-EMB	-16.35	0.04	14.5%	-1.37	3.79	2.9%	1.57	4.60	8.09	0%	-50.89	9Y.4M
EEM-VNQ-EMB	-12.99	0.24	14.5%	-1.74	3.44	2.9%	0.62	4.55	8.07	0%	-49.04	10Y.10M
MTUM-EEM-VNQ-EMB-GLD	-7.89	1.69	8.9%	0.59	4.60	0%	2.44	5.89	8.06	0%	-39.56	6Y.3M
SCZ-EMB-GLD	-7.11	-1.11	18.5%	-0.70	1.95	1.1%	1.50	4.86	8.06	0%	-32.71	11Y.6M
EEM-VNQ-EMB-TLT-GLD	-9.66	0.78	11.4%	-2.13	2.33	4%	1.60	5.21	8.05	0%	-31.33	12Y.3M
SCZ-EMB-TLT	-12.69	2.37	8.6%	-3.55	4.53	7.2%	1.44	5.13	8.04	0%	-38.63	11Y.8M
IJS-EEM-VNQ-EMB-GLD	-8.60	0.86	11.7%	0.01	3.80	0%	2.26	5.23	8.04	0%	-39.11	7Y.8M
SCZ-VNQ-EMB-TLT-GLD	-8.99	1.18	9.5%	-1.88	3.56	2.9%	2.23	5.28	8.03	0%	-30.68	10Y.6M
SCZ-EEM-VNQ-EMB-GLD	-8.76	-0.64	18.8%	-0.65	2.67	0.7%	1.13	4.76	8.03	0%	-41.81	9Y.10M
MTUM-SCZ-VNQ-EMB-TLT	-10.95	2.17	12.9%	-0.88	5.13	1.1%	3.02	6.02	8.03	0%	-39.19	8Y.9M

Order by **Median 15Y Return** - **Last 60 Years** (from 1963-12 to 2023-11)

Portfolio	3Y Rolling Annualized Return (%)			7Y Rolling Annualized Return (%)			15Y Rolling Annualized Return (%)				Max Draw-down (%)	Long Neg Period (Y.M)
	Worst	Base	%Fail	Worst	Base	%Fail	Worst	Base	Median ▼	%Fail		
IJS	-18.25	4.44	9.2%	-2.35	6.98	1.7%	5.15	8.94	14.42	0%	-54.13	8Y.1M
IJS-VTV	-17.40	2.52	10.7%	-2.09	6.05	1.3%	5.74	8.13	12.63	0%	-54.38	10Y.11M
VTI-IJS	-16.60	3.35	10.2%	-2.10	6.62	1.6%	6.05	8.30	12.39	0%	-51.92	9Y.9M
IJS-VNQ	-21.37	3.97	8.9%	-1.59	6.48	1.1%	5.43	9.04	12.08	0%	-60.63	7Y.8M
IJS-VTV-VNQ	-19.75	3.73	8%	-1.57	6.35	0.9%	5.39	8.56	12.07	0%	-58.66	8Y.6M
VTI-IJS-VNQ	-19.16	4.28	8.3%	-1.71	6.77	1.3%	5.58	8.90	11.94	0%	-57.10	8Y.7M
VTI-IJS-VTV	-16.60	2.81	11%	-2.35	5.97	1.4%	5.63	7.75	11.81	0%	-52.88	10Y.11M
VTI-IJS-VTV-VNQ	-18.52	3.71	9.6%	-1.89	6.22	1.1%	5.43	8.31	11.73	0%	-56.51	9Y.9M
VTI-IJS-VTV-VNQ-GLD	-11.08	5.58	4.5%	2.53	7.65	0%	6.14	8.85	11.51	0%	-43.67	5Y.2M
IJS-VTV-TLT	-7.65	4.22	5.3%	-0.18	6.89	0.2%	6.79	8.49	11.43	0%	-31.90	7Y.1M
IJS-TLT	-4.94	4.83	3.4%	0.94	7.72	0%	6.53	8.95	11.36	0%	-29.71	6Y.6M
IJS-VNQ-TLT	-10.35	4.33	6.4%	0.20	7.15	0%	6.40	9.07	11.29	0%	-37.77	6Y.8M
IJS-VTV-VNQ-TLT	-11.67	4.68	6.7%	0.44	6.68	0.2%	6.56	8.65	11.28	0%	-41.99	7Y.5M
IJS-VTV-IEI	-8.40	4.15	5.4%	0.69	6.31	0%	5.82	7.40	11.28	0%	-34.39	6Y.6M
IJS-IEI	-4.77	4.94	2.8%	2.15	6.40	0%	5.30	7.42	11.24	0%	-22.74	6Y.4M
IJS-LQD	-8.39	4.84	4.8%	0.94	6.43	0%	5.67	7.74	11.24	0%	-31.41	6Y.8M
VTI-IJS-VTV-GLD	-7.82	5.70	4.5%	3.16	7.87	0%	6.44	8.54	11.23	0%	-37.61	5Y.1M
IJS-VTV-BND	-9.49	3.99	5.8%	0.69	6.10	0%	5.73	7.35	11.20	0%	-36.83	6Y.6M
IJS-VTV-VNQ-IEI	-12.29	4.92	6.9%	0.20	6.21	0%	5.84	7.97	11.19	0%	-43.73	6Y.8M
VTI-IJS-TLT	-7.23	4.47	5.3%	-0.25	7.25	0.2%	7.31	8.66	11.18	0%	-31.32	7Y.1M
VTI-IJS-VTV-TLT	-9.25	4.00	8.3%	-0.81	6.73	0.3%	6.86	8.23	11.17	0%	-36.27	7Y.5M

Order by **Median 15Y Return** - **Last 60 Years** (from 1963-12 to 2023-11) - **US Infl. Adjusted**

Portfolio	3Y Rolling Annualized Return (%)			7Y Rolling Annualized Return (%)			15Y Rolling Annualized Return (%)				Max Draw-down (%)	Long Neg Period (Y.M)
	Worst	Base	%Fail	Worst	Base	%Fail	Worst	Base	Median ▼	%Fail		
IJS	-20.02	0.29	14.6%	-8.11	3.86	5.5%	3.14	6.39	9.73	0%	-57.83	11Y.5M
IJS-VTV	-19.19	-0.93	16.1%	-7.46	2.64	5.8%	2.41	4.73	8.60	0%	-55.29	11Y.8M
IJS-VNQ	-23.08	-0.19	15.3%	-7.40	3.13	6.1%	2.87	5.51	8.48	0%	-62.26	11Y.7M
VTI-IJS	-18.59	-0.23	15.5%	-7.82	2.57	6.6%	1.90	4.62	8.18	0%	-54.31	11Y.9M
IJS-VTV-VNQ	-21.49	0.05	14.6%	-7.20	2.57	6.4%	2.18	4.98	8.15	0%	-59.49	11Y.8M
IJS-VNQ-GLD	-10.62	0.93	12.1%	1.40	3.99	0%	3.34	5.31	8.00	0%	-38.59	5Y.11M
VTI-IJS-VNQ	-20.91	0.29	14.3%	-7.48	2.79	6.3%	1.85	5.03	7.97	0%	-57.97	11Y.7M
IJS-VNQ-TLT	-13.48	-0.03	15%	-5.49	2.47	6.1%	1.43	4.79	7.91	0%	-40.40	11Y.9M
VTI-IJS-VTV-VNQ	-20.29	-0.37	16.1%	-7.46	2.29	7.2%	1.31	4.55	7.80	0%	-57.38	11Y.9M
IJS-TLT	-11.68	0.03	14.6%	-4.80	2.81	5%	1.33	4.71	7.71	0%	-39.25	13Y.4M
VTI-IJS-VTV	-18.40	-0.57	16.6%	-7.75	2.08	6.9%	1.16	3.91	7.67	0%	-53.82	13Y.8M
IJS-VTV-VNQ-TLT	-13.59	-0.11	15%	-6.10	2.18	5.7%	1.01	4.97	7.63	0%	-43.41	12Y.10M
VTI-IJS-VNQ-TLT	-14.53	0.06	14.9%	-6.16	2.33	6.1%	0.79	5.15	7.49	0%	-42.74	13Y.8M
IJS-GLD	-6.91	0.78	12%	1.05	3.67	0%	2.23	4.79	7.49	0%	-33.07	5Y.7M
VNQ	-26.58	-2.46	23.2%	-7.33	0.76	11.5%	0.14	4.35	7.44	0%	-69.76	14Y.11M
IJS-VTV-VNQ-GLD	-12.09	1.50	10.1%	-0.48	4.36	0.2%	3.68	5.99	7.44	0%	-42.80	7Y.5M
VTI-IJS-GLD	-7.03	1.83	8.8%	1.50	4.76	0%	3.50	6.07	7.38	0%	-33.09	6Y.4M
VTI-IJS-VNQ-GLD	-11.68	1.33	9.6%	-0.46	4.53	0.2%	3.80	6.09	7.37	0%	-41.86	7Y.5M
IJS-VTV-GLD	-7.52	1.88	9.9%	1.43	4.70	0%	3.57	6.01	7.37	0%	-34.29	6Y.4M
IJS-VTV-TLT	-12.45	-0.25	15.8%	-5.85	2.42	5%	0.80	5.08	7.37	0%	-43.11	13Y.11M
VTI-IJS-VNQ-TLT-GLD	-7.38	1.35	10.7%	-1.00	4.26	0.6%	3.50	5.48	7.30	0%	-30.97	8Y.11M

Order by **Median 15Y Return - All data** (from 1871/1927 to 2023-11)

Portfolio	3Y Rolling Annualized Return (%)			7Y Rolling Annualized Return (%)			15Y Rolling Annualized Return (%)				Max Draw-down (%)	Long Neg Period (Y.M)
	Worst	Base	%Fail	Worst	Base	%Fail	Worst	Base	Median ▼	%Fail		
IJS	-49.09	1.17	13%	-7.75	5.98	4.3%	0.44	9.17	14.53	0%	-88.57	14Y.9M
IJS-VTV	-46.12	0.51	14.3%	-7.72	5.37	4%	0.39	8.18	12.74	0%	-86.54	14Y.9M
VTI-IJS	-46.41	0.86	13.9%	-7.15	5.74	4.1%	0.75	8.49	12.73	0%	-86.65	14Y.8M
VTI-IJS-VTV	-45.31	0.37	14.3%	-7.42	5.31	4.1%	0.53	7.91	12.04	0%	-85.89	14Y.9M
VTI-IJS-VTV-VNQ	-40.10	1.38	13%	-6.07	5.55	2.8%	0.82	8.09	11.40	0%	-81.44	14Y.6M
IJS-VTV-VNQ	-38.86	1.67	12%	-5.82	5.46	2.7%	1.15	8.08	11.33	0%	-80.31	14Y.4M
VTI-IJS-VNQ	-39.20	1.77	12.2%	-5.45	5.76	2.9%	1.35	8.41	11.27	0%	-80.53	14Y.4M
IJS-VNQ	-36.96	1.75	12.5%	-4.86	5.51	2.8%	1.70	8.44	11.07	0%	-78.32	14Y.4M
VTI-IJS-VTV-GLD	-34.52	2.95	9.3%	-2.86	7.05	1.6%	2.15	8.39	10.86	0%	-74.99	13Y.6M
VTI-IJS-VTV-SHY	-33.43	1.72	11.9%	-3.29	5.29	2.3%	2.04	7.16	10.65	0%	-73.77	13Y.7M
VTI-IJS-VTV-BND	-33.48	1.92	11.9%	-3.15	5.75	2%	2.35	7.50	10.65	0%	-73.86	13Y.5M
VTI-IJS-VTV-IEI	-33.49	1.95	11.8%	-3.16	5.80	1.9%	2.35	7.55	10.64	0%	-73.86	13Y.5M
VTI-VTV	-43.48	-0.28	15.3%	-7.64	4.15	5.2%	-0.66	6.42	10.64	0.3%	-84.44	15Y.7M
VTV	-43.29	-0.19	15.3%	-8.41	3.75	5.9%	-1.07	6.25	10.63	1.1%	-84.40	15Y.7M
IJS-VTV-IEI	-29.97	2.62	9.8%	-1.97	5.83	1%	2.80	7.46	10.63	0%	-69.24	13Y.1M
VTI-IJS-IEI	-30.26	2.87	9.7%	-1.57	6.25	0.7%	3.07	7.71	10.62	0%	-69.44	12Y.10M
VTI-IJS-VTV-TLT	-34.01	1.98	12.2%	-3.34	6.25	2.3%	2.39	7.96	10.61	0%	-74.51	13Y.5M
IJS-VTV-BND	-29.96	2.45	10.1%	-1.97	5.75	1%	2.81	7.40	10.61	0%	-69.23	13Y.0M
VTI-IJS-BND	-30.25	2.64	10%	-1.56	6.11	0.7%	3.08	7.65	10.59	0%	-69.43	12Y.10M
VTI-IJS-VTV-LQD	-33.55	1.95	12.1%	-3.17	5.71	2.2%	2.40	7.52	10.59	0%	-73.94	13Y.5M
VTI-IJS-SHY	-30.18	2.55	10.2%	-1.75	5.59	0.7%	2.70	7.11	10.58	0%	-69.30	13Y.1M

Order by **Median 15Y Return - All data** (from 1871/1927 to 2023-11) - **US Infl. Adjusted**

Portfolio	3Y Rolling Annualized Return (%)			7Y Rolling Annualized Return (%)			15Y Rolling Annualized Return (%)				Max Draw-down (%)	Long Neg Period (Y.M)
	Worst	Base	%Fail	Worst	Base	%Fail	Worst	Base	Median ▼	%Fail		
IJS	-45.05	-1.91	17.5%	-8.11	3.63	6%	0.72	6.44	10.61	0%	-85.57	14Y.8M
IJS-VTV	-41.85	-2.29	18.5%	-7.46	2.65	7.2%	0.66	4.65	8.95	0%	-83.01	14Y.8M
VTI-IJS	-42.15	-2.53	18.1%	-7.82	2.67	7.3%	1.04	4.62	8.75	0%	-83.15	14Y.5M
VTI-IJS-VTV	-40.98	-2.58	18.9%	-7.75	2.21	8.1%	0.38	3.83	8.10	0%	-82.18	14Y.8M
IJS-VNQ	-31.96	-0.86	17%	-7.40	3.04	4.8%	0.07	4.98	7.98	0%	-72.62	15Y.5M
IJS-VTV-VNQ	-34.02	-0.91	16.9%	-7.20	2.61	5.5%	0.21	4.41	7.86	0%	-75.13	14Y.3M
VTI-IJS-VNQ	-34.38	-0.67	17.1%	-7.48	2.85	5.3%	0.23	4.41	7.79	0%	-75.41	14Y.3M
VTI-IJS-VTV-VNQ	-35.34	-1.56	18.4%	-7.46	2.47	6.7%	0.29	3.98	7.67	0%	-76.56	14Y.6M
VTI-IJS-GLD	-26.27	0.71	13.6%	-1.50	4.48	1.3%	2.89	5.33	7.25	0%	-63.58	12Y.9M
IJS-VTV-GLD	-25.93	0.52	13.9%	-1.57	4.17	1.4%	2.78	5.21	7.17	0%	-63.30	13Y.0M
VTI-IJS-VTV-TLT	-28.78	-1.48	18.3%	-6.44	2.67	4.7%	0.29	3.54	7.06	0%	-67.81	14Y.3M
VTI-IJS-VTV-GLD	-29.33	0.08	14.8%	-1.90	3.88	1.5%	2.01	5.25	7.05	0%	-68.42	13Y.4M
VTI-IJS-TLT	-25.48	-0.64	17%	-5.92	3.21	3.7%	0.51	3.89	7.01	0%	-62.61	14Y.2M
VTI-IJS-VNQ-TLT	-23.60	-0.55	16%	-6.16	2.70	4.2%	0.27	3.54	7.01	0%	-60.16	13Y.11M
IJS-VTV-TLT	-25.19	-0.82	16.9%	-5.85	2.83	3.3%	0.80	3.78	6.98	0%	-62.40	13Y.11M
IJS-TLT	-18.33	-0.48	16.1%	-4.80	3.40	3.4%	1.33	4.42	6.98	0%	-49.74	13Y.4M
VTI-IJS-VTV-VNQ-TLT	-26.52	-0.68	16.9%	-6.52	2.52	4.7%	0.30	3.37	6.94	0%	-64.95	13Y.11M
VTI	-39.36	-2.49	20.7%	-8.51	0.77	12.6%	-2.10	2.40	6.93	2.5%	-80.55	26Y.4M
IJS-VTV-VNQ-TLT	-23.32	-0.34	16%	-6.10	2.41	4%	0.21	3.61	6.91	0%	-59.89	15Y.2M
VTI-IJS-VTV-LQD	-28.28	-1.29	17.7%	-6.38	2.58	5.1%	0.49	3.61	6.87	0%	-67.09	14Y.2M
IJS-GLD	-19.57	-0.28	16.1%	-1.46	3.52	1.6%	2.23	4.47	6.85	0%	-51.62	8Y.3M

The Most Famous Lazy Portfolios

After examining a wide range of equally weighted allocations, let's now discuss the most famous and traditional Lazy Portfolios.

The strategy remains the same: start with the goal, examine the metrics most crucial for that goal, study, and decide whether to invest.

You will find these portfolios on *LazyPortfolioEtf.com*, along with many others. The statistics presented here are updated as of November 2023.

Total US Market Portfolio

We have often been 'accused' of including such a portfolio among the Lazy Portfolios.

It's not necessary for a Lazy Portfolio to contain numerous ETFs. The key is to adhere to the passive investing philosophy that we have described.

Creating an accumulation plan with a U.S. equity ETF is a very common investment strategy worldwide. It perfectly reflects the logic of passive investing: simplicity, diversification, low management costs, and virtually no required effort.

The chart below, if you are a finance enthusiast, you have likely seen dozens of times. It is one of the most famous charts, demonstrating the beauty of long-term pure equity investment.

	1M	6M	1Y	5Y	10Y	30Y	MAX (~153Y)
US Stocks Portfolio	9.42	10.04	12.72	11.71	11.16	9.90	9.08
US Inflation Adjusted return	9.42	8.77	9.07	7.34	8.12	7.19	6.82

Many investors are dazzled by such returns but sell everything at the first sign of turbulence.

However, you already know the detailed metrics: you have already seen them in the analysis of the VTI ETF in the single-asset portfolios. Therefore, you already know what could happen, and you can assess whether you feel capable of managing the situation.

Data Source: 1871-01 - 2023-11 Metric	Last 30Y	Last 60Y	Since 1871-01
Worst 3Y Rolling Return (%)	-16.22	-16.22	-43.81
Baseline 3Y Rolling Return (%)	-1.94	1.87	-0.56
%Fail 3Y Rolling Return	16.9%	12.6%	15.9%
Worst 7Y Rolling Return (%)	-2.98	-3.00	-9.49
Baseline 7Y Rolling Return (%)	3.78	4.15	3.29
%Fail 7Y Rolling Return	2.2%	1.7%	4.2%
Worst 15Y Rolling Return (%)	4.37	4.37	-0.35
Baseline 15Y Rolling Return (%)	5.30	6.49	5.49
Median 15Y Rolling Return (%)	7.55	10.48	8.60
%Fail 15Y Rolling Return	0%	0%	0.1%
Maximum Drawdown (%)	-50.84	-50.84	-84.60
Longest Negative Period (Y.M)	11Y.7M	11Y.7M	15Y.8M

Data Source: 1871-01 - 2023-11 Metric - US Inflation Adjusted	Last 30Y	Last 60Y	Since 1871-01
Worst 3Y Rolling Return (%)	-18.24	-18.54	-39.36
Baseline 3Y Rolling Return (%)	-4.37	-2.55	-2.49
%Fail 3Y Rolling Return	20%	20.6%	20.7%
Worst 7Y Rolling Return (%)	-5.40	-8.51	-8.51
Baseline 7Y Rolling Return (%)	1.18	0.01	0.77
%Fail 7Y Rolling Return	6.9%	14.9%	12.6%
Worst 15Y Rolling Return (%)	2.16	-1.47	-2.10
Baseline 15Y Rolling Return (%)	2.90	2.39	2.40
Median 15Y Rolling Return (%)	5.14	6.97	6.93
%Fail 15Y Rolling Return	0%	2.2%	2.5%
Maximum Drawdown (%)	-51.59	-54.53	-80.55
Longest Negative Period (Y.M)	13Y.5M	18Y.1M	26Y.4M

These numbers clearly show us that, in the short term, such a portfolio can present challenges.

Considering all the available data from 1871 onwards, the probability of experiencing a negative nominal return over a 3-year period has been around 16%. Even the baseline return is negative.

In the long term, as expected, the values are excellent. Despite a 0.1% chance of loss, the baseline return over 15 years has been over 5% nominal.

The price to pay was a severe drawdown of -84% (1929 crisis - The Great Depression) and even a longest negative period of over 15 years (always considering nominal returns).

You might be wondering: why are the worst returns and drawdowns, considering inflation, sometimes higher than those without inflation? Examining the entire available history, so from 1871 onwards, covers the period of the 1929 crisis: during that time, the collapses were the most severe ever recorded, but U.S. inflation was negative (meaning prices fell). For this reason, the inflation-adjusted returns for that period are higher than nominal returns.

The 60/40 Portfolio

It is the classic example of a 'balanced' or 'moderate' portfolio, allocating 60% to stocks and 40% to bonds.

It represents the simplest form of diversification that aims to balance the pursuit of returns with risk mitigation.

Depending on the risk one is willing to take, the equity portion can be adjusted. With a higher allocation to stocks, it can also prove to be an effective long-term portfolio.

It is suitable for those seeking simplified management: with only 2 assets, it ensures absolute ease during rebalancing.

A mix of this kind (stocks-bonds) is so common that there are now ETFs that internally replicate this strategy and handle rebalancing without any action required from the investor. The most renowned ETFs of this kind are issued by Vanguard (LifeStrategy line).

In the simplest version, which we present below and is also available on *LazyPortfolioEtf.com*, the composition of the 60/40 portfolio is defined as follows:

60% U.S. Total Stock Market

40% U.S. Total Bond Market

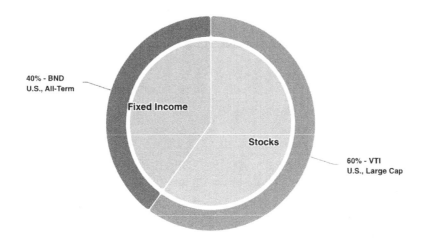

40% - BND
U.S., All-Term

Fixed Income

Stocks

60% - VTI
U.S., Large Cap

Below, we present the main metrics:

Data Source: 1871-01 - 2023-11 **Metric**	**Last 30Y**	**Last 60Y**	**Since 1871-01**
Worst 3Y Rolling Return (%)	-6.40	-6.40	-25.23
Baseline 3Y Rolling Return (%)	1.88	3.68	1.83
%Fail 3Y Rolling Return	9.5%	7.7%	9.4%
Worst 7Y Rolling Return (%)	0.82	0.56	-2.67
Baseline 7Y Rolling Return (%)	4.95	5.28	4.06
%Fail 7Y Rolling Return	0%	0%	0.7%
Worst 15Y Rolling Return (%)	5.21	5.21	2.25
Baseline 15Y Rolling Return (%)	5.93	6.50	5.30
Median 15Y Rolling Return (%)	7.10	9.22	7.17
%Fail 15Y Rolling Return	0%	0%	0%
Maximum Drawdown (%)	-30.55	-30.55	-62.03
Longest Negative Period (Y.M)	9Y.2M	9Y.2M	12Y.10M

Data Source: 1871-01 - 2023-11	Last	Last	Since
Metric - US Inflation Adjusted	**30Y**	**60Y**	**1871-01**
Worst 3Y Rolling Return (%)	-8.50	-12.03	-19.29
Baseline 3Y Rolling Return (%)	-0.99	-1.46	-0.93
%Fail 3Y Rolling Return	19.1%	21.8%	18.1%
Worst 7Y Rolling Return (%)	-1.70	-5.15	-6.22
Baseline 7Y Rolling Return (%)	2.22	0.92	1.42
%Fail 7Y Rolling Return	1.8%	12.1%	9.4%
Worst 15Y Rolling Return (%)	2.98	-1.04	-2.07
Baseline 15Y Rolling Return (%)	3.50	2.98	2.33
Median 15Y Rolling Return (%)	4.70	5.51	5.45
%Fail 15Y Rolling Return	0%	3.1%	2.6%
Maximum Drawdown (%)	-31.61	-38.92	-52.05
Longest Negative Period (Y.M)	11Y.0M	18Y.2M	21Y.11M

Continuing to focus on nominal returns, over the entire historical period, the probability of experiencing a negative return over 3 years has been around 9%, but the baseline return is positive. The situation improves when considering at least a 7-year time horizon.

When you hear that the 60/40 portfolio is a balanced portfolio with 'moderate' risk, now you also know that the worst drawdowns have been around 30% over the last 60 years, with nearly decade-long longest negative periods.

Harry Browne - Permanent Portfolio

Harry Browne was a well-known American author, economist, and politician. He is especially renowned for his 'Permanent Portfolio,' a long-term investment strategy he conceived in the 1980s and presented in 1999 in the book 'Fail-Safe Investing: Lifelong Financial Security in 30 Minutes'.

This portfolio was designed to be stable and resilient to market fluctuations, offering investors a simple and 'controlled' risk solution.

Browne's 'Permanent Portfolio' consists of four main diversified assets. It is an equally weighted portfolio, so we could have indeed encountered it in our simulations.

The difference lies in the fact that Browne did not arrive at this solution after conducting all the simulations we have done, but rather devised the asset allocation based on macro-economic concepts, which we'll explore below.

The 4 components of the 'Permanent Portfolio' each have a weight of 25%. The portfolio, in its original version, is allocated to U.S. assets. However, there are infinite local variations, especially regarding the bond/cash component."

Stocks: This part of the portfolio is designed to benefit from periods of economic growth.

Long-Term Bonds: This component provides stability and protection during economic recessions.

Gold: It serves as a "safe haven" against economic instability and inflation.

Cash: In the form of cash or similar, it provides liquidity and stability.

If we want to translate these assets into ETFs, the composition is as follows:

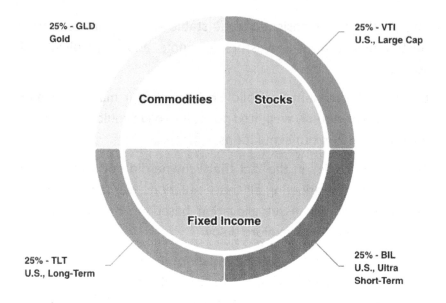

25% - GLD
Gold

25% - VTI
U.S., Large Cap

Commodities

Stocks

Fixed Income

25% - TLT
U.S., Long-Term

25% - BIL
U.S., Ultra
Short-Term

Since these 4 asset classes react differently to economic changes, the Permanent Portfolio can withstand a wide range of market scenarios without incurring significant losses.

It's a simple and conservative investment approach, although it's important to note that no investment strategy is completely immune to risk.

These are the main metrics:

Data Source: 1871-01 - 2023-11 Metric	Last 30Y	Last 60Y	Since 1871-01
Worst 3Y Rolling Return (%)	-1.50	-1.50	-10.10
Baseline 3Y Rolling Return (%)	3.31	3.83	2.58
%Fail 3Y Rolling Return	1.2%	0.6%	2.1%
Worst 7Y Rolling Return (%)	3.19	3.19	0.58
Baseline 7Y Rolling Return (%)	5.04	5.65	3.46
%Fail 7Y Rolling Return	0%	0%	0%
Worst 15Y Rolling Return (%)	5.07	5.07	2.64
Baseline 15Y Rolling Return (%)	6.61	6.77	3.83
Median 15Y Rolling Return (%)	7.18	7.83	4.93
%Fail 15Y Rolling Return	0%	0%	0%
Maximum Drawdown (%)	-15.92	-15.92	-30.61
Longest Negative Period (Y.M)	3Y.4M	3Y.4M	6Y.8M

Data Source: 1871-01 - 2023-11 Metric - US Inflation Adjusted	Last 30Y	Last 60Y	Since 1871-01
Worst 3Y Rolling Return (%)	-6.86	-6.86	-12.87
Baseline 3Y Rolling Return (%)	1.00	0.55	-0.07
%Fail 3Y Rolling Return	7.7%	10.5%	15.3%
Worst 7Y Rolling Return (%)	0.14	0.04	-7.21
Baseline 7Y Rolling Return (%)	2.66	2.62	0.84
%Fail 7Y Rolling Return	0%	0%	11.5%
Worst 15Y Rolling Return (%)	2.61	2.20	-2.93
Baseline 15Y Rolling Return (%)	4.28	3.41	1.01
Median 15Y Rolling Return (%)	4.85	4.64	3.54
%Fail 15Y Rolling Return	0%	0%	8%
Maximum Drawdown (%)	-23.32	-23.32	-45.48
Longest Negative Period (Y.M)	7Y.9M	7Y.9M	28Y.5M

Considering nominal returns, the portfolio is suitable for almost 'indefinite' use, independent of the time horizon. The metrics are satisfactory even in the short term (3 years) and are certainly better than those of the 60/40 Portfolio.

The Permanent Portfolio is counted among the best 'defensive' portfolios, yet it still ensures an acceptable return even in the long term.

Ray Dalio - All Weather Portfolio

Ray Dalio, founder of the world's largest hedge fund, Bridgewater Associates, is known for his theories on economic cycles and his ability to navigate through them.

He devised the All Weather Portfolio, made famous by Anthony Robbins' book 'Money: Master the Game'.

As the name suggests, the All Weather Portfolio is designed to be resilient even during market downturns and in all seasons (it is often also called All Seasons).

According to Dalio, using only stocks and bonds does not achieve optimal diversification. For this reason, his portfolio also includes gold and commodities.

The All Weather Portfolio is one of the most well-known and replicated globally, although Dalio himself acknowledges that in an ever-evolving economic world, it is sometimes advisable to reassess the asset allocation.

Below are the assets present in the portfolio:

30% U.S. Stocks: these can be shares of large companies, included in the S&P 500 index.

40% U.S. Long-Term Government Bonds.

15% U.S. Medium-Term Government Bonds.

7.5% Commodities: a diversified basket of commodities.

7.5% Gold.

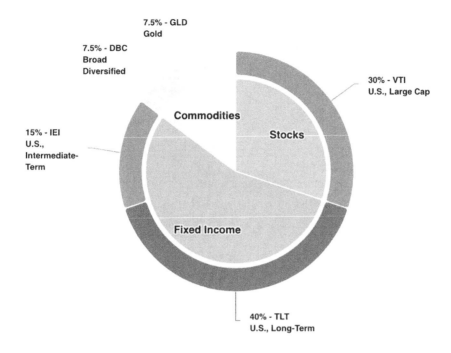

7.5% - GLD
Gold

7.5% - DBC
Broad
Diversified

30% - VTI
U.S., Large Cap

15% - IEI
U.S.,
Intermediate-
Term

Commodities

Stocks

Fixed Income

40% - TLT
U.S., Long-Term

What guarantees does a portfolio like this offer? For which strategies is it preferable? Let's examine the usual metrics.

Data Source: 1871-01 - 2023-11 Metric	Last 30Y	Last 60Y	Since 1871-01
Worst 3Y Rolling Return (%)	-2.92	-2.92	-12.66
Baseline 3Y Rolling Return (%)	4.54	4.48	2.56
%Fail 3Y Rolling Return	1.8%	1.8%	3.4%
Worst 7Y Rolling Return (%)	3.15	3.15	-0.03
Baseline 7Y Rolling Return (%)	6.37	6.76	3.52
%Fail 7Y Rolling Return	0%	0%	0.1%
Worst 15Y Rolling Return (%)	5.58	5.58	2.25
Baseline 15Y Rolling Return (%)	7.03	7.48	4.10
Median 15Y Rolling Return (%)	7.80	9.13	5.60
%Fail 15Y Rolling Return	0%	0%	0%
Maximum Drawdown (%)	-20.58	-20.58	-37.02
Longest Negative Period (Y.M)	3Y.10M	4Y.9M	7Y.0M

Data Source: 1871-01 - 2023-11 Metric - US Inflation Adjusted	Last 30Y	Last 60Y	Since 1871-01
Worst 3Y Rolling Return (%)	-8.18	-8.18	-14.36
Baseline 3Y Rolling Return (%)	2.51	-0.08	-0.26
%Fail 3Y Rolling Return	5.2%	15.3%	16.2%
Worst 7Y Rolling Return (%)	-0.36	-1.82	-7.47
Baseline 7Y Rolling Return (%)	4.26	1.13	0.59
%Fail 7Y Rolling Return	0.7%	4.9%	10.5%
Worst 15Y Rolling Return (%)	3.11	-0.24	-3.18
Baseline 15Y Rolling Return (%)	4.81	3.39	1.26
Median 15Y Rolling Return (%)	5.51	5.69	4.02
%Fail 15Y Rolling Return	0%	1.3%	4.4%
Maximum Drawdown (%)	-27.79	-27.79	-47.73
Longest Negative Period (Y.M)	8Y.9M	18Y.0M	28Y.5M

The same considerations as the Permanent Portfolio, mentioned earlier, apply here. There is a slightly higher minimum risk, as seen from the short-term metrics and slightly worse drawdowns, but in return, the long-term gains are higher.

Tyler - Golden Butterfly Portfolio

The Golden Butterfly portfolio is a strategy aimed at achieving a balance between long-term returns and stability.

It was developed by Tyler, a member of the Bogleheads forum, an online community dedicated to investments and devoted to the principles of John C. Bogle, the founder of Vanguard Group and an advocate of passive investing.

Tyler is also the creator of the *PortfolioCharts.com* website, a spectacular site that inspired us in the creation of ours. The composition of the Golden Butterfly portfolio is as follows:

20% U.S. Stocks

20% Small-Cap Value Stocks

20% U.S. Long-Term Government Bonds

20% U.S. Short-Term Government Bonds

20% Gold

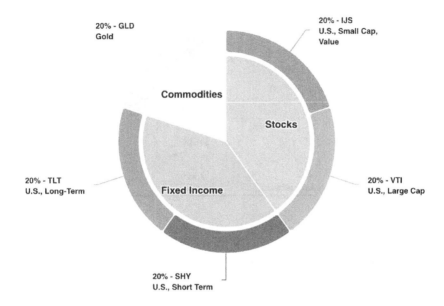

The Golden Butterfly portfolio is also a portfolio that could work well for almost any purpose: all metrics, both for short-term goals and long-term objectives, are remarkable.

Data Source: 1927-01 - 2023-11 Metric	Last 30Y	Last 60Y	Since 1927-01
Worst 3Y Rolling Return (%)	0.58	0.58	-17.91
Baseline 3Y Rolling Return (%)	4.71	5.25	4.12
%Fail 3Y Rolling Return	0%	0%	4.4%
Worst 7Y Rolling Return (%)	4.29	4.29	1.97
Baseline 7Y Rolling Return (%)	6.33	7.07	5.90
%Fail 7Y Rolling Return	0%	0%	0%
Worst 15Y Rolling Return (%)	5.98	5.98	3.74
Baseline 15Y Rolling Return (%)	7.47	8.00	6.72
Median 15Y Rolling Return (%)	8.12	9.53	8.30
%Fail 15Y Rolling Return	0%	0%	0%
Maximum Drawdown (%)	-17.79	-17.79	-48.31
Longest Negative Period (Y.M)	3Y.3M	3Y.3M	6Y.2M

Data Source: 1927-01 - 2023-11 Metric - US Inflation Adjusted	Last 30Y	Last 60Y	Since 1927-01
Worst 3Y Rolling Return (%)	-4.79	-4.79	-11.40
Baseline 3Y Rolling Return (%)	2.36	2.02	0.97
%Fail 3Y Rolling Return	5.5%	7.2%	11.3%
Worst 7Y Rolling Return (%)	0.73	0.30	-1.69
Baseline 7Y Rolling Return (%)	4.06	3.81	2.87
%Fail 7Y Rolling Return	0%	0%	1.8%
Worst 15Y Rolling Return (%)	3.52	3.20	1.09
Baseline 15Y Rolling Return (%)	5.13	4.83	3.80
Median 15Y Rolling Return (%)	5.79	6.03	5.39
%Fail 15Y Rolling Return	0%	0%	0%
Maximum Drawdown (%)	-23.38	-24.09	-34.73
Longest Negative Period (Y.M)	5Y.11M	6Y.5M	12Y.7M

Looking at nominal returns, in the last 60 years, there has never been a negative return over a 3-year period (%Fail = 0%). However, the longest negative period is slightly over 3 years. It may seem counterintuitive, but there are rare combinations that can make even this happen. In any case, the Golden Butterfly is a living example of a resilient portfolio, with remarkable metrics across all time horizons and excellent long-term returns.

Gyroscopic Investing - Desert Portfolio

The user Desert, on the Gyroscopic Investing forum, created this simple and effective portfolio.

It is one of our favorite portfolios because, like the Golden Butterfly, it is well-suited for both short and long-term goals. Moreover, it is very simple to implement and maintain as it consists of only 3 straightforward assets.

30% U.S. Stocks

60% U.S. Medium-Term Government Bonds

10% Gold

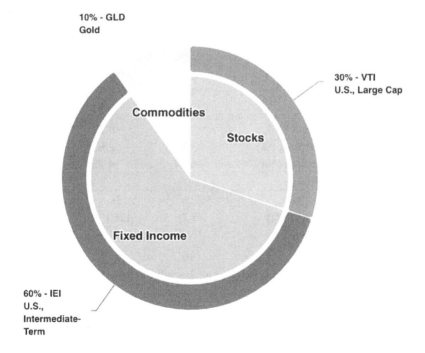

It is among the portfolios with the best return/drawdown ratio.

Data Source: 1871-01 - 2023-11 Metric	Last 30Y	Last 60Y	Since 1871-01
Worst 3Y Rolling Return (%)	0.35	0.11	-10.95
Baseline 3Y Rolling Return (%)	4.03	4.59	2.84
%Fail 3Y Rolling Return	0%	0%	2.1%
Worst 7Y Rolling Return (%)	4.04	4.04	0.61
Baseline 7Y Rolling Return (%)	5.23	5.97	3.79
%Fail 7Y Rolling Return	0%	0%	0%
Worst 15Y Rolling Return (%)	4.92	4.92	2.35
Baseline 15Y Rolling Return (%)	6.03	6.58	4.23
Median 15Y Rolling Return (%)	6.62	8.35	5.86
%Fail 15Y Rolling Return	0%	0%	0%
Maximum Drawdown (%)	-14.72	-14.72	-33.15
Longest Negative Period (Y.M)	3Y.2M	3Y.3M	6Y.8M

Data Source: 1871-01 - 2023-11 Metric - US Inflation Adjusted	Last 30Y	Last 60Y	Since 1871-01
Worst 3Y Rolling Return (%)	-5.11	-5.11	-13.19
Baseline 3Y Rolling Return (%)	2.07	0.63	0.10
%Fail 3Y Rolling Return	5.5%	11.8%	14.7%
Worst 7Y Rolling Return (%)	0.50	-1.01	-7.17
Baseline 7Y Rolling Return (%)	3.11	1.31	0.81
%Fail 7Y Rolling Return	0%	2.2%	9.4%
Worst 15Y Rolling Return (%)	2.47	0.35	-2.83
Baseline 15Y Rolling Return (%)	3.81	2.89	1.34
Median 15Y Rolling Return (%)	4.34	4.73	4.08
%Fail 15Y Rolling Return	0%	0%	3.5%
Maximum Drawdown (%)	-20.97	-20.97	-46.37
Longest Negative Period (Y.M)	6Y.2M	13Y.10M	28Y.2M

We are at Golden Butterfly levels: excellent metrics from every perspective.

The fact that it consists of only 3 assets makes it accessible to everyone, even with limited budgets.

Classic Lazy Portfolios

On the *LazyPortfolioEtf.com* website, you can find dozens of portfolios, many of which are designed by renowned economists or industry experts.

Below, we present the rankings of Lazy Portfolios on the site, organized based on the metrics we have already discussed.

We have chosen the so-called 'classic' Lazy Portfolios, which have a longer history, at least 30 years.

In this case as well, if you prefer, you can focus only on those with a deeper history (60 years or more).

We invite you to explore, on our website, all the Lazy Portfolios, in search of the one that inspires you the most.

Ranking: Baseline 3Y Return

Order by **Baseline 3Y Return - Last 30 Years** (from 1993-12 to 2023-11)

Portfolio	3Y Rolling Annualized Return (%)			7Y Rolling Annualized Return (%)			15Y Rolling Annualized Return (%)				Max Draw-down (%)	Long Neg Period (Y.M)
	Worst	Base ▼	%Fail	Worst	Base	%Fail	Worst	Base	Median	%Fail		
Shield Strategy	-5.00	5.05	3.7%	4.31	6.67	0%	6.31	7.48	8.43	0%	-19.36	3Y.8M
Golden Butterfly	0.58	4.71	0%	4.29	6.33	0%	5.98	7.47	8.12	0%	-17.79	3Y.3M
All Weather Portfolio	-2.92	4.54	1.8%	3.15	6.37	0%	5.58	7.03	7.80	0%	-20.58	3Y.10M
Stocks/Bonds 20/80 Momentum	-4.27	4.25	4.6%	1.99	5.20	0%	4.03	5.41	5.90	0%	-17.91	4Y.5M
Aim comfortable trip	-1.22	4.14	1.2%	4.49	6.07	0%	5.25	6.78	7.60	0%	-20.15	3Y.3M
Talmud Portfolio	-10.82	4.06	7.1%	1.35	6.15	0%	5.75	7.16	7.91	0%	-40.17	5Y.5M
Late Sixties and Beyond	-9.76	4.05	7.4%	2.45	6.19	0%	4.95	6.93	7.88	0%	-41.80	5Y.2M
Desert Portfolio	0.35	4.03	0%	4.04	5.23	0%	4.92	6.03	6.62	0%	-14.72	3Y.2M
Stocks/Bonds 20/80	-2.58	3.97	3.4%	2.21	4.60	0%	3.93	5.05	5.58	0%	-16.57	4Y.2M
One-Decision Portfolio	-7.87	3.90	6.8%	1.40	5.06	0%	4.80	5.83	6.47	0%	-31.96	5Y.4M
Marc Faber Portfolio	-3.16	3.80	1.2%	3.58	5.46	0%	4.95	6.92	8.61	0%	-28.82	3Y.5M
Dynamic 60/40 Income	-12.45	3.74	6.8%	-0.10	5.05	0.4%	4.43	5.82	6.67	0%	-41.44	7Y.3M
Aim Bold Strategy	-7.69	3.74	7.1%	3.86	6.53	0%	5.99	6.97	8.05	0%	-30.09	4Y.5M
All Country World 20/80	-2.75	3.74	4.9%	1.75	4.59	0%	3.53	5.23	6.07	0%	-17.97	4Y.4M
LifeStrategy Income Fund	-2.77	3.66	4.6%	1.81	4.51	0%	3.62	5.11	5.67	0%	-16.61	4Y.4M
In Saecula Saeculorum	-2.08	3.65	2.2%	3.64	6.09	0%	6.06	6.74	7.34	0%	-20.39	3Y.7M
Simplified Permanent Portfolio	-1.62	3.60	1.2%	3.15	5.07	0%	5.26	7.00	7.77	0%	-16.43	3Y.4M
Sheltered Sam 50/50	-5.25	3.58	3.4%	3.12	5.17	0%	4.21	5.48	6.54	0%	-28.23	4Y.5M
Dynamic 40/60 Income	-7.96	3.58	4%	1.44	5.28	0%	4.34	5.60	6.67	0%	-29.84	5Y.9M
Developed World ex-US 20/80	-3.44	3.51	6.5%	1.32	4.37	0%	3.40	5.00	6.01	0%	-16.80	4Y.11M
Sheltered Sam 40/60	-3.15	3.50	1.2%	3.26	4.70	0%	3.84	5.02	6.12	0%	-22.05	4Y.2M

Order by **Baseline 3Y Return - Last 30 Years** (from 1993-12 to 2023-11) - **US Infl. Adjusted**

Portfolio	3Y Rolling Annualized Return (%)			7Y Rolling Annualized Return (%)			15Y Rolling Annualized Return (%)				Max Draw-down (%)	Long Neg Period (Y.M)
	Worst	Base ▼	%Fail	Worst	Base	%Fail	Worst	Base	Median	%Fail		
All Weather Portfolio	-8.18	2.51	5.2%	-0.36	4.26	0.7%	3.11	4.81	5.51	0%	-27.79	8Y.9M
Golden Butterfly	-4.79	2.36	5.5%	0.73	4.06	0%	3.52	5.13	5.79	0%	-23.38	5Y.11M
Stocks/Bonds 20/80 Momentum	-9.45	2.19	6.8%	-1.46	2.80	4.7%	1.60	3.24	3.67	0%	-28.68	9Y.9M
Desert Portfolio	-5.11	2.07	5.5%	0.50	3.11	0%	2.47	3.81	4.34	0%	-20.97	6Y.2M
Aim comfortable trip	-3.36	2.06	9.5%	1.45	4.06	0%	2.79	4.50	5.20	0%	-22.06	6Y.5M
LifeStrategy Income Fund	-8.03	2.01	8%	-1.63	2.60	6.1%	1.20	2.95	3.49	0%	-25.42	11Y.1M
All Country World 20/80	-8.01	2.00	8.6%	-1.71	2.81	6.9%	1.11	3.07	3.85	0%	-26.16	11Y.1M
Stocks/Bonds 20/80	-7.85	1.81	7.1%	-1.25	2.37	5.1%	1.50	2.87	3.31	0%	-25.05	9Y.10M
Shield Strategy	-7.29	1.78	12%	1.63	4.00	0%	4.06	4.99	6.00	0%	-24.25	8Y.11M
Larry Portfolio	-6.89	1.65	6.8%	-1.91	2.36	7.2%	1.06	3.15	4.73	0%	-25.06	12Y.3M
Simplified Permanent Portfolio	-6.96	1.62	6.2%	0.10	2.98	0%	2.82	4.65	5.45	0%	-23.93	7Y.3M
Sheltered Sam 40/60	-5.25	1.47	11.1%	0.21	2.64	0%	1.42	2.98	3.81	0%	-23.25	7Y.7M
Developed World ex-US 20/80	-7.99	1.46	9.5%	-2.14	2.52	7.6%	0.98	2.66	3.75	0%	-25.75	11Y.2M
High Yield Bonds Income	-9.14	1.41	11.1%	-2.29	2.95	6.9%	1.53	3.68	5.03	0%	-30.40	11Y.8M
Dynamic 40/60 Income	-9.95	1.40	13.5%	-1.09	2.77	1.4%	1.91	3.50	4.38	0%	-31.05	9Y.2M
Rob Arnott Portfolio	-5.49	1.40	8.9%	-0.56	2.97	1.1%	1.77	3.53	4.72	0%	-23.93	9Y.5M
Marc Faber Portfolio	-5.24	1.32	8%	0.56	3.05	0%	2.49	4.41	6.12	0%	-29.75	6Y.3M
Robo Advisor 20	-5.92	1.29	7.1%	-1.48	1.69	7.2%	0.36	2.00	2.92	0%	-20.60	13Y.1M
Edge Select Conservative	-5.74	1.20	8.6%	-0.95	2.21	5.8%	0.94	2.39	2.84	0%	-20.50	10Y.0M
GAA Global Asset Allocation	-5.91	1.18	9.5%	0.06	3.85	0%	1.99	4.09	4.99	0%	-26.03	8Y.9M
Sheltered Sam 30/70	-4.13	1.16	8%	-0.47	2.24	1.4%	1.02	2.46	3.36	0%	-18.48	9Y.8M

Order by **Baseline 3Y Return** - Last 60 Years (from 1963-12 to 2023-11)

Portfolio	3Y Rolling Annualized Return (%)			7Y Rolling Annualized Return (%)			15Y Rolling Annualized Return (%)				Max Draw-down (%)	Long Neg Period (Y.M)
	Worst	Base ▼	%Fail	Worst	Base	%Fail	Worst	Base	Median	%Fail		
Golden Butterfly	0.58	5.25	0%	4.29	7.07	0%	5.98	8.00	9.53	0%	-17.79	3Y.3M
In Saecula Saeculorum	-2.08	4.62	1.2%	3.55	6.48	0%	6.06	7.16	8.90	0%	-20.39	3Y.7M
Desert Portfolio	0.11	4.59	0%	4.04	5.97	0%	4.92	6.58	8.35	0%	-14.72	3Y.3M
All Weather Portfolio	-2.92	4.48	1.8%	3.15	6.76	0%	5.58	7.48	9.13	0%	-20.58	4Y.9M
One-Decision Portfolio	-7.87	4.38	4.7%	1.40	5.43	0%	4.80	6.42	9.20	0%	-31.96	5Y.4M
Talmud Portfolio	-10.82	4.17	6.9%	0.39	5.82	0%	5.75	7.49	9.81	0%	-40.17	6Y.3M
Simplified Permanent Portfolio	-1.62	4.06	0.7%	3.15	6.11	0%	5.26	7.42	8.52	0%	-16.43	3Y.4M
Stocks/Bonds 20/80	-2.58	4.03	1.6%	2.21	5.02	0%	3.93	5.42	7.67	0%	-16.57	4Y.2M
Stocks/Bonds 40/60	-2.41	3.88	1.8%	2.10	5.36	0%	5.22	6.06	8.48	0%	-19.17	4Y.2M
Permanent Portfolio	-1.50	3.83	0.6%	3.19	5.65	0%	5.07	6.77	7.83	0%	-15.92	3Y.4M
Stocks/Bonds 60/40	-6.40	3.68	7.7%	0.56	5.28	0%	5.21	6.50	9.22	0%	-30.55	9Y.2M
Simple Path to Wealth	-9.99	3.23	10.5%	-0.70	4.97	0.3%	5.00	6.60	9.70	0%	-38.53	10Y.2M
Stocks/Bonds 80/20	-11.24	3.09	10.8%	-1.13	4.86	0.6%	4.90	6.63	9.87	0%	-41.09	10Y.2M
Total Bond US	-5.59	2.53	2.6%	-0.23	4.05	0.3%	2.36	4.28	7.03	0%	-17.28	7Y.6M
Warren Buffett Portfolio	-13.74	2.27	12.6%	-2.48	3.81	1.4%	4.09	5.85	10.01	0%	-45.52	11Y.0M
10-year Treasury	-7.79	2.14	6.1%	-1.15	3.83	1.3%	2.09	4.59	7.58	0%	-23.18	10Y.6M
US Stocks	-16.22	1.87	12.6%	-3.00	4.15	1.7%	4.37	6.49	10.48	0%	-50.84	11Y.7M
Robo Advisor 0	-1.33	1.52	2.3%	0.47	1.55	0%	1.02	2.49	6.61	0%	-8.48	4Y.1M
Short Term Treasury	-1.26	1.29	2.3%	0.39	1.39	0%	0.87	2.34	6.67	0%	-8.52	3Y.11M
Gold	-15.32	-6.07	32.9%	-6.75	-2.30	29.7%	-3.63	-1.12	7.05	19.6%	-61.78	27Y.5M

Order by **Baseline 3Y Return** - Last 60 Years (from 1963-12 to 2023-11) - **US Infl. Adjusted**

Portfolio	3Y Rolling Annualized Return (%)			7Y Rolling Annualized Return (%)			15Y Rolling Annualized Return (%)				Max Draw-down (%)	Long Neg Period (Y.M)
	Worst	Base ▼	%Fail	Worst	Base	%Fail	Worst	Base	Median	%Fail		
Golden Butterfly	-4.79	2.02	7.2%	0.30	3.81	0%	3.20	4.83	6.03	0%	-24.09	6Y.5M
Simplified Permanent Portfolio	-6.96	0.80	9.8%	-0.33	2.71	0.2%	1.81	3.63	5.14	0%	-25.58	9Y.1M
Desert Portfolio	-5.11	0.63	11.8%	-1.01	1.31	2.2%	0.35	2.89	4.73	0%	-20.97	13Y.10M
Permanent Portfolio	-6.86	0.55	10.5%	0.04	2.62	0%	2.20	3.41	4.64	0%	-23.32	7Y.9M
Talmud Portfolio	-12.75	0.04	14.9%	-5.31	1.24	10.1%	-0.16	3.88	6.04	0.7%	-42.36	16Y.5M
All Weather Portfolio	-8.18	-0.08	15.3%	-1.82	1.13	4.9%	-0.24	3.39	5.69	1.3%	-27.79	18Y.0M
One-Decision Portfolio	-10.46	-0.16	15.5%	-4.14	1.36	9.6%	0.20	3.02	4.83	0%	-34.04	14Y.5M
In Saecula Saeculorum	-6.04	-0.17	15.5%	-2.33	1.96	3.8%	0.29	3.76	5.35	0%	-26.94	14Y.2M
Stocks/Bonds 20/80	-7.85	-1.23	18.4%	-4.05	-0.24	15.9%	-1.56	1.77	3.82	8.9%	-30.21	18Y.9M
Stocks/Bonds 40/60	-9.10	-1.27	21%	-3.85	0.66	12.2%	-1.10	2.66	4.54	6.5%	-30.32	18Y.8M
Robo Advisor 0	-6.71	-1.41	36.1%	-3.41	-0.81	27.5%	-1.43	0.02	2.33	14.6%	-24.64	25Y.2M
Stocks/Bonds 60/40	-12.03	-1.46	21.8%	-5.15	0.92	12.1%	-1.04	2.98	5.51	3.1%	-38.92	18Y.2M
Short Term Treasury	-6.65	-1.57	36.2%	-3.25	-0.94	28.1%	-1.59	-0.10	2.29	16.8%	-23.89	25Y.8M
Total Bond US	-10.69	-1.75	25.1%	-4.53	-0.74	19.9%	-2.30	0.30	3.30	11.8%	-35.11	20Y.8M
Simple Path to Wealth	-14.36	-1.79	20.9%	-6.34	0.75	12.9%	-1.14	2.93	6.11	2.4%	-45.02	18Y.1M
Stocks/Bonds 80/20	-15.17	-1.96	20.4%	-6.75	0.67	13%	-1.19	2.85	6.31	2.4%	-46.99	18Y.0M
10-year Treasury	-13.24	-2.26	26.3%	-6.12	-1.45	23.6%	-3.52	0.40	3.98	13.7%	-45.61	21Y.5M
US Stocks	-18.54	-2.55	20.6%	-8.51	0.01	14.9%	-1.47	2.39	6.97	2.2%	-54.53	18Y.1M
Warren Buffett Portfolio	-16.24	-3.11	23.8%	-7.74	-0.52	18.1%	-2.09	2.10	6.51	9.4%	-50.04	18Y.8M
Gold	-20.28	-9.47	51.1%	-11.38	-5.24	44.3%	-7.77	-4.24	3.96	33.1%	-82.57	43Y.11M*

Order by **Baseline 3Y Return** - **All data** (from 1871/1927 to 2023-11)

Portfolio	3Y Rolling Annualized Return (%)			7Y Rolling Annualized Return (%)			15Y Rolling Annualized Return (%)				Max Draw-down (%)	Long Neg Period (Y.M)
	Worst	Base ▼	%Fail	Worst	Base	%Fail	Worst	Base	Median	%Fail		
Golden Butterfly	-17.91	4.12	4.4%	1.97	5.90	0%	3.74	6.72	8.30	0%	-48.31	6Y.2M
Stocks/Bonds 20/80	-5.37	3.02	1.7%	1.80	3.78	0%	2.76	4.13	5.14	0%	-18.94	5Y.1M
One-Decision Portfolio	-17.20	2.89	8.2%	-0.37	4.77	0.1%	1.95	5.74	6.96	0%	-47.77	12Y.10M
Desert Portfolio	-10.95	2.84	2.1%	0.61	3.79	0%	2.35	4.23	5.86	0%	-33.15	6Y.8M
Talmud Portfolio	-21.82	2.69	9.4%	-1.75	4.74	0.9%	1.47	5.91	7.86	0%	-57.05	13Y.4M
Permanent Portfolio	-10.10	2.58	2.1%	0.58	3.46	0%	2.64	3.83	4.93	0%	-30.61	6Y.8M
All Weather Portfolio	-12.66	2.56	3.4%	-0.03	3.52	0.1%	2.25	4.10	5.60	0%	-37.02	7Y.0M
Stocks/Bonds 40/60	-15.47	2.52	3.9%	-0.11	4.09	0.1%	2.53	4.88	6.22	0%	-43.68	7Y.1M
In Saecula Saeculorum	-18.75	2.34	5.6%	-1.08	3.81	0.1%	2.31	4.69	6.79	0%	-50.22	8Y.9M
Total Bond US	-5.59	2.15	1.6%	-0.23	2.57	0.1%	1.40	2.67	4.00	0%	-17.28	7Y.6M
Simplified Permanent Portfolio	-9.97	1.91	3.9%	0.56	2.83	0%	2.01	3.67	4.97	0%	-30.22	6Y.8M
Stocks/Bonds 60/40	-25.23	1.83	9.4%	-2.67	4.06	0.7%	2.25	5.30	7.17	0%	-62.03	12Y.10M
Robo Advisor 0	-1.33	1.56	1.1%	0.47	1.57	0%	1.00	2.22	4.38	0%	-8.48	4Y.1M
Short Term Treasury	-1.26	1.46	1.1%	0.39	1.52	0%	0.87	2.11	4.40	0%	-8.52	3Y.11M
10-year Treasury	-7.79	1.29	6.1%	-1.15	1.80	0.5%	0.98	2.14	4.04	0%	-23.18	10Y.6M
Simple Path to Wealth	-32.34	0.98	12.7%	-4.94	3.91	2.2%	1.52	5.50	7.75	0%	-72.36	13Y.7M
Stocks/Bonds 80/20	-34.67	0.72	13.4%	-5.77	3.81	2.6%	1.19	5.55	7.93	0%	-75.27	13Y.10M
Warren Buffett Portfolio	-38.18	0.02	14.9%	-5.83	3.11	3.1%	-0.02	5.32	8.03	0.1%	-79.29	15Y.1M
US Stocks	-43.81	-0.56	15.9%	-9.49	3.29	4.2%	-0.35	5.49	8.60	0.1%	-84.60	15Y.8M
Gold	-15.32	-1.61	23.9%	-6.75	-1.32	22.2%	-3.63	-0.50	0.05	21.3%	-61.78	62Y.0M

Order by **Baseline 3Y Return** - **All data** (from 1871/1927 to 2023-11) - **US Infl. Adjusted**

Portfolio	3Y Rolling Annualized Return (%)			7Y Rolling Annualized Return (%)			15Y Rolling Annualized Return (%)				Max Draw-down (%)	Long Neg Period (Y.M)
	Worst	Base ▼	%Fail	Worst	Base	%Fail	Worst	Base	Median	%Fail		
Golden Butterfly	-11.40	0.97	11.3%	-1.69	2.87	1.8%	1.09	3.80	5.39	0%	-34.73	12Y.7M
Desert Portfolio	-13.19	0.10	14.7%	-7.17	0.81	9.4%	-2.83	1.34	4.08	3.5%	-46.37	28Y.2M
Permanent Portfolio	-12.87	-0.07	15.3%	-7.21	0.84	11.5%	-2.93	1.01	3.54	8%	-45.48	28Y.5M
All Weather Portfolio	-14.36	-0.26	16.2%	-7.47	0.59	10.5%	-3.18	1.26	4.02	4.4%	-47.73	28Y.5M
In Saecula Saeculorum	-12.96	-0.26	16.1%	-6.92	1.32	8.1%	-2.73	1.99	4.72	2.5%	-45.23	23Y.5M
Simplified Permanent Portfolio	-13.46	-0.41	16.3%	-8.12	0.32	12.3%	-3.95	0.80	3.74	8.8%	-49.37	33Y.9M
Talmud Portfolio	-15.62	-0.56	16.2%	-5.31	1.27	8.3%	-0.52	2.02	4.93	1%	-45.76	18Y.9M
One-Decision Portfolio	-10.63	-0.59	16.9%	-4.14	1.12	8.7%	0.17	1.72	4.14	0%	-34.04	14Y.5M
Stocks/Bonds 40/60	-12.93	-0.73	17.4%	-6.68	0.81	11.1%	-2.37	1.54	4.26	3.9%	-45.57	23Y.5M
Stocks/Bonds 20/80	-13.27	-0.78	17.7%	-7.21	-0.25	15.9%	-2.77	0.61	3.27	8%	-46.65	28Y.4M
Stocks/Bonds 60/40	-19.29	-0.93	18.1%	-6.22	1.42	9.4%	-2.07	2.33	5.45	2.6%	-52.05	21Y.11M
Simple Path to Wealth	-26.97	-1.25	18.8%	-6.34	1.57	9.9%	-1.97	2.62	6.11	2.3%	-65.10	20Y.6M
Stocks/Bonds 80/20	-29.49	-1.56	18.8%	-6.75	1.50	10.1%	-1.98	2.64	6.29	2.2%	-68.77	20Y.6M
Robo Advisor 0	-12.40	-1.95	29.9%	-7.12	-1.34	25.6%	-3.23	-0.52	1.89	19.3%	-45.36	52Y.0M
Short Term Treasury	-12.29	-2.01	30.1%	-7.07	-1.41	25.7%	-3.27	-0.49	1.90	19.8%	-45.12	52Y.1M
Total Bond US	-13.89	-2.23	26.6%	-7.81	-1.23	25.1%	-3.27	-0.65	2.01	21.8%	-48.08	51Y.10M
10-year Treasury	-13.92	-2.32	28.7%	-8.73	-1.77	29%	-4.52	-1.17	2.36	28.1%	-58.48	85Y.5M
Warren Buffett Portfolio	-33.28	-2.46	20.5%	-7.74	0.68	12.6%	-2.12	2.23	6.43	4.7%	-73.85	20Y.4M
US Stocks	-39.36	-2.49	20.7%	-8.51	0.77	12.6%	-2.10	2.40	6.93	2.5%	-80.55	26Y.4M
Gold	-20.28	-5.84	58.4%	-11.38	-4.43	56.9%	-7.77	-3.77	-0.10	50.5%	-82.57	132Y.3M

Ranking: Maximum Drawdown

Order by **Maximum Drawdown - Last 30 Years** (from 1993-12 to 2023-11)

Portfolio	3Y Rolling Annualized Return (%)			7Y Rolling Annualized Return (%)			15Y Rolling Annualized Return (%)				Max Draw-down (%) ▼	Long Neg Period (Y.M)
	Worst	Base	%Fail	Worst	Base	%Fail	Worst	Base	Median	%Fail		
Short Term Treasury	-1.26	0.52	4.9%	0.39	0.72	0%	0.87	1.83	2.71	0%	-5.36	3Y.11M
Robo Advisor 0	-1.33	0.62	4.9%	0.47	0.87	0%	1.02	1.98	2.85	0%	-5.86	4Y.1M
Sheltered Sam 0/100	-1.65	0.77	7.1%	0.55	1.34	0%	1.59	2.64	3.81	0%	-8.61	4Y.1M
Robo Advisor 10	-0.80	1.75	4%	1.24	2.13	0%	1.99	3.11	3.91	0%	-8.91	3Y.9M
Sheltered Sam 10/90	-0.58	1.78	1.2%	1.58	2.22	0%	2.31	3.38	4.31	0%	-9.93	3Y.5M
Sheltered Sam 20/80	0.42	2.53	0%	2.32	3.12	0%	2.98	3.98	4.86	0%	-11.24	2Y.11M
Conservative Income	-2.23	2.02	4.6%	0.90	2.43	0%	2.55	3.61	4.51	0%	-11.50	4Y.4M
Robo Advisor 20	-0.68	2.73	2.2%	1.96	3.35	0%	2.76	4.12	5.05	0%	-12.16	3Y.9M
Edge Select Conservative	-0.39	3.23	1.5%	2.52	4.10	0%	3.34	4.53	5.05	0%	-12.44	3Y.3M
Dimensional Retirement Income Fund	0.33	2.84	0%	2.41	3.66	0%	3.44	4.40	5.09	0%	-12.91	2Y.10M
Desert Portfolio	0.35	4.03	0%	4.04	5.23	0%	4.92	6.03	6.62	0%	-14.72	3Y.2M
US Inflation Protection	-2.68	1.49	6.2%	0.61	2.34	0%	2.51	3.78	5.31	0%	-14.76	6Y.5M
Total Bond Developed World ex-US	-4.35	3.16	6.2%	0.18	3.98	0%	3.31	4.85	5.62	0%	-14.88	6Y.5M
Permanent Portfolio	-1.50	3.31	1.2%	3.19	5.04	0%	5.07	6.61	7.18	0%	-15.92	3Y.4M
Larry Portfolio	-1.57	3.48	2.2%	1.53	4.05	0%	3.48	5.19	6.90	0%	-15.96	4Y.4M
Simplified Permanent Portfolio	-1.62	3.60	1.2%	3.15	5.07	0%	5.26	7.00	7.77	0%	-16.43	3Y.4M
Stocks/Bonds 20/80	-2.58	3.97	3.4%	2.21	4.60	0%	3.93	5.05	5.58	0%	-16.57	4Y.2M
Sheltered Sam 30/70	-1.11	2.93	0.3%	2.83	3.97	0%	3.43	4.52	5.53	0%	-16.58	3Y.5M
LifeStrategy Income Fund	-2.77	3.66	4.6%	1.81	4.51	0%	3.62	5.11	5.67	0%	-16.61	4Y.4M
Developed World ex-US 20/80	-3.44	3.51	6.5%	1.32	4.37	0%	3.40	5.00	6.01	0%	-16.80	4Y.11M
Total Bond US	-5.59	2.05	5.5%	-0.23	2.60	0.7%	2.36	3.62	4.64	0%	-17.28	7Y.6M

Order by **Maximum Drawdown - Last 30 Years** (from 1993-12 to 2023-11) - **US Infl. Adjusted**

Portfolio	3Y Rolling Annualized Return (%)			7Y Rolling Annualized Return (%)			15Y Rolling Annualized Return (%)				Max Draw-down (%) ▼	Long Neg Period (Y.M)
	Worst	Base	%Fail	Worst	Base	%Fail	Worst	Base	Median	%Fail		
Sheltered Sam 20/80	-5.02	0.95	7.1%	-1.17	1.41	6.1%	0.58	1.86	2.74	0%	-17.92	12Y.6M
Dimensional Retirement Income Fund	-4.32	1.08	7.7%	-0.40	1.59	1.8%	1.04	2.31	2.94	0%	-18.08	10Y.9M
Sheltered Sam 30/70	-4.13	1.16	8%	-0.47	2.24	1.4%	1.02	2.46	3.36	0%	-18.48	9Y.8M
Sheltered Sam 10/90	-5.98	0.23	12.6%	-1.88	0.47	7.6%	-0.06	1.22	2.22	0.5%	-18.86	16Y.0M
Robo Advisor 10	-6.19	0.28	11.1%	-2.12	0.41	8.3%	-0.37	0.98	1.84	8.8%	-19.07	17Y.1M
Sheltered Sam 0/100	-7.00	-0.85	30.8%	-2.61	-0.48	21.3%	-0.76	0.52	1.74	8.8%	-20.07	21Y.3M
Edge Select Conservative	-5.74	1.20	8.6%	-0.95	2.21	5.8%	0.94	2.39	2.84	0%	-20.50	10Y.0M
Robo Advisor 20	-5.92	1.29	7.1%	-1.48	1.69	7.2%	0.36	2.00	2.92	0%	-20.60	13Y.1M
Eliminate Fat Tails	-5.15	1.06	10.2%	-0.88	1.56	4%	0.53	2.42	3.70	0%	-20.64	12Y.10M
Desert Portfolio	-5.11	2.07	5.5%	0.50	3.11	0%	2.47	3.81	4.34	0%	-20.97	6Y.2M
Aim comfortable trip	-3.36	2.06	9.5%	1.45	4.06	0%	2.79	4.50	5.28	0%	-22.06	5Y.5M
Robo Advisor 0	-6.71	-1.25	46.8%	-2.84	-0.86	32.9%	-1.43	-0.14	0.79	23.2%	-22.33	25Y.2M
Conservative Income	-7.52	0.28	11.7%	-2.54	0.78	8.3%	0.16	1.48	2.43	0%	-22.37	15Y.11M
Sheltered Sam 40/60	-5.25	1.47	11.1%	0.21	2.64	0%	1.42	2.98	3.81	0%	-23.25	7Y.7M
Permanent Portfolio	-6.86	1.00	7.7%	0.14	2.66	0%	2.61	4.28	4.85	0%	-23.32	7Y.9M
Golden Butterfly	-4.79	2.36	5.5%	0.73	4.06	0%	3.52	5.13	5.79	0%	-23.38	5Y.11M
US Inflation Protection	-7.96	-0.43	20.3%	-2.39	0.10	13.7%	0.17	1.68	3.23	0%	-23.74	15Y.9M
Short Term Treasury	-6.65	-1.40	47.4%	-2.90	-1.02	35.4%	-1.59	-0.29	0.65	29.8%	-23.76	25Y.8M
Rob Arnott Portfolio	-5.49	1.40	8.9%	-0.56	2.97	1.1%	1.77	3.53	4.72	0%	-23.93	9Y.5M
Simplified Permanent Portfolio	-6.96	1.62	6.2%	0.10	2.98	0%	2.82	4.65	5.45	0%	-23.93	7Y.3M
In Saecula Saeculorum	-4.44	0.60	12.6%	1.06	3.11	0%	3.59	4.29	4.97	0%	-23.97	8Y.6M

Order by **Maximum Drawdown - Last 60 Years** (from 1963-12 to 2023-11)

Portfolio	3Y Rolling Annualized Return (%)			7Y Rolling Annualized Return (%)			15Y Rolling Annualized Return (%)				Max Draw-down (%) ▼	Long Neg Period (Y.M)
	Worst	Base	%Fail	Worst	Base	%Fail	Worst	Base	Median	%Fail		
Robo Advisor 0	-1.33	1.52	2.3%	0.47	1.55	0%	1.02	2.49	6.61	0%	-8.48	4Y.1M
Short Term Treasury	-1.26	1.29	2.3%	0.39	1.39	0%	0.87	2.34	6.67	0%	-8.52	3Y.11M
Desert Portfolio	0.11	4.59	0%	4.04	5.97	0%	4.92	6.58	8.35	0%	-14.72	3Y.3M
Permanent Portfolio	-1.50	3.83	0.6%	3.19	5.65	0%	5.07	6.77	7.83	0%	-15.92	3Y.4M
Simplified Permanent Portfolio	-1.62	4.06	0.7%	3.15	6.11	0%	5.26	7.42	8.52	0%	-16.43	3Y.4M
Stocks/Bonds 20/80	-2.58	4.03	1.6%	2.21	5.02	0%	3.93	5.42	7.67	0%	-16.57	4Y.2M
Total Bond US	-5.59	2.53	2.6%	-0.23	4.05	0.3%	2.36	4.28	7.03	0%	-17.28	7Y.6M
Golden Butterfly	0.58	5.25	0%	4.29	7.07	0%	5.98	8.00	9.53	0%	-17.79	3Y.3M
Stocks/Bonds 40/60	-2.41	3.88	1.8%	2.10	5.36	0%	5.22	6.06	8.48	0%	-19.17	4Y.2M
In Saecula Saeculorum	-2.08	4.62	1.2%	3.55	6.48	0%	6.06	7.16	8.90	0%	-20.39	3Y.7M
All Weather Portfolio	-2.92	4.48	1.8%	3.15	6.76	0%	5.58	7.48	9.13	0%	-20.58	4Y.9M
10-year Treasury	-7.79	2.14	6.1%	-1.15	3.83	1.3%	2.09	4.59	7.58	0%	-23.18	10Y.6M
Stocks/Bonds 60/40	-6.40	3.68	7.7%	0.56	5.28	0%	5.21	6.50	9.22	0%	-30.55	9Y.2M
One-Decision Portfolio	-7.87	4.38	4.7%	1.40	5.43	0%	4.80	6.42	9.20	0%	-31.96	5Y.4M
Simple Path to Wealth	-9.99	3.23	10.6%	-0.70	4.97	0.3%	5.00	6.60	9.70	0%	-38.53	10Y.2M
Talmud Portfolio	-10.82	4.17	6.9%	0.39	5.82	0%	5.75	7.49	9.81	0%	-40.17	6Y.3M
Stocks/Bonds 80/20	-11.24	3.09	10.8%	-1.13	4.86	0.6%	4.90	6.63	9.87	0%	-41.09	10Y.2M
Warren Buffett Portfolio	-13.74	2.27	12.6%	-2.48	3.81	1.4%	4.09	5.85	10.01	0%	-45.52	11Y.0M
US Stocks	-16.22	1.87	12.6%	-3.00	4.15	1.7%	4.37	6.49	10.48	0%	-50.84	11Y.7M
Gold	-15.32	-6.07	32.9%	-6.75	-2.30	29.7%	-3.63	-1.12	7.05	19.6%	-61.78	27Y.5M

Order by **Maximum Drawdown - Last 60 Years** (from 1963-12 to 2023-11) - **US Infl. Adjusted**

Portfolio	3Y Rolling Annualized Return (%)			7Y Rolling Annualized Return (%)			15Y Rolling Annualized Return (%)				Max Draw-down (%) ▼	Long Neg Period (Y.M)
	Worst	Base	%Fail	Worst	Base	%Fail	Worst	Base	Median	%Fail		
Desert Portfolio	-5.11	0.63	11.8%	-1.01	1.31	2.2%	0.35	2.89	4.73	0%	-20.97	13Y.10M
Permanent Portfolio	-6.86	0.55	10.5%	0.04	2.62	0%	2.20	3.41	4.64	0%	-23.32	7Y.9M
Short Term Treasury	-6.65	-1.57	36.2%	-3.25	-0.94	28.1%	-1.59	-0.10	2.29	16.8%	-23.89	25Y.8M
Golden Butterfly	-4.79	2.02	7.2%	0.30	3.81	0%	3.20	4.83	6.03	0%	-24.09	6Y.5M
Robo Advisor 0	-6.71	-1.41	36.1%	-3.41	-0.81	27.5%	-1.43	0.02	2.33	14.6%	-24.64	25Y.2M
Simplified Permanent Portfolio	-6.96	0.80	9.8%	-0.33	2.71	0.2%	1.81	3.63	5.14	0%	-25.58	9Y.1M
In Saecula Saeculorum	-6.04	-0.17	15.5%	-2.33	1.96	3.8%	0.29	3.76	5.35	0%	-26.94	14Y.2M
All Weather Portfolio	-8.18	-0.08	15.3%	-1.82	1.13	4.9%	-0.24	3.39	5.69	1.3%	-27.79	18Y.0M
Stocks/Bonds 20/80	-7.85	-1.23	18.4%	-4.05	-0.24	15.9%	-1.56	1.77	3.82	8.9%	-30.21	18Y.9M
Stocks/Bonds 40/60	-9.10	-1.27	21%	-3.85	0.66	12.2%	-1.10	2.66	4.54	6.5%	-30.32	18Y.8M
One-Decision Portfolio	-10.46	-0.16	15.5%	-4.14	1.36	9.6%	0.20	3.02	4.83	0%	-34.04	14Y.5M
Total Bond US	-10.69	-1.75	25.1%	-4.53	-0.74	19.9%	-2.30	0.30	3.30	11.8%	-35.11	20Y.8M
Stocks/Bonds 60/40	-12.03	-1.46	21.8%	-5.15	0.92	12.1%	-1.04	2.98	5.51	3.1%	-38.92	18Y.2M
Talmud Portfolio	-12.75	0.04	14.9%	-5.31	1.24	10.1%	-0.16	3.88	6.04	0.7%	-42.36	16Y.5M
Simple Path to Wealth	-14.36	-1.79	20.9%	-6.34	0.75	12.9%	-1.14	2.93	6.11	2.4%	-45.02	18Y.1M
10-year Treasury	-13.24	-2.26	26.3%	-6.12	-1.45	23.6%	-3.52	0.40	3.98	13.7%	-45.61	21Y.5M
Stocks/Bonds 80/20	-15.17	-1.96	20.4%	-6.75	0.67	13%	-1.19	2.85	6.31	2.4%	-46.99	18Y.0M
Warren Buffett Portfolio	-16.24	-3.11	23.8%	-7.74	-0.52	18.1%	-2.09	2.10	6.51	9.4%	-50.04	18Y.8M
US Stocks	-18.54	-2.55	20.6%	-8.51	0.01	14.9%	-1.47	2.39	6.97	2.2%	-54.53	18Y.1M
Gold	-20.28	-9.47	51.1%	-11.38	-5.24	44.3%	-7.77	-4.24	3.96	33.1%	-82.57	43Y.11M*

Order by **Maximum Drawdown** - **All data** (from 1871/1927 to 2023-11)

Portfolio	3Y Rolling Annualized Return (%)			7Y Rolling Annualized Return (%)			15Y Rolling Annualized Return (%)				Max Drawdown (%) ▼	Long Neg Period (Y.M)
	Worst	Base	%Fail	Worst	Base	%Fail	Worst	Base	Median	%Fail		
Robo Advisor 0	-1.33	1.56	1.1%	0.47	1.57	0%	1.00	2.22	4.38	0%	-8.48	4Y.1M
Short Term Treasury	-1.26	1.46	1.1%	0.39	1.52	0%	0.87	2.11	4.40	0%	-8.52	3Y.11M
Total Bond US	-5.59	2.15	1.6%	-0.23	2.57	0.1%	1.40	2.67	4.00	0%	-17.28	7Y.6M
Stocks/Bonds 20/80	-5.37	3.02	1.7%	1.80	3.78	0%	2.76	4.13	5.14	0%	-18.94	5Y.1M
10-year Treasury	-7.79	1.29	6.1%	-1.15	1.80	0.5%	0.98	2.14	4.04	0%	-23.18	10Y.6M
Simplified Permanent Portfolio	-9.97	1.91	3.9%	0.56	2.83	0%	2.01	3.67	4.97	0%	-30.22	6Y.8M
Permanent Portfolio	-10.10	2.58	2.1%	0.58	3.46	0%	2.64	3.83	4.93	0%	-30.61	6Y.8M
Desert Portfolio	-10.95	2.84	2.1%	0.61	3.79	0%	2.35	4.23	5.86	0%	-33.15	6Y.8M
All Weather Portfolio	-12.66	2.56	3.4%	-0.03	3.52	0.1%	2.25	4.10	5.60	0%	-37.02	7Y.0M
Stocks/Bonds 40/60	-15.47	2.52	3.9%	-0.11	4.09	0.1%	2.53	4.88	6.22	0%	-43.68	7Y.1M
One-Decision Portfolio	-17.20	2.89	8.2%	-0.37	4.77	0.1%	1.95	5.74	6.96	0%	-47.77	12Y.10M
Golden Butterfly	-17.91	4.12	4.4%	1.97	5.90	0%	3.74	6.72	8.30	0%	-48.31	6Y.2M
In Saecula Saeculorum	-18.75	2.34	5.6%	-1.08	3.81	0.1%	2.31	4.69	6.79	0%	-50.22	8Y.9M
Talmud Portfolio	-21.82	2.69	9.4%	-1.75	4.74	0.9%	1.47	5.91	7.86	0%	-57.05	13Y.4M
Gold	-15.32	-1.61	23.9%	-6.75	-1.32	22.2%	-3.63	-0.50	0.05	21.3%	-61.78	62Y.0M
Stocks/Bonds 60/40	-25.23	1.83	9.4%	-2.67	4.06	0.7%	2.25	5.30	7.17	0%	-62.03	12Y.10M
Simple Path to Wealth	-32.34	0.98	12.7%	-4.94	3.91	2.2%	1.52	5.50	7.75	0%	-72.36	13Y.7M
Stocks/Bonds 80/20	-34.67	0.72	13.4%	-5.77	3.81	2.6%	1.19	5.55	7.93	0%	-75.27	13Y.10M
Warren Buffett Portfolio	-38.18	0.02	14.9%	-5.83	3.11	3.1%	-0.02	5.32	8.03	0.1%	-79.29	15Y.1M
US Stocks	-43.81	-0.56	15.9%	-9.49	3.29	4.2%	-0.35	5.49	8.60	0.1%	-84.60	15Y.8M

Order by **Maximum Drawdown** - **All data** (from 1871/1927 to 2023-11) - **US Infl. Adjusted**

Portfolio	3Y Rolling Annualized Return (%)			7Y Rolling Annualized Return (%)			15Y Rolling Annualized Return (%)				Max Drawdown (%) ▼	Long Neg Period (Y.M)
	Worst	Base	%Fail	Worst	Base	%Fail	Worst	Base	Median	%Fail		
One-Decision Portfolio	-10.63	-0.59	16.9%	-4.14	1.12	8.7%	0.17	1.72	4.14	0%	-34.04	14Y.5M
Golden Butterfly	-11.40	0.97	11.3%	-1.69	2.87	1.8%	1.09	3.80	5.39	0%	-34.73	12Y.7M
Short Term Treasury	-12.29	-2.01	30.1%	-7.07	-1.41	25.7%	-3.27	-0.49	1.90	19.8%	-45.12	52Y.1M
In Saecula Saeculorum	-12.96	-0.26	16.1%	-6.92	1.32	8.1%	-2.73	1.99	4.72	2.5%	-45.23	23Y.5M
Robo Advisor 0	-12.40	-1.95	29.9%	-7.12	-1.34	25.6%	-3.23	-0.52	1.89	19.3%	-45.36	52Y.0M
Permanent Portfolio	-12.87	-0.07	15.3%	-7.21	0.84	11.5%	-2.93	1.01	3.54	8%	-45.48	28Y.5M
Stocks/Bonds 40/60	-12.93	-0.73	17.4%	-6.68	0.81	11.1%	-2.37	1.54	4.26	3.9%	-45.57	23Y.5M
Talmud Portfolio	-15.62	-0.56	16.2%	-5.31	1.27	8.3%	-0.52	2.02	4.93	1%	-45.76	18Y.9M
Desert Portfolio	-13.19	0.10	14.7%	-7.17	0.81	9.4%	-2.83	1.34	4.08	3.5%	-46.37	28Y.2M
Stocks/Bonds 20/80	-13.27	-0.78	17.7%	-7.21	-0.25	15.9%	-2.77	0.61	3.27	8%	-46.65	28Y.4M
All Weather Portfolio	-14.36	-0.26	16.2%	-7.47	0.59	10.5%	-3.18	1.26	4.02	4.4%	-47.73	28Y.5M
Total Bond US	-13.89	-2.23	26.6%	-7.81	-1.23	25.1%	-3.27	-0.65	2.01	21.8%	-48.08	51Y.10M
Simplified Permanent Portfolio	-13.46	-0.41	16.3%	-8.12	0.32	12.3%	-3.95	0.80	3.74	8.8%	-49.37	33Y.9M
Stocks/Bonds 60/40	-19.29	-0.93	18.1%	-6.22	1.42	9.4%	-2.07	2.33	5.45	2.6%	-52.05	21Y.11M
10-year Treasury	-13.92	-2.32	28.7%	-8.73	-1.77	29%	-4.52	-1.17	2.36	28.1%	-58.48	85Y.5M
Simple Path to Wealth	-26.97	-1.25	18.8%	-6.34	1.57	9.9%	-1.97	2.62	6.11	2.3%	-65.10	20Y.6M
Stocks/Bonds 80/20	-29.49	-1.56	18.8%	-6.75	1.50	10.1%	-1.98	2.64	6.29	2.2%	-68.77	20Y.6M
Warren Buffett Portfolio	-33.28	-2.46	20.5%	-7.74	0.68	12.6%	-2.12	2.23	6.43	4.7%	-73.85	20Y.4M
US Stocks	-39.36	-2.49	20.7%	-8.51	0.77	12.6%	-2.10	2.40	6.93	2.5%	-80.55	26Y.4M
Gold	-20.28	-5.84	58.4%	-11.38	-4.43	56.9%	-7.77	-3.77	-0.10	50.5%	-82.57	132Y.3M

Ranking: Longest Negative Period

Order by **Longest Negative Period** - **Last 30 Years** (from 1993-12 to 2023-11)

Portfolio	3Y Rolling Annualized Return (%)			7Y Rolling Annualized Return (%)			15Y Rolling Annualized Return (%)				Max Draw-down (%)	Long Neg Period (Y.M) ▲
	Worst	Base	%Fail	Worst	Base	%Fail	Worst	Base	Median	%Fail		
Dimensional Retirement Income Fund	0.33	2.84	0%	2.41	3.66	0%	3.44	4.40	5.09	0%	-12.91	2Y.10M
Sheltered Sam 20/80	0.42	2.53	0%	2.32	3.12	0%	2.98	3.98	4.86	0%	-11.24	2Y.11M
Desert Portfolio	0.35	4.03	0%	4.04	5.23	0%	4.92	6.03	6.62	0%	-14.72	3Y.2M
Eliminate Fat Tails	-0.99	2.64	1.2%	1.81	3.42	0%	2.94	4.44	5.91	0%	-18.42	3Y.2M
Golden Butterfly	0.58	4.71	0%	4.29	6.33	0%	5.98	7.47	8.12	0%	-17.79	3Y.3M
Aim comfortable trip	-1.22	4.14	1.2%	4.49	6.07	0%	5.25	6.78	7.60	0%	-20.15	3Y.3M
Edge Select Conservative	-0.39	3.23	1.5%	2.52	4.10	0%	3.34	4.53	5.05	0%	-12.44	3Y.3M
Simplified Permanent Portfolio	-1.62	3.60	1.2%	3.15	5.07	0%	5.26	7.00	7.77	0%	-16.43	3Y.4M
Permanent Portfolio	-1.50	3.31	1.2%	3.19	5.04	0%	5.07	6.61	7.18	0%	-15.92	3Y.4M
Marc Faber Portfolio	-3.16	3.80	1.2%	3.58	5.46	0%	4.95	6.92	8.61	0%	-28.82	3Y.5M
Sheltered Sam 30/70	-1.11	2.93	0.3%	2.83	3.97	0%	3.43	4.52	5.53	0%	-16.58	3Y.5M
Sheltered Sam 10/90	-0.58	1.78	1.2%	1.58	2.22	0%	2.31	3.38	4.31	0%	-9.93	3Y.5M
In Saecula Saeculorum	-2.08	3.65	2.2%	3.64	6.09	0%	6.06	6.74	7.34	0%	-20.39	3Y.7M
Shield Strategy	-5.00	5.05	3.7%	4.31	6.67	0%	6.31	7.48	8.43	0%	-19.36	3Y.8M
GAA Global Asset Allocation	-3.09	3.27	3.1%	3.59	5.70	0%	4.44	6.42	7.34	0%	-24.91	3Y.9M
Robo Advisor 20	-0.68	2.73	2.2%	1.96	3.35	0%	2.76	4.12	5.05	0%	-12.16	3Y.9M
Robo Advisor 10	-0.80	1.75	4%	1.24	2.13	0%	1.99	3.11	3.91	0%	-8.91	3Y.9M
All Weather Portfolio	-2.92	4.54	1.8%	3.15	6.37	0%	5.58	7.03	7.80	0%	-20.58	3Y.10M
Stocks/Bonds 40/60 Momentum	-3.20	2.05	3.4%	3.39	5.78	0%	5.33	6.19	7.26	0%	-21.11	3Y.10M
Weird Portfolio	-6.05	3.47	3.1%	3.14	6.35	0%	5.80	7.87	10.02	0%	-32.97	3Y.11M
Short Term Treasury	-1.26	0.52	4.9%	0.39	0.72	0%	0.87	1.83	2.71	0%	-5.36	3Y.11M

Order by **Longest Negative Period** - **Last 30 Years** (from 1993-12 to 2023-11) - **US Infl. Adjusted**

Portfolio	3Y Rolling Annualized Return (%)			7Y Rolling Annualized Return (%)			15Y Rolling Annualized Return (%)				Max Draw-down (%)	Long Neg Period (Y.M) ▲
	Worst	Base	%Fail	Worst	Base	%Fail	Worst	Base	Median	%Fail		
Aim comfortable trip	-3.36	2.06	9.5%	1.45	4.06	0%	2.79	4.50	5.28	0%	-22.06	5Y.5M
Golden Butterfly	-4.79	2.36	5.5%	0.73	4.06	0%	3.52	5.13	5.79	0%	-23.38	5Y.11M
Pinwheel	-8.93	0.11	13.9%	1.18	3.45	0%	2.01	4.11	5.31	0%	-37.86	6Y.1M
Desert Portfolio	-5.11	2.07	5.5%	0.50	3.11	0%	2.47	3.81	4.34	0%	-20.97	6Y.2M
Marc Faber Portfolio	-5.24	1.32	8%	0.56	3.05	0%	2.49	4.41	6.12	0%	-29.75	6Y.3M
Sheltered Sam 50/50	-7.30	0.55	13.2%	0.55	2.87	0%	1.79	3.43	4.17	0%	-29.33	6Y.3M
Six Ways from Sunday	-10.30	0.54	14.2%	0.63	3.57	0%	2.36	3.89	5.28	0%	-39.85	6Y.3M
Sandwich Portfolio	-6.58	0.55	13.2%	0.71	3.72	0%	2.11	4.23	4.94	0%	-30.05	6Y.6M
Simplified Permanent Portfolio	-6.96	1.62	6.2%	0.10	2.98	0%	2.82	4.65	5.45	0%	-23.93	7Y.3M
Sheltered Sam 40/60	-5.25	1.47	11.1%	0.21	2.64	0%	1.42	2.98	3.81	0%	-23.25	7Y.7M
Edge Select Moderately Conservative	-5.54	0.69	12%	0.42	3.01	0%	2.08	3.57	4.05	0%	-24.60	7Y.7M
Ultimate Buy&Hold	-8.66	-0.05	15.4%	0.22	3.20	0%	1.47	3.61	5.09	0%	-35.24	7Y.7M
Simple Money Portfolio	-8.43	-0.10	15.4%	0.57	3.08	0%	1.65	3.78	5.04	0%	-33.42	7Y.7M
Robo Advisor 50	-7.48	0.37	13.5%	0.35	3.77	0%	1.84	4.21	5.04	0%	-31.78	7Y.8M
Permanent Portfolio	-6.86	1.00	7.7%	0.14	2.66	0%	2.61	4.28	4.85	0%	-23.32	7Y.9M
Big Rocks Portfolio	-9.32	0.07	14.5%	0.31	2.53	0%	1.76	3.42	4.35	0%	-34.81	8Y.1M
In Saecula Saeculorum	-4.44	0.60	12.6%	1.06	3.11	0%	3.59	4.29	4.97	0%	-23.97	8Y.6M
Late Sixties and Beyond	-11.72	0.54	13.2%	-0.10	3.67	0.4%	2.51	4.78	5.63	0%	-42.69	8Y.6M
Lifepath Fund	-5.47	0.51	12.3%	0.26	2.96	0%	1.90	3.44	3.91	0%	-24.57	8Y.6M
Sheltered Sam 60/40	-9.40	0.47	13.9%	0.01	2.98	0%	2.12	3.80	4.46	0%	-35.13	8Y.6M
Stocks/Bonds 40/60 Momentum	-8.46	-0.19	16.9%	0.62	3.04	0%	2.88	3.86	5.08	0%	-27.84	8Y.6M

Order by **Longest Negative Period** - **Last 60 Years** (from 1963-12 to 2023-11)

Portfolio	3Y Rolling Annualized Return (%)			7Y Rolling Annualized Return (%)			15Y Rolling Annualized Return (%)				Max Draw-down (%)	Long Neg Period (Y.M)
	Worst	Base	%Fail	Worst	Base	%Fail	Worst	Base	Median	%Fail		
Golden Butterfly	0.58	5.25	0%	4.29	7.07	0%	5.98	8.00	9.53	0%	-17.79	3Y.3M
Desert Portfolio	0.11	4.59	0%	4.04	5.97	0%	4.92	6.58	8.35	0%	-14.72	3Y.3M
Simplified Permanent Portfolio	-1.62	4.06	0.7%	3.15	6.11	0%	5.26	7.42	8.52	0%	-16.43	3Y.4M
Permanent Portfolio	-1.50	3.83	0.6%	3.19	5.65	0%	5.07	6.77	7.83	0%	-15.92	3Y.4M
In Saecula Saeculorum	-2.08	4.62	1.2%	3.55	6.48	0%	6.06	7.16	8.90	0%	-20.39	3Y.7M
Short Term Treasury	-1.26	1.29	2.3%	0.39	1.39	0%	0.87	2.34	6.67	0%	-8.52	3Y.11M
Robo Advisor 0	-1.33	1.52	2.3%	0.47	1.55	0%	1.02	2.49	6.61	0%	-8.48	4Y.1M
Stocks/Bonds 20/80	-2.58	4.03	1.6%	2.21	5.02	0%	3.93	5.42	7.67	0%	-16.57	4Y.2M
Stocks/Bonds 40/60	-2.41	3.88	1.8%	2.10	5.36	0%	5.22	6.06	8.48	0%	-19.17	4Y.2M
All Weather Portfolio	-2.92	4.48	1.8%	3.15	6.76	0%	5.58	7.48	9.13	0%	-20.58	4Y.9M
One-Decision Portfolio	-7.87	4.38	4.7%	1.40	5.43	0%	4.80	6.42	9.20	0%	-31.96	5Y.4M
Talmud Portfolio	-10.82	4.17	6.9%	0.39	5.82	0%	5.75	7.49	9.81	0%	-40.17	6Y.3M
Total Bond US	-5.59	2.53	2.6%	-0.23	4.05	0.3%	2.36	4.28	7.03	0%	-17.28	7Y.6M
Stocks/Bonds 60/40	-6.40	3.68	7.7%	0.56	5.28	0%	5.21	6.50	9.22	0%	-30.55	9Y.2M
Simple Path to Wealth	-9.99	3.23	10.5%	-0.70	4.97	0.3%	5.00	6.60	9.70	0%	-38.53	10Y.2M
Stocks/Bonds 80/20	-11.24	3.09	10.8%	-1.13	4.86	0.6%	4.90	6.63	9.87	0%	-41.09	10Y.2M
10-year Treasury	-7.79	2.14	6.1%	-1.15	3.83	1.3%	2.09	4.59	7.58	0%	-23.18	10Y.6M
Warren Buffett Portfolio	-13.74	2.27	12.6%	-2.48	3.81	1.4%	4.09	5.85	10.01	0%	-45.52	11Y.0M
US Stocks	-16.22	1.87	12.6%	-3.00	4.15	1.7%	4.37	6.49	10.48	0%	-50.84	11Y.7M
Gold	-15.32	-6.07	32.9%	-6.75	-2.30	29.7%	-3.63	-1.12	7.05	19.6%	-61.78	27Y.5M

Order by **Longest Negative Period** - **Last 60 Years** (from 1963-12 to 2023-11) - **US Infl. Adjusted**

Portfolio	3Y Rolling Annualized Return (%)			7Y Rolling Annualized Return (%)			15Y Rolling Annualized Return (%)				Max Draw-down (%)	Long Neg Period (Y.M) ▲
	Worst	Base	%Fail	Worst	Base	%Fail	Worst	Base	Median	%Fail		
Golden Butterfly	-4.79	2.02	7.2%	0.30	3.81	0%	3.20	4.83	6.03	0%	-24.09	6Y.5M
Permanent Portfolio	-6.86	0.55	10.5%	0.04	2.62	0%	2.20	3.41	4.64	0%	-23.32	7Y.9M
Simplified Permanent Portfolio	-6.96	0.80	9.8%	-0.33	2.71	0.2%	1.81	3.63	5.14	0%	-25.58	9Y.1M
Desert Portfolio	-5.11	0.63	11.8%	-1.01	1.31	2.2%	0.35	2.89	4.73	0%	-20.97	13Y.10M
In Saecula Saeculorum	-6.04	-0.17	15.5%	-2.33	1.96	3.8%	0.29	3.76	5.35	0%	-26.94	14Y.2M
One-Decision Portfolio	-10.46	-0.16	15.5%	-4.14	1.36	9.6%	0.20	3.02	4.83	0%	-34.04	14Y.5M
Talmud Portfolio	-12.75	0.04	14.9%	-7.74	1.24	10.1%	-0.16	3.88	6.04	0.7%	-42.36	16Y.5M
All Weather Portfolio	-8.18	-0.08	15.3%	-1.82	1.13	4.9%	-0.24	3.39	5.69	1.3%	-27.79	18Y.0M
Stocks/Bonds 80/20	-15.17	-1.96	20.4%	-6.75	0.67	13%	-1.19	2.85	6.31	2.4%	-46.99	18Y.0M
Simple Path to Wealth	-14.36	-1.79	20.9%	-6.34	0.75	12.9%	-1.14	2.93	6.11	2.4%	-45.02	18Y.1M
US Stocks	-18.54	-2.55	20.6%	-8.51	0.01	14.9%	-1.47	2.39	6.97	2.2%	-54.53	18Y.2M
Stocks/Bonds 60/40	-12.03	-1.46	21.8%	-5.15	0.92	12.1%	-1.04	2.98	5.51	3.1%	-38.92	18Y.2M
Stocks/Bonds 40/60	-9.10	-1.27	21%	-3.85	0.66	12.2%	-1.10	2.66	4.54	6.5%	-30.32	18Y.8M
Warren Buffett Portfolio	-16.24	-3.11	23.8%	-7.74	-0.52	18.1%	-2.09	2.10	6.51	9.4%	-50.04	18Y.8M
Stocks/Bonds 20/80	-7.85	-1.23	18.4%	-4.05	-0.24	15.9%	-1.56	1.77	3.82	8.9%	-30.21	18Y.9M
Total Bond US	-10.69	-1.75	25.1%	-4.53	-0.74	19.9%	-2.30	0.30	3.30	11.8%	-35.11	20Y.8M
10-year Treasury	-13.24	-2.26	26.3%	-6.12	-1.45	23.6%	-3.52	0.40	3.98	13.7%	-45.61	21Y.5M
Robo Advisor 0	-6.71	-1.41	36.1%	-3.41	-0.81	27.5%	-1.43	0.02	2.33	14.6%	-24.64	25Y.2M
Short Term Treasury	-6.65	-1.57	36.2%	-3.25	-0.94	28.1%	-1.59	-0.10	2.29	16.8%	-23.89	25Y.8M
Gold	-20.28	-9.47	51.1%	-11.38	-5.24	44.3%	-7.77	-4.24	3.96	33.1%	-82.57	43Y.11M*

Order by **Longest Negative Period** - **All data** (from 1871/1927 to 2023-11)

Portfolio	3Y Rolling Annualized Return (%)			7Y Rolling Annualized Return (%)			15Y Rolling Annualized Return (%)				Max Draw-down (%)	Long Neg Period (Y.M) ▲
	Worst	Base	%Fail	Worst	Base	%Fail	Worst	Base	Median	%Fail		
Short Term Treasury	-1.26	1.46	1.1%	0.39	1.52	0%	0.87	2.11	4.40	0%	-8.52	3Y.11M
Robo Advisor 0	-1.33	1.56	1.1%	0.47	1.57	0%	1.00	2.22	4.38	0%	-8.48	4Y.1M
Stocks/Bonds 20/80	-5.37	3.02	1.7%	1.80	3.78	0%	2.76	4.13	5.14	0%	-18.94	5Y.1M
Golden Butterfly	-17.91	4.12	4.4%	1.97	5.90	0%	3.74	6.72	8.30	0%	-48.31	6Y.2M
Desert Portfolio	-10.95	2.84	2.1%	0.61	3.79	0%	2.35	4.23	5.86	0%	-33.15	6Y.8M
Permanent Portfolio	-10.10	2.58	2.1%	0.58	3.46	0%	2.64	3.83	4.93	0%	-30.61	6Y.8M
Simplified Permanent Portfolio	-9.97	1.91	3.9%	0.56	2.83	0%	2.01	3.67	4.97	0%	-30.22	6Y.8M
All Weather Portfolio	-12.66	2.56	3.4%	-0.03	3.52	0.1%	2.25	4.10	5.60	0%	-37.02	7Y.0M
Stocks/Bonds 40/60	-15.47	2.52	3.9%	-0.11	4.09	0.1%	2.53	4.88	6.22	0%	-43.58	7Y.1M
Total Bond US	-5.59	2.15	1.6%	-0.23	2.57	0.1%	1.40	2.67	4.00	0%	-17.28	7Y.6M
In Saecula Saeculorum	-18.75	2.34	5.6%	-1.08	3.81	0.1%	2.31	4.69	6.79	0%	-50.22	8Y.9M
10-year Treasury	-7.79	1.29	6.1%	-1.15	1.80	0.5%	0.98	2.14	4.04	0%	-23.18	10Y.6M
One-Decision Portfolio	-17.20	2.89	8.2%	-0.37	4.77	0.1%	1.95	5.74	6.96	0%	-47.77	12Y.10M
Stocks/Bonds 60/40	-25.23	1.83	9.4%	-2.67	4.06	0.7%	2.25	5.30	7.17	0%	-62.03	12Y.10M
Talmud Portfolio	-21.02	2.69	9.4%	-1.75	4.74	0.9%	1.47	5.91	7.86	0%	-57.05	13Y.4M
Simple Path to Wealth	-32.34	0.98	12.7%	-4.94	3.91	2.2%	1.52	5.50	7.75	0%	-72.36	13Y.7M
Stocks/Bonds 80/20	-34.67	0.72	13.4%	-5.77	3.81	2.6%	1.19	5.55	7.93	0%	-75.27	13Y.10M
Warren Buffett Portfolio	-38.18	0.02	14.9%	-5.83	3.11	3.1%	-0.02	5.32	8.03	0.1%	-79.29	15Y.1M
US Stocks	-43.81	-0.56	15.9%	-9.49	3.29	4.2%	-0.35	5.49	8.60	0.1%	-84.60	15Y.8M
Gold	-15.32	-1.61	23.9%	-6.75	-1.32	22.2%	-3.63	-0.50	0.05	21.3%	-61.78	62Y.0M

Order by **Longest Negative Period** - **All data** (from 1871/1927 to 2023-11) - **US Infl. Adjusted**

Portfolio	3Y Rolling Annualized Return (%)			7Y Rolling Annualized Return (%)			15Y Rolling Annualized Return (%)				Max Draw-down (%)	Long Neg Period (Y.M) ▲
	Worst	Base	%Fail	Worst	Base	%Fail	Worst	Base	Median	%Fail		
Golden Butterfly	-11.40	0.97	11.3%	-1.69	2.87	1.8%	1.09	3.80	5.39	0%	-34.73	12Y.7M
One-Decision Portfolio	-10.63	-0.59	16.9%	-4.14	1.12	8.7%	0.17	1.72	4.14	0%	-34.04	14Y.5M
Talmud Portfolio	-15.62	-0.56	16.2%	-5.31	1.27	8.3%	-0.52	2.02	4.93	1%	-45.76	18Y.9M
Warren Buffett Portfolio	-33.28	-2.46	20.5%	-7.74	0.68	12.6%	-2.12	2.23	6.43	4.7%	-73.85	20Y.4M
Simple Path to Wealth	-26.97	-1.25	18.8%	-6.34	1.57	9.9%	-1.97	2.62	6.11	2.3%	-65.10	20Y.6M
Stocks/Bonds 80/20	-29.49	-1.56	18.8%	-6.75	1.50	10.1%	-1.98	2.64	6.29	2.2%	-68.77	20Y.6M
Stocks/Bonds 60/40	-19.29	-0.93	18.1%	-6.22	1.42	9.4%	-2.07	2.33	5.45	2.6%	-52.05	21Y.11M
In Saecula Saeculorum	-12.96	-0.26	16.1%	-6.92	1.32	8.1%	-2.73	1.99	4.72	2.5%	-45.23	23Y.5M
Stocks/Bonds 40/60	-12.93	-0.73	17.4%	-6.68	0.81	11.1%	-2.37	1.54	4.26	3.9%	-45.57	23Y.5M
US Stocks	-39.36	-2.49	20.7%	-8.51	0.77	12.6%	-2.10	2.40	6.93	2.5%	-80.55	26Y.4M
Desert Portfolio	-13.19	0.10	14.7%	-7.17	0.81	9.4%	-2.83	1.34	4.08	3.5%	-46.37	28Y.2M
Stocks/Bonds 20/80	-13.27	-0.78	17.7%	-7.21	-0.25	15.9%	-2.77	0.61	3.27	8%	-46.65	28Y.4M
Permanent Portfolio	-12.87	-0.07	15.3%	-7.21	0.84	11.5%	-2.93	1.01	3.54	8%	-45.48	28Y.5M
All Weather Portfolio	-14.36	-0.26	16.2%	-7.47	0.59	10.5%	-3.18	1.26	4.02	4.4%	-47.73	28Y.5M
Simplified Permanent Portfolio	-13.46	-0.41	16.3%	-8.12	0.32	12.3%	-3.95	0.80	3.74	8.8%	-49.37	33Y.9M
Total Bond US	-13.89	-2.23	26.6%	-7.81	-1.23	25.1%	-3.27	-0.65	2.01	21.8%	-48.08	51Y.10M
Robo Advisor 0	-12.40	-1.95	29.9%	-7.12	-1.34	25.6%	-3.23	-0.52	1.89	19.3%	-45.36	52Y.0M
Short Term Treasury	-12.29	-2.01	30.1%	-7.07	-1.41	25.7%	-3.27	-0.49	1.90	19.8%	-45.12	52Y.1M
10-year Treasury	-13.92	-2.32	28.7%	-8.73	-1.77	29%	-4.52	-1.17	2.36	28.1%	-58.48	85Y.5M
Gold	-20.28	-5.84	58.4%	-11.38	-4.43	56.9%	-7.77	-3.77	-0.10	50.5%	-82.57	132Y.3M

Ranking: Baseline 7Y Return

Order by Baseline 7Y Return - Last 30 Years (from 1993-12 to 2023-11)

Portfolio	3Y Rolling Annualized Return (%)			7Y Rolling Annualized Return (%)			15Y Rolling Annualized Return (%)				Max Draw-down (%)	Long Neg Period (Y.M)
	Worst	Base	%Fail	Worst	Base ▼	%Fail	Worst	Base	Median	%Fail		
Shield Strategy	-5.00	5.05	3.7%	4.31	6.67	0%	6.31	7.48	8.43	0%	-19.36	3Y.8M
Yale Endowment	-9.18	2.78	7.1%	2.97	6.62	0%	5.46	7.41	8.12	0%	-39.48	5Y.2M
Aim Bold Strategy	-7.69	3.74	7.1%	3.86	6.53	0%	5.99	6.97	8.05	0%	-30.09	4Y.5M
All Weather Portfolio	-2.92	4.54	1.8%	3.15	6.37	0%	5.58	7.03	7.80	0%	-20.58	3Y.10M
Weird Portfolio	-6.05	3.47	3.1%	3.14	6.35	0%	5.80	7.87	10.02	0%	-32.97	3Y.11M
Golden Butterfly	0.58	4.71	0%	4.29	6.33	0%	5.98	7.47	8.12	0%	-17.79	3Y.3M
Global Market Portfolio	-3.75	3.20	4.6%	3.09	6.30	0%	4.69	6.68	7.40	0%	-25.90	4Y.2M
Family Taxable Portfolio	-8.72	2.41	8.9%	3.08	6.29	0%	5.10	6.73	7.57	0%	-38.46	5Y.1M
Lazy Portfolio	-9.56	2.84	8%	2.61	6.20	0%	5.01	6.78	7.63	0%	-40.89	5Y.2M
Late Sixties and Beyond	-9.76	4.05	7.4%	2.45	6.19	0%	4.95	6.93	7.88	0%	-41.80	5Y.2M
Talmud Portfolio	-10.82	4.06	7.1%	1.35	6.15	0%	5.75	7.16	7.91	0%	-40.17	5Y.2M
Mid-Fifties	-11.17	3.08	10.2%	2.16	6.11	0%	4.90	7.05	7.97	0%	-46.21	5Y.3M
In Saecula Saeculorum	-2.08	3.65	2.2%	3.64	6.09	0%	6.06	6.74	7.34	0%	-20.39	3Y.7M
Aim comfortable trip	-1.22	4.14	1.2%	4.49	6.07	0%	5.25	6.78	7.60	0%	-20.15	3Y.3M
Stocks/Bonds 60/40 Momentum	-6.27	0.17	14.2%	2.39	5.99	0%	5.99	6.79	8.52	0%	-32.52	4Y.5M
Seven Value	-9.49	2.40	10.5%	2.86	5.98	0%	5.09	6.38	7.48	0%	-41.22	5Y.0M
Sandwich Portfolio	-4.49	3.36	1.5%	4.24	5.97	0%	4.55	6.39	7.34	0%	-28.96	4Y.2M
Couch Potato	-5.41	3.23	4%	2.22	5.96	0%	5.76	6.48	7.01	0%	-27.04	5Y.2M
Edge Select Moderate	-5.06	2.32	6.8%	2.57	5.90	0%	4.97	6.11	6.77	0%	-29.58	4Y.4M
Robo Advisor 50	-5.43	3.14	2.8%	3.86	5.87	0%	4.27	6.34	7.39	0%	-30.72	4Y.5M
Tilt Toward Value	-7.65	2.66	7.4%	2.02	5.87	0%	5.02	6.50	7.01	0%	-34.63	5Y.2M

Order by Baseline 7Y Return - Last 30 Years (from 1993-12 to 2023-11) - US Infl. Adjusted

Portfolio	3Y Rolling Annualized Return (%)			7Y Rolling Annualized Return (%)			15Y Rolling Annualized Return (%)				Max Draw-down (%)	Long Neg Period (Y.M)
	Worst	Base	%Fail	Worst	Base ▼	%Fail	Worst	Base	Median	%Fail		
All Weather Portfolio	-8.18	2.51	5.2%	-0.36	4.26	0.7%	3.11	4.81	5.51	0%	-27.79	8Y.9M
Yale Endowment	-11.15	-0.62	16.9%	0.40	4.21	0%	3.00	5.02	5.83	0%	-40.41	9Y.2M
Golden Butterfly	-4.79	2.36	5.5%	0.73	4.06	0%	3.52	5.13	5.79	0%	-23.38	5Y.11M
Aim comfortable trip	-3.36	2.06	9.5%	1.45	4.06	0%	2.79	4.50	5.28	0%	-22.06	5Y.5M
Global Market Portfolio	-7.63	0.72	11.4%	-0.40	4.01	0.7%	2.24	4.31	5.07	0%	-28.40	8Y.9M
Shield Strategy	-7.29	1.78	12%	1.63	4.00	0%	4.06	4.99	6.00	0%	-24.25	8Y.11M
Weird Portfolio	-8.09	0.79	10.8%	-0.38	3.96	0.7%	3.33	5.40	7.44	0%	-34.00	8Y.9M
GAA Global Asset Allocation	-5.91	1.18	9.5%	0.06	3.85	0%	1.99	4.09	4.99	0%	-26.03	8Y.9M
Robo Advisor 50	-7.48	0.37	13.5%	0.35	3.77	0%	1.84	4.21	5.04	0%	-31.78	7Y.8M
Aim Bold Strategy	-9.91	0.97	12.9%	1.27	3.75	0%	3.51	4.62	5.70	0%	-31.16	9Y.4M
Sandwich Portfolio	-6.56	0.55	13.2%	0.71	3.72	0%	2.11	4.23	4.94	0%	-30.05	6Y.6M
Talmud Portfolio	-12.75	0.88	12%	-1.18	3.69	0.7%	3.18	4.78	5.55	0%	-42.36	9Y.10M
Mid-Fifties	-13.10	-0.29	16%	-0.39	3.68	0.4%	2.46	4.73	5.66	0%	-47.03	9Y.8M
Late Sixties and Beyond	-11.72	0.54	13.2%	-0.10	3.67	0.4%	2.51	4.78	5.63	0%	-42.69	8Y.6M
Lazy Portfolio	-11.52	-0.29	16%	0.05	3.66	0%	2.57	4.41	5.31	0%	-41.79	9Y.2M
Seven Value	-11.45	0.26	14.5%	0.29	3.64	0%	2.64	4.12	5.21	0%	-42.13	9Y.2M
Six Ways from Sunday	-10.30	0.54	14.2%	0.63	3.57	0%	2.36	3.89	5.28	0%	-39.85	6Y.3M
Family Taxable Portfolio	-10.69	-0.60	17.5%	0.51	3.53	0%	2.66	4.40	5.16	0%	-39.41	9Y.8M
Late Thirties to Early Forties	-13.74	-1.03	16.6%	-0.71	3.48	0%	2.37	4.39	5.37	0%	-49.07	10Y.11M
Tilt Toward Value	-9.65	-0.88	17.5%	-0.52	3.46	0.7%	2.58	4.04	4.70	0%	-35.63	10Y.1M
Pinwheel	-8.93	0.11	13.9%	1.18	3.45	0%	2.01	4.11	5.31	0%	-37.86	6Y.1M

Order by **Baseline 7Y Return - Last 60 Years** (from 1963-12 to 2023-11)

Portfolio	3Y Rolling Annualized Return (%)			7Y Rolling Annualized Return (%)			15Y Rolling Annualized Return (%)				Max Draw-down (%)	Long Neg Period (Y.M)
	Worst	Base	%Fail	Worst	Base ▼	%Fail	Worst	Base	Median	%Fail		
Golden Butterfly	0.58	5.25	0%	4.29	7.07	0%	5.98	8.00	9.53	0%	-17.79	3Y.3M
All Weather Portfolio	-2.92	4.48	1.8%	3.15	6.76	0%	5.58	7.48	9.13	0%	-20.58	4Y.9M
In Saecula Saeculorum	-2.08	4.62	1.2%	3.55	6.48	0%	6.06	7.16	8.90	0%	-20.39	3Y.7M
Simplified Permanent Portfolio	-1.62	4.06	0.7%	3.15	6.11	0%	5.26	7.42	8.52	0%	-16.43	3Y.4M
Desert Portfolio	0.11	4.59	0%	4.04	5.97	0%	4.92	6.58	8.35	0%	-14.72	3Y.3M
Talmud Portfolio	-10.82	4.17	6.9%	0.39	5.82	0%	5.75	7.49	9.81	0%	-40.17	6Y.3M
Permanent Portfolio	-1.50	3.83	0.6%	3.19	5.65	0%	5.07	6.77	7.83	0%	-15.92	3Y.4M
One-Decision Portfolio	-7.87	4.38	4.7%	1.40	5.43	0%	4.80	6.42	9.20	0%	-31.96	5Y.4M
Stocks/Bonds 40/60	-2.41	3.88	1.8%	2.10	5.36	0%	5.22	6.06	8.48	0%	-19.17	4Y.2M
Stocks/Bonds 60/40	-6.40	3.68	7.7%	0.56	5.28	0%	5.21	6.50	9.22	0%	-30.55	9Y.2M
Stocks/Bonds 20/80	-2.58	4.03	1.6%	2.21	5.02	0%	3.93	5.42	7.67	0%	-16.57	4Y.2M
Simple Path to Wealth	-9.99	3.23	10.5%	-0.70	4.97	0.3%	5.00	6.60	9.70	0%	-38.53	10Y.2M
Stocks/Bonds 80/20	-11.24	3.09	10.8%	-1.13	4.86	0.6%	4.90	6.63	9.87	0%	-41.09	10Y.2M
US Stocks	-16.22	1.87	12.6%	-3.00	4.15	1.7%	4.37	6.49	10.48	0%	-50.84	11Y.7M
Total Bond US	5.50	2.63	2.6%	-0.23	4.05	0.3%	2.36	4.28	7.03	0%	-17.28	7Y.6M
10-year Treasury	-7.79	2.14	6.1%	-1.15	3.83	1.3%	2.09	4.59	7.58	0%	-23.18	10Y.6M
Warren Buffett Portfolio	-13.74	2.27	12.6%	-2.48	3.81	1.4%	4.09	5.85	10.01	0%	-45.52	11Y.0M
Robo Advisor 0	-1.33	1.52	2.3%	0.47	1.55	0%	1.02	2.49	6.61	0%	-8.48	4Y.1M
Short Term Treasury	-1.26	1.29	2.3%	0.39	1.39	0%	0.87	2.34	6.67	0%	-8.52	3Y.11M
Gold	-15.32	-6.07	32.9%	-6.75	-2.30	29.7%	-3.63	-1.12	7.05	19.6%	-61.78	27Y.5M

Order by **Baseline 7Y Return - Last 60 Years** (from 1963-12 to 2023-11) - **US Infl. Adjusted**

Portfolio	3Y Rolling Annualized Return (%)			7Y Rolling Annualized Return (%)			15Y Rolling Annualized Return (%)				Max Draw-down (%)	Long Neg Period (Y.M)
	Worst	Base	%Fail	Worst	Base ▼	%Fail	Worst	Base	Median	%Fail		
Golden Butterfly	-4.79	2.02	7.2%	0.30	3.81	0%	3.20	4.83	6.03	0%	-24.09	6Y.5M
Simplified Permanent Portfolio	-6.96	0.80	9.8%	-0.33	2.71	0.2%	1.81	3.63	5.14	0%	-25.58	9Y.1M
Permanent Portfolio	-6.86	0.55	10.5%	0.04	2.62	0%	2.20	3.41	4.64	0%	-23.32	7Y.9M
In Saecula Saeculorum	-6.04	-0.17	15.5%	-2.33	1.96	3.8%	0.29	3.76	5.35	0%	-26.94	14Y.2M
One-Decision Portfolio	-10.46	-0.16	15.5%	-4.14	1.36	9.6%	0.20	3.02	4.83	0%	-34.04	14Y.5M
Desert Portfolio	-5.11	0.63	11.8%	-1.01	1.31	2.2%	0.35	2.89	4.73	0%	-20.97	13Y.10M
Talmud Portfolio	-12.75	0.04	14.9%	-5.31	1.24	10.1%	-0.16	3.88	6.04	0.7%	-42.36	16Y.5M
All Weather Portfolio	-8.18	-0.08	15.3%	-1.82	1.13	4.9%	-0.24	3.39	5.69	1.3%	-27.79	18Y.0M
Stocks/Bonds 60/40	-12.03	-1.46	21.8%	-5.15	0.92	12.1%	-1.04	2.98	5.51	3.1%	-38.92	18Y.2M
Simple Path to Wealth	-14.36	-1.79	20.9%	-6.34	0.75	12.9%	-1.14	2.93	6.11	2.4%	-45.02	18Y.1M
Stocks/Bonds 80/20	-15.17	-1.96	20.4%	-6.75	0.67	13%	-1.19	2.85	6.31	2.4%	-46.99	18Y.0M
Stocks/Bonds 40/60	-9.10	-1.27	21%	-3.85	0.66	12.2%	-1.10	2.66	4.54	6.5%	-30.32	18Y.8M
US Stocks	-18.54	-2.55	20.6%	-8.51	0.01	14.9%	-1.47	2.39	6.97	2.2%	-54.53	18Y.1M
Stocks/Bonds 20/80	-7.85	-1.23	18.4%	-4.05	-0.24	15.9%	-1.56	1.77	3.82	8.9%	-30.21	18Y.9M
Warren Buffett Portfolio	-16.24	-3.11	23.8%	-7.74	-0.52	18.1%	-2.09	2.10	6.51	9.4%	-50.04	18Y.8M
Total Bond US	-10.69	-1.75	25.1%	-4.53	-0.74	19.9%	-2.30	0.30	3.30	11.8%	-35.11	20Y.8M
Robo Advisor 0	-6.71	-1.41	36.1%	-3.41	-0.81	27.5%	-1.43	0.02	2.33	14.6%	-24.64	25Y.2M
Short Term Treasury	-6.65	-1.57	36.2%	-3.25	-0.94	28.1%	-1.59	-0.10	2.29	16.8%	-23.89	25Y.5M
10-year Treasury	-13.24	-2.26	26.3%	-6.12	-1.45	23.6%	-3.52	0.40	3.98	13.7%	-45.61	21Y.5M
Gold	-20.28	-9.47	51.1%	-11.38	-5.24	44.3%	-7.77	-4.24	3.96	33.1%	-82.57	43Y.11M*

Order by **Baseline 7Y Return - All data** (from 1871/1927 to 2023-11)

Portfolio	3Y Rolling Annualized Return (%)			7Y Rolling Annualized Return (%)			15Y Rolling Annualized Return (%)				Max Draw-down (%)	Long Neg Period (Y.M)
	Worst	Base	%Fail	Worst	Base ▼	%Fail	Worst	Base	Median	%Fail		
Golden Butterfly	-17.91	4.12	4.4%	1.97	5.90	0%	3.74	6.72	8.30	0%	-48.31	6Y.2M
One-Decision Portfolio	-17.20	2.89	8.2%	-0.37	4.77	0.1%	1.95	5.74	6.96	0%	-47.77	12Y.10M
Talmud Portfolio	-21.82	2.69	9.4%	-1.75	4.74	0.9%	1.47	5.91	7.86	0%	-57.05	13Y.4M
Stocks/Bonds 40/60	-15.47	2.52	3.9%	-0.11	4.09	0.1%	2.53	4.88	6.22	0%	-43.68	7Y.1M
Stocks/Bonds 60/40	-25.23	1.83	9.4%	-2.67	4.06	0.7%	2.25	5.30	7.17	0%	-62.03	12Y.10M
Simple Path to Wealth	-32.34	0.98	12.7%	-4.94	3.91	2.2%	1.52	5.50	7.75	0%	-72.36	13Y.7M
In Saecula Saeculorum	-18.75	2.34	5.6%	-1.08	3.81	0.1%	2.31	4.69	6.79	0%	-50.22	8Y.9M
Stocks/Bonds 80/20	-34.67	0.72	13.4%	-5.77	3.81	2.6%	1.19	5.55	7.93	0%	-75.27	13Y.10M
Desert Portfolio	-10.95	2.84	2.1%	0.61	3.79	0%	2.35	4.23	5.86	0%	-33.15	6Y.8M
Stocks/Bonds 20/80	-5.37	3.02	1.7%	1.80	3.78	0%	2.76	4.13	5.14	0%	-18.94	5Y.1M
All Weather Portfolio	-12.66	2.56	3.4%	-0.03	3.52	0.1%	2.25	4.10	5.60	0%	-37.02	7Y.0M
Permanent Portfolio	-10.10	2.58	2.1%	0.58	3.46	0%	2.64	3.83	4.93	0%	-30.61	6Y.8M
US Stocks	-43.81	-0.56	15.9%	-9.49	3.29	4.2%	-0.35	5.49	8.60	0.1%	-84.60	15Y.8M
Warren Buffett Portfolio	-38.18	0.02	14.9%	-5.83	3.11	3.1%	-0.02	5.32	8.03	0.1%	-79.29	15Y.1M
Simplified Permanent Portfolio	-9.97	1.91	3.9%	0.56	2.83	0%	2.01	3.67	4.97	0%	-30.22	6Y.8M
Total Bond US	-5.59	2.15	1.6%	-0.23	2.57	0.1%	1.40	2.67	4.00	0%	-17.28	7Y.6M
10-year Treasury	-7.79	1.29	6.1%	-1.15	1.80	0.5%	0.98	2.14	4.04	0%	-23.18	10Y.6M
Robo Advisor 0	-1.33	1.56	1.1%	0.47	1.57	0%	1.00	2.22	4.38	0%	-8.48	4Y.1M
Short Term Treasury	-1.26	1.46	1.1%	0.39	1.52	0%	0.87	2.11	4.40	0%	-8.52	3Y.11M
Gold	-15.32	-1.61	23.9%	-6.75	-1.32	22.2%	-3.63	-0.50	0.05	21.3%	-61.78	62Y.0M

Order by **Baseline 7Y Return - All data** (from 1871/1927 to 2023-11) - **US Infl. Adjusted**

Portfolio	3Y Rolling Annualized Return (%)			7Y Rolling Annualized Return (%)			15Y Rolling Annualized Return (%)				Max Draw-down (%)	Long Neg Period (Y.M)
	Worst	Base	%Fail	Worst	Base ▼	%Fail	Worst	Base	Median	%Fail		
Golden Butterfly	-11.40	0.97	11.3%	-1.69	2.87	1.8%	1.09	3.80	5.39	0%	-34.73	12Y.7M
Simple Path to Wealth	-26.97	-1.25	18.8%	-6.34	1.57	9.9%	-1.97	2.62	6.11	2.3%	-65.10	20Y.6M
Stocks/Bonds 80/20	-29.49	-1.56	18.8%	-6.75	1.50	10.1%	-1.98	2.64	6.29	2.2%	-68.77	20Y.6M
Stocks/Bonds 60/40	-19.29	-0.93	18.1%	-6.22	1.42	9.4%	-2.07	2.33	5.45	2.6%	-52.05	21Y.11M
In Saecula Saeculorum	-12.96	-0.26	16.1%	-6.92	1.32	8.1%	-2.73	1.99	4.72	2.5%	-45.23	23Y.5M
Talmud Portfolio	-15.62	-0.56	16.2%	-5.31	1.27	8.3%	-0.52	2.02	4.93	1%	-45.76	18Y.9M
One-Decision Portfolio	-10.63	-0.59	16.9%	-4.14	1.12	8.7%	0.17	1.72	4.14	0%	-34.04	14Y.5M
Permanent Portfolio	-12.87	-0.07	15.3%	7.21	0.84	11.5%	-2.93	1.01	3.54	8%	-45.48	28Y.5M
Desert Portfolio	-13.19	0.10	14.7%	-7.17	0.81	9.4%	-2.83	1.34	4.08	3.5%	-46.37	28Y.2M
Stocks/Bonds 40/60	-12.93	-0.73	17.4%	-6.68	0.81	11.1%	-2.37	1.54	4.26	3.9%	-45.57	23Y.5M
US Stocks	-39.36	-2.49	20.7%	-8.51	0.77	12.6%	-2.10	2.40	6.93	2.5%	-80.55	26Y.4M
Warren Buffett Portfolio	-33.28	-2.46	20.5%	-7.74	0.68	12.6%	-2.12	2.23	6.43	4.7%	-73.85	20Y.4M
All Weather Portfolio	-14.36	-0.26	16.2%	-7.47	0.59	10.5%	-3.18	1.26	4.02	4.4%	-47.73	28Y.5M
Simplified Permanent Portfolio	-13.46	-0.41	16.3%	-8.12	0.32	12.3%	-3.95	0.80	3.74	8.8%	-49.37	33Y.9M
Stocks/Bonds 20/80	-13.27	-0.78	17.7%	-7.21	-0.25	15.9%	-2.77	0.61	3.27	8%	-46.65	28Y.4M
Total Bond US	-13.89	-2.23	26.6%	-7.81	-1.23	25.1%	-3.27	-0.65	2.01	21.8%	-48.08	51Y.10M
Robo Advisor 0	-12.40	-1.95	29.9%	-7.12	-1.34	25.6%	-3.23	-0.52	1.89	19.3%	-45.36	52Y.0M
Short Term Treasury	-12.29	-2.01	30.1%	-7.07	-1.41	25.7%	-3.27	-0.49	1.90	19.8%	-45.12	52Y.1M
10-year Treasury	-13.92	-2.32	28.7%	-8.73	-1.77	29%	-4.52	-1.17	2.36	28.1%	-58.48	85Y.5M
Gold	-20.28	-5.84	58.4%	-11.38	-4.43	56.9%	-7.77	-3.77	-0.10	50.5%	-82.57	132Y.3M

Ranking: Baseline 15Y Return

Order by **Baseline 15Y Return - Last 30 Years** (from 1993-12 to 2023-11)

Portfolio	3Y Rolling Annualized Return (%)			7Y Rolling Annualized Return (%)			15Y Rolling Annualized Return (%)				Max Draw-down (%)	Long Neg Period (Y.M)
	Worst	Base	%Fail	Worst	Base	%Fail	Worst	Base ▼	Median	%Fail		
Weird Portfolio	-6.05	3.47	3.1%	3.14	6.35	0%	5.80	7.87	10.02	0%	-32.97	3Y.11M
Shield Strategy	-5.00	5.05	3.7%	4.31	6.67	0%	6.31	7.48	8.43	0%	-19.36	3Y.8M
Golden Butterfly	0.58	4.71	0%	4.29	6.33	0%	5.98	7.47	8.12	0%	-17.79	3Y.3M
Yale Endowment	-9.18	2.78	7.1%	2.97	6.62	0%	5.46	7.41	8.12	0%	-39.48	5Y.2M
Stocks/Bonds 80/20 Momentum	-10.64	-0.93	16.6%	1.09	5.76	0%	5.92	7.22	9.54	0%	-43.61	9Y.4M
Talmud Portfolio	-10.82	4.06	7.1%	1.35	6.15	0%	5.75	7.16	7.91	0%	-40.17	5Y.5M
US Stocks Momentum	-15.43	-3.44	19.1%	-0.57	5.24	0.7%	5.61	7.13	10.08	0%	-53.85	10Y.6M
Mid-Fifties	-11.17	3.08	10.2%	2.16	6.11	0%	4.90	7.05	7.97	0%	-46.21	5Y.3M
All Weather Portfolio	-2.92	4.54	1.8%	3.15	6.37	0%	5.58	7.03	7.80	0%	-20.58	3Y.10M
Simplified Permanent Portfolio	-1.62	3.60	1.2%	3.15	5.07	0%	5.26	7.00	7.77	0%	-16.43	3Y.4M
Aim Bold Strategy	-7.69	3.74	7.1%	3.86	6.53	0%	5.99	6.97	8.05	0%	-30.09	4Y.5M
Late Sixties and Beyond	-9.76	4.05	7.4%	2.45	6.19	0%	4.95	6.93	7.88	0%	-41.80	5Y.2M
Marc Faber Portfolio	-3.16	3.80	1.2%	3.58	5.46	0%	4.95	6.92	8.61	0%	-28.82	3Y.5M
Late Thirties to Early Forties	-11.83	2.71	12.3%	1.83	5.84	0%	4.81	6.90	7.73	0%	-48.28	5Y.3M
Sheltered Sam 100/0	-16.64	1.84	13.2%	-0.40	5.23	0.7%	5.08	6.80	7.77	0%	-54.91	9Y.8M
Stocks/Bonds 60/40 Momentum	-6.27	0.17	14.2%	2.39	5.99	0%	5.99	6.79	8.52	0%	-32.52	4Y.5M
Aim comfortable trip	-1.22	4.14	1.2%	4.49	6.07	0%	5.25	6.78	7.60	0%	-20.15	3Y.3M
Lazy Portfolio	-9.56	2.84	8%	2.61	6.20	0%	5.01	6.78	7.63	0%	-40.89	5Y.2M
In Saecula Saeculorum	-2.08	3.65	2.2%	3.64	6.09	0%	6.06	6.74	7.34	0%	-20.39	3Y.7M
Mid-Twenties	-12.28	2.39	12.9%	1.72	5.72	0%	4.69	6.73	7.61	0%	-49.50	5Y.3M
Family Taxable Portfolio	-8.72	2.41	8.9%	3.08	6.29	0%	5.10	6.73	7.57	0%	-38.46	5Y.1M

Order by **Baseline 15Y Return - Last 30 Years** (from 1993-12 to 2023-11) - **US Infl. Adjusted**

Portfolio	3Y Rolling Annualized Return (%)			7Y Rolling Annualized Return (%)			15Y Rolling Annualized Return (%)				Max Draw-down (%)	Long Neg Period (Y.M)
	Worst	Base	%Fail	Worst	Base	%Fail	Worst	Base ▼	Median	%Fail		
Weird Portfolio	-8.09	0.79	10.8%	-0.38	3.96	0.7%	3.33	5.40	7.44	0%	-34.00	8Y.9M
Golden Butterfly	-4.79	2.36	5.5%	0.73	4.06	0%	3.52	5.13	5.79	0%	-23.38	5Y.11M
Yale Endowment	-11.15	-0.62	16.9%	0.40	4.21	0%	3.00	5.02	5.83	0%	-40.41	9Y.2M
Shield Strategy	-7.29	1.78	12%	1.63	4.00	0%	4.06	4.99	6.00	0%	-24.25	8Y.11M
All Weather Portfolio	-8.18	2.51	5.2%	-0.36	4.26	0.7%	3.11	4.81	5.51	0%	-27.79	8Y.9M
US Stocks Momentum	-17.26	-5.53	23.4%	-3.05	2.60	2.2%	3.37	4.81	7.64	0%	-54.55	12Y.5M
Stocks/Bonds 80/20 Momentum	-12.58	-4.00	22.8%	-1.43	3.16	1.1%	3.68	4.80	7.03	0%	-44.47	11Y.1M
Late Sixties and Beyond	-11.72	0.54	13.2%	-0.10	3.67	0.4%	2.51	4.78	5.63	0%	-42.69	8Y.6M
Talmud Portfolio	-12.75	0.88	12%	-1.18	3.69	0.7%	3.18	4.78	5.55	0%	-42.36	9Y.10M
Mid-Fifties	-13.10	-0.29	16%	-0.39	3.68	0.4%	2.46	4.73	5.66	0%	-47.03	9Y.8M
Simplified Permanent Portfolio	-6.96	1.62	6.2%	0.10	2.98	0%	2.82	4.65	5.45	0%	-23.93	7Y.3M
Aim Bold Strategy	-9.91	0.97	12.9%	1.27	3.75	0%	3.51	4.62	5.70	0%	-31.16	9Y.4M
Stocks/Bonds 60/40 Momentum	-8.30	-2.36	21.2%	-0.16	3.25	0.4%	3.74	4.52	6.14	0%	-33.56	9Y.11M
Aim comfortable trip	-3.36	2.06	9.5%	1.45	4.06	0%	2.79	4.50	5.28	0%	-22.06	5Y.5M
Lazy Portfolio	-11.52	-0.29	16%	0.05	3.66	0%	2.57	4.41	5.31	0%	-41.79	9Y.2M
Marc Faber Portfolio	-5.24	1.32	8%	0.56	3.05	0%	2.49	4.41	6.12	0%	-29.75	6Y.3M
Family Taxable Portfolio	-10.69	-0.60	17.5%	0.51	3.53	0%	2.66	4.40	5.16	0%	-39.41	9Y.8M
Late Thirties to Early Forties	-13.74	-1.03	16.6%	-0.71	3.48	0.7%	2.37	4.39	5.37	0%	-49.07	10Y.11M
Sheltered Sam 100/0	-18.44	-0.20	15.7%	-2.88	3.07	1.4%	2.53	4.38	5.36	0%	-55.61	11Y.9M
Sheltered Sam 90/10	-16.09	0.06	14.8%	-2.04	3.23	1.1%	2.80	4.34	5.21	0%	-50.88	11Y.7M
Global Market Portfolio	-7.63	0.72	11.4%	-0.40	4.01	0.7%	2.24	4.31	5.07	0%	-28.40	8Y.9M

Order by **Baseline 15Y Return** - **Last 60 Years** (from 1963-12 to 2023-11)

Portfolio	3Y Rolling Annualized Return (%)			7Y Rolling Annualized Return (%)			15Y Rolling Annualized Return (%)				Max Draw-down (%)	Long Neg Period (Y.M)
	Worst	Base	%Fail	Worst	Base	%Fail	Worst	Base ▼	Median	%Fail		
Golden Butterfly	0.58	5.25	0%	4.29	7.07	0%	5.98	8.00	9.53	0%	-17.79	3Y.3M
Talmud Portfolio	-10.82	4.17	6.9%	0.39	5.82	0%	5.75	7.49	9.81	0%	-40.17	6Y.3M
All Weather Portfolio	-2.92	4.48	1.8%	3.15	6.76	0%	5.58	7.48	9.13	0%	-20.58	4Y.9M
Simplified Permanent Portfolio	-1.62	4.06	0.7%	3.15	6.11	0%	5.26	7.42	8.52	0%	-16.43	3Y.4M
In Saecula Saeculorum	-2.08	4.62	1.2%	3.55	6.48	0%	6.06	7.16	8.90	0%	-20.39	3Y.7M
Permanent Portfolio	-1.50	3.83	0.6%	3.19	5.65	0%	5.07	6.77	7.83	0%	-15.92	3Y.4M
Stocks/Bonds 80/20	-11.24	3.09	10.8%	-1.13	4.86	0.6%	4.90	6.63	9.87	0%	-41.09	10Y.2M
Simple Path to Wealth	-9.99	3.23	10.5%	-0.70	4.97	0.3%	5.00	6.60	9.70	0%	-38.53	10Y.2M
Desert Portfolio	0.11	4.59	0%	4.04	5.97	0%	4.92	6.58	8.35	0%	-14.72	3Y.3M
Stocks/Bonds 60/40	-6.40	3.68	7.7%	0.56	5.28	0%	5.21	6.50	9.22	0%	-30.55	9Y.2M
US Stocks	-16.22	1.87	12.6%	-3.00	4.15	1.7%	4.37	6.49	10.48	0%	-50.84	11Y.7M
One-Decision Portfolio	-7.87	4.38	4.7%	1.40	5.43	0%	4.80	6.42	9.20	0%	-31.96	5Y.4M
Stocks/Bonds 40/60	-2.41	3.88	1.8%	2.10	5.36	0%	5.22	6.06	8.48	0%	-19.17	4Y.2M
Warren Buffett Portfolio	-13.74	2.27	12.6%	-2.48	3.81	1.4%	4.09	5.85	10.01	0%	-45.52	11Y.0M
Stocks/Bonds 20/80	-2.58	4.03	1.6%	2.21	5.02	0%	3.93	5.42	7.67	0%	-16.57	4Y.2M
10-year Treasury	-7.79	2.14	6.1%	-1.15	3.83	1.3%	2.09	4.59	7.58	0%	-23.18	10Y.6M
Total Bond US	-5.59	2.53	2.6%	-0.23	4.05	0.3%	2.36	4.28	7.03	0%	-17.28	7Y.6M
Robo Advisor 0	-1.33	1.52	2.3%	0.47	1.55	0%	1.02	2.49	6.61	0%	-8.48	4Y.1M
Short Term Treasury	-1.26	1.29	2.3%	0.39	1.39	0%	0.87	2.34	6.67	0%	-8.52	3Y.11M
Gold	-15.32	-6.07	32.9%	-6.75	-2.30	29.7%	-3.63	-1.12	7.05	19.6%	-61.78	27Y.5M

Order by **Baseline 15Y Return** - **Last 60 Years** (from 1963-12 to 2023-11) - **US Infl. Adjusted**

Portfolio	3Y Rolling Annualized Return (%)			7Y Rolling Annualized Return (%)			15Y Rolling Annualized Return (%)				Max Draw-down (%)	Long Neg Period (Y.M)
	Worst	Base	%Fail	Worst	Base	%Fail	Worst	Base ▼	Median	%Fail		
Golden Butterfly	-4.79	2.02	7.2%	0.30	3.81	0%	3.20	4.83	6.03	0%	-24.09	6Y.5M
Talmud Portfolio	-12.75	0.04	14.9%	-5.31	1.24	10.1%	-0.16	3.88	6.04	0.7%	-42.36	16Y.5M
In Saecula Saeculorum	-6.04	-0.17	15.5%	-2.33	1.96	3.8%	0.29	3.76	5.35	0%	-26.94	14Y.2M
Simplified Permanent Portfolio	-6.96	0.80	9.8%	-0.33	2.71	0.2%	1.81	3.63	5.14	0%	-25.58	9Y.1M
Permanent Portfolio	-6.86	0.55	10.5%	0.04	2.62	0%	2.20	3.41	4.64	0%	-23.32	7Y.9M
All Weather Portfolio	-8.18	-0.08	15.3%	-1.82	1.13	4.9%	-0.24	3.39	5.69	1.3%	-27.79	18Y.0M
One-Decision Portfolio	-10.46	-0.16	15.5%	-4.14	1.36	9.6%	0.20	3.02	4.83	0%	-34.04	14Y.5M
Stocks/Bonds 60/40	-12.03	-1.46	21.8%	-5.15	0.92	12.1%	-1.04	2.98	5.51	3.1%	-38.92	18Y.2M
Simple Path to Wealth	-14.36	-1.79	20.9%	-6.34	0.75	12.9%	-1.14	2.93	6.11	2.4%	-45.02	18Y.1M
Desert Portfolio	-5.11	0.63	11.8%	-1.01	1.31	2.2%	0.35	2.89	4.73	0%	-20.97	13Y.10M
Stocks/Bonds 80/20	-15.17	-1.96	20.4%	-6.75	0.67	13%	-1.19	2.85	6.31	2.4%	-46.99	18Y.0M
Stocks/Bonds 40/60	-9.10	-1.27	21%	-3.85	0.66	12.2%	-1.10	2.66	4.54	6.5%	-30.32	18Y.8M
US Stocks	-18.54	-2.55	20.6%	-8.51	0.01	14.9%	-1.47	2.39	6.97	2.2%	-54.53	18Y.1M
Warren Buffett Portfolio	-16.24	-3.11	23.8%	-7.74	-0.52	18.1%	-2.09	2.10	6.51	9.4%	-50.04	18Y.8M
Stocks/Bonds 20/80	-7.85	-1.23	18.4%	-4.05	-0.24	15.9%	-1.56	1.77	3.82	8.9%	-30.21	18Y.9M
10-year Treasury	-13.24	-2.26	26.3%	-6.12	-1.45	23.6%	-3.52	0.40	3.98	13.7%	-45.61	21Y.5M
Total Bond US	-10.69	-1.75	25.1%	-4.53	-0.74	19.9%	-2.30	0.30	3.30	11.8%	-35.11	20Y.8M
Robo Advisor 0	-6.71	-1.41	36.1%	-3.41	-0.81	27.5%	-1.43	0.02	2.33	14.6%	-24.64	25Y.2M
Short Term Treasury	-6.65	-1.57	36.2%	-3.25	-0.94	28.1%	-1.59	-0.10	2.29	16.8%	-23.89	25Y.5M
Gold	-20.28	-9.47	51.1%	-11.38	-5.24	44.3%	-7.77	-4.24	3.96	33.1%	-82.57	43Y.11M*

Order by **Baseline 15Y Return** - **All data** (from 1871/1927 to 2023-11)

Portfolio	3Y Rolling Annualized Return (%)			7Y Rolling Annualized Return (%)			15Y Rolling Annualized Return (%)				Max Draw-down (%)	Long Neg Period (Y.M)
	Worst	Base	%Fail	Worst	Base	%Fail	Worst	Base ▼	Median	%Fail		
Golden Butterfly	-17.91	4.12	4.4%	1.97	5.90	0%	3.74	6.72	8.30	0%	-48.31	6Y.2M
Talmud Portfolio	-21.82	2.69	9.4%	-1.75	4.74	0.9%	1.47	5.91	7.86	0%	-57.05	13Y.4M
One-Decision Portfolio	-17.20	2.89	8.2%	-0.37	4.77	0.1%	1.95	5.74	6.96	0%	-47.77	12Y.10M
Stocks/Bonds 80/20	-34.67	0.72	13.4%	-5.77	3.81	2.6%	1.19	5.55	7.93	0%	-75.27	13Y.10M
Simple Path to Wealth	-32.34	0.98	12.7%	-4.94	3.91	2.2%	1.52	5.50	7.75	0%	-72.36	13Y.7M
US Stocks	-43.81	-0.56	15.9%	-9.49	3.29	4.2%	-0.35	5.49	8.60	0.1%	-84.60	15Y.8M
Warren Buffett Portfolio	-38.18	0.02	14.9%	-5.83	3.11	3.1%	-0.02	5.32	8.03	0.1%	-79.29	15Y.1M
Stocks/Bonds 60/40	-25.23	1.83	9.4%	-2.67	4.06	0.7%	2.25	5.30	7.17	0%	-62.03	12Y.10M
Stocks/Bonds 40/60	-15.47	2.52	3.9%	-0.11	4.09	0.1%	2.53	4.88	6.22	0%	-43.68	7Y.1M
In Saecula Saeculorum	-18.75	2.34	5.6%	-1.08	3.81	0.1%	2.31	4.69	6.79	0%	-50.22	8Y.9M
Desert Portfolio	-10.95	2.84	2.1%	0.61	3.79	0%	2.35	4.23	5.86	0%	-33.15	6Y.8M
Stocks/Bonds 20/80	-5.37	3.02	1.7%	1.80	3.78	0%	2.76	4.13	5.14	0%	-18.94	5Y.1M
All Weather Portfolio	-12.66	2.56	3.4%	-0.03	3.52	0.1%	2.25	4.10	5.60	0%	-37.02	7Y.0M
Permanent Portfolio	-10.10	2.58	2.1%	0.58	3.46	0%	2.64	3.83	4.93	0%	-30.61	6Y.8M
Simplified Permanent Portfolio	-9.97	1.91	3.9%	0.56	2.83	0%	2.01	3.67	4.97	0%	-30.22	6Y.8M
Total Bond US	-5.59	2.15	1.6%	-0.23	2.57	0.1%	1.40	2.67	4.00	0%	-17.28	7Y.6M
Robo Advisor 0	-1.33	1.56	1.1%	0.47	1.57	0%	1.00	2.22	4.38	0%	-8.48	4Y.1M
10-year Treasury	-7.79	1.29	6.1%	-1.15	1.80	0.5%	0.98	2.14	4.04	0%	-23.18	10Y.6M
Short Term Treasury	-1.26	1.46	1.1%	0.39	1.52	0%	0.87	2.11	4.40	0%	-8.52	3Y.11M
Gold	-15.32	-1.61	23.9%	-6.75	-1.32	22.2%	-3.63	-0.50	0.05	21.3%	-61.78	62Y.0M

Order by **Baseline 15Y Return** - **All data** (from 1871/1927 to 2023-11) - **US Infl. Adjusted**

Portfolio	3Y Rolling Annualized Return (%)			7Y Rolling Annualized Return (%)			15Y Rolling Annualized Return (%)				Max Draw-down (%)	Long Neg Period (Y.M)
	Worst	Base	%Fail	Worst	Base	%Fail	Worst	Base ▼	Median	%Fail		
Golden Butterfly	-11.40	0.97	11.3%	-1.69	2.87	1.8%	1.09	3.80	5.39	0%	-34.73	12Y.7M
Stocks/Bonds 80/20	-29.49	-1.56	18.8%	-6.75	1.50	10.1%	-1.98	2.64	6.29	2.2%	-68.77	20Y.6M
Simple Path to Wealth	-26.97	-1.25	18.8%	-6.34	1.57	9.9%	-1.97	2.62	6.11	2.3%	-65.10	20Y.6M
US Stocks	-39.36	-2.49	20.7%	-8.51	0.77	12.6%	-2.10	2.40	6.93	2.5%	-80.55	26Y.4M
Stocks/Bonds 60/40	-19.29	-0.93	18.1%	-6.22	1.42	9.4%	-2.07	2.33	5.45	2.6%	-52.05	21Y.11M
Warren Buffett Portfolio	-33.28	-2.46	20.5%	-7.74	0.68	12.6%	-2.12	2.23	6.43	4.7%	-73.85	20Y.4M
Talmud Portfolio	-15.62	-0.56	16.2%	-5.31	1.27	8.3%	-0.52	2.02	4.93	1%	-45.76	18Y.9M
In Saecula Saeculorum	-12.96	-0.26	16.1%	-6.92	1.32	8.1%	-2.73	1.99	4.72	2.5%	-45.23	23Y.5M
One-Decision Portfolio	-10.63	-0.59	16.9%	-4.14	1.12	8.7%	0.17	1.72	4.14	0%	-34.04	14Y.5M
Stocks/Bonds 40/60	-12.93	-0.73	17.4%	-6.68	0.81	11.1%	-2.37	1.54	4.26	3.9%	-45.57	23Y.5M
Desert Portfolio	-13.19	0.10	14.7%	-7.17	0.81	9.4%	-2.83	1.34	4.08	3.5%	-46.37	28Y.2M
All Weather Portfolio	-14.36	-0.26	16.2%	-7.47	0.59	10.5%	-3.18	1.26	4.02	4.4%	-47.73	28Y.5M
Permanent Portfolio	-12.87	-0.07	15.3%	-7.21	0.84	11.5%	-2.93	1.01	3.54	8%	-45.48	28Y.5M
Simplified Permanent Portfolio	-13.46	-0.41	16.3%	-8.12	0.32	12.3%	-3.95	0.80	3.74	8.8%	-49.37	33Y.9M
Stocks/Bonds 20/80	-13.27	-0.78	17.7%	-7.21	-0.25	15.9%	-2.77	0.61	3.27	8%	-46.65	28Y.4M
Short Term Treasury	-12.29	-2.01	30.1%	-7.07	-1.41	25.7%	-3.27	-0.49	1.90	19.8%	-45.12	52Y.1M
Robo Advisor 0	-12.40	-1.95	29.9%	-7.12	-1.34	25.6%	-3.23	-0.52	1.89	19.3%	-45.36	52Y.0M
Total Bond US	-13.89	-2.23	26.6%	-7.81	-1.23	25.1%	-3.27	-0.65	2.01	21.8%	-48.08	51Y.10M
10-year Treasury	-13.92	-2.32	28.7%	-8.73	-1.77	29%	-4.52	-1.17	2.36	28.1%	-58.48	85Y.5M
Gold	-20.28	-5.84	58.4%	-11.38	-4.43	56.9%	-7.77	-3.77	-0.10	50.5%	-82.57	132Y.3M

238

Ranking: Median 15Y Return

Order by **Median 15Y Return** - **Last 30 Years** (from 1993-12 to 2023-11)

Portfolio	3Y Rolling Annualized Return (%)			7Y Rolling Annualized Return (%)			15Y Rolling Annualized Return (%)				Max Draw-down (%)	Long Neg Period (Y.M)
	Worst	Base	%Fail	Worst	Base	%Fail	Worst	Base	Median ▼	%Fail		
US Stocks Momentum	-15.43	-3.44	19.1%	-0.57	5.24	0.7%	5.61	7.13	10.08	0%	-53.85	10Y.6M
Technology	-38.68	-0.88	16.9%	-12.13	1.90	11.9%	0.35	5.73	10.05	0%	-81.08	14Y.6M
Weird Portfolio	-6.05	3.47	3.1%	3.14	6.35	0%	5.80	7.87	10.02	0%	-32.97	3Y.11M
Stocks/Bonds 80/20 Momentum	-10.64	-0.93	16.6%	1.09	5.76	0%	5.92	7.22	9.54	0%	-43.61	9Y.4M
Gold	-15.02	-6.98	33.9%	-6.20	-2.30	24.2%	3.86	6.28	8.84	0%	-42.91	12Y.1M
Marc Faber Portfolio	-3.16	3.80	1.2%	3.58	5.46	0%	4.95	6.92	8.61	0%	-28.82	3Y.5M
Stocks/Bonds 60/40 Momentum	-6.27	0.17	14.2%	2.39	5.99	0%	5.99	6.79	8.52	0%	-32.52	4Y.5M
Shield Strategy	-5.00	5.05	3.7%	4.31	6.67	0%	6.31	7.48	8.43	0%	-19.36	3Y.8M
Paul Boyer Portfolio	-3.66	2.49	5.2%	1.86	3.92	0%	4.14	6.72	8.22	0%	-18.04	4Y.2M
Golden Butterfly	0.58	4.71	0%	4.29	6.33	0%	5.98	7.47	8.12	0%	-17.79	3Y.3M
Yale Endowment	-9.18	2.78	7.1%	2.97	6.62	0%	5.46	7.41	8.12	0%	-39.48	5Y.2M
Aim Bold Strategy	-7.69	3.74	7.1%	3.86	6.53	0%	5.99	6.97	8.05	0%	-30.09	4Y.5M
Aggressive Global Income	-15.19	1.96	12.3%	0.34	5.37	0%	3.90	5.86	8.04	0%	-52.63	9Y.2M
Robust	-11.22	2.53	8.6%	3.26	5.20	0%	4.84	6.44	8.01	0%	-44.20	5Y.2M
Mid-Fifties	-11.17	3.08	10.2%	2.16	6.11	0%	4.90	7.05	7.97	0%	-46.21	5Y.3M
Ultimate Buy and Hold Strategy	-17.09	0.99	12.6%	2.03	4.75	0%	4.09	6.28	7.97	0%	-57.21	5Y.8M
US Stocks Minimum Volatility	-11.41	-0.75	15.7%	-1.54	4.45	0.7%	5.48	6.20	7.92	0%	-43.27	10Y.11M
Talmud Portfolio	-10.82	4.06	7.1%	1.35	6.15	0%	5.75	7.16	7.91	0%	-40.17	5Y.5M
Late Sixties and Beyond	-9.76	4.05	7.4%	2.45	6.19	0%	4.95	6.93	7.88	0%	-41.80	5Y.9M
All Weather Portfolio	-2.92	4.54	1.8%	3.15	6.37	0%	5.58	7.03	7.80	0%	-20.58	3Y.10M
Simplified Permanent Portfolio	-1.62	3.60	1.2%	3.15	5.07	0%	5.26	7.00	7.77	0%	-16.43	3Y.4M

Order by **Median 15Y Return** - **Last 30 Years** (from 1993-12 to 2023-11) - **US Infl. Adjusted**

Portfolio	3Y Rolling Annualized Return (%)			7Y Rolling Annualized Return (%)			15Y Rolling Annualized Return (%)				Max Draw-down (%)	Long Neg Period (Y.M)
	Worst	Base	%Fail	Worst	Base	%Fail	Worst	Base	Median ▼	%Fail		
US Stocks Momentum	-17.26	-5.53	23.4%	-3.05	2.60	2.2%	3.37	4.81	7.64	0%	-54.55	12Y.5M
Technology	-40.16	-3.06	19.4%	-14.39	-0.80	16.3%	-1.78	3.23	7.61	5%	-82.10	17Y.3M
Weird Portfolio	-8.09	0.79	10.8%	-0.38	3.96	0%	3.33	5.40	7.44	0%	-34.00	8Y.9M
Stocks/Bonds 80/20 Momentum	-12.58	-4.00	22.8%	-1.43	3.16	1.1%	3.68	4.80	7.03	0%	-44.47	11Y.1M
Gold	-15.87	-8.89	42.5%	-8.11	-4.32	30.3%	1.46	3.82	6.62	0%	-45.57	13Y.3M
Stocks/Bonds 60/40 Momentum	-8.30	-2.36	21.2%	-0.16	3.25	0.4%	3.74	4.52	6.14	0%	-33.56	9Y.11M
Marc Faber Portfolio	-5.24	1.32	8%	0.56	3.05	0%	2.49	4.41	6.12	0%	-29.75	6Y.3M
Shield Strategy	-7.29	1.78	12%	1.63	4.00	0%	4.06	4.99	6.00	0%	-24.25	8Y.11M
Yale Endowment	-11.15	-0.62	16.9%	0.40	4.21	0%	3.00	5.02	5.83	0%	-40.41	9Y.2M
Golden Butterfly	-4.79	2.36	5.8%	0.73	4.06	0%	3.52	5.13	5.79	0%	-23.38	5Y.11M
Aggressive Global Income	-17.03	-1.15	17.5%	-2.16	2.98	1.1%	1.48	3.83	5.79	0%	-53.35	9Y.4M
Paul Boyer Portfolio	-8.90	0.69	11.4%	-1.61	1.66	2.9%	1.71	4.27	5.79	0%	-27.85	12Y.3M
Aim Bold Strategy	-9.91	0.97	12.9%	1.27	3.75	0%	3.51	4.62	5.70	0%	-31.16	9Y.4M
Mid-Fifties	-13.10	-0.29	16%	-0.39	3.68	0.4%	2.46	4.73	5.66	0%	-47.03	9Y.8M
Late Sixties and Beyond	-11.72	0.54	13.2%	-0.10	3.67	0.4%	2.51	4.78	5.63	0%	-42.69	8Y.6M
US Stocks Minimum Volatility	-13.33	-3.23	19.7%	-4.00	1.74	2.5%	2.98	3.76	5.61	0%	-44.14	12Y.3M
Ultimate Buy and Hold Strategy	-18.88	-0.91	18.8%	-0.51	2.48	0.7%	1.67	4.20	5.60	0%	-57.87	11Y.7M
Talmud Portfolio	-12.75	0.88	12%	-1.18	3.69	0.7%	3.18	4.78	5.55	0%	-42.36	9Y.10M
Robust	-13.14	-0.38	15.7%	0.68	3.03	0%	2.40	4.24	5.53	0%	-45.06	8Y.9M
All Weather Portfolio	-8.18	2.51	5.2%	-0.36	4.26	0.7%	3.11	4.81	5.51	0%	-27.79	8Y.9M
Simplified Permanent Portfolio	-6.96	1.62	6.2%	0.10	2.98	0%	2.82	4.65	5.45	0%	-23.93	7Y.3M

239

Order by **Median 15Y Return - Last 60 Years** (from 1963-12 to 2023-11)

Portfolio	3Y Rolling Annualized Return (%)			7Y Rolling Annualized Return (%)			15Y Rolling Annualized Return (%)				Max Draw-down (%)	Long Neg Period (Y.M)
	Worst	Base	%Fail	Worst	Base	%Fail	Worst	Base	Median ▼	%Fail		
US Stocks	-16.22	1.87	12.6%	-3.00	4.15	1.7%	4.37	6.49	10.48	0%	-50.84	11Y.7M
Warren Buffett Portfolio	-13.74	2.27	12.6%	-2.48	3.81	1.4%	4.09	5.85	10.01	0%	-45.52	11Y.0M
Stocks/Bonds 80/20	-11.24	3.09	10.8%	-1.13	4.86	0.6%	4.90	6.63	9.87	0%	-41.09	10Y.2M
Talmud Portfolio	-10.82	4.17	6.9%	0.39	5.82	0%	5.75	7.49	9.81	0%	-40.17	6Y.3M
Simple Path to Wealth	-9.99	3.23	10.5%	-0.70	4.97	0.3%	5.00	6.60	9.70	0%	-38.53	10Y.2M
Golden Butterfly	0.58	5.25	0%	4.29	7.07	0%	5.98	8.00	9.53	0%	-17.79	3Y.3M
Stocks/Bonds 60/40	-6.40	3.68	7.7%	0.56	5.28	0%	5.21	6.50	9.22	0%	-30.55	9Y.2M
One-Decision Portfolio	-7.87	4.38	4.7%	1.40	5.43	0%	4.80	6.42	9.20	0%	-31.96	5Y.4M
All Weather Portfolio	-2.92	4.48	1.8%	3.15	6.76	0%	5.58	7.48	9.13	0%	-20.58	4Y.9M
In Saecula Saeculorum	-2.08	4.62	1.2%	3.55	6.48	0%	6.06	7.16	8.90	0%	-20.39	3Y.7M
Simplified Permanent Portfolio	-1.62	4.06	0.7%	3.15	6.11	0%	5.26	7.42	8.52	0%	-16.43	3Y.4M
Stocks/Bonds 40/60	-2.41	3.88	1.8%	2.10	5.36	0%	5.22	6.06	8.48	0%	-19.17	4Y.2M
Desert Portfolio	0.11	4.59	0%	4.04	5.97	0%	4.92	6.58	8.35	0%	-14.72	3Y.3M
Permanent Portfolio	-1.50	3.83	0.6%	3.19	5.65	0%	5.07	6.77	7.83	0%	-15.92	3Y.4M
Stocks/Bonds 20/80	-2.50	4.03	1.6%	2.21	5.02	0%	3.93	5.42	7.67	0%	-16.57	4Y.2M
10-year Treasury	-7.79	2.14	6.1%	-1.15	3.83	1.3%	2.09	4.59	7.58	0%	-23.18	10Y.6M
Gold	-15.32	-6.07	32.9%	-6.75	-2.30	29.7%	-3.63	-1.12	7.05	19.6%	-61.78	27Y.5M
Total Bond US	-5.59	2.53	2.6%	-0.23	4.05	0.3%	2.36	4.28	7.03	0%	-17.28	7Y.6M
Short Term Treasury	-1.26	1.29	2.3%	0.39	1.39	0%	0.87	2.34	6.67	0%	-8.52	3Y.11M
Robo Advisor 0	-1.33	1.52	2.3%	0.47	1.55	0%	1.02	2.49	6.61	0%	-8.48	4Y.1M

Order by **Median 15Y Return - Last 60 Years** (from 1963-12 to 2023-11) - **US Infl. Adjusted**

Portfolio	3Y Rolling Annualized Return (%)			7Y Rolling Annualized Return (%)			15Y Rolling Annualized Return (%)				Max Draw-down (%)	Long Neg Period (Y.M)
	Worst	Base	%Fail	Worst	Base	%Fail	Worst	Base	Median ▼	%Fail		
US Stocks	-18.54	-2.55	20.6%	-8.51	0.01	14.9%	-1.47	2.39	6.97	2.2%	-54.53	18Y.1M
Warren Buffett Portfolio	-16.24	-3.11	23.8%	-7.74	-0.52	18.1%	-2.09	2.10	6.51	9.4%	-50.04	18Y.8M
Stocks/Bonds 80/20	-15.17	-1.96	20.4%	-6.75	0.67	13%	-1.19	2.85	6.31	2.4%	-46.99	18Y.0M
Simple Path to Wealth	-14.36	-1.79	20.9%	-6.34	0.75	12.9%	-1.14	2.93	6.11	2.4%	-45.02	18Y.1M
Talmud Portfolio	-12.75	0.04	14.9%	-5.31	1.24	10.1%	-0.16	3.88	6.04	0.7%	-42.36	16Y.5M
Golden Butterfly	-4.79	2.02	7.2%	0.30	3.81	0%	3.20	4.83	6.03	0%	-24.09	6Y.5M
All Weather Portfolio	-8.18	-0.08	15.3%	-1.82	1.13	4.9%	-0.24	3.39	5.69	1.3%	-27.79	18Y.0M
Stocks/Bonds 60/40	-12.03	-1.46	21.8%	-5.15	0.92	12.1%	-1.04	2.98	5.51	3.1%	-38.92	18Y.2M
In Saecula Saeculorum	-6.04	-0.17	15.5%	-2.33	1.96	3.8%	0.29	3.76	5.35	0%	-26.94	14Y.2M
Simplified Permanent Portfolio	-6.96	0.80	9.8%	-0.33	2.71	0.2%	1.81	3.63	5.14	0%	-25.58	9Y.1M
One-Decision Portfolio	-10.46	-0.16	15.5%	-4.14	1.36	9.6%	0.20	3.02	4.83	0%	-34.04	14Y.5M
Desert Portfolio	-5.11	0.63	11.8%	-1.01	1.31	2.2%	0.35	2.89	4.73	0%	-20.97	13Y.10M
Permanent Portfolio	-6.86	0.55	10.5%	0.04	2.62	0%	2.20	3.41	4.64	0%	-23.32	7Y.9M
Stocks/Bonds 40/60	-9.10	-1.27	21%	-3.85	0.66	12.2%	-1.10	2.66	4.54	6.5%	-30.32	18Y.8M
10-year Treasury	-13.24	-2.26	26.3%	-6.12	-1.45	23.6%	-3.52	0.40	3.98	13.7%	-45.61	21Y.5M
Gold	-20.28	-9.47	51.1%	-11.38	-5.24	44.3%	-7.77	-4.24	3.96	33.1%	-82.57	43Y.11M*
Stocks/Bonds 20/80	-7.85	-1.23	18.4%	-4.05	-0.24	15.9%	-1.56	1.77	3.82	8.9%	-30.21	18Y.9M
Total Bond US	-10.69	-1.75	25.1%	-4.53	-0.74	19.9%	-2.30	0.30	3.30	11.8%	-35.11	20Y.8M
Robo Advisor 0	-6.71	-1.41	36.1%	-3.41	-0.81	27.5%	-1.43	0.02	2.33	14.6%	-24.64	25Y.2M
Short Term Treasury	-6.65	-1.57	36.2%	-3.25	-0.94	28.1%	-1.59	-0.10	2.29	16.8%	-23.89	25Y.8M

Order by **Median 15Y Return** - **All data** (from 1871/1927 to 2023-11)

Portfolio	3Y Rolling Annualized Return (%)			7Y Rolling Annualized Return (%)			15Y Rolling Annualized Return (%)				Max Draw-down (%)	Long Neg Period (Y.M)
	Worst	Base	%Fail	Worst	Base	%Fail	Worst	Base	Median ▼	%Fail		
US Stocks	-43.81	-0.56	15.9%	-9.49	3.29	4.2%	-0.35	5.49	8.60	0.1%	-84.60	15Y.8M
Golden Butterfly	-17.91	4.12	4.4%	1.97	5.90	0%	3.74	6.72	8.30	0%	-48.31	6Y.2M
Warren Buffett Portfolio	-38.18	0.02	14.9%	-5.83	3.11	3.1%	-0.02	5.32	8.03	0.1%	-79.29	15Y.1M
Stocks/Bonds 80/20	-34.67	0.72	13.4%	-5.77	3.81	2.6%	1.19	5.55	7.93	0%	-75.27	13Y.10M
Talmud Portfolio	-21.82	2.69	9.4%	-1.75	4.74	0.9%	1.47	5.91	7.86	0%	-57.05	13Y.4M
Simple Path to Wealth	-32.34	0.98	12.7%	-4.94	3.91	2.2%	1.52	5.50	7.75	0%	-72.36	13Y.7M
Stocks/Bonds 60/40	-25.23	1.83	9.4%	-2.67	4.06	0.7%	2.25	5.30	7.17	0%	-62.03	12Y.10M
One-Decision Portfolio	-17.20	2.89	8.2%	-0.37	4.77	0.1%	1.95	5.74	6.96	0%	-47.77	12Y.10M
In Saecula Saeculorum	-18.75	2.34	5.6%	-1.08	3.81	0.1%	2.31	4.69	6.79	0%	-50.22	8Y.9M
Stocks/Bonds 40/60	-15.47	2.52	3.9%	-0.11	4.09	0.1%	2.53	4.88	6.22	0%	-43.68	7Y.1M
Desert Portfolio	-10.95	2.84	2.1%	0.61	3.79	0%	2.35	4.23	5.86	0%	-33.15	6Y.8M
All Weather Portfolio	-12.66	2.56	3.4%	-0.03	3.52	0.1%	2.25	4.10	5.60	0%	-37.02	7Y.0M
Stocks/Bonds 20/80	-5.37	3.02	1.7%	1.80	3.78	0%	2.76	4.13	5.14	0%	-18.94	5Y.1M
Simplified Permanent Portfolio	-9.97	1.91	3.9%	0.56	2.83	0%	2.01	3.67	4.97	0%	-30.22	6Y.8M
Permanent Portfolio	-10.10	2.58	2.1%	0.58	3.46	0%	2.64	3.83	4.93	0%	-30.61	6Y.8M
Short Term Treasury	-1.26	1.46	1.1%	0.39	1.52	0%	0.87	2.11	4.40	0%	-8.52	3Y.11M
Robo Advisor 0	-1.33	1.56	1.1%	0.47	1.57	0%	1.00	2.22	4.38	0%	-8.48	4Y.1M
10-year Treasury	-7.79	1.29	6.1%	-1.15	1.80	0.5%	0.98	2.14	4.04	0%	-23.18	10Y.6M
Total Bond US	-5.59	2.15	1.6%	-0.23	2.57	0.1%	1.40	2.67	4.00	0%	-17.28	7Y.6M
Gold	-15.32	-1.61	23.9%	-6.75	-1.32	22.2%	-3.63	-0.50	0.05	21.3%	-61.78	62Y.0M

Order by **Median 15Y Return** - **All data** (from 1871/1927 to 2023-11) - **US Infl. Adjusted**

Portfolio	3Y Rolling Annualized Return (%)			7Y Rolling Annualized Return (%)			15Y Rolling Annualized Return (%)				Max Draw-down (%)	Long Neg Period (Y.M)
	Worst	Base	%Fail	Worst	Base	%Fail	Worst	Base	Median ▼	%Fail		
US Stocks	-39.36	-2.49	20.7%	-8.51	0.77	12.6%	-2.10	2.40	6.93	2.5%	-80.55	26Y.4M
Warren Buffett Portfolio	-33.28	-2.46	20.5%	-7.74	0.68	12.6%	-2.12	2.23	6.43	4.7%	-73.85	20Y.4M
Stocks/Bonds 80/20	-29.49	-1.56	18.8%	-6.75	1.50	10.1%	-1.98	2.64	6.29	2.2%	-68.77	20Y.6M
Simple Path to Wealth	-26.97	-1.25	18.8%	-6.34	1.57	9.9%	-1.97	2.62	6.11	2.3%	-65.10	20Y.6M
Stocks/Bonds 60/40	-19.29	-0.93	18.1%	-6.22	1.42	9.4%	-2.07	2.33	5.45	2.6%	-52.05	21Y.11M
Golden Butterfly	-11.40	0.97	11.3%	-1.69	2.87	1.8%	1.09	3.80	5.39	0%	-34.73	12Y.7M
Talmud Portfolio	-15.62	-0.56	16.2%	-5.31	1.27	8.3%	-0.52	2.02	4.93	1%	-45.76	18Y.9M
In Saecula Saeculorum	-12.96	-0.26	16.1%	-6.92	1.32	8.1%	-2.73	1.99	4.72	2.5%	-45.23	23Y.5M
Stocks/Bonds 40/60	-12.93	-0.73	17.4%	-6.68	0.81	11.1%	-2.37	1.54	4.26	3.9%	-45.57	23Y.5M
One-Decision Portfolio	-10.63	-0.59	16.9%	-4.14	1.12	8.7%	0.17	1.72	4.14	0%	-34.04	14Y.5M
Desert Portfolio	-13.19	0.10	14.7%	-7.17	0.81	9.4%	-2.83	1.34	4.08	3.5%	-46.37	28Y.2M
All Weather Portfolio	-14.36	-0.26	16.2%	-7.47	0.59	10.5%	-3.18	1.26	4.02	4.4%	-47.73	28Y.5M
Simplified Permanent Portfolio	-13.46	-0.41	16.3%	-8.12	0.32	12.3%	-3.95	0.80	3.74	8.8%	-49.37	33Y.9M
Permanent Portfolio	-12.87	-0.07	15.3%	-7.21	0.84	11.5%	-2.93	1.01	3.54	8%	-45.48	28Y.5M
Stocks/Bonds 20/80	-13.27	-0.78	17.7%	-7.21	-0.25	15.9%	-2.77	0.61	3.27	8%	-46.65	28Y.4M
10-year Treasury	-13.92	-2.32	28.7%	-8.73	-1.77	29%	-4.52	-1.17	2.36	28.1%	-58.48	85Y.5M
Total Bond US	-13.89	-2.23	26.6%	-7.81	-1.23	25.1%	-3.27	-0.65	2.01	21.8%	-48.08	51Y.10M
Short Term Treasury	-12.29	-2.01	30.1%	-7.07	-1.41	25.7%	-3.27	-0.49	1.90	19.8%	-45.12	52Y.1M
Robo Advisor 0	-12.40	-1.95	29.9%	-7.12	-1.34	25.6%	-3.23	-0.52	1.89	19.3%	-45.36	52Y.0M
Gold	-20.28	-5.84	58.4%	-11.38	-4.43	56.9%	-7.77	-3.77	-0.10	50.5%	-82.57	132Y.3M

'Multi-Horizon' Portfolios

And what if we wanted a portfolio that would be suitable for different time horizons? Are there interesting solutions?

Let's try to present another ranking, for the 'indecisive' who haven't chosen a specific time horizon or simply prefer to hold the portfolio for an indefinite period.

We sought an asset allocation that, in nominal terms, provided:

- 3Y Baseline return >= 3%
- 3Y %Fail <= 1%
- 7Y Baseline return >= 5%
- 15Y Baseline return >= 7.5%

We found this, considering the last 30 and 60 years.

Order by **Baseline 3Y Return - Last 30 Years** (from 1993-12 to 2023-11)

Portfolio	3Y Rolling Annualized Return (%)			7Y Rolling Annualized Return (%)			15Y Rolling Annualized Return (%)				Max Draw-down (%)	Long Neg Period (Y.M)
	Worst	Base ▼	%Fail	Worst	Base	%Fail	Worst	Base	Median	%Fail		
VTI-IJS-EMB-TLT-GLD	-0.87	5.63	0.9%	4.00	7.13	0%	6.32	8.36	9.58	0%	-21.87	3Y.3M
IJS-VTV-EMB-TLT-GLD	-1.18	5.23	0.6%	3.63	6.87	0%	6.02	8.04	9.52	0%	-19.80	3Y.3M
IJS-MTUM-EMB-IEI-GLD	-1.24	5.18	0.6%	4.52	7.04	0%	5.88	7.92	9.31	0%	-21.00	3Y.2M
VTI-IJS-BNDX-TLT-GLD	-0.16	5.04	0.6%	4.16	6.78	0%	6.44	7.87	8.67	0%	-19.46	3Y.3M
IJS-MTUM-BND-EMB-GLD	-1.88	5.03	0.9%	4.50	7.18	0%	5.87	7.99	9.25	0%	-21.83	3Y.3M
VTI-IJS-TLT-TIP-GLD	0.07	5.03	0%	4.31	6.69	0%	6.30	7.82	8.65	0%	-19.83	3Y.3M
IJS-MTUM-IEI-GLD	-1.31	5.00	0.9%	5.47	7.49	0%	6.49	8.26	8.95	0%	-22.67	3Y.2M
VTI-BNDX-EMB-CWB-GLD	-1.29	4.99	0.9%	4.62	6.43	0%	5.84	7.57	8.50	0%	-23.73	3Y.2M
IJS-VTV-BNDX-TLT-GLD	-0.46	4.99	0.3%	3.78	6.55	0%	6.13	7.66	8.53	0%	-17.40	3Y.3M
VTI-IJS-TLT-IEI-GLD	-0.07	4.96	0.3%	4.11	6.57	0%	6.22	7.80	8.52	0%	-18.99	3Y.3M

Order by **Baseline 3Y Return - Last 60 Years** (from 1963-12 to 2023-11)

Portfolio	3Y Rolling Annualized Return (%)			7Y Rolling Annualized Return (%)			15Y Rolling Annualized Return (%)				Max Draw-down (%)	Long Neg Period (Y.M)
	Worst	Base ▼	%Fail	Worst	Base	%Fail	Worst	Base	Median	%Fail		
VTI-IJS-TLT-GLD	-0.79	5.72	0.6%	5.09	7.77	0%	7.06	8.97	10.45	0%	-21.63	3Y.3M
VTI-IJS-TLT-LQD-GLD	-0.61	5.54	0.4%	4.18	7.33	0%	6.41	8.51	9.84	0%	-21.13	3Y.3M
VTI-IJS-TLT-IEI-GLD	-0.07	5.49	0.2%	4.11	7.33	0%	6.22	8.37	9.80	0%	-18.99	3Y.3M
VTI-IJS-BND-TLT-GLD	-0.36	5.47	0.3%	4.08	7.21	0%	6.22	8.35	9.76	0%	-19.78	3Y.3M
IJS-VTV-TLT-LQD-GLD	-0.70	5.32	0.9%	3.82	7.11	0%	6.11	8.33	9.87	0%	-19.07	3Y.3M
IJS-VTV-BND-TLT-GLD	-0.30	5.29	0.3%	3.71	6.99	0%	5.91	8.15	9.78	0%	-18.37	3Y.3M
VTI-IJS-IEI-GLD	-1.41	5.29	0.4%	4.47	7.45	0%	6.39	8.26	9.99	0%	-21.51	3Y.2M
IJS-VTV-TLT-IEI-GLD	-0.30	5.29	0.3%	3.73	6.96	0%	5.91	8.22	9.84	0%	-18.38	3Y.3M
VTI-IJS-LQD-GLD	-3.27	5.26	0.6%	4.67	7.61	0%	6.59	8.41	10.12	0%	-25.16	3Y.7M
VTI-IJS-TLT-SHY-GLD	0.58	5.25	0%	4.29	7.07	0%	5.98	8.00	9.53	0%	-17.79	3Y.3M

Considering only the assets with an 'extended' data source (up to 1871/1927), we didn't find anything that met the specified filters. To achieve results, we have to 'allow' a higher %Fail in the short term.

Order by **Baseline 3Y Return - All data** (from 1871/1927 to 2023-11)

Portfolio	3Y Rolling Annualized Return (%)			7Y Rolling Annualized Return (%)			15Y Rolling Annualized Return (%)				Max Draw-down (%)	Long Neg Period (Y.M)
	Worst	Base ▼	%Fail	Worst	Base	%Fail	Worst	Base	Median	%Fail		
VTI-IJS-IEI-GLD	-22.93	4.28	6%	1.05	6.45	0%	3.59	7.65	9.07	0%	-57.76	8Y.7M
VTI-IJS-TLT-GLD	-23.44	4.21	5.9%	0.92	6.49	0%	3.67	7.73	9.33	0%	-58.64	8Y.7M
VTI-IJS-BND-GLD	-22.93	4.14	6.1%	1.06	6.43	0%	3.59	7.64	9.04	0%	-57.75	8Y.7M
VTI-IJS-LQD-GLD	-23.00	4.09	6%	1.05	6.58	0%	3.64	7.70	9.07	0%	-57.86	8Y.7M
IJS-VTV-TLT-GLD	-23.20	4.07	6.3%	0.63	6.26	0%	3.46	7.65	9.23	0%	-58.45	8Y.7M
IJS-VTV-IEI-GLD	-22.68	4.04	6%	0.76	6.29	0%	3.38	7.51	9.02	0%	-57.54	8Y.7M
IJS-VTV-LQD-GLD	-22.74	3.98	6.4%	0.76	6.37	0%	3.43	7.63	9.01	0%	-57.65	8Y.7M
IJS-VTV-BND-GLD	-22.67	3.98	6%	0.77	6.31	0%	3.39	7.50	8.97	0%	-57.53	8Y.7M
IJS-IEI	-23.26	3.46	7.4%	0.89	6.04	0%	4.01	7.69	10.18	0%	-58.38	6Y.4M
IJS-BND	-23.25	3.36	7.9%	0.91	6.03	0%	4.02	7.55	10.19	0%	-58.36	6Y.4M

As you can see, by including the most 'disastrous' periods in the markets, the recorded drawdown was significantly higher.

If we want asset allocations that have never disappointed in the past, even in the short term (and therefore we want %Fail = 0% and Long Negative Period < 3 years), here's what we get:

Order by **Baseline 3Y Return - Last 30 Years** (from 1993-12 to 2023-11)

Portfolio	3Y Rolling Annualized Return (%)			7Y Rolling Annualized Return (%)			15Y Rolling Annualized Return (%)				Max Draw-down (%)	Long Neg Period (Y.M)
	Worst	Base	%Fail	Worst	Base	%Fail	Worst	Base ▼	Median	%Fail		
VTI-BNDX-GLD	0.16	3.75	0%	4.02	5.67	0%	6.10	7.32	8.07	0%	-20.64	2Y.11M
VTI-IJS-TLT-BIL-GLD	0.15	4.46	0%	4.48	6.16	0%	5.86	7.28	7.85	0%	-16.77	2Y.11M
VTV-MTUM-IEI-TIP-GLD	0.16	4.11	0%	5.27	6.43	0%	5.73	7.27	7.81	0%	-20.21	2Y.11M
IJS-BNDX-GLD	0.25	3.85	0%	3.05	5.42	0%	5.90	7.25	8.77	0%	-18.47	2Y.11M
VTI-IEI-GLD	0.21	3.39	0%	3.47	5.44	0%	5.75	7.19	7.86	0%	-16.66	2Y.9M
IJS-VTV-TLT-SHY-GLD	0.28	4.71	0%	3.89	6.17	0%	5.67	7.12	8.03	0%	-15.75	2Y.11M
IJS-MTUM-SHY-IEI-GLD	0.21	4.53	0%	4.74	6.32	0%	5.53	7.07	7.85	0%	-17.72	2Y.11M
VTV-LQD-GLD	0.31	3.64	0%	3.84	5.47	0%	5.69	7.06	7.92	0%	-22.18	2Y.11M
VTV-BNDX-GLD	0.69	3.97	0%	3.71	5.45	0%	5.69	6.96	7.89	0%	-20.54	2Y.11M
VTI-VTV-IEI-TIP-GLD	0.09	3.93	0%	4.49	6.14	0%	5.65	6.84	7.44	0%	-19.27	2Y.11M

Order by **Baseline 3Y Return** - **Last 60 Years** (from 1963-12 to 2023-11)

Portfolio	3Y Rolling Annualized Return (%)			7Y Rolling Annualized Return (%)			15Y Rolling Annualized Return (%)				Max Draw-down (%)	Long Neg Period (Y.M)
	Worst	Base	%Fail	Worst	Base	%Fail	Worst	Base ▼	Median	%Fail		
VTI-IJS-TLT-BIL-GLD	0.15	5.02	0%	4.48	6.91	0%	5.86	7.75	9.22	0%	-16.77	2Y.11M
VTI-IJS-SHY-IEI-GLD	0.12	5.13	0%	3.95	6.62	0%	5.44	7.36	9.20	0%	-16.78	2Y.11M
IJS-SHY-LQD-GLD	0.07	4.28	0%	2.78	5.84	0%	4.81	7.07	8.40	0%	-14.60	2Y.10M
IJS-BND-SHY-GLD	0.07	4.08	0%	2.58	5.61	0%	4.54	6.87	8.19	0%	-13.70	2Y.11M
IJS-IEI-LQD-BIL-GLD	0.30	4.05	0%	2.67	5.47	0%	4.25	6.58	7.84	0%	-12.87	2Y.11M
VTI-SHY-IEI-GLD	0.29	3.91	0%	2.72	5.43	0%	4.60	6.51	7.66	0%	-12.36	2Y.9M
VTI-LQD-BIL-GLD	0.30	3.88	0%	3.24	5.48	0%	4.78	6.37	7.28	0%	-16.57	2Y.10M
IJS-BND-IEI-BIL-GLD	0.30	3.97	0%	2.50	5.15	0%	4.02	6.36	7.68	0%	-11.75	2Y.10M
VTV-LQD-BIL-GLD	0.22	3.71	0%	3.16	5.22	0%	4.49	6.24	7.39	0%	-16.50	2Y.6M
IJS-SHY-LQD-BIL-GLD	0.05	3.97	0%	2.41	5.09	0%	4.01	6.20	7.50	0%	-11.61	2Y.10M

At this point, we leave to your imagination and experimentation any subsequent exploration, hoping to have provided you with interesting ideas.

Conclusion

Cultivate the calm and patient approach to investing. The stock market is designed to transfer money from the active to the patient.

WARREN BUFFETT

We are at the end of the journey: it's time for a nice summary of the investment strategy we have presented.

We wrote this book because we want to provide a method, as rigorous as possible, to help you identify the asset allocation that suits you and the most suitable tools to replicate it.

To outline the path to follow, these are the main phases of the process.

Phase 1: Analysis and Planning

- Clearly identify short-term, medium-term, and long-term financial goals. For example: retirement savings, home purchase, or children's education. In the end, each goal will correspond to a portfolio. For the more experienced, this is 'Goal-Based Investing'.

- Decide on the maximum predetermined time to achieve the goals. For example: 3 years, 7 years, 15 years, etc.

Phase 2: Identification of Suitable Metrics

- Choose metrics that best 'measure' a portfolio, based on the defined time horizon in the previous step. If you have little time available (for example, a maximum of 3-5 years), prefer metrics that measure 'risk' and completely ignore long-term returns. In general, however, it is never wrong to start with a risk assessment.

- The key metrics we have chosen are as follows, but choose others if you deem it appropriate:

	Objectives		
	Long Term ≥15Y	Medium Term ~7Y	Short Term ~3Y
Long term (15Y) rolling return			
Worst	O		
Baseline	X		
Median	X		
%fail	O		
Medium term (7Y) rolling return			
Worst		O	
Baseline		X	
%fail		O	
Short term (3Y) rolling return			
Worst			O
Baseline			X
%fail			O
Maximum drawdown	O	X	X
Longest Negative Period	O	X	X

X = recommended
O = optional

Phase 3: Selection of Asset Allocation

- Work with a sufficiently deep historical period, at least 30 years. If you feel more comfortable with traditional and 'classic' asset classes, consider a longer history (at least 50-60 years).

- Identify an asset allocation (here in the book or on the *LazyPortfolioEtf.com* simulator) that shows satisfactory values for the metrics identified earlier. Take into account inflation and, if necessary, currency exchange effects.

- Do not overdo the number of assets and do not adjust the percentage weights afterward to 'fine-tune' overall returns. Such an approach may lead you to choose asset allocations that are too 'tailored' to historical data, which may not perform as well in the future. This is the negative effect of the so-called *overfitting*.

Phase 4: Implement the Portfolio

- Always choose low-cost instruments (typically ETFs) when implementing such broad and generic assets. Active management, typical of investment funds, has not proven historically efficient in this case.

- Determine the budget to allocate to the portfolio. Purchase the identified instruments through your broker or bank. The amount of each asset relative to your budget must clearly respect the appropriate weight specified by the asset allocation.

Phase 5: Wait and Rebalance

- Respecting the time horizon, let the markets run their course. Performances come from the markets, not from investor activity.

- Periodically (for example, annually), rebalance the weights of the assets to restore them to their original percentage composition.

The Importance of Professional Assistance

Even if everything seems simple and straightforward, even if you feel calm and confident, consider whether it's worthwhile to seek support from a financial coach.

A financial coach provides an external and objective perspective on your financial situation. They can offer a more distant and pragmatic viewpoint while you may be emotionally involved in your financial decisions.

With a financial coach, you can save time in researching and managing your finances. This reduces the stress associated with complex financial decisions, allowing you to focus on other aspects of your life.

Clearly, with an awareness of the Lazy/Passive Investing approach, even with a coach, you will be able to evaluate performance yourself.

Stay lazy

What else to say? Throughout this book, we have explored the fascinating world of Passive Investing and Lazy Portfolios, highlighting the power of simple and consistent investment strategies in achieving long-term financial goals.

We have learned that the key to success in this approach lies in constructing a well-balanced portfolio based on understanding one's financial needs and careful analysis of suitable metrics.

Diversification across different assets and the selection of low-cost financial instruments have emerged as fundamental principles.

The concept of the 'Lazy Portfolio' has taught us that laziness, understood as reducing complexity and decision frequency, can be a powerful ally.

Simplifying the investment process does not mean compromising performance. It means, instead, focusing on a long-term strategy, resisting the temptations of market timing and excessive activity.

Following a well-defined strategy can lead to satisfying results in the long run.

May our financial journey be characterized by wisdom, resilience, and prosperity.

Appendix - Asset Allocation in EUR

In the current version of the *LazyPortfolioEtf.com* website, it is not yet possible to examine and test asset allocations in a currency other than the US dollar.

However, we already have some data for the Euro currency, which we present here in the book. In this case as well, you will find asset allocations with **1, 2, 3, 4, and 5 assets**, and finally, a mix of all. The data source spans thirty years (updated to November 2023). We will only present metrics calculated with nominal returns, so not adjusted for inflation.

In the analyses, we started with the same assets examined for USD portfolios but assumed them in the Euro version. For example, when we talk about 'VTI,' we imagine using a Euro-denominated equivalent ETF that replicates the US market. The case of covered currency exchange (hedged) is not analyzed, but we have calculated the metrics taking into account the actual EUR/USD exchange rate.

If you are interested in replicating similar asset allocations, it will be up to you to find an ETF in Euros that replicates the same benchmark as the US. We recommend always choosing a liquid and low-cost instrument.

If it can be of help, we guide you on how to retrieve what interests you on the specialized site *JustEtf.com*. Even if you use an equivalent site, the screening logic is generally the same.

Firstly, when you visit *JustEtf.com*, set the region of your interest and the language you prefer.

The main page for ETF search, which allows you to find ETFs, is the ETF Screener: https://www.justetf.com/en/find-etf.html

In the left menu (highlighted in the box), you can find various filters that allow you to select categories of your interest:

- Under "**Equity**", you can filter by "Region", "Country" and "Sector". Here you can find ETFs at the USA, Developed Markets, Emerging Markets, or Global levels.

- Under "**Bonds**", you can find "Bond Type", where you can further choose "Inflation Linked" (if you are interested in the TIP ETF) or "Convertible Bonds" (if you are inspired by the CWB ETF).

- Under "**Precious Metals**", you will find all ETFs related to gold (GLD). We recommend choosing those with physical replication (they have "physical" written in the name or something similar). In this case, the gold price replication will be more faithful and without extra costs.

- Under "**Matching Indices**", you can perform a more specific search: you can directly choose the benchmark that your ETF should replicate.

In any case, in the search bar at the top, you can enter the keywords you find appropriate, and you will get all the relevant ETFs as a result.

JustEtf.com provides a page that practically illustrates all the categories present on the site:https://www.justetf.com/en/etf-lists.html

Each section contains links that directly lead to the Screener page, already filtered for the chosen scenario, or to a very interesting detailed page.

For example, if you want to examine ETFs at the asset class level, this is the section:

List of ETFs by asset class

Bond ETFs   Multi-Asset ETFs

Commodity ETFs   Precious Metals ETFs

Equity ETFs   Real Estate ETFs

Money Market ETFs

Working on bonds, you can find this section:

Bond ETFs

All bond ETFs   Covered Bonds ETFs

Aggregate ETFs   Government ETFs

Convertible Bonds ETFs   Inflation-Linked ETFs

Corporate ETFs

If instead you prefer to focus on the main stock indices, in the section below you will find many options.

ETFs on popular indices

CAC 40 ETFs	MSCI ACWI IMI ETFs
DAX ETFs	MSCI Emerging Markets ETFs
Dow Jones Industrial Average ETFs	MSCI EMU ETFs
EURO STOXX 50 ETFs	MSCI Europe ETFs
EURO STOXX Select Dividend 30 ETFs	MSCI Japan ETFs
FTSE 100 ETFs	MSCI USA ETFs
FTSE All-World ETFs	MSCI World ETFs
FTSE Developed ETFs	Nasdaq 100 ETFs
FTSE Emerging ETFs	Nikkei 225 ETFs
FTSE MIB ETFs	Russell 2000 ETFs
JPX-Nikkei 400 ETFs	S&P 500 ETFs
MDAX ETFs	STOXX Europe 600 ETFs
MSCI ACWI ETFs	STOXX Global Select Dividend 100 ETFs

We have highlighted some indices that were the benchmark (or something very similar) for some ETFs examined in the book: All World, Developed World, Emerging Market, USA.

Be careful because the 'international' indices, in the US sense, do not include the USA themselves. On the contrary, very often, the international indices indicated in European ETFs include the USA.

One last note: the MSCI World index, despite its name, refers only to Developed Markets and not to the whole world. In contrast, the world global index is the MSCI ACWI or the FTSE All World.

EUR Single-Asset Lazy Portfolios

Order by **Baseline 3Y Return** - **Last 30 Years** (from 1993-12 to 2023-11)

Portfolio	3Y Rolling Annualized Return (%)			7Y Rolling Annualized Return (%)			15Y Rolling Annualized Return (%)				Max Draw-down (%)	Long Neg Period (Y.M)
	Worst	Base ▼	%Fail	Worst	Base	%Fail	Worst	Base	Median	%Fail		
VNQ	-27.23	2.76	10.2%	-6.90	4.58	3.3%	3.07	7.53	9.14	0%	-67.70	11Y.6M
EMB	-4.86	2.11	8.9%	0.14	5.78	0%	5.59	6.35	8.65	0%	-34.51	6Y.10M
TIP	-4.49	0.21	12.9%	-1.60	2.32	3.6%	3.02	3.84	5.05	0%	-21.03	8Y.6M
BNDX	-7.73	-0.76	19.7%	-3.37	1.06	10.1%	3.57	4.35	5.43	0%	-25.71	9Y.3M
LQD	-6.75	-1.00	20%	-3.52	1.96	9.8%	4.00	4.49	5.64	0%	-25.66	8Y.9M
IJS	-19.97	-1.23	18.2%	-7.14	3.84	4%	5.92	7.04	8.96	0%	-51.29	10Y.11M
TLT	-14.62	-1.28	17.5%	-3.61	1.62	7.9%	2.86	5.48	6.58	0%	-44.28	11Y.3M
IEI	-8.11	-1.32	23.1%	-2.91	0.82	7.6%	2.38	3.14	4.37	0%	-23.92	9Y.6M
SHY	-10.40	-1.35	24.9%	-4.59	0.49	13%	0.76	1.31	2.59	0%	-30.36	16Y.2M
HYG	-9.94	-1.36	17.5%	-4.66	2.00	9.4%	2.57	4.29	5.22	0%	-32.25	11Y.2M
BND	-8.81	-1.38	21.2%	-3.91	1.05	10.5%	2.66	3.23	4.56	0%	-27.21	10Y.1M
SCZ	-21.84	-1.61	19.1%	0.61	2.69	0%	1.52	5.64	7.68	0%	-60.57	9Y.3M
EEM	-18.01	-1.67	21.5%	-2.84	1.74	5.8%	1.00	4.74	6.92	0%	-56.31	10Y.10M
CWB	-14.87	-1.94	17.9%	-5.79	2.83	6.5%	3.97	5.18	7.28	0%	-42.39	11Y.1M
BIL	-11.97	-2.00	30.2%	-5.99	-0.76	18.4%	-0.55	0.19	1.60	10.5%	-35.71	21Y.4M
GLD	-10.73	-2.71	27.1%	-3.28	0.33	12.3%	3.80	7.22	8.24	0%	-36.80	11Y.8M
MTUM	-18.79	-6.17	20.6%	-5.90	2.08	9.4%	3.98	5.88	10.00	0%	-52.31	12Y.5M
VTI	-19.85	-6.60	20.9%	-8.07	0.25	14.4%	2.77	4.08	6.53	0%	-57.85	12Y.10M
VEA	-23.13	-6.88	22.2%	-4.45	1.12	4.7%	0.37	2.53	4.27	0%	-54.58	13Y.5M
VTV	-18.30	-7.15	21.5%	-8.25	1.66	9.8%	3.19	4.02	6.33	0%	-54.52	12Y.6M

Order by **Maximum Drawdown** - **Last 30 Years** (from 1993-12 to 2023-11)

Portfolio	3Y Rolling Annualized Return (%)			7Y Rolling Annualized Return (%)			15Y Rolling Annualized Return (%)				Max Draw-down (%) ▼	Long Neg Period (Y.M)
	Worst	Base	%Fail	Worst	Base	%Fail	Worst	Base	Median	%Fail		
TIP	-4.49	0.21	12.9%	-1.60	2.32	3.6%	3.02	3.84	5.05	0%	-21.03	8Y.6M
IEI	-8.11	-1.32	23.1%	-2.91	0.82	7.6%	2.38	3.14	4.37	0%	-23.92	9Y.6M
LQD	-6.75	-1.00	20%	-3.52	1.96	9.8%	4.00	4.49	5.64	0%	-25.66	8Y.9M
BNDX	-7.73	-0.76	19.7%	-3.37	1.06	10.1%	3.57	4.35	5.43	0%	-25.71	9Y.3M
BND	-8.81	-1.38	21.2%	-3.91	1.05	10.5%	2.66	3.23	4.56	0%	-27.21	10Y.1M
SHY	-10.40	-1.35	24.9%	-4.59	0.49	13%	0.76	1.31	2.59	0%	-30.36	16Y.2M
HYG	-9.94	-1.36	17.5%	-4.66	2.00	9.4%	2.57	4.29	5.22	0%	-32.25	11Y.2M
EMB	-4.86	2.11	8.9%	0.14	5.78	0%	5.59	6.35	8.65	0%	-34.51	6Y.10M
BIL	-11.97	-2.00	30.2%	-5.99	-0.76	18.4%	-0.55	0.19	1.60	10.5%	-35.71	21Y.4M
GLD	-10.73	-2.71	27.1%	-3.28	0.33	12.3%	3.80	7.22	8.24	0%	-36.80	11Y.8M
CWB	-14.87	-1.94	17.9%	-5.79	2.83	6.5%	3.97	5.18	7.28	0%	-42.39	11Y.1M
TLT	-14.62	-1.28	17.5%	-3.61	1.62	7.9%	2.86	5.48	6.58	0%	-44.28	11Y.3M
IJS	-19.97	-1.23	18.2%	-7.14	3.84	4%	5.92	7.04	8.96	0%	-51.29	10Y.11M
MTUM	-18.79	-6.17	20.6%	-5.90	2.08	9.4%	3.98	5.88	10.00	0%	-52.31	12Y.5M
VTV	-18.30	-7.15	21.5%	-8.25	1.66	9.8%	3.19	4.02	6.33	0%	-54.52	12Y.6M
VEA	-23.13	-6.88	22.2%	-4.45	1.12	4.7%	0.37	2.53	4.27	0%	-54.58	13Y.5M
EEM	-18.01	-1.67	21.5%	-2.84	1.74	5.8%	1.00	4.74	6.92	0%	-56.31	10Y.10M
VTI	-19.85	-6.60	20.9%	-8.07	0.25	14.4%	2.77	4.08	6.53	0%	-57.85	12Y.10M
SCZ	-21.84	-1.61	19.1%	0.61	2.69	0%	1.52	5.64	7.68	0%	-60.57	9Y.3M
VNQ	-27.23	2.76	10.2%	-6.90	4.58	3.3%	3.07	7.53	9.14	0%	-67.70	11Y.6M

Order by **Longest Negative Period - Last 30 Years** (from 1993-12 to 2023-11)

Portfolio	3Y Rolling Annualized Return (%)			7Y Rolling Annualized Return (%)			15Y Rolling Annualized Return (%)				Max Draw-down (%)	Long Neg Period (Y.M) ▲
	Worst	Base	%Fail	Worst	Base	%Fail	Worst	Base	Median	%Fail		
EMB	-4.86	2.11	8.9%	0.14	5.78	0%	5.59	6.35	8.65	0%	-34.51	6Y.10M
TIP	-4.49	0.21	12.9%	-1.60	2.32	3.6%	3.02	3.84	5.05	0%	-21.03	8Y.6M
LQD	-6.75	-1.00	20%	-3.52	1.96	9.8%	4.00	4.49	5.64	0%	-25.66	8Y.9M
BNDX	-7.73	-0.76	19.7%	-3.37	1.06	10.1%	3.57	4.35	5.43	0%	-25.71	9Y.3M
SCZ	-21.84	-1.61	19.1%	0.61	2.69	0%	1.52	5.64	7.68	0%	-60.57	9Y.3M
IEI	-8.11	-1.32	23.1%	-2.91	0.82	7.6%	2.38	3.14	4.37	0%	-23.92	9Y.6M
BND	-8.81	-1.38	21.2%	-3.91	1.05	10.5%	2.66	3.23	4.56	0%	-27.21	10Y.1M
EEM	-18.01	-1.67	21.5%	-2.84	1.74	5.8%	1.00	4.74	6.92	0%	-56.31	10Y.10M
IJS	-19.97	-1.23	18.2%	-7.14	3.84	4%	5.92	7.04	8.96	0%	-51.29	10Y.11M
CWB	-14.87	-1.94	17.9%	-5.79	2.83	6.5%	3.97	5.18	7.28	0%	-42.39	11Y.1M
HYG	-9.94	-1.36	17.5%	-4.66	2.00	9.4%	2.57	4.29	5.22	0%	-32.25	11Y.2M
TLT	-14.62	-1.28	17.5%	-3.61	1.62	7.9%	2.86	5.48	6.58	0%	-44.28	11Y.3M
VNQ	-27.23	2.76	10.2%	-6.90	4.58	3.3%	3.07	7.53	9.14	0%	-67.70	11Y.6M
GLD	-10.73	-2.71	27.1%	-3.28	0.33	12.3%	3.80	7.22	8.24	0%	-36.80	11Y.8M
MTUM	-18.79	-6.17	20.6%	-5.90	2.08	9.4%	3.98	5.88	10.00	0%	-52.31	12Y.5M
VTV	-18.30	-7.15	21.5%	-8.25	1.66	9.8%	3.19	4.02	6.33	0%	-54.52	12Y.6M
VTI	-19.85	-6.60	20.9%	-8.07	0.25	14.4%	2.77	4.08	6.53	0%	-57.85	12Y.10M
VEA	-23.13	-6.88	22.2%	-4.45	1.12	4.7%	0.37	2.53	4.27	0%	-54.58	13Y.5M
SHY	-10.40	-1.35	24.9%	-4.59	0.49	13%	0.76	1.31	2.59	0%	-30.36	16Y.2M
BIL	-11.97	-2.00	30.2%	-5.99	-0.76	18.4%	-0.55	0.19	1.60	10.5%	-35.71	21Y.4M

Order by **Baseline 7Y Return - Last 30 Years** (from 1993-12 to 2023-11)

Portfolio	3Y Rolling Annualized Return (%)			7Y Rolling Annualized Return (%)			15Y Rolling Annualized Return (%)				Max Draw-down (%)	Long Neg Period (Y.M)
	Worst	Base	%Fail	Worst	Base ▼	%Fail	Worst	Base	Median	%Fail		
EMB	-4.86	2.11	8.9%	0.14	5.78	0%	5.59	6.35	8.65	0%	-34.51	6Y.10M
VNQ	-27.23	2.76	10.2%	-6.90	4.58	3.3%	3.07	7.53	9.14	0%	-67.70	11Y.6M
IJS	-19.97	-1.23	18.2%	-7.14	3.84	4%	5.92	7.04	8.96	0%	-51.29	10Y.11M
CWB	-14.87	-1.94	17.9%	-5.79	2.83	6.5%	3.97	5.18	7.28	0%	-42.39	11Y.1M
SCZ	-21.84	-1.61	19.1%	0.61	2.69	0%	1.52	5.64	7.68	0%	-60.57	9Y.3M
TIP	-4.49	0.21	12.9%	-1.60	2.32	3.6%	3.02	3.84	5.05	0%	-21.03	8Y.6M
MTUM	-18.79	-6.17	20.6%	-5.90	2.08	9.4%	3.98	5.88	10.00	0%	-52.31	12Y.5M
HYG	-9.94	-1.36	17.5%	-4.66	2.00	9.4%	2.57	4.29	5.22	0%	-32.25	11Y.2M
LQD	-6.75	-1.00	20%	-3.52	1.96	9.8%	4.00	4.49	5.64	0%	-25.66	8Y.9M
EEM	-18.01	-1.67	21.5%	-2.84	1.74	5.8%	1.00	4.74	6.92	0%	-56.31	10Y.10M
VTV	-18.30	-7.15	21.5%	-8.25	1.66	9.8%	3.19	4.02	6.33	0%	-54.52	12Y.6M
TLT	-14.62	-1.28	17.5%	-3.61	1.62	7.9%	2.86	5.48	6.58	0%	-44.28	11Y.3M
VEA	-23.13	-6.88	22.2%	-4.45	1.12	4.7%	0.37	2.53	4.27	0%	-54.58	13Y.5M
BNDX	-7.73	-0.76	19.7%	-3.37	1.06	10.1%	3.57	4.35	5.43	0%	-25.71	9Y.3M
BND	-8.81	-1.38	21.2%	-3.91	1.05	10.5%	2.66	3.23	4.56	0%	-27.21	10Y.1M
IEI	-8.11	-1.32	23.1%	-2.91	0.82	7.6%	2.38	3.14	4.37	0%	-23.92	9Y.6M
SHY	-10.40	-1.35	24.9%	-4.59	0.49	13%	0.76	1.31	2.59	0%	-30.36	16Y.2M
GLD	-10.73	-2.71	27.1%	-3.28	0.33	12.3%	3.80	7.22	8.24	0%	-36.80	11Y.8M
VTI	-19.85	-6.60	20.9%	-8.07	0.25	14.4%	2.77	4.08	6.53	0%	-57.85	12Y.10M
BIL	-11.97	-2.00	30.2%	-5.99	-0.76	18.4%	-0.55	0.19	1.60	10.5%	-35.71	21Y.4M

Order by **Baseline 15Y Return - Last 30 Years** (from 1993-12 to 2023-11)

Portfolio	3Y Rolling Annualized Return (%)			7Y Rolling Annualized Return (%)			15Y Rolling Annualized Return (%)				Max Draw-down (%)	Long Neg Period (Y.M)
	Worst	Base	%Fail	Worst	Base	%Fail	Worst	Base ▼	Median	%Fail		
VNQ	-27.23	2.76	10.2%	-6.90	4.58	3.3%	3.07	7.53	9.14	0%	-67.70	11Y.6M
GLD	-10.73	-2.71	27.1%	-3.28	0.33	12.3%	3.80	7.22	8.24	0%	-36.80	11Y.8M
IJS	-19.97	-1.23	18.2%	-7.14	3.84	4%	5.92	7.04	8.96	0%	-51.29	10Y.11M
EMB	-4.86	2.11	8.9%	0.14	5.78	0%	5.59	6.35	8.65	0%	-34.51	6Y.10M
MTUM	-18.79	-6.17	20.6%	-5.90	2.08	9.4%	3.98	5.88	10.00	0%	-52.31	12Y.5M
SCZ	-21.84	-1.61	19.1%	0.61	2.69	0%	1.52	5.64	7.68	0%	-60.57	9Y.3M
TLT	-14.62	-1.28	17.5%	-3.61	1.62	7.9%	2.86	5.48	6.58	0%	-44.28	11Y.3M
CWB	-14.87	-1.94	17.9%	-5.79	2.83	6.5%	3.97	5.18	7.28	0%	-42.39	11Y.1M
EEM	-18.01	-1.67	21.5%	-2.84	1.74	5.8%	1.00	4.74	6.92	0%	-56.31	10Y.10M
LQD	-6.75	-1.00	20%	-3.52	1.96	9.8%	4.00	4.49	5.64	0%	-25.66	8Y.9M
BNDX	-7.73	-0.76	19.7%	-3.37	1.06	10.1%	3.57	4.35	5.43	0%	-25.71	9Y.3M
HYG	-9.94	-1.36	17.5%	-4.66	2.00	9.4%	2.57	4.29	5.22	0%	-32.25	11Y.2M
VTI	-19.85	-6.60	20.9%	-8.07	0.25	14.4%	2.77	4.08	6.53	0%	-57.85	12Y.10M
VTV	-18.30	-7.15	21.5%	-8.25	1.66	9.8%	3.19	4.02	6.33	0%	-54.52	12Y.6M
TIP	-4.49	0.21	12.9%	-1.60	2.32	3.6%	3.02	3.84	5.05	0%	-21.03	8Y.6M
BND	-8.81	-1.38	21.2%	-3.91	1.05	10.5%	2.66	3.23	4.56	0%	-27.21	10Y.1M
IEI	-8.11	-1.32	23.1%	-2.91	0.82	7.6%	2.38	3.14	4.37	0%	-23.92	9Y.6M
VEA	-23.13	-6.88	22.2%	-4.45	1.12	4.7%	0.37	2.53	4.27	0%	-54.58	13Y.5M
SHY	-10.40	-1.35	24.9%	-4.59	0.49	13%	0.76	1.31	2.59	0%	-30.36	16Y.2M
BIL	-11.97	-2.00	30.2%	-5.99	-0.76	18.4%	-0.55	0.19	1.60	10.5%	-35.71	21Y.4M

Order by **Median 15Y Return - Last 30 Years** (from 1993-12 to 2023-11)

Portfolio	3Y Rolling Annualized Return (%)			7Y Rolling Annualized Return (%)			15Y Rolling Annualized Return (%)				Max Draw-down (%)	Long Neg Period (Y.M)
	Worst	Base	%Fail	Worst	Base	%Fail	Worst	Base	Median ▼	%Fail		
MTUM	-18.79	-6.17	20.6%	-5.90	2.08	9.4%	3.98	5.88	10.00	0%	-52.31	12Y.5M
VNQ	-27.23	2.76	10.2%	-6.90	4.58	3.3%	3.07	7.53	9.14	0%	-67.70	11Y.6M
IJS	-19.97	-1.23	18.2%	-7.14	3.84	4%	5.92	7.04	8.96	0%	-51.29	10Y.11M
EMB	-4.86	2.11	8.9%	0.14	5.78	0%	5.59	6.35	8.65	0%	-34.51	6Y.10M
GLD	-10.73	-2.71	27.1%	-3.28	0.33	12.3%	3.80	7.22	8.24	0%	-36.80	11Y.8M
SCZ	-21.84	-1.61	19.1%	0.61	2.69	0%	1.52	5.64	7.68	0%	-60.57	9Y.3M
CWB	-14.87	-1.94	17.9%	-5.79	2.83	6.5%	3.97	5.18	7.28	0%	-42.39	11Y.1M
EEM	-18.01	-1.67	21.5%	-2.84	1.74	5.8%	1.00	4.74	6.92	0%	-56.31	10Y.10M
TLT	-14.62	-1.28	17.5%	-3.61	1.62	7.9%	2.86	5.48	6.58	0%	-44.28	11Y.3M
VTI	-19.85	-6.60	20.9%	-8.07	0.25	14.4%	2.77	4.08	6.53	0%	-57.85	12Y.10M
VTV	-18.30	-7.15	21.5%	-8.25	1.66	9.8%	3.19	4.02	6.33	0%	-54.52	12Y.6M
LQD	-6.75	-1.00	20%	-3.52	1.96	9.8%	4.00	4.49	5.64	0%	-25.66	8Y.9M
BNDX	-7.73	-0.76	19.7%	-3.37	1.06	10.1%	3.57	4.35	5.43	0%	-25.71	9Y.3M
HYG	-9.94	-1.36	17.5%	-4.66	2.00	9.4%	2.57	4.29	5.22	0%	-32.25	11Y.2M
TIP	-4.49	0.21	12.9%	-1.60	2.32	3.6%	3.02	3.84	5.05	0%	-21.03	8Y.6M
BND	-8.81	-1.38	21.2%	-3.91	1.05	10.5%	2.66	3.23	4.56	0%	-27.21	10Y.1M
IEI	-8.11	-1.32	23.1%	-2.91	0.82	7.6%	2.38	3.14	4.37	0%	-23.92	9Y.6M
VEA	-23.13	-6.88	22.2%	-4.45	1.12	4.7%	0.37	2.53	4.27	0%	-54.58	13Y.5M
SHY	-10.40	-1.35	24.9%	-4.59	0.49	13%	0.76	1.31	2.59	0%	-30.36	16Y.2M
BIL	-11.97	-2.00	30.2%	-5.99	-0.76	18.4%	-0.55	0.19	1.60	10.5%	-35.71	21Y.4M

EUR Lazy Portfolios with 2 equally weighted Assets

Order by **Baseline 3Y Return** - **Last 30 Years** (from 1993-12 to 2023-11)

Portfolio	3Y Rolling Annualized Return (%)			7Y Rolling Annualized Return (%)			15Y Rolling Annualized Return (%)				Max Draw-down (%)	Long Neg Period (Y.M)
	Worst	Base ▼	%Fail	Worst	Base	%Fail	Worst	Base	Median	%Fail		
IJS-GLD	-3.84	3.87	4.6%	2.07	6.59	0%	6.40	8.65	9.48	0%	-27.59	3Y.7M
VNQ-GLD	-7.08	3.20	5.2%	2.61	5.69	0%	5.15	8.37	9.58	0%	-27.99	5Y.0M
EMB-CWB	-8.11	3.17	8%	-0.81	5.53	1.8%	6.52	7.65	8.36	0%	-27.66	7Y.6M
MTUM-GLD	-8.57	2.97	10.8%	2.73	5.88	0%	6.74	8.02	10.04	0%	-29.16	5Y.5M
IJS-EMB	-11.41	2.84	8.6%	-1.95	5.63	1.4%	6.61	8.20	9.21	0%	-32.19	7Y.8M
CWB-GLD	-3.15	2.83	6.8%	2.84	5.20	0%	4.71	7.54	8.53	0%	-20.56	4Y.8M
VNQ-TIP	-11.72	2.83	8.3%	-1.99	4.45	2.2%	5.27	6.75	7.45	0%	-35.97	8Y.1M
SCZ-VNQ	-23.88	2.77	9.8%	-2.70	4.62	0.7%	2.85	6.92	8.93	0%	-62.16	8Y.8M
SCZ-TIP	-9.12	2.70	7.7%	2.13	4.88	0%	4.71	6.22	7.56	0%	-28.90	4Y.9M
VNQ-EMB	-14.21	2.67	8%	-1.49	5.25	0.7%	6.39	7.62	9.30	0%	-42.35	7Y.3M
VTI-GLD	-8.79	2.59	11.4%	1.60	4.12	0%	5.16	7.10	8.35	0%	-29.71	5Y.6M
SCZ-EMB	-11.43	2.56	9.2%	2.21	5.35	0%	5.52	7.09	9.51	0%	-36.23	4Y.4M
VTV-GLD	-6.49	2.56	12%	1.58	4.45	0%	5.31	7.11	8.17	0%	-27.96	5Y.1M
EEM-EMB	-6.49	2.27	6.8%	1.45	5.53	0%	4.13	6.53	9.07	0%	-44.47	5Y.1M
SCZ-IEI	-6.43	2.14	7.1%	2.55	4.62	0%	4.76	6.07	7.28	0%	-23.15	4Y.9M
EMB-GLD	-2.84	1.98	4.3%	1.80	4.44	0%	6.46	7.22	8.85	0%	-25.06	6Y.2M
VNQ-IEI	-10.02	1.96	9.5%	-1.86	4.11	1.8%	5.30	6.58	7.24	0%	-32.73	8Y.1M
SCZ-BNDX	-9.95	1.88	7.7%	0.99	4.70	0%	3.72	6.30	7.40	0%	-30.57	5Y.0M
SCZ-TLT	-5.85	1.87	9.2%	0.38	6.16	0%	5.74	7.84	8.99	0%	-27.57	6Y.8M
SCZ-LQD	-10.14	1.85	8.3%	0.93	4.87	0%	4.02	6.62	7.49	0%	-32.10	5Y.0M
EEM-VNQ	-18.95	1.82	10.2%	-1.15	5.37	0.7%	3.37	6.77	8.90	0%	-56.36	8Y.6M

Order by **Maximum Drawdown** - **Last 30 Years** (from 1993-12 to 2023-11)

Portfolio	3Y Rolling Annualized Return (%)			7Y Rolling Annualized Return (%)			15Y Rolling Annualized Return (%)				Max Draw-down (%) ▼	Long Neg Period (Y.M)
	Worst	Base	%Fail	Worst	Base	%Fail	Worst	Base	Median	%Fail		
HYG-GLD	-3.44	1.32	8.6%	2.11	3.45	0%	3.65	6.56	7.10	0%	-18.10	4Y.10M
TIP-HYG	-4.99	0.21	13.2%	-2.47	2.66	7.6%	3.52	4.41	5.35	0%	-18.21	9Y.1M
TIP-LQD	-5.41	-0.41	16.6%	-2.46	2.32	7.6%	3.62	4.24	5.43	0%	-18.95	8Y.7M
IEI-TIP	-6.30	-0.33	20%	-2.22	1.62	5.4%	2.73	3.58	4.74	0%	-19.29	8Y.7M
BNDX-TIP	-6.10	-0.15	16.6%	-2.39	1.74	8.7%	3.53	4.24	5.33	0%	-19.93	8Y.7M
BND-TIP	-6.64	-0.59	18.2%	-2.66	1.69	9%	2.93	3.59	4.82	0%	-20.36	8Y.8M
EMB-BIL	-5.16	0.58	10.2%	-0.67	2.21	1.4%	3.34	4.02	4.93	0%	-20.41	7Y.10M
CWB-GLD	-3.15	2.83	6.8%	2.84	5.20	0%	4.71	7.54	8.53	0%	-20.56	4Y.8M
IEI-CWB	-5.30	0.46	14.2%	-2.49	4.04	6.5%	4.13	5.43	6.44	0%	-20.89	9Y.1M
TLT-HYG	-5.78	-0.64	16.3%	-2.59	1.96	6.9%	5.03	5.62	6.46	0%	-21.15	8Y.7M
EMB-SHY	-4.37	0.74	10.2%	0.03	2.55	0%	3.90	4.52	5.41	0%	-21.21	6Y.8M
EMB-HYG	-6.39	1.07	10.8%	-0.94	3.54	1.1%	5.53	6.22	7.13	0%	-21.70	7Y.6M
BNDX-GLD	-4.50	0.96	8%	1.92	3.68	0%	3.92	6.40	6.99	0%	-21.95	6Y.0M
BND-EMB	-3.58	1.14	11.4%	0.25	3.16	0%	4.89	5.42	6.38	0%	-21.95	6Y.9M
SHY-GLD	-5.86	-0.23	16.9%	0.08	2.65	0%	3.94	4.89	5.65	0%	-22.05	6Y.10M
BIL-GLD	-6.59	-0.69	19.7%	0.00	1.98	0%	3.25	4.33	5.13	0%	-22.19	6Y.11M
TIP-CWB	-7.68	0.89	12.6%	-2.29	3.98	4.7%	4.19	5.68	6.64	0%	-22.26	8Y.10M
EMB-LQD	-4.33	1.11	10.5%	0.48	3.41	0%	5.60	6.09	6.97	0%	-22.29	6Y.10M
SHY-TIP	-7.44	-0.57	20.3%	-3.01	1.49	10.5%	1.92	2.68	3.87	0%	-22.30	10Y.10M
IEI-HYG	-6.43	0.02	14.8%	-3.20	2.00	8.7%	3.41	4.10	5.17	0%	-22.35	9Y.3M
EMB-IEI	-3.18	1.19	9.8%	0.34	3.27	0%	4.55	5.31	6.29	0%	-22.54	6Y.8M

Order by **Longest Negative Period** - Last 30 Years (from 1993-12 to 2023-11)

Portfolio	3Y Rolling Annualized Return (%)			7Y Rolling Annualized Return (%)			15Y Rolling Annualized Return (%)				Max Draw-down (%)	Long Neg Period (Y.M) ▲
	Worst	Base	%Fail	Worst	Base	%Fail	Worst	Base	Median	%Fail		
IJS-GLD	-3.84	3.87	4.6%	2.07	6.59	0%	6.40	8.65	9.48	0%	-27.59	3Y.7M
SCZ-EMB	-11.43	2.56	9.2%	2.21	5.35	0%	5.52	7.09	9.51	0%	-36.23	4Y.4M
EMB-TIP	-2.51	1.51	8.6%	0.89	3.79	0%	4.86	5.59	6.46	0%	-23.52	4Y.4M*
CWB-GLD	-3.15	2.83	6.8%	2.84	5.20	0%	4.71	7.54	8.53	0%	-20.56	4Y.8M
SCZ-TIP	-9.12	2.70	7.7%	2.13	4.88	0%	4.71	6.22	7.56	0%	-28.90	4Y.9M
SCZ-IEI	-6.43	2.14	7.1%	2.55	4.62	0%	4.76	6.07	7.28	0%	-23.15	4Y.9M
SCZ-BND	-8.07	1.67	7.7%	1.53	4.43	0%	4.30	6.07	7.08	0%	-27.35	4Y.10M
HYG-GLD	-3.44	1.32	8.6%	2.11	3.45	0%	3.65	6.56	7.10	0%	-18.10	4Y.10M
VNQ-GLD	-7.08	3.20	5.2%	2.61	5.69	0%	5.15	8.37	9.58	0%	-27.99	5Y.0M
SCZ-BNDX	-9.95	1.88	7.7%	0.99	4.70	0%	3.72	6.30	7.40	0%	-30.57	5Y.0M
SCZ-LQD	-10.14	1.85	8.3%	0.93	4.87	0%	4.02	6.62	7.49	0%	-32.10	5Y.0M
SCZ-SHY	-8.00	1.56	9.2%	1.23	3.71	0%	3.89	5.15	6.25	0%	-26.61	5Y.0M
VTV-GLD	-6.49	2.56	12%	1.58	4.45	0%	5.31	7.11	8.17	0%	-27.96	5Y.1M
EEM-EMB	-6.49	2.27	6.8%	1.45	5.53	0%	4.13	6.53	9.07	0%	-44.47	5Y.1M
CCM-TIP	-4.79	1.47	7.1%	2.28	4.40	0%	4.30	5.72	7.21	0%	-31.97	5Y.2M
EEM-IEI	-5.54	0.91	9.5%	1.75	4.46	0%	4.18	5.71	7.17	0%	-31.07	5Y.2M
EEM-BNDX	-6.37	0.79	10.8%	1.96	4.55	0%	3.72	5.98	7.22	0%	-33.11	5Y.2M
MTUM-GLD	-8.57	2.97	10.8%	2.73	5.88	0%	6.74	8.02	10.04	0%	-29.16	5Y.5M
VTI-GLD	-8.79	2.59	11.4%	1.60	4.12	0%	5.16	7.10	8.35	0%	-29.71	5Y.6M
EEM-LQD	-6.29	1.00	11.1%	1.83	4.72	0%	4.21	6.17	7.37	0%	-30.83	5Y.8M
EEM-BND	-6.70	0.54	11.4%	1.63	4.38	0%	4.07	5.59	6.94	0%	-30.51	5Y.8M

Order by **Baseline 7Y Return** - Last 30 Years (from 1993-12 to 2023-11)

Portfolio	3Y Rolling Annualized Return (%)			7Y Rolling Annualized Return (%)			15Y Rolling Annualized Return (%)				Max Draw-down (%)	Long Neg Period (Y.M)
	Worst	Base	%Fail	Worst	Base ▼	%Fail	Worst	Base	Median	%Fail		
IJS-GLD	-3.84	3.87	4.6%	2.07	6.59	0%	6.40	8.65	9.48	0%	-27.59	3Y.7M
SCZ-TLT	-5.85	1.87	9.2%	0.38	6.16	0%	5.74	7.84	8.99	0%	-27.57	6Y.8M
MTUM-GLD	-8.57	2.97	10.8%	2.73	5.88	0%	6.74	8.02	10.04	0%	-29.16	5Y.5M
IJS-EEM	-15.81	0.62	14.2%	-1.52	5.78	1.1%	4.80	7.13	8.44	0%	-49.11	8Y.6M
MTUM-EMB	-9.43	0.85	10.8%	-1.10	5.70	0.7%	6.94	8.29	9.67	0%	-28.00	8Y.7M
VNQ-GLD	-7.08	3.20	5.2%	2.61	5.69	0%	5.15	8.37	9.58	0%	-27.99	5Y.0M
IJS-EMB	-11.41	2.84	8.6%	-1.95	5.63	1.4%	6.61	8.20	9.21	0%	-32.19	7Y.8M
EEM-EMB	-6.49	2.27	6.8%	1.45	5.53	0%	4.13	6.53	9.07	0%	-44.47	5Y.1M
EMB-CWB	-8.11	3.17	8%	-0.81	5.53	1.8%	6.52	7.65	8.36	0%	-27.66	7Y.6M
EEM-TLT	-8.16	1.78	11.1%	-0.38	5.50	0.4%	5.29	7.59	9.07	0%	-32.02	8Y.9M
EEM-VNQ	-18.95	1.82	10.2%	-1.15	5.37	0.7%	3.37	6.77	8.90	0%	-56.36	8Y.6M
SCZ-EMB	-11.43	2.56	9.2%	2.21	5.35	0%	5.52	7.09	9.51	0%	-36.23	4Y.4M
MTUM-EEM	-18.14	-1.27	17.2%	-1.49	5.35	1.1%	5.01	6.81	8.69	0%	-51.14	9Y.8M
VTI-EMB	-9.55	1.02	11.7%	-2.34	5.34	2.9%	6.26	7.54	8.73	0%	-27.95	8Y.10M
VNQ-EMB	-14.21	2.67	8%	-1.49	5.25	0.7%	6.39	7.62	9.30	0%	-42.35	7Y.3M
CWB-GLD	-3.15	2.83	6.8%	2.84	5.20	0%	4.71	7.54	8.53	0%	-20.56	4Y.8M
VTV-EMB	-10.30	1.24	11.7%	-2.37	5.03	2.9%	6.36	7.33	8.27	0%	-31.44	8Y.7M
VNQ-TLT	-8.54	0.68	13.5%	-0.41	5.00	0.7%	6.13	8.13	8.68	0%	-32.23	7Y.5M
IJS-TLT	-5.91	1.16	12.9%	-1.29	4.98	2.9%	7.14	7.80	8.75	0%	-25.81	8Y.4M
SCZ-TIP	-9.12	2.70	7.7%	2.13	4.88	0%	4.71	6.22	7.56	0%	-28.90	4Y.9M
SCZ-LQD	-10.14	1.85	8.3%	0.93	4.87	0%	4.02	6.62	7.49	0%	-32.10	5Y.0M

Order by **Baseline 15Y Return** - **Last 30 Years** (from 1993-12 to 2023-11)

Portfolio	3Y Rolling Annualized Return (%)			7Y Rolling Annualized Return (%)			15Y Rolling Annualized Return (%)				Max Draw-down (%)	Long Neg Period (Y.M)
	Worst	Base	%Fail	Worst	Base	%Fail	Worst	Base ▼	Median	%Fail		
IJS-GLD	-3.84	3.87	4.6%	2.07	6.59	0%	6.40	8.65	9.48	0%	-27.59	3Y.7M
VNQ-GLD	-7.08	3.20	5.2%	2.61	5.69	0%	5.15	8.37	9.58	0%	-27.99	5Y.0M
MTUM-EMB	-9.43	0.85	10.8%	-1.10	5.70	0.7%	6.94	8.29	9.67	0%	-28.00	8Y.7M
IJS-EMB	-11.41	2.84	8.6%	-1.95	5.63	1.4%	6.61	8.20	9.21	0%	-32.19	7Y.8M
VNQ-TLT	-8.54	0.68	13.5%	-0.41	5.00	0.7%	6.13	8.13	8.68	0%	-32.23	7Y.5M
MTUM-VNQ	-21.24	-0.80	15.7%	-5.95	4.56	3.3%	6.55	8.12	9.63	0%	-56.39	9Y.11M
MTUM-GLD	-8.57	2.97	10.8%	2.73	5.88	0%	6.74	8.02	10.04	0%	-29.16	5Y.5M
SCZ-TLT	-5.85	1.87	9.2%	0.38	6.16	0%	5.74	7.84	8.99	0%	-27.57	6Y.8M
IJS-TLT	-5.91	1.16	12.9%	-1.29	4.98	2.9%	7.14	7.80	8.75	0%	-25.81	8Y.4M
IJS-VNQ	-23.45	1.27	11.7%	-6.83	4.51	3.3%	4.65	7.68	9.15	0%	-59.30	11Y.0M
EMB-CWB	-8.11	3.17	8%	-0.81	5.53	1.8%	6.52	7.65	8.36	0%	-27.66	7Y.6M
SCZ-GLD	-6.81	1.38	11.4%	-0.61	4.46	0.7%	3.73	7.64	9.22	0%	-30.01	9Y.5M
VNQ-EMB	-14.21	2.67	8%	-1.49	5.25	0.7%	6.39	7.62	9.30	0%	-42.35	7Y.3M
EEM-TLT	-8.16	1.78	11.1%	-0.38	5.50	0.4%	5.29	7.59	9.07	0%	-32.02	8Y.9M
CWB-GLD	-3.15	2.83	6.8%	2.84	5.20	0%	4.71	7.54	8.53	0%	-20.56	4Y.8M
VTI-EMB	-9.55	1.02	11.7%	-2.34	5.34	2.9%	6.26	7.54	8.73	0%	-27.95	8Y.10M
MTUM-SCZ	-19.33	-1.43	16.3%	-2.20	4.49	1.4%	5.61	7.38	8.81	0%	-54.47	9Y.10M
VTV-EMB	-10.30	1.24	11.7%	-2.37	5.03	2.9%	6.36	7.33	8.27	0%	-31.44	8Y.7M
IJS-SCZ	-20.49	1.59	12.6%	-2.79	4.72	1.8%	4.33	7.27	8.64	0%	-55.57	8Y.7M
IJS-MTUM	-18.22	-3.48	18.8%	-6.33	3.70	4.3%	5.95	7.23	9.67	0%	-49.11	11Y.1M
EMB-GLD	-2.84	1.98	4.3%	1.80	4.44	0%	6.46	7.22	8.85	0%	-25.06	6Y.2M

Order by **Median 15Y Return** - **Last 30 Years** (from 1993-12 to 2023-11)

Portfolio	3Y Rolling Annualized Return (%)			7Y Rolling Annualized Return (%)			15Y Rolling Annualized Return (%)				Max Draw-down (%)	Long Neg Period (Y.M)
	Worst	Base	%Fail	Worst	Base	%Fail	Worst	Base	Median ▼	%Fail		
MTUM-GLD	-8.57	2.97	10.8%	2.73	5.88	0%	6.74	8.02	10.04	0%	-29.16	5Y.5M
MTUM-EMB	-9.43	0.85	10.8%	-1.10	5.70	0.7%	6.94	8.29	9.67	0%	-28.00	8Y.7M
IJS-MTUM	-18.22	-3.48	18.8%	-6.33	3.70	4.3%	5.95	7.23	9.67	0%	-49.11	11Y.1M
MTUM-VNQ	-21.24	-0.80	15.7%	-5.95	4.56	3.3%	6.55	8.12	9.63	0%	-56.39	9Y.11M
VNQ-GLD	-7.08	3.20	5.2%	2.61	5.69	0%	5.15	8.37	9.58	0%	-27.99	5Y.0M
SCZ-EMB	-11.43	2.56	9.2%	2.21	5.35	0%	5.52	7.09	9.51	0%	-36.23	4Y.4M
IJS-GLD	-3.84	3.87	4.6%	2.07	6.59	0%	6.40	8.65	9.48	0%	-27.59	3Y.7M
MTUM-TLT	-8.71	-0.77	17.9%	-1.66	3.88	2.9%	5.99	7.16	9.47	0%	-27.79	9Y.6M
VNQ-EMB	-14.21	2.67	8%	-1.49	5.25	0.7%	6.39	7.62	9.30	0%	-42.35	7Y.3M
SCZ-GLD	-6.81	1.38	11.4%	-0.61	4.46	0.7%	3.73	7.64	9.22	0%	-30.01	9Y.5M
IJS-EMB	-11.41	2.84	8.6%	-1.95	5.63	1.4%	6.61	8.20	9.21	0%	-32.19	7Y.8M
IJS-VNQ	-23.45	1.27	11.7%	-6.83	4.51	3.3%	4.65	7.68	9.15	0%	-59.30	11Y.0M
EEM-TLT	-8.16	1.78	11.1%	-0.38	5.50	0.4%	5.29	7.59	9.07	0%	-32.02	8Y.9M
EEM-EMB	-6.49	2.27	6.8%	1.45	5.53	0%	4.13	6.53	9.07	0%	-44.47	5Y.1M
SCZ-TLT	-5.85	1.87	9.2%	0.38	6.16	0%	5.74	7.84	8.99	0%	-27.57	6Y.8M
MTUM-CWB	-15.37	-3.99	19.1%	-5.37	3.00	6.9%	4.23	5.98	8.94	0%	-43.15	11Y.6M
SCZ-VNQ	-23.88	2.77	9.8%	-2.70	4.62	0.7%	2.85	6.92	8.93	0%	-62.16	8Y.8M
EEM-VNQ	-18.95	1.82	10.2%	-1.15	5.37	0.7%	3.37	6.77	8.90	0%	-56.36	8Y.6M
EMB-GLD	-2.84	1.98	4.3%	1.80	4.44	0%	6.46	7.22	8.85	0%	-25.06	6Y.2M
EEM-GLD	-8.65	-1.12	18.8%	-1.56	2.02	3.6%	3.58	6.59	8.83	0%	-41.22	10Y.7M
MTUM-SCZ	-19.33	-1.43	16.3%	-2.20	4.49	1.4%	5.61	7.38	8.81	0%	-54.47	9Y.10M

EUR Lazy Portfolios with 3 equally weighted Assets

Order by **Baseline 3Y Return - Last 30 Years** (from 1993-12 to 2023-11)

Portfolio	3Y Rolling Annualized Return (%)			7Y Rolling Annualized Return (%)			15Y Rolling Annualized Return (%)				Max Draw-down (%)	Long Neg Period (Y.M)
	Worst	Base ▼	%Fail	Worst	Base	%Fail	Worst	Base	Median	%Fail		
IJS-EMB-GLD	-3.12	4.66	3.1%	2.32	6.89	0%	7.73	8.48	9.27	0%	-26.14	3Y.5M
IJS-VNQ-GLD	-11.41	3.99	6.2%	-0.51	7.12	0.4%	5.73	8.76	9.62	0%	-35.17	7Y.0M
IJS-SCZ-EMB	-14.27	3.81	9.2%	-0.48	5.69	0.7%	6.69	7.79	9.19	0%	-41.54	7Y.1M
IJS-SCZ-GLD	-9.15	3.80	5.8%	2.31	7.02	0%	5.29	8.34	9.27	0%	-29.94	4Y.9M
SCZ-VNQ-GLD	-11.37	3.69	5.8%	2.58	6.32	0%	4.36	8.01	9.45	0%	-37.02	5Y.3M
SCZ-EMB-GLD	-2.81	3.63	1.8%	3.71	6.27	0%	6.61	7.65	9.55	0%	-25.59	5Y.1M
EMB-CWB-GLD	-1.27	3.60	2.8%	3.06	6.25	0%	7.12	8.02	8.69	0%	-22.86	3Y.2M
SCZ-EMB-CWB	-12.17	3.60	8%	0.28	5.34	0%	6.57	7.64	8.59	0%	-36.85	6Y.11M
VTI-EMB-GLD	-2.50	3.52	4.6%	2.07	6.44	0%	7.13	8.14	8.94	0%	-22.67	4Y.4M
MTUM-VNQ-GLD	-9.76	3.45	10.8%	0.04	7.03	0%	6.97	8.86	9.90	0%	-32.19	4Y.5M
IJS-TIP-GLD	-2.56	3.29	4%	1.80	5.69	0%	6.15	7.36	8.13	0%	-20.89	3Y.11M
MTUM-IEI-GLD	-4.91	3.22	8.9%	1.54	4.97	0%	5.96	6.98	8.43	0%	-19.34	5Y.1M
VNQ-EMB-GLD	-5.21	3.20	4.3%	2.73	5.96	0%	6.98	7.96	9.41	0%	-23.71	3Y.7M
IJS-IEI-GLD	-3.63	3.18	3.4%	1.82	5.29	0%	6.12	7.24	7.96	0%	-21.39	3Y.11M
SCZ-VNQ-EMB	-16.22	3.17	8%	-0.25	5.36	0.7%	6.17	7.36	9.47	0%	-46.76	7Y.0M
SCZ-VNQ-TIP	-14.57	3.17	7.7%	-0.48	4.89	0.7%	4.52	6.95	8.27	0%	-42.84	7Y.10M
IJS-TLT-GLD	-2.56	3.15	2.8%	2.24	5.56	0%	7.02	8.29	9.00	0%	-20.60	3Y.11M
MTUM-TIP-GLD	-4.09	3.15	8.6%	2.02	5.68	0%	6.11	7.22	8.53	0%	-18.19	5Y.0M
EEM-VNQ-EMB	-12.85	3.14	6.5%	0.75	5.75	0%	5.69	7.07	9.48	0%	-40.85	4Y.11M
VTV-EMB-GLD	-1.99	3.13	3.4%	2.03	6.51	0%	7.25	7.99	8.67	0%	-23.17	3Y.8M
VNQ-EMB-CWB	-13.81	3.10	7.4%	-2.44	5.31	2.5%	6.86	7.93	8.77	0%	-40.00	7Y.11M

Order by **Maximum Drawdown - Last 30 Years** (from 1993-12 to 2023-11)

Portfolio	3Y Rolling Annualized Return (%)			7Y Rolling Annualized Return (%)			15Y Rolling Annualized Return (%)				Max Draw-down (%) ▼	Long Neg Period (Y.M)
	Worst	Base	%Fail	Worst	Base	%Fail	Worst	Base	Median	%Fail		
HYG-LQD-GLD	-4.15	1.58	6.8%	0.66	3.78	0%	3.98	6.01	6.68	0%	-15.11	4Y.8M
IEI-HYG-GLD	-4.70	1.65	7.4%	0.83	3.31	0%	4.24	5.61	6.34	0%	-15.49	4Y.8M
TIP-CWB-GLD	-2.68	2.66	4.9%	1.88	4.96	0%	5.05	6.62	7.67	0%	-15.89	4Y.6M
TLT-CWB-GLD	-3.01	2.82	7.7%	1.82	5.13	0%	5.93	7.61	8.39	0%	-16.00	4Y.7M
SCZ-BND-GLD	-2.62	2.48	2.5%	2.85	5.17	0%	4.36	6.93	7.92	0%	-16.33	5Y.3M
IEI-CWB-GLD	-3.80	2.84	7.4%	1.40	4.80	0%	5.02	6.46	7.40	0%	-16.35	4Y.8M
SCZ-IEI-GLD	-2.76	2.68	1.5%	2.86	5.13	0%	4.61	6.91	8.01	0%	-16.35	5Y.3M
BND-HYG-GLD	-4.95	1.67	7.4%	0.52	3.38	0%	4.02	5.61	6.33	0%	-16.38	4Y.10M
SCZ-LQD-GLD	-2.56	2.63	2.5%	2.77	5.30	0%	4.30	7.34	8.20	0%	-16.42	5Y.3M
SCZ-SHY-IEI	-3.11	1.41	5.5%	0.56	3.48	0%	4.55	5.16	5.81	0%	-16.63	4Y.0M
SCZ-TIP-GLD	-2.78	3.06	2.5%	3.12	5.35	0%	4.63	7.03	8.15	0%	-16.75	5Y.3M
SCZ-TLT-GLD	-2.46	2.71	3.4%	2.60	5.62	0%	5.56	7.90	9.17	0%	-16.86	5Y.2M
SCZ-SHY-TIP	-4.62	1.85	6.8%	1.04	3.77	0%	4.57	5.33	5.96	0%	-16.89	4Y.2M
SCZ-SHY-GLD	-2.91	2.39	3.4%	2.49	4.79	0%	4.05	6.38	7.31	0%	-17.07	5Y.3M
BNDX-HYG-GLD	-4.58	1.85	7.1%	0.72	3.68	0%	3.70	5.95	6.65	0%	-17.14	4Y.8M
SCZ-BND-IEI	-3.14	1.30	5.8%	0.76	3.86	0%	4.84	5.73	6.41	0%	-17.21	4Y.1M
TIP-CWB-LQD	-5.69	0.76	13.5%	-2.31	3.66	6.1%	4.24	5.42	6.35	0%	-17.22	8Y.9M
SCZ-TLT-SHY	-2.87	1.20	8.6%	0.92	3.95	0%	5.42	6.36	6.93	0%	-17.22	4Y.7M
TIP-HYG-GLD	-3.51	1.75	6.5%	1.25	3.54	0%	4.31	5.78	6.55	0%	-17.27	4Y.7M
SCZ-BND-TIP	-4.80	1.81	6.2%	1.24	4.27	0%	4.86	5.92	6.55	0%	-17.42	4Y.0M
BNDX-CWB-GLD	-3.72	2.69	8.3%	1.23	5.22	0%	4.46	6.70	7.64	0%	-17.45	4Y.8M

Order by **Longest Negative Period** - **Last 30 Years** (from 1993-12 to 2023-11)

Portfolio	3Y Rolling Annualized Return (%)			7Y Rolling Annualized Return (%)			15Y Rolling Annualized Return (%)				Max Draw-down (%)	Long Neg Period (Y.M) ▲
	Worst	Base	%Fail	Worst	Base	%Fail	Worst	Base	Median	%Fail		
EMB-CWB-GLD	-1.27	3.60	2.8%	3.06	6.25	0%	7.12	8.02	8.69	0%	-22.86	3Y.2M
EMB-HYG-GLD	-1.86	2.60	1.8%	2.84	4.48	0%	6.30	6.98	7.67	0%	-19.55	3Y.3M
IJS-EMB-GLD	-3.12	4.66	3.1%	2.32	6.89	0%	7.73	8.48	9.27	0%	-26.14	3Y.5M
BNDX-EMB-GLD	-2.44	2.46	3.4%	2.31	4.30	0%	6.14	6.78	7.71	0%	-22.12	3Y.6M
VNQ-EMB-GLD	-5.21	3.20	4.3%	2.73	5.96	0%	6.98	7.96	9.41	0%	-23.71	3Y.7M
VTV-EMB-GLD	-1.99	3.13	3.4%	2.03	6.51	0%	7.25	7.99	8.67	0%	-23.17	3Y.8M
VNQ-BNDX-GLD	-4.71	2.62	6.2%	1.40	5.39	0%	4.97	7.60	8.18	0%	-20.81	3Y.8M
EMB-LQD-GLD	-2.02	2.47	4%	2.47	4.27	0%	6.32	6.85	7.78	0%	-20.14	3Y.8M
EMB-TIP-GLD	-1.40	2.21	3.1%	2.30	4.17	0%	5.81	6.51	7.45	0%	-21.27	3Y.8M
BND-EMB-GLD	-2.81	1.80	4.3%	2.25	3.90	0%	5.80	6.42	7.41	0%	-19.93	3Y.8M
EMB-IEI-GLD	-2.57	1.74	4%	2.17	3.92	0%	5.51	6.34	7.48	0%	-20.31	3Y.8M
VNQ-LQD-GLD	-4.94	2.66	6.2%	1.31	5.41	0%	5.19	7.71	8.24	0%	-19.90	3Y.9M
VNQ-IEI-GLD	-2.90	2.63	5.2%	2.32	4.93	0%	5.54	7.28	7.88	0%	-18.99	3Y.9M
VEA-EMB-GLD	-2.09	2.52	4%	3.44	5.24	0%	6.08	6.92	7.90	0%	-21.94	3Y.9M
VNQ-BND-GLD	-3.59	2.38	5.2%	1.66	4.95	0%	5.30	7.30	7.85	0%	-18.61	3Y.9M
EMB-BIL-GLD	-3.85	1.79	4.9%	2.24	3.57	0%	4.84	5.47	6.41	0%	-19.07	3Y.10M
EMB-SHY-GLD	-3.35	1.69	4.3%	2.30	3.58	0%	5.21	5.78	6.79	0%	-19.61	3Y.10M
IJS-TIP-GLD	-2.56	3.29	4%	1.80	5.69	0%	6.15	7.36	8.13	0%	-20.89	3Y.11M
IJS-IEI-GLD	-3.63	3.18	3.4%	1.82	5.29	0%	6.12	7.24	7.96	0%	-21.39	3Y.11M
IJS-TLT-GLD	-2.56	3.15	2.8%	2.24	5.56	0%	7.02	8.29	9.00	0%	-20.60	3Y.11M
IJS-BNDX-GLD	-3.55	3.03	4.9%	0.96	5.44	0%	5.57	7.52	8.22	0%	-22.40	3Y.11M

Order by **Baseline 7Y Return** - **Last 30 Years** (from 1993-12 to 2023-11)

Portfolio	3Y Rolling Annualized Return (%)			7Y Rolling Annualized Return (%)			15Y Rolling Annualized Return (%)				Max Draw-down (%)	Long Neg Period (Y.M)
	Worst	Base	%Fail	Worst	Base ▼	%Fail	Worst	Base	Median	%Fail		
MTUM-SCZ-GLD	-7.72	2.77	9.8%	2.77	7.24	0%	6.23	8.44	9.43	0%	-29.08	4Y.4M
IJS-VNQ-GLD	-11.41	3.99	6.2%	-0.51	7.12	0.4%	5.73	8.76	9.62	0%	-35.17	7Y.0M
MTUM-VNQ-GLD	-9.76	3.45	10.8%	0.04	7.03	0%	6.97	8.86	9.90	0%	-32.19	4Y.5M
IJS-SCZ-GLD	-9.15	3.80	5.8%	2.31	7.02	0%	5.29	8.34	9.27	0%	-29.94	4Y.9M
MTUM-EMB-GLD	-1.45	3.03	4%	2.84	6.96	0%	7.57	8.70	9.57	0%	-19.25	4Y.4M
IJS-EMB-GLD	-3.12	4.66	3.1%	2.32	6.89	0%	7.73	8.48	9.27	0%	-26.14	3Y.5M
IJS-MTUM-GLD	-7.63	1.90	12.3%	-0.34	6.67	0.4%	7.25	8.36	9.94	0%	-29.82	7Y.0M
MTUM-EEM-GLD	-11.45	2.58	8.6%	3.42	6.66	0%	6.10	7.89	9.35	0%	-33.57	5Y.4M
SCZ-EMB-TLT	-4.68	2.85	8.3%	0.36	6.54	0%	6.55	7.72	9.27	0%	-22.93	6Y.8M
VTV-EMB-GLD	-1.99	3.13	3.4%	2.03	6.51	0%	7.25	7.99	8.67	0%	-23.17	3Y.8M
VTI-EMB-GLD	-2.50	3.52	4.6%	2.07	6.44	0%	7.13	8.14	8.94	0%	-22.67	4Y.4M
VNQ-CWB-GLD	-8.84	3.06	6.5%	0.31	6.42	0%	5.24	8.32	9.02	0%	-30.08	4Y.0M
EEM-VNQ-TLT	-8.41	1.40	9.2%	1.07	6.42	0%	5.76	7.89	9.52	0%	-30.33	4Y.7M
MTUM-EEM-EMB	-9.97	1.70	9.5%	0.59	6.41	0%	6.85	8.07	9.30	0%	-36.10	4Y.4M
IJS-EEM-TLT	-6.59	2.23	7.7%	1.34	6.40	0%	6.50	8.20	9.16	0%	-29.36	4Y.3M
IJS-CWB-GLD	-6.73	2.53	9.8%	-0.12	6.37	0.4%	5.83	7.76	8.97	0%	-28.54	7Y.0M
IJS-EEM-EMB	-10.94	3.04	5.8%	0.39	6.36	0%	6.58	7.58	9.25	0%	-36.00	6Y.11M
SCZ-VNQ-GLD	-11.37	3.69	5.8%	2.58	6.32	0%	4.36	8.01	9.45	0%	-37.02	5Y.3M
SCZ-EMB-GLD	-2.81	3.63	4.6%	3.71	6.27	0%	6.61	7.65	9.55	0%	-25.59	5Y.1M
EMB-CWB-GLD	-1.27	3.60	2.8%	3.06	6.25	0%	7.12	8.02	8.69	0%	-22.86	3Y.2M
IJS-EEM-GLD	-5.57	3.00	6.2%	3.23	6.25	0%	5.45	8.04	9.20	0%	-30.88	5Y.9M

Order by **Baseline 15Y Return - Last 30 Years** (from 1993-12 to 2023-11)

Portfolio	3Y Rolling Annualized Return (%)			7Y Rolling Annualized Return (%)			15Y Rolling Annualized Return (%)				Max Draw-down (%)	Long Neg Period (Y.M)
	Worst	Base	%Fail	Worst	Base	%Fail	Worst	Base ▼	Median	%Fail		
MTUM-VNQ-GLD	-9.76	3.45	10.8%	0.04	7.03	0%	6.97	8.86	9.90	0%	-32.19	4Y.5M
MTUM-VNQ-EMB	-14.71	2.19	8.6%	-2.66	5.54	1.8%	7.90	8.79	9.59	0%	-41.93	8Y.7M
IJS-VNQ-GLD	-11.41	3.99	6.2%	-0.51	7.12	0.4%	5.73	8.76	9.62	0%	-35.17	7Y.0M
MTUM-EMB-GLD	-1.45	3.03	4%	2.84	6.96	0%	7.57	8.70	9.57	0%	-19.25	4Y.4M
IJS-EMB-GLD	-3.12	4.66	3.1%	2.32	6.89	0%	7.73	8.48	9.27	0%	-26.14	3Y.5M
MTUM-SCZ-GLD	-7.72	2.77	9.8%	2.77	7.24	0%	6.23	8.44	9.43	0%	-29.08	4Y.4M
MTUM-SCZ-EMB	-13.13	1.84	10.8%	0.04	5.76	0%	7.34	8.42	9.29	0%	-39.93	7Y.9M
IJS-MTUM-EMB	-12.88	0.54	12.9%	-3.01	5.45	2.2%	7.24	8.41	9.80	0%	-36.43	8Y.7M
MTUM-VNQ-TLT	-10.54	0.02	14.8%	-1.72	5.83	1.4%	7.45	8.38	9.69	0%	-32.00	8Y.10M
MTUM-SCZ-TLT	-8.66	0.58	14.5%	1.07	5.98	0%	7.19	8.36	9.34	0%	-28.25	4Y.4M
IJS-MTUM-GLD	-7.63	1.90	12.3%	-0.34	6.67	0.4%	7.25	8.36	9.94	0%	-29.82	7Y.0M
IJS-SCZ-GLD	-9.15	3.80	5.8%	2.31	7.02	0%	5.29	8.34	9.27	0%	-29.94	4Y.9M
IJS-VNQ-EMB	-16.10	2.48	8%	-3.30	5.47	1.8%	6.78	8.34	9.36	0%	-44.78	7Y.11M
IJS-SCZ-TLT	-10.05	2.73	7.1%	0.62	6.14	0%	6.11	8.33	9.12	0%	-30.63	4Y.5M
VNQ-CWD-GLD	-8.84	3.06	6.5%	0.31	6.42	0%	5.24	8.32	9.02	0%	-30.08	4Y.2M
VNQ-TLT-GLD	-3.02	2.11	5.5%	2.27	5.45	0%	6.28	8.31	8.87	0%	-22.60	4Y.2M
IJS-TLT-GLD	-2.56	3.15	2.8%	2.24	5.56	0%	7.02	8.29	9.00	0%	-20.60	3Y.11M
IJS-VNQ-TLT	-12.15	2.03	9.5%	-2.41	5.77	2.2%	6.25	8.28	9.23	0%	-35.73	8Y.1M
IJS-EEM-TLT	-6.59	2.23	7.7%	1.34	6.40	0%	6.50	8.20	9.16	0%	-29.36	4Y.3M
MTUM-SCZ-VNQ	-21.29	1.55	12.9%	-3.51	4.62	2.2%	5.23	8.18	9.02	0%	-57.52	9Y.8M
VTI-VNQ-GLD	-9.86	2.21	11.4%	-0.72	6.03	0.4%	5.32	8.15	9.05	0%	-32.75	7Y.10M

Order by **Median 15Y Return - Last 30 Years** (from 1993-12 to 2023-11)

Portfolio	3Y Rolling Annualized Return (%)			7Y Rolling Annualized Return (%)			15Y Rolling Annualized Return (%)				Max Draw-down (%)	Long Neg Period (Y.M)
	Worst	Base	%Fail	Worst	Base	%Fail	Worst	Base	Median ▼	%Fail		
IJS-MTUM-GLD	-7.63	1.90	12.3%	-0.34	6.67	0.4%	7.25	8.36	9.94	0%	-29.82	7Y.0M
MTUM-VNQ-GLD	-9.76	3.45	10.8%	0.04	7.03	0%	6.97	8.86	9.90	0%	-32.19	4Y.5M
IJS-MTUM-EMB	-12.88	0.54	12.9%	-3.01	5.45	2.2%	7.24	8.41	9.80	0%	-36.43	8Y.7M
MTUM-VNQ-TLT	-10.54	0.02	14.8%	-1.72	5.83	1.4%	7.45	8.38	9.69	0%	-32.00	8Y.10M
IJS-MTUM-TLT	-8.80	-0.69	15.1%	-2.13	5.11	3.3%	6.89	7.82	9.63	0%	-28.45	9Y.3M
IJS-VNQ-GLD	-11.41	3.99	6.2%	-0.51	7.12	0.4%	5.73	8.76	9.62	0%	-35.17	7Y.0M
MTUM-VNQ-EMB	-14.71	2.19	8.6%	-2.66	5.54	1.8%	7.90	8.79	9.59	0%	-41.93	8Y.7M
MTUM-EMB-GLD	-1.45	3.03	4%	2.84	6.96	0%	7.57	8.70	9.57	0%	-19.25	4Y.4M
SCZ-EMB-GLD	-2.81	3.63	1.8%	3.71	6.27	0%	6.61	7.65	9.55	0%	-25.59	5Y.1M
VTI-MTUM-EMB	-11.80	-0.75	17.2%	-3.31	4.54	3.3%	5.69	7.21	9.52	0%	-34.60	9Y.8M
EEM-VNQ-TLT	-8.41	1.40	9.2%	1.07	6.42	0%	5.76	7.89	9.52	0%	-30.33	4Y.7M
EEM-VNQ-EMB	-12.85	3.14	6.5%	0.75	5.75	0%	5.69	7.07	9.48	0%	-40.85	4Y.11M
SCZ-VNQ-EMB	-16.22	3.17	8%	-0.25	5.36	0.7%	6.17	7.36	9.47	0%	-46.76	7Y.0M
EEM-VNQ-GLD	-7.10	2.35	5.8%	2.99	5.34	0%	4.73	7.54	9.47	0%	-32.43	5Y.8M
SCZ-VNQ-GLD	-11.37	3.69	5.8%	2.58	6.32	0%	4.36	8.01	9.45	0%	-37.02	5Y.3M
MTUM-SCZ-GLD	-7.72	2.77	9.8%	2.77	7.24	0%	6.23	8.44	9.43	0%	-29.08	4Y.4M
IJS-MTUM-VNQ	-20.74	-0.98	16%	-6.28	4.61	2.9%	6.45	7.96	9.43	0%	-54.47	9Y.10M
MTUM-EEM-TLT	-9.90	0.67	13.2%	1.60	5.70	0%	6.72	7.99	9.42	0%	-31.25	5Y.1M
VNQ-EMB-GLD	-5.21	3.20	4.3%	2.73	5.96	0%	6.98	7.96	9.41	0%	-23.71	3Y.7M
IJS-VNQ-EMB	-16.10	2.48	8%	-3.30	5.47	1.8%	6.78	8.34	9.36	0%	-44.78	7Y.11M
MTUM-EEM-GLD	-11.45	2.58	8.6%	3.42	6.66	0%	6.10	7.89	9.35	0%	-33.57	5Y.4M

EUR Lazy Portfolios with 4 equally weighted Assets

Order by **Baseline 3Y Return - Last 30 Years** (from 1993-12 to 2023-11)

Portfolio	3Y Rolling Annualized Return (%)			7Y Rolling Annualized Return (%)			15Y Rolling Annualized Return (%)				Max Draw-down (%)	Long Neg Period (Y.M)
	Worst	Base ▼	%Fail	Worst	Base	%Fail	Worst	Base	Median	%Fail		
IJS-SCZ-EMB-GLD	-7.16	4.92	4.3%	2.54	7.09	0%	7.06	8.16	9.43	0%	-25.20	3Y.9M
IJS-VNQ-EMB-GLD	-8.94	4.42	5.5%	0.39	6.88	0%	7.31	8.51	9.46	0%	-28.39	4Y.0M
SCZ-VNQ-EMB-GLD	-8.77	4.19	5.2%	2.79	6.56	0%	6.39	7.89	9.70	0%	-29.68	3Y.10M
IJS-EMB-TIP-GLD	-1.61	4.11	2.5%	2.05	5.65	0%	6.86	7.59	8.06	0%	-19.73	3Y.5M
VTI-SCZ-EMB-GLD	-6.01	4.04	4.6%	2.36	7.02	0%	6.57	8.37	8.97	0%	-23.50	3Y.8M
SCZ-EMB-CWB-GLD	-5.28	4.03	3.1%	3.11	6.84	0%	6.29	8.07	8.92	0%	-24.85	3Y.6M
VNQ-EMB-CWB-GLD	-6.95	3.97	5.2%	1.00	6.69	0%	6.91	8.35	8.99	0%	-24.20	3Y.11M
SCZ-VNQ-EMB-CWB	-15.51	3.94	8%	-1.31	5.33	0.7%	5.88	7.81	8.81	0%	-44.61	7Y.10M
IJS-EEM-EMB-GLD	-4.19	3.93	2.8%	3.26	6.53	0%	7.03	7.92	9.44	0%	-30.92	4Y.8M
IJS-SCZ-VNQ-EMB	-17.14	3.90	9.5%	-1.94	5.39	0.7%	6.22	7.91	9.31	0%	-47.92	7Y.10M
VTV-SCZ-EMB-GLD	-6.36	3.90	4.6%	2.32	6.76	0%	6.61	8.00	8.84	0%	-24.27	3Y.9M
SCZ-VNQ-TIP-GLD	-7.51	3.80	5.5%	2.53	6.18	0%	5.05	7.47	8.71	0%	-26.05	3Y.10M
IJS-EMB-LQD-GLD	-2.62	3.72	3.7%	1.35	5.61	0%	7.23	7.77	8.33	0%	-20.14	3Y.6M
MTUM-SCZ-EMB-GLD	-5.95	3.70	4.6%	2.93	7.23	0%	7.84	8.68	9.47	0%	-23.19	3Y.9M
IJS-EMB-IEI-GLD	-2.41	3.66	2.5%	2.08	5.44	0%	6.85	7.52	8.06	0%	-19.64	3Y.6M
IJS-EMB-CWB-GLD	-5.41	3.66	5.5%	0.67	7.06	0%	7.36	8.35	9.10	0%	-24.73	3Y.9M
IJS-EEM-VNQ-GLD	-10.32	3.63	6.2%	0.97	6.68	0%	5.31	8.25	9.40	0%	-35.45	4Y.8M
IJS-SCZ-VNQ-GLD	-13.54	3.63	5.8%	0.20	6.73	0%	4.99	8.32	9.39	0%	-40.02	5Y.0M
IJS-SCZ-TIP-GLD	-5.95	3.62	4.3%	2.25	6.67	0%	5.62	7.76	8.49	0%	-21.12	3Y.9M
VTI-EEM-EMB-GLD	-5.15	3.56	6.2%	3.02	6.53	0%	6.50	8.02	8.86	0%	-29.33	4Y.4M
VTV-VNQ-EMB-GLD	-8.10	3.55	6.2%	0.18	6.49	0%	6.93	8.31	8.96	0%	-28.07	4Y.0M

Order by **Maximum Drawdown - Last 30 Years** (from 1993-12 to 2023-11)

Portfolio	3Y Rolling Annualized Return (%)			7Y Rolling Annualized Return (%)			15Y Rolling Annualized Return (%)				Max Draw-down (%) ▼	Long Neg Period (Y.M)
	Worst	Base	%Fail	Worst	Base	%Fail	Worst	Base	Median	%Fail		
SCZ-IEI-BIL-GLD	-1.85	1.78	3.4%	2.35	4.27	0%	4.13	5.77	6.34	0%	-15.26	5Y.0M
SCZ-BND-HYG-GLD	-3.19	2.21	3.7%	2.32	4.85	0%	4.07	6.70	7.28	0%	-15.39	4Y.10M
SCZ-BND-SHY-GLD	-1.69	1.97	2.8%	2.44	4.46	0%	4.30	6.02	6.60	0%	-15.41	5Y.0M
IEI-CWB-LQD-GLD	-4.42	2.12	6.8%	0.19	4.60	0%	4.90	6.07	7.00	0%	-15.47	6Y.6M
TLT-SHY-CWB-GLD	-4.75	2.20	9.5%	0.24	4.03	0%	5.39	6.20	7.02	0%	-15.48	6Y.6M
SCZ-TIP-BIL-GLD	-1.86	1.91	3.1%	2.71	4.50	0%	4.16	5.91	6.44	0%	-15.55	5Y.0M
SCZ-SHY-LQD-GLD	-1.64	2.05	2.8%	2.52	4.69	0%	4.26	6.36	6.88	0%	-15.57	5Y.0M
SCZ-TLT-BIL-GLD	-1.61	1.77	2.8%	2.64	4.67	0%	4.83	6.61	7.17	0%	-15.63	4Y.10M
TLT-HYG-CWB-GLD	-3.96	1.79	8%	0.46	4.50	0%	5.21	6.93	7.66	0%	-15.64	4Y.8M
SCZ-SHY-HYG-GLD	-3.16	2.00	4%	2.16	4.64	0%	3.84	6.25	6.85	0%	-15.65	4Y.10M
SCZ-IEI-HYG-GLD	-2.33	2.32	1.8%	2.83	4.99	0%	4.27	6.71	7.33	0%	-15.66	4Y.10M
BND-TIP-CWB-GLD	-4.13	2.10	7.1%	0.45	4.54	0%	4.97	5.91	6.94	0%	-15.66	4Y.8M
SCZ-LQD-BIL-GLD	-1.70	1.80	3.7%	2.16	4.52	0%	3.90	6.04	6.60	0%	-15.68	5Y.0M
BND-TLT-CWB-GLD	-4.35	2.15	9.5%	0.40	4.29	0%	5.61	6.57	7.43	0%	-15.69	4Y.8M
SCZ-SHY-IEI-GLD	-1.79	2.27	2.2%	2.71	4.51	0%	4.48	6.00	6.62	0%	-15.70	5Y.0M
MTUM-IEI-TIP-GLD	-4.31	2.36	8.3%	0.84	5.01	0%	5.60	6.39	7.54	0%	-15.70	4Y.11M
SCZ-BND-LQD-GLD	-1.43	2.07	1.8%	2.68	4.96	0%	4.49	6.82	7.31	0%	-15.83	4Y.10M
TIP-CWB-LQD-GLD	-3.53	2.09	6.8%	0.55	4.80	0%	4.93	6.18	7.15	0%	-15.84	4Y.6M
MTUM-TIP-LQD-GLD	-4.11	1.68	8.9%	0.68	5.13	0%	5.79	6.64	7.87	0%	-15.84	4Y.11M
MTUM-TLT-LQD-GLD	-4.49	2.31	10.5%	0.62	4.36	0%	6.43	7.21	8.38	0%	-15.85	4Y.11M
TLT-CWB-LQD-GLD	-3.75	1.96	9.2%	0.50	4.57	0%	5.58	6.86	7.65	0%	-15.86	4Y.7M

Order by **Longest Negative Period** - Last 30 Years (from 1993-12 to 2023-11)

Portfolio	3Y Rolling Annualized Return (%)			7Y Rolling Annualized Return (%)			15Y Rolling Annualized Return (%)				Max Draw-down (%)	Long Neg Period (Y.M) ▲
	Worst	Base	%Fail	Worst	Base	%Fail	Worst	Base	Median	%Fail		
SCZ-EMB-IEI-GLD	-0.42	3.13	0.6%	3.03	5.54	0%	6.37	6.98	8.31	0%	-19.44	3Y.1M
SCZ-BND-EMB-GLD	-1.26	2.99	0.9%	2.97	5.64	0%	6.34	7.01	8.30	0%	-19.15	3Y.2M
SCZ-EMB-TIP-GLD	-1.29	3.38	1.5%	3.30	5.52	0%	6.39	7.07	8.36	0%	-19.73	3Y.3M
SCZ-EMB-LQD-GLD	-2.27	3.09	1.8%	3.09	5.79	0%	6.30	7.35	8.59	0%	-19.31	3Y.4M
SCZ-TLT-CWB-GLD	-1.94	2.64	3.7%	3.50	6.13	0%	5.51	8.26	8.86	0%	-17.44	3Y.4M
IJS-EMB-TIP-GLD	-1.61	4.11	2.5%	2.05	5.65	0%	6.86	7.59	8.06	0%	-19.73	3Y.5M
SCZ-EMB-CWB-GLD	-5.28	4.03	3.1%	3.11	6.84	0%	6.29	8.07	8.92	0%	-24.85	3Y.6M
IJS-EMB-LQD-GLD	-2.62	3.72	3.7%	1.35	5.61	0%	7.23	7.77	8.33	0%	-20.14	3Y.6M
IJS-EMB-IEI-GLD	-2.41	3.66	2.5%	2.08	5.44	0%	6.85	7.52	8.06	0%	-19.64	3Y.6M
IJS-BNDX-EMB-GLD	-2.46	3.53	4%	1.42	5.46	0%	7.08	7.75	8.32	0%	-19.95	3Y.6M
IJS-BND-EMB-GLD	-2.69	3.53	2.8%	1.60	5.35	0%	6.89	7.55	8.03	0%	-19.96	3Y.6M
SCZ-EMB-HYG-GLD	-4.41	3.36	2.5%	3.09	5.93	0%	5.85	7.27	8.43	0%	-20.78	3Y.6M
SCZ-TIP-CWB-GLD	-4.25	3.03	4%	2.78	6.27	0%	4.76	7.56	8.03	0%	-19.64	3Y.6M
SCZ-TIP-HYG-GLD	-3.21	2.57	3.1%	2.74	5.16	0%	4.28	6.81	7.45	0%	-16.16	3Y.6M
VNQ-CMD-ICI-GLD	-2.29	2.34	3.1%	2.44	5.20	0%	6.31	7.24	8.13	0%	-21.37	3Y.6M
IJS-BND-SHY-GLD	-3.09	3.46	3.1%	1.44	5.27	0%	6.40	7.08	7.63	0%	-20.16	3Y.7M
IJS-EEM-TLT-GLD	-2.71	3.06	3.7%	3.59	5.99	0%	6.41	8.26	9.25	0%	-24.80	3Y.7M
EMB-TIP-CWB-GLD	-1.70	3.05	3.4%	2.58	5.50	0%	6.48	7.12	7.86	0%	-19.09	3Y.7M
SCZ-IEI-CWB-GLD	-3.16	2.76	4%	2.92	6.07	0%	4.77	7.51	7.93	0%	-17.88	3Y.7M
VNQ-BNDX-EMB-GLD	-3.96	2.55	5.2%	1.76	5.52	0%	6.53	7.44	8.32	0%	-22.73	3Y.7M
SCZ-BND-CWB-GLD	-4.04	2.50	4.9%	2.38	5.99	0%	4.57	7.40	7.88	0%	-19.06	3Y.7M

Order by **Baseline 7Y Return** - Last 30 Years (from 1993-12 to 2023-11)

Portfolio	3Y Rolling Annualized Return (%)			7Y Rolling Annualized Return (%)			15Y Rolling Annualized Return (%)				Max Draw-down (%)	Long Neg Period (Y.M)
	Worst	Base	%Fail	Worst	Base ▼	%Fail	Worst	Base	Median	%Fail		
MTUM-SCZ-EMB-GLD	-5.95	3.70	4.6%	2.93	7.23	0%	7.84	8.68	9.47	0%	-23.19	3Y.9M
IJS-MTUM-EMB-GLD	-6.04	2.81	7.4%	0.51	7.20	0%	7.75	8.84	9.74	0%	-24.49	3Y.11M
IJS-MTUM-SCZ-GLD	-10.77	1.72	9.5%	0.36	7.10	0%	6.48	8.50	9.44	0%	-34.28	4Y.2M
IJS-SCZ-EMB-GLD	-7.16	4.92	4.3%	2.54	7.09	0%	7.06	8.16	9.43	0%	-25.20	3Y.9M
MTUM-EEM-EMB-GLD	-4.89	3.05	5.8%	3.58	7.07	0%	7.25	8.34	9.45	0%	-25.28	4Y.4M
IJS-EMB-CWB-GLD	-5.41	3.66	5.5%	0.67	7.06	0%	7.36	8.35	9.10	0%	-24.73	3Y.9M
MTUM-EMB-CWB-GLD	-4.14	2.50	9.8%	1.05	7.03	0%	6.89	8.19	9.39	0%	-21.70	4Y.8M
VTI-SCZ-EMB-GLD	-6.01	4.04	4.6%	2.36	7.02	0%	6.57	8.37	8.97	0%	-23.50	3Y.8M
MTUM-EEM-VNQ-GLD	-9.29	3.04	8.9%	1.30	7.01	0%	6.12	8.54	9.39	0%	-36.20	4Y.3M
IJS-MTUM-VNQ-GLD	-12.33	2.26	11.1%	-1.69	6.98	0.7%	6.86	8.72	9.79	0%	-36.45	8Y.7M
MTUM-VNQ-EMB-GLD	-7.60	3.40	5.5%	0.83	6.94	0%	8.21	8.94	9.63	0%	-25.78	4Y.0M
IJS-MTUM-EEM-GLD	-8.86	2.70	10.8%	1.01	6.93	0%	6.72	8.32	9.37	0%	-31.75	4Y.8M
MTUM-SCZ-VNQ-GLD	-12.42	3.37	8.6%	0.59	6.92	0%	5.87	8.76	9.55	0%	-38.82	4Y.4M
IJS-VNQ-EMB-GLD	-8.94	4.42	5.5%	0.39	6.88	0%	7.31	8.51	9.46	0%	-28.39	4Y.0M
SCZ-EMB-CWB-GLD	-5.28	4.03	3.1%	3.11	6.84	0%	6.29	8.07	8.92	0%	-24.85	3Y.6M
VTI-IJS-EMB-GLD	-6.14	2.74	8.3%	-0.08	6.77	0.4%	7.37	8.31	9.16	0%	-25.56	7Y.0M
VTV-SCZ-EMB-GLD	-6.36	3.90	4.6%	2.32	6.76	0%	6.61	8.00	8.84	0%	-24.27	3Y.9M
MTUM-SCZ-EEM-GLD	-9.83	2.68	8.9%	3.22	6.75	0%	5.37	8.02	9.05	0%	-35.90	4Y.9M
IJS-SCZ-VNQ-GLD	-13.54	3.63	5.8%	0.20	6.73	0%	4.99	8.32	9.39	0%	-40.02	5Y.0M
IJS-VTV-EMB-GLD	-6.50	2.42	7.7%	-0.13	6.70	0.4%	7.36	8.08	8.94	0%	-26.09	7Y.0M
MTUM-SCZ-TIP-GLD	-4.76	2.77	7.7%	2.61	6.70	0%	6.27	7.86	8.68	0%	-20.39	3Y.9M

Order by **Baseline 15Y Return** - **Last 30 Years** (from 1993-12 to 2023-11)

Portfolio	3Y Rolling Annualized Return (%)			7Y Rolling Annualized Return (%)			15Y Rolling Annualized Return (%)				Max Draw-down (%)	Long Neg Period (Y.M)
	Worst	Base	%Fail	Worst	Base	%Fail	Worst	Base ▼	Median	%Fail		
MTUM-VNQ-EMB-GLD	-7.60	3.40	5.5%	0.83	6.94	0%	8.21	8.94	9.63	0%	-25.78	4Y.0M
IJS-MTUM-EMB-GLD	-6.04	2.81	7.4%	0.51	7.20	0%	7.75	8.84	9.74	0%	-24.49	3Y.11M
MTUM-SCZ-VNQ-GLD	-12.42	3.37	8.6%	0.59	6.92	0%	5.87	8.76	9.55	0%	-38.82	4Y.4M
MTUM-SCZ-EMB-TLT	-7.21	1.57	10.2%	1.52	5.83	0%	7.86	8.72	9.39	0%	-23.13	4Y.3M
IJS-MTUM-VNQ-GLD	-12.33	2.26	11.1%	-1.69	6.98	0.7%	6.86	8.72	9.79	0%	-36.45	8Y.7M
MTUM-SCZ-VNQ-TLT	-12.84	1.19	12%	-0.55	6.03	0.7%	6.50	8.71	9.45	0%	-38.79	8Y.6M
MTUM-VNQ-EMB-TLT	-8.65	1.16	10.5%	-0.56	5.42	0.7%	7.92	8.69	9.34	0%	-25.99	7Y.2M
MTUM-SCZ-EMB-GLD	-5.95	3.70	4.6%	2.93	7.23	0%	7.84	8.68	9.47	0%	-23.19	3Y.9M
IJS-VNQ-TLT-GLD	-5.90	3.30	6.5%	0.95	6.11	0%	6.45	8.66	9.31	0%	-21.04	4Y.0M
MTUM-SCZ-TLT-GLD	-3.82	2.21	6.5%	3.61	6.63	0%	7.03	8.64	9.39	0%	-19.92	4Y.4M
MTUM-VNQ-TLT-GLD	-4.42	1.50	9.8%	1.41	6.29	0%	7.42	8.61	9.60	0%	-18.43	4Y.4M
IJS-SCZ-TLT-GLD	-3.96	3.22	2.2%	3.22	6.57	0%	6.20	8.59	9.22	0%	-21.03	3Y.8M
MTUM-EEM-VNQ-TLT	-10.33	1.00	12%	0.04	6.29	0%	6.82	8.58	9.38	0%	-34.33	7Y.9M
VTI-VNQ-EMB-GLD	-7.71	3.31	6.2%	0.24	6.63	0%	7.03	8.56	9.15	0%	-26.33	4Y.0M
MTUM-EEM-VNQ-GLD	-9.29	3.04	8.9%	1.30	7.01	0%	6.12	8.54	9.39	0%	-36.20	4Y.3M
IJS-MTUM-VNQ-EMB	-16.02	1.93	10.5%	-3.75	5.61	2.2%	7.85	8.53	9.65	0%	-44.38	8Y.8M
IJS-VNQ-EMB-GLD	-8.94	4.42	5.5%	0.39	6.88	0%	7.31	8.51	9.46	0%	-28.39	4Y.0M
IJS-MTUM-SCZ-GLD	-10.77	1.72	9.5%	0.36	7.10	0%	6.48	8.50	9.44	0%	-34.28	4Y.2M
MTUM-SCZ-VNQ-EMB	-16.23	2.91	8.9%	-1.50	5.63	0.7%	7.17	8.45	9.39	0%	-46.72	8Y.6M
IJS-VNQ-EMB-TLT	-9.87	2.27	7.7%	-1.07	5.60	0.7%	7.56	8.45	9.10	0%	-29.01	7Y.3M
IJS-MTUM-SCZ-EMB	-14.80	2.25	10.8%	-1.71	5.66	1.1%	7.76	8.41	9.37	0%	-42.84	8Y.7M

Order by **Median 15Y Return** - **Last 30 Years** (from 1993-12 to 2023-11)

Portfolio	3Y Rolling Annualized Return (%)			7Y Rolling Annualized Return (%)			15Y Rolling Annualized Return (%)				Max Draw-down (%)	Long Neg Period (Y.M)
	Worst	Base	%Fail	Worst	Base	%Fail	Worst	Base	Median ▼	%Fail		
IJS-MTUM-VNQ-GLD	-12.33	2.26	11.1%	-1.69	6.98	0.7%	6.86	8.72	9.79	0%	-36.45	8Y.7M
IJS-MTUM-EMB-GLD	-6.04	2.81	7.4%	0.51	7.20	0%	7.75	8.84	9.74	0%	-24.49	3Y.11M
SCZ-VNQ-EMB-GLD	-8.77	4.19	5.2%	2.79	6.56	0%	6.39	7.89	9.70	0%	-29.68	3Y.10M
IJS-MTUM-TLT-GLD	-3.99	2.04	10.2%	1.07	5.96	0%	7.45	8.31	9.66	0%	-24.03	4Y.8M
IJS-MTUM-VNQ-EMB	-16.02	1.93	10.5%	-3.75	5.61	2.2%	7.85	8.53	9.65	0%	-44.38	8Y.8M
MTUM-VNQ-EMB-GLD	-7.60	3.40	5.5%	0.83	6.94	0%	8.21	8.94	9.63	0%	-25.78	4Y.0M
IJS-MTUM-VNQ-TLT	-12.86	0.62	13.9%	-2.98	5.71	2.5%	7.28	8.40	9.62	0%	-36.68	8Y.11M
MTUM-VNQ-TLT-GLD	-4.42	1.50	9.8%	1.41	6.29	0%	7.42	8.61	9.60	0%	-18.43	4Y.4M
EEM-VNQ-EMB-GLD	-5.55	3.20	2.2%	3.48	5.91	0%	6.36	7.53	9.59	0%	-31.65	5Y.0M
VTI-MTUM-EMB-GLD	-5.43	2.00	11.7%	0.29	6.39	0%	6.59	7.93	9.59	0%	-23.18	5Y.0M
MTUM-SCZ-VNQ-GLD	-12.42	3.37	8.6%	0.59	6.92	0%	5.87	8.76	9.55	0%	-38.82	4Y.4M
MTUM-VNQ-CWB-GLD	-10.48	2.04	12.3%	-1.11	6.47	0.7%	6.48	8.05	9.54	0%	-32.83	8Y.7M
IJS-MTUM-EMB-TLT	-7.38	1.50	11.4%	-0.89	5.53	0.7%	7.46	8.38	9.53	0%	-23.37	7Y.10M
EEM-VNQ-TLT-GLD	-2.29	2.30	3.4%	2.65	5.74	0%	5.91	7.92	9.51	0%	-25.92	5Y.0M
VTI-MTUM-VNQ-GLD	-11.25	0.89	13.5%	-1.89	6.01	0.7%	6.40	7.84	9.49	0%	-34.96	9Y.2M
SCZ-VNQ-EMB-TLT	-9.65	2.71	10.2%	1.22	5.88	0%	6.99	7.88	9.48	0%	-30.19	4Y.7M
MTUM-SCZ-EMB-GLD	-5.95	3.70	4.6%	2.93	7.23	0%	7.84	8.68	9.47	0%	-23.19	3Y.9M
SCZ-VNQ-TLT-GLD	-5.54	3.15	4.3%	2.96	6.49	0%	5.57	8.30	9.46	0%	-21.52	3Y.9M
IJS-VNQ-EMB-GLD	-8.94	4.42	5.5%	0.39	6.88	0%	7.31	8.51	9.46	0%	-28.39	4Y.0M
SCZ-EEM-EMB-TLT	-5.59	3.02	7.1%	0.95	6.68	0%	5.66	7.41	9.46	0%	-27.78	6Y.0M
MTUM-EEM-EMB-GLD	-4.89	3.05	5.8%	3.58	7.07	0%	7.25	8.34	9.45	0%	-25.28	4Y.4M

EUR Lazy Portfolios with 5 equally weighted Assets

Order by **Baseline 3Y Return - Last 30 Years** (from 1993-12 to 2023-11)

Portfolio	3Y Rolling Annualized Return (%)			7Y Rolling Annualized Return (%)			15Y Rolling Annualized Return (%)				Max Draw-down (%)	Long Neg Period (Y.M)
	Worst	Base ▼	%Fail	Worst	Base	%Fail	Worst	Base	Median	%Fail		
IJS-SCZ-VNQ-EMB-GLD	-11.05	4.46	5.5%	0.85	6.69	0%	6.46	8.28	9.52	0%	-33.90	4Y.3M
IJS-SCZ-EMB-CWB-GLD	-8.26	4.28	5.5%	1.11	6.90	0%	6.65	8.31	9.04	0%	-26.88	3Y.11M
IJS-SCZ-EMB-TIP-GLD	-5.05	4.23	3.7%	2.39	6.46	0%	6.92	7.75	8.64	0%	-20.73	3Y.9M
IJS-VNQ-EMB-CWB-GLD	-9.59	4.08	6.2%	-0.56	6.68	0.4%	6.86	8.36	9.18	0%	-29.49	7Y.1M
SCZ-VNQ-EMB-CWB-GLD	-9.53	4.04	5.2%	1.34	6.57	0%	6.14	8.22	9.14	0%	-30.80	4Y.0M
IJS-EEM-VNQ-EMB-GLD	-8.45	4.00	4.6%	1.48	6.82	0%	6.69	8.12	9.52	0%	-29.32	3Y.9M
IJS-SCZ-EMB-IEI-GLD	-4.37	3.99	3.4%	2.46	6.28	0%	6.93	7.65	8.60	0%	-20.44	3Y.8M
IJS-VNQ-EMB-TIP-GLD	-6.47	3.98	5.8%	0.64	6.28	0%	6.99	7.89	8.55	0%	-21.00	4Y.0M
IJS-SCZ-EMB-LQD-GLD	-5.86	3.96	4.3%	1.83	6.48	0%	6.72	7.83	8.71	0%	-20.93	3Y.9M
IJS-SCZ-BNDX-EMB-GLD	-5.75	3.93	4.3%	1.87	6.35	0%	6.56	7.77	8.71	0%	-20.47	3Y.9M
IJS-SCZ-EMB-HYG-GLD	-7.57	3.90	4.9%	1.13	6.47	0%	6.25	7.74	8.64	0%	-24.39	3Y.10M
IJS-SCZ-BND-EMB-GLD	-5.05	3.83	3.7%	2.05	6.24	0%	6.76	7.64	8.50	0%	-20.99	3Y.9M
IJS-VNQ-EMB-LQD-GLD	-7.32	3.83	7.1%	0.07	6.20	0%	6.91	8.01	8.66	0%	-23.53	4Y.0M
IJS-SCZ-EMB-SHY-GLD	-5.02	3.82	3.7%	1.93	6.05	0%	6.58	7.30	8.17	0%	-21.17	3Y.9M
SCZ-VNQ-EMB-HYG-GLD	-8.84	3.81	5.2%	1.35	6.06	0%	5.74	7.54	8.83	0%	-28.76	3Y.11M
VTV-SCZ-EEM-EMB-GLD	-7.14	3.79	6.2%	2.91	6.37	0%	5.95	7.66	8.83	0%	-29.51	4Y.9M
IJS-SCZ-EEM-EMB-GLD	-7.48	3.78	4.3%	3.11	6.76	0%	6.37	7.77	9.38	0%	-29.55	4Y.10M
IJS-MTUM-EEM-EMB-GLD	-6.66	3.73	7.4%	1.52	7.29	0%	7.62	8.59	9.39	0%	-27.07	3Y.9M
SCZ-EEM-EMB-CWB-GLD	-6.23	3.73	3.4%	3.54	6.45	0%	5.66	7.73	8.88	0%	-30.25	5Y.1M
IJS-VNQ-EMB-IEI-GLD	-5.84	3.69	5.8%	0.69	5.97	0%	6.99	7.79	8.49	0%	-20.26	3Y.11M
VTI-SCZ-EEM-EMB-GLD	-6.86	3.66	5.8%	2.93	6.62	0%	5.88	7.93	8.86	0%	-28.67	4Y.9M

Order by **Maximum Drawdown - Last 30 Years** (from 1993-12 to 2023-11)

Portfolio	3Y Rolling Annualized Return (%)			7Y Rolling Annualized Return (%)			15Y Rolling Annualized Return (%)				Max Draw-down (%) ▼	Long Neg Period (Y.M)
	Worst	Base	%Fail	Worst	Base	%Fail	Worst	Base	Median	%Fail		
SCZ-SHY-HYG-LQD-GLD	-2.69	1.59	5.5%	1.29	4.50	0%	4.03	6.12	6.61	0%	-15.17	4Y.2M
SCZ-BND-IEI-BIL-GLD	-2.45	1.66	4.9%	1.12	3.87	0%	4.27	5.47	5.93	0%	-15.25	4Y.4M
SCZ-TLT-HYG-BIL-GLD	-2.48	1.17	5.5%	1.40	4.38	0%	4.50	6.34	6.83	0%	-15.25	4Y.4M
SCZ-TLT-SHY-BIL-GLD	-2.51	1.22	4.9%	1.24	4.06	0%	4.64	5.75	6.22	0%	-15.25	4Y.4M
SCZ-SHY-IEI-HYG-GLD	-1.97	1.78	4.3%	1.45	4.26	0%	4.21	5.95	6.41	0%	-15.27	4Y.2M
GCZ-IEI-LQD-BIL-GLD	-2.03	1.70	4.6%	1.20	4.04	0%	4.24	5.74	6.15	0%	-15.28	4Y.2M
SCZ-SHY-TIP-BIL-GLD	-2.21	1.53	4.3%	1.29	3.87	0%	4.12	5.22	5.69	0%	-15.29	4Y.2M
SCZ-BND-LQD-BIL-GLD	-2.30	1.57	4.9%	0.98	4.09	0%	4.10	5.68	6.16	0%	-15.37	4Y.2M
SCZ-BND-TIP-BIL-GLD	-2.08	1.72	4.3%	1.41	4.09	0%	4.30	5.58	6.03	0%	-15.39	4Y.2M
SCZ-BND-SHY-LQD-GLD	-1.73	1.60	4.3%	1.27	4.20	0%	4.38	5.64	6.37	0%	-15.41	3Y.11M
SCZ-BND-TLT-BIL-GLD	-2.38	1.39	5.8%	1.37	4.19	0%	4.82	6.11	6.57	0%	-15.45	4Y.2M
SCZ-BND-HYG-LQD-GLD	-2.71	1.58	4.9%	1.42	4.67	0%	4.21	6.50	6.96	0%	-15.46	3Y.10M
SCZ-BND-SHY-IEI-GLD	-1.88	1.78	3.7%	1.41	4.01	0%	4.55	5.72	6.17	0%	-15.51	4Y.2M
SCZ-TIP-LQD-BIL-GLD	-1.66	1.78	3.7%	1.49	4.26	0%	4.27	5.84	6.30	0%	-15.52	3Y.10M
MTUM-IEI-TIP-LQD-GLD	-4.64	1.94	7.4%	-0.01	4.29	0.4%	5.38	6.07	7.19	0%	-15.52	7Y.2M
SCZ-TIP-HYG-BIL-GLD	-2.40	1.36	6.5%	1.44	4.41	0%	3.95	5.78	6.28	0%	-15.55	4Y.2M
SCZ-BND-IEI-HYG-GLD	-1.85	1.63	4%	1.57	4.50	0%	4.40	6.27	6.75	0%	-15.57	3Y.11M
SCZ-TLT-LQD-BIL-GLD	-1.96	1.39	5.5%	1.44	4.34	0%	4.80	6.35	6.82	0%	-15.58	4Y.2M
SCZ-IEI-TIP-BIL-GLD	-1.82	1.94	4%	1.63	4.01	0%	4.44	5.59	6.03	0%	-15.62	4Y.2M
TIP-HYG-CWB-LQD-GLD	-3.81	1.57	9.5%	-0.28	4.48	0.7%	4.54	5.91	6.77	0%	-15.63	7Y.7M
SCZ-SHY-IEI-LQD-GLD	-1.46	1.66	3.4%	1.49	4.23	0%	4.52	5.97	6.40	0%	-15.64	3Y.10M

Order by **Longest Negative Period** - **Last 30 Years** (from 1993-12 to 2023-11)

Portfolio	3Y Rolling Annualized Return (%)			7Y Rolling Annualized Return (%)			15Y Rolling Annualized Return (%)				Max Draw-down (%)	Long Neg Period (Y.M) ▲
	Worst	Base	%Fail	Worst	Base	%Fail	Worst	Base	Median	%Fail		
SCZ-BND-EMB-IEI-GLD	-0.08	2.51	0.3%	2.50	4.94	0%	5.98	6.60	7.43	0%	-18.51	3Y.0M
SCZ-EMB-SHY-IEI-GLD	-0.23	2.47	0.3%	2.72	4.73	0%	5.58	6.23	7.02	0%	-18.31	3Y.0M
SCZ-EMB-IEI-TIP-GLD	-0.08	2.81	0.3%	2.76	4.93	0%	5.96	6.67	7.48	0%	-19.01	3Y.1M
SCZ-EMB-SHY-TIP-GLD	-0.50	2.58	1.2%	2.94	4.65	0%	5.60	6.32	7.10	0%	-18.54	3Y.1M
SCZ-BND-EMB-TIP-GLD	-0.49	2.54	0.9%	2.72	4.90	0%	5.99	6.70	7.47	0%	-18.77	3Y.1M
SCZ-BNDX-EMB-IEI-GLD	-0.42	2.54	0.6%	2.63	5.32	0%	6.01	6.74	7.62	0%	-19.83	3Y.1M
SCZ-EMB-IEI-BIL-GLD	-0.22	2.37	1.2%	2.83	4.58	0%	5.36	6.04	6.83	0%	-17.96	3Y.1M
SCZ-BND-EMB-SHY-GLD	-0.38	2.31	0.9%	2.68	4.79	0%	5.62	6.27	7.05	0%	-18.08	3Y.1M
IJS-EEM-EMB-IEI-GLD	-1.89	3.47	2.5%	3.03	5.87	0%	6.80	7.44	8.57	0%	-24.50	3Y.2M
EEM-EMB-TIP-CWB-GLD	-1.68	3.03	2.8%	3.37	5.55	0%	6.24	7.29	8.12	0%	-24.56	3Y.2M
EEM-EMB-IEI-CWB-GLD	-1.02	2.81	3.4%	3.45	5.56	0%	6.24	7.24	8.03	0%	-24.71	3Y.2M
EEM-EMB-TIP-HYG-GLD	-0.75	2.04	2.5%	2.98	4.52	0%	5.87	6.61	7.62	0%	-24.28	3Y.2M
EEM-EMB-CWB-LQD-GLD	-2.04	2.82	4%	2.83	5.83	0%	6.03	7.43	8.24	0%	-25.17	3Y.3M
EEM-EMB-HYG-LQD-GLD	-1.16	1.85	3.7%	2.77	4.83	0%	5.68	6.74	7.71	0%	-23.79	3Y.3M
IJS-EEM-BND-EMB-GLD	-2.53	3.35	3.1%	2.61	5.89	0%	6.77	7.43	8.53	0%	-24.75	3Y.4M
IJS-EEM-EMB-SHY-GLD	-2.39	3.24	3.4%	2.49	5.74	0%	6.54	7.08	8.14	0%	-24.92	3Y.4M
SCZ-BNDX-EMB-TIP-GLD	-1.34	2.64	1.5%	2.85	5.16	0%	6.03	6.85	7.66	0%	-20.07	3Y.4M
SCZ-EMB-TIP-LQD-GLD	-1.18	2.63	1.5%	2.82	5.12	0%	6.20	6.96	7.69	0%	-18.91	3Y.4M
SCZ-EMB-IEI-HYG-GLD	-2.19	2.60	1.8%	2.83	5.32	0%	5.86	6.87	7.71	0%	-18.27	3Y.4M
SCZ-EMB-IEI-LQD-GLD	-0.53	2.59	0.9%	2.61	5.28	0%	6.18	6.86	7.64	0%	-18.63	3Y.4M
SCZ-EMB-TIP-BIL-GLD	-0.97	2.56	1.2%	3.11	4.61	0%	5.37	6.14	6.91	0%	-18.20	3Y.4M

Order by **Baseline 7Y Return** - **Last 30 Years** (from 1993-12 to 2023-11)

Portfolio	3Y Rolling Annualized Return (%)			7Y Rolling Annualized Return (%)			15Y Rolling Annualized Return (%)				Max Draw-down (%)	Long Neg Period (Y.M)
	Worst	Base	%Fail	Worst	Base ▼	%Fail	Worst	Base	Median	%Fail		
IJS-MTUM-EEM-EMB-GLD	-6.66	3.73	7.4%	1.52	7.29	0%	7.62	8.59	9.39	0%	-27.07	3Y.9M
MTUM-EEM-VNQ-EMB-GLD	-7.74	3.46	6.8%	1.77	7.17	0%	7.40	8.50	9.56	0%	-29.84	3Y.9M
IJS-MTUM-SCZ-EMB-GLD	-8.79	3.27	5.8%	0.98	7.13	0%	7.69	8.79	9.47	0%	-28.94	4Y.0M
IJS-MTUM-SCZ-TLT-GLD	-6.11	2.43	8.6%	1.59	7.08	0%	7.03	8.66	9.44	0%	-23.59	3Y.10M
VTI-IJS-SCZ-EMB-GLD	-8.85	3.41	6.2%	0.51	7.01	0%	6.69	8.38	9.07	0%	-28.90	3Y.11M
IJS-MTUM-EMB-CWB-GLD	-7.34	1.95	10.2%	-0.49	6.99	0.4%	7.09	8.27	9.44	0%	-25.74	7Y.2M
MTUM-SCZ-EEM-EMB-GLD	-6.86	3.33	5.8%	3.37	6.98	0%	6.88	8.18	9.34	0%	-29.40	3Y.8M
VTI-MTUM-SCZ-EMB-GLD	-7.99	2.42	9.2%	0.81	6.96	0%	7.20	8.32	9.27	0%	-27.80	4Y.4M
IJS-EEM-EMB-CWB-GLD	-6.05	3.48	5.2%	1.67	6.94	0%	6.64	8.15	8.94	0%	-28.57	3Y.8M
IJS-MTUM-EEM-VNQ-GLD	-11.41	2.91	10.2%	-0.34	6.91	0.4%	6.26	8.68	9.38	0%	-37.78	7Y.0M
VTI-IJS-EEM-EMB-GLD	-6.68	3.31	8.3%	1.06	6.91	0%	6.87	8.27	8.98	0%	-28.33	3Y.11M
IJS-MTUM-VNQ-EMB-GLD	-10.11	3.48	6.8%	-0.70	6.90	0.7%	7.94	8.93	9.66	0%	-30.86	7Y.2M
IJS-SCZ-EMB-CWB-GLD	-8.26	4.28	5.5%	1.11	6.90	0%	6.65	8.31	9.04	0%	-26.88	3Y.11M
MTUM-EMB-CWB-GLD	-5.40	2.93	7.7%	1.93	6.89	0%	6.87	8.11	9.15	0%	-24.40	4Y.5M
MTUM-SCZ-VNQ-EMB-GLD	-10.07	3.61	5.2%	1.19	6.87	0%	7.21	8.72	9.56	0%	-32.70	4Y.0M
IJS-VTV-EEM-EMB-GLD	-6.96	3.14	7.7%	1.04	6.84	0%	6.84	8.06	8.84	0%	-28.65	3Y.9M
MTUM-SCZ-EMB-CWB-GLD	-7.37	2.88	8%	1.42	6.84	0%	7.21	8.41	9.23	0%	-25.94	3Y.10M
MTUM-SCZ-VNQ-TLT-GLD	-7.37	2.58	8.6%	1.82	6.83	0%	6.58	8.87	9.53	0%	-25.58	4Y.0M
IJS-EEM-VNQ-EMB-GLD	-8.45	4.00	4.6%	1.48	6.82	0%	6.69	8.12	9.52	0%	-29.32	3Y.9M
IJS-MTUM-SCZ-VNQ-GLD	-13.92	2.69	9.5%	-0.92	6.81	0.7%	6.03	8.68	9.53	0%	-41.16	7Y.10M
VTI-MTUM-VNQ-EMB-GLD	-9.19	2.22	11.1%	-0.84	6.81	0.7%	7.28	8.40	9.53	0%	-29.49	8Y.5M

267

Order by Baseline 15Y Return - Last 30 Years (from 1993-12 to 2023-11)

Portfolio	3Y Rolling Annualized Return (%)			7Y Rolling Annualized Return (%)			15Y Rolling Annualized Return (%)				Max Draw-down (%)	Long Neg Period (Y.M)
	Worst	Base	%Fail	Worst	Base	%Fail	Worst	Base ▼	Median	%Fail		
IJS-MTUM-VNQ-EMB-GLD	-10.11	3.48	6.8%	-0.70	6.90	0.7%	7.94	8.93	9.66	0%	-30.86	7Y.2M
MTUM-SCZ-VNQ-TLT-GLD	-7.37	2.58	8.6%	1.82	6.83	0%	6.58	8.87	9.53	0%	-25.58	4Y.0M
IJS-MTUM-SCZ-EMB-GLD	-8.79	3.27	5.8%	0.98	7.13	0%	7.69	8.79	9.47	0%	-28.94	4Y.0M
MTUM-VNQ-EMB-TLT-GLD	-3.87	2.11	6.2%	1.70	5.99	0%	8.10	8.74	9.30	0%	-19.25	3Y.9M
MTUM-SCZ-EMB-TLT-GLD	-2.62	2.47	3.7%	3.48	6.64	0%	8.09	8.72	9.39	0%	-17.75	3Y.9M
MTUM-SCZ-VNQ-EMB-GLD	-10.07	3.61	5.2%	1.19	6.87	0%	7.21	8.72	9.56	0%	-32.70	4Y.0M
IJS-MTUM-EMB-TLT-GLD	-2.76	2.26	5.5%	1.42	6.38	0%	7.76	8.72	9.45	0%	-20.79	3Y.9M
MTUM-SCZ-VNQ-EMB-TLT	-10.80	2.15	7.4%	0.20	6.04	0%	7.67	8.70	9.44	0%	-33.02	6Y.11M
IJS-MTUM-EEM-VNQ-GLD	-11.41	2.91	10.2%	-0.34	6.91	0.4%	6.26	8.68	9.38	0%	-37.78	7Y.0M
IJS-SCZ-VNQ-TLT-GLD	-8.45	3.40	5.2%	1.46	6.78	0%	5.83	8.68	9.37	0%	-27.40	4Y.0M
IJS-MTUM-SCZ-VNQ-GLD	-13.92	2.69	9.5%	-0.92	6.81	0.7%	6.03	8.68	9.53	0%	-41.16	7Y.10M
IJS-MTUM-SCZ-TLT-GLD	-6.11	2.43	8.6%	1.59	7.08	0%	7.03	8.66	9.44	0%	-23.59	3Y.10M
IJS-MTUM-EEM-VNQ-TLT	-12.25	1.40	11.4%	-1.23	6.57	0.7%	6.76	8.66	9.42	0%	-36.86	8Y.7M
MTUM-EEM-VNQ-TLT-GLD	-5.04	2.02	8.6%	2.40	6.72	0%	6.83	8.66	9.46	0%	-22.85	4Y.3M
IJS-MTUM-VNQ-TLT-GLD	-7.55	2.43	10.5%	-0.17	6.53	0.4%	7.28	8.66	9.69	0%	-24.27	7Y.0M
IJS-MTUM-SCZ-EMB-TLT	-9.74	1.90	7.7%	-0.03	6.00	0.4%	8.02	8.65	9.49	0%	-29.45	7Y.0M
IJS-MTUM-VNQ-EMB-TLT	-10.87	2.10	8.9%	-1.78	5.87	1.4%	7.98	8.64	9.57	0%	-31.21	8Y.0M
IJS-MTUM-EEM-EMB-GLD	-6.66	3.73	7.4%	1.52	7.29	0%	7.62	8.59	9.39	0%	-27.07	3Y.9M
IJS-MTUM-EEM-EMB-TLT	-7.70	1.43	10.5%	0.38	6.29	0%	7.54	8.58	9.43	0%	-26.24	4Y.1M
IJS-MTUM-EEM-TLT-GLD	-5.80	2.87	8.9%	2.12	6.58	0%	7.27	8.54	9.50	0%	-26.72	4Y.7M
IJS-MTUM-SCZ-VNQ-TLT	-14.27	1.74	10.8%	-1.84	5.95	1.1%	6.48	8.54	9.38	0%	-41.44	8Y.7M

Order by Median 15Y Return - Last 30 Years (from 1993-12 to 2023-11)

Portfolio	3Y Rolling Annualized Return (%)			7Y Rolling Annualized Return (%)			15Y Rolling Annualized Return (%)				Max Draw-down (%)	Long Neg Period (Y.M)
	Worst	Base	%Fail	Worst	Base	%Fail	Worst	Base	Median ▼	%Fail		
IJS-MTUM-VNQ-TLT-GLD	-7.55	2.43	10.5%	-0.17	6.53	0.4%	7.28	8.66	9.69	0%	-24.27	7Y.0M
IJS-MTUM-VNQ-EMB-GLD	-10.11	3.48	6.8%	-0.70	6.90	0.7%	7.94	8.93	9.66	0%	-30.86	7Y.2M
SCZ-EEM-VNQ-EMB-TLT	-9.57	2.87	7.7%	1.56	6.34	0%	6.31	7.58	9.61	0%	-31.23	4Y.7M
VTI-IJS-MTUM-EMB-GLD	-7.94	1.40	12.3%	-1.10	6.50	0.7%	6.90	8.10	9.58	0%	-27.38	8Y.7M
SCZ-EEM-VNQ-EMB-GLD	-8.61	3.40	4.6%	3.32	6.36	0%	5.82	7.42	9.58	0%	-32.44	5Y.2M
IJS-MTUM-VNQ-EMB-TLT	-10.87	2.10	8.9%	-1.78	5.87	1.4%	7.98	8.64	9.57	0%	-31.21	8Y.0M
MTUM-SCZ-VNQ-EMB-GLD	-10.07	3.61	5.2%	1.19	6.87	0%	7.21	8.72	9.56	0%	-32.70	4Y.0M
MTUM-EEM-VNQ-EMB-GLD	-7.74	3.46	6.8%	1.77	7.17	0%	7.40	8.50	9.56	0%	-29.84	3Y.9M
MTUM-SCZ-VNQ-TLT-GLD	-7.37	2.58	8.6%	1.82	6.83	0%	6.58	8.87	9.53	0%	-25.58	4Y.0M
IJS-MTUM-SCZ-VNQ-GLD	-13.92	2.69	9.5%	-0.92	6.81	0.7%	6.03	8.68	9.53	0%	-41.16	7Y.10M
MTUM-EEM-VNQ-EMB-TLT	-8.75	1.03	8.3%	0.66	6.27	0%	7.65	8.50	9.53	0%	-28.49	4Y.3M
VTI-MTUM-VNQ-EMB-GLD	-9.19	2.22	11.1%	-0.84	6.81	0.7%	7.28	8.40	9.53	0%	-29.49	8Y.5M
SCZ-EEM-VNQ-TLT-GLD	-5.86	2.48	3.7%	2.96	6.17	0%	5.29	7.88	9.52	0%	-25.53	5Y.2M
IJS-EEM-VNQ-EMB-GLD	-8.45	4.00	4.6%	1.48	6.82	0%	6.69	8.12	9.52	0%	-29.32	3Y.9M
IJS-SCZ-VNQ-EMB-GLD	-11.05	4.46	5.5%	0.85	6.69	0%	6.46	8.28	9.52	0%	-33.90	4Y.3M
IJS-MTUM-EEM-TLT-GLD	-5.80	2.87	8.9%	2.12	6.58	0%	7.27	8.54	9.50	0%	-26.72	4Y.7M
IJS-MTUM-SCZ-EMB-TLT	-9.74	1.90	7.7%	-0.03	6.00	0.4%	8.02	8.65	9.49	0%	-29.45	7Y.0M
SCZ-VNQ-EMB-TLT-GLD	-4.75	3.24	4.3%	2.44	6.57	0%	6.91	8.07	9.47	0%	-20.87	4Y.2M
IJS-MTUM-SCZ-EMB-GLD	-8.79	3.27	5.8%	0.98	7.13	0%	7.69	8.79	9.47	0%	-28.94	4Y.0M
MTUM-EEM-VNQ-TLT-GLD	-5.04	2.02	8.6%	2.40	6.72	0%	6.83	8.66	9.46	0%	-22.85	4Y.3M
MTUM-VNQ-TLT-CWB-GLD	-5.92	1.16	11.7%	0.32	6.22	0%	6.99	8.16	9.46	0%	-20.85	4Y.7M

EUR Lazy Portfolios (1-5 Assets)

Order by **Baseline 3Y Return** - **Last 30 Years** (from 1993-12 to 2023-11)

Portfolio	3Y Rolling Annualized Return (%)			7Y Rolling Annualized Return (%)			15Y Rolling Annualized Return (%)				Max Draw-down (%)	Long Neg Period (Y.M)
	Worst	Base ▼	%Fail	Worst	Base	%Fail	Worst	Base	Median	%Fail		
IJS-SCZ-EMB-GLD	-7.16	4.92	4.3%	2.54	7.09	0%	7.06	8.16	9.43	0%	-25.20	3Y.9M
IJS-EMB-GLD	-3.12	4.66	3.1%	2.32	6.89	0%	7.73	8.48	9.27	0%	-26.14	3Y.5M
IJS-SCZ-VNQ-EMB-GLD	-11.05	4.46	5.5%	0.85	6.69	0%	6.46	8.28	9.52	0%	-33.90	4Y.3M
IJS-VNQ-EMB-GLD	-8.94	4.42	5.5%	0.39	6.88	0%	7.31	8.51	9.46	0%	-28.39	4Y.0M
IJS-SCZ-EMB-CWB-GLD	-8.26	4.28	5.5%	1.11	6.90	0%	6.65	8.31	9.04	0%	-26.88	3Y.11M
IJS-SCZ-EMB-TIP-GLD	-5.05	4.23	3.7%	2.39	6.46	0%	6.92	7.75	8.64	0%	-20.73	3Y.9M
SCZ-VNQ-EMB-GLD	-8.77	4.19	5.2%	2.79	6.56	0%	6.39	7.89	9.70	0%	-29.68	3Y.10M
IJS-EMB-TIP-GLD	-1.61	4.11	2.5%	2.05	5.65	0%	6.86	7.59	8.06	0%	-19.73	3Y.5M
IJS-VNQ-EMB-CWB-GLD	-9.59	4.08	6.2%	-0.56	6.68	0.4%	6.86	8.36	9.18	0%	-29.49	7Y.1M
SCZ-VNQ-EMB-CWB-GLD	-9.53	4.04	5.2%	1.34	6.57	0%	6.14	8.22	9.14	0%	-30.80	4Y.0M
VTI-SCZ-EMB-GLD	-6.01	4.04	4.6%	2.36	7.02	0%	6.57	8.37	8.97	0%	-23.50	3Y.8M
SCZ-EMB-CWB-GLD	-5.28	4.03	3.1%	3.11	6.84	0%	6.29	8.07	8.92	0%	-24.85	3Y.6M
IJS-EEM-VNQ-EMB-GLD	-8.45	4.00	4.6%	1.48	6.82	0%	6.69	8.12	9.52	0%	-29.32	3Y.9M
IJS-SCZ-EMB-IEI-GLD	-4.37	3.99	3.4%	2.46	6.28	0%	6.93	7.65	8.60	0%	-20.44	3Y.8M
IJS-VNQ-GLD	-11.41	3.99	6.2%	-0.51	7.12	0.4%	5.73	8.76	9.62	0%	-35.17	7Y.0M
IJS-VNQ-EMB-TIP-GLD	-6.47	3.98	5.8%	0.64	6.28	0%	6.99	7.89	8.55	0%	-21.00	4Y.0M
VNQ-EMB-CWB-GLD	-6.95	3.97	5.2%	1.00	6.69	0%	6.91	8.35	8.99	0%	-24.20	3Y.11M
IJS-SCZ-EMB-LQD-GLD	-5.86	3.96	4.3%	1.83	6.48	0%	6.72	7.83	8.71	0%	-20.93	3Y.9M
SCZ-VNQ-EMB-CWB	-15.51	3.94	8%	-1.31	5.33	0.7%	5.88	7.81	8.81	0%	-44.61	7Y.10M
IJS-EEM-EMB-GLD	-4.19	3.93	2.8%	3.26	6.53	0%	7.03	7.92	9.44	0%	-30.92	4Y.8M
IJS-SCZ-BNDX-EMB-GLD	-5.75	3.93	4.3%	1.87	6.35	0%	6.56	7.77	8.71	0%	-20.47	3Y.9M

Order by **Maximum Drawdown** - **Last 30 Years** (from 1993-12 to 2023-11)

Portfolio	3Y Rolling Annualized Return (%)			7Y Rolling Annualized Return (%)			15Y Rolling Annualized Return (%)				Max Draw-down (%) ▼	Long Neg Period (Y.M)
	Worst	Base	%Fail	Worst	Base	%Fail	Worst	Base	Median	%Fail		
HYG-LQD-GLD	-4.15	1.58	6.8%	0.66	3.78	0%	3.98	6.01	6.68	0%	-15.11	4Y.8M
SCZ-SHY-HYG-LQD-GLD	-2.69	1.59	5.5%	1.29	4.50	0%	4.03	6.12	6.61	0%	-15.17	4Y.2M
SCZ-TLT-HYG-BIL-GLD	-2.48	1.17	5.5%	1.40	4.38	0%	4.50	6.34	6.83	0%	-15.25	4Y.4M
SCZ-BND-IEI-BIL-GLD	-2.45	1.66	4.9%	1.12	3.87	0%	4.27	5.47	5.93	0%	-15.25	4Y.4M
SCZ-TLT-SHY-BIL-GLD	-2.51	1.22	4.9%	1.24	4.06	0%	4.64	5.75	6.22	0%	-15.25	4Y.4M
SCZ-IEI-BIL-GLD	-1.85	1.78	3.4%	2.35	4.27	0%	4.13	5.77	6.34	0%	-15.26	5Y.0M
SCZ-SHY-IEI-HYG-GLD	-1.97	1.78	4.3%	1.45	4.26	0%	4.21	5.95	6.41	0%	-15.27	4Y.2M
SCZ-IEI-LQD-BIL-GLD	-2.03	1.70	4.6%	1.20	4.04	0%	4.24	5.74	6.15	0%	-15.28	4Y.2M
SCZ-SHY-TIP-BIL-GLD	-2.21	1.53	4.3%	1.29	3.87	0%	4.12	5.22	5.69	0%	-15.29	4Y.2M
SCZ-BND-LQD-BIL-GLD	-2.30	1.57	4.9%	0.98	4.09	0%	4.10	5.68	6.16	0%	-15.37	4Y.2M
SCZ-BND-TIP-BIL-GLD	-2.08	1.72	4.3%	1.41	4.09	0%	4.30	5.58	6.03	0%	-15.39	4Y.2M
SCZ-BND-HYG-GLD	-3.19	2.21	3.7%	2.32	4.85	0%	4.07	6.70	7.28	0%	-15.39	4Y.10M
SCZ-BND-SHY-LQD-GLD	-1.73	1.60	4.3%	1.27	4.20	0%	4.38	5.94	6.37	0%	-15.41	3Y.11M
SCZ-BND-SHY-GLD	-1.69	1.97	2.8%	2.44	4.46	0%	4.30	6.02	6.60	0%	-15.41	4Y.2M
SCZ-BND-TLT-BIL-GLD	-2.38	1.39	5.8%	1.37	4.19	0%	4.82	6.11	6.57	0%	-15.45	4Y.2M
SCZ-BND-HYG-LQD-GLD	-2.71	1.58	4.9%	1.42	4.67	0%	4.21	6.50	6.96	0%	-15.46	3Y.10M
IEI-CWB-LQD-GLD	-4.42	2.12	6.8%	0.19	4.60	0%	4.90	6.07	7.00	0%	-15.47	6Y.6M
TLT-SHY-CWB-GLD	-4.75	2.20	9.5%	0.24	4.03	0%	5.39	6.20	7.02	0%	-15.48	6Y.6M
IEI-HYG-GLD	-4.70	1.65	7.4%	0.83	3.31	0%	4.24	5.61	6.34	0%	-15.49	4Y.8M
SCZ-BND-SHY-IEI-GLD	-1.88	1.78	3.7%	1.41	4.01	0%	4.55	5.72	6.17	0%	-15.51	4Y.2M
SCZ-TIP-LQD-BIL-GLD	-1.66	1.78	3.7%	1.49	4.26	0%	4.27	5.84	6.30	0%	-15.52	3Y.10M

Order by **Longest Negative Period** - Last 30 Years (from 1993-12 to 2023-11)

Portfolio	3Y Rolling Annualized Return (%)			7Y Rolling Annualized Return (%)			15Y Rolling Annualized Return (%)				Max Draw-down (%)	Long Neg Period (Y.M) ▲
	Worst	Base	%Fail	Worst	Base	%Fail	Worst	Base	Median	%Fail		
SCZ-BND-EMB-IEI-GLD	-0.08	2.51	0.3%	2.50	4.94	0%	5.98	6.60	7.43	0%	-18.51	3Y.0M
SCZ-EMB-SHY-IEI-GLD	-0.23	2.47	0.3%	2.72	4.73	0%	5.58	6.23	7.02	0%	-18.31	3Y.0M
SCZ-EMB-IEI-GLD	-0.42	3.13	0.6%	3.03	5.54	0%	6.37	6.98	8.31	0%	-19.44	3Y.1M
SCZ-EMB-IEI-TIP-GLD	-0.08	2.81	0.3%	2.76	4.93	0%	5.96	6.67	7.48	0%	-19.01	3Y.1M
SCZ-EMB-SHY-TIP-GLD	-0.50	2.58	1.2%	2.94	4.65	0%	5.60	6.32	7.10	0%	-18.54	3Y.1M
SCZ-BND-EMB-TIP-GLD	-0.49	2.54	0.9%	2.72	4.90	0%	5.99	6.70	7.47	0%	-18.77	3Y.1M
SCZ-BNDX-EMB-IEI-GLD	-0.42	2.54	0.6%	2.63	5.32	0%	6.01	6.74	7.62	0%	-19.83	3Y.1M
SCZ-EMB-IEI-BIL-GLD	-0.22	2.37	1.2%	2.83	4.58	0%	5.36	6.04	6.83	0%	-17.96	3Y.1M
SCZ-BND-EMB-SHY-GLD	-0.38	2.31	0.9%	2.68	4.79	0%	5.62	6.27	7.05	0%	-18.08	3Y.1M
EMB-CWB-GLD	-1.27	3.60	2.8%	3.06	6.25	0%	7.12	8.02	8.69	0%	-22.86	3Y.2M
IJS-EEM-EMB-IEI-GLD	-1.89	3.47	2.5%	3.03	5.87	0%	6.80	7.44	8.57	0%	-24.50	3Y.2M
EEM-EMB-TIP-CWB-GLD	-1.68	3.03	2.8%	3.37	5.55	0%	6.24	7.29	8.12	0%	-24.56	3Y.2M
SCZ-BND-EMB-GLD	-1.26	2.99	0.9%	2.97	5.64	0%	6.34	7.01	8.30	0%	-19.15	3Y.2M
EEM-EMB-IEI-CWB-GLD	-1.02	2.81	3.4%	3.45	5.56	0%	6.24	7.24	8.03	0%	-24.71	3Y.2M
EEM-EMB-TIP-HYG-GLD	-0.75	2.04	2.5%	2.98	4.52	0%	5.87	6.61	7.62	0%	-24.28	3Y.2M
SCZ-EMB-TIP-GLD	-1.29	3.38	1.5%	3.30	5.52	0%	6.39	7.07	8.36	0%	-19.73	3Y.3M
EEM-EMB-CWB-LQD-GLD	-2.04	2.82	4%	2.83	5.83	0%	6.03	7.43	8.24	0%	-25.17	3Y.3M
EMB-HYG-GLD	-1.86	2.60	1.8%	2.84	4.48	0%	6.30	6.98	7.67	0%	-19.55	3Y.3M
EEM-EMB-HYG-LQD-GLD	-1.16	1.85	3.7%	2.77	4.83	0%	5.68	6.74	7.71	0%	-23.79	3Y.3M
IJS-EEM-BND-EMB-GLD	-2.53	3.35	3.1%	2.61	5.89	0%	6.77	7.43	8.53	0%	-24.75	3Y.4M
IJS-EEM-EMB-SHY-GLD	-2.39	3.24	3.4%	2.49	5.74	0%	6.54	7.08	8.14	0%	-24.92	3Y.4M

Order by **Baseline 7Y Return** - Last 30 Years (from 1993-12 to 2023-11)

Portfolio	3Y Rolling Annualized Return (%)			7Y Rolling Annualized Return (%)			15Y Rolling Annualized Return (%)				Max Draw-down (%)	Long Neg Period (Y.M)
	Worst	Base	%Fail	Worst	Base ▼	%Fail	Worst	Base	Median	%Fail		
IJS-MTUM-EEM-EMB-GLD	-6.66	3.73	7.4%	1.52	7.29	0%	7.62	8.59	9.39	0%	-27.07	3Y.9M
MTUM-SCZ-GLD	-7.72	2.77	9.8%	2.77	7.24	0%	6.23	8.44	9.43	0%	-29.08	4Y.4M
MTUM-SCZ-EMB-GLD	-5.95	3.70	4.6%	2.93	7.23	0%	7.84	8.68	9.47	0%	-23.19	3Y.9M
IJS-MTUM-EMB-GLD	-6.04	2.81	7.4%	0.51	7.20	0%	7.75	8.84	9.74	0%	-24.49	3Y.11M
MTUM-EEM-VNQ-EMB-GLD	-7.74	3.46	6.8%	1.77	7.17	0%	7.40	8.50	9.56	0%	-29.84	3Y.9M
IJS-MTUM-SCZ-EMB-GLD	-8.79	3.27	5.8%	0.98	7.13	0%	7.69	8.79	9.47	0%	-28.94	4Y.0M
IJS-VNQ-GLD	-11.41	3.99	6.2%	-0.51	7.12	0.4%	5.73	8.76	9.62	0%	-35.17	7Y.0M
IJS-MTUM-SCZ-GLD	-10.77	1.72	9.5%	0.36	7.10	0%	6.48	8.50	9.44	0%	-34.28	4Y.2M
IJS-SCZ-EMB-GLD	-7.18	4.92	4.3%	2.54	7.09	0%	7.06	8.16	9.43	0%	-25.20	3Y.9M
IJS-MTUM-SCZ-TLT-GLD	-6.11	2.43	8.6%	1.59	7.08	0%	7.03	8.66	9.44	0%	-23.59	3Y.10M
MTUM-EEM-EMB-GLD	-4.89	3.05	5.8%	3.58	7.07	0%	7.25	8.34	9.45	0%	-25.28	4Y.4M
IJS-EMB-CWB-GLD	-5.41	3.66	5.5%	0.67	7.06	0%	7.36	8.35	9.10	0%	-24.73	3Y.9M
MTUM-EMB-CWB-GLD	-4.14	2.50	9.8%	1.05	7.03	0%	6.89	8.19	9.39	0%	-21.70	4Y.9M
MTUM-VNQ-GLD	-9.76	3.45	10.8%	0.04	7.03	0%	6.97	8.86	9.90	0%	-32.19	4Y.5M
IJS-SCZ-GLD	-9.15	3.80	5.8%	2.31	7.02	0%	5.29	8.34	9.27	0%	-29.94	4Y.9M
VTI-SCZ-EMB-GLD	-6.01	4.04	4.6%	2.36	7.02	0%	6.57	8.37	8.97	0%	-23.50	3Y.8M
MTUM-EEM-VNQ-GLD	-9.29	3.04	8.9%	1.30	7.01	0%	6.12	8.54	9.39	0%	-36.20	4Y.3M
VTI-IJS-SCZ-EMB-GLD	-8.85	3.41	6.2%	0.51	7.01	0%	6.69	8.38	9.07	0%	-28.90	3Y.11M
IJS-MTUM-EMB-CWB-GLD	-7.34	1.95	10.2%	-0.49	6.99	0.4%	7.09	8.27	9.44	0%	-25.74	7Y.2M
IJS-MTUM-VNQ-GLD	-12.33	2.26	11.1%	-1.69	6.98	0.7%	6.86	8.72	9.79	0%	-36.45	8Y.7M
MTUM-SCZ-EEM-EMB-GLD	-6.86	3.33	5.8%	3.37	6.98	0%	6.88	8.18	9.34	0%	-29.40	3Y.8M

Order by **Baseline 15Y Return** - **Last 30 Years** (from 1993-12 to 2023-11)

Portfolio	3Y Rolling Annualized Return (%)			7Y Rolling Annualized Return (%)			15Y Rolling Annualized Return (%)				Max Draw-down (%)	Long Neg Period (Y.M)
	Worst	Base	%Fail	Worst	Base	%Fail	Worst	Base ▼	Median	%Fail		
MTUM-VNQ-EMB-GLD	-7.60	3.40	5.5%	0.83	6.94	0%	8.21	8.94	9.63	0%	-25.78	4Y.0M
IJS-MTUM-VNQ-EMB-GLD	-10.11	3.48	6.8%	-0.70	6.90	0.7%	7.94	8.93	9.66	0%	-30.86	7Y.2M
MTUM-SCZ-VNQ-TLT-GLD	-7.37	2.58	8.6%	1.82	6.83	0%	6.58	8.87	9.53	0%	-25.58	4Y.0M
MTUM-VNQ-GLD	-9.76	3.45	10.8%	0.04	7.03	0%	6.97	8.86	9.90	0%	-32.19	4Y.5M
IJS-MTUM-EMB-GLD	-6.04	2.81	7.4%	0.51	7.20	0%	7.75	8.84	9.74	0%	-24.49	3Y.11M
MTUM-VNQ-EMB	-14.71	2.19	8.6%	-2.66	5.54	1.8%	7.90	8.79	9.59	0%	-41.93	8Y.7M
IJS-MTUM-SCZ-EMB-GLD	-8.79	3.27	5.8%	0.98	7.13	0%	7.69	8.79	9.47	0%	-28.94	4Y.0M
IJS-VNQ-GLD	-11.41	3.99	6.2%	-0.51	7.12	0.4%	5.73	8.76	9.62	0%	-35.17	7Y.0M
MTUM-SCZ-VNQ-GLD	-12.42	3.37	8.6%	0.59	6.92	0%	5.87	8.76	9.55	0%	-38.82	4Y.4M
MTUM-VNQ-EMB-TLT-GLD	-3.87	2.11	6.2%	1.70	5.99	0%	8.10	8.74	9.30	0%	-19.25	3Y.9M
MTUM-SCZ-EMB-TLT-GLD	-2.62	2.47	3.7%	3.48	6.64	0%	8.09	8.72	9.39	0%	-17.75	3Y.9M
MTUM-SCZ-VNQ-EMB-GLD	-10.07	3.61	5.2%	1.19	6.87	0%	7.21	8.72	9.56	0%	-32.70	4Y.0M
MTUM-SCZ-EMB-TLT	-7.21	1.57	10.2%	1.52	5.83	0%	7.86	8.72	9.39	0%	-23.13	4Y.3M
IJS-MTUM-VNQ-GLD	-12.33	2.26	11.1%	-1.69	6.98	0.7%	6.86	8.72	9.79	0%	-36.45	8Y.7M
IJS-MTUM-EMB-TLT-GLD	-2.76	2.26	5.5%	1.42	6.38	0%	7.76	8.72	9.45	0%	-20.79	3Y.9M
MTUM-SCZ-VNQ-TLT	-12.84	1.19	12%	-0.55	6.03	0.7%	6.50	8.71	9.45	0%	-38.79	8Y.6M
MTUM-EMB-GLD	-1.45	3.03	4%	2.84	6.96	0%	7.57	8.70	9.57	0%	-19.25	4Y.4M
MTUM-SCZ-VNQ-EMB-TLT	-10.80	2.15	7.4%	0.20	6.04	0%	7.67	8.70	9.44	0%	-33.02	6Y.11M
MTUM-VNQ-EMB-TLT	-8.65	1.16	10.5%	-0.56	5.42	0.7%	7.92	8.69	9.34	0%	-25.99	7Y.2M
IJS-MTUM-EEM-VNQ-GLD	-11.41	2.91	10.2%	-0.34	6.91	0.4%	6.26	8.68	9.38	0%	-37.78	7Y.0M
MTUM-SCZ-EMB-GLD	-5.95	3.70	4.6%	2.93	7.23	0%	7.84	8.68	9.47	0%	-23.19	3Y.9M

Order by **Median 15Y Return** - **Last 30 Years** (from 1993-12 to 2023-11)

Portfolio	3Y Rolling Annualized Return (%)			7Y Rolling Annualized Return (%)			15Y Rolling Annualized Return (%)				Max Draw-down (%)	Long Neg Period (Y.M)
	Worst	Base	%Fail	Worst	Base	%Fail	Worst	Base	Median ▼	%Fail		
MTUM-GLD	-8.57	2.97	10.8%	2.73	5.88	0%	6.74	8.02	10.04	0%	-29.16	5Y.5M
MTUM	-18.79	-6.17	20.6%	-5.90	2.08	9.4%	3.98	5.88	10.00	0%	-52.31	12Y.5M
IJS-MTUM-GLD	-7.63	1.90	12.3%	-0.34	6.67	0.4%	7.25	8.36	9.94	0%	-29.82	7Y.0M
MTUM-VNQ-GLD	-9.76	3.45	10.8%	0.04	7.03	0%	6.97	8.86	9.90	0%	-32.19	4Y.5M
IJS-MTUM-EMB	-12.88	0.54	12.9%	-3.01	5.45	2.2%	7.24	8.41	9.80	0%	-36.43	8Y.7M
IJS-MTUM-VNQ-GLD	-12.33	2.26	11.1%	-1.69	6.98	0.7%	6.86	8.72	9.79	0%	-36.45	8Y.7M
IJS-MTUM-EMB-GLD	-6.04	2.81	7.4%	0.51	7.20	0%	7.75	8.84	9.74	0%	-24.49	3Y.11M
SCZ-VNQ-EMB-GLD	-8.77	4.19	5.2%	2.79	6.56	0%	6.39	7.89	9.70	0%	-29.68	3Y.10M
IJS-MTUM-VNQ-TLT-GLD	-7.55	2.43	10.5%	-0.17	6.53	0.4%	7.28	8.66	9.69	0%	-24.27	7Y.0M
MTUM-VNQ-TLT	-10.54	0.02	14.8%	-1.72	5.83	1.4%	7.45	8.38	9.69	0%	-32.00	8Y.10M
MTUM-EMB	-9.43	0.85	10.8%	-1.10	5.70	0.7%	6.94	8.29	9.67	0%	-28.00	8Y.7M
IJS-MTUM	-18.22	-3.48	18.8%	-6.33	3.70	4.3%	5.95	7.23	9.67	0%	-49.11	11Y.1M
IJS-MTUM-TLT-GLD	-3.99	2.04	10.2%	1.07	5.96	0%	7.45	8.31	9.66	0%	-24.03	4Y.8M
IJS-MTUM-VNQ-EMB-GLD	-10.11	3.48	6.8%	-0.70	6.90	0.7%	7.94	8.93	9.66	0%	-30.86	7Y.2M
IJS-MTUM-VNQ-EMB	-16.02	1.93	10.5%	-3.75	5.61	2.2%	7.85	8.53	9.65	0%	-44.38	8Y.8M
MTUM-VNQ-EMB-GLD	-7.60	3.40	5.5%	0.83	6.94	0%	8.21	8.94	9.63	0%	-25.78	4Y.0M
IJS-MTUM-TLT	-8.80	-0.69	15.1%	-2.13	5.11	3.3%	6.89	7.82	9.63	0%	-28.45	9Y.3M
MTUM-VNQ	-21.24	-0.80	15.7%	-5.95	4.56	3.3%	6.55	8.12	9.63	0%	-56.39	9Y.11M
IJS-MTUM-VNQ-TLT	-12.86	0.62	13.9%	-2.98	5.71	2.5%	7.28	8.40	9.62	0%	-36.68	8Y.11M
IJS-VNQ-GLD	-11.41	3.99	6.2%	-0.51	7.12	0.4%	5.73	8.76	9.62	0%	-35.17	7Y.0M
SCZ-EEM-VNQ-EMB-TLT	-9.57	2.87	7.7%	1.56	6.34	0%	6.31	7.58	9.61	0%	-31.23	4Y.7M

Appendix - Estimating Metrics Independently

You may find yourself evaluating a fund or a stock for which you don't have the in-depth metrics we've seen in the book.

Have you decided to focus on a niche ETF for which you can't find metrics on the web, or are you assessing the quality of an actively managed fund? Before investing, it's always essential to frame the investment based on your objective. The strategy from the book is always valid!

Never limit yourself to recent returns but estimate the rest independently. In particular, **rolling periods** and **drawdowns** are crucial.

Firstly, on the main reference websites (Morningstar, Yahoo Finance, or other specific sites), retrieve returns divided by periods. In the case of instruments listed on US markets, you are likely to find a wealth of information on *PortfolioVisualizer.com*, which practically includes all the metrics you've seen here.

Conversely, if you can't retrieve monthly returns for each instrument, at least consider quarterly or annual ones.

The next example is taken from Morningstar. After searching for the instrument of your interest, navigate to the 'Performance' tab.

Quote Chart Fund Analysis Performance Sustainability Risk Price Portfolio People Parent

On this page, you will find the returns for each year (sometimes, even returns for quarters).

Total Return %	2013	2014	2015	2016	2017	2018	2019	2020	2021	2022	YTD
Investment	20.50	10.37	0.41	7.01	16.50	-4.02	24.39	22.43	18.28	-18.19	21.60

In this case, the available history is limited, so the metrics derived are not very significant, but they are better than nothing. Clearly, there is a risk of starting from a very 'positive' time interval during which there were no strong periods of price stress.

If you want to calculate rolling returns over N years, you will need to consider all the series of consecutive N-year periods and calculate the overall returns.

The formula for the overall compound return is:

$[(1 + rend1/100) * (1 + rend2/100) * ... * (1 + rendN/100)] - 1$

If, for example, we wanted to calculate rolling returns over 3 years, for the three-year period 2013-2015, we would have:

$[(1 + 20.50/100) * (1 + 10.37/100) * (1 + 0.41/100)] - 1 =$

$[(1 + 0.205) * (1 + 0.1037) * (1 + 0.0041)] - 1 = 0.3354 = 33.54\%$

We conclude that, over the three-year period 2013-2015, the total return is 33.54%. The annualized return is:

$[(1 + 0.3354) \wedge (\frac{1}{3})] - 1 = 0.1012 = 10.12\%$

By calculating rolling returns over all series of consecutive 3-year periods, you will find the minimum value (Worst 3Y Rolling).

In the case of the example, the returns were all quite generous. One of the 'worst' cases was that of the last three years, for which we have the following total return:

[(1 + 18.28/100) * (1 - 18.19/100) * (1 + 21.60/100)] - 1 =

[(1 + 0.1828) * (1 - 0.1819) * (1 + 0.2160)] - 1 = 0.1766 = 17.66%

Online, you can find numerous resources that explain how to set up these calculations. If you're interested, on YouTube, we found an informative tutorial in a video (the interesting part starts at minute 3:30): https://www.youtube.com/watch?v=agLsHkkT7i4

If we want to get an idea of the worst drawdown in recent years, then we need to look for a series of "poor" or negative returns. In the example, we have a single strongly negative value: the -18.19% in 2022.

As you can see, even in such a generous series of returns, there was a year that would have tested your resilience as an investor. Can't "digest" such a negative return? Then you should allocate only a small portion of your capital to such investments or opt for more conservative instruments.

In addition to pure numerical calculations, always remember, when evaluating an instrument, to compare it to a benchmark reference. If a *US Total Stocks* portfolio, *US 60/40*, or a *Permanent Portfolio* perform better, carefully consider whether your investment choice is worthwhile.

Bibliography and Information Sources

Lazy Portfolio Etf (https://www.lazyportfolioetf.com/)

PortfolioCharts (https://portfoliocharts.com/)

PortfolioVisualizer (https://www.portfoliovisualizer.com/)

Dedalo Invest (https://www.dedaloinvest.com/)

Charlie Bilello (https://bilello.blog/)

Bogleheads Forum (https://bogleheads.org/forum/index.php)

Investing.com (https://www.investing.com/)

Trading Economics (https://tradingeconomics.com/)

Vanguard (https://www.vanguard.com/)

Investopedia (https://www.investopedia.com/)

ETF.com (https://www.etf.com/)

JustEtf.com (https://www.justetf.com/en/)

Curvo Backtest (https://curvo.eu/backtest/en)

World Government Bonds
(https://www.worldgovernmentbonds.com/)

Wikipedia (https://en.wikipedia.org/wiki/Main_Page)

Acknowledgements

As you already know, this book stems from the experience of the *LazyPortfolioEtf.com* website, which we built in 2019.

For at least a couple of years, the site had only a few daily visits, mostly from us and our friends. Being Italian, most of the traffic was local. Then something unexpected happened, and visibility skyrocketed globally.

Sites like Forbes, Nasdaq, Millionaire, SeekingAlpha and Investing started linking to our pages and mentioning us. Naturally, with such referrals, the audience quickly arrived.

Through social media, we finally emerged from anonymity, and there are numerous posts and videos that share our content. And we don't even have a social media account!

In particular, a huge thanks goes to Gabriele Bellelli, who, with great generosity, was the first to mention us multiple times in his online webinars and in his Facebook group 'Investire con Gabriele Bellelli' (Investing with Gabriele Bellelli). It has been an honor for us to be appreciated by such a recognized professional. Afterwards, as collaborators and partners of Gabriele, Francesco Brancatisano and Maurizio Papi joined, sharing our insights and 'numbers' with their audience on several occasions.

Simultaneously, thanks to Fulvio Marchese and his significant informative efforts, we also 'appeared' within another large financial community, which has its virtual 'home' in a Telegram group focused on financial e-learning. Here, we first met Carmine Covino, a financial coach and founder of <Aim-Ways>, and then Marco Foi, who involved us in the new project 'Cortile Finanziario' (Financial Courtyard).

Last but not least, simply because he is the last to have known in chronological order, a special thanks to Andrea Gonzali of Dedalo

Invest, who, for the Italian audience, had already created an extensive web portal dedicated to Lazy Portfolios (DedaloInvest.com), with statistics and calculations at a vastly superior level to ours. If you read something from us and then visit his site, it's like evolving from an abacus to a quantum supercomputer. Andrea, who already has experience in publishing books, provided us with valuable advice and a lot of online support.

And, lastly, thanks to you for reading and to the 2 thousand daily visitors to our website. Sooner or later, you will all be the ones to explain a particular metric to us, that we haven't mentioned in the book because we never understood it.

According to Google statistics, visits to our site increase when the sun is shining. There are two possibilities:

- it's nice weather, but passive investing and lazy portfolios are better than a walk outdoors
- it's raining outside, so you're experimenting with the real 'underwater period'

In both cases, we adore you.

Thanks to everyone.

Who we are

Agostino Carbone

I am passionate about personal finance, and I enjoy working with numbers. I delved into investments before the 2008 Subprime crisis. I took a hit, but I realized I needed to study and find a smarter approach to the markets. And since I'm also lazy, I build websites that process the data I need.

Cosimo Palma

I am an engineer passionate about the world of finance with a keen interest in investments. I am excited about reading and attempting to decipher the numbers of the complex and dynamic world of finance with an analytical mind. I ventured into the world of investments in 2007, and over the years, I have tried to understand financial dynamics and adapt to the changing market conditions. This journey has led me to appreciate Lazy Portfolios and, in general, the simplicity and passive management of the portfolio.

Contact Us

Online, you can find us at www.LazyPortfolioEtf.com, but you can also reach out to us via LinkedIn, where we have a dedicated page where we regularly share analyses and reflections:

Lazy Portfolio ETF
LazyPortfolioETF.com tracks the performances of the most famous "lazy" investing portfolios, replicating them with ETFs.

https://www.linkedin.com/company/lazy-portfolio-etf/

Made in the USA
Monee, IL
14 January 2025

76854998R00154